For Maryanne

from

Grandpa & Dammy

Happy Birthday april 30, 1977

70
Favorite Stories
for
Young Readers

READER'S DIGEST

70
Favorite Stories
for
Young Readers

The Reader's Digest Association, Inc.
Pleasantville, New York · Montreal · Sydney

The acknowledgments that appear on page 448 are
hereby made a part of this copyright page.

Library of Congress Catalog Card Number: 76-19444
Printed in the United States of America

INTRODUCTION

All children love a good story. And here is a book brimming with good stories—for your children to read and for you to read to them.

Teachers and librarians agree that children must be exposed to books in the home and to parents who read for their own enjoyment if they are to develop a true enjoyment and appreciation of reading. *70 Favorite Stories for Young Readers* provides you with a rich resource for family reading, both alone and aloud, that will help them to develop a lifetime reading habit and an enduring love of books.

Reading aloud brings pleasure to the parent and child alike. To the child it brings a special sense of closeness, reassurance and security. To the parent it brings a sense of personal satisfaction in one more act of devotion and tenderness. Although reading is usually a private activity—especially in later years—the act of reading aloud creates a special fellowship that thrives with the shared companionship and mutual enjoyment of characters met through the printed page, memorable scenes described, and beautiful language mutually savored.

What stories do parents choose to read to their children? Many will want to pick stories which were their favorites when they were young. This book gives ample opportunity: stories by Washington Irving, Nathaniel Hawthorne, O. Henry, Lewis Carroll and Richard Bennett are among the old favorites to be found here. And parents will be delighted to discover in this book little-known stories by authors of old favorites—such as the choices by Louisa May Alcott, Dorothy Canfield and Mary Mapes Dodge.

This collection will help you to make accessible to your children a selection of the best and most interesting stories for reading aloud. But it goes far beyond the preschooler or the beginning reader. Here are tales that satisfy the needs of young readers right up to the teens who want to curl up with a good book of almost endless variety. For this book provides a selection of stories from almost every category that appeals to children. Fantasy, magic and the fairy tale are well represented, with the incomparable "Many Moons," by James Thurber, "How to Tell Corn Fairies if You See 'Em," by Carl Sandburg, "The Griffin and the Minor Canon," by Frank R. Stockton, and many others. And here is a wealth of folk literature representing the many ethnic and national groups from around the world. In these tales you and your children can visit Pakistan, Burma, Finland, Italy, West Africa, Rumania, and sample one of the many facets of Jewish life in Isaac Bashevis Singer's beautiful "Menaseh's Dream."

You will find in these pages funny stories, animal tales, realistic stories of mystery and adventures past and present, stories with a spiritual message and scary stories like "Godfrey and the Werewolf," by Halina Gorska, "The Crow Child," by Mary Mapes Dodge, and "El Eñano," by Charles J. Finger. Just a word about these last: psychologists today agree that the tingle of anxiety such stories arouse is a pleasurable one because the safe return home of the child in the story only reinforces the young reader's own sense of a secure home and family.

But this is enough of introduction. In these *70 Favorite Stories For Young Readers* a world of enjoyment and adventure awaits you and your children. Read on!

—Mary Virginia Gaver

Past president American Library
Association; editor *Elementary
School Library Collection,*
Bro-Dart Foundation

CONTENTS

The Reindeer Slippers

*The slippers were now too small for
Alan's feet, but his mind and his imagination
had not yet outgrown them*

BARBARA WILLARD

The two suitcases were out on the beds. Alan and his mother were packing to go away for Christmas, trying to fit in not only their clothes but also presents for Uncle Jumbo and Auntie Sue and Sammy. Sammy was Alan's cousin, and he and his parents lived in the country. His father, Alan's Uncle Jumbo, was landlord of a very old inn beside a road that ran across the forest. As Alan's mother was a widow and had a job in London, Alan spent a lot of his holidays with Sammy. It did not matter that Sammy was a year younger, for he knew a lot of things that Alan could not know about, living in London as he did. Sammy knew very little about London, so the cousins were useful to one another.

Alan's mother kept putting things into his suitcase and then pulling them out again and trying to fit them in differently.

"Need you take these?" she asked, holding out a pair of slippers. "They take up so much room and anyway they're too small for you."

"They're all right," said Alan. "I must take them."

The slippers were made of reindeer hide. Uncle Stephen, who gave the best presents of anyone, had brought them back from a visit to Lapland, a little more than a year ago. Of course Alan's feet had grown a good deal in that time. He did know the slippers were getting too small for him, but he could not part with them and he would never admit that they were at all uncomfortable.

"Promise you'll be good about them, then," his mother said. "Don't go stuffing Sammy up with a lot of tales about them— you know how it annoys Auntie Sue."

11

"Okay," said Alan, not looking at her, pushing the slippers back into his suitcase.

There was a kind of magic about the reindeer slippers, but they were not by any means the first magic things Alan had possessed. He had a knack of finding such treasures. When he was very young there had been a mysterious bluish pebble which, at least in his own opinion, could make him invisible. Later, a couple of swan's feathers had had extraordinary powers—he could all but fly down the stairs when he was holding them. Then there was a wonderful double horse chestnut that everybody at school tried to get hold of, for such a thing had never been seen—that was strongly magic.

None of these things had been as good as the reindeer slippers.

Alan had been in the middle of measles when they came. When, hot and aching, he woke in the night, he put out his hand to touch the slippers of reindeer hide and he thought that a whole reindeer was there beside him. He felt the hard bones of the beast, like a strong framework over which the beautiful skin was fitted. Then he seemed to be riding on the reindeer's back, hanging on hard to the strong thick neck, sheltering behind the great antlers as he was carried many miles over snowy wastes beneath a huge sky sharp with stars. What is your name? he had asked the reindeer. My name is Swiftly, the creature had replied.

In the morning there were only the reindeer slippers, but night after night, Alan and Swiftly rode through deep forests together and across wide plains. As they went, Swiftly would tell Alan of life in the Arctic, of the herds moving darkly over the winter land, of battles when the clash of antlers rang for miles in the ice-bound distances; of the soft-eyed does and their fawns, stepping so lightly that their hoofs barely marked the ground. It was all ex-

actly as described in the book Uncle Stephen had given Alan at the same time as the slippers.

The box that the slippers had been packed in was kept on the high shelf in Alan's bedroom cupboard. It was a sort of magic museum—the pebble, the swan's feathers, the double chestnut, now shrivelled and small, were laid inside; and one day, no doubt, the reindeer slippers would find a place there, too.

Alan's various magical experiences had got him into trouble with Sammy's mother. Somehow Auntie Sue could only see Alan's tales of being invisible, flying downstairs, riding Swiftly over the snowy uplands, as a lot of silly fibs. Alan, she claimed, was teaching her Sammy to tell lies. At last Alan promised his mother that he would never speak to Sammy again about Swiftly or anything else of the kind. This promise he had already kept for months so he hardly needed his mother's warning to "be good" about the reindeer slippers this Christmas.

"The best idea," she said, as she watched him push the slippers back into his case, "would be to let Sammy have them. They'd be just about right for him."

"H'm," was all Alan said.

The inn where Sammy lived with his parents was called The Forester's Quarry. This was because, so some people said, there had been a quarry close by from which had come the soft-colored stone of which the house was built, and all the useful barns and stables and pig sties belonging to it, where Alan and Sammy were able to play in bad weather. Where's the quarry now, then? Uncle Jumbo would demand. He preferred the other kind of quarry, meaning something hunted—there had been wild boar roaming the forest once, and there were still deer and rabbits and game birds. He was always promising himself a new sign for the inn in place of

the dull old one that only had the name painted on it. Uncle Jumbo wanted a picture, a stag's head or a leaping deer, perhaps, or a hunter with bow and arrow.

There were not a great many trees in the forest. There were clumps and thickets of them, but mostly the forest was made up of rolling stretches of moorland where heather and gorse and bracken grew. There the wind swept bleakly in winter. Alan loved it then, for there was hardly a soul about. He and Sammy would go out for hours. Sammy was the best sort of companion at such times, for young as he was he knew a good deal about birds and animals. He was a good foresty boy, they said in the village. In the early dusk of December there was a mysterious blueness over all the forest and owls were out by half-past four. In the depth of the cold night foxes barked. Sometimes two or three deer passed quietly by, but mostly those were in the more wooded parts two miles or so away.

This Christmas was as good as all the others Alan and his mother had spent with Uncle Jumbo and Auntie Sue. Uncle Stephen drove down on Christmas Day and stayed the night. As usual, his presents were the best. Among them was a huge flat parcel for Uncle Jumbo. It was the new inn sign he had been talking about for so long and it was exactly what Uncle Jumbo wanted.

"The fitting screws still haven't come," Uncle Stephen explained. "They should arrive in the post any time. But I suppose you could always use the old ones."

On the day after Christmas, Boxing Day, the sky was black from early morning and anyone could see there was snow on the way. In the middle of the afternoon, Uncle Stephen decided he had better get back to London. Because she had to be at her job next day, Alan's mother went with him. As Alan and the others waved good-bye, the first careless flakes of snow were idly spinning through the dusk.

Alan hardly knew how to wait until the morning. He had never seen the forest

13

covered with snow. When he went to bed he put the reindeer slippers close beside him. In the darkness he put out his hand and felt the fine tough hide. Then he laughed to himself in a rather shamefaced way. Did he still expect the slippers to turn into a full-grown reindeer? Did he still think Swiftly might come to carry him over the snow? He was growing out of the reindeer slippers, so wasn't he perhaps growing out of Swiftly, too?

All night the snow fell. Next morning a grey swollen sky hung low over the stretches of forest. There was lots more snow to come but already everything was changed. Whole bushes had disappeared. The lower branches of the trees, bowed down under their load, had then been trapped and frozen to the ground. No bird was seen or heard. Up in the village the road was silent, for nothing on wheels could enter from any of the side-roads. Soon a wind came howling out of the gray sky and the snow started to fall again. By next morning it took shovels and spades to clear a pathway enough to leave the house.

Then the sky cleared, the sun shone. The snow, hard underneath, dry as powder on top, began to sparkle. Alan and Sammy went out in gumboots and thick gloves. They shouted and yelled in their excitement and their faces tingled with the sharpness of the air, their cheeks and noses turned red.

"Suppose we had a toboggan," Alan said.

"Make one," said Sammy.

All that afternoon they hunted about for something to make a toboggan. It was getting dark, a strange snowy dark like silver, when suddenly Alan saw hanging high up on the wall of the barn where the cars were kept the very thing they had been looking for.

"It is a toboggan, Sammy." Between them they hauled it down. The seats

needed a bit of repairing, but that was all.

When they had fixed the seats, they hid the toboggan behind bales of straw in the corner of the biggest barn. Then they went indoors and said nothing to a soul about what they had found.

Half a dozen times in the night Alan woke and heard the frost humming in the telephone wires. The reindeer slippers were close to his hand. Was it really too late for Swiftly to come and run beside the toboggan? Magic seemed easy because the whole world was under a spell. If there was indeed no Swiftly at such a time, then he would know he had gone for good. Then he would give the slippers to Sammy.

The night's frost had bound the snow as hard as cement. Where the snow had melted in yesterday's sunshine, dripping down the branches, there was now a film of ice. The glittering twigs tinkled when the wind blew them.

The two boys kept trying to escape with the toboggan, but there were jobs to be done. The snow meant that ordinary things were difficult and everyone was needing help. There was shopping to be fetched from the village, snow to be swept or shovelled, post to be collected because the van could not get round.

"Ask if there's a small parcel," Uncle Jumbo told the boys. "I could get the new sign up if only I'd got the fittings."

"Use the old ones as Stephen suggested," Auntie Sue said.

But for the toboggan, Alan would have wanted to help with the hanging of the new sign. The afternoon came and they had still not pulled the toboggan from its hiding place. Then without warning Alan heard Sammy shouting. "Now! Now!" He went pelting off to the barn without waiting for Alan to reply. Alan followed, snatching his duffle coat from behind the door and pulling it on as he went. He looked wildly around for his boots, but

Auntie Sue must have been tidying up again. There was no time to search. It was already after three. As soon as they were out of sight of home they were facing down a long shallow hillside and here they decided to give the toboggan its first run.

"I'll sit in front," Alan said. "You hang on to my middle." He sounded breathless.

"You've got your slippers on!" Sammy cried.

"They're my reindeer slippers, stupid."

"You'll get soaked! You'll die of frost-bite!"

"What's the good of a reindeer if its skin can't keep out the snow?"

At first it seemed as though the toboggan was not going to work. Then it began to move, slithering, slipping sideways, then settling to a straight course as it gathered speed. Suddenly the slope took it and pulled it, and at last Alan and Sammy were rushing over the snow, down the slope towards the hollow, shouting with excitement. Sammy yelled wordlessly, but Alan heard himself crying, "Swiftly! Swiftly!" in a loud excited voice. The toboggan was certainly not Swiftly, but it brought back some of his most magical memories and he felt wildly happy.

Now they were both enchanted. They dragged the toboggan up steep and steeper tracks. Soon Alan discovered how to make it swoop and swerve. It skimmed the snow, avoiding the sudden drifts against hidden bushes and humps of heather, leaping gullies that could have caught its nose and hurled them into a somersault.

The sun had vanished long ago, but the endless whiteness of the ground for miles kept the forest light and it was a surprise when a few flakes of snow came down on all the rest. The boys had been too busy to notice that the darkness in the sky was not night but clouds.

"Come on. Home," said Alan.

"One more!" Sammy cried. "If we go up there we're near a short cut to my home."

They toiled up as Sammy directed. When they reached the top they were looking over a part of the forest Alan had never seen before. It was not only the snow that made this seem unfamiliar territory. Dotted about the forest were various cottages and farms, lonely and cut off, with only well water for their supply. But here there were no roofs at all, only the open rolling plain, empty and mysterious.

"Where are we, Sammy?"

"I told you. Down to the bottom and then there's a short cut."

"But that's in the wrong direction. We go back that way," Alan said, turning and pointing.

"I tell you it's a short cut. I should know. Who lives here—me or you?"

"All right—if you're sure. Hop on. Buck up."

The toboggan shot off once more. But now neither of the boys shouted. They made the downhill run in silence, Sammy a bit sulky, Alan worried. The snow that had started to fall was very slight, but now the sky did indeed seem to grow darker.

Things Alan had been too much occupied to notice now became horribly obvious—that his feet were soaked and numb—that Auntie Sue would be getting worried and Uncle Jumbo would be getting furious—that Sammy should not have been allowed to come so far. And that no one knew where they had gone.

"Which way now?" he demanded, when they reached the bottom of the run.

"This way," said Sammy positively.

He plodded ahead and Alan followed, dragging the toboggan. Now his legs were soaked, as well as his feet. The snow was deeper here—it was over the top of Sammy's boots. The heads of low bushes broke the surface of the snow like swimmers in a choppy sea. The smoothness all around was crisscrossed with tiny tracks

15

where mice had run out from shelter, searched desperately for food, then scuttled for home. By the edge of a frozen pond, birds of all sizes had come and gone, frantic for water, patterning the snow with their delicate prints. A fox had come to the pond, too, and rabbits—Sammy knew all about such things and even now he stopped to look at the tracks and tell Alan which was which. Further on there was a patch where the snow was flattened and scattered, and there were some drops of blood and a few feathers.

"Fox caught a pheasant," Sammy said.

All these things made the forest seem wilder and lonelier than ever, given up to animals and birds, with no time or place for boys who had been silly enough to come so far from home.

Sammy was first at the top of the slope. He stood quite still with his back turned. The newly falling snow had given his red woolly cap a white top. Quite suddenly, in that expanse of snow and sky, he looked a very little boy, much more than a year younger than Alan. He needed to be looked after, rescued from danger.

"It looks different today," he said in a small voice, as Alan came up with him. He sat down on the toboggan, trying hard not to cry. "I thought I knew the way."

"Oh, we can't be far from home," Alan said jauntily. "I wish Swiftly was here. He'd take us."

They had not spoken about Swiftly since Alan made his promise, but for all that, Sammy remembered.

"But he's only a pretend reindeer. Mum says he's just a lot of imagination."

Alan looked about him. He had so often seen Swiftly in the past, had spoken to him so confidently. What had once been so easy was now quite impossible. He knew that the huge proud antlers he had seen were only dead upstanding branches; he knew that everything Swiftly had told him about

his home in the Arctic was what he remembered from books. He was too old; the magic had gone. But Sammy was younger—surely Swiftly was just the thing to help Sammy now.

"Come on," he said. "You'll freeze if you sit there. We'll leave the toboggan and fetch it another day. Oh, do come on. Swiftly may be waiting just ahead. He often shelters where there are trees. Look! There's a clump of gorse and stuff ahead. The quicker we get to it, the quicker we'll be home."

He pulled Sammy to his feet and hurried him along, hanging on to his hand.

Swiftly was not at the next clump of bushes nor at the next. By the time they reached the third clump Sammy was dragging behind, the snow was falling much faster and Alan could not pretend any longer that he was not afraid. What if they were really lost? The forest was so big. You could go for a comfortable walk of a mile or two, or what Uncle Jumbo called a real walk of ten, fifteen, twenty miles. What if they were on a real walk now?

"There are some trees, Sammy—look, I can just see them. Beside the track. Perhaps Swiftly likes trees better than just bushes."

"Don't you know if he does?" Sammy cried, bitter and disbelieving.

They reached the clump of trees. Snow whirled, not in big flakes but in little hard balls that blew over the white ground until it found a mound or ledge to stop it. It was difficult to see, but the trees seemed to offer some hope. They ringed a clump of snow-covered gorse, and here was another small frozen pond.

"He isn't here either," Sammy said. "Mum was right. Swiftly's just a made-up story. He's not a reindeer at all."

Alan did not answer. His throat felt hot and tight. He did not know what to do next. Around him he saw the tracks of animals that had come to drink and found the pond frozen—the same little mouse scratchings and bird patterns that Sammy had pointed out cheerfully enough earlier in the day. There were bigger tracks here, too, sharp, deep tracks that Alan recognized instantly.

He shook Sammy. "Look here, then! What did I tell you? Swiftly's been here! Here are his hoof marks!"

Sammy looked at the tracks and then at Alan. He gave a wobbly smile and sniffed hard.

"Are you sure it's him?"

"He's got tired of waiting for us and gone on," said Alan. "Quick! We've got to catch him up. It's easy to see the way he went."

The deep slots made by the deer's sharp hoofs led steadily onwards from the bushes up a steepish hill, like a chain of many links that might be dragging the boys to safety. In his eagerness Alan began to go faster, tugging poor Sammy along. He heard him crying out, but it was only when he fell flat that Alan allowed a halt.

He stooped beside the younger boy, trying to help him up.

"I can't," sobbed Sammy. "I can't—I can't. . . ."

Alan looked round him in terror. There seemed to be nothing but snow now, snow on the ground, snow in the air and in the sky, so that he hardly knew whether they had been walking or flying. The tracks were beginning to blur. He peered ahead, wondering how soon they would be lost altogether.

He saw something then that made his heart thump. He remembered all the stories he had ever read about people in deserts, people lost on moor and marshland—gazing ahead and thinking they saw what they most wanted to see . . .

"Sammy . . . Can you see something. . . . ?"

Sammy struggled up, dragging at Alan's hand. He, too, screwed up his eyes. Then he gave a shout.

"It's Swiftly," said Alan. "Isn't it?"

"It's Dad's new sign!" Sammy screeched. "He's got it up and it's lighted! It's a stag's head, look—the light's shining right through the eyes! It's The Forester's Quarry! We're home!"

First, there were the scoldings, then the huggings and kissings.

"What a stupid thing to do! Going off like that without telling anyone! You ought to be ashamed of yourselves. You might never have got home alive."

"Alan told me—" Sammy began. Then he changed what he had been going to say into, "Alan saw the tracks of a deer and we followed them, and they brought us all the way home."

"Yes, there's been an old stag nosing about," Uncle Jumbo agreed. "You seem to owe him quite a lot—I'll see he finds a bit of fodder." He looked at Alan. "You kept your wits about you. That was good."

Alan was not sure whether he felt pleased or sad. He would never forget the sudden sight of that proud, antlered head shining out over the snow. For an instant, until he saw that the antlers were the wrong shape, he had truly believed it was Swiftly who had brought them home.

Auntie Sue had the reindeer slippers in her hand. They were black and slimy with wet, as though they had been fished up from the bottom of a deep pond.

"Alan—I thought you were a sensible boy. Fancy going out into the snow in slippers!"

"Yes, but if I hadn't—" Alan began. And then, like Sammy, he stopped and said something else instead. "Will they dry all right?"

"They'll dry. But I doubt if you'll ever be able to get into them again."

They did dry—magically. The skin shrank back to the shape and size it had been when the slippers were new. That meant they were a whole year too small for Alan. There was nothing for it—he would have to give them to Sammy.

He waited until he was packing to go home.

"Here you are," he said. "If they fit you, you can have them."

Sammy looked at the slippers. Then he got busy rolling up some string he had found in his pocket.

"Don't you want them?" Alan cried.

"No, thanks. I don't want to be bothered with any old reindeer. We've got proper ones in the forest."

"Proper ones—" began Alan hotly. But it was no good trying to explain what he felt about Swiftly for he was not entirely sure himself. Was it Swiftly who had got them home, or was it the old stag nosing for food far from his usual haunts?

He gave the slippers a hard pressure, as though reassuring a friend, then thrust them back into his suitcase. He was relieved. Far better for Swiftly to have an honorable retirement and to join the other worn-out treasures in the magic museum, the shoe box safe on the shelf at home.

The Rat Who Made One Bargain Too Many

*He started out with a stick and ended
up with a bride. The bride was his mistake*

Ashraf Siddiqui and Marilyn Lerch

Once upon a time there was a plump rat who was very kind and also very shrewd. He was walking along the road one day when he found a thick branch under a pile of brush. He put it into his sack to use for winter kindling.

A short time later he came upon an old man trying in vain to light a fire. Around the man were clustered three little girls crying piteously. The rat, who never saw suffering without attempting to help, called out, "Poor fellow, is there anything I can do to aid you?"

"Perhaps you can, Mr. Rat. My children are hungry. The wood is wet from the spring rains, and I can't build a fire to cook their meager breakfast."

"See what I have," said the rat. "This dry stick will soon make a fine blaze."

To show his appreciation the poor man gave the rat a bit of dough.

The rat trotted off, thinking that he was very shrewd to have gotten a week's supply of food for one dry stick.

Further on, the rat heard a terrible noise. He entered the yard of a pottery maker and found two little boys crying as if their hearts would break.

"There, there, don't cry," said the kind-hearted rat. "Perhaps I can help you. Tell me what is the matter."

The eldest boy wiped the tears from his eyes and whimpered, "Our parents went to the village to get food, but they are late in returning, and we are hungry."

"Well, my children, take this bit of dough and bake it. In a few minutes everything will be all right."

The children thanked him a hundred times. "Here, Mr. Rat," said the eldest, "take this pot which my father made yesterday. We shall not forget your kindness."

The rat tottered off with the heavy pot on his back. It is a trifle cumbersome, he thought, but worth much more than a bit of dough. Yes, indeed, I am a shrewd hand.

By and by the rat came upon a funny scene. An old farmer was milking a buffalo, but as he did not have a pail, he was draining the milk into a pair of shoes. Now the rat was not only kind and shrewd, but also very clean.

19

"Mr. Farmer, when the milk comes from the buffalo, it is clean. You are making it dirty by using those shoes. A pail would be much better."

"A pail would be much better," said the farmer, mimicking the rat. "Of course, a pail would be better if I *had* one."

"Well, you do have one. Use mine. I cannot stand dirty milk."

The farmer thanked the rat and soon had the pot brimming full of clean milk. "Here, my little friend, have a taste of this."

The rat sat back on his haunches and pulled at his whiskers. "No, I deserve a better bargain than that. You could not have sold the milk because it was dirty, the buffalo was worth nothing to you. I think you should give me the buffalo."

The farmer laughed heartily. "And just what can a little fellow like you do with this huge animal?"

The rat drew up to his full stature and puffed out his chest. "Never mind. I'll handle the buffalo."

The farmer, who enjoyed jokes, tied the buffalo's halter around the rat's neck.

The rat set off in a cocky manner, but he had only walked a few yards when the rope began to choke him. Turning around, he saw that the buffalo had stopped by the roadside to graze. The rat pulled and shouted, but, of course, in vain.

Well, rationalized the rat, this monster is my property now, and I must take care of him. So I shall follow him. He knows better than I where the good grazing is.

All day long the buffalo wandered from one grassy spot to another, dragging the poor rat behind him. And you can imagine how fast the little rat's legs had to move in order to keep pace with the rambling buffalo. At twilight the buffalo lay down by a cool stream, and the weary rat gratefully sank down beside him.

A few minutes later a wedding procession stopped by the stream to rest. It seems that a prospective bride was being carried to meet her bridegroom. The four bride-bearers built a fire and began cooking a bit of rice.

"A fine thing," grumbled one of them, "to carry our heavy burden all day in the hot sun and then have only this bit of rice to eat."

The rat listened to every word. Suddenly an idea came to him.

"My friends," piped up the rat, "I know what it is to be hungry. Please take my buffalo and cook him for your supper."

The four bearers laughed and laughed at the thought of a rat owning a buffalo, but they were too hungry to argue. They killed the buffalo, and in a few minutes a large steak was sizzling over the fire. After they had gorged themselves on the tasty meat, they offered a morsel to the rat.

"Now, wait a minute," cried the rat, puffing out his chest. "I am a shrewd bargainer. Why only today I traded a stick for a week's supply of food. I traded the food for a pot. For the pot I received this buffalo. So, I shall take nothing less this time than the bride herself."

The bearers, realizing the trouble they had gotten into, shook with fear and decided that the best thing to do was flee, which they did in a great rush.

The rat, chuckling to himself, walked over to the covered litter and lifted the curtain. He drew back in amazement, for inside sat the loveliest lady he had ever seen. But the rat quickly regained his composure and in a sweet voice said, "My dear and lovely bride, you are mine now. Let me take you to my abode."

It was growing dark and the young bride, frightened at being alone in the great woods, gratefully accepted the rat's offer.

When they arrived at the rat's hole, he jumped in and graciously offered his hand to the bride. She giggled and did not move one inch.

"Come along," urged the rat. "You are mine now and must follow me."

The bride giggled again and said, "Do you expect me to squeeze into that tiny hole?"

The rat sat back on his haunches and pulled at his whiskers. At last he said, "Yes, it is obvious that you are overfed and that I must enlarge my hole in order to accommodate you. In the meantime you can sleep under this plum tree."

"I cannot sleep if I am hungry," complained the bride.

The rat, grumbling to himself that brides were terribly bothersome, disappeared into his hole and came up a few minutes later with two peas.

"Gracious," cried the bride, "do you expect me to clean house, cook and sew on two peas a day!"

The rat sighed and shook his head. It was more than he had bargained for. "Tonight I shall gather some wild plums, and tomorrow you can carry a basketful to market and sell them to buy the delicacies that you desire."

The next day, the bride, dressed in her lovely gown, wandered through the village streets selling plums. She came to the palace gates, and lo and behold! there was the bride's mother, the queen, running toward her. They embraced amid much weeping. Just then the rat appeared. "I demand my wife," he yelled, jumping up and down. "I traded a buffalo for her, and she belongs to me!"

The clever queen could scarcely keep from laughing. "My dear Son-in-law," she said sweetly, "do not be angry. We have just finished preparing a warm, spacious room for you. Come. Follow me!"

The rat, delighted beyond all measure, followed the queen. She led him to the stove, opened the oven door and announced, "Here it is, dear Son-in-law, hop in."

The rat did so in one leap, and bang! the oven door was slammed in his face. He sat there tugging at his whiskers and daydreaming about his good fortune. But the room was getting a bit stuffy. He rapped on the door and asked if a window could be raised. Outside, he heard the queen and the bride laughing hysterically. The room became hotter and hotter, and soon his tail began to sizzle.

"Oh! I have been tricked!" cried the rat. "I shall never, never, never make another bargain."

On hearing this, the queen opened the door, and the rat leaped out. He had learned his lesson, and he never, never, never made another bargain.

The Professor
and the Patagonian Giant

He was a most reasonable giant.
He offered to explain to Professor Muddlehed
exactly why it was all right for the professor
to be his—the giant's—dinner

TUDOR JENKS

Early one morning during my third visit to Patagonia, as I was strolling upon the banks of the River Chico, keeping a sharp lookout for a choice specimen of the Rutabaga Tremendosa, I saw what, at the time, I supposed to be a large and isolated cliff. It looked blue, and consequently I supposed it to be at some distance. Resuming my search for the beautiful saffron blossom which I have already named, my attention was for some moments abstracted. After pulling the plant up by the roots, however, I happened to cast my eyes again toward the supposed cliff, and you can conceive my extreme mortification and regret when I saw that it was not a cliff at all, but a giant, who was advancing at a run. Much annoyed at the interruption of my researches, I paused only long enough to deposit the Rutabaga securely in my botany box and then broke into an accelerated trot. Relying on the well-established

scientific probability that the giant was stupid, I expected therefore that my head would have an opportunity to save my heels.

It was not long before I saw the need of taking immediate steps to secure my specimens from destruction and myself from being eaten. He was certainly gaining upon me. As he foolishly ran with his mouth open, I noticed that his canine teeth were very well developed—not a proof, but strong evidence, that he was a cannibal. I redoubled my speed, in the hope that I might find some cave or crevice into which I could creep and thus obtain time enough to elaborate a plan of escape. I had not run far when I saw a most convenient cretaceous cave.

To ensconce myself within its mineral recesses was the work of but a moment, and it was fortunate for me that it took no longer. Indeed, as I rolled myself deftly beneath a shelving rock, the giant was so near that he pulled off one of my boots.

He sat down at the entrance and breathed with astonishing force and rapidity.

"Now, if he is as stupid as one of his race normally should be," I said to myself, "he will stay there for several hours, and I shall lose a great part of this beautiful day." The thought made me restless, and I looked about and discovered an outlet far above me. Fixing my hat more firmly upon my head, I began the ascent. It did not take long. Indeed, my progress was rather accelerated by the efforts of the attentive giant, who had secured a long and flexible switch—a young India-rubber tree, I think, though I did not notice its foliage closely—and was poking it with considerable violence into the cave. In fact, he lifted me several feet at every thrust.

It may easily be understood, therefore, that I was not long upon the way. When I emerged, I was much pleased with the situation. Speaking as a military expert, it was perfect. Standing upon a commodious ledge, which seemed to have been made for the purpose, my head and shoulders projected from an opening in the cliff, which was just conveniently out of the giant's reach.

As my head appeared, the giant spoke, "Aha, you're there, are you?"

"I suppose you think you're safe, don't you?"

"I know I'm safe," I answered, with an easy confidence calculated to please.

"Well," he replied, "tonight I am going to eat you for supper!"

"What, then," I asked, with some curiosity, "are you going to do for dinner?"

"Oh, if that troubles you," said he, "all you have to do is to come out at dinnertime and I will eat you then."

Evidently the giant was not a fool. His answers were apt. After a moment's reflection I concluded it was worth the effort to make an appeal to his better nature.

"Don't you know that it is wrong to eat your fellow beings?" I asked, with a happy mingling of austere reproach and sympathetic pain.

"Do you mean to come out soon?" asked the giant, seating himself upon an adjacent cliff, after tearing off such of the taller and stiffer trees as were in his way.

"It depends somewhat upon whether you remain where you are," I answered.

"Oh, I shall stay," said the giant, pleasantly. "Game is rare, and I haven't eaten a man for two weeks."

This remark brought me back to my appeal to his higher being. "Then I shall remain here, too, for the present," I answered, "though I should like to get away before sunset when it's likely to be humid here. But, to return to my question, have you never thought that it was immoral and selfish to eat your fellow creatures?"

"Why, certainly," said the giant, with a hearty frankness that was truly refreshing. "That is why," he went on, "I asked you whether you were coming out soon. If not, I would be glad to while the time away by explaining to you exactly how I feel about these matters. Of course I could smoke you out" (here he showed me an enormous boulder of flint and a long steel rod, the latter evidently a propeller shaft from some wrecked ocean steamer), "but I make it a rule seldom to eat a fellow mortal until he is fully convinced that I am justified in so doing."

The allusion to the smoking-out process convinced me that this was no hulking ignoramus of a giant, and I began to fear that my Rutabaga Tremendosa was lost to the world forever. But the latter part of his speech reassured me.

"If you can convince me that I ought to be eaten," I said, willing to be reasonable, "I shall certainly offer no objection. But I confess I doubt that you will succeed."

"I first discovered that I was a giant," he said, absently chewing the stem of the India-rubber tree, "at a very early age. I could not get enough to eat. I then lived in New York City, for I am an American, like yourself."

We bowed with mutual pleasure.

"I tried various sorts of work, but I could not earn enough at any of them to pay my food bills. I even exhibited myself in a museum, but had the same trouble.

"I consulted my grandfather, who was a man of matured judgment and excellent sense. His advice was to leave the city and try for work in the country. I did so, and after some little trouble found employment upon a farm. I stayed there three days. Then I was told that it cost more to keep me than I was worth, which was true. So I left. Then I went to work on a railroad. Here I did as much as twenty men. The result was a strike, and I was discharged."

"Is there much more autobiography?" I asked as politely as I could, for I was not at all interested in this unscientific memoir.

"Very little," he answered. "I can sum it up in a few words. Wherever I tried to get work, I was discharged because my food was too expensive. If I tried to do more work to make up for it, the other men were dissatisfied because it took the bread out of their mouths. Now, I put it to you, what was I to do?"

"Evidently, you were forced out of civilization," I answered, "and compelled to rely upon nature for your sustenance. That is, you had to become a hunter, trapper or fisherman—for of course, in your case, agriculture was out of the question, as you couldn't easily get down to the ground and would crush with your feet more crops than you could raise with your hands."

His eyes sparkled with joy at being so thoroughly understood. "Exactly," he said. "But the same trouble followed me there. Wherever I settled, the inhabitants complained that what I ate would support hundreds of other people."

"Very true," I answered, "but, excuse me, could you hand me a small rock to sit upon? It is tiresome to stand here."

"Come out," he said. "You have my word of honor, as a compatriot of George——"

"Say no more!" I broke in hastily.

I came out, and was soon, by his kind aid, perched upon the branch of a tree conveniently near.

"This argument," he said, sighing, "met me at every turn; and after much cogitation I could see no solution of the difficulty. No matter how far from the 'busy haunts of men' I proceeded, it was only to find that food grew scarcer as men were less numerous. At last I reached Patagonia and after a few years I have eaten it almost bare. Now, to what conclusion am I driven?"

I thought it over. At last I said, "I see the extremities to which you are reduced. But upon what principle do you proceed to the next step—cannibalism?"

"The greatest good to the greatest number," said he. "Whenever I eat an animal, I diminish the stock of food which supports mankind, but whenever I eat a man, I diminish the number to be supported. As all the wise men agree that it is the subsistence which is short, my course of action tends ultimately to the greater happiness of the race."

This seemed very reasonable and for a moment I was staggered. Then a happy thought came to me, and I suggested that if he should allow himself to die of starvation the demand for subsistence would be still more reduced.

He shook his head sadly. "I used to hope so myself. But the experience of some years, tabulated and reduced to most accurate statistics, has convinced me beyond a doubt that I can catch and eat enough

men, in a year, to more than make up for what would be saved if I should allow my own organism to cease its exertions."

I thought over these arguments carefully and was unable to pick a flaw in them.

"As a man of science," I said, after a pause, "I could wish that this interview might be reported to the world."

"Give yourself no uneasiness. It shall be done," said the giant.

"And I should also be glad to have the Rutabaga Tremendosa forwarded very soon to the New York Botanical Gardens," I said thoughtfully.

"With pleasure," said the giant.

There was no excuse for further delay.

"And are you convinced?" asked the giant, speaking kindly.

"Perfectly," I said, and kicked off the other boot.

[Note, by the giant—In accordance with Professor Muddlehed's last wishes I have reported our full conversation verbatim. In fact, much of the foregoing account was revised by the Professor himself before supper. He would have been glad, I have no doubt, to have gone over the paper again, but the bell rang and he was too considerate to keep the table waiting. He had many excellent tastes, and there was a flavor of originality about the man—a flavor I like. I enjoyed meeting him very much, and regret that my principles were such as to preclude a longer and less intimate acquaintance. I forwarded the specimen as directed and received in return an invitation to visit the Botanical Gardens in New York. Though I can not accept the kind invitation, I should find it gratifying to have the trustees at my own table.]

The Black Stallion and the Red Mare

*They were two magnificent creatures—
wild and free and proud—and young Donald found
that he must be a traitor to them*

GLADYS F. LEWIS

At first Donald lay still. Scarcely a muscle moved. The boulders and the low shrubs screened him from view. Excitement held him motionless. His hands gripped the short grass and his toes dug into the dry earth. Cautiously he raised himself on his elbows and gazed at the scene below him.

There, in his father's unfenced hay flats, was the outlaw band of wild horses. They were grazing quietly on the rich grass. Some drank from the small hillside stream. Donald tried to count them, but they suddenly began moving about and he could not get beyond twenty. He thought there might be two hundred.

Donald knew a good deal about that band of horses, but he had never had the good luck to see them. They were known over many hundreds of square miles. They had roamed at will over the grain fields and they had led away many a domestic horse to the wild life. Once in that band, a horse was lost to the farm.

There in the flats was the great black stallion, the hero or the villain of a hundred tales. Over the far-flung prairie and grass lands there was scarcely a boy who had not dreamed of wild rides with the great body of the stallion beneath him, bearing him clean through the air with the sharp speed of lightning.

There was the stallion now, moving among the horses with the sureness and ease of a master. As he moved about, teasingly kicking here and nipping there, a restlessness, as of a danger sensed, stirred through the band. The stallion cut to the outside of the group. At a full gallop he snaked around the wide circle, roughly bunching the mares and colts into the smaller circle of an invisible corral.

He was a magnificent creature, huge and proudly built. Donald saw the gloss of the black coat and the great curving muscles of the strong legs, the massive hoofs, the powerful arch of the neck, the proud crest of the head. Donald imagined he could see the flash of black intelligent eyes. Surely a nobler creature never roamed the plains!

Off-wind from the herd, a red mare came out from the fold of the low hills

27

opposite. She stood motionless a moment, her graceful head held high. Then she nickered. The black stallion drew up short in his herding, nickered eagerly, then bolted off in the direction of the mare. She stood waiting until he had almost reached her, then they galloped back to the herd together.

The shadows crept across the hay flats and the evening stillness settled down. A bird sang sleepily on one note. Donald suddenly became aware of the monotonous song and stirred from his intent watching. He must tell his father and help send news around the countryside. He was still intensely excited as he crept back from the brow of the hill and hurried home. All the time his mind was busy and his heart was bursting.

Donald knew that three hundred years ago the Spaniards had brought horses to Mexico. Descendants of these horses had wandered into the Great Plains. These horses he now was watching were of that Spanish strain. Thousands of them roamed the cattle lands north to the American boundary. This band now grazed wild over these park lands here in Canada—four hundred and fifty miles north of the boundary.

His father and the farmers for many miles around had determined to round up the horses and make an end of the roving band. As a farmer's son, Donald knew that this was necessary and right. But a certain respect for the band and the fierce loyalty that he felt toward all wild free creatures made him wish in his heart that they might never be caught, never be broken and tamed. He, who was so full of sympathy for the horses, must be traitor to them!

There had been conflicts in his heart before, but never had there been such a warring of two strong loyalties. He saw himself for the first time as a person of importance because he, Donald Turner, had the power to affect the lives of others. This power, because it could help or harm others, he knew he must use wisely.

When he stood before his father half an hour later, he did not blurt out his news. It was too important for that. But his voice and his eyes were tense with excitement. "That band of wild horses is in the hay hollow, west of the homestead quarter," he said. "There must be close to two hundred."

His father was aware of the boy's deep excitement. At Donald's first words he stopped his milking, his hands resting on the rim of the pail as he looked up.

"Good lad, Donald!" he said, quietly enough. "Get your supper and we'll ride to Smith's and Duncan's to start the word around. Tell Mother to pack lunches for tomorrow. We'll start at sunup." He turned to his milking again.

The other men were in the yard shortly after daylight.

Donald afterward wondered how long it would have taken ranch hands to round up the band of horses. These farmers knew horses, but not how to round up large numbers of them as the men of the ranch country knew so well. The farmers learned a good deal in the next two weeks.

Twenty men started out after the band as it thundered out of the hay flats, through the hills and over the country. The dust rose in clouds as their pounding hoofs dug the dry earth. The herd sped before the pursuers with the effortless speed of the wind. The black stallion led or drove his band and kept them well together. That first day only the young colts were taken.

At sunset the riders unsaddled and staked their horses by a poplar thicket, ate their stale lunches and lay down to sleep under the stars. Their horses cropped the short grass and drank from the stream. Some slept standing up; others lay down.

At dawn the herd was spied moving

westward. With the coming of night, they too had rested. For a mile or more they now sped along the rim of a knoll, swift as bronchos pulled in off the range after a winter out. The black stallion was a hundred feet ahead, running with a tireless, easy swing, his mane and tail streaming and his body stretched level as it cut through the morning mists. Close at his side but half a length behind him, ran the red mare. The band streamed after.

After the first day's chase and the night under the stars, Donald had ridden back home. Not that he had wanted to go back. He would have given everything that he owned to have gone on with the men. But there were horses and cattle and chores to attend to at home, and there was school.

The roundup continued. Each day saw the capture of more and more horses. As the men doubled back on their course, they began to see that the wild horses traveled in a great circle, coming back again and again over the same ground, stopping at the same watering holes and feeding in the same rich grass flats. Once this course became clear, fresh riders and mounts in relays were posted along the way while others drove on from behind. The wild band had still to press on with little chance for rest and feeding. The strain of the pursuit took away their desire for food, but they had a burning thirst and the black stallion would never let them drink their fill before he drove them on. Fatigue grew on them.

As the roundup continued, the whole countryside stirred with excitement. At every town where there was a grain elevator along the railroad, people repeated the latest news of the chase. On the farms the hay went unmowed or unraked, and the plows rested still in the last furrow of the summer fallow. At school the children played roundup at recess. Donald, at his desk, saw the printed pages of his books

but his mind was miles away, running with the now almost exhausted wild horses.

Near the end of the second week of the chase, Donald's father rode into the yard. Donald dropped the wood he was carrying to the house and ran to meet his father.

"Dad, they haven't got the black stallion and the red mare, have they?" Donald could scarcely wait for his father's slow reply.

"No, Donald, lad," he said. "Though those two are the only horses still free. They're back in the flats. We'll get them tomorrow."

Donald felt both relief and fear.

In the yellow lamplight of the supper table his father told of the long days of riding, of the farms where he had eaten and rested, of the adventures of each day.

"That was a gallant band, lad!" he said. "Never shall we see their equal! Those two that are left are a pair of great horses. Most wild horses show a weakening in the strain and grow up with little wind or muscle. But these two are sound of wind and their muscles are like steel. Besides that, they have intelligence. They would have been taken long ago but for that."

No one spoke. Donald felt that his father was on his side, the side of the horses. After a long pause, Mr. Turner continued.

"With his brains and his strength, that stallion could have got away in the very beginning. He could have got away a dozen times and would now be free south of the border. But that was his band. He stayed by them and he tried to get them to safety. This week, when his band had been rounded up, he stuck by that red mare. She is swift but she can't match his speed. It's curious the way they keep together! He stops and nickers. She nickers in reply and comes close to him, her nose touching his flank. They stand a moment. Then they are away again, she running beside him but not quite neck to neck. Day after day it is the same. They are no ordinary horseflesh, those two, lad!"

There was a lump in Donald's throat. He knew what his father meant. Those horses seemed to stand for something bigger and greater than himself. There were other things that made him feel the same—the first full-throated song of the meadowlark in the spring; ripe golden fields of wheat with the breeze rippling it in waves; the sun setting over the rim of the world in a blaze of rose and gold; the sun rising again in the quiet east; the smile in the blue depths of his mother's eyes; the still whiteness of the snow-bound plains, the story of Columbus dauntlessly sailing off into unknown seas.

These things were part of a hidden, exciting world. The boy belonged to these things in some strange way. He caught only glimpses of that hidden world, but those glimpses were tantalizing. Something deep within him leaped up in joy.

That night Donald dreamed of horses nickering to him but, when he tried to find them, they were no longer there. Then he dreamed that he was riding the great black stallion, riding over a far-flung range, riding along a hilltop road, the world spread below him on every side. He felt the powerful body of the horse beneath him. He felt the smooth curves of the mighty muscles. Horse and rider seemed as one.

A cold dawn shattered his glorious dream ride. With his father he joined the other horsemen. From the top of the slope from which Donald had first seen them, the pair of horses was sighted. They were dark moving shadows in the gray mists of the morning.

They had just finished drinking deep from the stream. Not for two weeks had the men seen the horses drink like that. Thirsty as they were, they had taken but one drink at each water hole. This last morning the two of them were jaded and

spent; they had thrown caution to the winds.

At first suspicion of close danger, they stood still, heads and tails erect. Then the two horses dashed toward the protecting hills. There the way forked.

It was then Donald saw happen the strange thing his father had described. At

the fork the stallion halted and nickered. The mare answered and came close. She touched his flank with her head. Then they bounded off and disappeared in the path that led northwest to the rougher country where the chase had not led before.

Along the way the horses had been expected to take, grain-fed horses had been stationed. These had now to move over northwest. But the men were in no hurry today. They were sure of the take before nightfall. The sun was low in the west when two riders spurred their mounts for the close in. The stallion and the mare were not a hundred yards ahead. They were dead spent. Their glossy coats were

flecked with dark foam. Fatigue showed in every line of their bodies. Their gallant spirits no longer could drive their spent bodies. The stallion called to the mare. He heard her answer behind him. He slowed down, turning wildly in every direction. She came up to him, her head drooped on his flank and rested there. In a last wild defiance, the stallion tossed his magnificent head and drew strength for a last mighty effort. Too late!

The smooth coils of a rope tightened around his feet. He was down, down and helpless. He saw the mare fall as the rope slipped over her body and drew tight around her legs. It maddened him. He struggled wildly to be free. The taut rope held. The stallion was conquered. In that last struggle something went out of him. Broken was his body and broken was his spirit. Never again would he roam the plains, proud and free, the monarch of his herd.

Donald saw it all. He felt it all. His hands gripped the pommel of the saddle and his knees pressed hard against his pony's side. Tears blinded his eyes and from his throat came the sound of a single sob. It was as if he himself were being broken and tied.

The sun dipped below the rim of the plains. The day was gone; the chase was ended. The men stood about smoking and talking in groups of two's and three's examining the two roped horses. Donald's father knelt close to the mare, watching her intently. Donald watched him. His father remained quiet for a moment, one knee still resting on the ground, in his hand his unsmoked pipe. Donald waited for his father to speak. At last the words came.

"Boys," he said, without looking up, and with measured words, "do you know, this mare is blind—stone blind!"

A week later, Donald and his father stood watching those two horses in the Turner corral. They were not the same spirited creatures, but they were still magnificent horses.

"I figured," his father said, turning to the boy, "that they had won the right to stay together. I've brought them home for you, Donald. They are yours, lad. I know you will be good to them."

How Old Stormalong Captured Mocha Dick

"Stormalong said he'd get Mocha Dick,
Aye, mates 'tis no lie,
But the Great White Whale just laughed in his face,
And spit right in his eye"

IRWIN SHAPIRO

There are many stories about who captured Mocha Dick, the Great White Whale, or Moby Dick, as he was sometimes called. But any sailorman worth his salt knows it was Old Stormalong—and he had to become a cowboy to do it.

Alfred Bulltop Stormalong was the greatest sailor who ever lived. He stood four fathoms tall in his stocking feet. His eyes were as blue as a calm sea. His hair was as black as a storm cloud. He could whistle shrill like the wind in the rigging; he could hoot like a foghorn; and he could talk ordinary, just like anyone else. Stormalong had one fault. He was always complaining that they didn't make ships big enough for him.

One windy night Stormalong was sitting in the Sailors' Snug Haven, the inn that served the best shark soup in the town of Nantucket. He sat cross-legged on the floor so that his head wouldn't bump the ceiling. He ate six dozen oysters, then called for some shark soup, which he drank from a dory. Beside him sat Captain Joshua Skinner of the good ship *Dolphin* and some members of the crew. Stormalong was to sail with them the next morning to catch whales in the Pacific.

"Captain Skinner," said Stormalong, "on this voyage I'm going to capture Mocha Dick."

"Hm," said Captain Skinner. "You've said that five times before. And five times the white whale escaped you."

"This time he won't escape!" shouted Stormalong, hooting like a foghorn. Then he added in an ordinary voice, "And I mean it, too."

"Hm," said Captain Skinner. "You meant it the other five times. And still Mocha Dick swims the seas."

"Aye, 'tis easy to capture the white whale—with words," said a little sailor with red whiskers, while all the other sailors laughed.

"Laugh while you may," said Stormalong angrily. "You'll be singing a different tune when the *Dolphin* comes back to port."

"If you are so sure of yourself," said the innkeeper, "write it down here." And he handed Stormalong one of the slates on which he kept accounts.

"Aye, that I will," said Stormalong. Picking up the slate, he wrote in big letters:

ON THIS VOYAGE OF THE DOLPHIN I WILL
CAPTURE MOCHA DICK.

SIGNED, ALFRED BULLTOP STORMALONG

The innkeeper hung the slate up over the fireplace for all to see.

"Aye, mateys!" roared Stormalong. "This time Mocha Dick will meet his doom!"

Stormalong finished his shark soup in one gulp. Then he whistled shrill like the wind in the rigging and left the inn.

The next morning a crowd of people was at the dock to say good-bye to the *Dolphin's* brave crew.

"Good luck, lads!" they shouted. "A short voyage and a greasy one! Fair winds, calm seas! Beware of Mocha Dick!"

"Let Mocha Dick beware, for Alfred Bulltop Stormalong is out to capture him!" said Stormalong, hooting like a foghorn.

"Belay there! Enough of your boasting!"

said Captain Skinner. Then he turned to the first mate and said, "Cast off!"

And a cheer went up as the *Dolphin* caught the wind in her sails and went out to the open sea.

For nine months the *Dolphin* sailed the Pacific Ocean. Wherever she went, there was always a lookout in the crow's nest high on the mast. Every time the lookout spied a whale, he would shout, "Blo-o-ows! Thar she blows!" And the men would jump into rowboats and give chase to the whale.

One day the lookout in the crow's nest called out, "Blo-o-ows! Thar she blows! Whale off the port side! Thar she blows and breaches! And Mocha Dick, at that!"

"Man the boats!" ordered the captain. "Lower away!"

The men set out over the side of the ship in little boats and rowed toward Mocha Dick. Stormalong stood in the stern of his boat, waving his harpoon in the air.

"After him, me hearties!" he shouted. "Faster, lads, faster! There he is now!"

And indeed they could see Mocha Dick's ugly face rising out of the sea. With a rumble and a roar the Great White Whale sent a spout of water high into the air. He was almost as big as the *Dolphin,* and he was the color of sea-foam in the light of a misty moon. As if to warn Stormalong, he opened his mouth and showed his great sharp teeth.

"After him, mateys!" cried Stormalong. "A dead whale or a stove boat!"

With a shout, Stormalong let his harpoon fly at Mocha Dick. It stuck in the whale's back. But Mocha Dick just gave himself a shake and began to swim away. The harpoon was attached to the boat by a long rope, and as Mocha Dick swam along he pulled the boat after him.

"Hold fast, mates!" said Stormalong. "Here we go on a sleigh ride!"

Swoosh! And off they went across the water. Faster and faster swam Mocha

Dick, with the little boat bobbing and bouncing after him. Soon they had left the *Dolphin* far behind.

Suddenly Mocha Dick stopped. He heaved himself into the air, and the rope broke with a snap. The harpoon remained in his back, a little bit of rope flying from it like a flag of victory. He dove below the water, gave a flip of his tail, and the boat overturned. With a splash, Stormalong and his mates tumbled into the sea.

"We are lost!" cried one of the sailors. "Mocha Dick is coming back! He will swallow us all!"

But Mocha Dick just pushed his way close to Stormalong and opened his mouth in a big grin. His body shook as though he were laughing. Then he spouted a stream of water right into Stormalong's face, grinned again and swam away.

"By my boots and breeches!" burst out the little sailor with a lot of red whiskers. "Mocha Dick laughed at Stormalong and spit in his eye!"

All the sailors began to laugh so hard that they almost went to the bottom of the sea. They laughed until their sides ached and then they laughed some more. They were still laughing when the *Dolphin* caught up with them.

"What's so funny?" asked Captain Skinner after the men had climbed on board.

"Mocha Dick laughed at Stormalong and spit in his eye!" said the little sailor.

Captain Skinner began to laugh so hard that the first mate had to grab him by the seat of his pants to keep him from falling overboard. Then the second mate had to grab the first mate to keep him from falling overboard.

"And Stormalong, the man who boasted that he would capture Mocha Dick!" sputtered the captain. "Ho, ho! Ha, ha!" "Ho, ho! Ha, ha! Har, har!" laughed the sailors. "Ho, har!" The little sailor with red whiskers began to sing:

"Stormalong said he'd get Mocha Dick,
    Aye, mates, 'tis no lie,
But the Great White Whale just
    laughed in his face,
    And spit right in his eye.
To my aye, aye, right in Stormalong's
    eye,
To my aye, aye, Mister Stormalong's
    eye."

Stormalong felt so ashamed that he went below and didn't come up on deck for a week.

For three more months, the *Dolphin* sailed the Pacific. Stormalong did his share of the work, but he never hooted like a foghorn or whistled shrill like the wind in the rigging. He hardly said a word.

When the *Dolphin* slid into the harbor at Nantucket, the sailors told everyone what had happened. Soon all Nantucket knew that Mocha Dick had laughed at Stormalong and spit in his eye. Poor Stormalong ran away to the beach where he could be alone. All day long he sat on the beach, sighing and sighing. He sighed so hard that the sea became choppy. At last Stormalong picked himself up and walked to the Sailors' Snug Haven. The first thing he saw when he entered the inn was the slate hanging over the fireplace. And on it were the words:

ON THIS VOYAGE OF THE DOLPHIN I WILL
    CAPTURE MOCHA DICK.
SIGNED, ALFRED BULLTOP STORMALONG

Below these words someone had written:

BUT THE GREAT WHITE WHALE JUST
    LAUGHED AT HIM AND SPIT
    IN HIS EYE.

Stormalong sat down and ordered some shark soup, which he drank from a dory. He topped it off with a keg of New England rum, then went over to Captain Skinner and said, "Captain, I've made my last voyage."

"Surely not, laddie," said Captain Skinner kindly. "Oh, no!"

"Aye, Captain, I'll never go to sea again. I'm going to be a farmer."

"A farmer!" said Captain Skinner. "You'll never be a farmer, my lad. You've got salt water in your veins. Wherever you go, you'll hear the sea calling to you."

"No," said Stormalong. "They don't build ships big enough for me. I can't get the kinks out of my muscles. And if I can't get the kinks out of my muscles, I can't capture Mocha Dick. And if I can't capture Mocha Dick, I'm no whaler. And if I'm no whaler, I'm no sailor. And if I'm no sailor, the sea is no place for me. I'm going off to be a farmer."

"Well, lad," said Captain Skinner, "if you must go, you must. Good luck to you, and may you reach a safe harbor. But you'll be coming back to sea some day. And when you do, old Captain Joshua Skinner will give you a berth."

"Thank you, Captain," said Stormalong. "Good-bye, Captain."

The next morning Stormalong left Nantucket for the mainland. His dufflebag over his shoulder, he walked down the road. In the light of the morning sun his shadow stretched before him, three counties long.

Stormalong rambled about the Hudson Valley, then stepped over the Allegheny Mountains and ambled about the Shenandoah Valley. He took a little side trip to the Cumberland Mountains and spent a day in the Tennessee Valley. He walked along the Ohio River, then over the rolling hills of Indiana and the prairies of Illinois. But not until he crossed the Mississippi River to Missouri did he find what he was looking for.

"Aye," said Stormalong, "this is a country where a full-sized man can get the kinks out of his muscles."

He was in a great forest, where men with axes were chopping down trees. Clong!

Clong! went the axes, and the trees crashed to the ground.

"Are you farmers, mateys?" asked Stormalong in his foghorn voice. All the men stopped their work to look at him.

"I reckon we are," said one of the men.

"That's good," said Stormalong. "I'm new to farming, and I'll thank you to tell me what to do."

"Right now we're clearing away the forest so we can grow our crops," he said.

Stormalong borrowed the biggest ax they had, then said, "Now mates, just sit down in the shade and rest a while. I mean to do some plain and fancy chopping to get the kinks out of my muscles."

Stormalong rolled up his sleeves and went to work. By nightfall he had cleared enough land for a hundred farms.

"Who are you?" asked the astonished farmers.

"Alfred Bulltop Stormalong is the name, mateys," said Stormalong. "They don't make ships big enough for me, so I can't get the kinks out of my muscles. If I can't get the kinks out of my muscles, I can't capture Mocha Dick. And if I can't capture Mocha Dick, I'm no whaler. And if I'm no whaler, then I'm no sailor. And if I'm no sailor, my place is on shore. So I came out here to be a farmer, and I'll thank you to tell me just what to do and how to do it."

And he hooted like a foghorn and whistled shrill like the wind in the rigging.

"The next thing is to clear out the stumps and stones and start planting," said the farmers. "But first you'd better build yourself a cabin to live in."

"A cabin it is, me hearties," said Stormalong. By the time the moon came out he had built himself a cabin.

The next morning Stormalong got up before the sun and started to plow. He didn't use a horse. He just pushed the plow along himself, while stones and stumps flew in all directions.

"Where's your horse?" asked the farmers, more astonished than ever. "We never heard tell of plowing without a horse, a mule or at least a team of oxen." They shook their heads.

"Didn't know you were supposed to have one," said Stormalong. "But no harm done. If you'll just toss these rocks and stumps into a pile, I'll finish this little job."

By evening, Stormalong had plowed enough land for a hundred farms.

"What's next, me hearties?" he asked. "For I've got the kinks out of my muscles and I'm rarin' to go."

"Plant the seed," said the farmers.

When the farmers got up the next morning, they found Stormalong stretched out under a tree.

"Glad you're up," he said. "I've planted all the seed. Nothing to it. What do I do now?"

"Just wait for the crops to start growing," said the farmers. "Unless you have some cows or chickens or pigs to look after."

"I can't look after cows or chickens or pigs," said Stormalong. "I'm too big for 'em. But I don't like this idea of waiting. I'll get kinks in my muscles."

It was hard for Stormalong to sit around doing nothing. At night he could hear the wind blowing through the trees of the forest. The leaves went hiss, swish, like the sound of the sea. The branches creaked like the rigging of a ship. Stormalong dreamt that he was a sailor again.

In the daytime Stormalong would climb the tallest tree in the forest. He would gaze out over the rolling hills, which looked like the waves of the sea. The tree swayed in the wind, and Stormalong imagined he was in the crow's nest of the *Dolphin*, keeping a sharp lookout for whales.

A big cloud floated past in the sky. To Stormalong it looked like Mocha Dick.

"Blo-o-ows!" he shouted. "Thar she blows! Whale off the starboard side! Thar she blows and breaches! A dead whale or a stove boat!"

Then one day a storm came up. The sky was as black as the bottom of a well. Lightning flashed, thunder roared, while the wind went howling through the forest like a madman.

"Hooray, a storm!" shouted Stormalong to the farmers. "Now I can get the kinks out of my muscles. Avast there, mateys! Storm ahead! All hands on deck!"

All of a sudden one of the farmers stuck his head out of the window of his cabin and looked at Stormalong.

"What's all the fuss?" he asked.

"Storm!" said Stormalong. "Pipe all hands on deck! What do farmers do in a storm, matey?"

"Let 'er storm," said the farmer. "Nothing else to do."

Stormalong was so surprised he couldn't say anything. He just stood there, the lightning flashing around his head, the rain dripping down his shoulders.

"I've had enough of this," he said at last. "I can't sit around and do nothing when there's a storm. I guess I just wasn't cut out to be a farmer."

He went to his cabin, threw his dufflebag over his shoulder, then waved good-bye to the farmers.

"So long," he said. "I'm going west to be a cowboy."

Stormalong rambled about the dusty plains of Texas, then ambled over to Oklahoma. He took a side trip to the Rocky Mountains and followed the Sweetwater River into Wyoming. He walked across the salt flats of Utah and the plateau of Arizona, but not until he came to New Mexico did he find what he was looking for.

"Aye," he said, "this is a country where a full-sized man can get the kinks out of his muscles."

Stormalong went into a store to buy himself a cowboy outfit.

"Matey," he said to the storekeeper, "I want a ten-gallon hat, chaps, a checkered shirt, Spanish boots with pointed toes, silver spurs and a pretty bandanna."

The storekeeper looked Stormalong up and down.

"Stranger," he said, "you're the biggest galoot that ever blew into this man's town. I can sell you what you want, but it will have to be made special."

It took eight weeks to make Stormalong's cowboy outfit. While he was waiting, Stormalong learned how to use a lariat. With his lariat Stormalong lassoed the wild mustangs that roamed the plains. A mustang was a little too small for Stormalong, but it was the biggest horse he could get.

Then Stormalong got a job as a cowboy on the Triple Star Ranch.

"Mateys," he said, "I've never been a cowboy before, and I'll thank you to tell me what to do."

"It's roundup time, pardner," said the cowboys. "First thing to do is round up the steers."

"Just sit down and rest yourself, me hearties," said Stormalong. "I'll round 'em up, just to get the kinks out of my muscles."

When evening came, Stormalong had rounded up all the steers.

"Who are you?" asked the astonished cowboys.

"Alfred Bulltop Stormalong is the name," answered Stormalong. "They don't make ships big enough for me, so I can't get the kinks out of my muscles. If I can't get the kinks out of my muscles, I can't capture Mocha Dick. And if I can't capture Mocha Dick, I'm no whaler. And if I'm no whaler, then I'm no sailor. And if I'm no sailor, my place is on shore. I tried to be a farmer, but I couldn't. So I came out here to be a cowboy, and I'll thank you to tell me what to do."

"The next thing to do is brand the steers," said the cowboys.

Stormalong got up before the sun the next morning and started to brand the steers. By the time the cowboys got up all the steers had been branded.

"What's next, me hearties?" asked Stormalong. "For I've got the kinks out of my muscles and I'm rarin' to go."

"Just ride around and keep an eye on the steers. We call it riding herd," they said.

Stormalong rode herd with the other cowboys. At night they sat around the campfire, playing the guitar and singing songs. Stormalong had a guitar made special, and when he played it the mountains would echo for miles around.

Stormalong soon began to get tired of being a cowboy. There wasn't enough to do, and he was getting kinks in his muscles. At night he would wake up and look around. In the moonlight the plain stretched out like a calm sea, while the mountains stood up like islands.

"Avast, mateys!" shouted Stormalong. "We're becalmed! More sail, more sail! Break out more sail for we must capture Mocha Dick, the Great White Whale!"

One day a huge black cloud filled the sky and the rain began. Lightning flashed, thunder boomed, and the wind raced across the plain like wild horses.

Stormalong waved his ten-gallon hat in the air and shouted, "All hands on deck!

Storm blowing up! All hands on deck!" And he hooted like a foghorn and whistled shrill like the wind in the rigging.

"What's the rumpus, pardner?" asked one of the cowboys.

"Storm!" said Stormalong. "What do cowboys do in a storm, matey? She's a-rippin' and a-snortin'."

"Let 'er rip and snort," said the cowboy. "Nothing else to do about it."

Stormalong sat down on a big rock. The wind howled around him, and the water dripped off his hat like a waterfall.

"I just can't sit around and do nothing when there's a storm," he said. "I guess I'm no more a cowboy than I was a farmer."

Stormalong seemed to hear the voice of Captain Skinner saying, "Aye, lad, you'll never be able to give up the sea. You've got salt water in your veins. Wherever you go, you'll hear the sea calling to you."

"You were right, Captain Skinner!" shouted Stormalong. "Maybe the ships are too small for a full-sized man. Maybe I'll get kinks in my muscles and won't be able to capture Mocha Dick. Maybe I'm no whaler, and maybe I'm no sailor. But I'll go back to sea if I have to be a cabin boy, for I'll never be happy anywhere else."

Stormalong turned his mustang loose on the plains. He threw his dufflebag over one shoulder and slung his guitar over the other.

"So long, mateys," he said to the cowboys. Then he started walking east, toward Nantucket and the sea.

It was a wet, misty morning when Stormalong got to Nantucket. For a long time he stood on a hill, sniffing in the salt sea air. He could see the harbor, with masts of ships sticking up into the sky. When he caught sight of the waves breaking on the shore, he hooted like a foghorn and whistled shrill like the wind in the rigging.

"The sea is the place for me," he said.

"And now for the Sailors' Snug Haven and some of that good shark soup."

When Stormalong got to the Sailors' Snug Haven he wiped the mist from his eyes and looked around. Everything was the same as it had been. Over the fireplace hung the slate with these words on it:

ON THIS VOYAGE OF THE DOLPHIN I WILL CAPTURE MOCHA DICK.

SIGNED, ALFRED BULLTOP STORMALONG

BUT THE GREAT WHITE WHALE JUST LAUGHED AT HIM AND SPIT IN HIS EYE.

"A cowboy in Nantucket!" said a voice behind him. "You're a long way from home, matey."

Stormalong turned around. There sat Captain Skinner.

"The sea is my home, Captain," said Stormalong, hooting like a foghorn and whistling shrill like the wind in the rigging.

"By my boots and breeches!" said the captain. "It's Stormalong, for there's no one else who can hoot like a foghorn and whistle shrill like the wind in the rigging."

"Aye," said Stormalong, "Alfred Bulltop Stormalong it is, and I'll never leave the sea again."

"I knew you'd be back, lad," said Captain Skinner. "Now sit down beside me and tell me your adventures."

Stormalong ordered some shark soup, which he drank from a dory. He told Captain Skinner all his adventures, and when he had finished he said, "And now, Captain, will you give me my old berth on the *Dolphin*?"

"Aye, laddie. But you used to complain that the *Dolphin* was too small for you. Well, she's still the same size, but you're bigger than ever."

"She'll be big enough for me," said Stormalong. "I'll go to sea in a washtub if I can't get anything else."

"Spoken like a true seaman!" laughed

Captain Skinner. "Well, I must leave you now. But we sail at six tomorrow morning. Be sure that you're on time."

When Captain Skinner stood up Stormalong saw that one of his legs was gone. In its place was a wooden pegleg.

"Your leg, Captain!" said Stormalong. "What happened?"

"It was bit off by Mocha Dick on my last voyage. The white whale bit off my leg and sent two of my crew to the bottom of the sea."

"Captain," cried Stormalong. "I won't rest until I've captured Mocha Dick."

"No, lad," said the captain. "Never again will I battle Mocha Dick. He's more fearful than ever. I'll lose no more of my men to the monster."

When Stormalong came on board the *Dolphin* the next morning, the crew began to laugh. He was still wearing his cowboy outfit, and he was so bowlegged from riding the mustangs that a ship could have sailed between his legs.

"Avast there, Stormalong!" said Captain Skinner. "Get below and put on some proper duds. Stormalong or no Stormalong, I'll have no cowboys on my ship."

"Captain, I'd like to do as you say, but this cowboy outfit was made special, and I'm going to keep on wearing it."

Captain Skinner grew red in the face.

"I'm captain of this ship, and you'll obey my orders!" he roared.

"Captain," said Stormalong, "I know you're the captain. But captain or no captain, I'm going to wear my cowboy outfit."

Stormalong began to hop up and down, so that the *Dolphin* rocked in the water.

"Belay there," shouted the sailors. "Sit down, you're rocking the boat!"

"Stop, Stormalong! You'll sink the ship!" cried the captain.

Stormalong kept hopping up and down.

"I won't stop until you say it's all right for me to wear my cowboy outfit," he said. "And you can lay to that!"

"Wear what you like, you stubborn walrus!" said the captain, and Stormalong stopped hopping up and down.

A crowd had gathered on shore to say good-bye to Captain Skinner and his crew.

"Good luck!" they called. "A short voyage and a greasy one!"

Captain Skinner was so angry that he didn't want to say good-bye to anyone.

"Cast off!" he bellowed.

The *Dolphin* was raring to go. She took the wind in her sails and made for the open sea.

It was not long before the lookout in the crow's nest sang out, "Blo-o-ows! Thar she blows! Whale off the port side!"

"Yippee!" shouted Stormalong, like a cowboy. Still dressed in his cowboy outfit, he jumped into his boat. It made Captain Skinner angry to see a cowboy in a whaling boat. But he didn't say anything. He was afraid Stormalong would start hopping up and down again.

Stormalong soon showed that he could still catch whales.

"By the Great Horn Spoon," said Captain Skinner to himself, "Stormalong is a real sailorman, even if he does dress like a cowboy."

Then one day the lookout in the crow's nest shouted, "Blo-o-ows! Thar she blows and breaches! And Mocha Dick, at that! It's the Great White Whale, mates!"

"All hands aloft!" ordered Captain Skinner. "Break out more sail. We're going to get away from these waters as fast as we can. I'll not battle Mocha Dick again."

"Captain," said Stormalong, "are you really going to let it be said that a Nantucket whaler ran away from a whale?"

"Mocha Dick is no ordinary whale. He is a monster, and I'll lose no more of my men to him," said Captain Skinner.

"Let me go after him," begged Stormalong. "He'll not laugh at me this time."

"Stow your chatter and help loose the sails," Captain Skinner bellowed. "I'm the captain of the *Dolphin*, Mr. Stormalong, and I forbid you to go after Mocha Dick. Now get aloft before I have you put in irons!"

But just then the lookout in the crow's nest gave a terrible cry.

"Mocha Dick is coming after us! He's going to bump the ship!"

Captain Skinner ran to the rail. There was Mocha Dick, roaring and snorting and plunging. He rushed straight at the *Dolphin*, and bump! the stern of the ship rose into the air.

"We are lost!" cried the sailors. "Mocha Dick will sink the ship. We are lost!"

"Not yet, mateys!" said Stormalong.

And leaping over the rail, he landed smack on Mocha Dick's back.

"Yippee!" shouted Stormalong, and he began to ride Mocha Dick like a cowboy riding a bucking broncho. He hung on with one hand and waved his ten-gallon hat with the other.

Mocha Dick thrashed about, trying to throw Stormalong off his back. Stormalong only laughed and waved his hat again.

"Ride him, cowboy!" cheered the sailors. "Ride him, Stormalong!"

Snorting with rage, the white whale leaped into the air. Then he dove deep under the water, trying to drown Stormalong. But Stormalong took a deep breath and held his nose. Mocha Dick heaved himself into the air again. He tossed and twisted and turned. Then he began to swim furiously about. He went zig-zagging

41

across the ocean so fast that the zigs and the zags became all mixed up. Captain Skinner and his crew grew dizzy watching them.

"Ride him, cowboy!" they yelled. "Ride him, Stormalong!"

"Yippee! Wahoo!" shouted Stormalong, hooting like a foghorn and whistling shrill like the wind in the rigging.

For three days Stormalong rode Mocha Dick. Once when he passed close to the ship he called, "I'm getting hungry, mates. How about coffee and a sandwich?"

The cook made him a washtub full of coffee and a sandwich three yards long. When Stormalong passed by again, a sailor stood on the jib boom and handed them to Stormalong.

On the third day Mocha Dick's strength was almost gone. But he made one great try to throw Stormalong off his back. He dove deep under the water. He turned somersaults. He tossed and twisted and rolled from side to side. He went around in circles, like a dog chasing his tail. Around and around he went, until the water foamed like milk. He leaped high into the air and came down with a tremendous splash. Then a shudder ran through his body and he was still.

"Hooray!" shouted the sailors. "Hooray for Stormalong!"

"This is the end of the Great White Whale," said a big sailor with a crooked nose. "He just wore himself out."

"No," said the little sailor with red whiskers, "he died of a broken heart."

"Hooray!" shouted the sailors again and again. "Hooray for Stormalong!"

"Aye, lads, you may well cheer," said Captain Skinner. "Stormalong has done a great thing. No more will Mocha Dick send honest seamen to their death."

Then the *Dolphin* dropped anchor beside the huge body of the white whale. The sailors cut him up and boiled the blubber for the sperm oil. In a few days the job was done, and they set sail for Nantucket.

"We're loaded to the hatches with oil. We'll all be rich," said Captain Skinner. He felt so happy that he danced a hornpipe across the deck. "Tappy, tappy, tap," went his pegleg.

Stormalong sat down on a hatch and rested his feet on the jib boom. He picked up his guitar and began to sing loud and gay.

"Twang, twang! Plunk, plunk! Plunkety, twang!" went the guitar. The deep notes sounded like a pipe organ and the high notes were as sweet as violins. Stormalong sang "Home on the Range" and "Bury Me Not on the Lone Prairie."

The crew came back with "Blow the Man Down." Stormalong topped them with "As I Walked out in the Streets of Laredo." Then they all chimed in with "Whiskey for My Johnnie."

The sound of their music was so sweet that all the fish lifted their heads out of the water to listen. Sea gulls flew after the ship, beating their wings in time to the music. All the way across the ocean the fish followed the *Dolphin*. In schools and shoals and droves they came, and the New England fishermen caught the greatest catch of seafish that was ever caught in all history.

When the *Dolphin* got into Nantucket, the crew was singing, each man jack louder than the next:

"Then give me a whaleman,
      wherever he be,
Who fears not a fish that can swim
      the salt sea;
Then give me a tight ship,
      and under snug sail,
And last lay me 'side the noble
      sperm whale;
   In the Indian Ocean,
   Or Pacific Ocean,
   No matter *what* ocean;
   Pull ahead, yo heave O!"

When the crowd at the dock heard about Mocha Dick they gave such a shout that the clouds scattered clear out of the sky.

Stormalong waved to the crowd and hurried to the Sailors' Snug Haven. He picked up the slate on which were the words:

ON THIS VOYAGE OF THE DOLPHIN I WILL CAPTURE MOCHA DICK.

SIGNED, ALFRED BULLTOP STORMALONG

BUT THE GREAT WHITE WHALE JUST LAUGHED AT HIM AND SPIT IN HIS EYE.

"No more he doesn't!" shouted Stormalong. He smashed the slate into a thousand pieces. "Mateys," he roared, "I captured Mocha Dick. If I captured Mocha Dick, I'm a whaler. And if I'm a whaler, then I'm a sailor. And if I'm a sailor, my place is on the sea. And the sea is no place for a cowboy. I'll never wear my cowboy outfit again, even though it was made special. And you can lay to that!"

Then Stormalong sat down and ate twelve dozen oysters, fifty-two codfish balls, sixty-seven lobsters, ten pounds of whale steak, a dory full of shark soup and another full of clam chowder. For dessert he had a New England boiled dinner, three or four apple pies and a nibble or two of maple-sugar candy. He washed it all down with a keg of New England rum, then hooted like a foghorn and whistled shrill like the wind in the rigging.

"Hooray for Old Stormalong!" shouted all the crew. "Hooray, hooray, hooray!"

ONAWANDAH

*Old Becky said
the ragged Indian boy was a spy.
"Send him away," she cried,
"or harm will come of it.
We shall all be scalped"*

<small>LOUISA M. ALCOTT</small>

Long ago, when Indians haunted the great forests, and every settlement had its fort for the protection of the inhabitants, in one of the towns on the Connecticut River lived Parson Bain and his little son and daughter. The wife and mother was dead; but an old servant took care of them, and did her best to make Reuben and Eunice good children. Her direst threat, when they were naughty, was, "The Indians will come and fetch you, if you don't behave." So they grew up in great fear of the red men. Even the friendly Indians, who sometimes came for food or powder, were regarded with suspicion by the people. No man went to work without his gun nearby. On Sundays, when they trudged to the rude meeting house, all carried the trusty rifle on the shoulder.

One autumn night, when the first heavy rains were falling and a cold wind whistled through the valley, a knock came at the minister's door and, opening it, he found an Indian boy, ragged, hungry and footsore, who begged for food and shelter. In his broken way, he told how he had fallen ill and been left to die by enemies who had taken him from his own people, months before; how he had wandered for days till almost sinking; and that he had come now to ask for help, led by the hospitable light in the parsonage window.

"Send him away, Master, or harm will come of it. He is a spy, and we shall all be scalped by the murdering Injuns who are waiting in the wood," said old Becky, harshly, while little Eunice hid in the old servant's ample skirts and twelve-year-old Reuben laid his hand on his crossbow, ready to defend his sister if need be.

But the good man drew the poor lad in, saying, with his friendly smile, "Shall not a Christian be as hospitable as a godless savage? Come in, child, and be fed; you sorely need rest and shelter."

Leaving his face to express the gratitude he had no words to tell, the boy sat by the comfortable fire and ate like a famished wolf, while Becky muttered her forebodings and the children eyed the dark youth at a safe distance. Something in his pinched face, wounded foot and eyes full of dumb pain and patience, touched the little girl's tender heart, and, yielding to a pitiful impulse, she brought her own basin of new milk and, setting it beside the stranger, ran to hide behind her father.

"That was well done, little daughter. Thou shalt love thine enemies and share thy bread with the needy. See, he is smiling; and he wishes us to be his friends."

But Eunice ventured no more that night and quaked in her little bed at the thought of the strange boy sleeping on a blanket before the fire below. Reuben hid his fears better and resolved to watch while others slept, but was off as soon as his curly head touched the pillow.

Next day, neighbors came to see the waif, and one and all advised sending him away as soon as possible, since he was doubtless a spy, as Becky said.

"When he is well, he may go wherever he will; but while he is too lame to walk and worn out with weariness, I will harbor him. He cannot feign suffering and starvation like this. I shall do my duty and leave the consequences to the Lord," answered the parson, with such pious firmness that the neighbors said no more.

But they kept a close watch upon Onawandah when he went among them, silent and submissive, but with the proud air of a captive prince, and sometimes a fierce flash in his black eyes when the other lads taunted him with his red skin. He was very lame for weeks, and could only sit in the sun, weaving pretty baskets for Eunice and shaping bows and arrows for Reuben. The children were soon his friends, for with them he was always gentle, trying in his soft language and expressive gestures to show his goodwill and gratitude.

When he was able to walk, he taught Reuben to shoot and trap the wild creatures of the wood, to find fish where others failed and to guide himself in the wilderness by star and sun, wind and water. To Eunice he brought little offerings of bark and feathers; taught her to make moccasins of skin, belts of shells or pouches gay with porcupine quills and colored grass. He would not work for old Becky—who plainly showed her distrust—saying, "A brave does not grind corn and bring wood; that is squaw's work. Onawandah will hunt and fish and fight for you, but no more." And even the request of the parson could not win obedience in this, though the boy would have died for the good man.

"We cannot tame an eagle as we can a barnyard fowl. Let him remember only kindness of us, and so we turn a foe into a friend," said Parson Bain, stroking the sleek, dark head, that always bowed before him with a docile reverence shown to no other living creature.

Winter came, and the settlers fared hardly through the long months when the drifts rose to the eaves of their low cabins, and the stores, carefully harvested, failed to supply even their simple wants. But the minister's family never lacked wild meat, for Onawandah proved himself a better hunter than any man in the town, and the boy of sixteen led the way on his snowshoes when they went to track a bear to its den, chase the deer for miles or shoot the wolves that howled about their homes.

But he never joined in their games and sat apart when the young folk made merry as if he scorned such childish pastimes and longed to be a man in all things. Why he stayed when he was well again, no one could tell, unless he waited for spring to make his way to his own people. But Reuben and Eunice rejoiced to keep him, for while he taught them many things, he was their pupil also, learning English rapidly and proving himself a very affectionate and devoted friend and servant.

"Be of good cheer, little daughter; I shall be gone but three days, and our brave Onawandah will guard you well," said the parson, one April morning, as he mounted his horse to visit a distant settlement where the bitter winter had brought sickness and death to more than one household.

The boy showed his white teeth in a bright smile as he stood beside the children, while Becky croaked, with a shake of the head, "I hope you mayn't find you've warmed a viper in your bosom, Master."

Two days later, it seemed as if Becky was a true prophet, and that the confiding minister had been terribly deceived; for Onawandah went away to hunt, and that night the awful war whoop woke the sleeping villagers to find their houses burning, while the hidden Indians shot at them by the light of the fires. In terror and confusion the whites flew to the fort; and, while the men fought bravely, the women held blankets to catch arrows and bullets, or bound up the hurts of their defenders.

It was all over by daylight, and the red men sped away up the river with several prisoners and such booty as they could plunder from the deserted houses. Not till all fear of a return of their enemies was over did the poor people venture to leave the fort and seek their ruined homes. Then it was discovered that Becky and the parson's children were gone.

Suddenly the smothered voice of Becky was heard by a party of visitors, calling dolefully. "I am here, betwixt the beds. Pull me out, neighbors, for I am half dead with fright and smothering."

The old woman was quickly extricated from her hiding-place, and with much energy declared that she had seen Onawandah, disguised with war paint, among the Indians, and that he had torn away the children from her arms.

"He chose his time well, when they were defenseless, dear lambs! Spite of all my warnings, Master trusted him, and this is the thanks we get. Oh, my poor Master!"

Then the sound of a horse's hoofs was heard and the parson came down the hilly road like one riding for his life. He had seen the smoke afar off, guessed the sad truth and hurried on to find his home in ruins and to learn by his first glance at the faces around him that his children were gone.

When he had heard all there was to tell, he sat down upon his door-stone with his head in his hands, praying for strength to bear a grief too deep for words. The wounded and weary men tried to comfort him with hope, and the women wept with him as they hugged their own babies closer to their hearts.

Suddenly a stir went through the mournful group as Onawandah came from the wood with a young deer upon his shoulders, and amazement in his face as he saw the desolation before him. Dropping his burden, he stood an instant looking with eyes that kindled fiercely; then he came bounding toward them, undaunted by the hatred, suspicion and surprise plainly written on the countenances before him. He asked but one question, "The boy? the little squaw?—where gone?"

His answer was a rough one, for the men seized him and poured forth the tale, heaping reproaches upon him for such treachery. He bore it all in proud silence till they pointed to the poor father whose dumb sorrow was more eloquent than all their wrath. Onawandah looked at him, and the fire died out of his eyes as if quenched by the tears he would not shed. Shaking off the hands that held him, he went to his good friend, saying with passionate earnestness, "Onawandah is not traitor! Onawandah remembers. Onawandah grateful! You believe?"

The poor parson looked up at him and could not doubt his truth, for genuine love and sorrow ennobled the dark face, and he had never known the boy to lie.

"I believe and trust you still, but others will not. Go, you are no longer safe here, and I have no home to offer you," said the parson sadly, feeling that he cared for none unless his children were restored to him.

"Onawandah goes; but he comes again to bring the boy, the little squaw."

Few words, but they were so solemnly spoken that the most unbelieving were impressed, for the youth laid one hand on the gray head bowed before him and lifted the other toward heaven as if calling the Great Spirit to hear his vow.

A relenting murmur went through the crowd, but the boy paid no heed as he turned away, and with no arms but his hunting knife and bow, no food but such as he could find, no guide but the sun by day, the stars by night, plunged into the pathless forest and was gone.

Then the people drew a long breath and muttered to one another, "He will never do it, yet he is a brave lad for his years."

"Only a shift to get off with a whole skin, I warrant you," added Becky, sourly.

The parson alone believed and hoped, though weeks and months went by, and his children did not come.

Meantime, Reuben and Eunice were far away in an Indian camp, resting as best they could after the long journey that followed that dreadful night. Their captors were not cruel to them, for Reuben was a stout fellow and, thanks to Onawandah,

could hold his own with the boys who would have tormented him if he had been feeble or cowardly. Eunice also was a hardy creature for her years, and when her first fright and fatigue were over, made herself useful among the squaws.

Life in a wigwam was not a life of ease, and fortunately the children were accustomed to simple habits and the hardships that all endured in those early times. But they mourned for home till their young faces were pathetic with the longing, and their pillows of dry leaves were often wet with tears in the night. Their clothes grew ragged, their hair unkempt, their faces tanned by sun and wind. Scanty food and exposure to all weathers tried the strength of their bodies, and uncertainty as to their fate saddened their spirits; yet they bore up bravely and said their prayers faithfully, sure that God would bring them home to father in His own good time.

One day, when Reuben was snaring birds in the wood, he heard the cry of a quail and followed it deeper and deeper into the forest till it ceased, and, with a sudden rustle, Onawandah rose up from the brakes, his finger on his lips to prevent any exclamation that might betray him to other ears and eyes.

"I come for you and little Laraka," (the name he gave Eunice, meaning "Wild Rose"). "I take you home. Not know me yet. Go and wait."

He spoke low and fast; but the joy in his face told how glad he was to find the boy after his long search, and Reuben clung to him, trying not to disgrace himself by crying like a girl in his surprise and delight.

Lying hidden in the tall brakes they talked in whispers while one told of the capture and the other of a plan to escape; for, though a friendly tribe, these Indians were not Onawandah's people and they must not suspect that he knew the children, else they might be separated at once.

"Little squaw betray me. You watch her. Tell her not to cry out, not speak me any time. When I say come, we go—fast—in the night. Not ready yet."

These were the orders Reuben received, and, when he could compose himself, he went back to tell the good news to Eunice.

Fear had taught her self-control, and the poor child stood the test well, working off her relief and rapture by pounding corn in the stone mortar till her little hands were blistered and her arms ached for hours afterward.

Not till the next day did Onawandah make his appearance, and then he came limping into the village, weary, lame and half-starved after his long wandering in the wilderness. He was kindly welcomed and his story believed, for he told only the first part and said nothing of his life among the white men. He hardly glanced at the children when they were pointed out to him by their captors and scowled at poor Eunice, who forgot her part in her joy and smiled as she met the dark eyes that till now had always looked kindly at her. A touch from Reuben warned her, and she was glad to hide her confusion by shaking her long hair over her face.

Onawandah took no further notice of them, but seemed to be very lame with the old wound in his foot, which prevented his being obliged to hunt with the men. He was resting and slowly gathering strength for the hard task he had set himself. The children understood, but the suspense proved too much for little Eunice, and she pined with impatience to be gone. She lost appetite and color and cast such appealing glances at Onawandah that he could not seem quite indifferent and gave her a soft word now and then or did such acts of kindness as he could perform unsuspected. When she lay awake at night thinking of home, a cricket would chirp outside the wigwam and a hand slip in a leaf full of berries or a bark-cup of fresh water for the feverish little mouth. Sometimes it was only a caress or a whisper of encouragement that reassured the childish heart and sent her to sleep with a comfortable sense of love and protection, like a sheltering wing over a motherless bird.

Reuben stood it better and entered heartily into the excitement of the plot, for he had grown tall and strong in these trying months and felt that he must prove himself a man to sustain and defend his sister. Quietly he put away each day a bit of dried meat, a handful of parched corn or a well-sharpened arrowhead, as provision for the journey, while Onawandah seemed to be amusing himself with making moccasins and a little vest of deerskin for an Indian child about the age of Eunice.

At last, in the early autumn, all the men went off on the warpath, leaving only boys and women behind. Then Onawandah's eyes began to kindle, and Reuben's heart to beat fast, for both felt that their time for escape had come.

All was ready, and one moonless night two trembling children crept out to follow the tall shadow that flitted noiselessly before them into the darkness of the wood. Not a broken twig, a careless step or a whispered word betrayed them, and they vanished as swiftly and silently as hunted deer flying for their lives.

Till dawn they hurried on, Onawandah carrying Eunice, whose strength soon failed, and Reuben manfully shouldering the hatchet and the pouch of food. At sunrise they hid in a thicket by a spring and rested while waiting for the friendly night to come again. Then they pushed on, and fear gave wings to their feet so that by another morning they were far enough away to venture to travel more slowly and sleep at night.

If the children had learned to love and trust the Indian boy in happier times, they adored him now and came to regard him as an earthly Providence, so faithful, brave and tender was he. He never seemed to sleep, ate the poorest morsels or went without any food when provisions failed; let no danger daunt him, no hardship wring complaint from him; but went on through the wild forest, led by guides invisible to them, till they began to hope that home was near.

Twice he saved their lives. Once, when he went in search of food, leaving Reuben to guard his sister, the children, being very hungry, ignorantly ate some poisonous berries which looked like wild cherries and were deliciously sweet. The boy generously gave most of them to Eunice and soon was terror-stricken to see her grow pale and cold and deathly ill. Not knowing what to do, he could only rub her hands and call wildly for Onawandah.

The name echoed through the silent wood, and, though far away, the keen ear of the Indian heard it, his fleet feet brought him back in time, and his knowledge of wild roots and herbs made it possible to save the child. Within instants he was able to locate the plant that would counteract the poison.

"Eat, eat, while I make drink. All safe now," cried Onawandah as he came leaping toward them, his hands full of green leaves and his dark face shining with joy.

The boy was soon relieved, but for hours they hung over the girl, who suffered sadly till she grew unconscious and lay as if dead. Reuben's courage failed then, and he cried bitterly, thinking how hard it would be to leave the dear little creature under the pines and go home alone to Father. Even Onawandah lost hope for a while and sat like a bronze statue of despair.

Suddenly he rose, stretched his arms to the west where the sun was setting splendidly and in his own musical language prayed to the Great Spirit. The Christian boy fell upon his knees, feeling that the only help was in the Father Who saw and heard them even in the wilderness. Both were comforted, and when they turned to Eunice there was a faint tinge of color on the pale cheeks as if the evening red kissed her, the look of pain was gone and she slept quietly.

"He hears! He hears!" cried Onawandah, and for the first time Reuben saw tears in his keen eyes as the Indian boy turned his face to the sky full of gratitude.

All night, Eunice lay peacefully sleeping, and the moon lighted Onawandah's lonely watch, for Reuben was worn out with suspense and slept beside his sister.

In the morning she was safe, and great was the rejoicing; but for two days the little invalid was not allowed to continue the journey, much as they longed to hurry on. It was a pretty sight, the bed of hemlock boughs spread under a green tent of woven branches, and on the pillow of moss the pale child watching the flicker of sunshine through the leaves, listening to the babble of a brook close by or sleeping tranquilly, lulled by the murmur of the pines. She was so patient, loving and grateful that it was a pleasure to serve her, and both the lads were faithful nurses.

Onawandah cooked birds for her to eat and made a pleasant drink of the wild raspberry leaves to quench her thirst. Reuben snared rabbits that she might have nourishing food and longed to shoot a deer for provisions that she might not suffer hunger again on their journey. This boyish desire led him deeper in the wood than it was wise for him to go alone, for it was near nightfall and wild creatures haunted the forest in those days. The fire, which Onawandah kept constantly burning, guarded their little camp where Eunice lay; but Reuben, with no weapon but his bow and hunting knife, was beyond this protection when he at last gave up his vain hunt and turned homeward. Suddenly, the sound of stealthy steps startled him, but he could see nothing through the dusk at first and hurried on, fearing that some treacherous Indian was following him. Then he remembered his sister and resolved not to betray her resting place if he could help it, for he had learned courage of Onawandah and longed to be as brave and generous as his dusky hero.

So he paused to watch and wait, and soon saw the gleam of two fiery eyes, not behind, but above him, in a tree. Then he knew that it was an "Indian devil," as they called a species of fierce wildcat that lurked in the thickets and sprang on its prey like a small tiger.

"If I could only kill it alone, how proud Onawandah would be of me," thought Reuben, burning for the good opinion of his friend.

It would have been wiser to hurry on and give the beast no time to spring; but the boy was overbold and, fitting an arrow to the string, aimed at the bright eyeball and let fly. A sharp snarl showed that some harm was done, and, rather daunted by the savage sound, Reuben raced away, meaning to come back next day for the prize he hoped he had secured.

But soon he heard the creature bounding after him, and he uttered one ringing shout for help, feeling too late that he had been foolhardy. Fortunately he was nearer camp than he thought. Onawandah heard him and was there in time to receive the wildcat as, mad with the pain of the wound, it sprang at Reuben. There was no time for words, and the boy could only watch in breathless interest and anxiety the fight which went on between the brute and the Indian.

It was sharp but short, for Onawandah had his knife, and as soon as he could get the snarling, struggling beast down, he killed it with a skillful stroke. But not before it had torn and bitten him more dangerously than he knew, for the dusk hid the wounds and excitement kept him from feeling them at first. Reuben thanked him heartily and accepted his few words of warning with docility; then both hurried back to Eunice, who till next day knew nothing of her brother's danger.

Onawandah made light of his scratches, as he called them, got their supper and sent Reuben early to bed, for tomorrow they were to start again.

Excited by his adventure, the boy slept lightly and waking in the night saw by the flicker of the fire Onawandah binding up a deep wound in his breast with wet moss and his own belt. A stifled groan betrayed how much he suffered; but when Reuben went to him, he would accept no help, said it was nothing and sent him back to bed, preferring to endure the pain in stern silence with true Indian pride.

Next morning, they set out and pushed on as fast as Eunice's strength allowed. But it was evident that Onawandah suffered much, though he would not rest, forbade the children to speak of his wounds and pressed on with feverish haste as if he feared that his strength might not hold out. Reuben watched him anxiously, for there was a look in his face that troubled the boy and filled him with alarm as well as with remorse and love. Eunice would not let him carry her as before, but trudged bravely behind him, though her feet ached and her breath often failed as she tried to keep up; and both children did all they could to comfort and sustain their friend.

In three days they reached the river and, as if Heaven helped them in their greatest need, found a canoe left by some hunter near the shore. In they sprang and let the swift current bear them along, Eunice kneeling in the bow like a little figurehead of Hope, Reuben steering with his paddle and Onawandah sitting with arms tightly folded over his breast as if to control the sharp anguish of the neglected wound. He knew that it was past help now and only cared to see the children safe.

Hour after hour they floated down the great river, looking eagerly for signs of home, and when at last they entered the familiar valley, while the little girl cried for joy and the boy paddled as he had never done before, Onawandah sat erect with his haggard eyes fixed on the dim distance and sang his death song in a clear, strong voice—though every breath was pain—bent on dying like a brave.

At last they saw the smoke from the cabins on the hillside and, hastily mooring the canoe, all sprang out, eager to be at home after their long and perilous wandering. But as his foot touched the land, Onawandah felt that he could do no more and stretching his arms toward the parsonage, the windows of which glimmered as hospitably as they had done when he first saw them, he said, with a pathetic sort of triumph in his broken voice, "Go. I cannot.—Tell the good father, Onawandah not lie, not forget. He keep his promise."

Then he dropped upon the grass and lay as if dead while Reuben, bidding Eunice keep watch, ran as fast as his tired legs could carry him to bring help.

The little girl did her part tenderly, carrying water in her hands to wet the white lips, tearing up her ragged skirt to lay fresh bandages on the wound that had been bleeding the brave boy's life away and, sitting by him, gathered his head into her arms, begging him to wait till father came.

But poor Onawandah had waited too long; now he could only look up into the dear, loving, little face bent over him and whisper wistfully, "Wild Rose will remember Onawandah?" as the light went out of his eyes and his last breath was a smile for her.

When the parson and his people came hurrying up full of wonder, joy and good will, they found Eunice weeping bitterly, and the Indian boy lying like a young warrior smiling at death.

"Ah, my neighbors, the savage has taught us a lesson we never can forget. Let us imitate his virtues and do honor to his memory," said the pastor as he held his little daughter close and looked down at the pathetic figure at his feet, whose silence was more eloquent than any words.

All felt it, and even old Becky had a remorseful sigh for the boy who had kept his word so well and given back her darlings safe.

They buried him where he lay, and for years the lonely mound under the great oak was kept green by loving hands. Wild roses bloomed there, and the murmur of the Long River of Pines was a fit lullaby for faithful Onawandah.

Paul Bunyan
and the Baby Rainstorm

*Ol' Paul couldn't believe his eyes.
It was true. Any way he looked at it. The rain
was coming straight up instead of down*

GLEN ROUNDS

One spring, a good many years back, Ol' Paul Bunyan had him a logging camp on the headwaters of the River That Ran Sidewise. He'd had a profitable winter and the landings were jammed full of logs decked up waiting for the spring floods to float them down to the mills.

Finally the weather turned warm and the snow started to melt. A few more days and the ice would break up so they could get the drive under way. Then one morning the men woke up to find it was raining. Now rain is not so unusual at that time of year, but this was no ordinary rain!

As everybody knows, ordinary rain falls down, but this rain fell UP! All over camp, and for as far around as anyone could see, streams of big raindrops were squirting up out of the ground, sailing straight up in the air and disappearing in the clouds overhead!

And that brought trouble. For, like I say, folks are used to the kind of rain that comes down and build their houses to take care of that kind, seldom giving the other kind a thought. And that was the case with Ol' Paul's camp. The buildings all had tight roofs that water couldn't come through,

53

but the floors, on the other hand, were made with wide cracks so that water and mud tracked in by the lumberjacks would run through to the ground below.

But now, with the rain coming up, the floors leaked like sieves and the water gathered on the ceilings and couldn't leak out. By the time the men woke up there were four feet of water on the underside of the ceiling of every bunkhouse in camp, and it was getting deeper every minute. The men as they got up had to duck their heads to keep from bumping into the water.

One of the loggers hotfooted it over to Paul's office to tell him about it.

"Paul!" he hollered when he could get his breath. "The rain is a-comin' straight up this morning!"

"Yuh mean it's a-clabberin' up to rain, don't yuh?" Paul asked, as he hunted for his socks. "Why the Sam Hill don't yuh learn to say what yuh mean."

"Nossir!" the lumberjack insisted. "I meant jest what I said, that the rain is a-comin' straight up outta the ground and yuh kin take a look fer yerself!"

And to prove it he hauled back the big bearskin rug that had been keeping the rain from coming up through the floor of Paul's office. When he did that, streams of water shot up through the cracks and started spattering on the ceiling overhead. Before he could put it back, Paul's bed and his clothes were all soaked and he knew he had a sure enough problem on his hands this time.

Ol' Paul and the lumberjack sat in the middle of the rug where it was fairly dry, and thought about what to do. Every so often Paul would stomp over to the window and look out. He couldn't seem to believe his eyes, and he tried looking out with the window closed, and he tried looking out with the window open, and later he even went outside for a good close look.

But any way he looked at it, the rain was sure enough coming straight up!

Meanwhile, the lumberjacks over in the bunkhouses, and the stable bucks and the bull cooks and the mess hall flunkeys were all in a very bad humor. The cooks were in a bad humor too, but camp cooks are almost always that way, so nobody noticed any particular difference in them.

After a while a delegation came to Ol' Paul and told him that he'd better do something about this business pretty soon or they'd all quit and go to work for Sowbelly Burke, his hated rival.

Ol' Paul assured them that he'd get to the bottom of the mystery as soon as possible, but pointed out that it would take time, since nothing like it had ever happened before. That being the case, there was of course nothing written in the books about how to deal with it, so he'd have to figure it all out by himself.

"Besides," he told them, "think of the stories you can tell in the towns this summer, about how you got your drive out in spite of the rain that fell straight up!"

But they were still mad and going to quit, so he saw he'd have to take measures, and pretty quick, at that.

After a spell of unusually heavy thinking he sent the lumberjack to get Johnny Inkslinger, his surveyor, and to have him bring a mail-order catalogue from his favorite mail-order house.

When Johnny got there Paul started looking through the catalogue while he explained to Johnny that a feller's clothes were made for ordinary rain, sorta like he was shingled over.

When Johnny looked kind of undecided, Paul went on to explain that a feller's hat stuck out over his collar to keep the rain from running down his neck, and his coat overlapped his britches and his britches overlapped his boots. But with rain like this, falling up instead of down, it fell straight up his britches legs, straight up his sleeves, and up under his coat and hat. It was no wonder the lumberjacks were in such a bad humor.

Johnny agreed with that, but couldn't see what could be done about it beyond putting all their clothes on upside down, and that didn't seem to be practical.

Paul told him he had the answer. He wanted an order sent off right away for bumbershoots, enough for two for every man in camp, including the stable bucks and bull cooks. And he showed Johnny the picture in the catalogue. Johnny told him what he was looking at was "umbrellas," and that anyway they would do no good being as they were for rain that fell down, while this rain was falling up.

Paul allowed he knew as well as the next man what bumbershoots were used for but he wanted them ordered, and marked "Rush" at that.

A couple days later the bumbershoots came, two for every man jack in camp, and you should have heard the lumberjacks roar. No self-respecting lumberjack had ever been known to carry one of the sissy things and they weren't going to start it now. They might be all right for city dudes, but not for reg'lar he-lumber-jacks! No sir! They'd quit first.

Ol' Paul goes on helping Ole open the boxes and tells the lumberjacks to keep their shirts on a minute till they see what he has in mind.

As fast as the bumbershoots are unpacked the little chore boy opens them up and Ol' Paul takes his jackknife and cuts the handles off short inside and fastens on a couple of snowshoe loops instead. When he has them all fixed up he has Johnny call the roll. As each logger comes up Paul hands him a couple of the remodeled bumbershoots and tells him to slip his feet in the loops. The first fellers are a mite shy about

the business, but after they put them on and straddle off, like they were wearing snowshoes, they find that the durn things do keep the rain from coming up their pant legs. And from then on the men push and holler for the line ahead to hurry up so they can get theirs.

"See there," says Ol' Paul. "I guess I knowed what I was doing. Don't reckon there is anything sissy about wearin' bumbershoots on your feet. An' anyways we'll call 'em bumbershoes from now on, jest to be sure!"

The men all cheered again, and decided not to quit after all.

The next morning a friendly Indian, Chief Rinktumdiddy by name, came tearing into camp wanting to see Paul. He told Ol' Paul that he and another Indian were out hunting the day before and camped by the mouth of a cave out on the prairie a way. After they'd eaten their supper they decided to explore this cave, so they took along some pine knots for torches, and started out. They go back through the narrow twisting passages for about half a mile, as near as they can judge, when all of a sudden they hear the goshawfullest noise they've ever laid an ear next to. They don't stop to argue, but tear outta there as fast as they can hyper. They figger that by going in there they've made the Great Spirit mad, and that it was him they heard hollering. So now this Indian wants Paul to see if he can talk the Great Spirit out of his mad.

Ol' Paul is plumb curious, but from what the Chief tells him he knows, the cave is too small for him to get into, and he hasn't his ox, Babe, along to burrow for him, so he sits still and thinks for a spell. Finally he allows as how that maybe two fellers listening together could listen far enough back to hear the noise from the mouth of the cave. That sounded like a good idea, but the Indian was plumb scared to go back, so Paul called Chris Crosshaul to come along instead.

The cave wasn't hard to find, and when they got there they both listened as hard as they could and sure enough, they could just hear the noise. But when they tried listening separately they couldn't hear a sound.

For a while Paul listens to the rumpus he can hear going on back in the cave, and a very curious sound it is, too. It's sorta mixed up with whimpering and whining like a lost puppy, mixed in with dribbling, splashing sounds, and a sort of pattering, and now and again a hollow booming like lightning might sound if it was shut in a cellar.

After a spell of especially hard listening that left them both red in the face and out of breath, Paul turns to Chris and allows that what they hear is nothing in the wide world but a baby rainstorm that's got itself lost back in the cave, and is bellering for his maw!

"Yuh don't say," says Chris, doubtful-like.

"Yessir!" says Paul, "An' by lookin' at my pocket compass I've discovered that the noise is a-comin' from right under our lumbercamp! The way I figger it, that little feller got separated from the rest of the herd and got in here by mistake a while back. Now, he's lost and scared. You jest heerd him whimperin' and thunderin' his little heart out back in there. Chances are he's got all upset in the dark and is rainin' straight up instead of down and don't know it. We gotta get him outta there."

"Yeah?" says Chris Crosshaul. "It sounds reasonable, but how the Sam Hill we gonna git him out?"

"Well, here's the way I see it," says Ol' Paul, when they had their pipes going good. "The only way to git that critter outta there is to call him out. It's a cinch we can't drag him out because there's no way to get a-hold of a critter like that. And

nobody ever had any luck tryin' to chase a rainstorm anywheres that I ever heard tell about."

"Reckon you're right that fur, Paul," says Chris, "but I never heard tell of anyone that can call a rainstorm, neither."

"That's the beauty of the whole thing," says Paul. "We'll be the first ones to ever do such a thing."

"Jest how do you figger to go about it," Chris wants to know. "Yuh don't mean to tell me you kin holler like rainstorms, do yuh?"

"Not right now, I can't," says Paul. "But I figger I kin durn soon learn. Yuh see, I know a feller in Kansas City that will rent yuh all kinds of disguises. I'll git him to disguise me up to look like a rainstorm, then I'll go out and live with a tribe of them and learn their language. Should be simple enough, shouldn't it?"

And that's just what he did. He went and got himself duded up in a rainstorm suit till you wouldn't have known him. Then he went out into Iowa where most of the rainstorms summered. He fell in with a big tribe of them, and his disguise was so perfect that they just figgered he was a strange rainstorm, maybe blowed up from Texas way, and invited him to stay with them as long as he liked.

He had a mighty fine time all summer, helping them rain out open-air political rallies and the like, although I think he took an unfair advantage at times, being as how he always got the crowd he was with to rain out the fellers he didn't want to see elected, while they stayed away from the rallies of the fellers he liked.

But anyways, late in the summer he came back. Just to show off, he was all the time throwing rainstorm words into his talk, until the lumberjacks hardly knew what he was talking about. Then one day he went over to the mouth of the cave where the rainstorm was, and getting down on his hands and knees he put his face up close to the entrance of the cave and imitated the cry a mother rainstorm makes when she is calling her young ones.

As soon as he did that, the noise and thundering and blubbering stopped sudden. There wasn't a sound to be heard, and the rain, for the first time all summer, stopped coming up around camp.

"See that," says Paul, with a big grin. And then he hollered the rainstorm holler again, and that little rainstorm came atearing outta that cave like he'd been sent for and couldn't come. He was just a little feller compared to what some rainstorms are, and a mite puny looking from being shut in the dark for so long. He jumps into Ol' Paul's arms and licks his face and rains all over him like an excited puppy dog.

Ol' Paul pets him and talks to him soothing like, till he kinda quiets down, then sends him off down to Iowa where the rest of the rainstorms are. The last we saw of him he was just a little cloud over in the next county, and plumb busted out with rainbows, he was so tickled.

Gears and Gasoline

*His mother had warned the little green car
against taxicabs when he left the old home plant in
Detroit, and now he knew why*

CAROLINE EMERSON

The small green car ran as quickly and quietly as he could down the avenue. It was five o'clock of a dreary winter's day. The little car was wet and cold. He closed his windows and turned on his heater, but the damp seemed to creep through his body just the same. It had been snowing earlier in the day. The air was chill and the road was wet and slippery.

"My gears-and-gasoline!" sighed the small green car as he ran carefully along the wet pavement. "How I wish I were safe at home in my own garage!"

Cars whisked past him on both sides. There were big cars, little cars, buses and taxicabs. He seemed to move in a sea of hurrying cars. He was not used to all this noise and bustle. His home was in the country, and he hated the sight and sound of the city.

"I never knew there were so many cars in the world," murmured the small green car to himself. "My gears-and-gadgets, where are they all hurrying to?"

But there was no one to answer him.

The long avenue ahead stretched before him like a gleaming fairy lane, but the small green car was too anxious to notice it. Gold lights lined the pavement, and above them shone green traffic lights. On the wet pavement below each light lay a shimmering pool of green or gold. The red taillights of the horde of cars darted here and there like fireflies.

Suddenly, all down the avenue the green lights vanished as though by magic. For a second there was gold only. Then on flashed the red, and the reflections on the pavement changed to pools of fire.

The small green car put on his brakes carefully. The road was slippery, and he wished to have no accidents. The cars around him came gently to a stop with quiet dignity. There they all crouched about him, dark forms ready to spring forward at a touch. Before them lay the road, empty and open. No chain or gate held them back, but not a car moved, not even a taxicab.

Then, suddenly, the enchantment was broken. Lights flashed from red to green. Away darted the cars. The little green car moved slowly forward. There was an impatient taxi just behind him.

"Oh, hurry up! Hurry up! Hurry up!" honked the taxi. "Get started, can't you! Don't go to sleep in the middle of the road!"

It made the small green car nervous to be honked at. He tried to hurry, but he shifted his gears too quickly. The next thing that he knew he had stalled his engine. He could hear the taxi panting angrily behind him.

"You ought not to be out alone," snarled the taxi. "You ought to have a nursemaid to push you!"

The small car started up his engine as quickly as he could and crept on down the avenue. If only that taxi would pass him and leave him in peace! But both lanes of traffic on either side were filled with hurrying cars. There was no way to escape. The small car could feel the hot impatient breath of the taxicab on his license plate. It made him feel nervous and uncomfortable. He hated to hurry on a wet night like this, but he did his best.

Then a dreadful thing happened. He was so confused by the taxicab that he never noticed when the lights flashed from green to red. On went the little green car, right past a red light. He had never done such a thing in all his life before! He heard a gasp of horror from the other cars. Then he slammed on his brakes, but it was all too late. There he stood helpless and alone. All the eyes of the world were upon him!

There came the long shrill whistle of the traffic cop.

"Where do you think you're going?" he shouted. *"Who do you think you are?"*

The small green car could think of nothing to say.

"Get back there to your place!" ordered the traffic cop.

The small green car wished with all his parts that he were safely away from all this crowd and home in his own garage. But wishes won't take you home, and there was nothing for him to do but to back miserably to his place in the line. The headlights of the crosstown traffic glared at him like the eyes of hungry wolves. He wished that he could sink through a manhole and be done with it!

The taxicab greeted him with a low laugh.

"Well, well, well," he cried, "are you color-blind, or what's the matter with you?"

"Oh, leave the little fellow alone," said a big car to the right. "You're enough to burst an inner tube!"

But there was no more time for talk. The lights flashed green, and away the cars sped. The small green car felt as though his gasoline had turned to water. He felt as though there was no air in his tires or power in his battery, but he managed to keep running. He grated his gears and he nearly choked his engine, but at least he kept on going.

But the taxicab was growing more and more impatient. He tried again and again to pass the small green car. He nosed this way and that, trying to slip over into the next lane, but with no luck. Then at last he saw his chance. The car at the right turned off on a side street. Quick as a flash the taxi pressed on his gas and darted ahead. But he was too fast. The car next in line was slowing up, and the taxi could not stop. He was just abreast of the small green car. He put on his brakes too quickly. The pavement was wet and his back wheels skidded.

There came a crash and the sound of bent metal and splintered wood. The small green car felt himself shoved aside. The taxicab had skidded into him! All down the avenue brakes screamed as cars came to a stop. People jumped out of cars and came running across the road. The small green car felt bruised and miserable, but there was nothing to do but switch off his engine and wait to see what would happen.

There seemed to be people everywhere.

"Anyone hurt?" asked a traffic officer.

"No, no one hurt," was the answer. "Only a bent mudguard and a broken wheel."

"Only a bent mudguard and a broken wheel!" exclaimed the small green car. "I'd like to have people know what it feels like to have a bent mudguard and a broken wheel! If anything happens to them, they make a great fuss and call for an ambulance and everything, but if it's a car, it's *'only a bent mudguard!'"*

Men pulled the taxi and the small green car apart. The taxi was not badly hurt. It takes a great deal to hurt a taxi, and the more bumps a taxi has the prouder he is. Stop by a taxi line any time at a quiet hour and listen to the old cars talking together. They'll be telling tales of their accidents and counting their dents. And now and again you'll hear the low chant of the old taxicabs:

> Kick them up,
> Pick them up,
> If they won't let you pass,
> Yo-ho-ho, and a gallon of gas!

It takes a great deal to hurt a taxicab! His bumper was off and his fender was smashed but his engine still ran, and the taxi moved off down the street under his own power.

Not so the small green car! His wheel was broken and he stood helpless and miserable.

"Oh, my carburetor!" moaned the small green car. "What's to become of me!"

When the traffic officer had written down a great many things in a little book, he said, "We need a wrecking car with a derrick."

In a few minutes, the wrecking car arrived.

"Well, little brother," called the derrick to the small green car. "Was the city too much for you?"

The derrick was tactless. He had a kind heart, but he never knew when not to joke.

"A taxi skidded into me," muttered the small green car.

"Oh, well," cried the derrick, "we all have our taxis sooner or later! They're like the measles."

He backed up to the little car. Chains were fastened under the small car's spring.

"Now, here we go!" cried the derrick cheerily.

Slowly and gently he raised the small car. He was a blustering fellow, but his heart was tender. He lifted up the front wheels as carefully as he could.

But at best it was a terrible position to be in. It made the small green car feel dizzy. His headlights stared blankly at the night sky. All his gasoline ran out of his feed pipe.

"Come along with me," called the derrick. "This will soon be over."

Down the avenue they went.

"Careful, now, at the corner," warned the derrick.

At last they reached a big garage. The doors stood open. The wrecking car turned carefully in through the opening and towed the small green car to a dark corner. Then the derrick was lowered. The wrecking car backed away. The small green car was left alone in his misery.

For a week the small green car stayed in the garage. No one touched him, but people came and looked at him and wrote down things in notebooks. There was one man called "The Insurance Man" who came very often. The owner of the small green car came with him. There was much talk.

Then one day the small green car saw his owner step into a *new* green car. Off his owner went in the new green car and left the old car behind.

"What do you think of that!" moaned the small green car. "Why don't they throw me out on the dump and be done with it!"

Day after day went by, and week after week passed. The small green car grew more and more lonely and disconsolate. Other cars came and went in the garage, but he did not trouble to talk to them. He crouched in his dark corner with his bent mudguard and his broken wheel.

"I wish they'd throw me out on the dump," was his only thought. "There'd at least be other wrecks there. We could tell our adventures through the long nights while we waited for rain and rust to wear us away."

Even the derrick stopped trying to cheer him up as he went by.

The winter passed, and at last the first breath of spring came into the garage through the gasoline fumes. There was a new smell in the air. It made the small green car think of cement roads that wound up hills toward the sky. It made him think of four-lane traffic routes and express highways. It made even the little old battered car dream of high-test in his gasoline tank. It made him dream of red-and-orange gasoline pumps by country roads, and thick yellow oil gurgling through his works. Oh, would the day ever come when he would feel the road beneath his wheels once more?

"If I ever get out of this garage," sighed the small green car, "I'll keep away from taxicabs for the rest of my life!"

His mother had warned him against taxicabs when he left the old home plant in Detroit, and now he knew why. He gave a long, low moan. It was a long, long day since he had left the factory with his paint all new and his engine stiff!

Then one day two boys came into the garage. They walked over to the small green car and stood looking at it.

"They've just come in here to make fun of me," the car said to himself. "I wish they'd go away!"

But the boys were not laughing at him. They began to look him over with care. Then the garageman joined them.

"How much do you want for it?" asked one of the boys.

"You can have it for thirty," said the garageman, "and I could put it in order for you for fifty, if you'd do some of the work on it yourself."

For a few minutes the boys talked with the man, and the car could not hear what they said. He ached to know what they were talking about, for way, way down in his old dead battery, a tiny ray of hope was beginning to stir.

Again the boys walked around the car looking carefully at this and that. Then the car heard one of them say, "We want to drive out to California and camp on the way. Do you think it would make it?"

The small green car hardly dared listen to the answer. What would it be?

"*California?*" answered the garageman. "*Sure!* The engine's as good as new. That car could run to California and back three times over."

"*Bless his carburetor!*" sighed the small green car.

The next day workmen came. Before the little car knew what was happening he was jacked up, and a new wheel was put on him. Then he was pushed into the workshop, and a thousand and one things were done to him. At first he felt very stiff and

cramped to be up on four wheels, after standing stooped over for so long, but the men greased him up and tightened his bolts and before he knew it he felt as gay as this year's model.

In the paint shop, the men sprayed him with fresh paint. At last he was ready. The boys climbed into the seat. The small green car could scarcely believe his luck. A summer in the open! Wide miles of road ahead! Two boys and a camping kit! Nights under the desert sky with only the stars above! Mountains to climb! For a moment doubt came into the generator of the small green car. Could he do it? Was he really well and strong again?

The boy at the wheel stepped on the starter. The small green car felt the electricity from his new battery flash through his wires. The engine started. Every cylinder was ready to do its best. Out into the bright fresh air ran the small green car.

It was glorious, glorious, glorious to be out on the road again. The small green car heard one of the boys say, "It certainly can go!"

"*I certainly can!*" laughed the small green car.

But just as they left the city a strange thing happened. A taxicab drew up beside the small green car.

"Get out of my way!" honked the taxicab.

The small green car saw red.

"I'll do no such thing!" he snorted, and he cut right across in front of the taxicab.

The taxicab was astonished. He put on his brakes so hard that he nearly stood up straight on his hind wheels.

"What do you think you're doing?" screamed the taxicab.

"I don't care what I'm doing," cried the small green car. *"I'm going to California. Get out of my way!"*

Then he backfired at the taxicab and ran on down the avenue.

"Well," thought the small green car, "they say that man made the city and God made the country. I wonder who it was that ever started making taxicabs!"

Then off and away he went, leaving taxicabs and city streets behind. Off he went to California with the open road ahead. There was power in his battery, air in his tires and gasoline in his tank, and the smell of spring in the air.

63

THE SAMPLER

*The cross-stitch sampler was more than
one hundred years old, yet in some mysterious way
when Sarah picked it up, she became the little girl
who had embroidered it*

DOROTHY CLEWES

The new chest of drawers sat comfortably between the two casement windows. It wasn't new in the sense that it had come straight from a shop, but new as far as Sarah was concerned.

"You do really need more room for your clothes," her mother had said—and the chest of drawers that had stood in the attic for so long had been the answer. Cleaned and polished, its brass handles gleaming, it waited now for her to fill it.

"And I've put a roll of wallpaper on your bed that will do for lining the drawers," her mother had said.

Patterned paper was so much more fun than plain white—and when Sarah unrolled it she recognized it at once. It was the same as the one decorating her bedroom walls but the rosebuds were more freshly pink against the white background which on Sarah's bedroom wall was now faded to a soft cream. This was the way it had been when it was new, Sarah thought. Perhaps the chest of drawers had looked different, too, when it had been new, its wood not so satin smooth, the color not so deep.

It was fun lining the drawers, cutting the paper the right shape to fit, first the two top small drawers and then the two long ones underneath. There was room enough to hold other things besides clothes in the bottom drawer. It was deeper than the others and should have been as empty as they were. But when Sarah lifted the old lining paper an envelope stared up at her. It was yellow with age, and long and narrow—but fat. She picked it up and drew out a paper parcel.

The paper wasn't soft like the tissue paper she wrapped presents up in, but crisp as if it had dried up lying folded for so long in the envelope. But the something inside was soft. A roll of material, it looked like. Sometimes her mother saved pieces of silk left over from an extra special party dress but this was firmer than silk—and stitched all over. It was a piece of embroidery. Tails of silk of all colors of the rainbow hung from it in a fringe, some lengths short, some long. It was a moment before Sarah realized that she was looking at it on the wrong side. She turned it over, unfolding it until it lay flat on the rug she was kneeling on.

It should have been a picture, but it wasn't. It was letters. And figures. They ran in long straight lines of cross-stitches over the sandy-colored linen. The alphabet first in capital letters and then when it came to Z it started all over again in small letters. Then the figures began, from 1 to 9, finishing with a round 0. And in between the rows were little lines of flowers, daisies, forget-me-nots, buttercups. After that there was a sentence: *BE GOOD, SWEET MAID, AND LET WHO WILL BE CLEVER*, it read. And right at the bottom of the work a name was embroidered in the same tiny cross-stitches: *SARAH SERAPHINA*, Aged 11, 1844.

It was startling to see her own name staring up at her, and her own age, too—but the date was a hundred and thirty years ago. Sarah turned it over wonderingly.

"All those untidy ends," a voice said. "I'm always telling you, the back of a piece of work should be as neat as the front. It should be difficult to tell the difference."

"But a knot is so much easier," Sarah said—and if you couldn't tell the back from the front all the letters on the wrong side would read backwards, she thought, but she didn't say so aloud because it was rude to contradict.

"And I do declare, you are only as far as N," the voice said.

Sarah looked down at the piece of embroidery. She was so sure it was finished, but now she could see that she was holding a needle in her hand. It was threaded with green silk that she had just pulled through the canvas after making the tiny cross that completed the letter N.

"And you aren't wearing your thimble. You'll wear a hole in your finger end."

Sarah looked at the second finger on her right hand. It was peppered all over with tiny punctures and as rough as sandpaper, but the silver thimble that should have sat on the end of her finger like a little hat felt clumsy and made her finger hot.

"Drawing-room hands, that's what young ladies should have. Put it away now. Master Graham has called." The name was spoken with a disapproving sniff.

Graham lived next door. He was thirteen, two years older than Sarah was, and her friend. If he had called it must mean that something nice was going to happen. All the nicest things that happened to her happened with Graham. She was already at the nursery door, her hand on the knob.

"—but not before we've washed our hands," Nanny Grose checked her, "and brushed our hair."

Such a waste of time. She had been made to wash her hands before she started up the embroidery and she had had her hair brushed until her scalp tingled only an hour ago. Sarah stood impatiently twisting first on one foot and then on the other while Nanny lifted a handful of hair and re-tied the black velvet bow.

"And if you're playing with Master Graham we'd best leave your overall on."

Sarah looked down at the starched and crimped white overall covering a black velvet frock with lace collar and cuffs and wondered why she had expected to see blue jeans and a yellow cardigan.

"And try and behave like a little lady," Nanny Grose's voice followed her racing footsteps down the stairs, "though it will be difficult with *that* young man."

"I'm glad I wasn't born a girl," Graham said as she jumped the last two stairs and landed unsteadily at his side. "Don't do this and don't do that, how do you stand it? I'd run away but you're a girl and so you can't."

"One day I will," Sarah promised him because if Graham thought running away

was a good thing, that was exactly what she would do.

"Nanny Grose would catch you before you got to the end of the road," Graham told her. "You haven't got a chance. You'll do as you're told until someone comes along and marries you, and if no one does you'll stay at home doing needlework until you die."

"I won't, I won't," Sarah shouted him down—but deep inside her she had an awful feeling that what he was saying was true. She wasn't even very good at needlework, she had to remind herself, thinking of how long it was taking her to fill the sandy-colored squares.

"What will you do, then?"

"I don't know," Sarah said, miserably—because there really wasn't very much she could do, "—but I'll think of something before I grow up. What are we going to play at?"

"We're not going to play. I'm building a house in a tree and I need you to hand me up the wood and the nails."

"A house in a tree—?" Sarah's eyes were wide with astonishment. Graham was a great builder of things. There had been the

time when he had built a wheeled carriage out of an old tea chest. He had taken the wheels from the platform of a fine rocking horse he never played with. He had fixed two seats inside and they had gone careering down the slope of his parents' lawn to end up bruised and bleeding on the rockery because he had not thought to fix a brake. One snowy winter he had built a toboggan which had ended in equal disaster: Sarah had proudly carried the scar on her forehead from that adventure for days. She was only ever allowed to be mate to his master, but when the job was completed he always

rewarded her patience and worshiping admiration by letting her be the first to try it out.

It was an old spreading beech tree and to reach the first giant branch Graham had fixed up a rope ladder.

"Like on a ship," he explained. "When you're in the house you can pull in the ladder and no one can follow you up."

He scrambled up the swaying rope footholds and sat straddled over the huge branch. "Now heave me up the wood—and the saw—and the nails."

At the end of an hour there was enough

floor space to hold them both. "Come on up," Graham called down to Sarah. "You can see for miles."

The rope ladder was much more difficult to climb up than it had seemed watching Graham. It wouldn't stay still and the hard bark of the tree scuffed the toes of her shoes and took the skin off her knuckles, but she wasn't going to let Graham think she couldn't do it. He pulled her up the last few inches, the rope ladder after her—and she was in another world. It was a shadowed, sun-speckled, secret world with surprising glimpses of the very prim Mrs. Webb next door hanging out frilled and beribboned knickers and voluminous petticoats where they couldn't be seen from neighboring windows. And there was the very pompous manservant who belonged to Mr. Soames who lived in the house next door to Mrs. Webb, sitting outside the kitchen door—in his shirt-sleeves, nodding over a large tankard.

"I always knew he wasn't as superior as he made out to be," Graham gloated. "What do you bet I couldn't wake him up?" He reached into his trouser pocket.

"Oh, Graham—the slingshot." Sarah covered her mouth to stifle her giggles.

Graham put the dried pea in the sling, drew back the elastic to its full stretch and took careful aim. Two gardens away Mr. Soames' manservant leapt into the air with a yelp of astonishment.

So engrossed were they in the antics of Mr. Soames' manservant trying to decide what was attacking him and from where the attacks were coming that they never heard the sound of voices approaching across the lawn.

"—and this tree was here long before the house was built," Graham's father's voice boomed. "A fine copper beech. It could shelter an army."

Sarah jumped, almost as startled as the manservant, overbalanced, missed her footing on the platform and shot down through the sheltering branches to land in a shower of leaves on Graham's father's best silk topper. Following in her wake, no less startled and too swiftly to use the rope ladder, came Graham.

It was hard to face Nanny Grose with the velvet frock and pinafore torn beyond repair, but at least Sarah was only bruised and shaken. Graham had fared much worse. "This time—boarding school," his angry father had pronounced as soon as he had recovered his breath.

Nanny Grose received the news triumphantly. "And not before time. Discipline is what that young man needs."

"But it was going to be such a beautiful tree house," Sarah said sadly.

"Oh—a clever young man, I grant you," Nanny Grose said, "but wild and not fit to play with young ladies. 'Be good, sweet maid, and let who will be clever.' The quotation will do very well, I think, to stitch into your sampler."

Sarah picked up the sampler with a heavy heart. Graham was going to school and out of her life. He was right, girls didn't have a chance. She would sit stitching at samplers for the rest of her life.

"Sarah Seraphina, Aged 11, 1844." It was finished at last. Sarah made the last cross-stitch and threaded the silk end neatly through the back of the stitch and put the needle away in its case.

"I wondered what had happened to you, you were so quiet," Sarah's mother said from the door.

Startled, Sarah sat back on her heels, her cheeks pinkly flushing.

Her mother looked over her shoulder. "Why—what have you got there?"

Sarah held up the sampler. "It was in the bottom drawer," she said. "It's my name— but it says 1844."

Sarah's mother took it from her. "Well—for heaven's sake, that's your great-great-grandmother's. You were named after her."

"So she did get married."

Sarah's mother looked at her questioningly and then laughed. "Of course she got married; you wouldn't be here if she hadn't. As a matter of fact she was a very remarkable person. Young ladies in those days were supposed to stay at home, help around the house, arrange the flowers, do needlework. She rebelled. She actually left home to follow another remarkable person whose name you must have heard of: Florence Nightingale."

"She nursed soldiers—in the Crimean War," Sarah was thinking. At school, only a few weeks ago, she had had to write an essay about Florence Nightingale. "She was the first real nurse and hospitals are the way they are today because of her."

"That's right," Sarah's mother said. "Soldiers were dying miles away from home in a strange land with no one to care for them properly. Florence Nightingale called for thirty-eight other nurses to go with her out to a place called Scutari. Your great-great-grandmother was one of the thirty-eight."

Thoughts were stirring in Sarah's head, thoughts mixed up with other thoughts. "—and Graham—was—my great-great-grandfather?"

Sarah's mother nodded. "It was really very romantic. As children they'd lived next door to each other and had been close friends. Then Graham was sent to boarding school, the family moved away, and they never met again—until Scutari. Graham was one of the wounded soldiers in the barrack hospital there."

"Didn't she have a mother?" Sarah asked, her mind on that other Sarah.

"Of course she did—but in those days boys and girls didn't see as much of their parents as they do now. Sarah would have had a nanny."

Sarah ran her fingers gently over the tiny stitches of the quotation. She spoke it softly under her breath: *Be good, sweet maid, and let who will be clever.* Aloud she said: "I'm glad she didn't take any notice of the words."

"Oh, but she did," Sarah's mother corrected her. She paused a moment, thinking. "Maybe it was the poem that started her mind working—or have you forgotten how the rest of it goes?"

For a moment Sarah had but now it was coming back to her. She said with excitement in her voice: "'Do noble deeds, not dream them, all day long.' And she didn't spend the rest of her life doing needlework. I'm so glad."

Sarah's mother laughed. "As far as I know that was the only piece of needlework she ever did; she was always too busy doing all those noble deeds." She began to fold up the sampler again, smoothing out the yellow, brittle tissue paper.

"Oh, please may I have it?" Sarah pleaded. "After all—in a way—it is mine."

"Well—of course. Why not? And it certainly makes no sense to put it back in the drawer again; but it would be a pity for it to get crumpled and soiled. Perhaps we could get it framed and then you can hang it on your wall as a picture."

It would be much more than a picture hanging on her wall, Sarah thought. It would be a kind of secret between herself and that other Sarah Seraphina who had once been the same age as herself.

THE MAGIC BOX

Do this, do that, do the other thing, people
advised him. But in the end Tonio
took the advice of the mad herdboy and went to
the old gypsy who made magic

RUTH SAWYER

In one of the fertile valleys of the Italian Apennine mountains—north in Emilia —long ago there lived a rich farmer. He had much land. His vineyards were the best pruned and yielded the best vintage; his olive grove was watched over with the utmost care and never suffered a frost. His fields of grain harvested more than his neighbors'; his cattle were sleeker and his sheep gave more wool at the spring shearings. On market- and fair-days his neighbors would wag their thumbs at him and say "There goes Gino Tomba. His sons will be very rich men one day."

He had two sons. The older was a daredevil who handled a rapier better than a pruning knife and could swing a broadsword with steadier aim than a mattock. Tonio, the younger, was an easy going, pleasure-loving rascal who knew more about fiddling than he did about winnowing grain. "If I had a third son, he might have been a farmer," old Tomba used to say when he came bringing his skins of wine to the inn to sell. "But we must make the most of what the good Virgin pro-

vides," and so he let his older son march off to the wars and set about making Tonio ready to look after his lands when he had gone.

"Hearken to me, boy; I am leaving you a fine inheritance. See that you keep a sharp eye on it and render it back with increase to your brother. Some day he will grow tired of fighting Spain and the French and come marching home."

In less than a twelvemonth old Tomba was dead. Tonio came from the burying, turned himself once about the farm to make sure it was all there and settled down to easy living. He made what you call good company. It was Tonio, come to the fair; and Tonio, stay longer at the inn; and Tonio, drink with this one; and Tonio, dance with that. He could step the tarantella as well as any man in the north and he could fiddle as he danced. So it was here and there and anywhere that a feast was spread or a saint's day kept; and Tonio, the younger son of old Tomba, danced late and drank deep and was the last to stop when the dawn broke. Often he slept until the sun was already throwing late shadows on the foothills.

The time came when his thrifty neighbors took him soundly to task for idling away his days and wasting what his father had saved. Then he would laugh, braggadocio, "Am I a sheep to graze in the pasture or a grain of wheat to be planted and stay in my fields all day and every day? The lands have grown rich for my father for fifty years; let them grow rich for me for fifty more. That is all I ask—that, and for my neighbors to prune their tongues when next they prune their vineyards."

But Tonio had asked too much. A place with a master is one thing, but without a master it is quite different. The *banditti* came down from the mountains and stole his cattle while the herdsmen slept; wolves ravaged his sheep; the bad little oil-fly came in swarms and spoiled the olives as they ripened; the grapes hung too long, and the wine turned thin and sour. And so it went—a little here, a little there, each year. The laborers took to small thieving— a few lambs from the spring dropping before they were driven in from the pastures for counting, a measure of wheat, a skin of wine, that would never be missed. The barns were not fresh-thatched in time, and the fall rains mildewed much of the harvest; the rats got in and ate their share. So, after years of adding one misfortune to another misfortune, there was a mountain of misfortune—large enough for even Tonio to see.

Over one night he became like a crazy man, for over one night he had remembered his brother. Any day he might be returning. At the inn the day before there had been two soldiers fresh from the wars, drinking and bragging of their adventures. Another night and who might not come? Once home, the older brother would be master. First, he would ask for an accounting. And what then? As master he could

have him, Tonio, flogged or flung into prison. More final than that, he could run him through with his clever rapier, and no one would question his right to do it. The more Tonio thought about it, the more his terror grew. He began running about the country like a man with fever in his brain. First he ran to the inn and asked the landlord what he should do, and the landlord laughed aloud. "Sit down, Tonio, and drink some of my good Chianti. Why worry about your brother now, when he may be lying in a strange country, stuck through the ribs like a pig?"

He ran to a neighbor, who laughed louder than the landlord. "Take up your fiddle and see if you cannot play your cattle back into the pasture."

He ran on to his favorite, Lisetta. She cocked her pretty head at him like a saucy macaw. "Let me see," she laughed, "you have forgotten your brother for ten years, yes? Then come to the inn tonight and dance the tarantella with me, and I will make you forget him for another ten years."

After that he ran to the priest and found him finishing Mass. He did not laugh, the priest. Instead he shook his head sorrowfully and told him to burn candles for nine days before the shrine of Saint Anthony of Padua and pray for wisdom. On the way to the shrine he met the half-witted herdboy Zeppo, who laughed foolishly when he saw his master's face and tapped his own forehead knowingly. "Master, you are so frightened it has made you quite mad, like me." Then he put his lips to Tonio's ear. "Hearken, I will tell you what to do. Go to the old gypsy woman of the grotto. She has much wisdom and she makes magic of all kinds."

In the end it was the advice of the mad herdboy that Tonio took. He climbed the first spur of the mountain to a deep grotto that time or magic had hollowed out of the

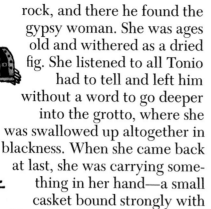

rock, and there he found the gypsy woman. She was ages old and withered as a dried fig. She listened to all Tonio had to tell and left him without a word to go deeper into the grotto, where she was swallowed up altogether in blackness. When she came back at last, she was carrying something in her hand—a small casket bound strongly with bands of brass, and in the top a hole so small it could hardly be seen in the pattern of the carving. She put the box into Tonio's hand and fixed him with eyes that were piercing as two rapier points. When she spoke, it was as if her voice rumbled out, not from her, but from deep in the rocks.

"Every morning, while the dew still lies heaviest, shake one grain of dust from the box in every corner of your lands—barns, pastures and vineyards.

See to it that no spot is left forgotten. Do this, and you will prosper as your father prospered. But never let one morning pass, and never till the day you die break the bands or look inside. If you do, the magic will be gone."

That night Tonio neither fiddled nor danced with Lisetta at the inn. He went to bed when the fowls went to roost and·was up at the crowing of the first cock. With the magic box under his arm, he went first to his barns to sprinkle the precious grains; but he found the men still asleep and the cattle unfed. Out of their beds he drove them with angry words until they began the day's work. From the barns he went to the fields and found the grain half cut and none of it stacked. The scythes were left rusting on the ground and the men still asleep in their huts. Tonio scattered more dust and then drove the reapers to their work.

And so it was in the olive grove, the vineyards and the pastures. Everywhere he found the men sleeping and the work half done. "Holy Mother, defend us!" the men said among themselves after Tonio had gone. "The master is up early and looking about for himself, even as the old master did. We shall have to keep a sharper watch."

After that, every morning Tonio was abroad before the sun, shaking the dust from his magic box into every corner of his lands. And every morning he was seeing something new that was needing care. In a little time the inn and the marketplace knew him no more, and Lisetta had to find a new dancing partner. A twelvemonth passed, and the farm of old Gino Tomba was prospering again. When Tonio came to the marketplace to sell his grain and wine, his neighbors would wag their thumbs at him as they had wagged them at his father and they would say, "There goes Tonio Tomba. His sons—when they are born—will be very rich men."

And in the end what happened? The older brother never came home to claim his inheritance. He must have been killed in the wars; at any rate, all the lands were Tonio's for the keeping. He married the daughter of his richest neighbor and had two sons of his own, even as his father had had. And when the time came for him to die he called them both to his side and commanded young Gino to bring him the casket and break the bands. Raising the lid he looked in, eager, for all his dying, to discover the magic that the box had held all those years.

What did he find? Under the lid were written these words: "Look you—the master's eye is needed over all." In the bottom were a few grains of sand left, the common kind any wayfarer can gather from the road that climbs to the Apennines.

The Fool of the World
and the Flying Ship

The Fool of the World set off with his bag
over his shoulder, singing as he went, for he was off
to seek his fortune and marry the Czar's daughter

ARTHUR RANSOME

There were once upon a time an old peasant and his wife, and they had three sons. Two of them were clever young men who could borrow money without being cheated, but the third was the Fool of the World. He was as simple as a child, simpler than some children, and he never did anyone a harm in his life.

Well, it always happens like that. The father and mother thought a lot of the two smart young men; but the Fool of the World was lucky if he got enough to eat.

However it was with his father and mother, this is a story that shows that God loves simple folk and turns things to their advantage in the end.

For it happened that the Czar of that country sent out messengers along the highroads and the rivers, even to huts in the forest like ours, to say that he would give his daughter, the Princess, in marriage to anyone who could bring him a flying ship—that should sail through the blue sky like a ship sailing on the sea.

"This is a chance for us," said the two clever brothers, and that same day they set off together.

And their father blessed them and gave them finer clothes than ever he wore himself. And their mother made them up hampers of food for the road: soft white rolls, and several kinds of cooked meats and bottles of corn brandy. And what happened to them I do not know, for they were never heard of again.

"I'd like to go too," says the Fool of the World, "and eat good meat, with soft white rolls, and drink corn brandy and marry the Czar's daughter."

"Stupid fellow," says his mother, "what's the good of your going? Why, if you were to stir from the house you would walk into the arms of a bear."

But the Fool of the World would not be held back by words.

"I am going. I am going. I am going. I am going," says he, till his mother saw there was nothing to be done and was glad to get

73

him out of the house. So she put some food in a bag for him to eat by the way. She put in the bag some crusts of dry black bread and a flask of water.

No matter. The Fool of the World set off with his bag over his shoulder, singing as he went, for he was off to seek his fortune and marry the Czar's daughter. He was sorry his mother had not given him any corn brandy, but he sang merrily for all that. He would have liked white rolls instead of the dry black crusts; but, after all, the main thing on a journey is to have something to eat.

He had not gone very far when he met an ancient old man with a bent back, and a long beard and eyes hidden under his bushy eyebrows.

"Good-day, young fellow," says the ancient old man.

"Good-day, grandfather," says the Fool of the World.

"And where are you off to?" says the ancient old man.

"What!" says the Fool, "haven't you heard? The Czar is going to give his daughter to anyone who can bring him a flying ship."

"And you can really make a flying ship?" says the ancient old man.

"No, I do not know how."

"Then what are you going to do?"

"God knows," says the Fool of the World.

"Well," says the ancient, "if things are like that, sit you down here. We will rest together and have a bite of food. Bring out what you have in your bag."

"I am ashamed to offer you what I have here. It is good enough for me, but it is not the sort of meal to which one can ask guests."

"Never mind that. Out with it. Let us eat what God has given."

The Fool of the World opened his bag and could hardly believe his eyes. Instead of black crusts he saw fresh white rolls and cooked meats. He handed them out to the ancient, who said, "You see how God loves simple folk. Let's have a sip at the corn brandy . . ."

The Fool of the World opened his flask, and instead of water there came out corn brandy, and that of the best. So the Fool and the ancient made merry, eating and drinking; and when they had done, the ancient says to the Fool:

"Listen to me. Off with you into the forest. Go up to the first big tree you see. Make the sacred sign of the cross three times before it. Strike it a blow with your little hatchet. Fall backwards on the ground and lie there, full length on your back, until somebody wakes you up. Then you will find the ship made, all ready to fly. Fly in it but be sure on the way to give a lift to everyone you meet."

The Fool of the World thanked the ancient old man, said good-bye to him and went off to the forest. He walked up to a tree, the first big tree he saw, made the sign of the cross three times before it, swung his hatchet round his head, struck a mighty blow on the tree trunk and instantly fell backwards flat on the ground.

A little time went by, and it seemed to the Fool as he slept that somebody was jogging his elbow. He woke up and opened his eyes. His hatchet, worn out, lay beside him. The big tree was gone, and in its place there stood a little ship, ready and finished. The Fool did not stop to think. He jumped into the ship and seized the tiller. Instantly the ship leapt up into the air and sailed over the tops of the trees.

The little ship answered the tiller as readily as if she were sailing in water, and the Fool steered for the highroad and sailed along above it.

He flew on and on and looked down, and saw a man lying in the road below him with his ear on the damp ground.

"Good-day to you, uncle," cried the Fool. "What are you doing down there?"

"I am listening to all that is being done in the world."

"Take your place in the ship with me."

The Listener was willing enough and sat down in the ship with the Fool, and they flew on singing songs. They flew on and on and looked down, and there was a man on one leg, with the other tied up to his head.

"Good-day, uncle," says the Fool. "Why are you hopping along on one foot?"

"If I were to untie the other I should move too fast. I should be stepping across the world in a single stride."

"Sit down with us," says the Fool.

The Swift-goer sat down with them in the ship, and they flew on singing songs.

They flew on and on and looked down, and there was a man with a gun, and he was taking aim, but what he was aiming at they could not see.

"Good health to you, uncle," says the Fool. "What are you shooting at? There isn't a bird to be seen."

"What!" says the man. "If there were a bird that you could see, I should not shoot at it. A bird or a beast a thousand miles away, that's the sort of mark for me."

"Take your seat with us," says the Fool.

The Far-shooter sat down with them in the ship, and they flew on. Louder and louder rose their songs.

They flew on and on and looked down, and there was a man with a sack of bread.

"Good health to you, uncle," says the Fool, sailing down. "And where are you off to?"

"I am going to get bread for my dinner."

"But you've got a full sack on your back."

"That—that little scrap! Why, that's not enough for a single mouthful."

"Take your seat with us," says the Fool.

The Eater sat down with them in the ship, and they flew on, singing loudly.

They flew on and on and looked down, and there was a man walking round and round a lake.

"Good health to you, uncle," says the Fool. "What are you looking for?"

"I want a drink, and I can't find any water."

"But there's a whole lake in front of your eyes. Why can't you drink from that?"

"That little drop!" says the man. "Why, there's not enough water there to wet the back of my throat if I were to drink it at one gulp."

"Take your seat with us," says the Fool.

The Drinker sat down with them, and again they flew on, singing in chorus.

They flew on and on and looked down, and there was a man walking towards the forest, with a fagot of wood on his shoulders.

"Good-day, uncle," says the Fool. "Why are you taking wood to the forest?"

"This isn't simple wood," says the man.

"What is it, then?" says the Fool.

"If it is scattered about, a whole army of soldiers leaps up out of the ground."

"There's a place for you with us," says the Fool.

The man sat down with them, and the ship rose up into the air.

They flew on and on and looked down, and there was a man carrying straw.

"Good-day, uncle," says the Fool, "and where are you taking your straw?"

"To the village."

"Why, are they short of straw in your village?"

"No, but this is such straw that if you scatter it abroad in the very hottest of the summer, instantly the weather turns cold, and there is snow and frost."

"There's a place here for you too," says the Fool.

"Very kind of you," says the man and

steps in and sits down, and away they all sail together, singing like to burst their lungs.

They did not meet anyone else, and presently came flying up to the palace of the Czar. They flew down and cast anchor in the courtyard.

Just then the Czar was eating his dinner. He heard their loud singing and looked out of the window and saw the ship come sailing down into his courtyard. He sent his servant out to ask who was the great prince who had brought him the flying ship.

The servant came up to the ship and saw the Fool of the World and his companions sitting there cracking jokes. He saw they were all simple peasants sitting in the ship; so he did not stop to ask questions, but came back quietly and told the Czar that there were no gentlemen in the ship at all, but only a lot of dirty peasants.

Now the Czar was not at all pleased with the idea of giving his daughter to a simple peasant, and he began to think how he could get out of his bargain. Thinks he to himself, "I'll set them such tasks that they will not be able to perform, and they'll be glad to get off with their lives, and I shall get the ship for nothing."

So he told his servant to go to the Fool and tell him that before the Czar had finished his dinner the Fool was to bring him some of the magical water of life.

Now, while the Czar was speaking, the Listener, the first of the Fool's companions, was listening, and heard the words of the Czar and repeated them to the Fool.

"What am I to do now?" says the Fool. "In a year, in a whole century, I never could find that water. And he wants it before he has finished his dinner."

"Don't you worry about that," says the Swift-goer, "I'll deal with that for you."

The servant came and announced the Czar's command.

"Tell him he shall have it," says the Fool.

His companion, the Swift-goer, untied his foot from beside his head, put it to the ground, wriggled it a little to get the stiffness out of it, ran off and was out of sight almost before he had stepped from the ship. Quicker than I can tell it to you in words he had come to the water of life and put some of it in a bottle.

"I shall have plenty of time to get back," thinks he, and down he sits under a windmill and goes off to sleep.

The royal dinner was coming to an end, and there wasn't a sign of him. There were no songs in the flying ship. Everybody was watching for the Swift-goer.

The Listener jumped out and laid his right ear to the damp ground, listened a moment, and said, "What a fellow! He has gone to sleep under the windmill. I can hear him snoring. And there is a fly buzzing with its wings, perched on the mill."

"This is my affair," says the Far-shooter, and he picked up his gun from between his knees, aimed at the fly on the windmill and woke the Swift-goer with the thud of the bullet on the wood of the mill close by his head. The Swift-goer leapt up and ran and in less than a second had brought the magic water of life and given it to the Fool. The Fool gave it to the servant, who took it to the Czar. The Czar had not yet left the table, so his command had been fulfilled as exactly as could be.

"What fellows these peasants are," thought the Czar. "There is nothing for it but to set them another task." So the Czar said to his servant, "Go to the captain of the flying ship and give him this message, 'If you are such a cunning fellow, you must have a good appetite. Let you and your companions eat at a single meal twelve oxen roasted whole and as much bread as can be baked in forty ovens!'"

The Listener heard the message and told the Fool what was coming. The Fool was terrified and said, "I can't get through even a single loaf at a sitting."

"Don't worry about that," said the Eater. "It won't be more than a mouthful to me, and I shall be glad to have a little snack in place of my dinner."

The servant came and announced the Czar's command.

"Good," says the Fool. "Send the food along. We'll know what to do with it."

So they brought twelve oxen roasted whole and as much bread as could be baked in forty ovens, and the companions had scarcely sat down to the meal before the Eater had finished the lot.

"Why," said the Eater, "what a little! They might have given us a decent meal."

The Czar told his servant to tell the Fool that he and his companions were to drink forty barrels of wine, with forty bucketfuls in every barrel.

The Listener told the Fool what message was coming.

"Why," says the Fool, "I never in my life drank more than one bucket at a time."

"Don't worry," says the Drinker. "You forget that I am thirsty."

They brought the forty barrels of wine and tapped them, and the Drinker tossed them down one after another, one gulp for each barrel. "Little enough," says he. "Why, I am thirsty still."

"Very good," says the Czar to his servant, when he heard that they had eaten all the food and drunk all the wine. "Tell the fellow to get ready for the wedding, and let him go and bathe himself in the bathhouse. But let the bathhouse be made so hot that the man will stifle and frizzle as soon as he sets foot inside. It is an iron bathhouse. Let it be made red-hot."

The Listener heard all this and told the Fool, who stopped short with his mouth open in the middle of a joke.

"Don't you worry," says the peasant with the straw.

Well, they made the bathhouse red-hot and called the Fool, and the Fool went along to wash himself, and with him went the peasant with the straw.

They shut them both into the bathhouse and thought that that was the end of them. But the peasant scattered his straw before them as they went in, and it became so cold in there that the Fool of the World had scarcely time to wash himself before the water in the cauldrons froze to solid ice. They lay down on the very stove itself and spent the night there, shivering.

In the morning the servants opened the bathhouse, and there were the Fool of the World and the peasant, alive and well, lying on the stove and singing songs.

They told the Czar, and the Czar raged with anger. "There is no getting rid of this fellow," says he. "But go and tell him that I send him this message, 'If you are to marry my daughter, you must show that you are able to defend her. Let me see that you have at least a regiment of soldiers.'" Thinks he to himself, "How can a simple peasant raise a troop? He will find it hard enough to raise a single soldier."

The Listener told the Fool of the World, and the Fool began to lament. "This time," says he, "I am done indeed. You, my brothers, have saved me from misfortune more than once, but this time, alas, there is nothing to be done."

"Oh, what a fellow you are!" says the peasant with the fagot of wood. "I suppose you've forgotten about me. Remember that I am the man for this little affair."

The Czar's servant came along and gave his message.

"Very good," says the Fool, "but tell the Czar that if after this he puts me off again, I'll make war on his country and take the Princess by force."

And then, as the servant went back with the message, the whole crew on the flying ship set to their singing again.

During the night, while the others slept, the peasant with the fagot of wood went hither and thither, scattering his sticks. Instantly where they fell there appeared a gigantic army. Nobody could count the number of soldiers in it—cavalry, foot soldiers, yes, and guns, and all the guns new and bright.

In the morning, as the Czar woke and looked from the windows of the palace, he found himself surrounded by troops upon troops of soldiers, and generals in cocked hats bowing in the courtyard and taking orders from the Fool of the World, who sat there joking with his companions in the flying ship. Now it was the Czar's turn to be afraid. As quickly as he could he sent his servants to the Fool with presents of rich jewels and fine clothes and invited him to come to the palace.

The Fool of the World put on the fine clothes and stood there as handsome a young man as a princess could wish for a husband. He presented himself before the Czar, fell in love with the Princess and she with him, married her the same day, received with her a rich dowry and became so clever that all the court repeated everything he said. The Czar and the Czarina liked him very much, and as for the Princess, she loved him to distraction.

The Ransom of Red Chief

*The boy had turned the tables on them.
He was supposed to be their prisoner, but
he was having the time of his life*

O. HENRY

It looked like a good thing, but wait till I tell you. We were down south, in Summit, Alabama—Bill Driscoll and myself—when this kidnaping idea struck us.

Bill and me had a joint capital of about six hundred dollars and we needed just two thousand dollars more to pull off a town-lot scheme in western Illinois.

We selected for our victim the only child of a prominent local citizen named Ebenezer Dorset. The father was respectable and tight, a mortgage fancier and a stern, upright collection-plate passer and fore-closer. The kid was a boy of ten, with bas-relief freckles and hair the color of the cover of the magazine you buy at the newsstand when you want to catch a train. Bill and me figured that Ebenezer would melt down for a ransom of two thousand dollars to a cent. But wait till I tell you.

About two miles from Summit was a little mountain covered with a dense cedar brake. On the mountain's rear elevation was a cave. There we stored provisions.

One evening after sundown, we drive in a buggy past old Dorset's house. The kid was in the street, throwing rocks at a kitten on the opposite fence.

"Hey, little boy!" says Bill, "would you like to have a bag of candy and a ride?"

The boy catches Bill neatly in the eye with a piece of brick.

That boy put up a fight like a welter-weight cinnamon bear, but at last we got him down in the bottom of the buggy and drove away. We took him up to the cave, and I hitched the horse in the cedar brake. After dark I drove the buggy to the little village three miles away where we had hired it, and walked back to the mountain.

Bill was pasting court plaster over the scratches and bruises on his features. There was a fire burning behind the big rock at the entrance of the cave, and the boy was watching a pot of boiling coffee with two buzzard-tail feathers stuck in his red hair.

He points a stick at me when I come up, and says, "Ha! cursed paleface, do you dare to enter the camp of Red Chief, the terror of the plains?"

"He's all right now," says Bill, rolling up his trousers and examining some bruises on his shins. "We're playing Indian. I'm Old Hank the Trapper, Red Chief's captive, and I'm to be scalped at daybreak. By Geronimo! That kid can kick hard."

Yes, sir, that boy seemed to be having the time of his life. The fun of camping out in a cave had made him forget that he was a captive himself. He immediately christened me Snake-eye the Spy and announced that when his braves returned from the warpath I was to be broiled at the stake at the rising of the sun.

Then we had supper; and he filled his mouth full of bacon and bread and gravy, and began to talk. He made a during-dinner speech something like this:

"I like this fine. I never camped out before; but I had a pet 'possum once, and I was nine last birthday. I hate to go to school. Rats ate up sixteen of Jimmy Talbot's aunt's speckled hen's eggs. Are there any real Indians in these woods? I want some more gravy. Does the trees moving make the wind blow? We had five puppies. What makes your nose so red, Hank? My father has lots of money. Are the stars hot? I whipped Ed Walker twice, Saturday. I don't like girls. You dassent catch toads unless with a string. Do oxen make any noise? Why are oranges round? Have you got beds to sleep on in this cave? Amos Murray has got six toes. A parrot can talk, but a monkey or a fish can't. How many does it take to make twelve?"

Every few minutes he would remember that he was a pesky redskin, and pick up his stick rifle and tiptoe to the mouth of the cave to rubber for the scouts of the hated paleface. Now and then he would let out a war whoop that made Old Hank the Trapper shiver. That boy had Bill terrorized from the start.

"Red Chief," says I to the kid, "would you like to go home?"

"Aw, what for?" says he. "I don't have any fun at home. I hate to go to school. I like to camp out. You won't take me back home again, Snake-eye, will you?"

"Not right away," says I. "We'll stay here in the cave a while."

"All right!" says he. "That'll be fine. I never had such fun in all my life."

We went to bed about eleven o'clock. We spread down some wide blankets and quilts and put Red Chief between us. We weren't afraid he'd run away. He kept us awake for three hours, jumping up and reaching for his rifle and screeching, "Hist! pard" in mine and Bill's ears as the fancied crackle of a twig or the rustle of a leaf revealed to his young imagination the stealthy approach of the outlaw band. At last I fell into a troubled sleep and dreamed that I had been kidnaped and chained to a tree by a ferocious pirate with red hair.

Just at daybreak, I was awakened by a series of awful screams from Bill. They weren't yells, or howls, or shouts, or whoops or yawps, such as you'd expect from a manly set of vocal organs—they were simply indecent, terrifying, humiliating screams, such as women emit when they see ghosts or caterpillars. It's an awful thing to hear a strong, desperate fat man scream in a cave at daybreak.

I jumped up to see what the matter was. Red Chief was sitting on Bill's chest, with one hand twined in Bill's hair. In the other he had the sharp case knife we used for slicing bacon; and he was realistically trying to take Bill's scalp, according to the sentence that had been pronounced upon him the evening before.

I got the knife away from the kid and made him lie down again. But from that moment Bill's spirit was broken. He lay down on his side of the bed, but he never closed an eye again in sleep as long as that boy was with us. I dozed off for a while but along toward sun-up I remembered that

Red Chief had said I was to be burned at the stake at the rising of the sun. I wasn't nervous or afraid, but I sat up and lit my pipe and leaned against a rock.

"What you getting up so soon for, Sam?" asked Bill.

"Me?" says I. "Oh, I got a kind of a pain in my shoulder. I thought sitting up would rest it."

"You're a liar!" says Bill. "You're afraid. You was to be burned at sunrise, and you was afraid he'd do it. And he would, too, if he could find a match. Ain't it awful, Sam? Do you think anybody will pay out money to get a little imp like that back?"

"Sure," said I. "A rowdy kid like that is just the kind that parents dote on. Now, you and the Chief get up and cook breakfast while I go reconnoiter."

I went up on the peak of the little mountain and ran my eye over the contiguous vicinity. Over toward Summit I expected to see the sturdy yeomanry of the village armed with scythes and pitchforks beating the countryside for the dastardly kidnapers. But what I saw was a peaceful landscape dotted with one man plowing with a dun mule. Nobody was dragging the creek, no couriers dashed hither and yon bringing tidings of no news to the distracted parents. There was a sylvan attitude of somnolent sleepiness pervading that section of the external outward surface of Alabama that lay exposed to my view. "Perhaps," says I to myself, "it has not yet been discovered that the wolves have borne away the tender lambkin from the fold. Heaven help the wolves!" says I, and I went down the mountain to breakfast.

When I got to the cave I found Bill backed up against the side of it, breathing hard, and the boy threatening to smash him with a rock half as big as a coconut.

"He put a red-hot boiled potato down my back," explained Bill, "and then mashed it with his foot, and I boxed his ears. Have you got a gun about you, Sam?"

I took the rock away from the boy and kind of patched up the argument. "I'll fix you," says the kid to Bill. "No man ever yet struck Red Chief but what he got paid for it. You better beware!"

After breakfast the kid takes a piece of leather with strings wrapped around it out of his pocket and goes outside the cave unwinding it.

"What's he up to now?" says Bill anxiously. "Do you think he'll run away?"

"No fear of it," says I. "He don't seem to be much of a home body. But we've got to fix up some plan about the ransom. There don't seem to be much excitement around Summit on account of his disappearance, but maybe they haven't realized yet that he's gone. His folks may think he's spending the night with Aunt Jane or one of the neighbors. Anyhow, he'll be missed today. Tonight we must get a message to his father, demanding the two thousand dollars for his return."

Just then we heard a kind of war whoop, such as David might have emitted when he knocked out the champion Goliath. It was a sling that Red Chief had pulled out of his pocket, and he was whirling it around his head.

I dodged, and heard a heavy thud and a kind of a sigh from Bill, like one a horse gives out when you take his saddle off. A rock the size of an egg had caught Bill just behind his left ear. He loosened himself all over and fell in the fire across the frying pan of hot water for washing the dishes. I dragged him out and poured cold water on his head for half an hour.

By and by, Bill sits up and feels behind his ear and says, "Sam, do you know who my favorite Biblical character is?"

"Take it easy," says I. "You'll come to your senses presently."

"King Herod," says he. "You won't leave me here all alone, will you, Sam?"

I went out and caught that boy and shook him until his freckles rattled.

"If you don't behave," says I, "I'll take you straight home."

"I was only funning," says he sullenly. "I didn't mean to hurt Old Hank. But what did he hit me for? I'll behave, Snake-eye, if you won't send me home and if you'll let me play the Black Scout today.

"I don't know the game," says I. "That's for you and Mr. Bill to decide. He's your playmate for the day. I'm going away for a while on business. Now, you come in and say you are sorry for hurting him, or home you go at once."

I made him and Bill shake hands, and then I took Bill aside and told him I was going to Poplar Cove, a little village three miles from the cave, and find out what I could about how the kidnaping had been regarded in Summit. Also, I thought it best to send the ransom letter to old man Dorset that day.

"You know, Sam," says Bill, "I've stood by you without batting an eye in earthquake, fire and flood—poker games, dynamite outrages, police raids, train robberies and cyclones. I never lost my nerve yet till we kidnaped that two-legged skyrocket. He's got me going. You won't leave me long with him, will you, Sam?"

"I'll be back some time this afternoon," says I. "You must keep the boy amused and quiet till I return. And now we'll write the letter to Old Dorset."

Bill and I got paper and pencil and worked on the letter while Red Chief, with a blanket wrapped around him, strutted up and down, guarding the mouth of the cave. Bill begged me tearfully to make the ransom fifteen hundred dollars instead of two thousand. "I ain't attempting," says he, "to decry the celebrated moral aspect of parental affection, but we're dealing with humans, and it ain't human for anybody to give up two thousand dollars for that forty-pound chunk of freckled wildcat. I'm willing to take a chance at fifteen hundred dollars. You can charge the difference up to me."

So, to relieve Bill, I acceded, and we collaborated a letter that ran this way:

Ebenezer Dorset, Esq:

We have your boy concealed in a place far from Summit. It is useless for you or the most skillful detectives to attempt to find him. Absolutely the only terms on which you can have him restored to you are these: We demand fifteen hundred dollars in large bills for his return, the money to be left at midnight tonight at the same spot and the same box as your reply—as hereinafter described. If you agree to these terms, send your answer in writing by a solitary messenger tonight at half-past eight o'clock. After crossing Owl Creek, on the road to Poplar Cove, there are three large trees about a hundred yards apart, close to the fence of the wheat field on the right-hand side. At the bottom of the fence post, opposite the third tree, will be found a small pasteboard box.

The messenger will place the answer in this box and return immediately to Summit.

If you attempt any treachery or fail to comply with our demand as stated, you will never see your boy again.

If you pay the money as demanded, he will be returned to you safe and well within three hours. These terms are final, and if you do not accede to them, no further communication will be attempted.

Two Desperate Men

I addressed this letter to Dorset and put it in my pocket. As I was about to start, the kid comes up to me and says, "Aw, Snake-eye, you said I could play the Black Scout while you was gone."

"Ah, of course," says I. "Mr. Bill will play with you. What kind of a game is it?"

"I'm the Black Scout," says Red Chief, "and I have to ride to the stockade to warn the settlers that the Indians are coming. I'm tired of playing Indian myself. I want to be the Black Scout."

"All right," says I. "It sounds harmless to me. I guess Mr. Bill will help you foil the pesky savages."

"What am I to do?" asks Bill, looking at the kid suspiciously.

"You are the hoss," says Black Scout. "Get down on your hands and knees. How can I ride to the stockade without a hoss?"

"You'd better keep him interested," said I, "till we get the scheme going. Loosen up, Bill."

Bill gets down on his all fours, and a look comes in his eyes like a rabbit's when you catch it in a trap.

"How far is it to the stockade, kid?" he asks, in a husky manner of voice.

"Ninety miles," says the Black Scout "And you have to hump yourself to get there on time. Whoa, now!"

The Black Scout jumps on Bill's back and digs his heels in his side.

"For Heaven's sake," says Bill, "hurry back, Sam, as soon as you can. I wish we hadn't made the ransom more than a thousand. Say, you quit kicking me, or I'll get up and warm you good."

I walked over to Poplar Cove and sat around the post office and store, talking with the chawbacons that come in to trade. One whiskerando says that he hears Summit is all upset on account of Elder Ebenezer Dorset's boy having been lost or stolen. That was all I wanted to know. I bought some smoking tobacco, referred casually to the price of black-eyed peas, posted my letter surreptitiously and came away. The postmaster said the mail carrier would come by in an hour to take the mail on to Summit.

When I got back to the cave, Bill and the boy were not to be found. I explored the vicinity of the cave and risked a yodel or

two, but there was no response. So I lighted my pipe and sat down on a mossy bank to await further developments.

In about half an hour I heard the bushes rustle, and Bill wobbled out into the little glade in front of the cave. Behind him was the kid, stepping softly like a scout, with a broad grin on his face. Bill stopped, took off his hat and wiped his face with a red handkerchief. The kid stopped about eight feet behind him.

"Sam," says Bill, "I suppose you'll think I'm a renegade, but I couldn't help it. I'm a grown person with masculine proclivities and habits of self-defense, but there is a time when all systems of egotism and predominance fail. The boy is gone. I have sent him home. All is off. There was martyrs in old times," goes on Bill, "that suffered death rather than give up the particular graft they enjoyed. None of 'em ever was subjugated to such supernatural tortures as I have been. I tried to be faithful to our articles of depredation, but there came a limit."

"What's the trouble, Bill?" I asks him.

"I was rode," says Bill, "the ninety miles to the stockade, not barring an inch. Then when the settlers was rescued, I was given oats. Sand ain't a palatable substitute. And then, for an hour I had to try to explain to him why there was nothin' in holes, how a road can run both ways and what makes the grass green. I tell you, Sam, a human can only stand so much. I takes him by the neck of his clothes and drags him down the mountain. On the way he kicks my legs black-and-blue from the knees down, and I've got two or three bites on my thumb and hand cauterized."

"But he's gone"—continues Bill—"gone home. I showed him the road to Summit and kicked him about eight feet nearer there at one kick. I'm sorry we lose the ransom, but it was either that or Bill Driscoll to the madhouse."

"Bill," says I, "there isn't any heart disease in your family, is there?"

"No," says Bill "nothing chronic except malaria and accidents. Why?"

"Then you might turn around," says I, "and have a look behind you."

Bill turns and sees the boy, and loses his complexion and sits down plump on the ground and begins to pluck aimlessly at grass and little sticks. For an hour I was afraid for his mind. And then I told him that my scheme was to put the whole job through immediately and that we would get the ransom and be off with it by midnight if old Dorset fell in with our proposition. So Bill braced up enough to give the kid a weak sort of a smile and a promise to play the Russian in a Japanese war with him as soon as he felt a little better.

I had a scheme for collecting that ransom without danger of being caught by counterplots that ought to commend itself to professional kidnapers. The tree under which the answer was to be left—and the money later on—was close to the road fence with big, bare fields on all sides. If a gang of constables should be watching for anyone to come for the note they could see him a long way off crossing the fields or in the road. But no, siree! At half-past eight I was up in that tree as well hidden as a tree toad, waiting for the messenger to arrive.

Exactly on time, a half-grown boy rides up the road on a bicycle, locates the pasteboard box at the foot of the fence post, slips a folded piece of paper into it and pedals away again back toward Summit.

I waited an hour and then concluded the thing was square. I slid down the tree, got the note, slipped along the fence till I struck the woods and was back at the cave in another half an hour. I opened the note, got near the lantern and read it to Bill. It was written with a pen in a crabbed hand, and the sum and substance of it was:

Two Desperate Men

GENTLEMEN: I received your letter today by post in regard to the ransom you ask for the return of my son. I think you are a little high in your demands, and I hereby make you a counter-proposition, which I am inclined to believe you will accept. You bring Johnny home and pay me two hundred and fifty dollars in cash, and I agree to take him off your hands. You had better come at night, for the neighbors believe he is lost, and I couldn't be responsible for what they would do to anybody they saw bringing him back.

Very respectfully,
Ebenezer Dorset

"Great pirates of Penzance!" says I. "Of all the impudent——"

But I glanced at Bill and hestitated. He had the most appealing look in his eyes I ever saw on the face of a dumb or a talking brute.

"Sam," says he, "what's two hundred and fifty dollars, after all? We've got the money. One more night of this kid will send me to a bed in Bedlam. Besides being a thorough gentleman, I think Mr. Dorset is a spendthrift for making us such a liberal offer. You ain't going to let the chance go, are you?"

"Tell you the truth, Bill," says I, "this little he ewe lamb has somewhat got on my nerves, too. We'll take him home, pay the ransom and make our getaway."

We took him home that night. We got him to go by telling him that his father had bought a silver-mounted rifle and a pair of moccasins for him, and we were going to hunt bears the next day.

It was just twelve o'clock when we knocked at Ebenezer's front door. Just at the moment when I should have been abstracting the fifteen hundred dollars from the box under the tree, according to the original proposition, Bill was counting out two hundred and fifty dollars into Dorset's hand.

When the kid found out we were going to leave him at home he started up a howl like a calliope and fastened himself as tight as a leech to Bill's leg. His father peeled him away gradually, like a porous plaster.

"How long can you hold him?" asks Bill.

"I'm not so strong as I used to be," says old Dorset, "but I think I can promise you ten minutes."

"Enough," says Bill. "In ten minutes I shall cross the Central, Southern and Middle Western States and be legging it trippingly for the Canadian border."

And, as dark as it was, and as fat as Bill was, and as good a runner as I am, he was a good mile and a half out of Summit before I could catch up with him.

The Lilac in the Lake

The Grydale Singers were a local legend.
From the bottom of the lake—so the story went—they
would lament their sister's death till a man would walk
into Grydale Water for love of them

JOAN AIKEN

There was this old boy, Enoch Dibben, the schoolmaster at a little place at the back of beyond. Grydale, it's called. Likely you'll not have heard of it. The lads at that village are terrible teasers, to a boy. Sure as one of them looks you in the eye, it's because he's dropped a live eel in your lunch-bucket, or loosed a sackful of grasshoppers inside your car or tied your shoelaces together so that you fall over when you try to walk. Teasers, and artful, they are, but not an ounce of vice in them. Indeed, Mr. Dibben rather enjoyed their goings-on. He was such a dreamy old fellow, wandering about the dale with his hands behind his back and his head in the clouds, that it was some way pleasant for him to feel folk noticed he was there to the extent of filling his inkwell with golden syrup, as Charlie Herdman did one Friday

afternoon. For he was a single man and sometimes felt a bit lonely, with no one to warm his slippers, or fry his bacon or bake him a bit of parkin for a Sunday treat.

It's a quiet little place, Grydale, thirty miles from the nearest railway. Up above it on each side the mountains climb out of sight. After the sun goes down you can hear a pheasant cluck in Grassy Woods, five miles off, or a dog barking in Shipton, down at the foot of the valley.

Sometimes at night in his little stone cottage Mr. Dibben, snug in bed, would think he heard a tapping at the door. Specially of a milky summer night, when you could hardly tell if the noise that broke the silence was the stream whispering or your own heart beating, he used to think somebody quietly knocked at his door; he used to think he could hear voices calling: "Mr. Dibben! Mr. Dibben! Please come down and let us in! We're so lonely and cold! Let us in, and we'll cook for you and clean for you. We'll dig your garden and darn your socks. We'll wash your shirts and tidy your papers and bake your bread and sharpen your pencils!"

Mr. Dibben, though, took no notice of this, except maybe to burrow deeper in the bedclothes. "It's those naughty boys," he would think, shutting his eyes tight. "They want me to come down and open the door; then a bucket of potato peelings will probably fall on my head while they run off up to the village laughing themselves into hiccups. I'm not such a fool as that!"

Sometimes of a morning when he opened his eyes and the blue day came rushing in he'd wonder if he had dreamed the voices. Sometimes he'd resolve that next time he heard them he'd go down to the door and open it. But somehow he never did.

There were only three cars in Grydale; Mr. Dibben's old Rattler was one of them. The boys left his car alone; whatever else they did, they never played any of their tricks on Rattler; when you live so cut-off you get to treat cars with respect. So, on fine weekends and summer evenings, Mr. Dibben was a great wanderer. You might come across him anywhere about the countryside from Mickle Fell to Spurn Head. What was he doing? Hunting for legends. If he heard tell of a village where they'd a bewitched bakehouse, or where the hares danced in a ring on Midsummer Eve, or where the ghost of King Richard sat eating gooseberries in the churchyard, first free moment Mr. Dibben had he'd be off, fast as old Rattler could make it at a galloping eighteen miles an hour. And once there, he'd get the whole take out of the oldest inhabitant—or the youngest—or whoever had a fancy to sit in the sun spinning tall tales. Mr. Dibben wrote them all down on sheets of paper with holes at one side and stuck them in a book. Bigger than the Bible it would be, when finished, and he was that proud of it! "When it's published," he used to say, "my name will be known throughout the length and breadth of England." But there were some in the village used to think he'd better get a move on, sending it to a publisher, or one of these days he'd find himself knocking at St. Peter's gate with all his bits of paper still under his arm.

Mr. Dibben was well occupied, chasing far and wide like a pup after bumblebees, and it wasn't till he'd been in Grydale nigh on ten years that he found, with all his questings and questionings, he'd clean missed one of the best tales of all and that on his own doorstep, the tale of the Grydale Singers.

Charlie Herdman told it to him then, one hot sleepy afternoon after school. Charlie had a reason for this: he wanted to keep Mr. Dibben distracted and out of the way up in the schoolhouse while some friends of his prepared a little surprise. So he said to the old boy, as they were tidying up the Infants' books—Charlie was monitor that week, "I wonder you aren't afeared to live in that house of yourn, all on your own down below the village, Mester Dibben. Don't you never think the Grydale Singers might spirit you away?"

"Grydale Singers?" says Mr. Dibben, all agog at once. "What are they? Grydale Singers, I don't believe I've ever heard of them. Leave rubbing the blackboard, my boy—I'll do that—now you tell me about these Grydale Singers."

And he commences rubbing at the board with his handkerchief.

"Well," artful Charles says, thoroughly enjoying himself now, "it's a tale we have in the village about these seven sisters who lived here in my grandfather's time, or it may have been in *his* granfer's time. I ain't so special sure, but it was in the days when folk rode horseback and the summers was always hot, and mushrooms grew on the village green and lasses wore their hair hanging long and loose."

"Seven sisters—yes, yes," Mr. Dibben he says. "Just a minute, Charlie, while I give the tape recorder a bit of a bang—it's stuck again."

For Mr. Dibben had this tape recorder he used for taking down the stories he collected.

"Right, Charlie, I've got it going again —now tell me about those seven sisters. What were their names?"

"Why," Charlie says, "there's some believe it wasn't seven sisters but three, or maybe four, but the way I heard it there's seven of 'em, and their names was Mary, Mercy, Marila, Martha, Marian, Marjorie and Marigold, and they was the blacksmith's lasses, Mr. Artingstall it was then, and pretty as a podful of young peas. Fair hair, blue eyes and all that. Half the lads in the village was after them. They lived in the blacksmith's cottage, that's the one you

have now, Mr. Dibben, afore my granda's grandad bought it up, and they used to help their dad with blowing the bellows and suchlike. Pretty as they were, they was that uppish and standoffish they'd sworn none of them 'ud ever marry, not a one of them could abide the male sex. Spinsters to their deathbeds they declared they'd be, on account of all the teasing they'd gone through at school, the lads in Grydale—as you know—being fond of a lark."

"Seven sisters sworn not to marry—yes, yes," Mr. Dibben says, setting light to the blackboard rubber instead of his pipe. "This is most interesting, Charlie, go on. What happened to them?"

"They used to sing a lot—any party or wedding, funeral or christening there was in the village the Artingstall lasses would be on hand obliging with a bit of Stainer or whatever was suitable. And of an evening they'd sit under the lilac bush in the garden—the same one that's still there now, Mr. Dibben—singing away like a sipkin of thrushes. Well, about the time Mary, that's the eldest one, was getting on for twenty-three and folk had started to think maybe they'd stick to their word and really would end up as old maids, people began to notice that when they sang a chorus, one of 'em was always flat. And next thing they found was that Mary had been secretly running off to meet a young fellow, name of Huxtable, kind of a wandering peddler who came up to the village once a month with ribbons and saucepans; and next thing was, he and Mary had got wed. Well, the other sisters put a good face on it, they sang at her wedding, but they felt she'd let the family down. They swore *they'd* never do such a thing. In fact, it made them more set against men than ever; they reckoned Huxtable had fair bewitched her. I forget whether he took her to Scunthorpe or Skegness or Scarborough for the honeymoon, but anyhow, not long after they got back they went out one day fishing on Grydale Water, in a rowboat, and Mary somehow got her long hair caught in the anchor chain, was pulled overboard with it, down to the bottom, and drowned. Her husband was fair mazed with grief, some say he jumped right overboard after her and that was the end of him, others that he joined the French Foreign Legion and was seen in Whitby twenty years after, declaring that he was the Emperor Boneypart. Anyway, he never came back to Grydale."

"What became of the other sisters?"

"The very night after she was drowned they went out to the lilac tree for the last time and sang a lament for her. Folk who heard it said it was so sad that the owls in the churchyard elms were boo-hooing too, and the lilac tree dropped all its blossom for pity. And when they'd done, they all got up and walked into Grydale Water and that was the end of them."

"Really?" says Mr. Dibben, absentmindedly putting his pen in his mouth and his lighted pipe in his pocket. "Dear me, what a remarkable tale. Is that the end of it, Charlie?"

"Not quite," Charlie says. "For there's folk as says that from that day to this, every night from half past eleven to twelve midnight, those sisters can be heard under the lilac tree singing their lament—only they won't do it if there's a man within earshot because they're still fell set against the whole flaysome race. It's said they'll go on lamenting till trout swim Grassy Wood, or till a man can be found that'll walk into Grydale Water for love of them."

"Dear me," Mr Dibben said again. "So they won't sing when a man's about? Are there ladies in the village that have heard them, then?"

"My mam says she has, many a time," Charlie says. "When she's been coming home late from the Ladies' Glee Club or the Bingo Drive."

"I must go and see your good mother without delay," says Mr. Dibben, trying to lock up his desk with a bit of blackboard chalk.

Mr. Dibben then hurried off to ask all the womenfolk in the village if they'd ever heard the Grydale Singers. Some said yes, some said no, some said they didn't believe in such foolishness. Time Mr. Dibben went home it was getting towards dusk, the swifts had stopped scooping for flies and gone to roost in the eaves.

He opened his gate, gave a bit of a glance at the historic lilac bush, never noticed the hedge, which heaved and shook with giggles because half the boys of the village were lodged in it, and went on to open his front door, which led straight into the little parlor. He found the door uncommon hard to shift, and when at last he got it open, about a ton of water rushed out at him. The boys had been busy ever since school finished, filling his room full of river through a hosepipe led from Grydale Falls. Mr. Dibben's cottage, the only house below the falls, was well downhill from the village, so it was easy enough to do.

The old chap wasn't angry, only astonished. He stood scratching his head, while the water pushed past him down the garden path like brown coffee suds.

"Dear have mercy!" says he to himself. "Can I have left the kitchen tap on?"

So like an old puzzled bird he looked, as he stood there on one leg, scratching his head, an old bird with its feathers all ruffled up, that the boys, who were as good-natured a set of young addlepates as you could hope to find, hadn't the heart to leave him to clear up the mess. They came bursting out of the hedge, half choked with laughing, patted Mr. Dibben, picked him up, carried him into his kitchen, which was still dry, and started mopping down the parlor floor.

"Eh, dear, Mr. Dibben, didn't you ever guess?" Charlie said to him. "Didn't you ever wonder why I was keeping you so long at the school?"

"But then, that story you told me about the singers—was that not a true tale?"

"The Grydale Singers? Yes, that was a lively tale enough," Charlie told him. "I dare say they'd be singing away now if we wasn't about."

Relieved to hear this, which was the only thing that had worried him, Mr. Dibben went to his bed, leaving the boys to get on with swabbing down the parlor. Next day the place was still damp enough, and he thought it right to go along to Farmer Herdman, who was his landlord, and explain what had happened. Farmer Herdman shook his head over the tale (though he couldn't forbear a grin, having been a boy himself once) and offered to give them all a dusting if Mr. Dibben wished. But the old boy shook his head.

"I don't hold it agen them. Young blood will out. I only thought fit to mention it, Mr. Herdman, to explain how the house came to be so uncommon damp."

"As to that," Farmer Herdman he says, "the house'll be damper still soon enough. I was going to come and see you, Mester Dibben, about that very thing."

Then he began explaining something about the new dam at Shipton to the schoolmaster, who didn't hear a single word he said. For a grand notion had just come into Mr. Dibben's head: why not try to get a recording of the Grydale Singers on his tape machine? Likely enough the young ladies had never heard of a tape recorder and would have no suspicions of it, might not even notice it quietly spinning away, if he hid it under the grass and leaves. And if they did happen to spot it—well, a tape recorder's not the same as a man, is it, no reason why that should stop them singing? As you might imagine, Mr.

Dibben, who used to sing himself when he was young, baritone in the Bottlewell Male Voice Choir, was mortal keen to be the first man to hear those poor sorrowful singers, and he thought he had hit on the very answer to the problem. The only snag was that he himself would have to clear out for a night and go well away so that his presence wouldn't put a cramp in the business. Where could he go? he wondered, and then he remembered his Auntie Sarah in York. She would put him up, and willing.

"So do you want to see about getting the furniture shifted, or will you leave it to me?" says Farmer Herdman, finishing his long explanation, and Mr. Dibben, who hadn't taken in a word of it, quickly says, "Oh, I will, I'll look after it, thank'e," for he didn't want anybody meddling around the cottage while he was away and maybe upsetting the Singers. He put his hat on inside out and bustled off home to pack up a few things.

Late that night, about twenty past eleven, he set off, first hiding the tape recorder under the lilac tree in a clump of fern where he hoped the ghostly sisters wouldn't notice it. The tape was a two-hour one, so he calculated there would be enough and to spare for recording the lament.

Away he drove, along the side of the valley, past Grydale Water, glimmering in the hazy moonlight, and made his way to York city, where, as it chanced, he found his Auntie Sarah, nigh on a hundred, on her deathbed.

"Don't forget to wind the clock when I'm gone, Enoch Dibben," she croaked at him. "I've left you all my money, Enoch, on condition you have this house turned into a cats' home. Now I must be on my way—I'm ten minutes late already. My old crony Nancy Thorpe is waiting for me up there in Paradise; I promised to take her all the latest knitting patterns," and with that she took and died. Mr. Dibben was a bit put out, since he was now obliged to stay in York, make arrangements for the funeral, see to moving the pusses into their new home, not to mention winding the clock. A fortnight it took him getting everything straight, and a marble slab for Auntie Sarah with half a cherub on it. He was in a fret, too, about how his tape recorder was standing the weather, though he'd left it in a waterproof cover.

As soon as the cats were in, and a caretaker to feed them and wind the clock, he was off, hotfoot, back to Grydale, where things had not been standing still as you shall hear.

It was late night again when Mr. Dibben drove back up the daleside; the mist stood in the bottom of the valley like clumps of thistledown, and the night was so quiet that old Rattler's chug-chug sounded louder than cannonfire. Mr. Dibben felt a bit lonesome thinking of the cats all snug together in their new home and Auntie Sarah so cosy up in Paradise a-chatting with Mrs. Thorpe over their plain-and-pearl, while he had only his cold empty cottage waiting for him.

When he reached the track turning down off the main road to his own house he was a bit perplexed because there seemed to be water across the road, though with all the mist lying it was hard to be sure.

"Dang it," says Mr. Dibben, "are my eyes deceiving me? Surely to gracious the lake can't have risen all that much? There's not been a drop of rain in York for the last fortnight. Can it be those boys, up to their tricks again?"

He stopped in the middle of the track, got out and ambled forward on foot.

"My eyes must be deceiving me," he says then. "It must be some kind of a mirage. Because if the water is up here, where I think I see it, then my house is under the lake up to the chimney pots—which is out of the question. For if my house is under water up to the chimneys, then my tape recorder would be under water also —which is not to be thought of. I am having a hallucination, but I will ignore it."

On he goes, up to his ankles first, then up to his knees. Then he was wading with his belt under water, then his chin was covered, and at last Mr. Dibben was clean gone under the water, plodding forward in search of his tape recorder and naught left visible but a trail of bubbles.

Well! When he got to his front gate a perfect chorus of voices greeted him.

"Evening, Mr. Dibben!"

"Welcome home, then, Mr. Dibben!"

"We've got your slippers a-warming, Mr. Dibben!"

"And a pot of tea mashed!"

"And a rasher of bacon frying!"

"And a lovely bit of parkin in the oven!"

"And the best cheesecakes and marmalade this side of Doncaster!"

Then they all said together, "Oh, Mr. Dibben, we're so pleased you've come home!"

Mr. Dibben was fair bewildered, as you can imagine, by such a welcome, but he couldn't help being pleased too, not a doubt of that. It was plain that the Artingstall lasses had grown tired of their solitary life and wanted someone to take care of. The only thing that worried him was, what had become of his recording of the lament, under all that lake water, but Mercy Artingstall told him, "To tell you the truth, Mr. Dibben, we was so cast down and low-spirited the night we thought you'd gone off and left us that we never sang a note. But, we'll make up for that now!"

Of course, next day in Grydale village they was fair upset to find Mr. Dibben's old Rattler standing on the edge of the new reservoir, and him nowhere to be seen.

"I blame myself, that I do!" says Farmer

Herdman. "I should have made certain sure that he knew about the dam they was building at valley-foot, and how the reservoir would cover his cottage. I should have moved his furniture myself into the new little house I had ready for him up in the village. I ought to have remembered what an absentminded old chap he was. I'm right downhearted, and that's the truth."

As for Charlie Herdman, he went about the place with a face as long as an eight-day clock. And Farmer Herdman said he'd have the book of tales (which they found in old Rattler) printed up in big print, with fine colored pictures, at his own expense as a memorial.

But they needn't have worried about keeping Mr. Dibben's memory green. Punctual that night at half past eleven, the Grydale Singers started up over the lake, over the lilac bush that was now drowned eighteen feet deep in Grydale Water—and this time they'd a baritone with them as well. And no nonsense about not singing if there were men within earshot—the noise they made, with a rousing good rendering of the Hallelujah Chorus, was enough to fetch the whole village out of its beds, and it was the same each night after and ever since.

In fact, though there's no denying it draws the tourist business, coaches come from as far afield as Hull, some of the folk in Grydale are beginning to grumble about the nightly choruses, and have even complained to the County Council.

But the Council says that nothing can be done.

Jimmy's Made-to-Order Story: Anchor House

*About a little boy and a ship's anchor
and a library full of old books and a woodchuck
and a bed and a doorknob*

DOROTHY CANFIELD

"What I like best about your stories," said Jimmy, "is that there isn't any moral to them."

"Nor any sense," said a grown-up.

"Yes, that *is* another nice thing about them," said Jimmy and continued, "Seems as though we haven't had any made-to-order stories for quite a while, and I'm sort of hungry for one."

"All right," said I. "Have you settled yet what you want to have in it this time?"

"As you haven't told me one for three whole days, the things I want have piled up and *piled* up!"

"Let's hear what they are."

"A little boy and a ship's anchor and a library full of old books and a woodchuck and a spider and a bed and a doorknob."

"Not on your life!" said I. "That's three days' worth, not one. There are too many."

"All right, I'll leave out the spider," said Jimmy. "I didn't want him in so very much, anyhow. It would probably turn out that he spun his web over the mouth of a cave and saved the life of somebody hiding inside. And I'd hate that."

Jimmy's choice of what to put in a story is not as wild and haphazard as it seems. He has one fixed aim, to avoid certain stale old combinations that make him groan in printed stories. For instance, he never has put into a story either a millionaire or an orphan child; but if he did, I know that nothing could make him put them into the same story. He would be afraid that the orphan couldn't help turning out to be the long lost child of the millionaire. To prevent such a vexing thing, he would, I am sure, put the millionaire in with a cake of soap and have the orphan child in the story with a hippopotamus.

"No," said Jimmy once again, "we'll leave the spider out."

"Well, without the spider, it is, of course, the story about the little boy whose brothers and sisters got the measles, and the family weren't sure whether he'd been exposed, so they sent him off to Anchor House, which was the name of his old uncle's house down by the seashore."

"Was it in school time?" asked Jimmy.

"Yes, right in the first part of May."

"Didn't he have the luck!" commented Jimmy.

"Oh, I don't know. Anchor House was 'way out on a sandy point, with no children in any of the farmhouses around. His uncle was a retired sea captain, pretty deaf and awfully fat, who only wanted to read his newspaper all day and snore all night. And the old cook who did for them was as cross as two sticks and hated little boys in the kitchen. So he had to invent games to play all by himself. Mostly he played with the books in the library which were big and thick and made splendid walls for forts. His uncle didn't mind, and the old cook didn't know anything about it because she never went into the wing of the house where the library was. It was a good way from the kitchen, and she had rheumatism in her knee.

Well, one night the little boy woke up and remembered that he had carried a lot of the books out on the porch to build a rampart there and hadn't taken them back in. It was a nice clear night; but you never know for sure about the weather, so he thought he'd better go down and carry them back into the library, in case of rain.

It was lovely and warm, so he didn't need anything but his pajamas; and he'd been going barefoot daytimes, so he didn't stop for slippers. He trotted downstairs and along the hall into the library and out on the porch that was back of the main part of the house. The books were a little damp, already, from the night air, so he was glad he had come down. He carried them into the library, armful after armful, dozens and dozens of armfuls it seemed to him. It took him a long, long time even though he didn't try to put them back on the shelves but just piled them up anywhere. He was pretty tired when he finally got the last one in, and started back up the stairs.

He was yawning and stretching and thinking how nice it would be to get into bed and snuggle down and doze off, when he noticed that the door to his room stood open. This gave him rather a turn, for he was sure that he had shut it very carefully. But that was nothing compared to what he found when he stepped inside his room.

For his bed was gone!

Yes, just like that. The headboard was leaned up against the wall, and the footboard lay on the floor, and the bedclothes were tossed over the back of a chair; but the springs and mattress had disappeared! Not a sign nor a smitch of them was to be seen.

Of course, the little boy knew at once that this couldn't be so. Whatever else might get carried away out of a house at night, it wouldn't be a *bed*.

So he went out into the hall, shut his door behind him, waited a minute and then opened it quick, expecting surely to see his bed all there, just as he'd left it.

95

But it wasn't, only just the headboard leaned up against the wall, and the footboard lying on the floor.

You can't imagine how *queer* the little boy felt. Not scared, for there wasn't anything to be scared of, but so queer-feeling that he sat down quick in a chair.

"Let me think," he said to himself. "Let me *think*." But every thought he tried to think was perfectly impossible. How *could* his bed be gone, and he away for only a few minutes from his room, and not a soul awake in the house? And anyhow, why would anybody *want his bed?* Burglars didn't steal beds. He decided he would go and tell Uncle Peter and find out—Oh mercy! suppose that Uncle Peter had disappeared, too, like the bed! This did scare him, really and truly, so that he could barely stagger across the hall to his uncle's door and turn the knob.

Uncle Peter always kept a little nightlight burning, and by its light the little boy could see him plainly. He was oh so beautifully, comfortably asleep as only deaf people can sleep, and snoring so loudly and so enjoyably as only old sea captains can snore. It made the little boy all right again, just in a minute, only to look at him. Nothing much could be the matter with Uncle Peter hitting the pillow like that.

He drew a long breath, stepped out again into the hall and shut the door behind him. It would be a sin to wake up anybody who was having such a sleep as that. But all the same, it didn't get him back his bed.

Then he had another idea that explained everything perfectly. This was all a dream, and he'd wake up in the morning just as usual. That was the way all the stories in books ended. The best thing for him to do was to turn over, curl up, drop off to sleep more soundly, and—

But how could he do all that without any bed to do it in?

Mercy! This was getting worse and worse. He put his hand up to his head to see if it were still on his neck and in the right place. It was. But that was all the good it did him.

Of course, he could have wrapped the bedclothes around him and lain down on the floor, but although he wasn't scared—not *really* scared—he wouldn't have lain down between that headboard and footboard, not for a million dollars. Suppose whatever it was that had carried off the bed should carry him off to the same place. Not, of course, you know, that he really believed for a minute that his bed was gone. How could it be?

He began to feel a little chilly and went in to get his blanket. The phosphorescent hands of his alarm clock showed him that it was nearly three o'clock. It would soon be day. He had an idea. He'd take his blanket and go out of doors for the rest of the night. He'd never seen dawn begin, and all the nature books said that the animals got out and played more and moved around more just at dawn than at any other time. He wrapped the blanket around him and started out of the front door to go down to a big rock by the brook. There were woodchucks in the field beyond. Maybe he'd see them out feeding when it got light. He was sure of one thing! He wouldn't miss them from dropping off to sleep. He felt as though he never, never would sleep again—if, as a matter of fact, he wasn't asleep all this whole time!

As he stepped down the front path he saw something white lying there. And what do you suppose it was? The knob of his door. He recognized it because it was cracked in a funny way, with lines that made a triangle. He stooped over it to make sure, but you'd better believe he didn't pick it up or touch it. No, sir! All this was too queer for *him*. He stepped wide around it, left it lying there and kept turn-

ing his head over his shoulder as he went on down the path. It wouldn't have surprised him to see it begin to roll along after him. But he was pretty sure that he could run faster than a doorknob—although, of course, he had never tried.

It seemed awfully good to get away from the house altogether and out on the rock, where he lay down with his blanket. The rock was hard and humpy, but he loved all the humps. They felt so natural and real. In a few minutes, as his eyes got used to the light, he saw that dawn was almost there. The sky was lighter in the east and the trees and bushes began to look gray. A big maple tree stood over the rock, and he heard a bird rustling around in the leaves and by and by it said *"Queet! queet!"* in a sleepy little voice.

And then, right under where the little boy lay, not two feet from his face, he saw something move and come slowly out of a hole. It was a woodchuck's head. It looked around an instant and then dodged back so quickly that the little boy was afraid he had moved and frightened it, though he had hardly breathed for fear of making a noise. But in a minute, out it came again and looked all around, very cautiously. Then the whole woodchuck came out, and, behind it, four baby woodchucks, little soft, furry, gray things, all roly-poly and round. They toddled along after their mother for a few steps. Then, as she began to eat, they began to play—just like a family of puppies or kittens, rolling each other over and over, squealing and running around or standing up on their hind legs to push each other. The little boy could hardly keep back his laughing to see them, they were so jolly.

After a while, their mother took them down to the brook for a drink, and he could hear them going on with their fun, pushing for the best place, falling into the water, squalling, and shaking themselves and starting another roughhouse the minute one was finished. They came racing back up the slope to the rock, bouncing along with their mother back of them. And now it was almost daylight so the little boy could really see them. He had never seen wild animals close at hand before when they were not frightened or angry, and he never forgot the gay look of fun on their bright little faces as they came scampering along toward him.

Something dreadful happened then. A

97

shadow—or what the little boy had taken for a shadow—sprang up from beside the rock, pounced on the first of the baby woodchucks and pinned it to the ground, with a horrid noise of snarling and craunching, like the noise a cat makes over a mouse. The mother woodchuck heard it too and never hesitated an instant. The brave mother made one great jump and landed on top of the animal, whatever it was—weasel perhaps—that had killed her baby. And then there was a frightful fight, a snarling, snapping, growling ball rolling over and over, with sharp yells when somebody got bitten, and a gnashing click-click of angry teeth snapping together that sounded to the little boy ever so much fiercer than the roaring of any lion at the zoo.

The little boy grabbed up a stick and stood over them, trying to see where to hit, for he didn't want to hurt the woodchuck. For a minute they didn't notice him, they were so set on tearing each other to pieces; but all of a sudden they must have caught a glimpse of him, for—whiz! flash! In a jiff, they had both vanished, the woodchuck back into the hole and the weasel off into the bushes. There was the little boy, left alone, with the sun just up over the horizon, and the poor little woodchuck lying with its head bent under it, all limp.

He picked it up to be sorry for it and thought he felt its heart still beating. Oh, perhaps he could save its life and have it for a pet! He left his blanket on the rock and ran back into the house to the kitchen. There was an old box there, with straw in it and wire netting on two sides, that somebody had brought a setting hen in the day before. He lifted the top, laid the woodchuck in on the straw and got a cup of water to sprinkle on its face, in case it had just fainted.

Old Mary came in as he was running back to the box, and when he told her about it, she advised him to see if they couldn't get a little milk down the poor thing's throat.

By the time they had some milk in a saucer, with a bit of cloth to let it drip from, the woodchuck had come to, had got up on its feet and backed off into a corner. The little boy was so glad of this and knelt down in front of the box to put his face close up to the netting to see how the new pet looked. The woodchuck sprang at him so savagely, clicking its teeth so horridly that he pulled away in a hurry. It made him feel bad to have the little creature hate him so; but, of course, it didn't surprise him. Just caught and imprisoned, it couldn't know who was its friend. But he'd tame it; he'd be so good to it, it would have to learn to love him! That's what he told his uncle at the breakfast table, where he set the box with the little captive up beside him. His uncle said that he didn't think anybody ever *had* tamed a woodchuck, but the little boy was sure *he* could.

Well, he certainly tried his best. For the next two days he didn't think of another thing. He sat right beside the cage by the hour so that the little wild thing would get used to him. He tried everything he could think of to make it eat—from fresh clover to angleworms and sugar. But it wouldn't even look at any of the foods, and snarled and jumped wickedly at his hand whenever he put something new into the box. And when he sat still and looked in lovingly at it, it would glare back at him, hating him so that the little boy could scarcely stand it.

Of course, not eating anything, it soon grew weak and could barely stand on its feet. But even lying down and panting for breath, it still had strength enough to stare hatefully at the little boy if he came near.

The second night after he'd caught it, he couldn't sleep for thinking of it and finally got up to light a candle and go to look at it again. It was crouched together in a corner, its fur every which way, looking miserably sick; but as the little boy came up with his candle, it staggered to its feet and made a feeble little spring toward him, gnashing its teeth and glaring. Then it fell over weakly on its side. But still it stretched its neck around to keep its hot eyes on the boy.

He remembered then how he had seen it playing and joking so happily with its brothers and sisters. He picked up the box in a great hurry and ran with all his might out to the big rock. There he opened the box, took the little woodchuck out and laid it down on the ground in front of the hole. As soon as it felt the earth under it, it struggled up to its feet, and without once looking at the boy, it let itself slowly down into the hole. The last the little boy saw was a tiny black-striped hind leg, trembling with eagerness, as the little wild baby went home.

Jimmy drew a long breath. "I'm glad he let him go," he said softly and fell into a dreaming silence.

I started to move away but was recalled by an indignant yell from Jimmy, "But what about that bed?"

"Oh," said I, "that turned out not to be interesting at all. One of the neighbors, going home late at night, had had an automobile accident around the turn of the road and his wife sprained her ankle. They came up to Uncle Peter's house to ask for a bedspring to carry her home on, and Uncle Peter stuck his head out of his door to say, sure, yes, they could have the one in the bedroom on the right-hand side of the landing. They made a mistake and took the left-hand room. That was all.

"And as for the doorknob, that was loose and came off in the hand of one of the men, and he was so excited he didn't think about it till he got downstairs and out on the path."

The Gorgon's Head

*Instead of locks of hair it had
a hundred twisting, venomous snakes. And if you
looked at it, you changed to lifeless stone*

Nathaniel Hawthorne

Perseus was the son of Danaë, who was the daughter of a king. And when Perseus was a very little boy, some wicked people put his mother and himself into a chest and set them afloat upon the sea. The wind blew freshly and drove the chest away from the shore, and the uneasy billows tossed it up and down while Danaë clasped her child to her bosom and dreaded that some big wave would dash its foamy crest over them both. The chest sailed on, however, until, when night was coming, it floated so near an island that it got entangled in a fisherman's nets and was drawn out high and dry upon the sand. The island was called Seriphus and it was reigned over by King Polydectes, who happened to be the fisherman's brother.

The fisherman, I am glad to tell you, was an exceedingly humane and upright man. He showed great kindness to Danaë and her little boy, and continued to befriend them until Perseus had grown to be a handsome youth, very strong and active, and skillful in the use of arms. Long before this time, King Polydectes had seen the two strangers—the mother and her child—who had come to his dominions in a floating chest. As he was not good and

kind like his brother the fisherman, but extremely wicked, he resolved to send Perseus on a dangerous enterprise in which he would probably be killed, and then to do some great mischief to Danaë herself. So this bad-hearted king spent a long while in considering what was the most dangerous thing that a young man could possibly undertake to perform. At last, having hit upon an enterprise, he sent for the youthful Perseus.

The young man came to the palace and found the king sitting upon his throne.

"Perseus," said King Polydectes, smiling craftily upon him, "you are grown up a fine young man. You and your good mother have received a great deal of kindness from myself as well as from my worthy brother the fisherman, and I suppose you would not be sorry to repay some of it."

"Please your Majesty," answered Perseus, "I would willingly risk my life."

"Well, then," continued the king, with a cunning smile on his lips, "I have a little adventure to propose to you; as you are a brave and enterprising youth, you will doubtless look upon it as a great piece of good luck to have so rare an opportunity of distinguishing yourself. You must know, my good Perseus, I think of getting married to the beautiful Princess Hippodamia; and it is customary, on these occasions, to make the bride a present of some far-fetched and elegant curiosity. I have been a little perplexed, I must honestly confess, where to obtain anything likely to please a princess of her exquisite taste. But, this morning, I flatter myself, I have thought of precisely the article."

"And can I assist your Majesty in obtaining it?" cried Perseus eagerly.

"You can, if you are as brave a youth as I believe you to be," replied King Polydectes, with the utmost graciousness. "The bridal gift which I have set my heart on presenting to the beautiful Hippodamia is the head of the Gorgon Medusa, with the snaky locks; and I depend on you, my dear Perseus, to bring it to me."

"I will set out tomorrow morning," answered Perseus.

"Pray do so, my gallant youth," replied the king. "And, Perseus, in cutting off the Gorgon's head, be careful to make a clean stroke so as not to injure its appearance. You must bring it home in the very best condition in order to suit the exquisite taste of the beautiful Princess Hippodamia."

Perseus left the palace, but was scarcely out of hearing before Polydectes burst into a laugh, being greatly amused—wicked king that he was—to find how readily the young man fell into the snare. The news quickly spread abroad that Perseus had undertaken to cut off the head of Medusa with the snaky locks. Everybody was rejoiced, for most of the inhabitants of the island were as wicked as the king himself and would have liked nothing better than to see some enormous mischief happen to Danaë and her son. The only good man in this unfortunate island of Seriphus appears to have been the fisherman. As Perseus walked along, therefore, the people pointed after him, and made mouths, and winked to one another and ridiculed him.

"Ho, ho!" cried they, "Medusa's snakes will sting him soundly!"

Now, there were three Gorgons alive at that period, and they were the most strange and terrible monsters that had ever been seen since the world was made, or that have been seen in afterdays, or that are likely to be seen in all time to come. I hardly know what sort of creature or hobgoblin to call them. They were three sisters and seem to have borne some distant resemblance to women, but were really a very frightful and mischievous species of dragon. It is, indeed, difficult to imagine what hideous beings these three sisters were. Why, instead of locks of hair, if you can believe me, they had each of them a hundred enormous snakes growing on their heads, all alive, twisting, wriggling, curling, and thrusting out their venomous tongues with forked stings at the end! The teeth of the Gorgons were terribly long tusks; their hands were made of brass; and their bodies were all over scales, which, if not iron, were something as hard and impenetrable. They had wings, too, and exceedingly splendid ones, I can assure you, for every feather in them was pure, bright, glittering, burnished gold, and they looked very dazzling, no doubt, when the Gorgons were flying about in the sunshine.

But when people happened to catch a glimpse of their glittering brightness, aloft in the air, they seldom stopped to gaze but ran and hid themselves as speedily as they could. You will think, perhaps, that they were afraid of being stung by the serpents that served the Gorgons instead of hair—or of having their heads bitten off by their ugly tusks—or of being torn all to pieces by their brazen claws. Well, to be sure, these were some of the dangers, but by no means the greatest nor the most difficult to avoid. For the worst thing about these abominable Gorgons was that, if once a poor mortal fixed his eyes full upon one of their faces, he was certain, that very instant, to be changed from warm flesh into cold and lifeless stone!

Thus, as you will easily perceive, it was a very dangerous adventure that the wicked King Polydectes had contrived for this innocent young man. Perseus himself, when he had thought over the matter, could not help seeing that he had very little chance of coming safely through it and that he was far more likely to become a stone image than to bring back the head of Medusa with the snaky locks. For, not to speak of other difficulties, there was one which it would have puzzled an older man than Perseus to get over. Not only must he fight with and slay this golden-winged, iron-scaled, long-tusked, brazen-clawed, snaky-haired monster, but he must do it with his eyes shut or, at least, without so much as a glance at the enemy with whom he was contending. Else, while his arm was lifted to strike, he would stiffen into stone and stand with that uplifted arm for centuries until time, and the wind and weather, should crumble him quite away.

So disconsolate did these thoughts make him that Perseus could not bear to tell his mother what he had undertaken to do. He therefore took his shield, girded on his sword and crossed over from the island to the mainland, where he sat down in a solitary place and hardly refrained from shedding tears.

But, while he was in this sorrowful mood, he heard a voice close behind him.

"Perseus," said the voice, "why are you sad?"

He lifted his head from his hands in which he had hidden it, and behold! all alone as Perseus had supposed himself to be, there was a stranger in the solitary place. It was a brisk, intelligent and re-markably shrewd-looking young man, with a cloak over his shoulders, an odd sort of cap on his head, a strangely-twisted staff in his hand, and a short and very crooked sword hanging by his side. He was exceedingly light and active in his figure, like a person much accustomed to gymnastic exercises and well able to leap and run. Above all, the stranger had such a cheerful, knowing and helpful aspect (though it was certainly a little mischievous into the bargain) that Perseus could not help feeling his spirits grow livelier as he gazed at him. Besides, being really a courageous youth, he felt greatly ashamed that anybody should have found him with tears in his eyes, like a timid little schoolboy, when, after all, perhaps there might be no occasion for despair. So Perseus wiped his eyes and answered the stranger pretty briskly, putting on as brave a look as he could.

"I am not sad," he said, "only thoughtful about an adventure I have undertaken."

"Oho!" answered the stranger. "Well, tell me all about it, and possibly I may be of service to you. I have helped a good many young men through adventures that looked difficult enough beforehand. Perhaps you may have heard of me. I have more names than one but the name of Quicksilver suits me as well as any other. Tell me your trouble, and we will talk the matter over and see what can be done."

The stranger's words and manner put Perseus into quite a different mood from his former one. He resolved to tell Quicksilver all his difficulties, since he could not easily be worse off than he already was, and very possibly his new friend might give him some advice that would turn out well in the end. So he let the stranger know precisely what the case was and that he was afraid of being turned into stone.

"And that would be a great pity," said Quicksilver, with his mischievous smile. "You would make a very handsome marble statue, it is true, and it would be a considerable number of centuries before you crumbled away; but, on the whole, one would rather be a young man for a few years than a stone image for a great many."

"O, far rather!" exclaimed Perseus, with the tears again in his eyes. "And, besides, what would my dear mother do if her beloved son were turned into a stone?"

"Well, well, let us hope that the affair will not turn out so very badly," replied Quicksilver. "I am the very person to help you if anybody can. My sister and myself will do our utmost to bring you safe through the adventure."

"Your sister?" repeated Perseus.

"Yes, my sister," replied the stranger. "She is very wise, I promise you, and as for myself, I generally have all my wits about me, such as they are. If you show yourself bold and cautious, and follow our advice, you need not fear being a stone image yet awhile. But, first of all, you must polish your shield till you can see your face in it as distinctly as in a mirror."

This seemed to Perseus rather an odd beginning of the adventure, for he thought it of far more consequence that the shield should be strong enough to defend him from the Gorgon's brazen claws than that it should be bright enough to show him the reflection of his face. However, concluding that Quicksilver knew better than himself, he scrubbed the shield with so much diligence and goodwill that it very quickly shone like the moon at harvest time. Quicksilver looked at it with a smile and nodded his approbation. Then, taking off his own short and crooked sword, he girded it about Perseus instead of the one which he had before worn.

"No sword but mine will answer your purpose," observed he, "the blade has a most excellent temper and will cut through iron and brass as easily as through the slenderest twig. And now we will set

out. The next thing is to find the Three Gray Women, who will tell us where to find the Nymphs."

"The Three Gray Women!" cried Perseus, to whom this seemed only a new difficulty in the path of his adventure. "Pray who may the Three Gray Women be? I never heard of them before."

"They are three very strange old ladies," said Quicksilver, laughing. "They have but one eye among them, and only one tooth. Moreover, you must find them out by starlight or in the dusk of the evening, for they never show themselves by the light either of the sun or moon."

"But," said Perseus, "why should I waste my time with these Three Gray Women? Would it not be better to set out at once in search of the terrible Gorgons?"

"No, no," answered his friend. "There are other things to be done before you can find your way to the Gorgons. There is nothing for it but to hunt up these old ladies; and when we meet them, you may be sure that the Gorgons are not a great way off. Come, let us be stirring!"

Perseus, by this time, felt so much confidence in his companion's sagacity that he made no more objections and professed himself ready to begin the adventure immediately. They accordingly set out, and walked at a pretty brisk pace—so brisk, indeed, that Perseus found it rather difficult to keep up with his nimble friend Quicksilver. To say the truth, he had a singular idea that Quicksilver was furnished with a pair of winged shoes which, of course, helped him along marvelously. And then, too, when Perseus looked sideways at him, out of the corner of his eye, he seemed to see wings on the side of his head although, if he turned a full gaze, there were no such things to be perceived, but only an odd kind of cap. But, at all events, the twisted staff enabled Quicksilver to proceed so fast that Perseus, though a remarkably active young man, began to be out of breath.

"Here!" cried Quicksilver, at last—for he knew well enough, rogue that he was, how hard Perseus found it to keep pace with him—"take you the staff, for you need it a great deal more than I. Are there no better walkers on the island of Seriphus?"

"I could walk pretty well," said Perseus, glancing slyly at his companion's feet, "if I had only a pair of winged shoes."

"We must see about getting you a pair," answered Quicksilver.

But the staff helped Perseus along so bravely that he no longer felt the slightest weariness. In fact, the stick seemed to be alive in his hand and to lend some of its life to Perseus. He and Quicksilver now walked onward at their ease, talking very sociably together, and Quicksilver told so many pleasant stories about his former adventures and how well his wits had served him on various occasions that Perseus began to think him a very wonderful person. He evidently knew the world, and nobody is so charming to a young man as a friend who has that kind of knowledge.

At last, he happened to recollect that Quicksilver had spoken of a sister, who was to lend her assistance in the adventure which they were now bound upon.

"Where is she?" he inquired. "Shall we not meet her soon?"

"All at the proper time," said his companion. "But this sister of mine, you must understand, is quite a different sort of person than myself. She is very grave and prudent, seldom smiles, never laughs and makes it a rule not to utter a word unless she has something particularly profound to say. Neither will she listen to any but the wisest conversation."

"Dear me!" ejaculated Perseus. "I shall be afraid to say a syllable."

"She is a very accomplished person, I assure you," continued Quicksilver, "and has all the arts and sciences at her fingers' ends. In short, she is so immoderately wise that many people call her wisdom personified. But to tell you the truth, she has hardly vivacity enough for my taste, and I think you would scarcely find her so pleasant a traveling companion as myself. She has her good points nevertheless, and you will find the benefit of them in your encounter with the Gorgons."

By this time it had grown quite dusk. They were now come to a very wild and desert place, overgrown with shaggy bushes and so silent and solitary that nobody seemed ever to have dwelt or journeyed there. All was waste and desolate in the grey twilight, which grew every moment more obscure. Perseus looked about him disconsolately and asked Quicksilver whether they had much further to go.

"Hist! hist!" whispered his companion. "Make no noise! This is just the time and place to meet the Three Gray Women. Be careful that they do not see you before you see them; for, though they have but a single eye among the three, it is as sharp-sighted as half-a-dozen common eyes."

"But what must I do," asked Perseus, "when we meet them?"

Quicksilver explained to Perseus how the Three Gray Women managed with their one eye. They were in the habit, it seemed, of changing it from one to another, as if it had been a pair of spectacles, or—which would have suited them better—a quizzing glass. When one of the three had kept the eye a certain time, she took it out of the socket and passed it to one of her sisters, whose turn it might happen to be, and who immediately clapped it into her own head and enjoyed a peep at the visible world. Thus it will easily be understood that only one of the Three Gray Women could see, while the other two were in utter darkness; and, moreover, at the instant when the eye was passing from hand to hand, none of the poor old ladies was able to see a wink.

"You will soon find out whether I tell the truth or no," observed Quicksilver "Hark! hush! hist! hist! There they come now!"

Perseus looked earnestly through the dusk of the evening, and there, sure enough, at no great distance off, he descried the Three Gray Women. The light being so faint, he could not well make out what sort of figures they were—only he discovered that they had long gray hair; and, as they came nearer, he saw that two of them had but the empty socket of an eye in the middle of their foreheads. But, in the middle of the third sister's forehead, there was a very large, bright and piercing eye, which sparkled like a great diamond in a ring; and so penetrating did it seem to be that Perseus could not help thinking it must possess the gift of seeing in the darkest midnight just as perfectly as at noonday.

Thus the three old dames got along about as comfortably, upon the whole, as if they could all see at once. She who chanced to have the eye in her forehead led the other two by the hands, peeping sharply about her all the while—insomuch that Perseus dreaded lest she should see right through the thick clump of bushes behind which he and Quicksilver had hidden themselves. My stars! it was positively terrible to be within reach of so very sharp an eye!

But before they reached the clump of bushes, one of the Three Gray Women spoke, "Sister! Sister Scarecrow!" cried she, "you have had the eye long enough. It is my turn now!"

"Let me keep it a moment longer, Sister Nightmare," answered Scarecrow. "I thought I had a glimpse of something behind that thick bush."

"Well, and what of that?" retorted Nightmare peevishly. "Can't I see into a thick bush as easily as yourself? The eye is mine as well as yours, and I know the use of it as well as you or maybe a little better. I insist upon taking a peep immediately!"

But here the third sister, whose name was Shakejoint, began to complain and said it was her turn to have the eye, and that Scarecrow and Nightmare wanted to keep it all to themselves. To end the dispute, old Dame Scarecrow took the eye out of her forehead and held it forth in her hand.

"Take it, one of you," cried she, "and quit this foolish quarreling. For my part, I shall be glad of a little thick darkness. Take it quickly, however, or I must clap it into my own head again!"

Accordingly, both Nightmare and Shakejoint put out their hands, groping eagerly to snatch the eye out of the hand of Scarecrow. But, being both alike blind, they could not easily find where Scarecrow's hand was; and Scarecrow, being now just as much in the dark as Shakejoint and Nightmare, could not at once meet either of their hands, in order to put the eye into it. Thus (as you will see with half an eye, my wise little auditors), these good old dames had fallen into a strange perplexity. For, though the eye shone and glistened like a star, as Scarecrow held it out, yet the Gray Women caught not the least glimpse of its light.

Quicksilver was so much tickled at beholding Shakejoint and Nightmare both groping for the eye and each finding fault with Scarecrow and one another that he could scarcely help laughing aloud.

"Now is your time!" he whispered to Perseus. "Quick, quick, before they can clap the eye into either of their heads. Rush out upon the old ladies and snatch it.

In an instant, while the three Gray

Women were still scolding each other, Perseus leaped from behind the clump of bushes and made himself master of the prize. The marvelous eye, as he held it in his hand, shone very brightly and seemed to look up into his face with a knowing air and an expression as if it would have winked had it been provided with a pair of eyelids for that purpose. But the Gray Women knew nothing of what had happened, and, each supposing that one of her sisters was in possession of the eye, they began their quarrel anew. At last, as Perseus did not wish to put these respectable dames to greater inconvenience than was really necessary, he thought it right to explain the matter.

"My good ladies," said he, "pray do not be angry with one another. If anybody is at fault, it is myself; for I have the honor to hold your very brilliant and excellent eye in my own hand!"

"You! you have our eye! And who are you then?" screamed the Three Gray Women all in a breath; for they were terribly frightened, of course, at hearing a strange voice and discovering that their eyesight had gone into the hands of they could not guess whom. "O! what shall we do, sisters? We are all in the dark! Give us our one, precious, solitary eye! You have two of your own! Give us our eye!"

"Tell them," whispered Quicksilver to Perseus, "that they shall have back the eye as soon as they direct you where to find the Nymphs who have the flying slippers, the magic wallet and the helmet of darkness."

"My dear, good admirable old ladies,"

ger!—whoever you may be, give it back!"

All this while, the Three Gray Women were groping with their outstretched hands and trying their utmost to get hold of Perseus. But he took good care to keep out of their reach.

"My respectable dames," said he—for his mother had taught him always to use the greatest civility—"I hold your eye fast in my hand and shall keep it safely for you until you please to tell me where to find these Nymphs. The Nymphs, I mean, who keep the enchanted wallet, the flying slippers and the—what is it?—the helmet of invisibility."

"Mercy on us, sisters! what is the young man talking about?" exclaimed Scarecrow, Nightmare and Shakejoint one to another with great appearance of astonishment. "A pair of flying slippers, quoth he! His heels would quickly fly higher than his head if he were silly enough to put them on. And a helmet of invisibility! How could a helmet make him invisible, unless it were big enough for him to hide under it? And an enchanted wallet! What sort of a contrivance may that be, I wonder? No, no, good stranger! we can tell you nothing of these marvelous things. You have two eyes of your own, and we but a single one amongst us three. You can find out such wonders better than three blind old creatures like us."

Perseus, hearing them talk in this way, began really to think that the Gray Women knew nothing of the matter; and, as it grieved him to have put them to so much trouble, he was just on the point of restoring their eye and asking pardon for his rudeness in snatching it away. But Quicksilver caught his hand.

"Don't let them make a fool of you!" said he. "These Three Gray Women are the only persons in the world that can tell you where to find the Nymphs; and, unless you get that information, you will never

said Perseus, addressing the Gray Women, "there is no occasion for putting yourselves into such a fright. I am by no means a bad young man. You shall have back your eye, safe and sound and as bright as ever, the moment you tell me where to find the Nymphs."

"The Nymphs! Goodness me, sisters! what Nymphs does he mean?" screamed Scarecrow. "There are a great many Nymphs, people say, some that go a-hunting in the woods, and some that live inside of trees and some that have a comfortable home in fountains of water. We know nothing at all about them. We are three unfortunate old souls, that go wandering about in the dusk, and never had but one eye amongst us, and that one you have stolen away. O, give it back, good stranger!

succeed in cutting off the head of Medusa with the snaky locks. Keep fast hold of the eye, and all will go well."

As it turned out, Quicksilver was in the right. There are but few things that people prize so much as they do their eyesight; and the Gray Women valued their single eye as highly as if it had been half-a-dozen, which was the number they ought to have had. Finding that there was no other way of recovering it, they at last told Perseus what he wanted to know. No sooner had they done so than he immediately, and with the utmost respect, clapped the eye into the vacant socket of one of their fore-heads, thanked them for their kindness and bade them farewell. Before the young man was out of hearing, however, they had got into a new dispute because he happened to have given the eye to Scarecrow, who had already taken her turn of it when their trouble with Perseus commenced.

It is greatly to be feared that the Three Gray Women were very much in the habit of disturbing their mutual harmony by bickerings of this sort, which was the more pity as they could not conveniently do without one another. As a general rule, I would advise all people, whether sisters or brothers, old or young, who chance to have but one eye amongst them, to cultivate forebearance and not all insist upon peeping through it at once.

Quicksilver and Perseus, in the mean-time, were making the best of their way in quest of the Nymphs. The old dames had given them such particular directions that they were not long in finding them out. They proved to be very different persons from Nightmare, Shakejoint and Scare-crow for, instead of being old, they were young and beautiful and instead of one eye amongst the sisterhood, each Nymph had two exceedingly bright eyes of her own, with which she looked very kindly at Per-seus. They seemed to be acquainted with Quicksilver, and when he told them the adventure which Perseus had undertaken, they made no difficulty about giving him the valuable articles that were in their cus-tody. In the first place, they brought out what appeared to be a small purse, made of deerskin and curiously embroidered, and bade him be sure and keep it safe. This was the magic wallet. The Nymphs next produced a pair of shoes, or slippers, with a nice little pair of wings at the heel of each.

"Put them on, Perseus," said Quick-silver. "You will find yourself as light-heeled as you can desire for the remainder of our journey."

When Perseus had got on both of these wonderful slippers, he was altogether too buoyant to tread on earth. Making a step or two, lo, and behold! upward he popped into the air, high above the heads of Quicksilver and the Nymphs, and found it very difficult to clamber down again. Winged slippers and all such high-flying contrivances are seldom quite easy to manage until one grows a little accus-tomed to them. Quicksilver laughed at his companion's involuntary activity and told him that he must not be in so desperate a hurry, must wait for the invisible helmet.

The good-natured Nymphs had the hel-met, with its dark tuft of waving plumes, all in readiness to put upon his head. And now there happened about as wonderful an incident as anything that I have yet told you. The instant before the helmet was put on, there stood Perseus, a beautiful young man, with golden ringlets and rosy cheeks, the crooked sword by his side and the brightly-polished shield upon his arm—a figure that seemed all made up of courage, sprightliness and glorious light. But when the helmet had descended over his white brow, there was no longer any Perseus to be seen! Nothing but empty air! Even the helmet that covered him with its invisibility had vanished!

"Where are you, Perseus?" asked Quicksilver.

"Why, here, to be sure!" answered Perseus, very quietly, although his voice seemed to come out of the transparent atmosphere. "Just where I was a moment ago. Don't you see me?"

"No, indeed!" answered his friend. "You are hidden under the helmet. But, if I cannot see you, neither can the Gorgons. Follow me, therefore, and we will try your dexterity in using the winged slippers."

With these words, Quicksilver's cap spread its wings as if his head were about to fly away from his shoulders; but his whole figure rose lightly into the air, and Perseus followed. By the time they had ascended a few hundred feet, the young man began to feel what a delightful thing it was to leave the dull earth so far beneath him and to be able to flit about like a bird.

It was now deep night. Perseus looked upward and saw the round, bright, silvery moon, and thought that he should desire nothing better than to soar up thither and spend his life there. Then he looked downwards again and saw the earth, with its seas and lakes, and the silver courses of its rivers, and its snowy mountain peaks, and the breadth of its fields, and the dark cluster of its woods and its cities of white marble; and, with the moonshine sleeping over the whole scene, it was as beautiful as the moon or any star could be. And, among other objects, he saw the island of Seriphus, where his dear mother was. Sometimes, he and Quicksilver approached a cloud that at a distance looked as if it were made of fleecy silver although, when they plunged into it, they found themselves chilled and moistened with gray mist. So swift was their flight, however, that in an instant they emerged from the cloud into the moonlight again. Once, a high-soaring eagle flew right against the invisible Perseus. The bravest sights were the meteors that gleamed suddenly out as if a bonfire had been kindled in the sky and made the moonshine pale for as much as a hundred miles around them.

As the two companions flew onward, Perseus fancied that he could hear the rustle of a garment close by his side; and it was on the side opposite to the one where he beheld Quicksilver, yet only Quicksilver was visible.

"Whose garment is this," inquired Perseus, "that keeps rustling close beside me?"

"O, it is my sister's!" answered Quicksilver. "She is coming along with us as I told you she would. We could do nothing without the help of my sister. You have no idea how wise she is. She has such eyes, too! Why, she can see you at this moment just as distinctly as if you were not invisible, and I'll venture to say she will be the first to discover the Gorgons."

By this time, in their swift voyage through the air, they had come within sight of the great ocean and were soon flying over it. Far beneath them, the waves tossed themselves tumultuously in mid-sea, or rolled a white surf line upon the long beaches or foamed against the rocky cliffs with a roar that was thunderous in the lower world although it became a gentle murmur, like the voice of a baby half asleep, before it reached the ears of Perseus. Just then a voice spoke in the air close by him. It seemed to be a woman's voice and was melodious though not exactly what might be called sweet, but grave and mild.

"Perseus," said the voice, "there are the Gorgons."

"Where?" exclaimed Perseus. "I cannot see them."

"On the shore of that island beneath you," replied the voice. "A pebble,

dropped from your hand, would strike in the midst of them."

"I told you she would be the first to discover them," said Quicksilver to Perseus. "And there they are!"

Straight downward, two or three thousand feet below him, Perseus perceived a small island, with the sea breaking into white foam all around its rocky shore, except on one side where there was a beach of snowy sand. He descended toward it and, looking earnestly at a cluster or heap of brightness at the foot of a precipice of black rocks, behold, there were the terrible Gorgons! They lay fast asleep, soothed by the thunder of the sea for it required a tumult that would have deafened everybody else to lull such fierce creatures into slumber. The moonlight glistened on their steely scales and on their golden wings, which drooped idly over the sand. Their brazen claws, horrible to look at, were thrust out and clutched the wave-beaten fragments of rock while the sleeping Gorgons dreamed of tearing some poor mortal all to pieces. The snakes that served them instead of hair seemed likewise to be asleep although, now and then, one would writhe, and lift its head, and thrust out its forked tongue, emitting a drowsy hiss, and then let itself subside among its sister snakes.

The Gorgons were more like an awful, gigantic kind of insect—immense, golden-winged beetles, or dragonflies, or things of that sort—at once ugly and beautiful—than like anything else, only that they were a thousand and a million times as big. And, with all this, there was something partly human about them, too. Luckily for Perseus, their faces were completely hidden from him by the posture in which they lay for, had he but looked one instant at them, he would have fallen heavily out of the air, an image of senseless stone.

"Now," whispered Quicksilver as he hovered beside Perseus, "now is your time to do the deed! Be quick; if one of the Gorgons should awake, you are too late!"

"Which shall I strike at?" asked Perseus, drawing his sword and descending a little lower. "They all three look alike. Which of the three is Medusa?"

It must be understood that Medusa was the only one of these dragon-monsters whose head Perseus could possibly cut off. As for the other two, let him have the sharpest sword that ever was forged, and he might have hacked away by the hour together, without doing them the least harm.

"Be cautious," said the calm voice which had before spoken to him. "One of the Gorgons is stirring in her sleep and is just about to turn over. That is Medusa. Do not look at her! The sight would turn you to stone! Look at the reflection of her face and figure in the bright mirror of your shield."

Perseus now understood Quicksilver's motive for so earnestly exhorting him to polish his shield. In its surface he could safely look at the reflection of the Gorgon's face. And there it was—that terrible countenance—mirrored in the brightness of the shield, with the moonlight falling over it and displaying all its horror. The snakes, whose venomous nature could not altogether sleep, kept twisting themselves over the forehead. It was the fiercest and most horrible face that ever was seen or imagined, and yet with a strange, fearful and savage kind of beauty in it. The eyes were closed, and the Gorgon was still in a deep slumber, but there was an unquiet expression disturbing her features as if she was troubled with an ugly dream. She gnashed her white tusks and dug into the sand with her brazen claws.

The snakes, too, seemed to feel Medusa's dream and to be made more restless by it. They twisted themselves into tumultuous knots, writhed fiercely and uplifted a hundred hissing heads without opening their eyes.

"Now, now!" whispered Quicksilver, who was growing impatient. "Make a dash at the monster!"

"But be calm," said the grave, melodious voice at the young man's side. "Look in your shield as you fly and take care that you do not miss your first stroke."

Perseus flew cautiously downward, still keeping his eyes on Medusa's face as reflected in his shield. The nearer he came, the more terrible did the snaky visage and metallic body of the monster grow. At last, hovering over her within arm's length, Perseus uplifted his sword, while at the same instant each separate snake upon the Gorgon's head stretched threateningly up-

ward and Medusa unclosed her eyes. But she awoke too late. The sword was sharp; the stroke fell like a lightning flash; and the head of the wicked Medusa tumbled from her body!

"Admirably done!" cried Quicksilver. "Make haste and clap the head into your magic wallet."

To the astonishment of Perseus, the small, embroidered wallet, which he had hung about his neck and which had hitherto been no bigger than a purse, grew all at once large enough to contain Medusa's head. As quick as thought, he snatched it up, with the snakes still writhing upon it, and thrust it in.

"Your task is done," said the calm voice. "Now fly, for the other Gorgons will do their utmost to take vengeance for Medusa's death."

It was, indeed, necessary to take flight; for Perseus had not done the deed so quietly but that the clash of his sword, and the hissing of the snakes and the thump of Medusa's head as it tumbled upon the sea-beaten sand awoke the other two monsters. There they sat for an instant, sleepily rubbing their eyes with their brazen fingers, while all the snakes on their heads reared themselves on end with surprise and with venomous malice against they knew not what. But when the Gorgons saw the scaly carcass of Medusa, headless, and her golden wings all ruffled and half out on the sand, it was really awful to hear what yells and screeches they set up. And then the snakes! They sent forth a hundredfold hiss with one consent, and Medusa's snakes answered them out of the magic wallet.

No sooner were the Gorgons broad awake than they hurtled upward into the air, brandishing their brass talons, gnashing their horrible tusks and flapping their huge wings so wildly that some of the golden feathers were shaken out and floated down upon the shore. And there, perhaps, those very feathers lie scattered till this day. Up rose the Gorgons, as I tell you, staring horribly about in hopes of turning somebody to stone. Had Perseus looked them in the face or had he fallen into their clutches, his poor mother would never have kissed her boy again! But he took good care to turn his eyes another way; and, as he wore the helmet of invisibility, the Gorgons knew not in what direction to follow him, nor did he fail to make the best use of the winged slippers by soaring upward a mile or so. At that height, when the screams of those abominable creatures sounded faintly beneath him, he made a straight course for the island of Seriphus.

I have no time to tell you of several marvelous things that befell Perseus on his way homeward such as his killing a hideous sea-monster just as it was on the point of devouring a beautiful maiden, nor how he changed an enormous giant into a mountain of stone merely by showing him the head of the Gorgon. If you doubt this latter story, you may make a voyage to Africa, some day or other, and see the very mountain, which is still known by the ancient giant's name.

Finally, our brave Perseus arrived at the island, where he expected to see his dear mother. But, during his absence, the wicked king had treated Danaë so very ill that she was compelled to make her escape and had taken refuge in a temple, where some good old priests were extremely kind to her. These praiseworthy priests, and the kind-hearted fisherman who had first shown hospitality to Danaë and little Perseus when he found them afloat in the chest, seem to have been the only persons on the island who cared about doing right. All the rest of the people, as well as King Polydectes himself, were remarkably ill-behaved and deserved no better destiny

than that which was now about to happen.

Not finding his mother at home, Perseus went straight to the palace and was immediately ushered into the presence of the king. Polydectes was by no means rejoiced to see him, for he had felt almost certain, in his own evil mind, that the Gorgons would have torn the poor young man to pieces and have eaten him up out of the way. However, seeing him safely returned, he put the best face he could upon the matter and asked Perseus how he had succeeded.

"Have you performed your promise?" inquired he. "Have you brought me the head of Medusa, with the snaky locks? If not, young man, it will cost you dear, for I must have a bridal present for the beautiful Princess Hippodamia and there is nothing else that she would admire so much."

"Yes, please your Majesty," answered Perseus in a quiet way, as if it were no very wonderful deed for such a young man as he to perform. "I have brought you the Gorgon's head, snaky locks and all!"

"Indeed! Pray let me see it," quoth King Polydectes. "It must be a very curious spectacle if all that travelers tell about it be true!"

"Your Majesty is right," replied Perseus. "It is really an object that will be pretty certain to fix the regards of all who look at it. And, if your Majesty think fit, I would suggest that a holiday be proclaimed and that all your Majesty's subjects be summoned to behold this wonderful curiosity. Few of them, I imagine, have seen a Gorgon's head before and perhaps never may again!"

The king well knew that his subjects were an idle set of reprobates and very fond of sight-seeing as idle persons usually are. So he took the young man's advice and sent out heralds and messengers in all directions to blow the trumpet at the street corners, and in the marketplaces and wherever two roads met, and summon everybody to court. Thither, accordingly, came a great multitude of good-for-nothing vagabonds, all of whom, out of pure love of mischief, would have been glad if Perseus had met with some ill-hap in his encounter with the Gorgons. If there were any better people in the island (as I really hope there may have been, although the story tells nothing about any such), they stayed quietly at home, minding their own business and taking care of their little children. Most of the inhabitants, at all events, ran as fast as they could to the palace, and shoved and pushed and elbowed one another in their eagerness to get near a balcony on which Perseus showed himself, holding the embroidered wallet in his hand.

On a platform, within full view of the balcony, sat the mighty King Polydectes, amid his evil counsellors and with his flattering courtiers in a semicircle round about him. Monarch, counsellors, courtiers and subjects, all gazed towards Perseus.

"Show us the head! Show us the head!" shouted the people, and there was a fierceness in their cry as if they would tear Perseus to pieces unless he should satisfy them. "Show us the head of Medusa with the snaky locks!"

A feeling of sorrow and pity came over the youthful Perseus.

"O King Polydectes," cried he, "and ye, many people, I am very loth to show you the Gorgon's head!"

"Ah, the villain and coward!" yelled the people, more fiercely than before. "He is making game of us! He has no Gorgon's head! Show us the head if you have it, or we will take your own head for a football!"

The evil counsellors whispered bad advice in the king's ear, the courtiers murmured with one consent that Perseus had shown disrespect to their royal lord and master, and the great King Polydectes himself waved his hand and ordered Perseus on his peril, to produce the head.

"Show me the Gorgon's head, or I will cut off your own!"

And Perseus sighed.

"This instant," repeated Polydectes, "or you die!"

"Behold it, then!" cried Perseus, in a voice like the blast of a trumpet.

And, suddenly holding up the head, not an eyelid had time to wink before the wicked King Polydectes, his evil counsellors and all his fierce subjects were no longer anything but the mere images of a monarch and his people. They were all fixed forever in the look and attitude of that moment! At the first glimpse of the terrible head of Medusa, they whitened into marble! And Perseus thrust the head back into his wallet and went to tell his dear mother that she need no longer be afraid of the wicked King Polydectes.

THE   GIFT

*It was the boy's first trip in a rocket,
and the date was Christmas Eve in the year 2052*

RAY BRADBURY

Tomorrow would be Christmas, and even while the three of them rode to the rocket port the mother and father were worried. It was the boy's first flight into space, his very first time in a rocket, and they wanted everything to be perfect. So when, at the customs table, they were forced to leave behind his gift which exceeded the weight limit by no more than a few ounces and the little tree with the lovely white candles, they felt themselves deprived of the season and their love.

The boy was waiting for them in the Terminal room. Walking toward him after their unsuccessful clash with the Interplanetary officials, the mother and father whispered to each other.

"What shall we do?"

"Nothing, nothing. What *can* we do?"

"Silly rules!"

"And he so wanted the tree!"

The siren gave a great howl and people pressed forward into the Mars Rocket. The mother and father walked at the very last, their small pale son between them.

"I'll think of something," said the father.

"What . . . ?" asked the boy.

And the rocket took off and they were flung headlong into dark space.

The rocket moved and left fire behind and left Earth behind on which the date was December 24, 2052, heading out into a place where there was no time at all, no month, no year, no hour. They slept away the rest of the first "day." Near midnight, by their Earth-time New York watches, the boy awoke and said, "I want to go look out the porthole."

There was only one port, a "window" of immensely thick glass of some size, up on the next deck.

"Not quite yet," said the father. "I'll take you up later."

"I want to see where we are and where we're going."

"I want you to wait for a reason," said the father.

He had been lying awake, turning this way and that, thinking of the abandoned gift, the problem of the season, the lost tree and the white candles. And at last, sitting up, no more than five minutes ago, he believed he had found a plan. He need only carry it out and this journey would be fine and joyous indeed.

"Son," he said, "in exactly one half hour it will be Christmas."

"Oh," said the mother, dismayed that he had mentioned it. Somehow she had rather hoped that the boy would forget.

The boy's face grew feverish and his lips trembled. "I know, I know. Will I get a present, will I? Will I have a tree? You promised—"

"Yes, yes, all that, and more," said the father.

The mother started. "But—"

"I mean it," said the father. "I really mean it. All and more, much more. Excuse me, now. I'll be back."

He left them for about twenty minutes. When he came back he was smiling. "Almost time."

"Can I hold your watch?" asked the boy, and the watch was handed over and he held it ticking in his fingers as the rest of the hour drifted by in fire and silence and unfelt motion.

"It's Christmas now! It's Christmas! Where's my present?"

"Here we go," said the father and took his boy by the shoulder and led him from the room, down the hall, up a rampway, his wife following.

"I don't understand," she kept saying.

"You will. Here we are," said the father.

They had stopped at the closed door of a large cabin. The father tapped three times and then twice in a code. The door opened and the light in the cabin went out and there was a whisper of voices.

"Go on in, son," said the father.

"It's dark."

"I'll hold your hand. Come on, Mama."

They stepped into the room and the door shut, and the room was very dark indeed. And before them loomed a great glass eye, the porthole, a window four feet high and six feet wide, from which they could look out into space.

The boy gasped.

Behind him, the father and the mother gasped with him, and then in the dark room some people began to sing.

"Merry Christmas, son," said the father.

And the voices in the room sang the old, the familiar carols, and the boy moved forward slowly until his face was pressed against the cool glass of the port. And he stood there for a long long time, just looking and looking out into space and the deep night at the burning and the burning of ten billion billion white and lovely candles. . . .

Ebenezer Never-Could-Sneezer

*Poor Ebenezer. Even with his wonderful
new wooden nose, he wasn't able to sneeze*

GILBERT S. PATTILLO

Ebenezer Never-Could-Sneezer was a wonderful old French soldier. Years long gone he had been retired from Napoleon's army with a pension of one cheese a week for as long as he lived. He was a great favorite with the children in his village. He could do anything. He could tell stories by the hour. He never seemed to end a story. But he could tell them all the same. All the children loved to listen. He told them stories of little boys and girls he had seen when he had been a soldier in Napoleon's armies: little boys and girls in Spain; little boys and girls in Italy; little boys and girls in Austria; little boys and girls in Egypt; little boys and girls in Russia.

But in spite of the fact that Ebenezer could do anything, and tell stories by the hour, there was one thing he could not do. He simply could not sneeze. You might suppose it was because he never shook pepper in his soup. But no, it wasn't that. He sometimes did shake pepper in his soup. The reason he couldn't sneeze was because he had no nose to sneeze with. What! No nose! How did that happen?

Ebenezer had a nose when he was a baby. He had a nose when he was a small boy. He had a nose when he was a young man. He had a nose when he marched away with Napoleon's army to fight for France. He had a nose before the battle of Austerlitz. But after the battle of Austerlitz his nose was gone. A cannonball tweaked it off and took it away. And that's why he never could sneeze. It wasn't because he never caught cold. It wasn't because he never shook pepper in his soup. It was because he had no nose to sneeze with.

Now the strangest part was that sometimes Ebenezer wanted to sneeze very badly. Though his nose had been tweaked off by a cannonball, still, sometimes, he could feel his nose itching. And oh, how he wanted to sneeze. He could throw back his head, open his mouth, close his eyes and say, "Ah-ah-ah-," or he could say, "Ker-ker-ker-," just as well as you or anyone else. But he could not say a single "Choo!" Just imagine getting ready to say a good, satisfying "Choo!" and then not being able to say it. It was dreadful.

One morning Ebenezer had what he thought was a very brilliant idea. He would make himself a wooden nose. In the woodpile he found just the piece of wood he needed. With his pocketknife he whittled out a nose in wood that looked very much like the nose he had before the battle of Austerlitz. It was a very large nose, but that suited Ebenezer's purpose so much the better. In the end of it where the nostrils would naturally be, he bored a hole as large as the mouth of a bottle. Into this hole he fitted a cork-stopper just as you would in a bottle. He fastened his wooden nose in place with glue, put a corkscrew in one of his pockets and sat down in the sun to wait until he should feel like sneezing.

Presently, sure enough, Ebenezer felt a sneeze coming and trembled all over with excitement. Soon he would know whether his new wooden nose were a success or a failure. Hopefully he threw back his head, opened his mouth, closed his eyes and said, "Ah-ah-ah-!" Oh dear, oh dear, where had he put that corkscrew? In which pocket was it hiding? As fast as his fingers could fly he hunted in his coat pockets. The cork-screw wasn't there. And all the time he kept saying, "Ah-ah-ah-!" Then he hunted in his vest pockets. The day was saved. There was the corkscrew. He screwed it into the cork-stopper in the end of his nose, and just at the end of another, "Ah-ah-ah-," he gave it a quick pull and out it came with a loud "Pop!"

He tried it again. "Ah-ah-ah-POP!" "Ker-ker-ker-POP!" Well, that was something. But after all, it was a disappointment. He couldn't really feel satisfied with an "Ah-ah-ah-POP!" or a "Ker-ker-ker-POP!" when what he wanted with all his heart was a good loud "Ah-ah-ah-CHOO!" or a "Ker-ker-ker-CHOO!" "I am afraid," he said to himself in despair, "that I shall never, never sneeze again." So he threw away the corkscrew. He threw away the cork-stopper. And he threw away the wooden nose.

But even at that moment of his greatest disappointment, affairs were shaping in the world outside his village that were going to bring Ebenezer a very happy surprise. There came a rumor that the new railroad from Paris to the sea would run right smack through the village. With a yawn and a stretch the sleepy little town woke up and began to buzz with talk. "A railroad! What do you think of that!" said everybody to everybody else. "We'll have a station, too," they said, "where trains will arrive and depart just as they do in Paris." So it went. Buzz, buzz, buzz; how their tongues ran on. The more they talked of the railroad, the more excited they became. The Town Fathers renamed the streets for famous boulevards of Paris. The Mayor began to carry a cane and wear a silk hat. The Jack-of-all-trades mended the clock in the town hall steeple, and for the first time in half a century people could tell what time it was once more.

For months the rumors flew. For months the rumors were confirmed. For months they worked on plans. For months they worked on the tracks. For months they worked on the station. Until finally the day of the first train arrived. No one in the village had ever seen a railroad train, or a railroad engine, so they made a gala day of it and flocked to the station. And of course Ebenezer was there, too.

The new station shone like a dandelion in its fresh coat of yellow paint. The new tracks disappeared in one direction toward Paris and in the other direction toward the sea. The people were so excited that half of them were talking and half of them were laughing. Then the half that had been talking began to laugh and the half that had been laughing began to talk, until they were so mixed up that everyone was talking out of one side of his mouth and laughing out of the other side of his mouth at the same time. You never heard such a bedlam! In the midst of it the town hall clock struck eleven. The train was due.

"H-ooooooo—h-ooooooo—hoo-hoo!"

117

Right on the dot the train whistled. Right on the dot it appeared in sight. Right on the dot it drew up at the station, bell ringing, steam escaping, engine panting, brakes grinding. Everybody shouted. Babies screamed and dogs barked. People waved from everywhere on the station platform. Ebenezer waved both hands at once. "Rat-tat-tat" down the steps of the car came the Conductor's heels with the Conductor after them, throwing out his swelling chest as he came. He bowed. He beamed. He strutted. He shook hands with the Station Agent. He shook hands with the Mayor. He shook hands with the Mayor's new cane. He shook hands with everybody, including Ebenezer, until it was time for the train to depart.

Oh, that was a big moment for Ebenezer! Just as the Conductor shouted, "A-llllll aboard!" just as the engine bell began to ring, just as the Engineer put his hand on the throttle, Ebenezer felt a sneeze coming. Back flew his head. Open flew his mouth. Tight shut his eyes. "Ah-ah-ah-," said Ebenezer. "CHOO!" said the engine. "Ker-ker-ker-," said Ebenezer. "CHOO!" said the engine. Oh, it was a great big whacker of a choo, a delicious choo, the noisiest, juiciest CHOO you ever

heard. "Ah-ah-ah-CHOO!" Ker-ker-ker-CHOO!" The first good, satisfying sneeze Ebenezer had had since before the battle of Austerlitz! He kept it up as long as the train was in sight.

From that day on, Ebenezer saved all his sneezes for train time. He knew when every train would depart and never missed a train. He would wait until the Conductor called, "A-llllll aboard!" He would wait until the engine bell rang and the Engineer put his hand on the throttle. Then he would throw back his head, open his mouth, shut his eyes and say, "Ah-ah-ah-" and "CHOO!" would say the engine.

"Ker-ker-ker-," he would say. "CHOO!" would say the engine. Ah-ah-ah-choo-choo! Ker-ker-ker-choo-choo-! Ah-ker-choo-choo-choo! Ah-ker-choo-choo-choo! Ah-ker-choo-choo! Ah-ker-choo! Ah-ker-choo! Ah-ker-choo! Ahkerchoo, ahkerchoo, ahkerchoo-ahkerchoo-ahkerchoo-ahkerchoo!

There, now if you have your breath again after all that sneezing, here's the end of it. To this very day when the little boys and girls in that village hear the trains leaving the station, they laugh and say, "There goes Ebenezer-Never-Could-Sneezer's Nose."

MANY MOONS

*Princess Lenore was wiser than the
Lord High Chamberlain, the Royal Wizard
and the Royal Mathematician. It took
the Court Jester to figure that out*

JAMES THURBER

Once upon a time, in a kingdom by the sea, there lived a little Princess named Lenore. She was ten years old, going on 11. One day Lenore fell ill of a surfeit of raspberry tarts and took to her bed.

The Royal Physician came to see her and took her temperature and felt her pulse and made her stick out her tongue. He was worried, and sent for the King, Lenore's father, and the King came to see her.

"I will get you anything your heart desires," the King said. "Is there anything your heart desires?"

"Yes," said the Princess. "I want the moon. If I can have the moon, I will be well again."

Then the King went to the throne room and pulled a bell cord, three long pulls and a short pull, and presently the Lord High Chamberlain came into the room. He was a large, fat man with thick glasses which made his eyes seem twice as large as they really were. This made the Lord High Chamberlain seem twice as wise as he really was.

"I want you to get the moon for the Princess Lenore," said the King. "If she can have the moon, she will get well again. Get it tonight, tomorrow at the latest."

The Lord High Chamberlain wiped his forehead with a handkerchief and then blew his nose loudly. "I have got a great many things for you in my time, Your Majesty," he said. "It just happens that I have with me a list of those things." He pulled a long scroll of parchment out of his pocket. "Let me see, now." He glanced at the list, frowning. "I have got ivory, apes and peacocks; rubies, opals and emeralds; black orchids, pink elephants and blue poodles; hummingbirds' tongues, angels' feathers and unicorns' horns; giants, midgets and mermaids; frankincense, ambergris and myrrh; a pound of butter, two dozen eggs and a sack of sugar—sorry, my wife wrote that in there."

"Never mind," said the King. "What I want now is the moon."

"The moon," said the Lord High Chamberlain, "is out of the question. It is 35,000 miles away and it is bigger than the room the Princess lies in. Furthermore it is made of molten copper. I cannot get the moon for you. Blue poodles, yes; the moon, no."

The King flew into a rage and told the

120

Lord High Chamberlain to leave the room and to send the Royal Wizard to him. The Royal Wizard was a little, thin man with a long face. He wore a high red peaked hat covered with silver stars and a long blue robe covered with golden owls. He grew very pale when the King told him he wanted the moon for his little daughter, and that he expected the Royal Wizard to get it.

"I have worked a great deal of magic for you in my time, Your Majesty," he said. "I just happen to have in my pocket a list of the wizardries I have performed for you. Now let's see. I have squeezed blood out of turnips for you, and turnips out of blood. I have produced rabbits out of silk hats, and silk hats out of rabbits. I have conjured up flowers, tambourines and doves out of nowhere, and nowhere out of flowers, tambourines and doves. I have brought you divining rods, magic wands, and crystal spheres in which to behold the future. I have made you my own special mixture of wolfsbane, nightshade and eagles' tears, to ward off witches, demons and things that go bump in the night. I have given you seven-league boots, the golden touch and a cloak of invisibility—"

"The cloak of invisibility didn't work," said the King. "I kept bumping into things the same as ever."

"The cloak is supposed to make you invisible," said the Royal Wizard. "It is not supposed to keep you from bumping into things." He looked at his list again. "I got you," he said, "horns from Elfland, sand from the Sandman and gold from the rainbow. Also a spool of thread, a paper of needles and a lump of beeswax—sorry, those are things my wife wrote down for me to get her."

"What I want you to do now," said the King, "is to get me the moon. The Princess Lenore wants the moon, and when she gets it, she will be well again."

"Nobody can get the moon," said the Royal Wizard. "It is 150,000 miles away, and it is made of green cheese, and it is twice as big as this palace."

The King flew into another rage and sent the Royal Wizard back to his cave. Then he summoned the Royal Mathematician, a baldheaded, nearsighted man, with a skullcap on his head and a pencil behind his ear.

"I don't want to hear a long list of all the things you have figured out for me since 1907," the King said to him. "I want you to figure out right now how to get the moon for the Princess Lenore."

"I am glad you mentioned all the things I have figured out for you since 1907," said the Royal Mathematician. "It happens that I have a list of them with me. I have figured out for you the distance between the horns of a dilemma, night and day, and A and Z. I have computed how far is Up, how long it takes to get to Away, and what becomes of Gone. I have discovered the length of the sea serpent, the price of the priceless, and the square of the hippopotamus. I know where you are when you are at Sixes and Sevens, how much Is you have to have to make an Are, and how many birds you can catch with the salt in the ocean— 187,796,132, if it would interest you to know."

"There aren't that many birds," said the King. "And anyway, what I want is the moon."

"The moon is 300,000 miles away," said the Royal Mathematician. "It is round and flat like a coin, only it is made of asbestos, and it is half the size of this kingdom. Furthermore it is pasted on the sky. Nobody can get the moon."

The King flew into still another rage and sent the Royal Mathematician away. Then he rang for the Court Jester, who came bounding into the room in his cap and bells, and sat at the foot of the throne.

"What can I do for you, Your Majesty?"

"The Princess Lenore wants the moon," said the King mournfully, "and she cannot be well till she gets it, but nobody can get it for her. Every time I ask anybody for the moon, it gets larger and farther away. There is nothing you can do for me except play on your lute. Something sad."

"How big do they say the moon is," asked the Court Jester, "and how far away?"

"The Lord High Chamberlain says it is 35,000 miles away, and bigger than the Princess Lenore's room," said the King. "The Royal Wizard says it is 150,000 miles away, and twice as big as this palace. The Royal Mathematician says it is 300,000 miles away, and half the size of this kingdom."

The Court Jester strummed on his lute for a while. "They are all wise men," he said, "and so they must all be right. If they are all right, then the moon must be just as large and as far away as each person thinks it is. The thing to do is to find out how big the Princess Lenore thinks it is, and how far away."

"I never thought of that," said the King.

"I will go and ask her, Your Majesty."

The Princess Lenore was glad to see the Court Jester, but her face was very pale and her voice was very weak.

"Have you brought the moon to me?" she asked.

"Not yet," said the Court Jester, "but I will get it for you right away. How big do you think it is?"

"It is just a little smaller than my thumbnail," she said, "for when I hold my thumbnail up at the moon it just covers it."

"And how far away is it?" asked the Court Jester.

"It is not as high as the big tree outside my window," said the Princess, "for sometimes it gets caught in the top branches."

"I will climb the tree tonight when the moon gets caught in the top branches and bring it to you," said the Court Jester. Then he thought of something else. "What is the moon made of, Princess?" he asked.

"Oh," she said, "it's made of gold, of course, silly."

The Court Jester went to see the Royal Goldsmith and had him make a tiny round golden moon just a little smaller than the thumbnail of the Princess Lenore. Then he had him string it on a golden chain so the Princess could wear it around her neck.

"What is this thing I have made?" asked the Royal Goldsmith.

"You have made the moon," said the Court Jester. "That is the moon."

"But the moon," said the Royal Goldsmith, "is 500,000 miles away and it is made of bronze and is round like a marble."

"That's what you think," said the Court Jester as he went away with the moon.

The Court Jester took the moon to the Princess, and she was overjoyed. The next day she was well again and could get up and go out in the gardens to play.

But the King knew that the moon would shine in the sky again that night, and if the Princess should see it, she would know that the moon she wore on a chain was not the real moon. So he said to the Lord High Chamberlain, "We must keep the Princess from seeing the moon tonight. Think of something."

The Lord High Chamberlain tapped his forehead with his fingers. "We can make some dark glasses for the Princess."

This made the King very angry. "If she wore dark glasses, she would bump into things," he said, "and then she would be ill again." So he called the Royal Wizard, who stood on his hands and then stood on his head and then stood on his feet again.

"I know what we can do," he said. "We can stretch some black velvet curtains on poles to cover all the palace gardens like a circus tent."

The King was so angry that he waved his arms around. "Black curtains would keep out the air," he said, "and the Princess Lenore would be ill again." He summoned the Royal Mathematician.

The Royal Mathematician walked around in a circle, and then he walked around in a square and then he stood still. "I have it!" he said. "We can set off fireworks in the garden every night. We will make a lot of silver fountains and golden cascades, and when they go off, they will fill the sky with so many sparks that it will be as light as day and the Princess Lenore will not be able to see the moon."

The King flew into such a rage that he began jumping up and down. "Fireworks would keep the Princess awake," he said, "and she would be ill again." So he sent the Royal Mathematician away.

When he looked up again, it was dark outside and the bright rim of the moon was just peeping over the horizon. He jumped up in a great fright and rang for the Court Jester. "Play me something very sad," he said, "for when the Princess sees the moon, she will be ill again."

The Court Jester strummed on his lute. "What do your wise men say?"

"They can think of no way to hide the moon that will not make the Princess ill," said the King.

The Court Jester played another song very softly. "If your wise men cannot hide the moon, then it cannot be hidden," he said. "But who could explain how to get the moon? It was the Princess Lenore. Therefore the Princess Lenore is wiser than your wise men and knows more about the moon than they do. So I will ask *her*." And before the King could stop him, he slipped quietly out of the throne room and up the wide marble staircase to the Princess Lenore's bedroom.

The Princess was in bed, but she was wide awake and she was looking out the window at the moon shining in the sky. Shining in her hand was the moon the Court Jester had got for her. He looked very sad, and there seemed to be tears in his eyes.

"Tell me, Princess Lenore," he said mournfully, "how can the moon be shining in the sky when it is hanging on a golden chain around your neck?"

The Princess looked at him and laughed. "That is easy, silly," she said. "When I lose a tooth, a new one grows in its place, doesn't it? And when the Royal Gardener cuts the flowers in the garden, other flowers come to take their place."

"I should have thought of that," said the Court Jester, "for it is the same way with the daylight."

"And it is the same way with the moon," said the Princess Lenore. "I guess it is the same way with everything." Her voice became very low and faded away, and the Court Jester saw that she was asleep. Gently he tucked the covers in around her.

But before he left the room, he went over to the window and winked at the moon, for it seemed to the Court Jester that the moon had winked at him.

Pies of the Princess

*The King
was in a rage.
Why, when she had
golden dolls and
ivory cats and jade balls
to play with,
did the Princess
prefer to make
mud pies?*

ARTHUR B. CHRISMAN

Three plump mandarins hid behind a single tiny rose bush. The chancellor crawled under a chair. All courtiers fell upon their chins, and shivering, prayed that soft words might prevail.

For no slight reason did they shiver and hide and pray. King Yang Lang was angry. And he was an old-fashioned monarch, living in the long ago. Nowadays, any greasy kitchen lout may tweak a King's beard and go forth to boast of his bravery. But then-a-days, Kings were Kings, and their swords were ever sharp.

King Yang Lang was such a ruler—and more angry than is good to see. His face was purple, and his voice boomed like a battle drum. "Keeper of the Treasury, has all my gold been used to make weights for fishing lines?"

Time after time the treasurer knocked his head against the paving. "Most Glorious and Peaceful Monarch, your gold is so plentiful that seven years must pass before I can finish counting the larger bars—ten years more for the smaller."

That was rather pleasant news. The King's voice lost some of its harshness. "What of the ivory? Has all my ivory been burned for firewood, a pot to boil?"

The treasurer continued to knock his head. "Supreme Ruler of The World and The Stars, your ivory completely fills a hundred large and closely guarded vaults."

The King hadn't dreamed that his wealth was so vast. His voice was not more than moderately furious as he asked, "For what reason have you disposed of my jade? Do you mean to say that my jade has been used to build a stable?"

Tap, tap, tap, went the treasurer's head on marble paving: "Oh, Powerful Potentate, the store of green jade grows larger each day. Your precious white jade is worth more than green, and gold, and ivory combined. It is all quite safe, under lock and key and watchful spears."

The King was astonished and put in somewhat better humor. His voice was no louder than thunder as he again questioned the treasurer. "Then why, tell me why is my daughter, the Princess Chin Uor, not given suitable toys? If the treasury holds gold and ivory and jade, why is my daughter compelled to use toys of clay?"

The treasurer could not explain: "Monarch whose word compels the sun to rise, we have pleaded with the wee Princess Chin Uor. We have given her a thousand dolls of solid gold, with silver cradles for each, cradles set with rubies—and the dolls have eyes of lustrous black pearl. For the princess we have made ivory cats, and ivory mice for the cats to catch—two thousand of each. For the princess we have fashioned from jade lovely tossing balls,

wonderful dishes and puppy dogs that bark and come when called. Yet, the princess ignores these things . . . and makes mud pies—MUD PIES. Mightiest Majesty, I do not know why, unless it may be that the princess is a girl as well as a princess."

A trifle relieved, King Yang Lang passed into the garden. Beside the river bank he found his daughter, the Princess Chin Uor, or Princess Many Dimples—for that is the meaning of Chin Uor. Nurses standing near kept watch upon the wheelbarrows spilling over with golden dolls. But Chin Uor had no thought for such toys. Her royal hands shaped the tastiest of mud pies. Very pretty pies they were—made of white clay.

The King said, "Littlest and most beautiful daughter, the golden dolls are longing for your touch. Why do you not please them? It is not seemly for a princess to dabble in clay. Then why do you make pies?"

The princess had a very good answer ready. "Because, Daddy, I want to make pies. This nice large one is for your dinner."

The King was so shocked that he could say nothing more. Mud pies for a King's dinner? Such nonsense. His Majesty was scandalized at the thought. He departed in haste.

But the Princess Chin Uor smiled and kneaded more and more pies. And when she had made enough she placed them in a wheelbarrow and trundled them to the palace.

And now the story changes. Far away to the west, in a mountain named Huge Rocks Piled, the famous dragon, Oo Loong, made his home. This fierce dragon was a creature of consuming greed. He was ever hungry and anxious to dine. A rabbit or an elephant—nothing was too large, nothing was too hard, nothing too soft. A man he considered fine eating. Boys he liked somewhat better. Girls? Girls were far superior to boys—in the dragon's opinion.

Much sorrow this ferocious *loong* had created in His Majesty's kingdom. A reward of one hundred silver pieces had been offered for the dragon's horns, two hundred for his ears. Magicians had worked charms to slay him—only themselves to be slain. Hunters had loaded their jingals with yellow paper and had fired where the dragon was thickest, fired where he was thinnest—only to be eaten—their guns with them. Made angry by the loss of so many people, King Yang Lang marched an army into the Mountain of Huge Rocks Piled. And the army was well armed with thumping drums and fifes and smoking guns.

Then the dragon became doubly furious and ferocious. To punish King Yang Lang, he resolved to visit the palace. That, he knew, would cause the army to be withdrawn. Accordingly, at the hour of deepest slumber, darksome mid of night, he prowled round Yang Lang's palace, seeking entrance. He had no easy task. Upon the king's door were pictures, also the word "Chi," written in gold. And so that door was well protected. The Queen's door likewise was dragon proof. It was covered with whole sentences taken from the black book of Hu Po, master magician. The door that led to where Princess Chin Uor slept was made strong by magic words and symbols. More of Hu Po's sorcery. Useless to prowl there. Dangerous to prowl there. The dragon was a knowing beast and prudent. The signs were against him. Hence, he tarried not, but crawled down the hallway in leaving.

A wheelbarrow stood in his path. He could not pass to the right. To the left he could not pass. Nor could he leap over the obstruction. But the dragon was not one to be baffled by such a weak and wooden contrivance. His huge mouth opened and his white hot breath rushed forth. In a twinkling the wooden barrow vanished. Like a butter cake dropped upon the summer sun it melted, burned to a cinder of nothingness.

Now the wheelbarrow thus destroyed was property of the little Princess Chin Uor. In it had been golden dolls, dolls of the princess. The dolls were dolls no longer. Under the dragon's fiery breath they changed to a pool of liquid gold. The hard gold became soft and flowing.

In the barrow had been pretty mud pies, pies of the princess. Under the dragon's burning breath they were changed to discs of stony hardness. The soft clay took on a hardness as of flint. The princess had wished her pies to dry. And her wish had been granted.

Next morning, the palace, from presence room to pantry, buzzed with excitement. Oo Loong had dared intrude within the royal dwelling. It could not be doubted. He had left his footprints in the molten gold, and the gold, in hardening, had preserved his tracks.

Witches and wizards came to make more able charms. Messengers galloped away to summon the distant army. The King raged and roared. Said His Majesty, "Let that reprobate dragon return, if he dares. If he dares, let that reprobate dragon return." The courtiers trembled and gasped: "Pray may the wicked *loong* never return. Never, never return." But little Princess Many Dimples played with her pies and was happy. Her pies had been baked to a queen's taste—or rather to the taste of a princess. Beside the river she worked faithfully in wet white clay. Such beautiful pies. "I do hope that the nice *loong* will return," said Princess Chin Uor. "He is such a fine oven. I shall make a hundred more pies for his baking."

Pie after pie. Even the nurses helped.

Instead of saying, "Please, will your Royal Highness not play with this lovely doll?" they said, "Please, is this one rounded enough?" and "Please, shall I scallop the edges a trifle deeper?" and "Shall I imagine that this one contains cherries, or radishes?" or whatever it may be that makers of pies would say in a royal kitchen. So, a hundred pies were made and wheeled to the palace. In reality, they numbered a hundred and one, but the odd one was so thick that it must be called a cake. Howbeit, that is not important.

Night followed day—a habit most nights have. The soldiers slept—as they had been ordered not to do. The hour approached when clock hands point to the highest sky. Midnight came, and with it the mountainous mountain *loong*. Unseen by those whose duty was seeing, the dragon entered King Yang Lang's courtyard. And there he was perplexed and paused. The King's door was a hodgepodge of magic signs, plastered with yellow paper. Vain to think of entering there. The Queen's door was upside down—best charm of all. To think of entering was vain. The door that led to Princess Chin Uor's sleeping chamber was written thick with words to still a dragon's heart, circles to dizzy his head. Say what you please, the witches and wizards had done good work upon that door. Their charms were written with clearness and force. The *loong* dared not take a second glance. He felt his limbs grow weak. Wisely hastened he from the spell-guarded threshold.

Now in the reign of the Emperor Ming, a crazed and knavish fellow known to the world as Wing Dow, invented a contrivance called by him "Look-through-the-wall," but which we of today call a "Window." His invention gave the Emperor Ming a severe cold, and Wing Dow came within a sword's width of losing his ears—but more of that later. Here it is necessary to say only that Look-through-the-walls became popular, and many such were to be found in King Yang Lang's palace. In the Princess Chin Uor's room were many wing-dows (or windows), and—hard to believe—those wing-dows were unguarded either by charm or by apple wood beam, which is as good as a charm. Could the dragon pass by such a fine chance? Could he pass the wing-dow and not have a try? When he had come with purpose to do harm? It is easy to imagine the thing that happened. And yet not so easy as may seem.

The dragon's lumpish head entered the wing-dow. His deer horns, his rabbit eyes, his snake tongue, all entered, and easily enough. A ponderous sofa-cushion foot he placed upon the window ledge . . .

Crash and smash and clatter. . . .

The nurses awoke and screamed, "Save us."

The Princess Chin Uor awoke and said, "Shoo."

Soldiers in the courtyard awoke and lighted green fires as they smote their drums, saying: "Come if you dare. Help. Help."

The dragon was already awake—awake to the danger. Promptly he vanished. Such noise he could not abide.

King Yang Lang came with a golden torch. Greatly he was pleased that the *loong* had been routed.

But Princess Chin Uor was far from pleased. Indeed, she was fretful. From the floor she took a sliver of flint-hard clay. "My pies are all broken. All. All are broken," mourned Princess Many Dimples. "I have placed them in the wing-dow. And the dragon knocked them down and broke them." And beyond doubt so had he done. There were the pieces.

Still the King remained cheerful. His little daughter's sadness passed unnoticed. His Majesty said: "Your pies, my daughter, are excellent food—let no one deny it—but even better are they to give warning of the dragon's nearness. Your pies have provided me with a wonderful idea. Hereafter we need have no more fear of the *loong*. . . . Ho! General. Awaken your soldiers. Let them march to the river."

For a week the King's army did no other labor than make mud pies. And like it. The pies were given heat in giant ovens, were baked into stony hardness. Then they were placed throughout the palace, in windows, upon tables, chairs, upon chests and shelves, high and low and everywhere. Even on the chimney tops were rows of glistening pies. The slightest misstep by a prowling dragon would have caused a din most tremendous.

The royal dining table was a shining whiteness, covered with mud pies. So numerous were the pies of the princess that no room remained for food. But that was no cause for worry. The King merely ordered that his rice be placed upon a baked clay pie. Mandarins who visited the palace were much surprised at what they saw—a King eating from common clay. Nevertheless, their own tables were soon covered with Princess Chin Uor's pies. For the King, of course, set all fashions.

And so, we modern peoples speak of our plates and cups and saucers as "China." China? Is it? Yes, and no. China is merely our way of pronouncing Chin Uor. Our plates are merely thin copies of Princess Chin Uor's pies.

The Birch and the Star

*The boy remembered a large birch tree
and the girl remembered a star. Together
these memories would lead them home*

ZACHARIAS TOPELIUS

About two hundred years ago, there was sorrow with great want in Old Finland. War raged on all sides. Cities and villages were in flames. Growing things were trampled down. People, thousands and thousands of them, were lost by the sword, by famine, by sickness and by exile.

Nothing was seen or heard on all sides but sighs and tears, sorrow and groans, ashes and blood. Then, too, families were scattered. Some were carried to the enemy's land. Others fled to the woods and desert places. Others found their way to faraway Sweden. Wives lost their husbands; brothers their sisters. Fathers and mothers were separated from their children and did not know whether they were alive or dead.

During this long war two children, a brother and sister, were carried off to a strange land. There some kind folk found them and cared for them.

The years rolled by. The children grew up. They had everything they needed, but they could not forget their father and mother and dear home. They felt like captives far from their own land.

At last news came that peace was made, and all the captives who so wished might return to their homes in Finland. When the children heard this, they could bear to stay no more in that strange land, and they longed to return home.

The strangers who cared for them smiled and said, "Go home? Poor children! Do you know how far you will have to go? Over seven hundred miles!"

"That makes no difference," said the children. "Only let us go!"

"Have you not a home here with us?" said the strangers. "You have fruit to eat, milk to drink, warm clothes to wear and a pretty house to live in. Yes, and have you not kind friends here, who love you? What more do you want?"

"Yes!" said the children. "But we want to go home."

"In your own home is great poverty," said the strangers. "Moss will be your bed, and a hut of twigs your house. Cold winds and frosts will always be with you, and your bread will be the bark of trees. Your father and mother, your brothers and sisters and all your friends died long ago. Where your hut once stood you will find traces of wolves in the snowdrifts that have swept over the mountains."

"Yes!" said the children. "But we want to go home."

"Ten years have passed since you were

carried away," said the strangers. "Then you were a little brother of five and a little sister of four. Now you are fifteen and fourteen. You have forgotten the way home and forgotten your father and mother. They, too, have forgotten you."

"Yes!" said the children. "But we want to go home."

"Who will show you the way?" asked the strangers.

"God!" said the boy. "Besides, I remember a large birch tree that stands in our father's garden, where many beautiful birds sing in the morning sun."

"And I remember," said the girl, "that in the evenings a beautiful star shines down through the leaves of the birch."

"Foolish children!" said the strangers. "What you ask is folly and ruin. Think no more about going."

But the more they forbade them, the more the children thought about home. There was a longing and a desire in their hearts to go home, which the children could not help. At last one night as the boy lay awake and could not sleep because of these thoughts, he said to his sister, "Are you asleep?"

"No!" she said. "I cannot sleep because I am thinking of home."

"So am I," said the boy. "Come, let us tie up our best clothes and start for home. I feel as if God were whispering all the time in my heart, 'Go home! Go home!' and what God tells us to do cannot be wrong."

"That is so!" said the sister.

And they quietly left the house.

The moon was silvering every hill and silent path. When they had gone a little distance, the girl said, "Brother, I am afraid that we shall not find our way home."

"Let us keep to the northwest," said the brother. "It is there we see the sun set in the evenings. Our home is that way. And when we see the old birch and the star

shining through its leaves, we shall know our home."

Again after a while the sister said, "Dear Brother, I am so afraid that wild beasts and robbers will hurt us."

"God will protect us," said the brother. "Do you not remember the prayer we used to say at home, when we were little:

'Let what will in life betide me,
God's own hand shall lead and
    guide me.'"

"Yes!" said the girl. "God will send angels to lead us through this strange land."

Thus they went on their way. The boy cut a strong oak stick to defend himself and his sister if evil befell them.

One day they came to a place where two roads met. They did not know which to take. Two little birds were singing by the road that led to the left.

"Come," said the brother, "to the left is the road we should follow. I know it by the twittering of the birds."

"Yes!" said the girl. "These birds are more than ordinary birds. God's angels have taken the form of birds to lead us to our home."

So they went along. The birds flew before them from branch to branch, just fast enough for the children to follow.

Wild fruit and berries were their food, and little springs that gushed from the rocks here and there gave them water. In quiet nooks on soft moss they slept at night. How strange it seemed, for during the day wherever they went, they found food, and at night they always found a quiet place for rest.

And whenever the children saw the little birds, they cried, "See the little angels leading us!"

Thus they went on their way.

And after many many days and many

many nights, the girl grew tired and said to her brother, "When shall we begin to look for the old birch?"

"Not before we hear people speaking the language our parents spoke."

And again they walked on many, many, weary long miles to the north and west. The summer began to draw to its close. The woods began to feel damp and chilly. And the girl said, "May we not look for our birch?"

"Not yet," answered the boy.

The country around them began to change. They had been passing over wide plains. Now there were hills and mountains and large lakes.

"How are we to climb over these steep mountains?" asked the girl.

"I will help you," said the boy.

"But how are we to cross the big rivers and lakes?"

"We will row across them."

And so they did, for they found boats waiting as though provided for them.

One day they walked from early morning till evening. They were very tired and hungry. They came to a lonely place where there was a new hut of logs, built on the ashes of a ruined house. In the garden a little girl stood peeling a turnip.

"Will you please give us one of your turnips?" asked the boy.

"Yes, come in," said the child. "Mother will give you something to eat."

Then the boy clapped his hands. He kissed the child and cried for joy.

"Why are you so happy, Brother?" asked the sister.

"Should I not be happy? This little one speaks the language of our father and mother. Now we may look for our birch and our star."

They went into the hut and the people asked them from where they came.

The boy said, "We come from a foreign land to seek our home. We will know it by a large birch in our father's garden, where the birds sing in the mornings, and where a beautiful star shines through the tree in the evenings."

"Poor children!" explained the people sorrowfully. "There are thousands of birches growing everywhere. Many thousands of stars shine in the heavens. How will you ever find the right ones?"

"God will lead us!" said both the children. "Have not His angels led us all this long way, through strange lands to our own land? Are we not halfway home?"

"Finland is great," said the people, and shook their heads.

"But God is greater still!" said the boy.

And so the children thanked the people and went on.

Happily now they did not have to eat and sleep in the woods. They went from place to place. Often great distances and wild heaths lay between one hut and another, and everywhere there was poverty. Yet they always found food and shelter, for people took pity on them. But the birch and star they could not find. Many birches and many stars they saw, but not the right ones.

"Alas!" said the girl. "Finland is so large, and we are so small! We shall never be able to find our home."

"Do you believe in God?" said the brother.

"Yes!"

"Then you know what wonderful things have happened. When the Wise Men came to see the Savior in Bethlehem, a star went before them. A star will lead us, if we will but believe."

"Yes!" said the sister as she always did to her brother.

And they went on looking for the birch and star.

It was the second year of their wanderings. One evening they came to a lonely farmhouse. It was the evening before Whitsunday, in the latter part of May. The first leaves were beginning to burst forth.

As the children passed through the gate, they saw in the garden a large birch with spreading branches and tender young leaves. And in the early twilight shone through the leaves the most beautiful evening star. It was the only star to be seen, for it was larger than any other.

"There is our birch!" cried the boy.

"And there is our star!" cried the sister.

And they put their arms around each other's neck, and thanked God with tears of joy.

"Here is the place where our father used to lead in the horses!" said the boy.

"And I remember this well where Mother used to water the cows!" said the girl.

"Here are two crosses under the birch trees," said the boy. "What do they mean?"

"I am afraid to go into the house," said the girl. "Suppose Mother and Father are no more! Suppose they do not know us! You go first, Brother!"

"Let us both peep in the door, first," said the brother with fast-beating heart.

In the house sat an old man and his wife. They were not old in years, but sorrow had wrinkled their brows.

"Yes, it is Pentecost," said the husband, "when God sent the Comforter down to sorrowing hearts. But to us no comfort comes. All our four children are gone. Two sleep beneath the birch. Two are far away and will never come back."

"Is not God all-powerful," said the wife, "and of infinite goodness? He who led the Children of Israel out of bondage can give us back our children if He thinks it is best. How old would our youngest child be now?"

"The boy sixteen, and the girl fifteen. But we do not deserve such a blessing from the Lord, as to get our children back."

As he spoke, the door opened. A boy and girl stepped in.

"We have come a long way," they said. "May we have a bite of bread?"

"Come nearer, children," cried the father, "and be with us this night. You are just the size our own children would be could they have stayed with us."

"What handsome children!" exclaimed the mother. "Just like our children could they have stayed with us!"

Both parents began to weep. The two children could not restrain themselves longer. They threw themselves weeping into their parents' arms, and exclaimed, "Do you not know us? We are your lost children. God has wonderfully led us back from a strange land to our home!"

The parents kissed their children with joy and love too great for words. Then with the children they fell on their knees and poured out their hearts in thanksgiving to God, who on this very Pentecost had sent them deep joy and comfort.

After that the children had to tell their story. The father and mother told theirs. Though they had all suffered sorrow and distress, sorrow was changed to joy. The father rejoiced as he felt the strong arms of his boy. The mother smoothed the brown locks of her daughter and kissed her rosy cheeks a hundred times.

"Yes," cried the mother in childlike glee, "I thought something would happen! Today I heard two strange birds singing so sweetly in the birch."

"Oh, I know them!" said the girl. "They are two angels in bird form who led us on our way. They now rejoice that we have found our home."

"Come, Sister," said the boy, "let us look once more at the birch and the star. See, Sister, see! There sleep our little brother and sister. If it were we who were sleeping there beneath the green sod, and our brother and sister were standing here, what should we be?"

"Surely you would be angels in heaven," said the mother gently.

"Now I know!" said the girl. "The little angel birds that led us on our way and sang of our coming today are our little brother and sister. It was they who ever whispered in our hearts, 'Go home! Go home! Comfort Father and Mother!' It was they who led us through desert places and kept us from starving, who provided us with beds of moss and had the boats ready for us to cross the rivers and lakes. It was they, too, who told us that this was the right birch and the right star among so many thousands. Thanks be to our little brother and sister! Thanks be to the great and good God!"

"See!" said the boy. "See how clear the star shines through the leaves of the birch. Now we have found our home! Now our wanderings are over."

Under Cover
of Apologies

*A fifteen-year-old boy becomes
a secret agent and has the adventure
of his young life as he steals
back a stolen government treaty*

GEOFFREY HOUSEHOLD

When the draft of the naval pact was stolen from the archives of the Foreign Office in London, during the 1930s, the American ambassador and the British officials despaired. They knew who had it—Cosmo Casals, the popular but unscrupulous first secretary of a foreign embassy—but they could not hope to get it back. Embassies may not be raided, and diplomats cannot be prosecuted.

In a Knightsbridge apartment two young men sat gloomily in front of an array of empty dishes, digesting their breakfast and reading their mail. They had every right to be gloomy, for the work of years had been undone by the daring coup of Mr. Casals. The owner of the apartment was Oscar Lund, an attaché of the American Embassy. All Lund's duties were obscure; nothing was expected of him except that he should have information on every subject when the ambassador wanted it. His guest was Lord Reginald Bathgate, a tall, hatchet-faced, monocled Englishman, who, so far as London society knew, did

nothing at all for a living and did it very gracefully. But on the continent of Europe various mysterious travelers knew him only as Number 4X. He was an unsuspected chief of the British secret service.

"Casals is leaving for his own country today," said the American. "He'll carry a diplomatic mailbag, and the pact will be inside it. Can't you stage a holdup?"

"I could, old chap," answered the Englishman, "but I daren't risk it. If Casals were a spy, I could do anything to him short of murder. If he were a criminal, I could set the police on him. But since he's a diplomat, his person is sacred."

"Oh, all right!" said Lund wearily and went on reading his mail. He slit open a pale blue envelope and glanced through the enclosed letter.

"Just listen to this, Bats," he groaned, turning to his friend.

"Dear Mr. Lund: I *do* hate to trouble you again, but I know you will forgive me, as we are such *old* friends. My

little Teddy is leaving London for his school in Switzerland, and I can't *bear* to think of him traveling alone. Would you send him in charge of one of your charming diplomatic friends, so that he doesn't get frightened and has no trouble with the customs? Please tell your friend to see that he has a glass of milk at eleven and keeps his throat *well* covered up on the boat. . . ."

"And two pages more of the same," said Lund. "But that's nothing. I once had to forward her Pekingese to a dog show!"

"Who is this mother's darling?" asked Bats.

"Teddy van Ness. The first time he was over here he ran away and joined a Paris circus. Then his tutor lost him in Constantinople, and he turned up as the Wonder Boy Drummer in a German cabaret. He knows Europe better than I do, and I'm supposed to nurse him."

"Send him with Casals!" snorted Lord Reginald.

"That's an idea!" the American exclaimed.

Bats screwed his monocle well home and stared at his friend.

"Are you serious?" he asked.

"Sure! Listen here! If young Teddy steals the bag, nobody can say he's one of your agents. He'll be taken for a spoiled, mischievous child playing at being a gangster. You people over here believe anything of our American boys."

"But can he keep his mouth shut?"

"Can he?" answered Lund. "That kid could keep his mouth shut if he had a hot potato in it. I'll call him over and you can judge for yourself."

Lund telephoned Teddy at his hotel, and the boy promised to be right over. Then the attaché telephoned Cosmo Casals.

"Mayfair 1756, please. Hello, is that you, Cosmo? Sorry to call you so early, old man. . . . I hear you're leaving us today. . . . Isn't that just too bad! What's a London season without our Cosmo? I wonder if you'll do me a favor? Will you take a fifteen-year-old pet of the embassy as far as Lausanne with you? . . . That's fine! He won't give you any trouble. Momma says keep his throat well covered—he's that kind of boy."

Bats, who was seldom deceived by appearances, liked Teddy at first sight. There was a suggestion of a thoroughbred greyhound about Theodore van Ness. When he was bored he looked a pampered pet; but when he was aroused his pale face became keen and remarkably intelligent, and the sleek young muscles tautened all over his lanky body. Deep down in his eyes was a wicked sense of humor—unless Teddy was suspected of wrongdoing, when they were blue, innocent and appealing.

"Teddy," said Lund, "we've a job for you. Promise me on your honor that you will keep to yourself what I'm to tell you."

"On my honor," replied Teddy.

"In the event of any nation declaring war on another," Lund explained, "the United States and Great Britain have agreed to pool their naval and air forces to prevent it. The pact hasn't been ratified by the Senate or by Parliament, but it will be if we can choose our moment to get it passed. Other countries are pretty sure that the unofficial agreement exists, but they daren't say so unless they have an authentic copy of it. Teddy, Cosmo Casals has such a copy. He will show it to his government and then to the newspapers; the whole world will ring with it prematurely, and it will never be signed.

"Now, then! Mr. Casals, at your mother's request, has consented to escort you as far as Lausanne and to give you your glass of milk at eleven."

Teddy grinned broadly.

"Be the nastiest kind of spoiled child you can imagine. Watch him closely. Note who talks to him. And keep your eyes on his mailbag."

"Shall I grab it if I can?" asked Teddy.

"This is where I chip in," interrupted Lord Reginald. "Get the bag if you can, and bring it to Mr. Lund. But remember— there would be a first-class international row if it were known that we were behind you. So if you're caught, you must pretend you did it for a lark."

"And if I succeed?" asked Teddy. He had grown serious.

"If you succeed," answered Lund, "I shall have to disown you and apologize for you, and probably the ambassador will send you home in disgrace."

"Gee!" Teddy gasped. "Then I get it in the neck both ways."

"You do," admitted Lord Reginald. "That's why there are very few men in the world brave enough to be secret agents."

"I don't know about brave," said Teddy, "but I do love excitement. How soon can I start?"

"This morning," answered Lund, putting his hands on Teddy's shoulders. "Our men will be near you, though they can't help you much. If anyone addresses you as Mr. Thwaite, show no particular interest, but listen to what he has to say."

Teddy spent a frantically busy hour at his hotel and then returned to Lund's apartment, where he was handed over to the care of Casals, an exquisite young diplomat, dark, slim and beautifully dressed.

When the diplomat saw Teddy he wished to Heaven that he had not been so obliging. The boy looked sulky, he was bad-mannered, he had an indecent quantity of baggage. Although it was a warm spring day, the fur collar of his overcoat was turned up to his ears.

"Well, well, my little man! So you're going back to school!" remarked Casals, as soon as they were settled on the gorgeous cherry-colored cushions of the boat train and roaring smoothly from London to Dover.

"Don't want to!" replied Teddy, and started to kick the mahogany paneling.

"I wouldn't do that, if I were you," said the diplomat firmly.

"Why wouldn't you?" asked Teddy, continuing to kick.

There was a strained silence for some minutes. Then Teddy, pointing rudely at the small white mail sack with the arms of Mr. Casals' country stamped on the outside, asked, "What's in that bag?"

"Just letters and reports," said Casals politely.

"Huh!" Teddy grunted. "If it's got money in it, be careful I don't steal it!"

Mr. Casals, sighing, called the attendant and ordered lunch for them both.

"Soup, sir?" the attendant asked, turning to the sulky boy.

"No," said Teddy. "I want a big cream puff. Right away!"

"That isn't very good for you," suggested Mr. Casals. "Try a—"

"I want a cream puff!" Teddy repeated in a loud voice.

Mr. Casals glanced nervously at his grinning fellow passengers, and ordered one.

"Make it four," said Teddy to the attendant.

The attendant made it four. On top of them Teddy ate a whole lobster and a pound of strawberries. He then lay back in his corner, munching a candy bar. Casals lighted a dainty cigarette and then looked at the boy with disgust.

At Dover two blue-jerseyed porters seized their hand baggage and led them through the dungeon-like vestibules under the station and out upon the windy pier. While one of them escorted Casals to his stateroom, the other, who appeared to be nothing more than one of the regular porters, touched his cap to Teddy.

"Hope you have a smooth crossing, Mr. Thwaite," he said. "Stand in the corridor when your train leaves Calais."

The boat churned up the water and stood out of the harbor for the distant gray hills of France. Teddy joined Casals in his stateroom. He made himself a nuisance by examining all the fittings of the tiny cabin, leaving the port open so that it banged and losing the soap under Casals' chair.

"Will you please sit down!" ordered the diplomat, who by now was calculating how many more hours he would have to spend in the company of this beastly boy.

Teddy obediently sat down. The boat began to roll in the ceaseless swell of the Channel. The boy's face took on an injured expression. He was so quiet that Casals actually managed to read three pages of his book.

"Mr. Casals!" cried Teddy suddenly. "Oh, Mr. Casals!"

"What is it?"

"Mr. Casals, I think I'm going to be seasick!"

He clutched the unfortunate diplomat, and gave a heartrending hiccup. Casals led him firmly to the side of the boat, but he was too late. Teddy had had the greatest difficulty in making himself seasick, and having succeeded, he wasn't going to waste his efforts.

Casals, cursing in four languages, mopped his exquisite trousers with an inadequate silk handkerchief and returned to his stateroom. Teddy chuckled to himself. Casals had actually left the bag unguarded while he rushed the boy to the open air. Teddy rightly guessed that by this time he had got so thoroughly on the diplomat's nerves that the man had forgotten everything except his hatred of him.

The desolate-looking town of Calais came racing up from the horizon, and soon the boat nosed alongside the jetty. Casals

137

showed his diplomatic passport, and the two walked serenely through the customs and on to the station platform. Gold-laced, bearded and magnificent, the stationmaster led them to their reserved compartment on the Simplon-Orient Express. A narrow corridor ran along one side of the coach, and out of it opened luxurious little rooms. Casals dropped dejectedly into the corner nearest the corridor, with the precious bag on the seat beside him. Teddy sulked in the corner by the window. The famous express slid silently out of the station and settled down to its seventy miles an hour.

Teddy pushed past Casals' legs and went out into the corridor. Two men, looking like solid English manufacturers, edged past him.

"I hear, Mr. Thwaite," said one, apparently speaking to the other, "that there's a slight obstacle on the line. The train will slow up in five minutes."

Teddy returned to the compartment. "Feeling better now!" he announced. "I guess I could eat another candy bar."

He pulled a half-melted bar from his pocket and started to eat it noisily. The trick worked. Casals got up and stood at the entrance to the compartment, his back to Teddy. The bag remained on the seat. Teddy banged the window down and thrust his head out. Casals glanced around, saw the boy's shoulders heaving, and looked away again, hoping fiercely that the revolting child would fall out. Anything to get rid of him!

As they passed outside the port of Boulogne, the brakes jarred on quietly. Teddy thrust his legs through the open window and balanced on the sill. The speed of the train dropped to ten miles an hour. He leaned back, grabbed the mail sack and slid, feet foremost, to the track. The bag and his heavy coat broke the fall, and in an instant he was up and skidding down the embankment. At the bottom he shed his coat and sprinted across the open fields toward the outskirts of Boulogne.

Teddy was no mean runner. He had done the 100 yards in 10 seconds, which was well for the two great countries whose plans depended on his legs. He took a low hedge in his stride and dropped on one knee behind it to see what was happening. Casals was standing on the embankment, raving. Some of the train crew and passengers were pounding after the fugitive, strung out like a pack of hounds.

"Au voleur!" they yelled. "Stop thief!"

Teddy sprang up and skimmed over the ground toward a narrow, cobbled street that seemed to promise dark corners and yards where he might hide. He was nearly in it when out shot a mob of honest citizens, headed by a blue-cloaked French policeman. Teddy swerved, but he was too late. The flic caught him by the collar.

"I arrest you in the name of the law!" he said.

He led Teddy down the street at a rapid walk, surrounded by the excited crowd.

Suddenly he stopped and looked the crowd over, twirling his glorious moustaches with his free hand.

"Circulez!" he ordered grandly. "Circulez donc!"

The crowd obediently dispersed, but followed at a distance. The policeman turned a corner and with a catlike spring leaped into a tiny, dark cottage, dragging Teddy after him.

"That was a close shave, Mr. Thwaite!" he said in English.

"Gosh!" exclaimed Teddy. "Are you a Mr. Thwaite, too?"

"Exactly!" replied the policeman.

He hurled his cloak, uniform and moustaches into a corner and slipped on a loud tweed suit. In an instant he was transformed into a middle-class English tourist spending a jolly weekend in Boulogne.

"If anyone catches us," he said, "say that you escaped from the police. I wish I could help you more, old boy. But you've got to play a lone hand. They told you that, I suppose?"

"Sure!" Teddy grinned. "I don't know there are such things as secret agents."

He dressed Teddy in the blue jersey and trousers of a French fishing boy, and tanned his face. The mail sack he dropped into a stout paper bag and covered it with rolls of bread.

"Off No. 2 pier," he said, "is my motor launch, the *Baby Mine*. She's fast and seaworthy, in spite of her disgusting name. Steal her. Make Folkestone, not Dover, if you can. Your course is due west till the tide starts running down channel, then northwest. I'll have to make an awful row when I find she's gone, but I'll delay pursuit as long as I can."

The two shook hands with a single swift grip. Teddy left the cottage and strolled through the streets toward the port. He saw Casals standing outside the telegraph office and shot hastily around a corner. Nobody took any interest in him. He might have been a boy from any of the brown-sailed fishing smacks that worked the coast from Ostend to Dieppe.

He got himself rowed out to the *Baby Mine* on the pretense of delivering stores. Standing with his back to the man in the dinghy so that the movements of his hands were hidden, he started the motor. It roared into life, and before the boatman could recover from his surprise, Teddy had slipped the moorings and was tearing out to sea at a speed absolutely prohibited by the port of Boulogne.

He settled down at the wheel and relaxed. He had the gift of trusting to his luck when there was nothing else to trust to.

The *Baby Mine* purred into the sunset at twenty knots an hour. The misty shores of England gradually took on definite shape, and a white cliff gave him a landmark. He found that he was drifting down channel and altered his course to the northwest. The lights of Folkestone winked in the dusk and he aimed straight for the harbor.

"'Eave to, and stop yer engines!" came a sharp command.

Teddy, gazing fixedly into the growing darkness, had not noticed the coast-guard cutter that foamed up on his port quarter. He disobeyed the order, trusting to his superior speed. Three times he was challenged; then a fountain of water deluged him as a one-pounder shot plumped into the sea a yard ahead of the *Baby Mine*.

"The next un'll knock yer 'ead off," remarked a grieved voice through a megaphone. "I don't want ter 'ave ter do it."

Teddy promptly hove to and the cutter came alongside.

"Aye!" said the captain. "This 'ere's the boat wot was pinched from Boulong 'arbor. Come aboard, young un!"

"But I'm Mr. Thwaite," protested Teddy firmly.

"I don't care if yer the bloomin' Prince of Wales," replied the captain. "Come on quietly now!"

Teddy went aboard, and the cutter, taking his boat in tow, ran into Folkestone.

With a seaman on each side of him, he was marched along the jetty to the port offices, still clutching his paper bag, and deposited in a whitewashed and depressing cell. Teddy sat there dejectedly, hoping that his unknown friend in Boulogne had been able to wire Lord Reginald that he was on the way. It was maddening to think that all his work might be undone by the clumsy questioning of the police.

After a short wait he was escorted to the

charge room, where a stern inspector looked him up and down disdainfully.

"Name?" asked the inspector.

"Theodore van Ness."

"Nationality?"

"United States citizen."

"Did you steal the launch *Baby Mine* from Boulogne Harbor?"

"I did," answered Teddy calmly.

The inspector snorted and looked over a telegram lying on his desk. Then he pulled a bell at his side. A stout and helmeted police sergeant answered the ring.

"Sergeant Hawkins," ordered the inspector, "we have instructions from the Foreign Office to send this boy under arrest to No. 6 Clarendon Crescent in London, where an attaché of the American Embassy will hold him for inquiries. Take him there. Resist any attempt at rescue, and above all, see that his baggage is not disturbed. Where's your baggage?" he asked Teddy.

"Here," said Teddy, indicating the paper bag and trying hard not to show his delight.

"Balmy!" exclaimed the inspector. "That's what they are, balmy! Still, it's no business of mine. Sergeant Hawkins, you'll just make the boat train if you run."

At Victoria Station, in London, the sergeant led his prisoner to a taxi and they drove out into the murky London night. A drizzling fog shrouded the great city. The street lamps were pale yellow globes dimly reflected in the soaking pavement. The taxi crawled toward Clarendon Crescent through a maze of wide, elegant squares and terraces, deserted at this hour.

A powerful Rolls-Royce pulled up alongside them.

"Hand over your prisoner, sergeant," said a quiet voice with a slight accent.

Sergeant Hawkins jumped. He was looking down the barrel of a revolver. A second was trained on Teddy, while a third man

covered the taxi driver. The car stopped with a jerk.

"Nah then!" said Sergeant Hawkins calmly, reaching for his whistle. "Yer can't do this in London, yer know."

"No?" answered Casals' agent. "If you blow that whistle, you're a dead man."

"Here's your bag!" interrupted Teddy sulkily. "I only took it for a joke."

He opened the door of the taxi, stepped onto the running board and offered the bag to the man who had spoken. The secret agent grasped it eagerly. At the same instant Teddy jerked the bottom. The wet paper gave way, leaving the mailsack in Teddy's hands. He hurled himself sideways under a shower of stale rolls and ducked behind the back of the car. Two tongues of fire spat at him. A bullet ripped through his sleeve. Another cut a part through his hair. In a fraction of a second he was up and zigzagging through the fog—an impossible target. He heard Sergeant Hawkins blow his whistle, heard it answered at once from the next block. The Rolls-Royce whizzed around a corner on two wheels and disappeared.

Teddy jumped the railings of one of the little gardens that line the residential terraces of London, and took cover in some shrubbery. His first impulse was to make a dash for Lund's apartment, but then decided that he should appear to be brought there against his will. The police were scattering through the adjoining street and gardens in search of him. He marked the burly figure of friendly Sergeant Hawkins, to whom he wished to give the honor of his recapture, dashed across the road in front of him and tripped deliberately over the curb. The sergeant grabbed him in triumph.

"Well," he remarked, "that there was the queerest rescue I ever did see. 'Ang me if them furriners h'acted like yer friends!"

He waited for an explanation, but Teddy offered none and allowed himself to be led in stony silence to No. 6 Clarendon Crescent and handed over to Mr. Lund. The attaché looked so sternly at Teddy that Sergeant Hawkins felt positively sorry for the boy.

As soon as the sergeant had left, Lord Reginald, who had kept discreetly out of sight, appeared from the bedroom. Teddy was overwhelmed by his reception. The diplomats, apparently mad with joy, danced around him, cheering incoherently and slapping him on the back.

"Well done! Well done, my Thwaiteling!" yelled Bats. "Lord! I can't and I won't let this boy go without credit! You'll have to wait till the pact is signed, Teddy, but then I'm going to let this tale leak out where it will do you the most good!"

He ripped open the bag and removed a simple, typewritten document, each paragraph initialed in several hands.

"That's it!" he said, pocketing the document. "They'll miss it, but they can't say anything. Why, our efficient police even recovered the bag for them within a mere eight hours!"

"And now your lordship had better shut up and take itself down the backstairs." said Lund. "I'll deliver the bag to Casals' chief with many apologies for our spoiled American children. Whatever made you do such a shocking thing, Van Ness?"

Teddy opened his big blue eyes and pretended to be on the verge of tears. "I guess I must have seen too many gangster films!" he whimpered.

THE TRAMP

Mother had a rule about feeding tramps.
She always asked them to do a bit of work first

ANNE LITTLEFIELD LOCKLIN

When Grandfather Wib was a boy, tramps often came to the back door to ask for a bite to eat. There was a railroad junction a mile north, and the tramps followed along the tracks and stopped for food at houses on the way. Wib's mother never seemed to be the least bit afraid of any of the tramps. She always found something to spare them, but she always asked them to do some work for her before she fed them—and they always did it, even the toughest-looking ones. She said the work was good for their self-respect. Wib did not much understand what that meant, but the work part of it suited him fine. He was

quite willing that all the chores should be done that way.

One day, toward the end of March, Cousin Ned and Wib and Shorty had an argument on the way home from school. It was about tramps.

It seemed that one of the older boys, Lank Smith, had said that tramps who stop at your house have a way of leaving signs behind them so that all the tramps who come along will know whether your house is a good one to stop at.

"Do you believe that?" Ned wanted to know.

Shorty said, "It must be so. Why old

142

Missus Peele boasts that no tramp has entered her gate in twenty years. She's too stingy to give away a bread crust, and I bet anything the tramps all know it beforehand."

Wib said he didn't believe it, and he wanted to know what the signs looked like. "I've never seen a tramp make any marks around our house, and you know how many stop there," he said. "I'm glad of it. Why every now and then I don't have a stick of kindling to split, and I remember once I got out of dipping water from the rain barrel and lugging it into the house on washday. I like tramps."

"Huh," Shorty said and he kicked at a hunk of melting snow with his rubber boots and sent it flying in a fine spray, just by way of emphasis, "liking 'em doesn't prove anything. We were talking about signs."

"Oh, well," Ned said, "don't get het up about it. The old tramps will be coming back pretty soon and then we'll see who is right." Most of the tramps in that region were like robins—they went south in the winter and came back in the spring. "Let's cut across lots and see if the pussywillows are out," he added.

They always looked for the first pussywillows along the brook, just west of the tracks. The brook, now swollen with melting snow, was swift and deep—and so wide that the boys could hardly jump it in their heavy rubber boots. The pussywillows were not really out, they found. Only a few had burst their red-brown sheaths. It would be another week before most of them showed their furry gray coats. Wib cut one or two to let his mother know how far along they were. She was fond of growing things.

Then the boys followed the brook down through the orchard to the footbridge. Wib was proud to see that the bridge still held despite the high water. The snow had pretty well gone off in the open, except for places where drifts had been—the brook would not get much higher. They crossed, stopped for a drink all around at the spring, then sloshed up the path to the house. A delicious aroma of hot molasses and spice came through the open kitchen window.

"Cookies," Ned said. "Aunt Annie is at it again." They made a rush for the back door. But they stopped long enough in the back room to take off their caps and to wipe their feet—they were well trained that way.

All the boys thought that Wib's mother made the best things to eat. There were doughnuts and pies to make your mouth water. But cookies were her specialty—and she could make every kind you ever heard of. Molasses cookies, sugar cookies, hermits, ginger puffs and raisin cookies—the big brown crock was never empty.

Now as the boys unwound their mufflers and unbuttoned their coats, she took a great pan of golden brown cookies from the oven. "I don't blame the tramps for stopping at your house," Shorty said as he watched her.

Mother Annie smiled and her blue-gray eyes twinkled. "Do you remember last year when I gave a tramp some molasses cookies?"

Wib and Ned knew the story, but Shorty had not heard it. So Wib's mother told it again. First she put two sticks of wood in the stove and fixed the draft. Then she began. "About this time last spring, a big burly old tramp stopped to ask if I could spare him a bite to eat. I told him if he would fetch a pail of water from the spring, I would see. And while he was getting the water, I fixed him a big plate of cookies. It so happened it was April first and I had been making some molasses cookies about like these, only I put cotton batting inside one or two of them to fool the boys." Wib and Ned grinned—they remembered the cookies. "Of course the cotton didn't show once they were baked," she went on, "and somehow I got hold of one of those April Fool cookies and put it on the plate with the others. You should have seen the surprised look on that big fellow's face when he bit into the cotton. I couldn't help laughing."

"And what did the tramp do?" Shorty wanted to know.

"Oh, he laughed too," Mother Annie said. "Laughed till I thought he'd burst the last button on his coat."

It made the boys laugh just to think of it, and Mother Annie joined in. She was like that. She always loved a joke.

Now she gave them a plateful of hot cookies and a couple of russet apples apiece and they went out to eat by the back door where the wind didn't hit and the last bit of sun did. It was warm out there on the flat stone that served as a doorstep. There was silence for a full minute while the boys crunched and munched.

The afternoon shadows were purple-black, but the sun had that peculiar yellow brilliance that spring sunshine seems to have about that time of day. It searched out the patch on Wib's short trousers where he had torn them on the picket fence, and the darns on the knees of Ned's black stockings now faded to a greenish hue, and the tiny mended moth holes in Shorty's gray coat. It revealed every crack and cranny in the granite stone they were sitting on. Wib knew them all by heart anyway—he could have found them in the dark. There was a worn spot by the doorsill where folks stepped in and out of the house—there was a big seam split by the frost—and there was the spoon-shaped hollow he and Fred had hammered out so that they could crack their butternuts more easily. He wished he had brought out

a handful of butternuts to eat with their apples.

He began to shine one of the russets on his trousers. Russets are a bronzy apple speckled all over like Shorty's nose in midsummer. They're the best keepers of all the New Hampshire apples, but they never take a very high shine.

"I've been thinking," Shorty said. "What if that big old tramp had got mad at your mother?"

"Huh," Wib said. "She's not afraid of tramps!" and he bit a worm hole out of his apple and spit it out scornfully.

"I know—my mother says, the usual tramp is perfectly harmless," Ned put in. "But what I'd like to know is how you going to tell which is which?"

Wib stood up. "Pooh! No tramp ever hurt a flea," he said. "I'd just like to see one that could scare me!" and he puffed out his chest like a young tom turkey.

All this time Mother Annie was in the pantry cutting out more cookies. She had the window open a crack and she stood before it working. When Wib looked up and saw her smiling and her eyes twinkling, he didn't think anything of it, only how pretty she looked standing there with her almost black hair combed back smoothly from her forehead and her cheeks all rosy from baking—sort of like a picture in a frame. He didn't mind that there was a smooch of flour over one eyebrow.

There wasn't much more time for their arguing. All three of the boys had chores to do before supper and the sun was dropping fast. Wib knew with all that baking his mother had done the kitchen woodbox would take a sight of wood, and he set to work to fill it.

A few days later when Wib came home from school and ran in to get a bite to eat he found a tramp sitting in the middle of the kitchen warming himself at the stove. He didn't think it strange to see a tramp there, they always came with the spring, but it was strange that his mother was nowhere about. Perhaps she was upstairs getting something of his father's for the tramp to wear—he was certainly ragged enough and all slumped down as if he were worn out. So he called "Mother" loudly. There was no answer.

The tramp did not speak, but he raised his head and looked at Wib. Wib did not feel nearly so sure about tramps as he had a few days before. This was the roughest-looking tramp Wib had seen in a long time. He had black bushy whiskers and fierce black eyebrows and his hat was jammed down over one eye. And when he looked at Wib with one visible eye, a chill chased down Wib's spine. He was just ready to back out of the kitchen and shut the door after him. Then he thought, "No, I can't just run out and leave a tramp in the house and nobody home." A good deal was expected of a boy going on nine years.

So he screwed up his courage and tried to make his voice sound very big. "What are you doing in my mother's kitchen, sir?" The tramp didn't even look up this time.

"I'm hungry," he said, and his voice sounded awfully gruff.

Wib said, "My mother always asks the men who come for food," and he was very careful to be polite and not say tramps, "to do some work for her before she feeds them." The old fellow shook his head. "My mother says that's only just," Wib urged, hoping that the tramp would play fair. But the tramp just sat huddled down in his chair.

"Got rheumatism," he grunted and still didn't look up.

Just then Wib remembered that he had left his bank on the kitchen table. He could not see whether it was still there, for his mother had set her tins of bread dough on the table to rise and covered them over with a big cloth. He wanted desperately to go and look under the cloth. There was a lot of money in that bank—boat money it was. Ever since fall when old Breshnahan had told them about his boat, Wib had been saving for one of his own. It came to ninety-three cents when he had counted it at noon. He remembered that Ned's mother said that the usual tramp was perfectly honest, but he was quite sure that this was not a usual tramp.

What was Wib to do? He wanted to be rid of the fellow. He thought the tramp would go as soon as he was fed and he knew there was plenty of bread and butter and cookies. Yet he felt he should stick to the rule his mother always followed. He would try once more and be extra polite. "I'm sorry about the rheumatism," Wib said, "and I'm sure Mother would be. If you would just fetch one small pail of water from the spring, I'm sure she wouldn't mind if I gave you something to eat."

"Good for you, Wibbie," the tramp said. And before Wib could move in his tracks, that tramp pulled off his hat, jerked off his whiskers and eyebrows and there sat his mother. "April Fool," she said and began to laugh. Of course, it was April first. Wib had forgotten for the moment. He ran and hugged her and they both laughed and laughed until they cried.

"As We Forgive Those"

*A story about a bargain, made between a young boy
and a President of the United States*

T. Morris Longstreth

The brothers Ripley were as different in nearly every way as the rapids and still pools of a mountain stream. Perhaps that is why they loved each other in a degree not usually meant by "brotherly love."

Will Ripley was the still pool. He was thoughtful to drowsiness, honest as daylight, mild-tempered, and twenty. He was in Pennsylvania somewhere, either alive or dead, for the date of this story is July 7th, 1863, which means that the terrible slaughter of the battle of Gettysburg was just over. The Ripleys, on their farm near the Soldiers' Home, outside of Washington, had not heard from him.

Although Will was no soldier at heart—it hurt him even to stick pigs—he had responded to Lincoln's call for more men two years before, leaving his young brother Dan at home to help his father and mother. Dan was now fourteen, a high-strung, impetuous, outspoken lad of quick actions and hasty decisions. He was the laughing rapid. But for all his hastiness, he had a head and a heart that could be appealed to, usually. The only thing to which he could not reconcile himself was the separation from Will. Even Will's weekly letters—which never missed their date except when

the army was in retreat, and which always sent messages of love to Dan, coupled with encouragement to stay on the farm as the best way he could aid the cause—scarcely kept Dan from running off and hunting up his brother. Dan knew that he and his collie, Tam, were needed to look after the sheep; he knew that the President had asked the loyal to raise all the wool possible; he knew that his father was little more than an invalid since he had been hurt some time before by an accident on the farm. But to see the soldiers marching down Pennsylvania Avenue set him wild to be away with them. In fact, Tam seemed to be the anchor that held him; Dan sometimes even thought that he loved Tam next to Will.

The summer of '63 had been unbearably hot. Then there had been an increasingly ominous list of military disasters. Even the loyal were beginning to murmur against Lincoln's management of the war. Then Will's letters had ceased, and Mr. Ripley could get no satisfaction from headquarters. Even Will's uncle, a Colonel Scott, of Illinois, and a friend of Lincoln's, after repeated efforts to influence some officials at the War Department to aid him in securing news, had not been able to see the

President, who was the last resort of everybody in those days of tribulation.

Dan was nearly sick with the heat and tension.

The climax to this state came from an unforeseen event. Tam, either crazed by the heat or some secret taste for blood, ran amuck one night, stampeded the sheep and did grievous damage. Farmer Ripley doubtless acted on what he considered the most merciful course by having Tam done away with and buried before Dan got back from an errand to the city. But to Dan it seemed, in the first agony of his broken heart, an unforgivable thing. Weariness, worry, and now this knife-sharp woe changed the boy into a heartsick being who flung himself on the fresh mound behind the barn and stayed there the whole day.

He shed no tears; tears would have been dried up by the waves of hot anger against his father. That evening his mother carried some food out to him. He did not touch it; he would not talk to her.

Sometime later, as the night wore on, he stole into the house, did up some clothes into a bundle, took the food at hand and crept from his home. Once more he went to the grave of Tam. What he said there, aloud but quietly, need not be told. Sufficient it is to know that a burning resentment toward his father filled him, coupled with a sickening longing to be with his brother Will. Ill with his hasty anger, he thought that Will was the only one in the world who loved or understood him. In the wee hours of morning he left the farm, forever, as he thought, and turned down the wood road which led to the Soldiers' Home, where he hoped to find someone who could tell him how to get to Will's regiment. The sultry, starless heat of a Washington midsummer enclosed him; the wood was very dark and breathless; his head throbbed. But he pushed on, high-tempered, unforgiving; he would show

them all! Suddenly he recollected that he had not said the Lord's Prayer that night. Dan had been strictly raised. He tried saying it, walking. But that seemed sacrilegious. He kneeled in the dark and tried. But when he got to "as we forgive those who trespass against us," he balked, for he was an honest soul. And this new gulf of mental distress was too much for him; it brought the tears.

There in the dark by the roadside, Dan cried himself to sleep.

At the same hour another worn soul, a tall, lean-faced man with eyes full of unspeakable sorrow, was pacing the chamber of the White House. The Rebellion had reached its flood tide at Gettysburg three days before; the President had stayed the flood, bearing in tireless sympathy the weight of countless responsibilities. Now, all day long there bore down upon him decisions that concerned not only armies but races; not only races, but principles of human welfare. He was grief-stricken still from his son Willie's death, and his secretary in the room downstairs, listened unconsciously to the steady march of steps overhead. Lincoln had given special instructions that no one was to interrupt him. He was having one of his great spiritual battles.

Finally, shortly before dawn, the footsteps stopped, the secretary's door opened, and the gaunt, gray face looked in. "Stoddard, do you want anything more from me tonight?"

The secretary rose. "I want you in bed, sir. Mrs. Lincoln should not have gone away; you are not fair with her or us."

"Don't reproach me, Stoddard," said Lincoln, kindly. "It had to be settled, and, with God's help, it has been. Now I can sleep. But I must have a breath of air first. There's nothing?"

"Only the matter of those deserters, sir, and that can wait."

The President passed his hands over his deep-lined face. "Only!" he murmured. "Only! How wicked this war is. It leads us to consider lives by the dozen, by the bale, wholesale. How many in this batch, Stoddard?"

The secretary turned some papers, "Twenty-four, sir. You remember the interview with General Scanlon yesterday."

Lincoln hesitated, saying, "Twenty-four! Yes, I remember. Scanlon said that lenience to the few was injustice to the many. He is right, too." Lincoln held out his hand for the papers; then drew it back and looked up at Stoddard. "I can't decide," he said in a low voice, "not now. Stoddard, you see a weak man. But I want to thresh this out a little longer. I must walk. These cases are killing me; I must get out."

"Let me call an attendant, Mr. Lincoln."

"They're all asleep. No, I'll take my chances with God. If anybody wants to kill me, he will do it. You must go to bed, Stoddard."

The two men, each concerned for the other, shook hands in good night, and Lincoln slipped out into the dark, his long legs bearing him rapidly westward. During the heat he usually slept at the Soldiers' Home, being escorted thither by cavalry with sabers drawn. But he hated the noise of it, and during Mrs. Lincoln's visit in New York, was playing truant to her rules. When he neared the Home he turned into the woods, drawn by the need of companionship with elements as calm and benign as forest trees. The sky at his back began to lighten.

By the time dawn showed the ruts in the road, Lincoln realized that he was tired. "Abe, Abe," he said half aloud, "they tell me you used to be a whale at splitting rails, and now a five-mile stroll before breakfast— By jings!" It was his usual swear, that "by

jings!" and this time it was occasioned by his nearly stepping on a lone youngster lying in the road. The boy raised his head from a bundle of clothes; the tall man stooped with tenderness, saying, "Hello, sonny. So you get old Mother Earth to make your bed for you! How's the mattress?"

Dan sat up and rubbed his eyes. "What are you doin'?" he asked.

"I appear to be waking you, and making a bad job of it," said Lincoln.

"You didn't come to take me, then," said Dan, relieved. "I wouldn't 'a' gone," he added defiantly.

Lincoln looked at him sharply, his interest aroused by the trace of tears in the boy's eyes and the bravado in his voice. "There's a misunderstanding here," continued Lincoln, "almost as bad a misunderstanding as Mamie and her mother had over Mr. Riggs, who was the undertaker back home." Here the gaunt man gave a preliminary chuckle. "Ever hear that story, sonny?"

Dan shook his head, wondering how such a homely man could sound so likable. Lincoln seated himself on a fallen tree trunk. "Well, it was this way. Back home there was an old chap used to drive an old rig around collecting rags. And one day when Mamie's ma was inside dusting the parlor, Mr. Riggs, whose job was undertaking, as I said, drops by for a friendly call, and Mamie sings out, country style, 'Ma, here's Mr. Riggs'; and her ma, thinking she'd said the man for the rags, called back, 'Tell him we haven't anything for him today.'"

The joke broke on Dan after one look at his friend's face, and his quick impetuous laugh might have disturbed the early-rising birds. Lincoln joined in, and for an instant Dan clean forgot Tam dead and home deserted; and for the same fleet instant Lincoln forgot his troubles in Dan's laugh. "Tell him we haven't anything for him today!" repeated the boy, "I'll sure have to tell that to Fa—" He didn't finish, remembering with a pang that he was not going to see his father again.

Lincoln had caught the swift change on his face and it was his turn to wonder. He knew better than to ask questions. You can't fish for a boy's heart with question marks, neat little fishhooks though they be. So he said, "Our sitting here when we ought to be getting back home reminds me of another story."

"Tell me," said Dan, well won already to this man, despite the gray, lined cheeks and the sadness that colored his voice. Dan didn't know yet who he was. He'd not seen the cartoons that flooded the country during election, he was too young to go in to the inauguration, and the idea of the President of the United States sitting with him in the woods was too preposterous to cross his mind.

"You and I are pretty lazy, son," said the kindly man; "but we aren't as lazy as the two young soldiers in the battle of Chancellorsville. The order came to retire, but those two were too lazy to move. Presently 'Ping!' a bullet had hit the canteen of one of them. 'Brother,' said the second, 'I reckon we ought to be a-movin'.' 'I reckon we ought,' said the first; but they didn't move. And it wasn't long before the hat of the second was shot clean off. 'Mercy sakes! I reckon we just ought to be a-movin',' exclaimed the other soldier and he half rose to go; but it was too much exertion. 'Mebbe,' he said, 'if we hang aroun' a while longer, we kin git ourselves carried away.'"

When Dan had got over that story, Lincoln said, "Well, since there's no one to carry us away, sonny, I reckon we just ought to be a-moving, don't you?"

"Are you going to the war, too?" asked Dan. "I am."

"You!" exclaimed Lincoln, "why you're no bigger than my own Tadpole, and he's only a wriggler yet. Does your father know?"

"I reckon he does by now," said the boy, darkly. "Father's an early riser. You see, he killed my dog without my knowin', and so I lit out without his knowin'."

The hardness of the boy's voice hurt Lincoln, who said, "What's your father's name, sonny?"

"William Ripley, that's senior. Will, that's junior, is my brother, off at the war. I'm Dan. I'm going to find my brother. I don't care if I never come back. I loved Tam better than—than—" His voice choked.

Lincoln put his hand on his shoulder. He was getting the situation. "Tam was your dog?" asked the big man, as gently as a mother.

"Yeh. And Father shouldn't 'a' killed him unbeknownst to me. I'll never forgive him that, never!"

"Quite right," said the wise man, walking with him. "Don't you ever forgive him, Dan. Or don't ever forget it—under one certain condition."

"What's that?" asked the boy, a trifle puzzled.

"Why, that you also never forget all the kind and just things that your father has done for you. Why did he kill the dog, Dan?"

"Well—he—killed—some sheep," said the boy.

"How old are you, Dan?"

"Fourteen, going on fifteen."

"That's quite a heap," said Lincoln, musingly, "quite a heap! In fourteen years a father can pile up a lot of good deeds. But I suppose he's done a lot of mean ones to cancel 'em off, has he?"

"No," admitted Dan.

His frankness pleased the President. "I congratulate you, Dan. You're honest. I want to be honest with you and tell you

149

a story that isn't funny, for we're both in the same boat, as I size up this proposition—yes, both in the same boat. I am in the army, in a way; at least, I'm called Commander-in-Chief, and occasionally they let me meddle a little with things."

"Honest?" said Dan, opening his eyes very wide. He had been so absorbed in his own disasters that he had accepted this curious, friendly acquaintance, without questions. But now, the misty background of his consciousness was trying to make him compare this man with a certain picture in the family album, with another one pasted on the dining-room-cupboard door, the same loose-hung person, only this one had a living rawness—maybe it was bigness—about him that the pictures didn't give, like a tree, perhaps. But it couldn't be the President talking to him, Dan. If it was, what would the folks at home—And again his thought stopped. There were to be no more "folks at home" for him.

"Honest Injin, Dan. But sometimes they yell when I do meddle. There's a case on now. Last night I pretty nearly had twenty-four men shot."

"Whew!"

"But I hadn't quite decided, and that's the reason I came out here in God's own woods. And I'm glad I came, for you've helped me decide."

"I have!" said Dan, astonished, "to shoot them?"

"No! Not to. You showed me the case in a new light. Here you are, deserting home, deserting your father, bringing sorrow to him and to your mother, who have sorrows enough with Will in danger and all; you're punishing your father because he did one deed that he couldn't very well help, just as if he'd been a mean man all his life. And it's like that with my twenty-four deserters, Dan, very like that. They've served years, faithfully. Then can any one thing they do

be so gross, so enormously bad, as to blot out all the rest, including probably a lifetime of decent living? I think not. Is a man to blame for having a pair of legs that play coward once? I think not, Dan. I tell you what, sonny," and the tall man stopped, a new light shining in his cavernous, sad eyes. "I'll make a bargain with you. If you'll go home and forgive your father, I'll go home and forgive my twenty-four deserters."

The boy had been shaken, but it was difficult to change all at once. "It is hard to forgive," he murmured.

"Some day you'll find it hard not to," said the great man, putting out his huge palm for the boy to shake. "Isn't that a pretty good bargain, Dan? By going home, by ceasing to be a deserter yourself, you will save the lives of twenty-four men. Won't you be merciful? Perhaps God will remember sometime and forgive you some trespass even as you forgive now."

Something of last night's horror, when he could not say the prayer, and something of the melting gentleness of the new friend before him touched the boy. He took Lincoln's hand, saying, "All right. That's a go."

"Yes, a go home," smiled Lincoln. "I suppose I'll have to turn, now."

"Where's your home?" asked the boy, knowing, yet wishing to hear the truth, to be very sure; for now he could tell the folks at home.

"The White House," replied Lincoln, "but I wish I were going with you."

The boy's jaw was sagging. "Then you—are the President?"

Lincoln nodded, enjoying the boy's wonder. "And your servant, don't forget," added Lincoln. "You have been a help to me in a hard hour, Dan. Generals or no generals, I'll spare those men. Any time that I can do anything for you, drop in, now that you know where to find me. But

you'd better— Wait," and Lincoln began hunting through his pockets; "you'd better let me give you a latchkey. The man at the door's a sort of stubborn fellow, for the folks will pester the life out of him. Here—"

And finding a card and a stub of a pencil, he wrote:

Please admit Dan'l Ripley on demand.
A. Lincoln.

"Thank you," said Dan, as proud as a cockerel. "I reckon I should 'a' guessed it was you, but those stories you told kind o' put me off."

"That's sometimes why I tell them," and Lincoln smiled again. "It's not a bad morning's work—twenty-four lives saved before breakfast, Dan. You and I ought to be able to stow a mighty comfortable meal. Goodbye, sonny."

And so they parted. The man strode back the way he had come; the boy stood looking, looking, and then swiftly wheeled and sped. He had been talking to the President, to Abraham Lincoln, and hearing such talk as he never had heard before; but especially the words "You have been a help to me in a hard hour, Dan"—those words trod a regular path in his brain. He ran, eager to get to the very home he had been so eager to leave. Forgiveness was in his heart, but chiefly there was a warm and heady pride. He had been praised by Abraham Lincoln! Of this day he would talk to the end of time. Dan did not know that the major part of the day, the greatest in his life, was still to come.

Breathless and eye-bright with anticipation of telling his tale, he leaped the fences and plunged into his house. The kitchen was quiet. A misgiving ran over him; were they all out in search of him? Would he have to postpone his triumph?

In the dining room, a half-eaten meal was cooling. He explored on, and coming out on the spacious front of the house, found them—found them in an inexplicable group around a uniformed officer. Tears were streaming down his mother's cheeks. His father, still pale from his accident, looked ashen and shriveled. They turned at Dan's approach. He expected that this scene of anguish would turn to smiles upon his discovery. He was amazed to find that his return gave them the merest flurry of relief, and alleviated their sorrow not at all.

"Danny dear, where have you been?" asked his mother.

"The Lord must have turned you about and sent you home in answer to our prayers," said his father.

And then they turned back to the officer, pleading, weeping. Dan felt hurt. Did his return, his forgiveness mean so little to them? He might as well have gone on. Then he caught the officer's words. "Colonel Scott can do no more, Madam. The President cannot see him, and more pardons are not to be hoped for."

Mrs. Ripley turned and threw her arm across Dan's shoulders. "Danny—Danny—you are our only son now. Will was—" and she broke down completely.

"Will was found asleep while on duty, Dan, and—"

"Is he to be shot?" asked the boy. "I wonder if he was one of the twenty-four." They looked at him, not understanding.

"The Lord has restored you to us. If we could only pray in sufficient faith, he could restore Will," said Farmer Ripley, devoutly. "Dear, let us go in and pray."

Dan realized with a sudden clearness that his brother, his beloved, was to be taken from him as Tam had been taken. It shook his brain dizzy, but he knew that he must hold on to his wits—must think. There was Abraham Lincoln, his friend!

"You pray," he cried to his father, shrilly, "and I'll run."

"Run where, dear? Will is in Pennsylvania."

"To the White House, Mother. He said, 'Any time I can do anything for you, drop in.' *Anything*, Mother. Surely he'll—"

"Who?" cried both his parents.

"Why, the President, Mr. Lincoln!"

"But the President is busy, dear. This gentleman says that Cousin Andrew has not been able to see him, and he is a colonel, you know."

"He'll see me—I know he will!" said Dan. "Look! We have a secret together, the President and I have." And the boy showed his card and poured out his story.

The mother saw a break in her gray heaven, saw the bright blue of hope.

"We must go at once," she said. "Father, you pray here for us."

"Please take my horse and wagon," said the officer.

"Yes," said Dan, "Let's hurry. Oh, I'm glad, I'm so glad!"

"May God help you!" said the officer.

"He often does," said the boy, thinking.

It was high noon when the doorkeeper of the White House saw an impetuous youth leap from a light carriage and drag a woman up the portico steps toward him.

"In which room is the President?" asked Dan.

"He's very busy," said the doorkeeper. "Have you an appointment?"

"No, but he said drop in when I wanted; and what's more, here's my 'latchkey'" and Dan, trembling a little, showed him the card "A. Lincoln" had written.

The man looked quizzically at it and at him. "In that case," he said drily, "you'd better step into the waiting room there."

There must have been forty or fifty people crowded into the anteroom. Some were in uniform; all looked tired, impatient, important. Dan whispered to his mother and put her in a chair, then went up to the door-boy and asked if the President was in the next room. The boy admitted the fact, but would not admit anything further, including Dan. The looks on the faces of the waiting-room people deepened in annoyance. "Does this urchin" (said their looks) "expect to see the President today, when so many more important persons (such as we) are kept waiting?"

Death has small regard for persons, and, in this respect, boys come next to death. Dan slipped under the arm of the door-boy and bolted into the room.

Lincoln was standing by the window. He looked around in surprise at the noise of Dan Ripley's entry, recognized his walking partner, made a motion for the door-boy to withdraw, and said, "Why, Dan, I'm glad to see you so soon again. You're just in time to back me up. Let me introduce you to General Scanlon."

Dan looked into the amazed and angry eyes of a Union general who, practically ignoring the boy, went on to say, "Mr. President, I repeat, that unless these men are made an example of, the army itself may be in danger. Mercy to these twenty-four means cruelty to near a million."

The President, worn from his sleepless night and from incessant strain, looked grave, for the general spoke truth. He turned to Dan, "Did you go home, sonny?"

Dan nodded.

"Then I shall keep my half of the bargain. General, this boy and I each walked the woods half the night carrying similar troubles, trying to decide whether it was best to forgive. We decided that it was best, as the Bible says, even to seventy times seven. Dan, how did your folks take it?"

Dan spoke quickly. "It would 'a' killed them if I'd run off for good, for they just got word that my brother Will—you know I told you about him—is to be shot for sleeping on watch. I just know he was tired out—he didn't go to sleep on purpose. I told my mother that you wouldn't let him be shot, if you knew."

Lincoln groaned audibly and turned away to the window for a moment. The general snorted.

"I brought my mother in to see you, too," said Dan, "seeing as she wouldn't quite believe what I said about our agreement."

Lincoln looked at the boy, and his sunken eyes glistened. "I agreed for twenty-four lives," he said; "but I don't mind throwing in an extra one for you, Dan."

And this time the general groaned.

"Stoddard," added the President, "will you see if there is a Will Ripley on file?" The secretary left the room. Lincoln turned abruptly to the general. "You have heard me," he said. "I, with the help of God and this boy, threshed out the matter to a conclusion, and we only waste time to discuss it further. If I pardon these deserters, it surely becomes a better investment for the United States than if I had them shot—twenty-four live fighters in the ranks, instead of that many corpses underground. There are too many weeping widows now. Don't ask me to add to the number, for I won't do it!"

It was rarely that Lincoln was so stirred. There was a strange silence. Then the secretary entered with, "Yes, sir, a Will Ripley is to be executed tomorrow, for sleeping on duty. The case was buried in the files; it should have been brought to you earlier."

"Better for the case to be buried than the boy," said the President. "Give me the paper, Stoddard."

"Then you will!" said Dan, trembling with joy.

"I don't believe that shooting the boy will do him any good," said Lincoln, as the pen traced the letters of his name, beneath

this message. "Will Ripley is not to be shot until further orders from me."

Dan looked at it. "That's great! Oh, thank you!" he said. "Can I bring Mother in to see it—and to see you?" he asked.

The President looked down into the shining face and could not refuse. In a jiffy, Dan had dragged his mother into the presence. She was all confusion; the general was red with irritation.

She read the message; it didn't seem quite clear to her. "Is that a pardon? Does that mean that he won't be shot at all?"

"My dear Madam," replied Lincoln, kindly, "evidently you are not acquainted with me. If your son never looks on death till orders come from me to shoot him, he will live to be a great deal older than Methuselah!"

She stretched out both her hands, crying, "Thank you, sir. Oh, thank you!"

"Thank Dan here," said Lincoln. "If he had not let the warmth of forgiveness soften his heart, Will Ripley would have died. And perhaps, if I had not met him in the woods at dawn, I might have gone into eternity with the blood of these twenty-four men on my hands. Dan helped me."

The boy looked as one transfigured. Lincoln went on, "And all this only confirms my notion that it is selfish, stupid and destructive not to forgive if you've got a loophole for forgiveness left. It reminds me of a little story. Will you excuse me another moment, General?" The pink officer bowed stiffly and Lincoln said, "One of my neighbors back home was a Quaker named Silas Greene, and he was so forgiving that his wife could not even induce him to shoot the chickens which persisted in scratching up her garden. 'Consider, dear,' Silas used to say, 'consider the hen. Any creature that is so useful before it is born and after it is dead deserves a little consideration during its short lifetime, doesn't thee think?'"

Everybody in the room laughed but the general. The President concluded, "And that's the way I feel about these erring soldiers, Mrs. Ripley. We must consider what they have done and what they will do, as intently as we consider the wrong of the moment. Good-by, Dan, we shall both remember today with easy consciences."

The crowd in the anteroom could not understand, of course, why that intruder of a boy who had dragged the woman in to see the President should bring her out on his arm with such conscious pride. They could not understand why the tears were rolling down her cheeks at the same time that a smile glorified her face. But the dullest of them could see that the boy was radiant with a great happiness.

And if they could have looked past him through the door of the inner room with their wondering glances, they could have seen a reflection of Dan's joy still shining on the deep-lined face of the man who had again indulged himself—in mercy.

MIKE FINK

*He could crow like a rooster, fight
like a wildcat and with his trusty long-barreled gun
he could shoot the wings off a hummingbird*

ANNE MALCOLMSON

"I'm a Salt River roarer! I'm a ring-tailed squealer! Whoop! I'm half wild horse and half alligator and the rest of me is crooked snags an' red hot snappin' turtle . . . I can out-run, out jump, out-shoot, out-brag . . . any man on both sides the river from Pittsburgh to New Orleans and back again to St. Louee! Cock-a-doodle-doo!"

Mike Fink, the bad man of the Ohio River, was not at all modest when he made this famous boast. Whether or not he was as bad as he liked to think remains to be seen.

Mike started out as a keelboatman. In his day there were no steamboats to carry people and goods up and down the rivers. Instead there were long flat boats, like barges, which drifted downstream with the current and had to be pushed upstream by poles and oars. The men who worked on these keelboats were very strong. In order to get his job, Mike had to beat up the rest of the crew. When Baptiste, the French boss, saw him handing out black eyes and broken noses, he knew that Mike was the man for him.

Mike was as clever as he was wild. He could steer a boat in and out of the snags; he could make her dance over a falls like a lady at a ball. Before long, he was his own master and could lick any other captain between Pittsburgh and New Orleans, as he boasted. He became very famous.

One of the things for which he was best known was his skill with a rifle. With his long-barreled gun, Bang-All, he could shoot the wings off a hummingbird. He proved his skill once and for all when he was a young boy.

Farmer Neal, his friend, had a shooting match. As a prize he offered his best steer, a fat animal which would keep a family in food for several weeks. Anyone could come and shoot for twenty-five cents a chance. All the woodsmen from the countryside came to try their luck. Little Mike came, too, in spite of the laughter of the men. "What? Let a baby shoot with us?" they sneered. "You go back home to your mother and make mud-pies."

This made the youngster angry. All the money he had was one dollar and twenty-five cents. "I'll take five chances," he roared at the top of his voice. "I can shoot better than any of you. You'll see!"

The others laughed all the harder. He seemed to be a brave lad, however, so they agreed to let him take his turn at the end of the contest. One after another the grown men aimed their rifles at the target. By the time they had finished, it was chewed to pieces by bullet holes. Only a diamond-shaped hole showed where the bull's-eye had been.

Then up stepped young Fink. Slowly he raised Bang-All to his shoulder for the first of his five shots. He looked down the barrel at the target, taking his time. After what seemed to be an hour he pulled the trigger. Zing! Right through the center of the diamond flew his bullet.

The crowd roared. "That was only luck! You can't do that again! Move the target back a ways!"

"All right!" yelled back Mike. "Move the target. You haven't seen anything yet."

The target was nailed to another tree farther away. Again Mike took up Bang-All, looked down the barrel and pulled the trigger. Once more the bullet cut clean through the center of the diamond. The crowd said that the target should be moved even farther away.

After the fourth shot Farmer Neal himself bet that Mike couldn't do it again. "Leave the target where it is, this time, and let us see if you can hit it," he shouted. The boy grinned and lifted his gun. He didn't bother to take a careful aim. He just banged away.

"Hooray!" yelled the judges as they looked over the target. "You didn't even touch the paper. Who says you can shoot?"

"Missed it, indeed!" "I'll show you if I missed it." With that he took his knife and dug into the bark of the tree. Out came two flat bits of lead, one on top of the other. The fifth bullet had hit the fourth and driven it into the wood. The young marks-

man turned around to glare at the crowd. "Cock-a-doodle-doo!" he roared, beating his chest and flapping his arms. And before the astonished crowd he walked off with the prize steer.

From that day on Mike and Bang-All were the champions. Not many rivermen tried to beat him. Once Davy Crockett challenged Fink to a contest. Davy and Mike had long been friendly enemies; neither would admit that the other was better than *he* was! First Mike aimed Bang-All at a family of little pigs in a nearby pen. One after the other he shot off their tails. "Pooh!" sneered Davy, "you left them each a half-inch of tail. I'll finish the job." So he shot off the stubs as clean as a whistle.

Mike began to worry a little. He couldn't let the hunter from the Shakes of Tennessee win at his own game. Then the boatman saw his chance. Mrs. Fink, a patient woman, walked to the well. As she stood quietly drawing a pail of water, her husband raised his rifle. Bang! The pretty shell comb she wore in her hair broke into two perfect halves. One of them fell to the ground. Mrs. Fink didn't feel a thing.

"Let's see you knock the other half out!" Mike cried.

This was too much for Davy Crockett. No gentleman would shoot at a lady, no matter how well he handled a gun. "Consider it a draw, Mike," he said politely. "I won't try to beat that shot."

Not only was Mike famous for his shooting; he was famous for his mischief as well. When he saw something he wanted, he didn't bother to buy it properly. Neither would he stoop to stealing like a common thief. He usually got his way through trickery.

The keelboat was drifting down the Ohio River when Mike saw a flock of fat sheep grazing on the bank. He and his crew hadn't tasted fresh meat for a long time.

The sight made him hungry. "Well, boys," he roared, "it looks as though we'll be having a leg of lamb for dinner tonight. Tie the boat in to the shore."

It so happened that the keelboat was loaded with barrels of snuff bound for Natchez. Mike filled a bucket with the horrid brown stuff and carried it ashore. He picked out six of the best-looking animals and rubbed their faces in the bucket. Of course, the snuff made the sheep sneeze. Their eyes watered and grew red, and the unhappy beasts ran bleating around the pasture frightening the others. Then Mike called the farmer.

"Look here, friend," he said sadly, "your sheep are sick. They have the Black Murrain. It's a terrible disease. If you don't shoot them right away the whole flock will catch it and die. Why! I've seen thousands of sheep die of this very thing! I do feel sorry for you. To think of losing such fine fat animals!" With that he shed a crocodile tear, and the poor farmer looked worried. He had heard about the dreadful disease that killed whole flocks overnight.

"You'd better shoot them now," went on the boatman, "before they give it to the others. And be sure to throw their bodies into the river."

"Alas! Alas!" cried the farmer. "What shall I do? I could never shoot the sick ones without hitting the healthy ones. I'm not smart enough with a gun. Won't you shoot them for me?"

Mike pretended to feel badly about the whole thing. He shook his head until the farmer got down on his knees and begged. "If you'll do this for me," he sobbed, "I'll give you two jugs of my best peach brandy."

At last Mike Fink agreed. He shot the unfortunate sheep and dumped them into the river. The grateful farmer brought the jugs of brandy and said good night. As soon as it was dark, the boatmen fished up the

bodies of the sheep, had themselves a fine dinner and went on their way.

They thought they were safe. A little farther down the river they tried the trick over again. It worked, too. But before long the news got back to the first farmer. He saw that he had been robbed, and he went to the judge at Louisville.

When Mike and his gang returned from their trip down-river, they found that they were under arrest for stealing sheep. Every officer in the country was looking for them. For a long time they were able to hide in a cave beside the river. At last the governor offered a big reward for their capture. The poor sheriff, who needed the money, was a friend of Mike's. He knew where the boatmen were hiding, too, and he went to call on them in a friendly way.

After a long conversation he got Mike to give himself up and to come into court.

"On one condition," said the boatman. "I'm not at home on dry land. I have to have my boat under me to feel right. If I can come to court in my keelboat I'll be very glad to come. And you can have the reward money."

The sheriff, of course, thought that this was another of Mike's strange jokes. "Don't look so worried," snapped the boatman. "I'll fix it."

On the day of the trial, the judge and the townsfolk met in the courthouse on the top of the hill. Everyone wondered how Mike would come "in his boat." And then they all saw! The big keelboat was mounted on wheels and hitched to a team of oxen. All the boatmen stood in their places on the deck with their big poles in their hands. As the oxen puffed up the hill, Mike called out to the sheriff, "Is everything ready? I can't stay long."

The sheriff knew that the judge was angry. He tried to tell his friend about the judge's anger. But for all the faces he made, Mike and his boys rode merrily on into the courthouse square. What a sight they made as they jumped down from the boat and marched into the room in their red shirts, all shouting "Cock-a-doodle-doo!"

The boatmen sat down in the front row. The judge scowled at them over his glasses and began to read. "I charge you, Michael Fink, keelboatman, with stealing sheep," he read. All the people in the room scowled at the thieves. It was perfectly clear that Mike and his boys were going to be put into jail for their tricks.

All of a sudden, before the judge could catch his breath to say anything else, Mike jumped up from his chair. He blew a terrible blast on his horn. "To your places, boys," he yelled. "We're leaving." And with that the boatmen jumped out the window, took their oars in their hands, and pushed the boat, wheels and oxen and all, down into the water of the Ohio River. "We had a pleasant time," Mike called up to the judge and the worried sheriff. "We'll call on you again some day!"

That was the last time that anyone tried to arrest Mike Fink.

Once, it's true, Mike Fink bit off more than he could chew. He was so pleased with himself after his escape from the law that he thought he could do anything. At a river inn he met his old friend and enemy, Davy Crockett. Davy had been boasting about his wife, who wasn't afraid of anything under the sun.

"I'll scare her!" roared Fink. "I'll bet my Bang-All against your Betsy that I can scare the daylights out of Mrs. Crockett." The bet was made, and Mike crowed his old crow, "Cock-a-doodle-doo!" to settle the matter.

He searched through the swamps until he found an old alligator with a horrible face. He dressed himself up in the 'gator's skin and lay beside the road until Mrs. Crockett set out for her evening walk.

As she walked up to him, Mike opened the huge jaws of the 'gator right in her path. She stepped quietly aside as though he were nothing but an old stump. He swished his tail back and forth and crawled up beside her. She paid no attention at all. She certainly didn't look frightened.

This made Mike angry. He rose up on the 'gator's back legs and tried to give Mrs. Crockett an alligator hug. It didn't frighten her at all. Instead it made her angry. She turned around and looked at him with her worst look. Lightning flashed from her eyes. She was awfully mad!

Mike tried once more. He moved closer and tried to hug her again. "That's enough, you lowly worm!" she screamed. "Take that!" And with her toothpick she cut off the 'gator's head. Then, of course, she saw Mike inside the beast's skin.

"So that's your trick, is it?" cried Mrs. Davy Crockett, rolling up her sleeves. "I'll teach you to bother respectable women on their evening walks. Come out and fight like a man!"

Without another word she lit into the bad man. She swung her handbag and kicked and bit and pulled and punched. When the battle was over, she rolled down her sleeves again and went on her way. Poor Mike Fink! He lay there in the swamp, bleeding and sore. "I'm a Salt River roarer," he whispered to himself as he counted stars. "I'm half wild horse and half cock-eyed alligator . . ." But the word "alligator" in his boast sounded feeble. The great Mike Fink, who could crow like a rooster and fight like a wildcat, had been licked. Worse than that, he had been licked by a woman!

The Wild Birthday Cake

*The professor was Johnny's favorite friend
on the whole of Broomstick Hill, and here
he had forgotten all about his birthday*

Lavinia R. Davis

It was a spring morning in the country. The whole world looked fresh and rested after a good night's sleep. Johnny stood on the top of Broomstick Hill and took great, happy gulps of the sunny air. He could smell lilacs and apple blossoms, and the cool spring smell of new things growing.

Johnny stretched and wriggled his toes inside his new sneakers. Up and down Broomstick Hill the grown people began to work in their gardens. Johnny watched for a minute. Then he picked up his knapsack. Johnny was not going to garden on a morning like this. No, sir. Johnny was off for a hike and a day of adventure!

Johnny had on his bright plaid shirt, his khaki shorts and his hiking sneakers. Best of all, he had his brand-new knapsack that he had bought with his own money. Inside the knapsack were sandwiches, cookies, cake, and a bottle of Coke.

Johnny slung his knapsack over his shoulders and wriggled it comfortable. Then he dug his hands in his pockets and started down Broomstick Hill whistling a tune.

He walked on and on until he came to the Professor's house. Then he stopped. He stopped so short that the Coke bottle knocked against his shoulder blade.

He stopped short because he saw the turtles! The Professor carried a tinker turtle in his right hand. He carried a painted turtle in his left hand. He carefully carried those two live turtles away from his garden toward the woods beyond.

"Hi, Johnny!" said the Professor, and then he saw that Johnny was staring at his turtles and he grinned. "Moving day," he said. "I'm moving my turtles from their winter quarters in my garden pond out to the woods for the summer."

Johnny grinned back so that his freckles stretched. Winter or summer, spring or fall, the Professor was always doing something interesting. Sometimes he hatched out butterfly cocoons right in his own study. Sometimes he spent whole days getting snails for his aquarium. Once Johnny had come to the Professor's house when he was teaching his tame squirrel a new trick. Another time he had arrived there just as the Professor came home with a new pet crow. Johnny could never tell what the Professor would be doing next but it was sure to be something to do with birds, or bugs or animals. And it was absolutely sure to be fun.

"Can I help?" Johnny said, and he forgot all about his hike. "Can I help move the turtles?"

The Professor smiled at Johnny but he shook his head. "I'm all finished," he said. "I tidied up the pond bright and early. But don't forget you're coming down this evening to help me eat my birthday cake."

"Jeepers!" said Johnny. "Thanks, I'll be there, Professor."

With that, Johnny started down the hill. His heart clunked around inside his plaid shirt. Today was the Professor's seventy-fifth birthday, and Johnny had forgotten all about it. Worse than that, he had been so excited about his hike that he had forgotten to buy a card or a birthday present for the Professor, who was his very favorite friend on the whole of Broomstick Hill!

For a minute Johnny thought of rushing back home to empty his horse bank, but he remembered it was already empty. He had emptied it only a few days ago to buy the new knapsack which he was wearing on his back.

Johnny walked on down the hill and on to a little winding lane that led through the valley. He didn't stretch any more in the warm sunshine. He didn't take deep breaths any more or whistle. He didn't even feel the soft breeze that ruffled his hair. He was too busy thinking, and thinking, and THINKING what he could give the Professor for his seventy-fifth birthday.

Johnny walked on, and on, until he had passed through the Little Woodlot and come out on Penton's Pasture. It was a very wide, very rocky pasture. A lane ran through the middle of it all the way to the Big Woodlot and Penton's Pond. Johnny trudged along still thinking about the present. Suddenly he heard something. He heard it because it was a loud sound, and a queer sound. He heard it because it was right over his head and so sudden that it made him jump!

Johnny looked up. There, high above his head, was a long, whip-straight line of ducks. The ducks flew high and proud right through the blue spring sky. As Johnny watched them, he forgot about his hike. He forgot all about the Professor's birthday. He could only feel. And the way he felt was high, and proud and free, the way the ducks looked as they flew steadily past over his head.

The next moment the ducks had all dropped down out of sight in the Big Woodlot. Johnny trudged on again. The fine, high, proud feeling he had felt only a moment ago dropped away, too. Little beads of sweat stood out on Johnny's forehead and his back felt wet and itchy underneath the knapsack. He was hungry and thirsty, but he decided not to eat his lunch until he reached Penton's Pond.

He passed elm trees and maple trees and big solid oaks. Then he passed a silver birch and some of its bark was peeling. He picked off a piece and put it in his knapsack. Even if he could not find the Professor a birthday present at least he could make him a birthday card out of the birch bark.

Johnny walked on until he came to a grove of yellow willow trees. There, just beyond the willows, was the pond. And floating on top were all the ducks.

At least the ducks were there as Johnny reached the water. The very next second they flew off and the air rustled with the beating of their wings. They quacked loudly and proudly as they flew off. The deep woods crackled with the wild echo. Johnny shivered inside his plaid shirt. He wasn't cold. He was just excited at the sight of the ducks and the sound of their quacking.

Soon they had gone, and Johnny took off his knapsack. He moved over closer to the edge of the pond and then he saw that there was one duck left. There was just one lonely duck that struggled to fly after the others.

The duck struggled and struggled, and churned the water, but it could not fly. It couldn't even swim very fast, and after a moment it stopped trying and just floated on top of the water.

Johnny walked around to the other side of the pond to see better. As he drew near, the duck flapped and struggled again, but still nothing happened.

Johnny stood very still so the duck would not be frightened. He was so close he could see the speckly brown feathers on its back. He could see the neat line of clean white feathers that trimmed the shiny patches on its wings. He could even see its eyes and two little holes in its flat yellowish bill.

That duck didn't look hurt. It wasn't wounded or bloody. Johnny knelt down and then he saw that one side was twisted. Somehow that side had been sprained so that the duck could not fly and it could only swim slowly. But except for that it was a perfect duck. In fact, as Johnny watched it glide lazily on the surface of the water, he knew it was the most beautiful duck he had ever seen.

Johnny watched the duck for a long, long time. Then he stood up and moved back to his knapsack. The duck didn't struggle. The duck didn't flutter. It was beginning to get used to Johnny, so it just floated quietly near some rushes.

Johnny drank his Coke first because he was so thirsty. It felt cold and good at the back of his throat. He ate his sandwiches, all except the crusts. Then he walked back to the far side of the pond and dropped a bit of crust in the water in front of the duck. For an instant nothing happened.

Then the next second the duck's neck stretched down underwater. For a moment nothing showed except brown back feathers so that it looked like a turtle or a small brown log. The next moment its head came up again and that crust was all gone. The duck had gobbled it all up!

Johnny dropped another piece of bread and laughed out loud at what happened. The duck plunged headfirst after the breadcrust. It tipped over until it was upside down, like a boy standing on his head in a swimming pool. This time nothing showed except the fluffy white feathers underneath the duck's tail and its two webbed feet busily paddling. The next moment the duck bobbed up again with the bread crust down in its gullet.

Johnny walked back to his knapsack and ate his nut cookie. He drank his last drop of Coke and ate his chocolate cookie. He took a bite of his cake and then he had an idea!

It was a wonderful Fourth-of-July-sort-of-idea that exploded like a rocket right inside Johnny's head. He was going to catch that duck and bring it home! He would carry it home and take care of it, and make it so happy that it would never miss Penton's Pond or the other ducks. It was going to be his own duck to keep, the way the Professor kept the squirrel and the crow and the turtles.

Johnny stood up, and his heart beat so hard he was afraid the duck might hear it. But of course it didn't. The duck heard only a soft little splash as Johnny dropped a piece of cake in front of its bill.

The duck plunged after the cake and Johnny stepped nearer. He stepped off the bank of the pond and into the water right in his sneakers. The cold water stung his legs and soaked through his sneakers. Johnny hardly felt it. He held on to the clump of rushes with one hand and dropped his last piece of cake. The duck reached out its neck for the cake. Johnny let go of the rushes. Then he reached forward and grabbed the duck with both hands!

The duck fluttered, and Johnny almost let go. He almost let go, but he didn't. Instead he held tight and fell back onto the muddy bank of the pond with the duck in both arms.

After he had caught his breath Johnny stood up. He was very wet and very muddy, but what did that matter? He had the duck! He could feel its heart beat right through his plaid shirt. He held it gently but firmly with one arm and then soothed its ruffled feathers with his free hand. "Poor duck," he said. "Poor, beautiful duck. Did you want to fly after the others?"

The duck didn't make a sound. Johnny held its bony, feathery body close and leaned over for his knapsack. He managed to jerk his knapsack over one shoulder and then he started for home. "O.K., duck," he said. "Don't be frightened. I'll take care of you."

It was a long, hot walk. Johnny had to walk slowly and carefully, so he wouldn't drop his duck. He carried it out of the Big Woodlot, across Penton's Pasture, through the Little Woodlot and finally on the long trudge up Broomstick Hill.

Johnny was at the steepest part of the hill that led right up to his family's house. As he looked up at his house, he began to worry. He had worried before over his present for the Professor, but compared to his new worry that was nothing. Right now Johnny was worried sick over what his family would say about his duck.

Mother was waiting for him on the porch. "Johnny," she said. "Johnny boy, where have you been all this time?" And then she saw the duck. "Oh, Johnny," she said, "where did that come from?"

And as she spoke the worry inside Johnny grew so big it burst. It burst like a soap bubble, or a thunderstorm, or the tears that Johnny hadn't known he had locked up inside him.

"It's my duck," he sobbed. "It's my beautiful duck that I caught all by myself."

"Put it in the shed," Mother said, and she didn't sound cross but just hot and tired the way Johnny was himself. "But where in the world can we keep it?"

"Well," Johnny said, and he held out the duck so that mother could see the shiny feathers on its wings and the neat little holes in its bill. "Well," he said, "I think it would like to swim in my bathtub."

"No!" Mother shook her head. "No, I'm sorry, but the duck cannot come in the house. Put it in the tool shed and then change your clothes and go see the Professor. Daddy'll be home when you get back and perhaps he can get Mr. Potter to keep it for you."

Johnny did as he was told, but his heart felt heavy. It felt as heavy as his new knapsack loaded with stones. Mr. Potter was a farmer who lived in the valley below Broomstick Hill. He had chickens and he had ducks, but they were all waddling white barnyard ducks that looked fat and foolish and clumsy even when they swam around his muddy duckpond. Johnny knew that his duck, his beautiful dark wild duck, would never be happy there.

He changed his clothes and then he made the birthday card out of birch bark. He wrote "Happy Birthday," and "Professor" in blue letters, and his own name and the "to" and "from" in brown letters. He wanted to draw pictures of the crow, the turtles and the tame squirrel around the edge, but that didn't turn out very well, so he made Indian designs instead and they looked very fine indeed.

When he was all finished, he put away his crayons and went out to look at the duck. The duck was right where he had left it and it looked very unhappy. Its feathers were ruffled, and its bad wing draggled more than ever. "Poor duck," Johnny whispered. "Poor, poor lame duck."

The duck didn't even look at Johnny. It just sat droopily on top of an overturned peach basket and looked miserable.

Johnny sighed, and shook his head, and then, when he had shut the door of the shed, he started off for the Professor's. Usually when he went to the Professor's he scrambled over the stone walls, or hopped, skipped and jumped down the road because he was so glad to go there. But today he walked slowly, very, very slowly, worrying about his duck.

"Hi, Johnny," the Professor said. "I thought you'd never turn up. I have something to show you. A family of wrens moved into the house you helped me build last winter."

"Good," said Johnny, but he didn't feel very excited. He just wished his duck could live in something as small and neat as a wrenhouse.

The Professor showed Johnny the wrens. Then Johnny remembered his birthday card and gave it to the Professor.

"Why, this is great," the Professor said, and it was clear he meant it. "The nicest birthday card I ever had in my life and you made it all by yourself? Where did you get such a fine piece of birch bark?"

"On my hike," Johnny said, and it all seemed a long, long while ago. "On my hike down to Penton's Pond this morning."

The Professor put the card on his mantel next to a collection of shells and a gray wasp's nest. "Thank you a lot, Johnny," he said. "And after you've seen what's happened in my pond, we're going to eat my birthday cake. My sister sent it to me all the way from New York."

Johnny said nothing as he followed the Professor out of the house. Usually he liked seeing the Professor's pond, and he cer-

tainly liked cake. It was only that today, after everything that had happened, he felt sad because of his duck. He wanted to tell the Professor about it, but he knew he couldn't. When he had caught the duck, he had been so sure it was going to be the most wonderful pet in the world. And then nothing had turned out the way he had planned. When he thought of the duck shut up all by itself in the tool shed, he knew if he talked about it he would cry like a big baby.

The Professor reached the pond long before Johnny did. "Hurry up," he said, "and tell me what you think of them."

Them? For the first time Johnny was really interested. He ran forward and then he stopped short. There in front of him on the water of the Professor's lily pond were three baby ducks. They were dark, nearly black, with little touches of brownish yellow, and they could swim like anything. "Why, they're wild ducks," Johnny said. The Professor nodded.

"That's right. A friend of mine from Vermont brought them down to me. I wish I owned their mother. They look lonely."

For a long, long time Johnny stood and stared at the baby ducks without saying a word. As he stood there, an idea grew in his mind. It grew slowly, silently, but very surely, like a tulip pushing its way through the ground in the spring. This was a place where his duck would be happy, a place where his duck would feel at home.

Johnny frowned and dug his hands so deep into his pockets that he made a hole. Part of his idea was wonderful and easy but part of it was hard. It was harder than sticks, or stones or the ground before the frost had left it. The easy part of his idea was that his duck would love living in that pond. The hard part of his idea was that if the duck lived in that pond, it would have to be because it belonged to the Professor and not to Johnny himself.

"How do you like the baby ducks?" the Professor asked.

"Neat," said Johnny, and as he turned away from the pond, his mind was made up. He hurried across the fields and over the stone wall and through the vegetable garden back to his family's tool shed. He picked up his duck and ran all the way back to the Professor's pond.

"Here!" Johnny panted. "For you. For your birthday."

"A female mallard!" the Professor said. "Just like the young ones, and what a beauty. Are you sure you want to give her to me?"

"Yes," said Johnny. Then he told the Professor exactly how he had caught the duck and what had happened when he had brought it home.

"I see," said the Professor. "Thank you, Johnny. Thank you very much!" Then without another word he took the duck and lowered it gently down to the pond. The moment the duck reached the water it looked better. Its feathers didn't seem ruffled any more and you couldn't even see that it had a hurt wing. It looked cool and comfortable, and at home. When the Professor put the big duck into the water, the babies paddled away so fast that the water rippled in long arrows behind them. Then a few moments later they cruised in and out among the irises on the edge of the pond and looked at the big duck through curious, beady black eyes.

"Look!" said the Professor, and he sounded as pleased as Punch. "They're going to make friends. Let's leave them

alone while we eat some cake and then we'll come back and see how they are getting along."

So the Professor and Johnny went inside and ate cake until even Johnny couldn't hold another crumb. "There's still a lot of cake," said the Professor. "Shall we give some to the ducks?"

"Let's!" said Johnny, and this time he reached the pond ahead of the Professor.

The big duck and the little ones were swimming around as though that pond had always been their home. When Johnny saw that, a cheerful, comfortable feeling spread all over him and he settled down at the edge of the pond to watch. He felt cool, and full, and happy himself, just like the duck.

He dropped a bit of cake on the water and the duck plunged after it the way it had in Penton Pond. Then he dropped some crumbs of cake for the baby ducks and they plunged, too. "Look!" Johnny said, and he was as thrilled as when he had first caught the big duck. "Look! The baby ducks aren't a bit afraid of the big duck and they all love cake!"

"Good," said the Professor. "And I hope you'll come over every day to help me feed them. But now, what am I going to call the big one? The little ones were named before they came to me. The fat one is Stuffer, the one over there is Squeaker and the one who is standing on his head in the water is called Plunger. Those are perfectly good names, but I want an even better name for the one you gave me because she is such a beauty. Now what do you think?"

Johnny thought for a minute and then all of a sudden he knew!! "Birthday Cake!" he said. "Let's call her Birthday Cake because she came on your birthday and because I caught her with cake."

The Remarkable Rocket

*It was the evening of the Prince and Princess' wedding,
and fireworks were on the program—a magnificent display
that no one in the kingdom would ever forget*

OSCAR WILDE

The King's son was going to be married, so there were general rejoicings. He had waited a whole year for his bride, and at last she had arrived. She was a Russian Princess, and had driven all the way from Finland in a sledge drawn by six reindeer. The sledge was shaped like a great golden swan, and between the swan's wings lay the little Princess herself. Her long ermine cloak reached right down to her feet, on her head was a tiny cap of silver tissue, and she was as pale as the Snow Palace in which she had always lived. So pale was she that as she drove through the streets all the people wondered. "She is like a white rose!" they cried, and they threw down flowers on her from the balconies.

At the gate of the Castle the Prince was waiting to receive her. He had dreamy violet eyes, and his hair was like fine gold. When he saw her he sank upon one knee and kissed her hand.

"Your picture was beautiful," he murmured, "but you are more beautiful than your picture," and the little Princess blushed.

"She was like a white rose before," said a young page to his neighbor, "but she is like a red rose now," and the whole Court was delighted.

For the next three days everybody went about saying, "White rose, Red rose, Red rose, White rose," and the King gave orders that the Page's salary was to be doubled. As he received no salary at all this was not of much use to him but it was considered a great honor and was duly published in the Court Gazette.

When the three days were over the marriage was celebrated. It was a magnificent ceremony, and the bride and bridegroom walked hand in hand under a canopy of purple velvet embroidered with little pearls. Then there was a State Banquet, which lasted for five hours. The Prince and Princess sat at the top of the great Hall and drank out of a cup of clear crystal. Only true lovers could drink out of this cup, for if false lips touched it, it grew grey and dull and cloudy.

"It is quite clear that they love each other," said the little Page, "as clear as crystal!" and the King doubled his salary a second time.

"What an honor!" cried all the courtiers.

After the banquet there was to be a Ball. The bride and bridegroom were to dance the Rose Dance together, and the King had promised to play the flute. He played very badly, but no one had ever dared to tell him so because he was the King. Indeed, he knew only two airs, and was never quite certain which one he was playing; but it made no matter, for, whatever he did, everybody cried out, "Charming! charming!"

The last item on the program was a grand display of fireworks, to be set off exactly at midnight. The little Princess had never seen a firework in her life, so the King had given orders that the Royal Pyrotechnist should be in attendance on the day of her marriage.

"What are fireworks like?" she had asked the Prince, one morning, as she was walking on the terrace.

"They are like the Aurora Borealis," said the King, who always answered questions that were addressed to other people, "only much more natural. I prefer them to stars myself, as you always know when they are going to appear, and they are as delightful as my own flute playing. You must certainly see them."

So at the end of the King's garden a great stand had been set up, and as soon as the Royal Pyrotechnist had put everything in its proper place, the fireworks began to talk to each other.

"The world is certainly very beautiful," cried a little firecracker called a Squib. "Just look at those yellow tulips. Why! if they were real crackers they could not be lovelier. I am very glad I have traveled. Travel improves the mind wonderfully and does away with all one's prejudices."

"The King's garden is not the world, you foolish Squib," said a big Roman Candle. "The world is an enormous place, and it would take you three entire days to see it thoroughly."

"Any place you love is the world to you," exclaimed the pensive Catherine Wheel, who had been attached to an old pine box in early life and prided herself on her broken heart. "But love is not fashionable any more, the poets have killed it. They wrote so much about it that nobody believed them, and I am not surprised. True love suffers, and is silent. I remember myself once——But no matter now. Romance is a thing of the past."

"Nonsense!" said the Roman Candle, "Romance never dies."

Suddenly, a sharp, dry cough was heard, and they all looked round.

It came from a tall, supercilious-looking Rocket, who was tied to the end of a long stick. He always coughed before he made any observations so as to attract attention.

"Ahem! ahem!" he said and everybody listened except the poor Catherine Wheel, who was shaking her head and murmuring, "Romance is dead."

"Order! order!" cried out a Cracker. He was something of a politician and had always taken a prominent part in the local elections, so he knew the proper Parliamentary expressions to use.

"Quite dead," whispered the Catherine Wheel, and she went off to sleep.

As soon as there was perfect silence, the Rocket coughed a third time and began. He spoke with a very slow, distinct voice as if he were dictating his memoirs and always looked over the shoulder of the person to whom he was talking. In fact, he had a most distinguished manner.

"How fortunate it is for the King's son," he remarked, "that he is to be married on the very day on which I am to be let off! Really, if it had not been arranged beforehand it could not have turned out better for him, but then Princes are always lucky."

"Dear me!" said the little Squib, "I

thought it was quite the
other way, and that we were
to be let off in the Prince's honor."

"It may be so with you," he answered. "Indeed, I have no doubt that it is, but with me it is different. I am a very remarkable Rocket, and come of remarkable parents. My mother was the most celebrated Catherine Wheel of her day and was renowned for her graceful dancing. When she made her great public appearance she spun round nineteen times before she went out, and each time that she did so she threw into the air seven pink stars. She was three feet and a half in diameter and made of the very best gunpowder. My father was a Rocket like myself, and of French extraction. He flew so high that the people were afraid that he would never come down again. He did, though, for he was of a kindly disposition, and he made a most brilliant descent in a shower of golden rain. The newspapers wrote about his performance in very flattering terms. Indeed, the Court Gazette called him a triumph of Pylotechnic art."

"Pyrotechnic, Pyrotechnic, you mean," said a Bengal Light. "I know it is Pyrotechnic, for I saw it written on my own canister."

"Well, I said Pylotechnic," answered the Rocket in a severe tone of voice, and the Bengal Light felt so crushed that he began at once to bully the little Squibs in order to show that he was still a person of some importance.

"I was saying," continued the Rocket, "I was saying——What was I saying?"

"You were talking about yourself," replied the Roman Candle.

"Of course; I knew I was discussing some interesting subject when I was so rudely interrupted. I hate rudeness and bad manners of every kind, for I am extremely sensitive. No one in the whole world is so sensitive as I am, I am quite sure of that."

"What is a sensitive person?" said the Cracker to the Roman Candle.

"A person who, because he has corns himself, always treads on other people's toes," answered the Roman Candle in a low whisper; and the Cracker nearly exploded with laughter.

"Pray, what are you laughing at?" inquired the Rocket. "I am not laughing."

"I am laughing because I am happy," replied the Cracker.

"That is a very selfish reason," said the Rocket angrily. "What right have you to be happy? You should be thinking about others. In fact, you should be thinking about me. I am always thinking about myself, and I expect everybody else to do the same. That is what is called sympathy. It is a beautiful virtue, and I possess it in a high degree. Suppose, for instance, anything happened to me tonight, what a misfortune that would be for everyone! The Prince and Princess would never be happy again, their whole married life would be spoiled; and as for the King, I know he would not get over it. Really, when I begin to reflect on the importance of my position, I am almost moved to tears."

"If you want to give pleasure to others," cried the Roman Candle, "you had better keep yourself dry."

"Certainly," exclaimed the Bengal Light, who was now in better spirits, "that is only common sense."

"Common sense, indeed!" said the Rocket indignantly. "You forget that I am very uncommon and very remarkable. Why anybody can have common sense, provided that they have no imagination. But I have imagination, for I never think of things as they really are; I always think of them as being quite different. As for keeping myself dry, there is evidently no one here who can at all appreciate an emotional nature. Fortunately for myself, I don't care. The only thing that sustains one through life is the consciousness of the immense inferiority of everybody else, and this is a feeling I have always cultivated. But none of you have any hearts. Here you are laughing and making merry just as if the Prince and Princess had not just been married."

"Well, really," exclaimed a small Fire Balloon, "why not? It is a most joyful occasion, and when I soar up into the air I intend to tell the stars all about it. You will see them twinkle when I talk to them about the pretty bride."

"Ah! what a trivial view of life!" said the Rocket, "but it is only what I expected. There is nothing in you; you are hollow and empty. Why, perhaps the Prince and Princess may go to live in a country where there is a deep river, and perhaps they may have only one son, a little fair-haired boy with violet eyes like the Prince himself; and perhaps some day he may go out to walk with his nurse; and perhaps the nurse may go to sleep under a great elder-tree; and perhaps the little boy may fall into the deep river and be drowned. What a terrible misfortune! Poor people, to lose their only son! It is really too dreadful! I shall never get over it."

"But they have not lost their only son," said the Roman Candle. "No misfortune has happened to them at all."

"I never said that they had," replied the Rocket, "I said that they might. If they had lost their only son there would be no use in saying any more about the matter. I hate people who cry over spilt milk. But when I think that they might lose their only son, I certainly am very much affected."

"You certainly are!" cried the Bengal Light. "In fact, you are the most affected person I ever met."

"You are the rudest person I ever met," said the Rocket, "and you cannot understand my friendship for the Prince."

"Why, you don't even know him," growled the Roman Candle.

"I never said I knew him," answered the

Rocket. "I dare say that if I knew him I should not be his friend at all. It is a very dangerous thing to know one's friends."

"You had really better keep yourself dry," said the Fire Balloon. "That is the important thing."

"Very important for you, I have no doubt," answered the Rocket, "but I shall weep if I choose." He actually burst into tears, which flowed down his stick like raindrops and nearly drowned two little beetles who were just thinking of setting up house together and were looking for a nice dry spot to live in.

"He must have a truly romantic nature," said the Catherine Wheel, "for he weeps when there is nothing at all to weep about," and she heaved a deep sigh and thought about the pine box.

But the Roman Candle and the Bengal Light were quite indignant and kept saying, "Humbug! humbug!" at the top of their voices. They were extremely practical, and whenever they objected to anything they called it humbug.

Then the moon rose like a wonderful silver shield, and the stars began to shine and a sound of music came from the palace.

The Prince and Princess were leading the dance. They danced so beautifully that the tall white lilies peeped in at the window and watched them, and the great red poppies nodded their heads and beat time.

Then ten o'clock struck, and then eleven, and then twelve, and at the last stroke of midnight everyone came out on the terrace, and the King sent for the Royal Pyrotechnist.

"Let the fireworks begin," said the King, and the Royal Pyrotechnist made a low bow and marched down to the end of the garden. He had six attendants with him, each of whom carried a lighted torch at the end of a long pole.

It was certainly a magnificent display.

Whizz! Whizz! went the Catherine Wheel, as she spun round and round. Boom! Boom! went the Roman Candle. Then the Squibs danced all over the place, and the Bengal Lights made everything look scarlet. "Good-bye," cried the Fire Balloon, as he soared away, dropping tiny blue sparks. Bang! Bang! answered the Crackers, who were enjoying themselves immensely. Everyone was a great success except the Remarkable Rocket. He was so damped with crying that he could not go off at all. The best thing in him was the gunpowder, and that was so wet with tears that it was of no use. All his poor relations, to whom he would never speak except with a sneer, shot up into the sky like wonderful golden flowers with blossoms of fire. Huzza! Huzza! Huzza! cried the Court, and the little Princess laughed with pleasure.

"I suppose they are reserving me for some grand occasion," said the Rocket. "No doubt that is what it means," and he looked more supercilious than ever.

The next day the workmen came to put everything tidy.

"This is evidently a deputation," said the Rocket. "I will receive them with becoming dignity." So he put his nose in the air and began to frown severely as if he were thinking about some very important subject. But they took no notice of him at all till they were just going away. Then one of them caught sight of him. "Hullo!" he cried, "what a bad rocket!" and he threw him over the wall into the ditch.

"Bad Rocket? Bad Rocket?" he said, as he whirled through the air. "Impossible! Grand Rocket, that is what the man said. Bad and Grand sound very much the same, indeed they often are the same," and he fell into the mud.

"It is not comfortable here," he remarked, "but no doubt it is some fashionable watering place, and they have sent me away to regain my health. My nerves are certainly very much shattered, and I require rest."

Then a little Frog, with bright jeweled eyes and a green mottled coat, swam up and stopped beside him.

"A new arrival, I see!" said the Frog. "Well, after all there is nothing like mud. Give me rainy weather and a ditch, and I am quite happy. Do you think it will be a wet afternoon? I do hope so, but the sky is blue and cloudless. What a pity!"

"Ahem! ahem!" said the Rocket, and he began to cough.

"What a delightful voice you have!" cried the Frog. "Really it is quite like a croak, and croaking is, of course, the most musical sound in the world. You will hear our glee club this evening. We sit in the old duck pond close by the farmer's house, and as soon as the moon rises we begin. It is so entrancing that everybody lies awake to listen to us. In fact, it was only yesterday that I heard the farmer's wife say to her mother that she could not get a wink of sleep at night on account of us. It is most gratifying to find oneself so popular."

"Ahem! ahem!" said the Rocket angrily. He was very much annoyed that he could not get a word in.

"A delightful voice, certainly," continued the Frog. "I hope you will come over to the duck pond. I am off to look for my

daughters. I have six beautiful daughters, and I am so afraid the Pike may meet them. He is a perfect monster, and would have no hesitation in breakfasting off them. Well, goodbye; I have enjoyed our conversation very much, I assure you."

"Conversation, indeed!" said the Rocket. "You have talked the whole time yourself. That is not conversation."

"Somebody must listen," answered the Frog, "and I like to do all the talking myself. It saves time and prevents arguments."

"But I like arguments," said the Rocket.

"I hope not," said the Frog complacently. "Arguments are extremely vulgar, for everybody in good society holds exactly the same opinions. Good-bye a second time; I see my daughters in the distance," and the little Frog swam away.

"You are a very irritating person," said the Rocket, "and very ill-bred. I hate people who talk about themselves as you do, when one wants to talk about oneself as I do. It is what I call selfishness, and selfishness is a most detestable thing, especially to anyone of my temperament, for I am well known for my sympathetic nature. In fact, you should take example by me; you could not possibly have a better model. Now that you have the chance you had better avail yourself of it, for I am going back to Court almost immediately. I am a great favorite at Court; in fact, the Prince and Princess were married yesterday in my honor. Of course, you know nothing of these matters, for you are a provincial."

"There is no good talking to him," said a Dragonfly, who was sitting on the top of a large brown bulrush, "no good at all, for he has gone away."

"Well, that is his loss, not mine," answered the Rocket. "I am not going to stop talking to him merely because he pays no attention. I like hearing myself talk. It is one of my greatest pleasures. I often have long conversations all by myself, and I am so clever that sometimes I don't understand a single word I am saying."

"Then you should certainly lecture on Philosophy," said the Dragonfly, and he spread a pair of lovely gauze wings and soared away into the sky.

"How very silly of him not to stay here!" said the Rocket. "I am sure that he has not often got such a chance of improving his mind. However, I don't care a bit. Genius like mine is sure to be appreciated some day," and he sank down a little deeper into the mud.

After some time a large White Duck swam up to him. She had yellow legs and webbed feet, and was considered a great beauty on account of her waddle.

"Quack, quack, quack," she said. "What a curious shape you are! May I ask if you were you born like that, or is it the result of an accident?"

"It is quite evident that you have always lived in the country," answered the Rocket, "otherwise you would know who I am. However, I shall excuse your ignorance. It would be unfair to expect other people to be as remarkable as oneself. You will no doubt be surprised to hear that I can fly up into the sky and come down in a shower of golden rain."

"I don't think much of that," said the Duck, "as I cannot see what use it is to anyone. Now, if you could plough the fields

like the ox, or draw a cart like the horse or look after the sheep like the collie dog, that would be something."

"My good creature," cried the Rocket in a very haughty tone of voice, "I see that you belong to the lower orders. A person of my position is never useful. We have certain accomplishments, and that is more than sufficient. I have no sympathy myself with industry of any kind, least of all with such industries as you seem to recommend. Indeed, I have always been of opinion that hard work is simply the refuge of people who have nothing whatever to do."

"Well, well," said the Duck, who was of a very peaceful disposition and never quarreled with anyone, "everybody has different tastes. I hope, at any rate, that you are going to take up your residence here."

"Oh! dear no," cried the Rocket. "I am merely a visitor, a distinguished visitor. The fact is that I find this place rather tedious. There is neither society here nor solitude. In fact, it is essentially suburban. I shall probably go back to Court, for I know that I am destined to make a sensation in the world."

"I had thoughts of entering public life once myself," remarked the Duck. "There are so many things that need reforming. Indeed, I took the chair at a meeting some time ago, and we passed resolutions condemning everything that we did not like. However, they did not seem to have much effect. Now I go in for domesticity and look after my family."

"I am made for public life," said the Rocket, "and so are all my relations, even the humblest of them. Whenever we appear we excite great attention. I have not actually appeared myself, but when I do so it will be a magnificent sight. As for domesticity, it ages one rapidly and distracts one's mind from higher things."

"Ah! the higher things of life, how fine

they are!" said the Duck. "That reminds me how hungry I feel," and she swam away down the stream, saying, "Quack, quack, quack."

"Come back! come back!" screamed the Rocket, "I have a great deal to say to you," but the Duck paid no attention to him. "I am glad that she has gone," he said to himself, "she has a decidedly middle-class mind." He sank a little deeper still into the mud and began to think about the loneliness of genius, when suddenly two little boys in white smocks came running down the bank with a kettle and some sticks.

"This must be the deputation," said the Rocket, and he tried to look very dignified.

"Hullo!" cried one of the boys, "look at this old stick; I wonder how it came here." He picked the Rocket out of the ditch.

"Old Stick!" said the Rocket, "impossible! Gold Stick, that is what he said. Gold Stick is very complimentary. In fact, he mistakes me for a Court dignitary!"

"Let us put it into the fire!" said the other boy. "It will help to boil the kettle."

So they piled the sticks together, put the Rocket on top and lit the fire.

"This is magnificent," cried the Rocket, "they are going to let me off in broad daylight, so that everyone can see me."

"We will go to sleep now," they said, "and when we wake up the kettle will be boiled," and they lay down on the grass and shut their eyes.

The Rocket was very damp, so he took a long time to burn. At last, however, the fire caught him.

"Now I am going off!" he cried, and he made himself very stiff and straight. "I know I shall go much higher than the stars, much higher than the moon, much higher than the sun. In fact, I shall go so high that——"

Fizz! Fizz! Fizz! and he went straight up into the air.

"Delightful!" he cried, "I shall go on like this forever. What a success I am!"

But nobody saw him.

Then he began to feel a curious tingling sensation all over him.

"Now I am going to explode," he cried. "I shall set the whole world on fire and make such a noise that nobody will talk about anything else for a whole year." And he certainly did explode. Bang! Bang! Bang! went the gunpowder. There was no doubt about it.

But nobody heard him, not even the two little boys, for they were sound asleep.

Then all that was left of him was the stick, and this fell down on the back of a Goose who was taking a walk by the side of the ditch.

"Good heavens!" cried the Goose. "It is going to rain sticks," and she rushed into the water.

"I knew I should create a great sensation," gasped the Rocket, and he went out.

Godfrey and the Werewolf

*Could the hairy, ill-clad man
be a werewolf, one of those evil beings that
had assumed a human shape?
Godfrey hoped so*

Halina Gorska

A short time after the disappearance of the shepherd's pet goat, two other goats went astray, then a ram and four sheep, and last a large white cow, the pride of the whole herd.

The old herdsman brooded greatly over this loss and was particularly disconsolate over the cow. He was angry at the herd-boys because they had a mind for nothing but pranks, he said, and could not keep their animals from harm.

When, however, shortly after that, a bull was lost, too, a bull so strong and stubborn that he would have been a match for any wolf, the old man shook his head sadly and said, "Ah, boys, 'tis some unholy power and not the wolves. As long as only goats and sheep were lost, I thought it was your carelessness that was to blame, for it is well known that they are foolish, flighty and thoughtless creatures and likely to come to grief, so that they want careful watching. But with a cow it is an altogether different matter. And what a cow, mind you. Quiet, sedate, not at all given to pranks and frolic.

Still, I said to myself that even such a cow might be frightened into straying from the herd, and in the woods a mishap is easily met with. But a bull. Why, he would throw a wolf, and not the other way around."

He had scarce finished speaking when shepherds from the valley next to theirs came running and began to inquire if their neighbors had seen two cows from their own herd—one black, they said, and the other piebald.

They proceeded to complain and lament that things had been getting out of hand lately, so many cattle had disappeared under their very eyes. And not only that. Why, only yesterday two shepherds had gone into the woods to search for sheep and had not yet returned.

Likewise, they said, farmers from nearby villages have come to us to inquire about children. It appears that they went picking berries and were lost. But, stranger yet, yesterday at evenfall there came hurrying into our valley the wife of John the Sharp-shooter, who is known as the best shot of the neighborhood, and she told us, crying, that three days have gone by since he went chamois-chasing and he has not yet come home. No doubt about it, some mighty packs of hungry and very daring wolves must have come sneaking from the other side of the mountains.

The old herdsman listened to this tale in gloomy silence and then said, "Nay, not wolves; they are not wolves that go ravening hereabouts; it is a werewolf and his devilish crew. We shall all perish pitifully, we and our herds."

A great terror came over the shepherds. They all grew silent, casting fearful glances at one another. Godfrey, however, was not a whit alarmed. He began to inquire curiously about the werewolf and his crew who frightened everybody. But the old herdsman responded thus, "It does no good talking about it. Empty talk will avail nothing and calamity is easily invited. Be on your guard. Stay close to one another. Do not scatter and God grant that we somehow come through scatheless, for an evil creature does not like a crowd."

The herdboys obeyed him and none dared leave his companions to go picking raspberries, while at night they huddled together like frightened sheep. Laughter and gay talk ceased. Melancholy and fear came to reign among them. Godfrey alone did not lose his spirit, and his gay fiddling bore up his companions' hearts.

A few days passed in complete quiet and soon the shepherds began to take heart. Perhaps the evil was past.

First one, then another, made bold enough to stray from his companions in order to drive in a goat or to seek out some special tree for reeds.

But the wicked being did not sleep; it merely lay in wait, the better to deceive the watchful shepherds. And so it was that Jackie the Homeless, so nicknamed because he was an orphan and had no one in the world, disappeared one day without leaving a trace. He was Godfrey's dearest comrade, and Godfrey sought long and singly for his cherished companion, weeping and greatly sorrowing for him. Finally, when he returned to camp without finding the boy, he vowed in his heart he would destroy the monster. He said nothing about his decision to anyone but constantly kept thinking of how he was going to find the werewolf.

By chance he soon found an opportunity.

One day there arrived in the valley a farmer from a far-off village in the mountains. Bowing to the herdsman, he said that he had heard of the great fiddler from his shepherds and had come expressly to bid him to a wedding. This request did not surprise the herdsman and his boys, for the fame of Godfrey's fiddling had spread far and wide over the region and no wedding or christening could be held without his music.

The old herdsman prided himself upon having such a player among his herders and would gladly have given his permission. But something about this farmer did not please him; the man was shaggy like a wolf and all clothed in skins, he flashed his eyes like a wild beast, and his smile was sly and malevolent.

The old man was loath to let Godfrey go along with the stranger, therefore he took the boy aside and said, "I do not know what manner of man this is, but he has something evil in his eyes, and times are uncertain. Also, I heard my grandfather say that a werewolf can sometimes assume man's shape, the more easily to deceive people. I do not like to see you go off into the mountains and wild woods with this stranger, but it would be most painful for me to deny his request. After all, he may be a very good fellow, and, as he said himself, he has come a great distance."

Godfrey was well pleased to hear these words and thought, Grant God it is the werewolf and not a peasant from the far-away mountains. I do not know yet what I shall do, but one thing I do know: his fiendish mischief will not go unpunished.

To the herdsman he said aloud, "An old mountaineer who used to come to the valley for milk and cheese told me, too, how werewolves sometimes prowl about in human shape. But he also said they feel ill at ease in the skin of man and can easily be discovered then. For, to make themselves more comfortable, they often cast it off like an ill-suited garment, and in so doing flash a bloodshot eye or a wolf's claw. This man, however, does not act in that manner. Besides, why should he assume man's shape to lure away a little shepherd like me? Could he not, if he wished, just carry me off and do away with me as he has done with Jackie the Homeless? He is only a common peasant, and he is hairy and ill-clad as peasants from wild mountainous regions sometimes are. It would not be right, I think, to hurt him with such suspicions and refuse his request."

"Go along with him, then, if that is your will," said the herdsman. "I will not cross you, although some uneasiness is troubling me."

Godfrey thereupon took his fiddle and, bidding farewell to the old herdsman and the boys, set forth with the stranger.

They had not gone a long way when the stranger said to Godfrey, "The sun is scorching hot today. I must take off my cap and my sheepskin."

He removed his cap and there appeared from under it not hair, but something like a wolf's pelt.

He doffed his sheepskin and his shirt which was open on his chest revealed a body covered with hair like that of a wild beast.

He wiped his sweaty forehead with his hand and it was as if suddenly his hand had changed to a beast's paw.

Ho, ho! thought Godfrey, but he did not say a word.

They walked on and after a while Godfrey's companion began to complain that his shoes were greatly troubling him.

"Take them off, sir," said Godfrey, "and you will feel more comfortable."

To which the other answered, "I would take them off gladly, only I am afraid you might be frightened when you see my feet."

"Why should I be frightened?" asked Godfrey, feigning great surprise.

"Well—because my feet are not like those you are used to."

"Why?" said Godfrey, shrugging his shoulders. "Have you hoofs on your feet, or what?"

"Well, not quite hoofs. But constant walking in the mountains has given me corns and bumps which make them look like hoofs."

"I know well how the skin sometimes toughens from walking barefoot and I am not frightened by any such thing. My grandfather had such corns on his feet that they looked like two gnarled stumps. Why shouldn't yours look like hoofs? So take them off without another thought."

The stranger was greatly pleased. "You are a clever lad," he said. And sitting down on a stone he removed his shoes. Instead of toes on his feet there were hoofs just like those of devils, only so large that Godfrey was quite astonished. Yet he showed no sign of it but smiled and said, "Hah, you are a sissy, sir. My grandfather had larger bumps and did not groan as you do."

Thus he spoke while within him great anger welled up, and rage choked him, for he now knew for certain what kind of farmer this was. And he would have leaped at the werewolf's throat then and there, but he remembered Jackie the Homeless, and thought: No, dear comrade, you shall not be unavenged. This cruel monster shall inflict no more harm on mankind. I will not be done away with for nothing. I will wait for a favorable moment and hold my anger until I accomplish my design.

So they marched on all day and all night and at last they reached the devil's abode where the werewolf and his cronies, the witches and ogres, dwelt. It stood in the midst of steep and bare rocks, in a small and weirdly dismal glen. Godfrey was quite weary by the time they reached it, for the journey had been arduous, and the werewolf, once he had rid himself of his shoes which cumbered him greatly since he was unaccustomed to human footgear, had run so swiftly that Godfrey could hardly keep pace with him.

Therefore, when they came to the valley, Godfrey sat down on a stone and said, "You must let me rest awhile, sir."

"Rest yourself," replied the werewolf cheerfully. "Though it surprises me that it is only now you are feeling weary, because from here we can see the roofs of the houses, and the saying is that a horse runs faster once he sees the stable."

So they sat down together, and Godfrey peered about curiously, fixing in his mind every detail of this place.

But, to tell the truth, there was not much to see. It was a barren glen where nothing grew, and its black and hard soil suggested a big threshing floor. There was a small but deep lake almost at the far end of it, and beyond the lake there rose a hillock, huddled up against the rocks that enclosed the glen. On this very hillock the werewolf and his henchmen had put up their huts.

"What lake is that?" inquired Godfrey of the werewolf.

"That lake is called the Loch of the Drowned," returned the werewolf.

And Godfrey at once recalled what the old herdsman had told him about the lake:

"The water is deep even at the short end and its mysterious whirlpools draw in the best swimmers. Nobody has ever yet come out of the lake alive."

"Well, let us go," said the werewolf, rising. "It is a pity to waste time. Indoors you will rest and refresh yourself."

They skirted the lake and started to climb up the hill where the devils' huts stood. These did not differ much from the usual peasant huts except that they had no windows and their walls were not whitened with lime but were blackened with tar, since evil spirits do not like white.

Each of the huts was surrounded, as is common in the country, by a little garden. But they were queer gardens, indeed. Instead of sunflowers, cats' heads grew on tall stalks and peeped intently at passersby, blinking their gleaming green eyes. The trees had leaves shaped like outstretched human fingers which kept curling up and straightening out, and row on row, like neatly planted cabbage-heads, grew bearded muzzles of black bucks. About the porches coiled something that looked a bit like peas and a bit like wild vine. When, however, Godfrey looked at this plant more closely he noted that its climbing stalks moved continually like a tangle of green snakes, and its flowers, shaped like long red tongues, hid and showed again, smacking greedily.

Another lad would surely have fainted with terror at such a sight, but Godfrey knew no fear. He was merely seized with loathing and great disgust but he never so much as trembled, being well aware that the werewolf was watching him intently. At last the monster stopped in front of one of the cottages and, opening the gate, entered the garden. Here he was greeted by an old dame, lean as a rod, with a thick mop of bristling hair on her head. Godfrey gazed at her, wondering what sort of freak

this was, then realized that she was nothing but a plain broom prettily dressed in a skirt and bodice.

"This is the handmaid of my betrothed," said the werewolf. "She is an industrious and good girl."

And the broom began to wriggle coyly and preen herself and giggle, and veil herself with her apron as village maidens will do.

"I am going," she said, "to give the bats a drink, because evening is falling and our cattle will wake anon."

Meanwhile the werewolf entered the cottage, so Godfrey followed him.

The room was completely dark except for a fire that burned in the middle of it. In its red light Godfrey beheld a witch seated by the fire. Her face was yellow as a lemon, her eyes gleamed like those of a cat and she had a long hooked nose and one green tooth which stuck out of her hideous mouth and reached to her chin.

The werewolf at once presented Godfrey to her, saying he was the player who had been brought along for the next day's wedding.

"You must be very wayworn and hungry after so long a journey?" screeched the witch in a voice that resembled the squeak of ungreased wheels. "So be seated and eat, for the evening meal is ready."

And she brought forth some pots and cups which were like skulls of men and beasts and were filled with smoking food.

But Godfrey had no stomach for such devils' fare, wherefore he excused himself, saying that fatigue had got the better of his hunger. He lay down in one corner of the room and pretended to fall asleep. Yet, in real truth, he did not sleep at all, but listened closely to the conversation between the witch and the werewolf.

"Why do you take such pains with this one shepherd?" said the witch to the werewolf. "Could you not just snatch him,

bring him hither and force him to play, instead of going to all the trouble of putting on the guise of man?"

"Very troublesome it was indeed," answered the werewolf and, shedding the rest of his human guise, he suddenly turned into a huge wolf with shining bloodshot eyes and horse hoofs. "Phew! I can hardly breathe. Still, I could not do otherwise, for had I snatched the boy and dragged him hither, forcing him to play, he would scarcely be alive from fright and his music would not be very gay to dance to. Now, this is to be a wedding the like of which has not yet been witnessed. It isn't every day that a werewolf weds a witch."

Ho, ho, I will treat you to some wedding, thought Godfrey, still pretending to be asleep and even snoring occasionally.

"You are right," agreed the witch. "You have contrived this wisely. But tell me, what do you propose to do with him afterward?"

The werewolf broke into laughter, exhibiting his sharp white fangs, and retorted with a grin, "Me-thinks a roast of the fiddler would be no worse than any other. We will eat him together with that other herdboy whom I carried away from their valley last week."

"I have been trying to fatten him up but he is still as skinny as a lath," said the witch wryly.

At these words Godfrey was overjoyed and thought: So you are still alive, Jackie dear. Well, please God, I will set you free, and together we shall return safe and sound to the valley.

For he had already formed his scheme to destroy the ogres, witches and the werewolf and deliver the whole region of the devil-sent plague. So he kept listening to what the witch was whispering to the werewolf.

"We are talking too loud," she said. "The boy might hear us."

"Don't be silly," replied the werewolf. "See, he is fast asleep."

And he laughed again.

"He is not so clever. He has not the slightest notion of where he is. He is a frightfully stupid boy."

Godfrey listened no longer. Now that he knew all he wanted to learn, he resolved to rest awhile. He fell asleep and slept soundly not only through that night, but through nearly all the next day as well, so weary was he from the journey.

He was at length aroused by the preparations which the witch and the werewolf, aided by the broom, were making for the wedding.

"We shall have to clear the room," said the witch, "because once the dancing gets under way we will need every bit of space."

"That will not help much," sighed the werewolf. "The room is so small and the guests will be many."

"I know a way to avoid a crush," remarked Godfrey unexpectedly, for he had been listening closely to the conversation.

"Now, what would you suggest?" queried the werewolf.

"If you want my advice," said Godfrey, "then do not dance indoors, but down in the valley by the lake. It is going to be a moonlit night, there will be plenty of room for dancing, and since there are no bushes or stones and the ground is level and hard, you will be more comfortable than inside. You can dance in the valley on one side of the lake while I stand on the other, on the hill, and play for you. Because of the mountains all around, the music will be echoed loud and clear throughout the valley."

"By my dear devil!" exclaimed the werewolf, who had forgotten that he was supposed to be a peasant. "By my dear devil, the lad is right."

The witch, however, was possessed of more sagacity than the werewolf, so she said to Godfrey, "That is good advice. But tell me, why is it you want to stand on the other side of the lake when you play right amongst us in the valley?"

"I will explain," replied Godfrey. "You must have heard how, when I strike up a lively tune in my sweeping manner, nobody and nothing can stand still, but all must instantly start to dance and keep at it for as long as their breath holds. Well, if I should be standing in your midst, you would jostle me ever and again and hinder me from playing. And then, too, I would fain watch your dancing, and it will be much easier for me to see you from the hill than if I should stand in the middle of the crush, in the throng."

"Have it your way, then," acquiesced the witch, having dismissed her suspicions.

And straightway she ran off to invite the guests to the valley.

Ugh, 'twas a sight and something to wonder at when the guests assembled!

Horrible witches there were galore, those who will harm men in no time, and bogies which feed on human blood and goblins who lead travelers astray on foggy nights. In the bright moonlight Godfrey could see clearly from his hill as the gathering paired off for dancing. They were overjoyed at having such a fiddler to play for them, for usually at devils' weddings the only music is the whistling of the wind and the croaking of toads.

Well, thought Godfrey, with God's help this shall be your last dance. And he drew the bow across the strings.

Ho! So sprightly and rousing was the music which resounded through the valley that not only the ogres, witches and goblins, led by the werewolf, began to dance; but even the brooms, who, as is well known, are in attendance upon witches, ran out of the huts and started whirling with their mistresses.

And the dancing grew ever more frenzied, ever giddier, until the dancers' breath failed, sparks began to fly before their eyes, and reason left their heads.

The witches thrust their claws into one another and danced on.

The ogres and goblins took each other by the hand and spun about, howling and whistling with glee so loud that the wind scurried all over the valley and the bats, startled by the wild uproar, fled in swarms from the devils' huts.

The brooms lost their skirts and bodices and thrashed about with such fury that from sheer impetus one and then another slashed her mistress on the pate.

In the middle was the werewolf himself, dancing, stamping his hoofs, flashing his bloodshot eyes and showing his sharp fangs.

Ha, you will not rejoice long, son of the devil, thought Godfrey, and struck the strings even more violently.

And the whole fiendish lot surged forward in one solid mass, lured onward by the irresistible call of the dance music and unmindful of the bottomless lake that separated them from the fiddler.

Perhaps one or another would have come to his senses and stopped, but the dance-drunk crowd swept him forward and carried him along.

And the fiddle kept calling from the other shore of the lake, ever louder, ever more insistently.

Onward, onward, this way, this way, the music seemed to say.

Just at the water's edge, the crowd seemed to waver, but drunk with the music and completely senseless, it plunged straight into the lake.

Thus it was that Godfrey freed the whole region of the werewolf, the ogres, witches and goblins—the whole devilish crew. In one of the huts he found Jackie the Homeless and other shepherds whom the werewolf had kept imprisoned, all of whom his music had saved from death.

THE SNOW PARTY

*It started out with one little old woman
and one little old man. Before the evening was over,
there were 85 grownups, 17 children, 7 babies, 6 dogs,
a cat, a parakeet, a canary and a pet skunk*

BEATRICE SCHENK DE REGNIERS

There was this little old woman and this
little old man and they lived in a little
old farmhouse 'way out in Dakota. They
lived all alone with some chickens.

Outside it was snowing and snowing and
the wind was blowing.

And the little old woman said, "I'm
mighty lonely here with just you and the
chickens for company. I'd like to give me a
party and have plenty of folks in."

And the little old man said, "What's the
matter with you, woman? Are you daft?
We don't know a soul to invite to a party.
And if we did know a soul, who would
come to a party through all this wind and
snow?"

The little old woman looked out of the
window and she could see that outside it
was snowing and snowing. And she could
hear the wind blowing.

184

And she said, "I'd bake me a cake and put candles on it and I'd hire me a fiddler to fiddle a tune and there would be feasting and dancing and merrymaking. There would be high jinks and low jinks. It would be a fine party, I can tell you."

"Woman, are you daft?" said the little old man. "Even if we knew a soul to invite to a party and even if they came through the wind and the snow, we don't have a crust or a crumb of cake or a thimbleful of flour in the house to bake one."

Outside it was snowing and snowing and the wind was blowing.

Inside, the little old woman turned on all the lights so the house wouldn't look so lonely. And she turned on the radio so the house wouldn't sound so lonely.

The man on the radio was advertising the K-M Bakery. He was saying, "The next time you have a party, order K-M's lus-cious, delicious, delightful, and simply heavenly chocolate fudge cake. And re-member, the K-M Bakery delivers its de-licious cakes, bread, pies, cupcakes, cin-namon rolls and buns right to your door.

So when you hear that knock-knock-knock-knock-knock answer the door as fast as you can, 'cause knock-knock-knock-knock-knock means here comes the K-M man!

"Chocolate cake," the little old woman sighed. "Cinnamon rolls, buns . . ."

Then all of a sudden the wind blew hard and harder and it blew down the electric lines and the radio went off and the lights went out and it was dark in the little house. So the little old woman lit candles. She had a lot of candles and she lit them all and put them on the table.

185

The table looked like a big birthday cake, it had so many candles all around it.

"I wish it were a cake," said the little old woman. "I wish the table were a big cake and we were having a party."

"Hush, woman," said the little old man. "Wishes won't wash dishes and wishes won't stop the wind from blowing or the snow from snowing." And he put on his high galoshes and his overcoat and his hat and his earmuffs and his mittens.

"Where are you going in all this snow and wind?" asked the little old woman.

"We have three hundred baby chicks in the barn and I'm going to bring them into the house to keep them warm. Three hundred chirping chicks will be company enough."

"Well, bring in the chicks," said the little old woman, "but that's not the company I'm wishing for."

And the little old man went out the back door to the barn with the snow snowing and the wind blowing.

Listen!

There is a knock at the front door —knock-knock!

The little old woman hurries to the door. "Who could be knocking at our door," she says, "on a night like this with the snow snowing and the wind blowing?"

She opens the door and in comes a great blast of wind and snow and there stands a man saying, "My car is stuck in the snow with a carload of people. Would you be good enough, old woman, to let us come in out of the snow and the wind until the snowplow comes to clear the road?"

"Come in, come in," says the little old woman, "and bring your carload of people and welcome!" And she scoops up a panful of snow and puts it on the stove to boil to make a pot of hot tea.

The man goes to his car and brings back his wife and his mother and his three brothers-in-law. And his wife is carrying a tiny baby wrapped in a woolen blanket.

The little old man is bringing in a basket full of chirping chicks. He says, "Welcome, welcome. My little old woman was just wishing for company."

Then he picks up a box and goes out the back door again to bring in some more baby chicks.

Listen!

There is a knock at the front door —knock-knock!

The little old woman hurries to the door and there in the wind and the snow stand a man and his wife and their twin boys and another man and a big hunting dog.

Their car is stuck in the snow and they are waiting for the snowplow to come through and clear the road.

"Come in, come in," says the little old woman, "and welcome! There's plenty of hot tea to drink, though there's not a crust or a crumb of cake or bread in the house to eat with it."

The little old man is bringing in a basketful of chirping chicks. Now there are 11 grownups and 1 baby and 2 little boys and a big hunting dog in the house.

"Welcome, welcome," says the little old man. "My little old woman was wishing for company and now she has it." And once again he goes out the back door and into the wind and snow to bring in some more baby chicks.

Outside the snow is snowing and the wind is blowing and the strangers are glad to be inside.

But listen!

Someone is knocking at the front door —knock-knock!

The little old woman hurries to the door and there are three carloads of people. Their cars are stuck in the snow and they must wait for the snowplow to come through to clear the road.

"Come in, come in," says the little old woman, "and welcome!"

So now when the little old man comes in the back door with a box of chirping baby chicks, he counts 27 grownups, 5 children, 3 babies, 2 dogs and a parakeet.

"Welcome, welcome," says the little old man. "My little old woman was wishing for company and now she has it."

But listen!

Someone is knocking at the front door —knock-knock!

There is only one man standing at the door in the wind and the snow. He says, "The snow is snowing and the wind is blowing and my bus is stuck in the snow. May I wait inside till the snowplow comes?"

"Come in, come in," says the little old woman, "and welcome!"

So the bus driver goes back to the bus and comes back with 42 grownups, 7 children, 2 babies, 3 dogs, a canary and a little pet skunk.

"Welcome, welcome," says the little old man. "My little old woman was wishing for company and now she has it."

"If only," says the little old woman, "if only there were a crust or a crumb of cake or bread in the house."

Listen!

Someone is knocking at the front door —knock-knock! And someone is knocking at the back door—knock-knock!

The little old woman hurries to the front and the little old man goes to the back.

It is the snowplow man at the front door. "My snowplow got stuck in the snow," he says. So he comes in to wait till the other snowplows come.

At the back door there are more people who got stuck in the snow.

"Come in, come in," and "Welcome, welcome," say the little old woman and the little old man.

All night long people come knocking at the door.

Now there are 84 grownups, 17 children, 7 babies, 6 dogs, a cat, a parakeet, a canary bird and a little pet skunk in the little old house.

Outside it is snowing and snowing and the wind is blowing.

Inside, the babies are yowling, the dogs are yapping, the chicks are chirping, the mothers are scolding.

"It's a shame," says the little old woman, "it's a shame. All these people and no party. If only there were a crust or a crumb of cake or bread in the house or a bit of music."

But listen!

Someone is knocking at the door. It is a very special knock—

knock-knock-knock-knock-knock
knock-knock-knock-knock-knock

The little old woman hurries to open the door.

It is the K-M man, the man from the K-M Bakery.

His trailer truck is stuck in the snow right in front of the door.

"Come in, come in," says the little old woman, "and welcome."

The K-M man comes in and he looks around at all the people there and he says, "You look like mighty hungry people to me."

And the little old woman says, "There's not a crust or a crumb of bread or cake in the house, but you're welcome to come in out of the wind and the snow."

"Who will help me?" says the K-M man. "Who will help me unload my truck?" Then he chooses some of the children and some of the grownup men.

What a parade!

First come the trays full of rolls—crunchy crusty rolls, brown and shiny; soft fluffy rolls, white and powdery; poppyseed rolls, sesame seed rolls, little rolls braided like ribbons, smooth round rolls shaped just like a tiny baby's bottom.

Then come the trays of cinnamon buns. The cinnamon makes the air smell like perfume.

Now comes a special parade of pies—lemon meringue pies, cherry pies, apple pies, coconut custard pies, chocolate cream pies.

Now come the cupcakes—chocolate and vanilla with pink icing, white icing, rich chocolate icing.

The little old woman jumps up and down and claps her hands. "It's a party," she says. "It's a party sure enough."

"Ha," says the K-M man, "if it's a party, I'd better bring in my special-order chocolate fudge party cake."

So he brings it in and the little old woman puts candles all around it and somebody makes party hats out of newspapers and everyone eats to his heart's content.

Then the accordion player plays his accordion and he plays so gaily that no one can sit still. Everyone stamps his feet to the music. Even the babies wave their fat little hands and feet in time to the music.

Now the accordion player plays a waltz tune and the little old man grabs the little old woman around the waist and waltzes with her till they are both out of breath (which doesn't take very long) and everybody claps hands and begins to dance too.

The accordion player plays and plays. He plays "Turkey in the Hay, Turkey in the Straw" and he plays "Pop Goes the Weasel" and he plays "I Put My Left Foot In"—oh, he knows a hundred tunes and he plays them all!

It's a party, all right. There is feasting and dancing and merrymaking. There are high jinks and low jinks. It's a fine party, I can tell you.

The party lasts until noontime—when the snow stops snowing and the wind stops blowing and the snowplows come through and clear the road.

Everyone says good-bye to the little old woman and the little old man and they all say it is the best party they have ever been to.

The little old woman is so content and so happy and so tired and so sleepy that she lays her head on the table next to a coconut custard pie and falls fast asleep. . . .

Tom Chist and the Treasure Box

*Captain Kidd buries a treasure chest
on the shores of Delaware Bay and turns the whole
of Tom Chist's life topsy-turvy*

HOWARD PYLE

To tell about Tom Chist, and how he got his name, and how he came to be living at the little settlement of Henlopen, just inside the mouth of the Delaware Bay, the story must begin as far back as 1686, when a great storm swept the Atlantic coast from end to end. During the heaviest part of the hurricane a bark went ashore on the Hen-and-Chicken Shoals, just below Cape Henlopen and at the mouth of the Delaware Bay, and Tom Chist was the only soul of all those on board the ill-fated vessel who escaped alive.

This story must first be told, because it was on account of the strange and miraculous escape that happened to him at that time that he gained the name that was given to him.

Even as late as that time of the American colonies, the little scattered settlement at Henlopen, made up of English with a few Dutch and Swedish people, was still only a spot upon the face of the great American wilderness that spread away with swamp and forest no man knew how far to the westward. That wilderness was not only full of wild beasts, but of Indians who every fall would come in wandering tribes to spend the winter along the shores of the freshwater lakes below Henlopen. There for four or five months they would live upon fish and clams and wild ducks and geese, chipping their arrowheads and making their earthenware pots and pans under the lee of the sand hills and pine woods below the Capes.

Sometimes on Sundays, when the Rev. Hilary Jones would be preaching in the little log church back in the woods, these half-clad red men would come in from the cold and sit squatting in the back part of the church, listening stolidly to the words that had no meaning for them.

But about the wreck of the bark in 1686. Such a wreck was a godsend to the poor and needy settlers in the wilderness where so few good things ever came. For the vessel went to pieces during the night, and the next morning the beach was strewn with wreckage—boxes and barrels, chests and spars, timbers and planks, a plentiful and bountiful harvest to be gathered up by the settlers as they chose, with no one to forbid or prevent them.

The name of the bark, as found painted on some of the water barrels and sea chests,

189

was the *Bristol Merchant,* and she no doubt hailed from England.

As was said, the only soul who escaped alive off the wreck was Tom Chist.

A settler, a fisherman named Matt Abrahamson, and his daughter Molly found Tom. He was washed up on the beach among the wreckage in a great wooden box which had been securely tied around with a rope and lashed between two spars— apparently for better protection in beating through the surf. Matt Abrahamson thought he found something of more than usual value when he came upon this chest, but when he cut the cords and broke open the box with his broadax, he could not have been more astonished had he beheld a salamander instead of a baby of nine or ten months old lying half-smothered in the blankets that covered the bottom of the chest.

Matt Abrahamson's daughter Molly had had a baby who had died a month or so before. So when she saw the little one lying there in the bottom of the chest, she cried out in a great loud voice that the Good Man had sent her another baby in place of her own.

It was Parson Jones who gave the foundling his name. When the news came to his ears of what Matt Abrahamson had found he went over to the fisherman's cabin to see the child. He examined the clothes in which the baby was dressed. They were of fine linen and handsomely stitched, and the reverend gentleman opined that the foundling's parents must have been of quality. A kerchief had been wrapped around the baby's neck and under its arms and tied behind, and in the corner, marked with very fine needlework, were the initials T. C.

"What d'ye call him, Molly?" said Parson Jones. He was standing, as he spoke, with his back to the fire, warming his palms before the blaze. The pocket of the great-coat he wore bulged out with a big case bottle of spirits which he had gathered up out of the wreck that afternoon. "What d'ye call him, Molly?"

"I'll call him Tom, after my own baby."

"That goes very well with the initial on the kerchief," said Parson Jones. "But what other name d'ye give him? Let it be something to go with the C."

"I don't know," said Molly.

"Why not call him 'Chist,' since he was born in a chist out of the sea? 'Tom Chist' —the name goes off like a flash in the pan." And so "Tom Chist" he was called and "Tom Chist" he was christened.

So much for the beginning of the history of Tom Chist. The story of Captain Kidd's treasure box does not begin until the late spring of 1699.

That was the year that the famous pirate captain, coming up from the West Indies, sailed his sloop into the Delaware Bay, where he lay for over a month waiting for news from his friends in New York.

For he had sent word to that town asking if the coast was clear for him to return home with the rich prize he had brought from the Indian seas and the coast of Africa, and meantime he lay there in the Delaware Bay waiting for a reply. Before he left he turned the whole of Tom Chist's life topsy-turvy.

By that time Tom Chist had grown into a strong-limbed, thick-jointed boy of fourteen or fifteen. It was a miserable dog's life he lived with old Matt Abrahamson, for the old fisherman was in his cups more than half the time, and when he was so there was hardly a day passed that he did not give Tom a curse or a buffet or, as like as not, an actual beating. One would have thought that such treatment would have broken the spirit of the poor little foundling, but it had just the opposite effect upon Tom Chist, who was one of your stubborn, sturdy, stiff-willed fellows who only grow harder and more tough the more they are ill-treated. It had been a long time now since he had made any outcry or complaint at the hard usage he suffered from old Matt. At times Molly would interfere to protect her foster son, and then she and Tom would together fight the old man until they had wrenched the stick or the strap out of his hand. Then old Matt would chase them out of doors and around and around the house for maybe half an hour until his anger was cool, when he would go back again, and for a time the storm would be over.

Besides his foster mother, Tom Chist had a very good friend in Parson Jones, who used to come over every now and then to Abrahamson's hut upon the chance of getting a half dozen fish for breakfast. He always had a kind word or two for Tom, who during the winter evenings would go over to the good man's house to learn his letters, and to read and write and cipher a little, so that by now he was able to spell the words out of the Bible and the almanac and knew enough to change tuppence into four ha'pennies.

This is the sort of boy Tom Chist was, and this is the sort of life he led.

In the late spring or early summer of 1699 Captain Kidd's sloop sailed into the mouth of the Delaware Bay and changed the whole fortune of his life.

Old Matt Abrahamson kept the flat-bottomed boat in which he went fishing some distance down the shore and in the neighborhood of the old wreck that had been sunk on the Shoals. This was the usual fishing ground of the settlers, and here old Matt's boat generally lay drawn up on the sand.

There had been a thunderstorm that afternoon, and Tom had gone down the beach to bale out the boat in readiness for the morning's fishing.

It was full moonlight now as he was returning, and the night sky was full of floating clouds. Now and then there was a dull flash to the westward, and once a muttering growl of thunder, promising another storm to come.

All that day the pirate sloop had been lying just off the shore back of the Capes, and now Tom Chist could see the sails glimmering pallidly in the moonlight, spread for drying after the storm. He was walking up the shore homeward when he became aware that at some distance ahead of him there was a ship's boat drawn up on the little narrow beach, and a group of men clustered about it. He hurried forward with a good deal of curiosity to see who had landed, but it was not until he had come close to them that he could distinguish who and what they were. Then he knew that it must be a party who had come off the pirate sloop. They had evidently just landed, and two men were lifting out a chest from the boat. One of them was a black man, naked to the waist, and the other was white, in shirt sleeves, wearing petticoat breeches, a Monterey cap upon his head, a red bandanna handkerchief around his neck and gold earrings in his ears. He had a long, plaited queue hanging down his back and a great sheath knife dangling from his side. Another man, evidently the captain of the party, stood at a little distance as they lifted the chest out of the boat. He had a cane in one hand and a lighted lantern in the other, although the moon was shining as bright as day. He wore jackboots and a handsome laced coat, and he had a long, drooping mustache that curled down below his chin. He wore a fine, feathered hat, and his long black hair hung down upon his shoulders.

All this Tom Chist could see in the moonlight that glinted and twinkled upon the gilt buttons of his coat.

They were so busy lifting the chest from the boat that at first they did not observe

191

that Tom Chist had come up and was standing there. It was the man with the long, plaited queue and the gold earrings who spoke to him. "Boy, what do you want here, boy?" he said, in a rough, hoarse voice. "Where d'ye come from?" And then dropping his end of the chest, and without giving Tom time to answer, he pointed off down the beach and said, "You'd better be going about your own business if you know what's good for you; and don't you come back, or you'll find what you don't want waiting for you."

Tom saw in a glance that the pirates were all looking at him, and then, without saying a word, he turned and walked away. The man who had spoken to him followed him threateningly for some little distance as though to see that he had gone away as he was bidden to do. But presently he stopped, and Tom hurried on alone until the boat and the crew and all were dropped away behind and lost in the night. Then he himself stopped also, turned and looked back whence he had come.

There had been something very strange in the appearance of the men he had just seen, something very mysterious in their actions, and he wondered what it all meant and what they were going to do. He stood for a little while thus looking and listening. He could see nothing and could hear only the sound of distant talking. What were they doing on the lonely shore thus at night? Then, following a sudden impulse, he turned and cut off across the sand hummocks, skirting around inland, but keeping pretty close to the shore, his object being to spy upon them and to watch what they were about from the back of the low sand hills that fronted the beach.

He had gone along some distance in his circuitous return when he became aware of the sound of voices that seemed to be drawing closer to him as he came toward the speakers. He stopped and stood listening, and instantly, as he stopped, the voices stopped also. He crouched there silently in the bright, glimmering moonlight, surrounded by the silent stretches of sand, and the stillness seemed to press upon him like a heavy hand. Then suddenly the sound of a man's voice began again, and as Tom listened he could hear someone slowly counting. "Ninety-one," the voice began, "ninety-two, ninety-three, ninety-four,

ninety-five, ninety-six, ninety-seven, ninety-eight, ninety-nine, one hundred, one hundred and one"—the slow, monotonous count coming nearer and nearer— "one hundred and two, one hundred and three, one hundred and four," and so on in its monotonous reckoning.

Suddenly he saw three heads appear above the sand hill, so close to him that he crouched down quickly with a keen thrill close beside the hummock near which he stood. His first fear was that they might have seen him in the moonlight, but they had not, and his heart rose again as the counting voice went steadily on. "One hundred and twenty," it was saying—"and twenty-one, and twenty-two, and twenty-three, and twenty-four," and then he who was counting came out from behind the little sandy rise into the white and open level of shimmering brightness.

It was the man with the cane, the captain of the party who had landed. He carried his cane under his arm now and was holding his lantern close to something that he held in his hand and upon which he looked narrowly as he walked with a slow and measured tread in a perfectly straight line across the sand, counting each step as he took it. "And twenty-five, and twenty-six, and twenty-seven, and twenty-eight, and twenty-nine, and thirty."

Behind him walked two other figures; one was the half-naked black, the other the man with the plaited queue and the earrings, whom Tom had seen lifting the chest out of the boat. Now they were carrying the heavy box between them, laboring through the sand with shuffling tread as they bore it onward. As he who was counting pronounced the word "thirty," the two men set the chest down on the sand with a grunt, the white man panting and blowing and wiping his sleeve across his forehead. And immediately he who counted took out a slip of paper and marked something down upon it. They stood there for a long time, during which Tom lay behind the

sand hummock watching them, and for a while the silence was uninterrupted. In the perfect stillness Tom could hear the washing of the little waves beating upon the distant beach, and once the faraway sound of a laugh from one of those who stood by the ship's boat.

One, two, three minutes passed, and then the men picked up the chest and started on again; and then again the other man began his counting. "Thirty and one, and thirty and two, and thirty and three, and thirty and four"—he walked straight across the level open, still looking intently at that which he held in his hand—"and thirty and five, and thirty and six, and thirty and seven," and so on until the three figures disappeared in the little hollow between the two sand hills on the opposite side of the open, and still Tom could hear the sound of the counting voice.

Just as they disappeared behind the hill there was a sudden faint flash of light; and by and by, as Tom lay still listening to the counting, he heard, after a long interval, a faraway muffled rumble of distant thunder. He waited for a while and then arose and stepped to the top of the sand hummock behind which he had been lying. He looked all about him, but there was no one else to be seen. Then he stepped down from the hummock and followed in the direction which the pirate captain and the two men carrying the chest had gone. He crept along cautiously, stopping now and then to make sure that he still heard the counting voice, and when it ceased he lay down upon the sand and waited until it began again.

Presently, so following the pirates, he saw the three figures again in the distance, and, skirting around back of a hill of sand covered with coarse sedge grass, he came to where he overlooked a little open level space gleaming white in the moonlight.

The three had been crossing the level of sand and were now not more than twenty-five paces from him. They had again set down the chest, upon which the white man with the long queue and the gold earrings had seated to rest himself, the black standing close beside him. The moon shone as bright as day and full upon his face, which was looking directly at Tom Chist, every line as keen cut with white lights and black shadows as though it had been carved in ivory and jet. He sat perfectly motionless, and Tom drew back with a start, almost thinking he had been discovered. He lay silent, his heart beating heavily in his throat; but there was no alarm, and presently he heard the counting begin again, and when he looked once more he saw they were going away straight across the little open. A soft, sliding hillock of sand lay directly in front of them. They did not turn aside, but went straight over it, the leader helping himself up the sandy slope with his cane, still counting and still keeping his eyes fixed upon that which he held in his hand. Then they disappeared again behind the white crest on the other side.

So Tom followed them cautiously until they had gone almost half a mile inland. When next he saw them clearly it was from a little sandy rise which looked down like the crest of a bowl upon the floor of sand below. Upon this smooth, white floor the moon beat with almost dazzling brightness.

The white man who had helped to carry the chest was now kneeling, busied at some work, though what it was Tom at first could not see. He was whittling the point of a stick into a long wooden peg, and when, by and by, he had finished what he was about, he arose and stepped to where he who seemed to be the captain had stuck his cane upright into the ground as though to mark some particular spot. He drew the cane out of the sand, thrusting the stick down in its stead. Then he drove the long peg down with a wooden mallet which the black man handed to him. The sharp rapping of the mallet upon the top of the peg sounded loud in the perfect stillness, and Tom lay watching and wondering what it all meant. The man, with quick-repeated blows, drove the peg farther and farther down into the sand until it showed only two or three inches above the surface. As he finished his work there was another faint flash of light, and by and by another smothered rumble of thunder, and Tom, as he looked out toward the westward, saw the silver rim of the round and sharply outlined thundercloud rising slowly up into the sky and pushing the other and broken drifting clouds before it.

The two white men were now stooping over the peg, the black man watching them. Then presently the man with the cane started straight away from the peg, carrying the end of a measuring line with him, the other end of which the man with the plaited queue held against the top of the peg. When the pirate captain had reached the end of the measuring line he marked a cross upon the sand, and then again they measured out another stretch of space.

So they measured a distance five times over, and then, from where Tom lay, he could see the man with the queue drive another peg just at the foot of a sloping rise of sand that swept up beyond into a tall white dune marked sharp and clear against the night sky behind. As soon as the man with the plaited queue had driven the second peg into the ground they began measuring again and so, still measuring, disappeared in another direction which took them in behind the sand dune where Tom no longer could see what they were doing.

The black man still sat by the chest where the two had left him.

Presently from behind the hill there came, for the third time, the sharp rapping sound of the mallet driving still another peg, and then after a while the two pirates emerged from behind the sloping whiteness into the space of moonlight again.

They came direct to where the chest lay, and the white man and the black man lifting it once more, they walked away across the level of open sand and so on behind the edge of the hill and out of Tom's sight.

Tom Chist could no longer see what the pirates were doing, neither did he dare to cross over the open space of sand that lay between them and him. He lay there speculating as to what they were about, and meantime the storm cloud was rising higher and higher above the horizon with louder and louder mutterings of thunder following each dull flash from out the cloudy, cavernous depths. In the silence he could hear an occasional click as of some iron implement, and he opined that the pirates were burying the chest, though just where they were at work he could neither see nor tell.

Still he lay there watching and listening, and by and by a puff of warm air blew across the sand, and a thumping tumble of louder thunder leaped from out the belly of the storm cloud, which every minute was coming nearer and nearer. Still Tom Chist lay watching.

Suddenly, almost unexpectedly, the three figures reappeared from behind the sand hill, the pirate captain leading the way. They had gone about halfway across the white, sandy level between the hill and the hummock behind which Tom Chist lay when the white man stopped and bent over as though to tie his shoe.

This brought the black man a few steps in front of his companion.

That which then followed happened so suddenly, so unexpectedly, so swiftly that

195

Tom Chist had hardly time to realize what it all meant before it was over. As the black man passed him the white man arose suddenly and silently erect, and Tom Chist saw the white moonlight glint upon the blade of a great dirk knife which he now held in his hand. He took one, two silent, catlike steps, then there was a sweeping flash of the blade in the pallid light, and a blow, the thump of which Tom could distinctly hear even from where he lay stretched out upon the sand. There was an instant echoing yell from the black man, who ran stumbling forward, who stopped, who regained his footing and then stood for an instant as though rooted to the spot.

Tom had distinctly seen the knife enter his back and even thought that he had seen the glint of the point as it came out from the breast.

Meantime the pirate captain had stopped and now stood with his hand resting upon his cane looking impassively on.

Then the black man started to run. The white man stood for a while glaring after him; then he, too, started after his victim upon the run. The black man was not very far from Tom when he staggered and fell. He tried to rise, then fell forward again and lay at length. At that instant the first edge of the cloud cut across the moon, and there was a sudden darkness; but in the silence Tom heard the sound of another blow and a groan, and then presently a voice calling to the pirate captain that it was all over.

He saw the dim form of the captain crossing the level sand, and then, as the moon sailed out from behind the cloud, he saw the white man standing over a black figure that lay motionless upon the sand.

Then Tom Chist scrambled up and ran away, plunging down into the hollow of sand that lay in the shadows below. Over the next rise he ran and down again into the next black hollow, and so on over the sliding, shifting ground, panting and gasping. It seemed to him that he could hear footsteps following, and in the terror that possessed him he almost expected every instant to feel the cold knife blade slide between his own ribs in such a thrust from behind as he had seen given to the poor black man.

So he ran on like one in a nightmare. His feet grew heavy like lead, he panted and gasped, his breath came hot and dry in his throat. But still he ran and ran until at last he found himself in front of old Matt Abrahamson's cabin, gasping, panting and sobbing for breath, his knees relaxed and his thighs trembling with weakness.

As he opened the door and dashed into the darkened cabin (for both Matt and Molly were long ago asleep in bed) there was a flash of light, and even as he slammed to the door behind him there was an instant peal of thunder, heavy as though a great weight had been dropped upon the roof of the sky, so that the doors and windows of the cabin rattled.

Then Tom Chist crept to bed, trembling, shuddering, bathed in sweat, his heart beating like a trip-hammer and his brain dizzy from that long, terror-inspired race in which he had striven to outstrip he knew not what pursuing horror.

For a long, long time he lay awake, trembling and chattering with nervous chills, and when he did fall asleep it was only to drop into monstrous dreams in which he once again saw enacted, with various grotesque variations, the tragic drama which his waking eyes had beheld the night before.

Then came the dawning of the broad, wet daylight, and before the rising of the sun Tom was up and out of doors to find the young day dripping with the rain of overnight. His first act was to climb the nearest sand hill and to gaze out toward the offing where the pirate ship had been the day before.

It was no longer there.

Soon afterward Matt Abrahamson came out of the cabin and he called to Tom to go get a bite to eat, for it was time for them to be away fishing.

All that morning the recollection of the night before hung over Tom Chist like a great cloud of boding trouble. It filled the confined area of the little boat and spread over the entire wide spaces of sky and sea that surrounded them. Not for a moment was it lifted. Even when he was hauling in his wet and dripping line with a struggling fish at the end of it a recurrent memory of what he had seen would suddenly come upon him, and he would groan in spirit at the recollection. He looked at Matt Abrahamson's leathery face, at his lantern jaws cavernously and stolidly chewing at a tobacco leaf, and it seemed monstrous to him that the old man should be so unconscious of the black cloud that wrapped them all about.

When the boat reached the shore again he leaped scrambling to the beach, and as soon as his dinner was eaten he hurried away to find the Dominie Jones.

He ran all the way from Abrahamson's hut to the parson's house, hardly stopping once, and when he knocked at the door he was panting and sobbing for breath.

The good man was sitting on the back-kitchen doorstep smoking his long pipe of tobacco out into the sunlight, while his wife within was rattling about among the pans and dishes in preparation of their supper, of which a strong, porky smell already filled the air.

Then Tom Chist told his story, panting, hurrying, tumbling one word over another in his haste, and Parson Jones listened, breaking every now and then into an ejac-

ulation of wonder. The light in his pipe went out and the bowl turned cold.

"And I don't see why they should have killed the poor black man," said Tom, as he finished his narrative.

"Why, that is very easy enough to understand," said the good reverend man. "'Twas a treasure box they buried!"

In his agitation Mr. Jones had risen from his seat and was now stumping up and down, puffing at his empty tobacco pipe as though it were still alight.

"A treasure box!" cried out Tom.

"Aye, a treasure box! And that was why they killed the poor black man. He was the only one, d'ye see, besides they two, who knew the place where 'twas hid, and now that they've killed him out of the way, there's nobody but themselves knows. The villains—Tut, tut, look at that now!" In his excitement the dominie had snapped the stem of his tobacco pipe in two.

"Why, then," said Tom, "if that is so, 'tis indeed a wicked, bloody treasure, and fit to bring a curse upon anybody who finds it!"

"'Tis more like to bring a curse upon the soul who buried it," said Parson Jones, "and it may be a blessing to him who finds it. But tell me, Tom, do you think you could find the place again where 'twas hid?"

"I can't tell that," said Tom, "'twas all in among the sand humps, d'ye see, and it was at night into the bargain. Maybe we could find the marks of their feet in the sand," he added.

"'Tis not likely," said the reverend gentleman, "for the storm last night would have washed all that away."

"I could find the place," said Tom, "where the boat was drawn up on the beach."

"Why, then, that's something to start from, Tom," said his friend. "If we can find that, then maybe we can find whither they went from there."

"If I was certain it was a treasure box," cried out Tom Chist, "I would rake over every foot of sand betwixt here and Henlopen to find it."

"'Twould be like hunting for a pin in a haystack," said the Rev. Hilary Jones.

As Tom walked away home, it seemed as though a ton's weight of gloom had been rolled away from his soul. The next day he and Parson Jones were to go treasure-hunting together.

The next afternoon Parson Jones and Tom Chist started off together upon the expedition that made Tom's fortune forever. Tom carried a spade over his shoulder and the reverend gentleman walked along beside him with his cane.

As they jogged along up the beach they talked together about the only thing they could talk about—the treasure box. "And how big did you say 'twas?" quoth the good gentleman.

"About so long," said Tom Chist, measuring off upon the spade, "and about so wide, and this deep."

"And what if it should be full of money, Tom?" said the reverend gentleman, swinging his cane around and around in wide circles in the excitement of the thought as he strode along briskly. "Suppose it should be full of money, what then?"

"By Moses!" said Tom Chist, hurrying to keep up with his friend, "I'd buy a ship for myself, I would, and I'd trade to Injy and to Chiny to my own boot, I would. Suppose the chist was all full of money, sir, and suppose we should find it; would there be enough in it, d'ye suppose, to buy a ship?"

"To be sure there would be enough, Tom: enough and a good big lump over."

"And if I find it 'tis mine to keep, is it, and no mistake?"

"Why, to be sure it would be yours!" cried out the parson, in a loud voice. "To be sure it would be yours!" He knew nothing of the law, but the doubt of the question began at once to ferment in his brain, and he strode along in silence. "Whose else would it be but yours if you find it?" he burst out. "Can you tell me that?"

"If ever I have a ship of my own," said Tom Chist, "and if ever I sail to Injy in her, I'll fetch ye back the best chist of tea, sir, that ever was fetched from Cochin Chiny."

Parson Jones burst out laughing. "Thankee, Tom," he said, "and I'll thankee again when I get my chist of tea. But tell me, Tom, didst thou ever hear of the farmer girl who counted her chickens before they were hatched?"

It was thus they talked as they hurried along up the beach together and so came to a place at last where Tom stopped short and stood looking about him. "'Twas just here," he said, "I saw the boat last night. I know 'twas here, for I mind me of that bit of wreck yonder, and that there was a tall stake drove in the sand just where yon stake stands."

Parson Jones put on his spectacles and went over to the stake toward which Tom pointed. As soon as he had looked at it carefully he called out, "Why, Tom, this hath been just drove down into the sand. 'Tis a brand-new stake of wood, and the pirates must have set it here themselves as a mark, just as they drove the pegs you spoke about down into the sand."

Tom came over and looked at the stake. It was a stout piece of oak nearly two inches thick; it had been shaped with some care, and the top of it had been painted red. He shook the stake and tried to move it, but it had been driven or planted so deeply into the sand that he could not stir it. "Aye, sir," he said, "it must have been set here for a mark, for I'm sure 'twas not here yesterday or the day before." He stood looking about him to see if there were other signs of the pirates' presence.

At some little distance there was the corner of something white sticking up out of the sand. He could see that it was a scrap of paper, and he pointed to it, calling out, "Yonder is a piece of paper, sir. I wonder if they left that behind them?"

It was a miraculous chance that placed that paper there. There was only an inch of it showing, and if it had not been for Tom's sharp eyes, it would certainly have been overlooked and passed by. The next windstorm would have covered it up, and all that afterward happened never would have occurred. "Look, sir," he said, as he struck the sand from it, "it hath writing on it."

"Let me see it," said Parson Jones. He adjusted the spectacles a little more firmly astride of his nose as he took the paper in his hand and began conning it. "What's all this?" he said. "A whole lot of figures and nothing else." And then he read aloud, "'Mark—S.S.W.S. by S.' What d'ye suppose that means, Tom?"

"I don't know, sir," said Tom. "But maybe we can understand it better if you read on."

"'Tis all a great lot of figures," said Parson Jones, "without a grain of meaning in them so far as I can see, unless they be sailing directions." And then he began reading again, "'Mark—S.S.W. by S. 40, 72, 91, 130, 151, 177, 202, 232, 256, 271'—d'ye see, it must be sailing directions—'299, 335, 362, 386, 415, 446, 469, 491, 522, 544, 571, 598'—what a lot of them there be—'626, 652, 676, 695, 724, 851, 876, 905, 940, 967. Peg. S.E. by E. 269 foot. Peg. S.S.W. by S. 427 foot. Peg. Dig to the west of this six foot.'"

"What's that about a peg?" exclaimed Tom. "What's that about a peg? And then there's something about digging, too!" It was as though a sudden light began shining into his brain. He felt himself growing quickly very excited. "Read that over

again, sir," he cried. "Why, sir, you remember I told you they drove a peg into the sand. And don't they say to dig close to it? Read it again, sir—read it again!"

"Peg?" said the good gentleman. "To be sure it was about a peg. Let's look again. Yes, here it is. 'Peg S.E. by E. 269 foot.'"

"Aye!" cried out Tom Chist again, in great excitement. "Don't you remember what I told you, sir, 269 foot? Sure that must be what I saw 'em measuring with the line."

Parson Jones had now caught the flame of excitement that was blazing up so strongly in Tom's breast. He felt as though some wonderful thing was about to happen to them. "To be sure, to be sure!" he called out, in a great big voice. "And then they measured out 427 foot south-southwest by south, and they then drove another peg, and then they buried the box six foot to the west of it. Why, Tom—why, Tom Chist! if we've read this aright, thy fortune is made."

Tom Chist stood staring straight at the old gentleman's excited face, and seeing nothing but it in all the bright infinity of sunshine. Were they, indeed, about to find the treasure chest? He felt the sun very hot upon his shoulders, and he heard the harsh, insistent jarring of a tern that hovered and circled with forked tail and sharp white wings in the sunlight just above their heads; but all the time he stood staring into the good old gentleman's face.

It was Parson Jones who first spoke. "But what do all these figures mean?" And Tom observed how the paper shook and rustled in the tremor of excitement that shook his hand. He raised the paper to the focus of his spectacles and began to read again. "'Mark 40, 72, 91—'"

"Mark?" cried out Tom, almost screaming. "Why, that must mean the stake yonder; that must be the mark." And he pointed to the oaken stick with its red tip blazing against the white shimmer of sand behind it.

"And the 40 and 72 and 91," cried the old gentleman, in a voice equally shrill—"why, that must mean the number of steps the pirate was counting when you heard him."

"To be sure that's what they mean!" cried Tom Chist. "That is it, and it can be nothing else. Oh, come, sir—come, sir; let us make haste and find it!"

"Stay! stay!" said the good gentleman, holding up his hand, and again Tom Chist noticed how it trembled and shook. His voice was steady enough, though very hoarse, but his hand shook and trembled as though with a palsy. "Stay! stay! First of all, we must follow these measurements. And 'tis a marvelous thing," he croaked, after a little pause, "how this paper ever came to be here."

"Maybe it was blown here by the storm," suggested Tom Chist.

"Like enough; like enough," said Parson Jones. "Like enough, after the wretches had buried the chest and killed the poor black man, they were so buffeted and bowsed about by the storm that it was shook out of the man's pocket, and thus blew away from him without his knowing aught of it."

"But let us find the box!" cried out Tom Chist, flaming with his excitement.

"Aye, aye," said the good man, "only stay a little, my boy, until we make sure what we're about. I've got my pocket compass here, but we must have something to measure off the feet when we have found the peg. You run across to Tom Brooke's house and fetch that measuring rod he used to lay out his new barn. While you're gone I'll pace off the distance marked on the paper with my pocket compass."

Tom Chist was gone for almost an hour, though he ran nearly all the way and back, upborne as on the wings of the wind. When he returned, panting, Parson Jones was nowhere to be seen, but Tom saw his footsteps leading away inland, and he followed the scuffling marks in the smooth surface across the sand humps and down into the hollows, and by and by found the good gentleman in a spot he at once knew as soon as he laid his eyes upon it.

It was the open space where the pirates had driven their first peg, and where Tom Chist had afterward seen them kill the poor black man. Tom Chist gazed around as though expecting to see some sign of the tragedy, but the space was as smooth and as undisturbed as a floor, excepting where, midway across it, Parson Jones, who was now stooping over something on the ground, had trampled it all around about.

When Tom Chist saw him he was still bending over, scraping away from something he had found.

It was the first peg!

Inside of half an hour they had found the second and third pegs, and Tom Chist stripped off his coat and began digging like mad down into the sand, Parson Jones standing over him watching him. The sun was sloping well toward the west when the blade of Tom Chist's spade struck upon something hard.

If it had been his own heart that he had hit in the sand his breast could hardly have thrilled more sharply.

It was the treasure box!

Parson Jones himself leaped down into the hole and began scraping away the sand with his hands as though he had gone crazy. At last, with some difficulty, they tugged and hauled the chest up out of the sand to the surface, where it lay covered all over with the grit that clung to it. It was securely locked and fastened with a padlock, and it took a good many blows with the blade of the spade to burst the bolt. Parson Jones himself lifted the lid. Tom

Chist leaned forward and gazed down into the open box. He would not have been surprised to have seen it filled full of yellow gold and bright jewels. It was filled half full of books and papers, and half full of canvas bags tied safely and securely around and around with cords of string.

Parson Jones lifted out one of the bags, and it jingled as he did so. It was full of money.

He cut the string, and with trembling, shaking hands handed the bag to Tom, who, in an ecstasy of wonder and dizzy with delight, poured out with swimming sight upon the coat spread on the ground a cataract of shining silver money that rang and twinkled and jingled as it fell in a shining heap upon the coarse cloth.

Parson Jones held up both hands into the air, and Tom stared at what he saw, wondering whether it was all so, and whether he was really awake. It seemed to him as though he was in a dream.

There were two-and-twenty bags in all in the chest: ten of them full of silver money, eight of them full of gold money, three of them full of gold dust and one small bag with jewels wrapped up in wad cotton and paper.

"'Tis enough," cried out Parson Jones, "to make us both rich as long as we live."

The burning summer sun, though sloping in the sky, beat down upon them as hot as fire, but neither of them noticed it. Neither did they notice hunger nor thirst nor fatigue, but sat there as though in a trance, with the bags of money scattered on the sand around them, a great pile of money heaped upon the coat and the open chest beside them. It was an hour of sundown before Parson Jones had begun fairly to examine the books and papers in the chest.

Of the three books, two were evidently logbooks of the pirates who had been lying off the mouth of the Delaware Bay all this time. The other book was written in Spanish and was evidently the logbook of some captured prize.

It was then, sitting there upon the sand, the good old gentleman reading in his high, cracking voice, that they first learned from the bloody records in those two books who it was who had been lying inside the Cape all this time, and that it was the famous Captain Kidd. Every now and then the reverend gentleman would stop to exclaim, "Oh, the bloody wretch!" or, "Oh, the desperate, cruel villains!" and then would go on reading again a scrap here and a scrap there.

And all the while Tom Chist sat and listened, every now and then reaching out furtively and touching the heap of money still lying upon the coat.

One might be inclined to wonder why Captain Kidd had kept those bloody records. He had probably laid them away because they so incriminated many of the great people of the colony of New York that, with the books in evidence, it would have been impossible to bring the pirate to justice without dragging a dozen or more fine gentlemen into the dock along with him. If he could have kept them in his own possession they would doubtless have been a great weapon of defense to protect him from the gallows. Indeed, when Captain Kidd was finally brought to conviction and hung, he was not accused of his piracies, but of striking a mutinous seaman upon the head with a bucket and accidentally killing him. The authorities did not dare try him for piracy. He was really hung because he was a pirate, and we know that it was the logbooks that Tom Chist brought to New York that did the business for him; he was accused and convicted of manslaughter for killing his own ship carpenter with a bucket.

So Parson Jones, sitting there in the slanting light, read through these terrible records of piracy, and Tom, with the pile of gold and silver money beside him, sat and listened to him.

What a spectacle, if anyone had come upon them! But they were alone, with the vast arch of sky empty above them and the wide white stretch of sand a desert around them. The sun sank lower and lower, until there was only time to glance through the other papers in the chest.

They were nearly all goldsmiths' bills of exchange drawn in favor of certain of the most prominent merchants of New York. Parson Jones, as he read over the names, knew of nearly all the gentlemen by hearsay. Aye, here was this gentleman; he thought that name would be among 'em. What? Here is Mr. So-and-so. Well, if all they say is true, the villain has robbed one of his own best friends. "I wonder," he said, "why the wretch should have hidden these papers so carefully away with the other treasures, for they could do him no good?" Then, answering his own question, "Like enough because these will give him a hold over the gentlemen to whom they are drawn so that he can make a good bargain for his own neck before he gives the bills back to their owners. I tell you what it is, Tom," he continued, "it is you yourself shall go to New York and bargain for the return of these papers. 'Twill be as good as another fortune to you."

The majority of the bills were drawn in favor of one Richard Chillingsworth, Esquire. "And he is," said Parson Jones, "one of the richest men in the province of New York. You shall go to him with the news of what we have found."

"When shall I go?" said Tom Chist.

"You shall go upon the very first boat we can catch," said the parson. He had turned, still holding the bills in his hand, and was now fingering over the pile of money that yet lay tumbled out upon the coat. "I wonder, Tom," said he, "if you could spare me a score or so of these doubloons?"

"You shall have fifty score, if you choose," said Tom, bursting with gratitude and with generosity in his newly found treasure.

"You are as fine a lad as ever I saw, Tom," said the parson, "and I'll thank you to the last day of my life."

Tom scooped up a double handful of silver money. "Take it, sir," he said, "and you may have as much more as you want of it."

He poured it into the dish that the good man made of his hands, and the parson made a motion as though to empty it into his pocket. Then he stopped, as though a sudden doubt had occurred to him. "I don't know that 'tis fit for me to take this pirate money, after all," he said.

"But you are welcome to it," said Tom.

Still the parson hesitated. "Nay," he burst out, "I'll not take it; 'tis blood money." And as he spoke he chucked the whole double handful into the now empty chest, then arose and dusted the sand from his breeches. Then, with a great deal of bustling energy, he helped to tie the bags again and put them all back into the chest.

They reburied the chest in the place whence they had taken it, and then the parson folded the precious paper of directions, placed it carefully in his wallet, and his wallet in his pocket. "Tom," he said, for the twentieth time, "your fortune has been made this day."

And Tom Chist, as he rattled in his

breeches pocket the half dozen doubloons he had kept out of his treasure, felt that what his friend had said was true.

As the two went back homeward across the level space of sand Tom Chist suddenly stopped stock-still and stood looking about him. "'Twas just here," he said, digging his heel down into the sand, "that they killed the poor black man."

"And here he lies buried for all time," said Parson Jones, and as he spoke he dug his cane down into the sand. Tom Chist shuddered. He would not have been surprised if the ferrule of the cane had struck something soft beneath that level surface. But it did not, nor was any sign of that tragedy ever seen again. For, whether the pirates had carried away what they had done and buried it elsewhere, or whether the storm in blowing the sand had completely leveled off and hidden all sign of that tragedy where it was enacted, certain it is that it never came to sight again—at least as far as Tom Chist and the Rev. Hilary Jones ever knew.

This is the story of the treasure box. All that remains now is to conclude the story of Tom Chist and to tell of what came of him in the end.

He did not go back again to live with old Matt Abrahamson. Parson Jones had now taken charge of him and his fortunes, and Tom did not have to go back to the fisherman's hut.

Old Abrahamson talked a great deal about it and would come in his cups and harangue good Parson Jones, making a vast protestation of what he would do to Tom—if he ever caught him—for running away. But Tom on all these occasions kept carefully out of his way, and nothing came of the old man's threatenings.

Tom used to go over to see his foster mother now and then, but always when the old man was from home. And Molly Abra-

hamson used to warn him to keep out of her father's way. "He's in as vile a humor as ever I see, Tom," she said. "He sits sulking all day long, and 'tis my belief he'd kill ye if he caught ye."

Of course Tom said nothing, even to her, about the treasure, and he and the reverend gentleman kept the knowledge thereof to themselves. About three weeks later Parson Jones managed to get him shipped aboard of a vessel bound for New York town, and a few days later Tom Chist landed at that place. He had never been in such a town before, and he could not sufficiently wonder and marvel at the number of brick houses, at the multitude of people coming and going along the fine, hard, earthen sidewalk, at the shops and the stores where goods hung in the windows, and, most of all, the fortifications and the battery at the point, at the rows of threatening cannon, and at the scarlet-coated sentries pacing up and down the ramparts. All this was very wonderful, and so were the clustered boats riding at anchor in the harbor. It was like a new world, so different was it from the sand hills and the sedgy levels of Henlopen.

Tom Chist took up his lodgings at a coffeehouse near to the town hall, and thence he sent by the postboy a letter written by Parson Jones to Master Chillingsworth. In a little while the boy returned with a message, asking Tom to come up to Mr. Chillingsworth's house that afternoon at two o'clock.

Tom went thither with a great deal of trepidation, and his heart fell away altogether when he found it a fine, grand brick house, three stories high, and with wrought-iron letters across the front.

The counting house was in the same building, but Tom, because of Mr. Jones's letter, was conducted directly into the parlor, where the great rich man was awaiting his coming. He was sitting in a leather-covered armchair, smoking a pipe of tobacco, and with a bottle of fine old Madeira close to his elbow.

Tom had not had a chance to buy a new suit of clothes yet, and so he cut no very fine figure in the rough dress he had brought with him from Henlopen. Nor did Mr. Chillingsworth seem to think very highly of his appearance, for he sat looking sideways at Tom as he smoked.

"Well, my lad," he said, "and what is this great thing you have to tell me that is so mightily wonderful? I got what's-his-name—Mr. Jones's—letter, and now I am ready to hear what you have to say."

But if he thought but little of his visitor's appearance at first, he soon changed his sentiments toward him, for Tom had not spoken twenty words when Mr. Chillingsworth's whole aspect changed. He straightened himself up in his seat, laid aside his pipe, pushed away his glass of Madeira and bade Tom take a chair.

He listened without a word as Tom Chist told of the buried treasure, of how he had seen the poor man murdered and of how he and Parson Jones had recovered the chest again. Only once did Mr. Chillingsworth interrupt the narrative. "And to think," he cried, "that the villain this very day walks about New York town as though he were an honest man, ruffling it with the best of us! But if we can only get hold of these log-books you speak of . . . Go on; tell me more of this."

When Tom Chist's narrative was ended, Mr. Chillingsworth's bearing was as different as daylight is from dark. He asked a thousand questions, all in the most polite and gracious tone imaginable, and not only urged a glass of his fine old Madeira upon Tom, but asked him to stay to supper. There was nobody to be there, he said, but his wife and daughter.

Tom, all in a panic at the very thought of the two ladies, sturdily refused to stay even for the dish of tea Mr. Chillingsworth offered him.

He did not know that he was destined to stay there as long as he should live.

"And now," said Mr. Chillingsworth, "tell me about yourself."

"I have nothing to tell, Your Honor," said Tom, "except that I was washed up out of the sea."

"Washed up out of the sea!" exclaimed Mr. Chillingsworth. "Why, how was that? Come, begin at the beginning, and tell me all."

Thereupon Tom Chist did as he was bidden, beginning at the very beginning and telling everything just as Molly Abrahamson had often told it to him. As he continued, Mr. Chillingsworth's interest changed into an appearance of stronger and stronger excitement. Suddenly he jumped up out of his chair and began to walk up and down the room.

"Stop! stop!" he cried out at last, in the midst of something Tom was saying. "Stop! stop! Tell me; do you know the name of the vessel that was wrecked, and from which you were washed ashore?"

"I've heard it said," said Tom Chist, "'twas the *Bristol Merchant*."

"I knew it! I knew it!" exclaimed the great man, in a loud voice, flinging his hands up into the air. "I felt it was so the moment you began the story. But tell me this, was there nothing found with you with a mark or a name upon it?"

"There was a kerchief," said Tom, "marked with a T and a C."

"Theodosia Chillingsworth!" cried out the merchant. "I knew it! I knew it! Heavens! to think of anything so wonderful happening as this! Boy! boy! dost thou know who thou art? Thou art my own brother's son. His name was Oliver Chillingsworth, and he was my partner in business, and thou art his son." Then he ran out into the entryway, shouting and calling for his wife and daughter to come.

So Tom Chist—or Thomas Chillingsworth, as he now was to be called—did stay to supper, after all.

This is the story, and I hope you may like it. For Tom Chist became rich and great, as was to be supposed, and he married his pretty cousin Theodosia (who had been named for his own mother, drowned in the *Bristol Merchant*).

He did not forget his friends, but had Parson Jones brought to New York to live.

As to Molly and Matt Abrahamson, they both enjoyed a pension of ten pounds a year for as long as they lived, for now that all was well with him, Tom bore no grudge against the old fisherman for all the drubbings he had suffered.

The treasure box was brought on to New York, and if Tom Chist did not get all the money there was in it (as Parson Jones had opined he would) he got at least a good big lump of it.

And it is my belief that those logbooks did more to get Captain Kidd arrested in Boston town and hanged in London than anything else that was brought up against him.

The Giant
Who Rode on the Ark

Hurtali was a friendly giant. Without him, who knows what would have happened to Noah and the Ark?

ADRIEN STOUTENBURG

Long ago when the world was so new that the mountains had not been built, and the largest rivers were still unfinished, there were many more giants than there are now. In fact, it has been such a long time since anybody has seen a giant walking around that some people say there are no giants anymore. Maybe not. Since giants are so big, and usually clumsy and noisy, it's hard to know where they could hide without being seen.

Some people say that all the giants who were supposed to have lived thousands of years ago were drowned in the great flood the Bible tells about. That was when the rain fell day after day, night after night, until the entire earth was covered with water. The only human beings who survived were old man Noah and his family, because Noah had built a huge boat known as an ark.

Whether or not giants can be considered human beings is difficult to say. Many of them looked like human beings except for being ten or twenty or even a hundred times bigger. And some of them had two or more heads, and a few had an extra leg. Most of them were said to be horribly mean, and some even ate people for breakfast or dinner, or for a snack at bedtime.

But there were nice giants too. One of these was a freckle-faced giant called Hurtali. It was rather an odd name, but giants had odd names in those days, so Hurtali thought nothing about it. His great-grandfather, the very first giant, was called Chalbroth. His grandfather was Sarabroth. And his father was Faribroth. So, actually, Hurtali's name should have been Hurtalibroth, but that would have been a pretty long name even for a giant.

And Hurtali was truly a giant. He was so tall that his head was in the clouds most of the time, with the result that he often could not see his own toes. As for the ordinary people scrambling around below, he paid no more attention to them than if they had been ants. He had better things to do, like wading out into the ocean until he reached the middle, where the water was deep enough for him to swim. If he happened to be hungry after his swim, he would simply reach out and snatch a whale and hold it up to the sun to roast. When he wanted a green salad, he would pick up a tree and with one swipe of his hand strip off its juicy leaves. Naturally, it took more than one tree to satisfy Hurtali, so whenever he had a fine salad for himself, it meant the end of a whole forest.

Hurtali had no brothers or sisters, and there were no other giants around to be friends with, so at times he was very lonesome. He played games by himself, such as knocking off hunks of mountains and tossing them into the ocean to make a big splash. Or he would leap from cliff to cliff, jumping a mile or more in one leap. He would wade in the deepest rivers and race his own shadow under the sun until he was tired out. Then he would find a valley wide enough and long enough to hold him, and stretch out and sleep for days at a time, snoring so that it sounded like thunder to the little people on earth.

Before the flood began, there was real thunder. Lightning slashed the sky and clouds banged together like great gray ships in the air. The lions in the desert slunk to their caves. The elephants in the jungle huddled together and made deep trumpeting noises. The eagles stayed close to their high nests. None of the creatures knew what was happening, but Noah, who was very, very old, knew, and he and his three sons were working night and day to build a mighty ark. The ark had to be large enough not only for Noah and the others, but so large that it would hold one pair of every kind of animal in the world so that they would be saved from the flood.

Hurtali knew nothing about this. When the rain began to fall he was stretched out in a valley, busily sleeping. Even when he finally woke and felt the hard rain banging down on his freckled nose, he scarcely noticed. It seemed to him like nothing more than a fine mist. Anyhow, he liked water of all kinds, whether it was mist or rain or rivers or oceans. So he just yawned and stretched—accidentally knocking several hills out of place—and went back to sleep. When he woke again, several days later, he did notice that his feet, which were in a low part of the valley, felt rather damp. He looked down the length of his long legs and saw that there was a lake forming around his toes. Some of the tallest trees there were already covered. Hurtali sat up, splashing his feet in the water. It barely covered his ankles but it was pleasant, and the way the lake kept growing it looked as if it would soon be deep enough for a nice wading pool.

Hurtali stood up. The moment he did this his head and shoulders were above the clouds, and the sun shone on him. He strode along, shining from his armpits up, while the rest of him was surrounded by clouds and rain. As he walked and then ran toward the ocean—for he was very hungry for a whale—he noticed that the water in some places sloshed up over his ankles. In a couple of ravines that had always been dry before, it almost reached his knees. At this rate, he thought, he was going to have lots of wading pools. He felt so good about it that he made a two-mile leap across a valley and shouted, "Oggle-oh-bog!" which was his way of saying, "Hooray!"

The rain kept on falling for forty days and nights, and even then it did not cease. Valleys became lakes. The deserts were covered with water. Even many of the hills. In time, the only dry places left were the mountain peaks. For all that he loved swimming and wading, Hurtali began to think that maybe there was getting to be a little too much water. There was hardly a dry place left to stretch out in for a nap, and wherever there was a dry peak there were crowds of animals. It was no problem for Hurtali to flick a lion or even an elephant away with a snap of his little finger, but if he did that the animals would surely drown, and Hurtali liked animals. They were far too small for him to make pets of, but still he had spent many lonely hours watching the tiny antics of the elephants, giraffes and rhinoceroses. So there was nothing to do but try to make room for himself on a mountain peak and settle down among the restless lions, antelope, squirrels, porcupines, apes and birds. He took care not to crush them when he stretched himself out, but several times he accidentally knocked an elephant flat, and once he almost smashed a tiger with his elbow.

Life was becoming hard for Hurtali and he wished that the heavy mist would let up. But the rain-mist grew thicker and the clouds were so high and deep that even when he stood on tiptoe the sun touched only the top of his head.

One day, Hurtali was huddled up on one of the few mountaintops still above water, trying to get in a good snooze. The animals, as usual, were pressed all around him. Even though the lion's roar or the elephant's blare usually sounded only like squeaks to Hurtali, there were so many lions and elephants and other creatures milling around him now that all their snarls, barks, whines, whistles and grunts made a din loud enough to bother even him. It was partly because of the noise and partly because of waves and foam washing up as high as his waist that he woke after only about ten hours of sleep. He sat up, rubbing his eyes, grumbling over his short nap and wondering what he should do to amuse himself. There really wasn't much to do any more except swim. A couple of ravens and a thrush that had been resting on his head flew off with a squawk, looking for some other dry spot to roost.

Hurtali was still sitting, thinking, when suddenly he saw a strange object in the distance. He could see it clearly because it was as large as a blue whale—and except for him, blue whales were the largest creatures in the world. But this creature, or whatever it was, was made of wood. It seemed to be caught against the peak of a mountain that thrust up a little way above the floodwaters.

The young giant had never seen an ark before, but he had seen fallen trees stuck against river rocks just as this strange wooden object was. Often he had floated logs in streams for the fun of watching them, and when he could find a large enough log—which was very seldom—he would straddle it and have a ride.

Whatever the strange object out there in the water was, perhaps he could ride it! But first he would have to free it from the rocks. In his excitement over a new plaything he stood up so quickly that he knocked aside a whole troop of monkeys, a dozen zebras and a herd of buffalo.

"Jing-oh-juggy," said Hurtali, which was his way of saying, "I'm sorry." Then he dived into the water and swam with mighty strokes toward the ark. As he drew closer, he could see that it had windows all around and a roof with a square opening out of which came some puffs of smoke. When he was alongside the ark, he heard snarls, barks, whines, whistles and grunts, just like those back on the mountain peak. He glanced behind him, believing that the animals must have followed him. No, they were still where he had left them.

Hurtali scarcely knew what to think —and he had never liked to think much, anyhow. He set himself to trying to free the ark by rocking it back and forth. It went up and down like a huge teeter-totter, but it stuck fast on the rocks of the mountain peak. The animals inside squeaked and howled louder than ever. Along with their voices were sounds Hurtali had never heard before. They were faint chirping sounds, but not like the chirping of birds. Such chirping Hurtali knew well, for once a bluebird had built its nest in a rim of his ear.

Suddenly, something looked out at him from one of the window openings in the wooden whale, then ducked back. Hurtali was so startled at the sight that he gulped in a wave. When he spat it out, coughing and sputtering, the ark rocked as in a hurricane. The creature that had looked out at him had eyes and ears and a nose like his own, except that they were very tiny compared to his. He felt a leap of joy. Maybe he had found a baby giant! He turned five somersaults in the water, out of happiness, but during the fifth somersault he remembered that even when he had been a baby himself he had been a hundred times larger than the creature who had looked at him from the ark.

Hurtali wiped the ocean water and rainwater from his eyes and went back to work trying to free the ark. He decided at last that the best thing to do was to throw one leg over the object as if it were a log and see if he could push the contraption off the peak with a shove of his feet. He straddled it easily, though the wood creaked under his weight. Then, with one leg hanging down farther than the other, he groped with his bare toes, searching for a footing. There! Deep down there was a solid ridge of the mountain under his left foot. Hurtali gave a mighty shove. The ark trembled, wobbled, and then, with a rasping of its keel, lurched forward. Another lurch and it was free, bobbing crazily on all the waves Hurtali had stirred up. Hurtali paddled furiously with both feet and then saw that there was another mountain peak sticking up ahead. He leaned back, one hand clinging to the roof of the ark, the other thrust down into the waves. By flapping his hand

in the water like the tail of a fish, he managed to steer the ark safely past the mountain.

Now there was nothing but water ahead, stretching from sky to sky. Hurtali stopped paddling, letting the ark drift along through the rain and wind. It was really very pleasant to have something like this to ride, he thought, although he was growing terribly hungry after all his exercise.

He was wondering whether he could reach out and catch a whale to eat, when a head poked out of one of the windows slightly below his right knee. The head was the same as he had seen before, a long white beard hanging from its chin. The head was chirping up at him, though what it said Hurtali could not tell.

"Praise to thee, noble giant," old Noah was saying. "We thank thee for thy great help, I and my wife and my three sons, Shem, Ham and Japheth, and their three wives and all the host of animals that are with me from the flood."

Seven other heads popped out from seven other windows.

Hurtali could understand none of this, but the chirping voice, so low that he had to bend down to hear, had a friendly sound. Because it seemed impolite not to answer, he boomed a greeting, "Hingle-oh-hig!" in response. The sound shook the ship, started the animals shrieking and cawing again and made the eight heads all bob back inside the openings.

The little people remained hidden for a long while and Hurtali wondered what he had done wrong. His feelings were a bit hurt at the way the tiny people had scurried out of sight, and he was of half a mind to slip off the ark and let it take itself to wherever it was going. Also, he was becoming so hungry he was almost tempted to start gnawing on the gopher wood of the ark's roof. He sulked and brooded and now and then gave a good kick with his feet to make the ark jolt up and down. Partly he enjoyed the rocking motion; partly he wanted to remind the feeble little people below that he was still there.

He was about to swim away in search of a tasty whale when there was some movement near the square hole where he had seen puffs of smoke earlier. The hole was, in fact, an opening like a chimney above a hearth where Noah's family did its cooking. There, rising up through the hole, was the bearded old man, riding on the head of a giraffe. Long though the animal's spotted neck was, the giraffe had to stretch to put Noah on the roof beside Hurtali. The old man chirped something that Hurtali could scarcely hear; it was like a white-bearded cricket speaking. The giraffe lowered its

head, and in the shadows below, Hurtali could dimly see the tiny people scurrying about. The giraffe raised its head, stretched up on its hoofs again, and there on its nose was a huge platter of food. Noah removed the platter and placed it before Hurtali.

"We have brought much food," Noah said, "for the journey may be longer than we know. We are pleased to share it with thee."

Again the giraffe lowered its neck, then raised it once more with another bowl of food.

Hurtali was too surprised and grateful to exclaim more than "Og—!" before he began gulping the food. Time after time,

the giraffe lifted more bowls and platters. There were porridges and puddings, and shanks of meat, enough for a feast for a hundred ordinary human beings. Even so, when Hurtali had licked every plate and sucked the marrow out of the bones of roasted sheep, goats and steers, he was still hungry. So, when Noah had gone below again, Hurtali waited until a whale glided near the ark. He reached out and hauled it in. Since there was no sunlight, he shrugged and gobbled it raw.

The rain kept falling, that day and the next and the day thereafter. Even though there was no sunlight, there was a gray light by day. But at night, without moon or stars, the world of water and sky was totally black. Those were the loneliest times

for Hurtali, riding astride the ark, paddling it forward steadily, using his hand as a rudder. At the beginning, his feet would often brush the tops of drowned mountains. Now there was nothing but water. And in spite of the food the giraffe lifted to him each day, he was often hungry. He did not like to snatch whales when any of Noah's family was watching, for fear they would think he did not appreciate what they fed him. So he did most of his whale hunting at night, though it was hard to see. This, together with his work of paddling and steering the ark, meant that he had no chance to take the long naps he loved.

Once in a while he wondered about all the animals that had been left on the mountain peak where he had last slept. That mountain, like all others, would have been flooded over by now. But perhaps, somewhere, there were higher peaks where they had found safety. Often he thought he should leave the ark and go in search of those peaks, no matter how far he might have to swim. No ocean, in the past, had been too wide for him to cross. But something held him to the ark, even when his powerful legs grew tired and his steering hand numb from the cold sea.

Then one day there was a pale glimmer of light through the clouds. Up there, somewhere, the sun was shining. With a joyful shout, so loud that it made the people in the ark think that new thunder was booming, Hurtali reared up on his knees. He almost upset the ark as he did so, but as he straightened up, his shoulders cleared the clouds and he felt warm sunlight on his head and neck. He cried out, "Agra-oogh!"—the greatest expression of joy he knew. Below, Noah and Mrs. Noah, Shem, Ham and Japheth, and their three wives —and even some of the animals—all covered their ears to keep their eardrums from shattering from the boom of Hurtali's

voice. Then Noah and his family rushed to the eight windows, each peering out and up at the sky. They shouted so loudly in their excitement that even Hurtali could hear them, though his head was above the clouds.

The clouds began to fade away—Hurtali knocked some of them across the sky with his fists—and soon there was not even a scrap of a cloud to be seen. Sunlight gleamed and sparkled, danced and jigged, on every ripple. It flooded the ark and streamed through the windows, warming the people and the animals there.

Day by day, the water sank lower and a warm wind blew. Still there was no sight of land. But then, after more days had passed, one of Hurtali's paddling feet struck something hard. He looked down through the water and there, about a thousand feet below the ark, was a mountain peak. It was so wonderful to see a mountain again, even though it was underwater, that Hurtali gave a bounce of joy that nearly wrecked the ark's roof and sent all the kettles and pans in Mrs. Noah's kitchen clattering onto the floor. Old man Noah himself ran to his window and chirped up at Hurtali in an angry way.

The next time Hurtali's feet grazed a mountain peak—a peak that was much closer to the surface of the water than the other peak had been—he tried not to shout too loudly or bounce so hard. But the day he saw a mountain peak actually shining above the water he was so excited he fell right off the ark. The terrific splash he created nearly drowned everybody and everything in the ship.

"Jing-oh-juggy," he said as he climbed carefully back onto the ark's roof, trying to whisper that he was sorry. But even his whisper sounded like a roar.

More days went by, and finally hills began to show above the water, and then trees. Hurtali was able to reach out across the miles of water and pull up a few trees for the first fresh salad he had had in months. He yearned to swim toward the distant peaks and hills and go leaping about—or, even better, stretch himself out and sleep. For he was becoming very tired of paddling and steering the ark. Also, he was lonesome. He liked the little people below, but he could not talk to them. Yet, every time he decided to leave, something held him back. And so he kept rowing the ark onward; at the same time he kept watching the distant peaks and hills, hoping to see another giant like himself somewhere.

Then, a hundred and fifty days since the great flood had begun, something tall and mighty showed dimly on the horizon. Hurtali's heart knocked hard and fast, for the great object, he thought, must be a giant. It was about seventeen thousand feet high, certainly a giant big enough to talk to. Hurtali paddled his feet so swiftly that the ark seemed to fly across the water. Then he slowed down, slower and slower, until the ark was almost standing still. The thing standing high above the water was a giant of stone, being simply another mountain peak.

Even so, Hurtali could not give up his dream. The mountain was certainly big enough to hold a giant, and it had wonderful, wide places to sleep in—or would have as soon as the water went down. So he steered toward it, paddling swiftly again. Only when the ark came near the peak did he slow down. Carefully, he eased the ark toward a smooth shelf of the mountain. Then he slid from the roof as gently as possible and stood on the mountain's lower slope, with the water around his waist. He pushed the ark forward, and when its prow was almost against the rock shelf, he lifted it and set it softly on the dry land.

The people in the ark were all at the windows watching. And the animals, who had their own windows on the other side, were watching too. The giraffe had his long neck thrust out, the elephant was waving his trunk, and a lion and his mate were both trying to push their heads through one window at the same time.

But nobody left the ark, for half the mountain was still covered with water and there was not enough dry ground yet for all the animals to roam and leap and wander on. And there was nothing for the goats and cattle and sheep to graze on, since the lower slopes where grass, trees and other plants grew were still under the ocean. It was not very comfortable for Hurtali either, for when he stretched out on the peak for a snooze, the water sloshed around his hips. He managed to nap, anyhow, for about a week. When he woke, the water was down to his knees, which was a little better. He dozed off again, and the next time he opened his eyes, many days later, he saw old man Noah at his window, holding a dove in his hands. Noah tossed the dove into the air and the bird flew off.

It was all very strange to Hurtali. He put his head in his hands and tried to think. He was still thinking when, at the end of the day, the dove returned. In its beak was an olive leaf. Noah and his family chirped and babbled as if this was something to be very excited about. Hurtali thought some more. He thought so hard it kept him awake for almost two hours. Finally, he realized what was going on. He could look out and see the faraway hills rising above the water and all the olive trees glittering on them. But the tiny people could not look out over the world the way he could. They did not know that there were leaves and grass on some of the higher hills that were slowly rising above the floodwaters. Mount Ararat, where the ark was, was still only a great spire of rock without trees or grass.

There was no way that Hurtali could tell the little people that the green land was coming back all around. Anyhow, they could not swim and leap from one green hill to another as he could. They had to wait until all the water disappeared before they could walk out onto the land again.

Now that he no longer needed to take care of the ark, Hurtali waded through the lakes and what was left of the flood ocean, leaped from one mountaintop to another and kept searching for a giant friend as big as he. But whenever he was through with swimming, leaping and catching whales, he returned to the mountain where the ark stood. And so he was there seven days later, when Noah sent the dove flapping into the air again. The dove did not return—not that night or the next or the night after.

It was then that Noah and his wife, and Shem, Ham and Japheth and their wives walked out of the ark, for they knew that the dove had found a safe home in the new, green land, and that the waters were gone. Noah released the dove's mate so that the two doves could start nest-building to raise many more doves. Next, he opened the doors of the ark, and the animals began to stream out, blinking in the sunlight, leaping, hopping and flying down the mountainside to the green slopes at its base and toward the forests beyond.

Hurtali, standing nearby, squatted down to have a closer look at the creatures streaming out across the landscape. Many of them such as mosquitoes and ladybugs, wrens and caterpillars, were far too small for him to see. Even so, he realized that there was a mighty procession of its kind.

"We thank thee again, noble giant," Noah was chirping up at him. Hurtali did not understand, but he answered, "Laggle-oh-lig," in a sad voice. For he saw Noah and the other human beings turning away, following the creatures down the mountain, and a new sense of loneliness seized him.

At last there was nobody but Hurtali left on the mountain—he and the empty ark. He stood looking at it. Suddenly a beautiful light appeared in the sky. It shone over the world and then it rippled and flowed together to make the shape of a tremendous arch stretching from one end of the earth to the other. The colors of the arch were pink, yellow, lavender, green—all the colors of the rainbow, for that was what it was.

Hurtali had never seen a rainbow before. To him it appeared like a marvelous bridge, large enough for a giant to walk upon. Perhaps, he thought, it had even been built by a giant standing out of sight at the rainbow's end. But the end of the rainbow was very far away, too far even for a swimmer as strong as he. He looked at the ark again and then, with a gleeful shout, he picked it up, carried it down the mountain and across the green land to where the salty ocean foamed against the shore. He waded out until he had reached deep water. There he set the ark afloat and straddled it, paddling away once more with his feet.

Whether Hurtali found the end of the rainbow, or a giant friend there, nobody knows. Maybe. Maybe not. All that anyone knows for certain is that Noah's ark is gone from Mount Ararat, and that the rainbow that appeared at the end of the flood returns often when a rainstorm is over, like a shining promise.

How to Tell Corn Fairies
if You See 'Em

*Perhaps you didn't know it—or never thought
about it—but if there were no corn fairies, we wouldn't
have any fields of ripe, golden corn*

CARL SANDBURG

If you have ever watched the little corn begin to march across the black lands and then slowly change to big corn and go marching on from the little corn moon of summer to the big corn harvest moon of autumn, then you must have guessed who it is that helps the corn come along. It is the corn fairies. Leave out the corn fairies and there wouldn't be any corn.

All children know this. All boys and girls know that corn is no good unless there are corn fairies.

Have you ever stood in Illinois or Iowa and watched the late summer wind or the early fall wind running across a big cornfield? It looks as if a big, long blanket were being spread out for dancers to come and dance on. If you look close and if you listen close you can see the corn fairies come dancing and singing—sometimes. If it is a wild day and a hot sun is pouring down while a cool north wind blows—and this happens sometimes—then you will be sure to see thousands of corn fairies marching and countermarching in mocking grand marches over the big, long blanket of green

and silver. Then too they sing, only you must listen with your littlest and newest ears if you wish to hear their singing. They sing soft songs that go pla-sizzy pla-sizzy-sizzy, and each song is softer than an eye wink, softer than a Nebraska baby's thumb.

And Spink, who is a little girl living in the same house with the man writing this story, and Skabootch, who is another little girl in the same house—both Spink and Skabootch are asking the question, "How can we tell corn fairies if we see 'em? If we meet a corn fairy how will we know it?" And this is the explanation the man gave to Spink who is older than Skabootch, and to Skabootch who is younger than Spink:—

All corn fairies wear overalls. They work hard, the corn fairies, and they are proud. The reason they are proud is because they work so hard. And the reason they work so hard is because they have overalls.

But understand this. The overalls are corn gold cloth, woven from leaves of ripe corn mixed with ripe October corn silk. In the first week of the harvest moon coming

215

up red and
changing to yellow and silver
the corn fairies sit by thousands between
the corn rows weaving and stitching the
clothes they have to wear next winter, next
spring, next summer.

They sit cross-legged when they sew.
And it is a law among them each one must
point the big toe at the moon while sewing
the harvest moon clothes. When the moon
comes up red as blood early in the evening
they point their big toe slanting toward the
east. Then towards midnight when the
moon is yellow and halfway up the sky
their big toes are only half slanted as they
sit cross-legged sewing. And after midnight
when the moon sails its silver disk high
overhead and toward the west, then the
corn fairies sit sewing with their big toes
pointed nearly straight up.

If it is a cool night and looks like frost,
then the laughter of the corn fairies is
something worth seeing. All the time they
sit sewing their next year clothes they are
laughing. It is not a law they have to laugh.
They laugh because they are half-tickled
and glad because it is a good corn year.

And whenever the corn fairies laugh
then the laugh comes out of the mouth like
a thin gold frost. If you should be lucky
enough to see a thousand corn fairies sitting between the corn rows and all of them
laughing, you would laugh with wonder
yourself to see the gold frost coming from
their mouths.

Travelers who have traveled far and seen
many things say that if you know the corn

fairies with a real knowledge you can always tell by the stitches in their clothes what state they are from.

In Illinois the corn fairies stitch fifteen stitches of ripe corn silk across the woven corn-leaf cloth. In Iowa they stitch sixteen stitches, in Nebraska seventeen, and the farther west you go the more corn silk stitches the corn fairies have in the corn-cloth clothes they wear.

In Minnesota one year there were fairies with a blue sash of cornflowers across the breast. In the Dakotas the same year all the fairies wore pumpkin-flower neckties, yellow four-in-hands and yellow ascots. And in one strange year it happened in both the states of Ohio and Texas the corn fairies wore little wristlets of white morning glories.

The traveler who heard about this asked many questions and found out the reason why that year the corn fairies wore little wristlets of white morning glories. He said, "Whenever fairies are sad they wear white. And this year, which was long ago, was the year men were tearing down all the old zigzag rail fences. Now those old zigzag rail fences were beautiful for the fairies because a hundred fairies could sit on one rail and thousands and thousands of them could sit on the zigzags and sing pla-sizzy pla-sizzy, softer than an eyewink, softer than a baby's thumb, all on a moonlight summer night. And they found out that year was going to be the last year of the zigzag rail fences. It made them sorry and sad, and when they are sorry and sad they wear white. So they picked the wonderful white morning glories running along the zigzag rail fences and made them into little wristlets and wore those wristlets the next year to show they were sorry and sad."

Of course, all this helps you to know how the corn fairies look in the evening, the night time and the moonlight. Now we shall see how they look in the day time.

In the day time the corn fairies have their overalls of corn gold cloth on. And they walk among the corn rows and climb the corn stalks and fix things in the leaves and stalks and ears of the corn. They help it to grow.

Each one carries on the left shoulder a mouse brush to brush away the field mice. And over the right shoulder each one has a cricket broom to sweep away the crickets. The brush is a whisk brush to brush away mice that get foolish. And the broom is to sweep away crickets that get foolish.

Around the middle of each corn fairy is a yellowbelly-belt. And stuck in this belt is a purple moon shaft hammer. Whenever the wind blows strong and nearly blows the corn down, then the fairies run out and take their purple moon shaft hammers out of their yellowbelly-belts and nail down nails to keep the corn from blowing down. When a rain storm is blowing up terrible and driving all kinds of terribles across the cornfield, then you can be sure of one thing. Running like the wind among the corn rows are the fairies, jerking their purple moon shaft hammers out of their belts and nailing nails down to keep the corn standing up so it will grow and be ripe and beautiful when the harvest moon comes again in the fall.

Spink and Skabootch ask where the corn fairies get the nails. The answer to Spink and Skabootch is, "Next week you will learn all about where the corn fairies get the nails to nail down the corn if you will keep your faces washed and your ears washed till next week."

And the next time you stand watching a big cornfield in late summer or early fall, when the wind is running across the green and silver, listen with your littlest and newest ears. Maybe you will hear the corn fairies going pla-sizzy pla-sizzy-sizzy, softer than an eye wink, softer than a Nebraska baby's thumb.

217

Christmas
in the
Street of Memories

Any Christmas morning is exciting.
But this one was especially
joyous because they were going
to give the Prince
and Princess to Mrs. Lavendar

ELIZABETH RHODES JACKSON

The Prince and Princess lived with Mr. Lifsky on the street floor, and we live on the next floor, and old Mrs. Lavendar lives on the top floor.

We first got acquainted with Mrs. Lavendar by accident. The accident happened to Beany.

There are three of us. Jack is my older brother and Beany is my younger brother. I am Dee and I am just eleven.

We live on one of the oldest streets in Boston at the foot of Beacon Hill. The houses have alleys at the back or through their cellars, and we play tag in them. The alleys all run into each other and make a sort of maze. You run up an alley and climb over a couple of fences and down another alley and through a gate and there you are in another street. We were all playing one day after school, and Beany went to climb a fence and fell, right on his face. Beany would, you know. He's always the one of us that has the falls. He bruised his forehead and skinned his nose. He was very brave about it and didn't cry, although there were tears in his eyes.

We took him home, Jack and I, but when

we took Beany upstairs to our landing, the door was locked and Mother was out. Beany had been brave so long that he couldn't wait any longer, and while I was fumbling in the regular place for the key, he burst out into a long, sad wail. Then a lady on the floor above, who was a stranger to us, leaned over the banister and said, "Bring him up to me."

Her apartment was very lovely with beautiful old furniture and soft, thick rugs on the floor and huge silver candlesticks on the mantel. But there was no fire in the fireplace, though the day was cold, and she had on a beautiful white silk shawl with an embroidered border. She took Beany on her lap and washed the dirt off his face very gently. Then she held him in her arms and we sat on the rug, and she told us about her son when he was a little boy.

That was how we got acquainted with Mrs. Lavendar. And that was the way we came to find the Prince and the Princess.

Mother calls the street we live on the Street of Memories for two reasons. One is that memories of the past are still living there. Two blocks from our house, at the corner of Boston Common, is the spot where the British soldiers embarked the night that Paul Revere got ahead of them on his famous ride. Two blocks the other way Oliver Wendell Holmes used to live.

The other reason Mother calls it the Street of Memories is because of the antique shops all up and down the street. Some of them are very artistic, with nothing but two colonial chairs and a table in the window. But we like best the ones that have the windows crowded full of new and interesting things. Mr. Lifsky's is like that, on the street floor of our house. His show window is just jammed with three ship models and some colored bottles, and a battered old lantern, and andirons and silhouettes in tiny frames and an inlaid snuffbox and a pair of china dogs and a luster tea set, and hanging up are old engravings and faded samplers.

We were all three looking into Mr. Lifsky's window one day when Mrs. Lavendar came out and saw us there. We knew her very well by that time.

"Mrs. Lavendar, do see this ship's model," said Jack.

"It looks like all sorts of adventures," she said, and then she caught her breath a little.

"How long have those been here?" she said. "I haven't seen them before."

She was pointing to a pair of china figures, a lady and gentleman in elaborate old-fashioned dress. The lady had wide skirts and high powdered hair and flowers on her breast, and the gentleman had a ruffled shirt and knee breeches and buckled shoes. They were tiny but very perfect and delicate, and the faces were exquisitely beautiful.

"I'm sure those are mine," said Mrs. Lavendar very low. Then she walked into Mr. Lifsky's shop.

"She's going in to buy them," we said, but presently she came out without them.

We told Mother about it. "Why do you think she didn't buy them?" asked Jack.

"Probably Mr. Lifsky's price was too high," said Mother.

"Oh, but Mrs. Lavendar is rich," said Beany. "You ought to see her beautiful apartment."

"I'm afraid not," said Mother. "She used to have a great deal of money, but now she is old and poor and alone. Her son gave up his life in the war, you know."

"I wonder if that is why she doesn't have a fire in the fireplace," I said, for we often went up to see her now, and her apartment was usually cold. Of course, the house is supposed to be heated from the cellar, but we always have two log fires going in winter to help out. Our house is a beautiful old residence that has been made over into apartments, so the plumbing and heating are old-fashioned and often cause us trouble.

A week later we had cold weather. Cold weather in Boston is *very* cold. I don't believe even the North Pole is any colder than the Street of Memories in winter!

"I was going to suggest your going up to see Mrs. Lavendar," said Mother, when we came home from school, "but it is so cold, perhaps you'd better take a fire with you."

I followed her up the stairs and heard her saying, "Mrs. Lavendar, would it bother you if the children made a little call?"

"I'd love to have them," said Mrs. Lavendar, "only I'm afraid the room is rather cold. I can't seem to get enough heat."

"It's a frightful heating system, isn't it?" said Mother. "We've had to have a hearth-fire today. Jack will bring up some wood, if you don't mind the litter."

So soon we were on the way up, Jack with a basket of logs and Beany carrying the paper bag of kindling and I with the hearth brush. Beany, poor child, tripped over the rug and dropped the bag, which split open, but Mrs. Lavendar was very nice about it, and I swept up the debris and it was all right. Jack made a glorious fire and we were very cozy. Knowing Mother, I suspect she planned the whole thing just to get Mrs. Lavendar warm.

While we were all sitting there as happy as could be, Beany suddenly spoke up. Beany too frequently says things he shouldn't and what he said this time was, "Mrs. Lavendar, how did your china figures come to be in Mr. Lifsky's antique shop?"

We tried to hush him, but Mrs. Lavendar said, "I sold all the furnishings of my house some years ago, except what I have here, and the little Prince and Princess went with the rest."

"Are they a Prince and Princess?" I asked.

"That was the name my boy had for them when he was little." And somehow, from the way she said it, I knew that she missed the little china figures.

Then Beany piped up again. "Why did you have to sell your furniture, Mrs. Lavendar, when you have so much money?"

We couldn't hush him at all, but Mrs. Lavendar understood and she only smiled and said, "I haven't much money, dear. I had some, but it was taken from me. So I had to sell the furniture to get money to live on."

"How was it taken?" said Beany, all interest.

"It isn't a very pleasant story," said Mrs. Lavendar. "My investments were in a business that could not go on until the war was over."

Beany nodded, though he didn't understand. We did partly.

"My son's salary was enough for us till he went to war. Then we planned to sell our house and invest the money to take care of me till he came back."

"I see," said Beany.

"My son came in with the money from the sale one afternoon. He wouldn't take a check because sometimes checks can't be collected. He went to the bank with the man who bought the house, and the man drew the money in bills and gave it to him—forty thousand dollars. It was too late to take the money to my bank for deposit that day, so he brought it home to me, and it was taken that same day."

"Who took it?" we said together.

"I never knew," said Mrs. Lavendar. "Not the servants. They had been with me for years. Someone must have come in—but I don't know how. It has always been a mystery."

"Where was it?" we asked.

"In the Governor Winthrop desk," said

old Mrs. Lavendar. "That very desk there against the wall. My son said, 'I'll put it in here, Mother.' I saw him with his hand on the open leaf of the desk. I said, 'Yes, that's a perfectly safe place.' I went out to see my son off then, and I was so confused and troubled over parting with him that I forgot to lock it. And when I went to get the money next day to take it to the bank, it was not there."

"This very desk!" said Jack. We were all very much excited, for we knew that some of those old desks have secret drawers and false backs to the pigeonholes. It seemed perfectly clear to us that there were forty thousand dollars somewhere inside that solid square old piece of mahogany, and if we could find it, Mrs. Lavendar would be rich again. We told her so very excitedly, but she shook her head.

"I've known this desk all my life, dears," she said. "It was my great-grandfather's. I know every nook and corner of it. It has no secrets."

"May we look through it?" we said. "We might be able to find *something.*"

Of course, Mrs. Lavendar let us, and we took out all the papers and the drawers, and measured and tapped and pushed to find secret springs. But we had to give it up at last. If the money was still there, hidden in some secret place, it was too successfully hidden for us to find.

I noticed that the beautiful silver candlesticks were not on the mantel, and Mrs. Lavendar was wearing a little black sweater instead of the embroidered shawl. I was afraid Beany would notice and ask if she had to sell them, too, but he was too interested in the desk to ask questions about anything else.

For several days we talked about the money and then we forgot all about it for a while, because of Christmas. We were busy as could be, writing our Christmas wants and making things and counting our savings and going shopping for presents after school. We all painted cards for Mrs. Lavendar, of course, and it was while we were doing this, one snowy day, that I said, "Oh, dear, I wish we could buy the Prince and Princess and give them to Mrs. Lavendar for Christmas!"

"That's just like you, Dee," said Jack. "One of those brilliant ideas that there's no way of carrying out!"

I knew he didn't mean that to sound unpleasant. It was just that he wanted so much to do it and didn't see how we could.

"Let's ask Mr. Lifsky how much they are, anyway!" said Beany.

Beany is always so hopeful. Jack and I knew it was useless, because we had already spent all our money for Christmas. But Beany went down to ask Mr. Lifsky and came back soon to tell us.

"Seven dollars and fifty cents." He said it just as cheerfully as if we had seven dollars and fifty cents right there.

And then something very unexpected happened. We were playing tag in the back alley a few days later and by mistake we tipped over an ash barrel. When we went to pick up the junk we had spilled, we found some old bundles of letters tied with faded ribbon and photographs and some good camera films. Someone had just moved out of the house, and there was no one there but a cleaning woman. We showed her the films and asked if we could have them, and she said we could have anything we found in the back yard, but we must clean up any rubbish we spilled. There were four or five barrels in the yard and we dumped them all out, one after another, and found a number of very worthwhile articles. But the really important thing was two filled books of trading stamps, and when we saw those, we knew, after all, that there was hope of our buying the Prince and Princess.

We took the stamps home to Mother and she said they were worth two dollars for each book and that it would be all right for Jack to go and get the money for them, as otherwise they would be burned for rubbish. So while Jack hurried off across the Common to the department stores, Beany and I went back to dig again for buried treasure. We didn't find anything else in the barrels, but Beany spied a row of store milk bottles, and we gathered those up and took them back to the chain store. There were twenty-one of them, and that gave us a dollar and five cents, so when Jack came back with the trading stamp money, we had five dollars and five cents altogether.

"Perhaps Mr. Lifsky would come down," said Jack. "People always do bargain for antiques, you know."

So we took the five one-dollar bills and the nickel and showed them to Mr. Lifsky. We told him that was all the money we had and asked if he would sell us the pair of china figures. We couldn't pay another cent for them.

"For five dollars and five cents you ask for them!" said Mr. Lifsky indignantly. Seven-fifty is my price, and not one cent less than five-fifty."

"We haven't got five-fifty," said Jack.

"Five-fifty!" Mr. Lifsky said again, so we went out to talk it over.

"We almost have it," said Jack. "Only forty-five cents. Let's all think hard."

So we all thought hard. But it was Beany who thought of asking Mother to advance forty-five cents of our pocket money. There was a great shout of joy from us all when he came back with it. We went right in to Mr. Lifsky's and bought the Prince and Princess. They were a little bit dusty, and Jack thought we ought to put them into the bathtub and wash them. But Mother thought not, because we might chip them or wash off the color, and Mrs. Lavendar would know best how to clean

them. Then we started to wrap them in Christmas paper, but we were afraid that Mrs. Lavendar might break them in opening them. Besides it would be more fun to have her see them right away, the minute she opened the door.

Jack wanted to be the one to carry the Prince and I wanted to carry the Princess, and Beany felt very bad about it.

"It's just because I'm the youngest," he said. "I have to take turns with you filling the wood-basket and going to the store, but no one ever takes turns with me being the youngest. I thought how to get the last forty-five cents anyway. And Mrs. Lavendar was my friend first."

So we told him he could be the one to say, "Merry Christmas, Mrs. Lavendar; we've brought you a present." So it was settled.

Christmas Eve is very beautiful on Beacon Hill. All the houses are lighted with candles in every window, and the curtains are drawn back so that everyone can see the inside. The houses are all very beautiful to see, too, because most of them were built in early days and have winding staircases and paneled walls, and many of them have beautiful tapestries and paintings. A great crowd comes from all over Boston, so that you can hardly move through the streets, but everyone is quiet and reverent. It is almost like church outdoors, especially after the carols begin. Mother always takes us out for a little while, after we have lighted the candles in our own windows.

This Christmas Eve we asked Mrs. Lavendar to go out with us, but she thought she might get too tired. So when we came back, we three sang carols just for her—"Silent Night, Holy Night" and "The First Noel"—looking up at the candles in her windows.

It is such an exciting feeling to wake on Christmas morning and see the stockings all humpy. But this Christmas I had a specially joyous feeling, and I remembered we were going to take the Prince and Princess to Mrs. Lavendar.

Right after breakfast we went upstairs, Jack carrying the Prince and I carrying the Princess, just as we had planned. But half-way upstairs I caught a glimpse of Beany's face. He had a scratch across his chin where the grocer's cat had scratched him when he tried to pet her, and he had such a sad look that I was sorry for him. It must be hard to be the youngest. So I said, "Here, Beany, you can carry her," and handed him the Princess.

We got to the top of the stairs and Jack looked around and saw how it was, and he said, "Oh, well," and he put the Prince into my hands. So after all it was Jack who lifted the brass knocker and said, "Merry Christmas, Mrs. Lavendar; we've brought you a present."

But when she saw the Prince and Princess, she said, "Oh, you dear children!" very softly.

Then she said, "Their home is on the desk, dears, one on each side of my son's picture." I walked across the room and put the Prince on the desk very carefully, and Beany came next.

But then Beany slipped and down he came—crash!—on the floor. Beany *would!*

Mrs. Lavendar stooped over the pieces.

"I am sure we can mend the Princess," she was saying and then she gasped and picked up something from under the pieces.

It was a roll of bills that had been inside the hollow Princess.

"The money was not taken," she said slowly. "It was there all the time."

She sat down and her hands were trembling.

"I begin to understand," she said. "My son was standing by the desk. I never thought of the Princess. But of course he would put it there. From the time he was a baby he used to stow all sorts of little treasures through that hole in the base. He thought of course that I saw him putting it there and that no one else would know."

We had a great rejoicing after that, and since then Mrs. Lavendar hasn't gone out to do sewing any more. The silver candlesticks are back on the mantel and she wears the white silk shawl and has a fire, too, on cold days. And she has mended the Princess with china cement so you can't see the cracks at all unless you get up very close.

The Griffin
and the Minor Canon

*Whenever people in the town wanted anything done
for them, they went to the Minor Canon.
So who else but the young priest should save them
from the horrible Griffin?*

FRANK R. STOCKTON

Over the great door of an old, old church which stood in a quiet town of a far-away land there was carved in stone the figure of a large griffin. The old-time sculptor had done his work with great care, but the image he had made was not a pleasant one to look at. It had a large head, with enormous open mouth and savage teeth; from its back arose great wings, armed with sharp hooks and prongs; it had stout legs in front, with projecting claws; but there were no legs behind—the body running out into a long and powerful tail finished off at the end with a barbed point. This tail was coiled up under him, the end sticking up just back of his wings.

The sculptor, or the people who had ordered this stone figure, had evidently been very much pleased with it, for little copies of it, also in stone, had been placed here and there along the sides of the church, not very far from the ground.

A long, long distance from the town, in the midst of dreadful wilds scarcely known to man, there dwelt the Griffin whose image had been put up over the church door. In some way or other, the old-time sculptor had seen him and afterward, to the best of his memory, had copied his figure in stone. The Griffin had never known this until, hundreds of years afterward, he heard from a bird that there was a likeness of him on the old church in the distant town. Now, this Griffin had no idea how he looked. He had never seen a mirror, and the streams where he lived were so turbulent and violent that a quiet piece of water which would reflect the image of anything looking into it could not be found. Being, as far as could be ascertained, the very last of his race, he had never seen another griffin. Therefore when he heard of this stone image of himself, he determined to go and see for himself what manner of being he was. So he started off from the dreadful wilds and flew on and on

225

until he came to lands inhabited by men, where his appearance in the air created great consternation; but he alighted nowhere until he reached the suburbs of the town which had his image on its church. Here, late in the afternoon, he alighted in a green meadow and stretched himself on the grass to rest. His great wings were tired, for he had not made such a long flight in a century or more.

The news of his coming spread quickly over the town, and the people, frightened nearly out of their wits by the arrival of so extraordinary a visitor, fled into their houses and shut themselves up. The Griffin called loudly for someone to come to him, but the more he called, the more afraid the people were to show themselves. At length he saw two laborers hurrying through the fields, and in a terrible voice he commanded them to stop. Not daring to disobey, the men stood trembling.

"What is the matter with you all?" cried the Griffin. "Is there not a man in your town who is brave enough to speak to me?"

"I think," said one of the laborers, his voice shaking so that his words could hardly be understood, "that—perhaps— the Minor Canon—would come."

"Go, call him, then!" said the Griffin. "I want to see him."

The Minor Canon, who filled a subordinate position in the old church, had just finished the afternoon services and was coming out of a side door with three aged women who had formed the weekday congregation. He was a kind young man and very anxious to do good to the people of the town. Apart from his duties in the church, where he conducted services every weekday, he visited the sick and the poor, counseled and assisted persons who were in trouble and taught a school composed entirely of the bad children in the town with whom nobody else would have any-

thing to do. Whenever people wanted anything done for them, they always went to the Minor Canon. Thus it was that the laborer thought of the young priest.

The Minor Canon had not heard of the strange event and when he was informed of it and told that the Griffin had asked to see him, he was amazed and frightened. "Me!" he exclaimed. "He has never heard of me! Why should he want me?"

"Oh! you must go instantly!" cried the two men. "He is very angry now because he has been kept waiting so long."

The poor Minor Canon would rather have had his hand cut off than go out to meet an angry griffin; but it would be a woeful thing if injury should come to the people because he was not brave enough. So, pale and frightened, he started off.

"Well," said the Griffin, as soon as the young man came near, "I am glad to see that there is someone who has the courage to come to me."

The Minor Canon did not feel very courageous, but he bowed his head.

"Is this the town," said the Griffin, "where there is a church with a likeness of myself over one of the doors?"

The Minor Canon looked at the frightful figure of the Griffin and saw that it was, without doubt, exactly like the stone image on the church.

"Yes," he said, "you are right."

"Well, then," said the Griffin, "will you take me to it? I wish to see it."

The Minor Canon instantly thought that if the Griffin entered the town without the people knowing what he came for, some of them would probably be frightened to death, and so he sought to gain time to prepare their minds.

"It is growing dark, now," he said, very much afraid as he spoke that his words might enrage the Griffin, "and the objects on the front of the church cannot be seen clearly. It will be better to wait until morning if you wish to get a good view."

"That will suit me very well," said the Griffin. "I see that you are a man of good sense. I am tired, and I will take a nap here on this soft grass, while I cool my tail in the little stream that runs near me. The end of my tail gets red-hot when I am angry or excited, and it is quite warm now. So you may go, but be sure and come early to-morrow morning and show me the way to the church."

The Minor Canon was glad enough to take his leave and hurried into the town. In front of the church he found a great many people assembled to hear his report of his interview with the Griffin. When they found that he had not come to spread ruin and devastation, but simply to see his stony likeness on the church, they showed neither relief nor gratification, but began to upbraid the Minor Canon for consenting to conduct the creature into the town.

"What could I do?" cried the young man. "If I should not bring him he would come himself and, perhaps, end by setting fire to the town with his red-hot tail."

Still the people were not satisfied, and a great many plans were proposed to prevent the Griffin from coming into the town. Some elderly persons urged that the young men should go out and kill him, but the young men scoffed at such a ridiculous idea. Then someone said that it would be a good thing to destroy the stone image so that the Griffin would have no excuse for entering the town; and this idea was received with such favor that many of the people ran for hammers, chisels and crowbars with which to tear down and break up the stone griffin. But the Minor Canon resisted this plan with all the strength of his mind and body. He assured the people that this action would enrage the Griffin beyond measure, for it would be impossible to conceal from him that his image had been destroyed during the night. But the

people were so determined to break up the stone griffin that the Minor Canon saw that there was nothing for him to do but to stay there and protect it. All night he walked up and down in front of the church door, keeping away the men who brought ladders by which they might mount to the great stone griffin and knock it to pieces with hammers and crowbars. After many hours the people were obliged to give up their attempts and went home to sleep, but the Minor Canon remained at his post till early morning, and then he hurried away to the field where he had left the Griffin.

The monster had just awakened, and rising to his forelegs and shaking himself, he said that he was ready to go into the town. The Minor Canon, therefore, walked back, the Griffin flying slowly through the air at a short distance above the head of his guide. Not a person was to be seen in the streets, and they proceeded directly to the front of the church, where the Minor Canon pointed out the stone griffin.

The real Griffin settled down in the little square before the church and gazed earnestly at his sculptured likeness. For a long time he looked at it. First he put his head on one side, and then he put it on the other; then he shut his right eye and gazed with his left, after which he shut his left eye and gazed with his right. Then he moved a little to one side and looked at the image, then he moved the other way.

After a while he said to the Minor Canon, who had been standing by all this time, "It is, it must be, an excellent likeness! That breadth between the eyes, that expansive forehead, those massive jaws! I feel that it must resemble me. If there is any fault to find with it, it is that the neck seems a little stiff. But that is nothing. It is an admirable likeness—admirable!"

The Griffin sat looking at his image all the morning and all the afternoon. The Minor Canon had been afraid to go away

and leave him, and had hoped all through the day that he would soon be satisfied with his inspection and fly away home. But by evening the poor young man was utterly exhausted and felt that he must go away to eat and sleep. He frankly admitted this fact to the Griffin and asked him if he would not like something to eat. He said this because he felt obliged in politeness to do so, but as soon as he had spoken the words, he was seized with dread lest the monster should demand half a dozen babies or some such tempting repast.

"Oh, no," said the Griffin. "I never eat between the equinoxes. At the vernal and at the autumnal equinox I take a good meal, and that lasts me for half a year. I am extremely regular in my habits and do not think it healthful to eat at odd times. I will return to the soft grass where I slept last night and take another nap."

The next day the Griffin came again to the little square before the church and remained there until evening, steadfastly regarding the stone griffin. The Minor Canon came once or twice to look at him, and the Griffin seemed very glad to see him; but the young clergyman could not stay for he had many duties to perform. Nobody went to the church, but the people came to the Minor Canon's house and anxiously asked him how long the Griffin was going to stay.

"I do not know," he answered, "but I think he will soon be satisfied with regarding his stone likeness, and then he will go away."

But the Griffin did not go away. Morning

228

after morning he came to the church, but after a time he did not stay there all day. He seemed to have taken a great fancy to the Minor Canon and followed him about as he pursued his various activities. He would wait for him at the side door of the church, for the Minor Canon held services every day, morning and evening, though nobody came now. "If anyone should come," he said to himself, "I must be found at my post." When the young man came out, the Griffin would accompany him in his visits to the sick and the poor and would often look into the windows of the school-house where the Minor Canon was teaching his unruly scholars. All the other schools were closed, but the parents of the Minor Canon's scholars forced them to go to school because they were so bad the parents could not endure them all day at home—griffin or no griffin. But it must be said they generally behaved very well when the great monster sat up on his tail and looked through the schoolroom window.

When it was perceived that the Griffin showed no sign of going away, all the people who were able to do so left the town. The canons and the higher officers of the church had fled away during the first day of the Griffin's visit, leaving behind only the Minor Canon and some of the men who swept the church. All the citizens who could afford it traveled to distant parts, and only the working people and the poor were left behind. After a while these ventured to go about and attend to their business, for if they did not work they would starve.

Day by day the Griffin became more and more attached to the Minor Canon. This strange companionship was often burdensome to the Minor Canon; but, on the other hand, he could not deny that he derived a great deal of benefit and instruction from it. The Griffin had lived for hundreds of years and had seen much, and he told the Minor Canon many wonderful things.

"It is like reading an old book," said the young clergyman to himself, "but how many books I would have had to read before I would have found out what the Griffin has told me about the earth, the air, the water, about minerals and metals and growing things, and all the wonders of the world!"

Thus the summer went on and drew toward its close. And now the people of the town began to be very much troubled again.

"It will not be long," they said, "before the autumnal equinox is here, and then that monster will want to eat. He will be dreadfully hungry, for he has taken so much exercise since his last meal. He will devour our children. Without doubt, he will eat them all. What is to be done?"

To this question no one could give an answer, but all agreed that the Griffin must not be allowed to remain. After talking over the matter, a crowd of the people went to the Minor Canon at a time when the Griffin was not with him.

"It is all your fault," they said, "that that monster is among us. You brought him here, and you ought to see that he goes away. It is only on your account that he stays here at all, for, although he visits his image every day, he is with you the greater part of the time. If you were not here, he would not stay. It is your duty to go away and then he will follow you."

"Go away!" cried the Minor Canon. "Where shall I go? If I go to some other town, shall I not take this trouble there? Have I a right to do that?"

"No," said the people, "you must not go to any other town. There is no town far enough away. You must go to the dreadful wilds where the Griffin lives, and then he will follow you and stay there."

They did not say whether they expected

the Minor Canon to stay there also, and he did not ask them anything about it. He bowed his head and went into his house to think. The more he thought, the more clear it became to his mind that it was his duty to go away and thus free the town from the presence of the Griffin.

That evening he packed a leathern bag full of bread and meat and early the next morning he set out on his journey to the dreadful wilds. It was a long, weary and doleful journey, especially after he had gone beyond the habitations of men, but the Minor Canon kept on bravely and never faltered. The way was longer than he had expected, and his provisions soon grew so scanty that he was obliged to eat but a little every day, but he kept up his courage and pressed on, and, after many days of toilsome travel, he reached the dreadful wilds.

When the Griffin found that the Minor Canon had left the town he seemed sorry, but showed no disposition to go and look for him. After a few days had passed, he became much annoyed and asked some of the people where the Minor Canon had gone. But, although the citizens had been so anxious that the young clergyman should go to the dreadful wilds, thinking that the Griffin would immediately follow him, they were now afraid to mention the Minor Canon's destination, for the monster seemed angry already, and if he should suspect their trick he would, doubtless, become very much enraged. So everyone said he did not know, and the Griffin wandered about disconsolately. One morning he looked into the Minor Canon's schoolhouse, which was always empty now, and thought that it was a shame that everything should suffer on account of the young man's absence.

"It does not matter so much about the church," he said, "for nobody went there, but it is a pity about the school. I think

I will teach it myself until he returns."

It was just about school time, and the Griffin went inside and pulled the rope which rang the schoolbell. Some of the children who heard the bell ran in to see what was the matter, supposing it to be a joke of some one of their companions; but when they saw the Griffin they stood astonished and scared.

"Go tell the other scholars," said the monster, "that school is about to open, and that if they are not all here in ten minutes, I shall come after them."

In seven minutes every scholar was in place.

Never was seen such an orderly school. Not a boy or girl moved or uttered a whisper. The Griffin climbed into the master's seat, his wide wings spread on each side of him because he could not lean back in his chair while they stuck out behind, and his great tail coiled around in front of the desk, the barbed end sticking up, ready to tap any boy or girl who might misbehave. The Griffin now addressed the scholars, telling them that he intended to teach them while their master was away. In speaking he endeavored to imitate, as far as possible, the mild and gentle tones of the Minor Canon, but it must be admitted that in this he was not very successful. He had paid a good deal of attention to the studies of the school, and he now determined not to attempt to teach them anything new, but to review them in what they had been studying, so he called up the various classes and questioned them upon their previous lessons. The children racked their brains to remember what they had learned. They were so afraid of the Griffin's displeasure that they recited as they had never recited before. One of the boys, far down in his class, answered so well that the Griffin was astonished.

"I should think you would be at the head," said he. "I am sure you have never been in the habit of reciting so well. Why is this?"

"Because I did not choose to take the trouble," said the boy, trembling in his boots. He felt obliged to speak the truth, for all the children thought that the great eyes of the Griffin could see right through them.

"You ought to be ashamed of yourself," said the Griffin. "Go down to the tail of the class, and if you are not at the head in two days, I shall know the reason why."

The next afternoon the boy was number one.

It was astonishing how much these children now learned of what they had been studying. It was as if they had been educated over again. The Griffin used no severity toward them, but there was a look about him which made them unwilling to go to bed until they were sure they knew their lessons for the next day.

The Griffin now thought that he ought to visit the sick and the poor. The effect upon the sick was miraculous. All, except those who were very ill indeed, jumped from their beds when they heard he was coming and declared themselves quite well. To those who could not get up, he gave herbs and roots, which none of them had ever before thought of as medicines, but which the Griffin had seen used in various parts of the world; and most of them recovered. But, for all that, they afterward said that, no matter what happened, they hoped that they should never again have such a doctor feeling their pulses and looking at their tongues.

As for the poor, they seemed to have utterly disappeared. All those who had depended upon charity for their daily bread were now at work in some way or other, many of them offering to do odd jobs for their neighbors just for the sake of their meals—a thing which had been seldom heard of before in the town. The Griffin could find no one who needed his assistance.

The summer had now passed, and the autumnal equinox was rapidly approaching. The citizens were in a state of great alarm and anxiety. The Griffin showed no signs of going away but seemed to have settled himself permanently among them. In a short time, the day for his semi-annual meal would arrive, and then what would happen? The monster would devour all their children.

Now they greatly regretted and lamented that they had sent away the Minor Canon; he was the only one on whom they could have depended in this trouble, for he could talk freely with the Griffin and so find out what could be done. But it would not do to be inactive. Some step must be taken immediately. A meeting of the citizens was called, and two old men were appointed to go and talk to the Griffin. They were instructed to offer to prepare a splendid dinner for him on equinox day —one which would entirely satisfy his hunger. They would offer him the fattest mutton, the most tender beef, fish and game of various sorts and anything of the kind that he might fancy. If none of these suited, they were to mention that there was an orphan asylum in the next town.

"Anything would be better than to have our dear children devoured."

The old men went to the Griffin, but their propositions were not received with favor. "From what I have seen of the people of this town," said the monster, "I do not think I could relish anything that was ever prepared by them. They appear to be all cowards and, therefore, mean and selfish. As for eating one of them, old or young, I couldn't think of it for a moment. In fact, there was only one creature in the whole place for whom I could have had any appetite, and that is the Minor Canon.

231

He was brave and good and honest, and I think I would have relished him."

"Ah!" said one of the old men very politely, "in that case I wish we had not sent him to the dreadful wilds!"

"What!" cried the Griffin. "Explain instantly what you are talking about!"

The old man was obliged to tell how the Minor Canon had been sent away by the people in the hope that the Griffin might be induced to follow him.

When the monster heard this, he became furiously angry. He dashed away from the old men and, spreading his wings, flew backward and forward over the town. He was so much excited that his tail became red-hot and glowed like a meteor against the evening sky. When at last he settled down in the little field where he usually rested and thrust his tail into the brook, the steam arose like a cloud and the water of the stream ran hot through the town. The citizens were greatly frightened and bitterly blamed the old man for telling about the Minor Canon.

"It is plain," they said, "that the Griffin intended to go and look for him, and we should have been saved. Now who can tell what misery you have brought us."

The Griffin did not remain long in the little field. As soon as his tail was cool he flew to the town hall and rang the bell. The citizens knew that they were expected to come there, and they were afraid to stay away. The Griffin was on the platform at one end, flapping his wings and walking up and down, and the end of his tail was still so warm that it scorched the boards as he dragged it after him.

When everybody who was able to come was there, the Griffin stood still and addressed the meeting.

"I have had a contemptible opinion of you," he said, "ever since I discovered what cowards you were, but I had no idea that you were so ungrateful, selfish and cruel as I now find you to be. Here was your Minor Canon, who labored day and night for your good and thought of nothing else but how he might benefit you and make you happy; and as soon as you imagine yourselves threatened with a danger —for well I know you are dreadfully afraid of me—you send him off, caring not whether he returns or perishes, hoping thereby to save yourselves. Now, I had conceived a great liking for that young man and had intended, in a day or two, to go and look him up. But I have changed my mind about him. I shall go and find him, but I shall send him back here to live among you, and I intend that he shall enjoy the reward of his labor and his sacrifices. Go, some of you, to the officers of the church, who so cowardly ran away when I first came here, and tell them never to return to this town under penalty of death. And if, when your Minor Canon comes back to you, you do not put him in the highest place among you and serve and honor him all his life, beware of my terrible vengeance! There were only two good things in this town: the Minor Canon and the stone image of myself. One of these you have sent away, and the other I shall carry away myself."

With these words he dismissed the meeting, and it was time, for the end of his tail had become so hot that there was danger of his setting fire to the building.

The next morning, the Griffin came to the church and, tearing the stone image of himself from its fastenings over the great door, he grasped it with his powerful forelegs and flew up into the air. Then, after hovering over the town for a moment, he gave his tail an angry shake and took up his flight to the dreadful wilds. When he reached this desolate region, he set the stone griffin upon a ledge of a rock which rose in front of the dismal cave he called his home. There the image occupied a position somewhat similar to that it had had over the church door; and the Griffin, panting with the exertion of carrying such an enormous load to so great a distance, lay down upon the ground and regarded it with much satisfaction. When he felt somewhat rested he went to look for the Minor Canon. He found the young man, weak and half-starved, lying under the shadow of a rock. After picking him up and carrying him to his cave, the Griffin flew away to a distant marsh where he procured some roots and herbs. After eating these the Minor Canon was greatly revived and listened while the Griffin told him what had happened in the town.

"Do you know," said the monster when he had finished, "that I have had, and still have, a great liking for you?"

"I am very glad to hear it," said the Minor Canon, with his usual politeness.

"I am not at all sure that you would be," said the Griffin, "if you thoroughly understood the state of the case, but we will not consider that now. If some things were different, other things would be otherwise. I have been so enraged by discovering the manner in which you have been treated that I have determined that you shall at last enjoy the rewards and honors to which you are entitled. Lie down and have a good sleep, and then I will take you back to the town."

As he heard these words, a look of trouble came over the young man's face.

"You need not give yourself any anxiety," said the Griffin, "about my return to the town. Now that I have that admirable likeness of myself in front of my cave, where I can sit at my leisure and gaze upon its noble features and magnificent proportions, I have no wish to see that abode of cowardly and selfish people."

The Minor Canon, relieved from his fears, now lay back and dropped into a doze, and when he was sound asleep the Griffin took him up and carried him back to the town. He arrived just before daybreak, and putting the young man gently on the grass in the little field where he himself used to rest, the monster, without having been seen, flew back to his home.

When the Minor Canon made his appearance in the morning among the citizens, the enthusiasm with which he was received was truly wonderful. He was taken to a house which had been occupied by one of the banished high officers of the place, and everyone was anxious to do all that could be done for his health and comfort. The people crowded into the church when he held services, and the parents of the bad children determined to reform them at home, in order that he might be spared the trouble of keeping up his former school. The Minor Canon was appointed to the highest office of the old church, and before he died, he became a bishop.

During the first years after his return, the people of the town looked up to him as a man to whom they were bound to do honor and reverence; but they often, also, looked up to the sky to see if there were any signs of the Griffin coming back. However, in course of time, they learned to honor and reverence their former Minor Canon without the fear of being punished if they did not do so.

But they need never have been afraid of the Griffin. The autumnal equinox day came round, and the monster ate nothing. If he could not have the Minor Canon, he did not care for anything. So, lying down, with his eyes fixed upon the great stone griffin, he gradually declined and died. It was a good thing for some of the people of the town that they did not know this.

If you should ever visit the old town, you would still see the little griffins on the sides of the church; but the great stone griffin that was over the door is gone.

Modern Improvements
at the Peterkins'

*Their new house was marvelous—it had buttons
to sound a burglar alarm, summon the fire department,
a carriage or a telegraph boy. The only problem was—
which button did which*

LUCRETIA P. HALE

Agamemnon Peterkin felt that it became necessary for him to choose a profession. It was important on account of his little brothers. If he should make a trial of several different professions he could find out which would be the most likely to be successful, and it would then be easy to bring up the little boys in the right direction.

Elizabeth Eliza, his sister, agreed with this. She thought the family occasionally made mistakes and had come near disgracing themselves. Now was their chance to avoid this in the future by giving the little boys a proper education.

Solomon John was almost determined to become a doctor. From earliest childhood he had practiced writing prescriptions on little slips of paper. Mrs. Peterkin, to be sure, was afraid of infection. She could not bear the idea of his bringing one disease after the other into the family circle. Solomon John, too, did not like sick people. He thought he might manage it if he should not have to see his patients while they were sick. If he could only visit them when they were recovering and when the danger of infection was over, he would really enjoy making calls.

He should have a comfortable doctor's chaise and take one of the little boys to hold his horse while he went in, and he thought he could get through the conversational part very well, and feeling the pulse, perhaps looking at the tongue. He should read all the newspapers and so be acquainted with the news of the day to talk of. But he should not like to be waked up at night to visit. Mr. Peterkin thought that would not be necessary. He had seen signs on doors of "Night Doctor," and it should be as convenient to have a sign of "Not a Night Doctor."

Solomon John thought he might write his advice to those of his patients from whom there was danger of infection. And then Elizabeth Eliza agreed that his prescriptions would probably be so satisfactory that they would keep his patients well—not too well to do without a doctor, but needing his prescriptions.

Agamemnon was delayed, however, in his choice of a profession by a desire he had to become a famous inventor. If he could only invent something important and get out a patent, he would make himself known all over the country. If he could get out a patent he would be set up for life or at least as long as the patent lasted, and it would be well to be sure to arrange it to last through his natural life.

Indeed, he had gone so far as to make his invention. It had been suggested by their trouble with a key in their late moving to their new house. He had studied the matter over a great deal. He looked it up in the Encyclopedia, and had spent a day or two in the Public Library reading about Chubb's Lock and other patent locks.

But his plan was more simple. It was this: that all keys should be made alike! He wondered it had not been thought of before, but so it was, Solomon John said, with all inventions, with Christopher Columbus and everybody. Nobody knew the invention till it was invented, and then it looked very simple. With Agamemnon's plan you need have but one key that should fit everything! It should be a medium-sized key, not too large to carry. It ought to answer for a house door, but you might open a suitcase with it. How much less danger there would be of losing one's keys if there were only one to lose!

Mrs. Peterkin thought it would be inconvenient if their father were out and she wanted to open the jam closet for the little boys. But Agamemnon explained that he did not mean there should be but one key in the family, or in a town—you might have as many as you pleased, only they should all be alike.

Elizabeth Eliza felt it would be a great convenience—they could keep the front door always locked, yet she could open it with the key of her upper drawer; that she was sure to have with her. And Mrs. Peterkin felt it might be a convenience if they had one on each story so that they need not go up and down for it.

Mr. Peterkin studied all the papers to decide about the lawyer they should consult, and at last, one morning, they went into town to visit a patent agent.

Elizabeth Eliza took the occasion to make a call upon the lady from Philadelphia, but she came back hurriedly to her mother.

"I have had a delightful call," she said,

"but—perhaps I was wrong—I could not help, in conversation, speaking of Agamemnon's proposed patent."

"But where is the harm?" asked Mrs. Peterkin. "I'm sure you can trust the lady from Philadelphia."

Elizabeth Eliza then explained that the lady from Philadelphia had questioned the plan a little when it was told her and had suggested that "if everybody had the same key there would be no particular use in a lock."

"Did you explain to her," said Mrs. Peterkin, "that we were not all to have the same keys?"

"I couldn't quite understand her," said Elizabeth Eliza, "but she seemed to think that burglars and other people might come in if the keys were the same."

"Agamemnon would not sell his patent to burglars!" said Mrs. Peterkin.

"But about other people," said Elizabeth Eliza, "there is my upper drawer; the little boys might open it at Christmas time—and their presents in it!"

"And I am not sure that I could trust Amanda," said Mrs. Peterkin, considering.

Both she and Elizabeth Eliza felt that Mr. Peterkin ought to know what the lady from Philadelphia had suggested. Elizabeth Eliza then proposed going into town, but it would take so long she might not reach them in time. A telegram would be better, and she ventured to suggest using the Telegraph Alarm.

For, on moving into their new house, they had discovered it was provided with all the modern improvements. This had been a disappointment to Mrs. Peterkin, for she was afraid of them since their experience the last winter when their water pipes were frozen up. She had been originally attracted to the house by an old pump at the side, which had led her to believe there were no modern improvements. It had pleased the little boys, too.

They liked to pump the handle up and down, and agreed to pump all the water needed and bring it into the house.

There was an old well, with a picturesque well sweep, in a corner by the barn. Mrs. Peterkin was frightened by this at first. She was afraid the little boys would be falling in every day. It proved, however, that the well was dry. There was no water in it so she had some moss thrown down, and an old feather bed, for safety, and the old well was a favorite place of amusement.

The house, it had proved, was well furnished with bathrooms, and a hack-, telegraph- and fire alarm, with a little knob for each.

Mrs. Peterkin was very anxious. She feared the little boys would be summoning somebody all the time, and it was decided to conceal from them the use of the knobs, and the card of directions at the side was destroyed. Agamemnon had made one of his first inventions to help this. He had arranged a number of similar knobs to be put in rows in different parts of the house, to appear as if they were intended for ornament, and had added some of the original knobs. Mrs. Peterkin felt more secure, and Agamemnon thought of taking out a patent for this invention.

It was, therefore, with some doubt that Elizabeth Eliza proposed sending a telegram to her father. Mrs. Peterkin, however, was pleased with the idea. Solomon John was out, and the little boys were at school, and she herself would touch the knob while Elizabeth Eliza should write the telegram.

"I think it is the fourth knob from the beginning," she said, looking at one of the rows of knobs.

Elizabeth Eliza was sure of this. Agamemnon, she believed, had put three extra knobs at each end.

"But which is the end and which is the

beginning—the top or the bottom?" Mrs. Peterkin asked hopelessly.

Still she bravely selected a knob, and Elizabeth Eliza hastened with her to look out for the messenger. How soon should they see the telegraph boy?

They seemed to have scarcely reached the window when a terrible noise was heard and down the shady street the white horses of the fire brigade were seen rushing at a fatal speed.

It was a terrific moment!

"I have touched the fire alarm," Mrs. Peterkin exclaimed.

Both rushed to the front door. By this time the fire engines were approaching.

"Do not be alarmed," said the chief engineer. "The furniture shall be carefully covered, and we will move all that is necessary."

"Move again!" exclaimed Mrs. Peterkin, in agony.

Elizabeth Eliza strove to explain that she was only sending a telegram to her father, who was in Boston.

"It is not important," said the head engineer. "The fire will all be out before it could reach him."

And he ran upstairs, for the engines were beginning to play water upon the roof.

Mrs. Peterkin rushed to the knobs again hurriedly; there was more necessity for summoning Mr. Peterkin home.

"Write a telegram to your father," she said to Elizabeth Eliza, "to 'come home directly.'"

"That will take but three words," said Elizabeth Eliza with presence of mind, "and we need ten. I was just trying to make them out."

"What has come now?" exclaimed Mrs. Peterkin, and they hurried again to the window, to see a row of carriages coming down the street.

"I must have touched the carriage knob," cried Mrs. Peterkin, "and I pushed it half a dozen times I felt so anxious!"

Six hacks stood before the door. All the village boys were assembling. Even their own little boys had returned from school and were showing the firemen the way to the well.

Again Mrs. Peterkin rushed to the knobs, and a fearful sound arose. She had touched the burglar alarm!

The former owner of the house, who had a great fear of burglars, had invented a machine of his own, which he had connected with a knob. A wire attached to the knob moved a spring that could put in motion a number of watchmen's rattles, hidden under the eaves of the piazza.

All these were now set a-going, and their terrible din roused those of the neighborhood who had not before assembled around the house. At this moment Elizabeth Eliza met the chief engineer.

"You need not send for more help," he said. "We have all the engines in town here and have stirred up all the towns in the neighborhood. I can't find the fire yet, but we have water pouring all over the house."

Elizabeth Eliza waved her telegram in the air. "We are only trying to send a telegram to my father and brother, who are in town."

"If it is necessary," said the chief engineer, "you might send it down in one of the hackney carriages. I see a number standing before the door. We'd better begin to move the heavier furniture."

Mrs. Peterkin was ready to fall into hysterics. She controlled herself with a supreme power and hastened to touch another knob.

Elizabeth Eliza corrected her telegram and decided to take the advice of the chief engineer and went to the door to give her message to one of the hackmen, when she saw a telegraph boy appear. Her mother had touched the right knob. It was the fourth from the beginning, but the beginning was at the other end!

She went out to meet the boy, when, to her joy, she saw behind him her father and Agamemnon. She clutched her telegram and hurried toward them.

Mr. Peterkin was bewildered. Was the house on fire? If so, where were the flames?

He saw the row of carriages. Was there a funeral or a wedding? Who was dead? Who was to be married?

He seized the telegram that Elizabeth Eliza reached to him and read it aloud.

"Come to us directly—the house is not on fire!"

The chief engineer was standing on the steps.

"The house not on fire!" he exclaimed. "What are we all summoned for?"

"It is a mistake," cried Elizabeth Eliza, wringing her hands. "We touched the wrong knob; we wanted the telegraph boy!"

"We touched all the wrong knobs," exclaimed Mrs. Peterkin from the house.

The chief engineer turned directly to give counter-directions, with a few exclamations of disgust as the bells of distant fire engines were heard approaching.

Solomon John appeared at this moment and proposed taking one of the carriages and going for a doctor for his mother, for she was now nearly ready to fall into hysterics, and Agamemnon thought to send a telegram down by the boy, for the evening papers, to announce that the Peterkins' house had not been on fire.

The crisis of the commotion had reached its height. The beds of flowers, bordered with dark-colored leaves, were trodden down by the feet of the assembled crowd.

The chief engineer grew more and more indignant as he sent his men to order back the fire engines from the neighboring towns. The collection of boys followed the procession as it went away. The fire brigade hastily restored the furniture to their places and took away the ladders. Many neighbors remained, but Mr. Peterkin hastened into the house to attend to Mrs. Peterkin.

Elizabeth Eliza took an opportunity to question her father before he went in as to the success of their visit to town.

"We saw all the patent agents," answered Mr. Peterkin in a hollow whisper. "Not one of them will touch the patent or have anything to do with it."

Elizabeth Eliza looked at Agamemnon as he walked silently into the house. She would not now speak to him of the patent, but she recalled some words of Solomon John. When they were discussing the patent he had said that many an inventor had grown gray before his discovery was acknowledged by the public. Others might reap the harvest, but it came, perhaps, only when he was going to his grave.

Elizabeth Eliza looked at Agamemnon reverently and followed him silently into the house.

The
Four Young Men

*A story with not one, or two,
or three, or four—but five—tall tales and
an ending that will make you smile*

A Burmese Tale

In a certain village there lived four young men, and they could make up strange and impossible tales. One day they saw a traveler resting in the rest house outside the village, and he was wearing fine clothes. The four young men plotted to take these fine clothes away from him, so they went to the rest house and started a conversation.

After a while one of the young men suggested that they all join in a contest.

"Let each one of us tell about his most wonderful adventure," he said. "Anyone who doubts the truth of the story will become the slave of the man who tells it."

The traveler agreed to the idea, and the young men smiled to themselves, thinking him to be a fool. He did not look as though he could tell impossible stories, but even so they couldn't lose the contest if they merely said they believed his tale. On the other hand, they expected their own tales would be so thoroughly unbelievable that the traveler would have to protest. They did not really intend to make the traveler their slave, but merely to claim his clothes, since the property of a slave was the property of his master. So they went to the village and brought back the headman to act as a judge of the contest.

The first young man then began his wonderful adventure:

"Before I was born, my mother asked my father to pick some plums from the tree in front of the house, but my father replied that the tree was too high to climb. My mother asked my brothers, but they gave the same answer. I couldn't bear to see my mother disappointed, so I climbed the tree and picked the plums myself when no one was looking. I left them on the kitchen table. No one knew where the plums had come from, but my mother was very pleased."

The young man looked at the traveler, hoping that he would express doubt as to the truth of the story, but he merely nodded his head to show that he believed it. The other three young men also nodded their heads.

So it was the second young man's turn, and he said:

"When I was a week old, I took a walk in the forest and saw a large date tree with ripe fruit on it. As I was very hungry, I climbed up the tree swiftly and began eating dates. When I had eaten all I could hold, I was so heavy and sleepy that I couldn't climb down. So I went back to the village and brought a ladder. I propped it against the tree and came down by its rungs. If I hadn't found the ladder, I would still be up in the date tree."

He looked at the traveler, expecting to hear some protest, but the traveler merely nodded his head in agreement. The other

three young men also nodded their heads.

It was the third young man's turn to tell his impossible adventure:

"When I had reached the ripe old age of one year, I saw a rabbit running swiftly into the tall grass, and I chased it. When I caught up with it, I discovered that what I had been chasing was really a tiger. He opened his mouth to swallow me. I told him this was very unfair because what I was looking for was a rabbit and not a tiger. But he took no notice of my protests and opened his mouth even wider. Becoming annoyed at his rudeness, I caught hold of him with my left hand and broke him in two."

Again the young men looked expectantly at the traveler, waiting for him to deny the truth of the story. But he nodded his head in agreement. So the fourth young man told his story:

"Last year I went fishing in a boat, but I

241

couldn't catch a single fish. I asked the other fishermen, and they hadn't caught any fish either. I decided to see what was the matter at the bottom of the river. I dived out of my boat and swam down. After about three days I reached the bottom of the river, and I discovered a fish as large as a mountain there, eating all the small fish. I killed the great fish with one blow of my fist. After all this exercise I was beginning to feel a little hungry, so I decided to eat the fish right there. I lit a fire and after roasting the fish I ate it at one sitting. Then I floated back up to my boat and went home."

The young men waited for the traveler to laugh at this monstrous tale, or to cry out, "Oh, this is unbelievable!" but he merely nodded his head in agreement.

And then it was his turn to tell of an adventure. He began:

"Some years ago I had a farm. There was one fruit tree on my farm which grew differently than the others. It had four branches but no leaves. On the end of each branch, however, was a single fruit. When they were ripe, I picked the four fruits, and when I cut them open a young man jumped out of each one of them. As they came from my tree, they were legally my property—that is to say, my slaves. I made them work on my farm. But being lazy and much preferring to sit around and tell tales than to work, they ran away after only a few weeks. Since that time I have been traveling all over the country looking for them. And I am very gratified that now, here in this rest house, I have found them at last. Young men, you know very well that you are my runaway slaves. Come back with me to my farm, and don't give me any trouble."

The four young men couldn't say a word. They couldn't shake their heads one way or another. They were greatly embarrassed, for they were in a hopeless position. If they declared that the man's story was true, they would be acknowledging that they were his runaway slaves. If they said the story was false, they would lose the contest and become his slaves anyway. So they were silent.

The headman of the village asked them whether they believed the traveler's tale or not. They were silent. He asked them again. They would not speak. Once more he asked. They remained mute.

And so the headman declared that the stranger had won the contest. The traveler said to the young men, "Now you are my slaves. Since you are my slaves, your clothes belong to me. Take off your clothes and give them to me. After that I will give you your freedom."

The young men removed their clothes and gave them to him. The traveler tied the clothes in a bundle, put it on his back and resumed his journey, while the four clever young men stood naked in the rest house.

Shawneen and the Gander

*It was an uncommon egg
and from it hatched an uncommon gander.
Shawneen only hoped the leprechaun
had been right about everything*

RICHARD BENNETT

On top of a high green hill in Ireland there once lived a boy and his name was Shawneen. One bright warm day while his mother was washing out the clothes, she said, "The fire is out and there isn't a match in the house. Run down to Mrs. Murphy's shop like a good lad and buy a box. Here is a penny."

Indeed there was no need for a second word about that. Shawneen was always ready to go on errands to Mrs. Murphy's.

"I will, to be sure," said he, putting his cap on his head and the penny in his pocket.

Now at the foot of the hill there was a little village with a row of houses and shops up one side of the street and down the other.

Mrs. Murphy's was the prize of the lot. She sold everything.

If you wanted to buy a dress or if you wanted to buy a ham, Mrs. Murphy would be sure to have it.

When Shawneen arrived at her shop he was out of breath. He had been running down the hill, and it was a good way round when you came by the road.

Before opening the door, he stopped for a minute to look in the window.

The first shelf had the usual array of cups and saucers and the second shelf had nothing on it to talk about, but on the third shelf, right near the glass, Shawneen saw the most beautiful bugle he had ever seen in all his life.

It glistened so brightly in the sun that Shawneen could scarcely look at it.

It was all the color of gold and so shiny he could see himself seven times in it.

When Paddy the postman walked by the

window to deliver the letters, seven Paddys walked by in the bugle. It was that bright.

Around the middle was tied a blue-and-yellow cord with a silky tassel on each end as big as your hand.

Shawneen went into the shop.

"A box of matches, if you please, ma'am," said he to Mrs. Murphy; "and if it wouldn't be asking too much, may I have a toot on the bugle?"

"A toot, is it?" said Mrs. Murphy. "Indeed you may, my lad, two if you like. There is no harm in a good toot."

So Mrs. Murphy took the bugle out of the window and gave it to Shawneen. The end was cold and smooth and shaped so nicely that it fit snugly over his mouth.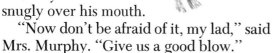

"Now don't be afraid of it, my lad," said Mrs. Murphy. "Give us a good blow."

Shawneen blew very gently at first, then a little louder and then so loud you could hear it down the street and over the hill and down by the sea.

Shawneen had never heard anything so fine in all his life.

"Ah, it's grand entirely," said he, stroking the tassels. "How much is it?"

"Ah, that's a very fine bugle," said Mrs. Murphy. "I couldn't let you have it for less than ten shillings and sixpence."

Shawneen blew on the bugle again but not so loud this time, then put it back on the counter.

Ten shillings and sixpence was a lot of money. Indeed a pair of shoes would cost as much as that.

Shawneen gave Mrs. Murphy the penny and put the box of matches in his pocket.

He walked slowly out the door and down the street.

He was thinking very hard to himself. How could he get ten shillings and six-

pence to buy the bugle in Mrs. Murphy's shopwindow?

There was no money at home to be spent for bugles. Indeed he was sure of that. Didn't his mother need a new shawl and the donkey a new harness and the window a new pane of glass? Wasn't his mother's teapot badly cracked and she often saying she wished she had the price of a new one? Weren't the soles of his own shoes so thin he decided to take a shortcut across the fields as the gravel on the road hurt his feet?

"No, indeed," said Shawneen to himself, "it will be no use asking for ten shillings and sixpence to buy a bugle."

He jumped over the ditch and began to climb the hedge.

The heather and moss at the top felt nice and soft so he sat down for a bit to think the matter over.

He was no sooner nicely settled when all of a sudden he saw a strange little man, dressed all in green, asleep under a furze bush only a few feet away. He was no more than a foot long and his suit was so much the color of the grass about him that indeed Shawneen had to look sharp to make him out at all.

"It's a Leprechaun surely," whispered Shawneen to himself, "and the very lad who can tell me how I can get ten shillings and sixpence to buy the bugle."

Before you could say two two's, Shawneen had the little fellow about the waist.

Now you may be sure it isn't every day you see a Leprechaun and when you do you have to keep your eyes on him or it's off he is in no time at all.

Shawneen lifted the little maneen out

from under the bush. The Leprechaun awoke with a great start and let such a yell out of him you wouldn't think he was equal to it. It was that loud.

"Ah, let me down now like a good lad," said the little fellow, kicking this way and that. "This is no way to be treating a gentleman."

"I will, faith," said Shawneen, "but first you must tell me how I can get ten shillings and sixpence to buy the bugle in Mrs. Murphy's shopwindow."

"Ah, that's easy enough," said the Leprechaun, "but you are hurting me now. Take your thumb off my stomach like a good lad."

Shawneen lifted his thumb a bit and then the Leprechaun began to stretch his arms and stretch his legs and rub his eyes at a great rate.

"This warm weather makes one very sleepy," said he.

"Never mind that now," said Shawneen; "how can I get ten shillings and sixpence to buy the bugle?"

"Ah, you are a very determined lad," said the Leprechaun. "Why, earn it, of course. You can't expect to get something for nothing."

"I know that well enough," said Shawneen, "but how can I earn all that money?"

The Leprechaun put one of his long bony fingers to the side of his nose and, leaning forward, whispered very mysteriously. "Not a word to a soul now," said he. "Hatch the egg and sell the gander."

"What egg?" said Shawneen, squeezing the little fellow tighter than ever.

The Leprechaun didn't say another word but pointed to the earth.

Before Shawneen stopped to think, he glanced down and there by the side of the ditch was the biggest goose egg he had ever seen in all his life.

I needn't tell you the Leprechaun was gone in a flash.

"Well, the egg is real enough, faith," said Shawneen, picking it up and putting it in his cap to keep it from breaking.

"An egg the size of this should make a big gander and a big gander should bring a good price at the Fair. I should have enough money in all to buy my mother a new shawl and a new dress and a silver teapot and have still enough left over to buy a bugle."

He was so excited he could hardly wait to get home.

The sooner the hatching began, the better.

When he reached home, his mother was hanging out the clothes.

"What have you there, my lad?" said she.

"A goose egg," said Shawneen.

"A goose egg, is it?" said his mother. "I have seen big eggs in my day but nothing the likes of that. Where did you find it?"

Now Shawneen remembered what the Leprechaun had said about keeping quiet.

"I was coming across the field," said he, "and there it was all by itself in the shelter of the ditch."

"And what will you do with an egg like that?" said his mother.

"Hatch it," said Shawneen. "Is there a hen setting?"

"There is, to be sure," said his mother. "Bring it into the shed."

She opened the henhouse door and pointed to a big brown hen in one corner.

"I am afraid she will find it a bit uncomfortable," said Shawneen, pushing the hen aside a bit.

"Oh, in a few days she will be so used to it she will never know it was there at all," said his mother.

Now, goodness knows, the egg did make the poor hen sit a bit crooked, to be sure. But she was a quiet, obliging bird and went on sitting as if nothing had happened.

There she sat with one side up and one

side down for days and days, a very mountain of patience.

Every morning Shawneen took a little peek under her wing to make sure all was going well and every now and then he went to have a look at the bugle in Mrs. Murphy's shopwindow. The bugle seemed to grow more beautiful every day and when Mrs. Murphy let him have a little toot on it now and then it sounded richer and sweeter as the days went by.

Well, the time passed as time will and soon the eggs were hatched—twelve yellow chicks and one yellow gosling. The chicks were fluffy and pretty as you may expect, but the gosling was a sight.

I don't think you could have found an uglier bird in the length and breadth of all Ireland.

His pinfeathers stuck out of him like the bristles of an old pig and his feet were so big and red and awkward he was forever stepping on his own toes.

His head was as big as a gosling twice his size and his poor little neck so thin and scrawny that it looked for all the world like a cabbage on the end of a broomstick.

"Ah, he is beautiful," said Shawneen to his mother; "may I raise him myself?"

"Indeed you may," said she. "I am sure I will have nothing to do with him. I have raised ducks and geese in my day but I have never seen anything come out of an egg the likes of that. Goodness knows what kind of gander he will make. He has altogether too knowing a look in his eye, to my notion. Faith, he looks at you as if he knew what you are thinking. Take my word, the sooner you fatten him up and send him off to the Fair the better."

Shawneen thought this was a good idea. The sooner he had the money in his pocket, the sooner he could buy his bugle.

So every day he fed his gander the best of this and the best of that. Shawneen thought nothing was too good for him. In no time at all the gander was as big as the hens and as big as the turkeys and soon as big as the geese themselves.

Indeed he grew so fast he became the talk of all the neighbors for lands around.

"That's no common gander," everyone began to say. "He comes from no common stock, I can tell you. Look at the way he carries himself! You would think he owned the world and all!"

Now all this talk and all this attention made the gander very proud. Oh, you have no idea. In fact, he was so carried away with himself that he would have nothing to do with the other birds of the barnyard. Like a king he walked before them.

The ducks thought he was very funny and laughed at him.

The hens had never seen his like before and were a bit afraid of him.

But the geese were so put about with his fine airs they couldn't stand the sight of him.

Now with the animals it was a different story.

"Oh, he is only a gander," said they, and went on about their business.

This didn't please the gander, you may be sure of that. Since they gave him no attention, he took great delight in teasing them every chance he could get.

Pulling the pigs' tails while they were eating supper was one of his favorite tricks.

"Faith, I will wring his neck if he goes on with that," said Shawneen's father.

"Maybe he doesn't like curly tails," said Shawneen; "he was just trying to straighten them out a bit."

"Straighten them out, indeed," said his father. "I'll straighten him out in short order if he goes on with any more of that nonsense."

One day the gander made faces at the

donkey and the poor little fellow was so frightened he backed the cart wheel over a boulder and upset two churns of milk and two fine baskets of eggs.

Another day he chased the goats over the young cabbages and the one little patch of potatoes. You can imagine the state of the garden.

One day Shawneen's mother decided to clean the house. She washed the windows and swept the floor and polished the pots and pans. When everything was nice and neat, she went out to get a pail of water.

Meanwhile, it started to rain. Over the half door flew the gander as easy as you please and made himself at home in front of the fireplace. He shook the rain off his feathers and flapped his wings, blowing the ashes and cinders all over the house.

"Oh, glory," said Shawneen's mother when she opened the door, "that bird will drive us out of house and home. I think the safest place for him is in the pot."

"Oh, no," said Shawneen, "he was just trying to be helpful and blow up the fire a bit. He is a very thoughtful gander."

"Thoughtful, indeed," said his mother. "It's a nice job he has given me with his thoughtfulness. Another trick like that and into the pot he goes."

I needn't tell you Shawneen was beginning to get worried when he heard this. The gander was acting very strange, to be sure. He would never get to the Fair at the rate he was going. But never a fear had the gander.

He made friends with all the hungry crows of the neighborhood and one evening invited them all in for supper. They ate up the grain in no time at all and the poor hens had to go to bed hungry. Oh, he was a holy terror.

There was no holding him.

Another day Shawneen's mother made some bread. She mixed the dough in a large pan and put it on the table near the fire while she hung out the clothes on the line.

It was a warm afternoon and the gander was feeling a bit drowsy. He jumped over the half door again, as familiar as you please, and settled himself for a nice comfortable nap in the very middle of the pan.

"Oh, glory," said Shawneen's mother when she opened the door. "This is too much. Tomorrow is Fair day. That gander goes with your father. Whatever price he will bring he will have to go. We can't put up with him a minute longer. There is something strange about that bird. Heaven knows what he may do to us all if he takes the notion.

"Sh, sh, sh, sh," said the gander, jumping out of the pan and leaping over the half door. He stood outside for a minute with his ear to the crack and heard the whole story. He knew very well that when ganders or geese went to the Fair they never came back. Oh, he was no fool.

That night he never slept a wink. He stood on one foot and then on the other. When the cock began to crow, his mind was made up. He would hide outside the garden wall until Shawneen's father was well out of sight.

Now as luck would have it, who should be sleeping outside the garden wall that very minute but Ned the Napper—the foxiest rogue in all Ireland. He was forever sneaking across the countryside, stealing everything he could lay his hands on.

Over the wall came the gander and landed squarely on top of his head. Feathers went flying. I can tell you. Such kicking and biting you never saw. For a while in the dim light you couldn't tell which was Ned and which was the gander. But I am sorry to say foxy Ned soon had the upper hand. He tucked the gander safely in his bag, tossed it over his shoulder and made off east the road.

That morning when Shawneen's father had hitched the donkey to the cart and was ready to be off, no gander could be found. They all looked high and they all looked low but no gander could they see. They looked behind this and they looked behind that, but not a feather of him was in sight.

"Well, gander or no gander," said Shawneen's father, "I can't wait any longer." So he slapped the lines over the donkey's back and set off to the Fair.

Shawneen watched the donkey cart rattling down the lane and through the gate. Soon it turned a bend of the road and was out of sight. He stood in the middle of the road, wondering what to do next. He had waited so long for the egg to hatch and for the gander to grow a bit. Indeed, it was a trial keeping him out of the pot with all his strange actions. Now he was ready for the Fair but nowhere to be found. Shawneen couldn't help but think of the bugle in Mrs. Murphy's shopwindow. It was likely to stay just where it was. Shining away for itself on the top shelf.

Shawneen ate his breakfast very slowly, thinking very hard to himself.

"Perhaps he has gone for a walk," said he to his mother.

"Very likely, indeed," said she. "Faith, he was liable to do most anything."

Shawneen decided to take a walk east the road. The gander might have gone in that direction.

Now Shawneen hadn't gone very far when he met two women gathering their washing off the hedges where it had been put out to dry.

"Did you see a big gander pass by here, by any chance?" said Shawneen.

"A gander, is it?" said one of the women very crossly. "No, indeed, but I would like a glimpse of the rogue that made off with my husband's new Sunday shirt."

Shawneen went on a little further until he came to a little cottage. Outside the door was an old woman spinning.

"Did you see a big gander pass by here, by any chance?" said Shawneen.

"A gander, is it?" said the old woman. "No, my child, but I would like to get a glimpse of my little teapot I put out to dry on the window sill. A fine, shiny little teapot it was. The fairies must have had their eyes on it."

Shawneen went on his way. Around another bend of the road he met two men cutting turf.

"Did you see a big gander pass by here, by any chance?" said Shawneen.

"A gander, is it?" said one of the men very crossly. "Indeed I didn't, but I would like to lay my hands on the rogue that made off with our coats and dinner pail when our backs were turned."

A little way further Shawneen came to a tinkers' van that was standing by the side of the road. Three of the tinkers were talking together in a very wild manner.

"Did you see a big gander pass by here, by any chance?" asked Shawneen.

"A gander, is it?" said one of the tinkers very crossly. "No, I didn't, but I would like to lay my hands on the rogue that made off with our finest pots and pans."

Now a little way further Shawneen came to a crossroads where some young people were dancing on a large flat stone by the side of the ditch.

"Did you see a big gander pass by here, by any chance?" cried Shawneen.

The young people were so busy laughing and dancing and the fiddler so busy playing and calling out the sets that no one paid any attention.

Shawneen said no more but continued.

"A flock of ganders could pass by that crowd and I am sure they would be none the wiser," said Shawneen to himself. "It's too busy dancing they are."

Now he hadn't gone many steps when he met two guards.

"Did you see a big gander pass by here, by any chance?" said Shawneen.

"A gander, is it?" said one of the guards. "No, my lad, but we would like to lay our hands on Ned the Napper. We heard he was around these parts."

Shawneen sat on a stone nearby and wondered what to do next. His hopes of finding the gander seemed less than ever. He would never get the bugle now.

Now during all this time great clouds had been rolling across the sky and soon big raindrops began to fall.

"I'll be drenched surely," said Shawneen, looking about for a bit of shelter. An old ruined castle at the top of a nearby hill was the only thing in sight. He climbed over the hedge and ran up the hill. He walked quickly across the yard and through the castle door.

It was dark and gloomy among the old walls and the ivy rustled and whispered in the wind. In the far corner of the first room Shawneen found a spot that was fairly dry in spite of the wind and rain.

Now he was no sooner nicely settled when all of a sudden he heard a strange noise in the next room.

"Sh, sh, sh, sh," it went very softly.

"Sh, sh, sh, sh," it went again a little louder than before.

"Rain or no rain, I'll stay here no longer," said Shawneen, starting for the door.

"Sh, sh, sh, sh," came the noise again, a little louder this time.

Shawneen stopped a bit. He had heard that sound before.

He tiptoed gently to the door of the next room and peeked in. You can well imagine his surprise. There on the floor was a fierce-looking man fast asleep. By his side was a big bag—and what in the world should be sticking out of the side of it but the gander's head.

The man stirred in his sleep. He began to rub his nose. He was going to wake up, there was no doubt about that. Shawneen held his breath.

Just then the gander leaned over and said, "Sh, sh," so softly in his ear the man went on sleeping as sound as ever.

Then the gander began to tear the sack very slowly with his strong bill.

As the hole became bigger and bigger, Shawneen suddenly remembered what the guards had said about Ned the Napper. Beyond a doubt this was the very lad the guards were after.

Without a word Shawneen tiptoed across the room. He ran out the door and down the hill.

His feet splashed in all the pools and the rain blinded him so badly he could hardly see. As luck would have it, the guards hadn't gone very far. Shawneen came running up, puffing and blowing. He was so excited he could hardly speak.

"Up there, up there!" shouted Shawneen, pointing to the castle.

"What's up there, my lad?" said one of the guards.

"Ned the Napper, I think, sir," said Shawneen.

Without another word they all ran up the hill. Before you could say two two's, the guards had the fierce-looking man safely between them.

With a few good bites, the gander stepped out of the bag and gave himself a good shake. He was as cross as two sticks. And indeed it's well he may be. To be tossed into a bag like an old cabbage head would be hard on anyone's dignity.

"This is a lucky day for you, my lad," said one of the guards to Shawneen. "It will be well worth your while to come down to the barracks with us. This is Ned the Napper all right, all right. It's a long chase he has given us. We will leave his bag here and take care of that later. It will be quite safe in this deserted place."

So down the hill they went—foxy Ned with a guard on each arm and Shawneen and the gander out before.

A few minutes later Shawneen and one of the guards walked out of the barracks door. Shawneen was carrying a little leather sack in one hand. In it was enough money to buy teapots and shoes and dresses and shawls. And bugles!

"Well indeed, my lad," said the guard; "you well deserve this reward for telling us about Ned the Napper. Now that the rain is over, let us go back to the castle and see what we can find in the bag."

So up the hill they went. When they reached the castle, the guard turned the bag upside down.

Coats and shirts and pots and pans came tumbling out on the floor.

"Why, this must be the old lady's teapot," said Shawneen, "all wrapped up in the turf cutter's coat, and here are the tinkers' pots and pans."

"Do you know who all these things belong to?" said the guard, scratching his head.

"Indeed I do," said Shawneen, rattling the money in the little sack. "It's scattered west the road they are—tinkers and turf cutters, old ones and young ones. Have a little patience now, your honor. I'll bring them all flying in short order."

Without another word he was down the hill and into Mrs. Murphy's shop. Before you could say two two's, he was out again and up the hill, blowing the fine shiny bugle for all he was worth. Ah, indeed, it's fine and clear it sounded, ringing out through all the countryside. Through all the lands around, its like was never heard before. All who heard it came running up the hill. The tinkers, the women, the turf cutters, the dancers—even the old woman left her spinning wheel and came as far as she could to see what was making such a sweet sound. Soon they all arrived. Shawneen lined them up before the castle door. When each received his bit, Shawneen blew a fine lively toot on the bugle. Then there was merry talk, you may be sure. A few minutes later they all went down the hill and west the road. The fiddler played and the young people sang and the gander strutted out before as if he owned the world and all.

"Oh, he is no common gander," everyone said. "It's easy to see that. There isn't a finer bird in the length and breadth of all Ireland."

Owl with the Great Head and Eyes

*Did you ever wonder why the owl cries
"hoot, hoot, hoot," or why the wolf and
the rabbit are not friends?*

CYRUS MACMILLAN

Long ago, when Glooskap was the ruler of the Indians in Eastern Canada and when the animals all worked for him and talked like men, Wolf was one of Rabbit's enemies. On the surface they seemed to be friends, but each was afraid of the other and each suspected the other of treachery. Rabbit was very faithful to his work as the forest guide who showed people the way to far places. But he was also a great trickster, and he delighted to play pranks on everyone he met. He liked more than all to pester Wolf, for he had a hatred for his cruel ways, and he was always able to outwit him.

It happened that Rabbit and Wolf lived close together, deep in the Canadian forest. Some distance from them, in a little house, lived a poor widow woman who had only one daughter. She was a very beautiful girl, with hair as black as the raven's wing and with eyes like the dark of the underwater. Rabbit and Wolf each fell in love with her, and each in his own way sought her as his wife. Rabbit tried hard to win her love. When he went to her house he always dressed himself in a soft brown coat, and he put a bangle around his neck and bells upon his feet. And often he played sweetly on his flute, hoping to charm her with his music, for he was a great player upon the Indian pipe. And he tried to grow a moustache to hide his split lip, but he had little success, for his whiskers would not grow thick, and he has the thin scraggy moustache of a few hairs to this day. But no matter what Rabbit did to adorn himself, the girl gave him cold looks, and old Wolf seemed to be deeper in her favor, for she liked his willowy form and his sleek and bashful ways. And poor Rabbit was sore distressed.

One fine day in the springtime Rabbit came upon the girl and her mother gathering mayflowers among the moss. He crept close to listen to their talk. He heard the

251

mother say, "I have no stomach for little Rabbit, but Wolf pleases me well. You must marry Wolf. They tell me he is a great hunter, and if you marry him we shall never want for food."

When Rabbit heard this he was very sad; he determined that on no account should Wolf marry the widow's daughter, and that he must use all his power to prevent it. That night he went alone to the girl's house. He spoke sneeringly of Wolf, saying with a bitter frown, "Wolf is no hunter; he never catches any game because he is lazy and he has no brains; I always have to feed him to keep him from starving. He is but a beast of burden. I always ride upon his back when I go to a far country, for he is good for nothing else."

The girl's mother wondered greatly, and she was very startled by this news, for she did not want her daughter to marry a good-for-nothing, but she was not sure that Rabbit spoke the truth, for she heard that sometimes he told great lies. So she said, "If you will ride Wolf over here I will believe you, and he shall not marry my daughter, and you shall marry her yourself." And Rabbit went home well pleased and sure of a happy ending to his trick.

The next day Rabbit purposely met Wolf in the forest, and he said, "Let us go together to see the widow's daughter." And Wolf was glad to go. They had not gone far when Rabbit began to cry. Then he lay down on the ground and rolled and moaned and rubbed his belly as if in great distress. "I have a sharp pain in my belly," he sobbed. "I cannot walk any farther. If I walk I shall surely die, and I cannot go unless you carry me on your back." Wolf willingly agreed, for he wanted to see the beautiful girl and he was very sorry for poor Rabbit in his pain, and Rabbit, laughing to himself, climbed on Wolf's back.

Wolf ran along not feeling the load, for Rabbit was very light. They had not gone far when Rabbit cried again and said, "I cannot ride without a saddle, for your bare back hurts me and gives me blisters." So they borrowed a little saddle from a field by the way and put it on Wolf's back. Soon Rabbit said, "This is fine fun; let us play that you are a horse and that I am a great rider. I should like to put a little bridle on you, and to wear spurs on my feet and to carry a whip." And Wolf, wishing to please Rabbit to make him forget his pain, gladly agreed. So they borrowed a little bridle and spurs and a whip from another field nearby and did as Rabbit asked, and together they went to the girl's home, Wolf trotting along like a little horse, and Rabbit laughing to himself, sitting in the saddle, with his spurs and his whip, holding the bridle reins.

When they drew near the house, Rabbit made a great noise so that the mother and her daughter might look out to see where the shouting came from. He called loudly, "Whoa! Whoa!" And the girl and her mother opened the door and looked out at them in wonder. Then, as they were looking on, Rabbit, chuckling to himself, struck Wolf a stinging blow with his whip and stuck his spurs deep into Wolf's sides and called him loudly a lazy beast. Wolf jumped and plunged and kicked because of the prick of the spurs and the sting of the whip; he was very cross, but he said nothing.

Some distance away, Rabbit tied Wolf to a tree, saying, "Stay here and I will send the girl to you." Then he went to the house and he said to the woman, "Now you will believe that Wolf is a beast of burden, for I have ridden here on his back." And the woman believed him. She told him to give Wolf some corn or grass. But Rabbit said, "He doesn't eat corn or grass; he eats only fresh meat," for he knew well that Wolf would be quite contented if he got a good meal of meat. Then she gave him some fresh meat, which he brought to Wolf. And Wolf was happy, and his anger disappeared, and he forgot the pain of the spurs and the whip, and he thought it was fine fun to get a good meal so easily.

The woman promised that Rabbit should marry her daughter, and when night fell Rabbit went home well pleased, leaving Wolf still tied to the tree. It was so dark that Wolf did not see him leaving the house, and for a long time he thought he was still inside, and he waited long in the starlight. At last he grew tired waiting, for he was hungry and he was cold standing still in the chill night air of early spring. He cut with his teeth the bridle rein that tied him to the tree, and then he went to the woman's house. But the woman would not let him in. She told him to go away, that she never wished to see him again, and she called him a lazy beast of burden. He went home in great anger, for he knew now that he had been tricked, and he swore that he would have vengeance on Rabbit.

The next day Rabbit learned from the woman that she had spurned Wolf from her door, and he knew that Wolf realized he had been deceived. He was somewhat frightened, for he dreaded Wolf's vengeance, and for several days he hid among the trees. Then hunger drove him out and he went forth to look for food. One evening he entered a garden in search of cabbage, and he was busy robbing it when the people who owned the garden spied him. And they said, "Here is the thief who has been stealing our vegetables. We will catch him and teach him a lesson." Before Rabbit knew it, they were upon him (for he was eating heartily, he was so hungry), and they caught him and bound him fast to a tree and went to get scalding water to pour upon his back to teach him not to rob their garden again.

But while they were away Wolf came along. He, too, was very hungry, for he had eaten no meal for many days, but he was glad when he saw Rabbit, for now he thought he would have his revenge. Rabbit saw him at a distance, and he resolved to try another trick on him, and to hail him as if he thought he was still his friend. And he cried out to him, "Help me, Wolf! Help me! The people here asked me to eat up a nice little lamb, and when I refused to do it, they tied me up to this tree and they have gone to bring the lamb to me."

Wolf was too hungry to be cautious and he forgot all about Rabbit's tricks, for spring lamb was his favorite food. And he said, "I will eat up the little lamb," and he smacked his lips as he spoke and thought of the nice tender meal he would have.

Then Rabbit said, "Untie me and take my place, for the people will soon be here with the lamb." So Wolf untied him, and Rabbit in turn bound Wolf fast to the tree and, laughing to himself because he had again outwitted stupid Wolf, he ran rapidly away. Far off he hid behind the trees to see what would happen.

Soon the people came back, carrying the pots of scalding water. Wolf saw them coming, and he was in high spirits, for he thought the lamb he was to eat was in one of the pots. It was moonlight, and in the shadow of the great tree the people could not see very clearly and they thought Wolf was Rabbit, still bound fast where they had left him. So they poured the scalding water on his back and kicked him and knocked him on the head with a big stick, and they said, "Now, thief, we have taught you how dangerous it is to rob gardens in the spring moonlight." Wolf howled with pain, for his back was blistered and his head was sore, and Rabbit heard him, and he sat on a log and shook with laughter because of the success of his prank.

Then the people untied Wolf and let him go. He went away wearily among the trees.

And he again swore vengeance on Rabbit, and he resolved to kill him as soon as he set eyes upon him, for he knew he had been tricked a second time. For several days he searched for his enemy. At last, one night of bright moonlight, he came upon Rabbit sitting in a patch of Indian tobacco plants eating his fill and contentedly chewing the tobacco leaves. Rabbit's mouth was full of tobacco, but he laughed loudly when he saw Wolf's back bound in bandages because of the blisters, and his sore head tied up in a cloth. But when he saw Wolf's angry eyes he was frightened and he ran away into the woods. The moon was shining in the forest and Wolf could catch a glimpse now and then of his brown coat among the trees, and he chased him for a long time. Rabbit tried all his tricks to shake him from his tracks, but without avail.

At last, when Rabbit was almost worn out, he took refuge in a hollow tree into which he slipped through a small hole where Wolf could not follow him. And Wolf said, "Now I have him in my power. I will kill him, but first I must go home to get my axe to cut down the tree and to chop off his head." Then he looked around for someone to keep watch over the tree while he was gone so that Rabbit could not escape. At last he saw Owl sitting quietly on a branch nearby. He called to him and said, "Watch by this hole until I get back, and do not let Rabbit get away." So Owl came down and sat by the hole and promised to keep guard over the prisoner, and Wolf went away to look for his axe.

But Rabbit was not caught yet; he had another trick left. After Wolf had gone away, he called to Owl sitting by the hole and said, "Owl, come and see what a nice little room I have here in the tree."

But Owl replied: "It is too dark, I cannot see."

Then Rabbit said, "Open your eyes wide

and put your face close to the hole, for I have a light here and you can see easily." Owl did as he was told, for he was a curious fellow. Rabbit had a great mouthful of tobacco juice from the Indian tobacco leaves he had been chewing, and when Owl put his face close to the hole, he squirted the juice into Owl's eyes. Owl screamed loudly, for his eyes were smarting and he was blinded by the juice; he ran around the tree and stamped and shrieked and rubbed his eyes, trying to relieve them of their pain. And while he was about it, Rabbit slipped out of the hole and ran away, and Owl did not know he was gone.

Soon Wolf came back, carrying his big sharp axe. And he said: "Now I shall kill him at last." And Owl was afraid to tell him about his sore eyes; they were still open wide and he could not close them. At once Wolf chopped down the hollow tree. Then he split it open from end to end, but there was no sign of Rabbit. Wolf then thought Owl had tricked him and that he had helped Rabbit to escape.

But Owl said he had not. He sat with his eyes wide open, staring stupidly and moaning and making strange noises because of his pain. Wolf thought he was laughing at him and taunting him, for he did not know the meaning of Owl's strange cries, and in his rage he fell to beating him over the head with his axe handle until poor Owl's head was swollen to a great size. And Owl cried, "Hoot, hoot, hoot!" and his eyes stared from his swollen head even larger than before.

Then Wolf went on his way, resolved to keep away from Rabbit. And since that time Owl has cried "Hoot, hoot, hoot!" at night, for he still remembers his pain, and his head is still swollen and bigger than that of other birds because of the beating Wolf gave him with his axe handle, and his eyes are still large and they stare stupidly, and he cannot look at light, and he is blind in the daylight because of the tobacco juice Rabbit squirted into his eyes. And since that night Rabbit and Wolf have avoided each other, and they have not lived in the same place, and they have never since been friends.

THE HEXER

*Cliff didn't believe John Brock when
he told them about hexing. "Let's prove there's
nothing to it," he said. "You two boys hex me.
Carve my face in the tree, drive in the nail
and we'll see what happens"*

THOMAS THOMPSON

No one introduced me to John Brock, the man who came out to get the team the night we moved to the new farm Dad had bought out there at the edge of the swamp. But then, you really didn't need to be introduced.

It was the first time I had ever seen a hunchback, but that wasn't what you noticed first. He had eyebrows as thick as horses' tails, and when he chewed tobacco, which was always, those eyebrows bounced up and down and his coal black eyes sort of glittered through them, snapping on and off the way stars do through trees on a windy night. I knew right off he was as different as this new land we had come to, and the land sure was different from the Texas Panhandle we were used to.

My dad always had been fiddle-footed, and we were used to moving, because he'd work for first one cow outfit and then another, but this time he really pulled up stakes.

He had been working for Mr. Charles Goodnight there in the Palo Duro, and he had just come back from trail driving a herd up to Dodge. I knew the minute I looked at him he had something big on his mind because he was grinning from ear to ear, but I don't guess any of us were ready for it when he said, "It's California, Mother. That's where we're headed!"

Far into that night Dad and Mother sat there in the kitchen, the lamp throwing a big circle of light on the maps and railroad folders Dad had brought back from Dodge. The big California gold rush was long past, but according to those railroad folders, the real gold was still there in the ground. All you had to do to get it was plow, put in seeds and sit back and watch 'em grow. In a place called the San Joaquin Valley, wheat and barley grew as high as a man on horseback, and there was always work for a good cowhand—which my dad was—because there were cattle on a thousand hills. My mother hinted we could just go up to Kansas and get some railroad land, but Dad said, "And face grasshoppers and blizzards and cattlemen tearing down your fences? No siree, Bob! It's California for us."

And that's the way it was. The land he took was in the swamp country along the Kaweah River in the San Joaquin Valley of California. As for John Brock, well, he just seemed to come along with the place.

John Brock was a Missouri man. He had fought in the War Between the States and been mixed up in the Kansas-Missouri border troubles. Some said he had gotten run out of there and couldn't go back. I don't know. All I knew for sure then was he was here in California, the same as us. Folks called him a swamp rat and he did odd jobs and that's about all we knew. But we were going to find out a whole lot more than that.

He was a man who could do almost anything. He could witch wells and make medicine out of green grapefruit and manzanita leaves and he was always digging up strange roots and drying different kinds of bark and nobody knew just what he did with those things. I was afraid to ask.

John was the only one who had ever really seen the ghost mare that lived out there in the swamp. Dad said it was just an old stray mare, but my brother Hamp and I weren't so sure. John told how he had seen her that night, fire squirting out of her nostrils, her chains rattling in the dark. . . . Dad said the Sutton boys had caught this old stray and tied a chain to her tail and turned her loose just as John was coming through the swamp one night. Some people believed that, but some didn't, and I was one of those who didn't. There was a ghost mare out there, all right. There were lots of strange things in the swamp you couldn't see, but you knew they were there.

It was a wonderful place to live. Mom

and Dad had a tenthouse with a wooden floor, and Hamp and I had a tent of our own, right under a big weeping willow tree. Cliff Price, who was a cousin of Dad's and just a little older than my brother, came to live with us, and bit by bit we got the ground cleared and the stumps pulled and the farm started taking shape.

The days were busy, with us burning brush and cutting bean poles, and finally the ground was ready to plant potatoes. Those were the good times, because John Brock came to help us, and that's when I started hearing all the stories he told. About how it had rained frogs in Missouri, and about the hoop snake that put its tail in its mouth and rolled along. It had a stinger so poisonous it would kill a tree right in front of your eyes. One time John had tried to straddle one with a team, and the hoop snake got its stinger caught in the wagon tongue. That wagon tongue swelled up and pushed the team right off the road.

There were other stories, too, as we sat there in the main tent house, cutting potatoes to the eye and getting the gunny sacks cut just right so they'd fit over your shoulder and you could drop the cut potatoes "eye side up" into the furrow.

We were just about ready to plant, but John Brock went out and looked at the moon and when he came back inside he shook his head. "Can't plant tomorrow," he said. "Moon ain't right. 'Taters will rot sure." We did what he said, because there was no doubt about it, John had a lot of magic powers. Cliff Price was the only one who didn't believe in him. Cliff laughed at everything John said, and that's what finally got him in big trouble.

It happened right after I got into a little bit of trouble myself. Dad sent me out to plant cantaloupes. It was a hot day and I'd walk along, dig with the hoe, drop in eight seeds, cover the hole and tamp it, take eight long steps and do it all over again.

After about three rows, I got tired. I don't know what ever made me do it, but I just dug one deep hole and put all the seeds I had left into it and covered it up. Then I wished I hadn't, because I knew those seeds would all come up in one spot and Dad would know what I had done and I'd be in real trouble . . . Well, that's when I went to John Brock, because I just didn't know where else to go.

What I had in mind was for John to hex those seeds so they wouldn't grow. Oh, he could hex, all right, but he didn't much like to talk about it. The way he explained it, the more you talk about hexing, the more your hexing loses its power. I remember how he sat there, chewing away on his Cotton Boll Twist, his eyebrows bouncing and his eyes glittering and finally he said, "I could hex the seeds, but it still wouldn't get rid of what you done wrong, would it?" I had to admit that was right, but I sure wanted out of this mess bad, so he finally said all right, that night we'd take care of it.

It was spooky out there in the canta-loupe patch, what with the frogs chunking and the mosquitoes buzzing and every time one bit me I got to worrying I'd get malaria sure and have to take calomel and then maybe even salivate . . . John had told me all about salivating, and it was awful. If you took calomel and then ate anything sour or sweet your teeth would fall out and your bones would get all soft. What you had to do was take Epsom salts to get rid of the calomel, and I guess there isn't anything tastes worse. What with the ghost mare out there roaming around, and me worried about salivating and John digging away in the ground just like he was digging a grave . . . well, I don't want to go through that night again.

Finally John had three buckets full of dirt. He packed two and I packed one and we went back to the tent where we could have some light. Of course we had to tell Cliff and Hamp what I had done, but they promised they wouldn't tell.

John made a sifter out of an old window screen and we set up most of the night, sifting out those seeds. I was so tired I would have gone to sleep, but I couldn't, because that was the night John told us the most about hexing. Hamp and I sat there bug-eyed and Cliff kept laughing and John's voice kept droning on and on. Once when I went outside, you could see their shadows climbing up the wall of the tent. The tule fog was swirling around my an-kles, and the sour smell of fresh-cut cotton-wood was in the air, mingling with the fragrance of the damp salt grass and the alkali. The swamp sounds were every-where. It wasn't hard to believe John could hex people.

Hamp and Cliff helped me get the can-taloupe seeds planted, and all the while we kept talking about hexing. Then all of a sudden Cliff said, "Let's try it." Hamp said he didn't know if we should or not, but Cliff said he would prove there was noth-ing to it. We could hex him.

I sure didn't want any part of it, but they were older than I was and after all, they had promised to keep still about me bury-ing all the seeds in one spot. They made me cross my heart and hope to die, and I went into the swamp with them.

Usually the swamp isn't too scary in daylight, but that day it was. The wild grapevines we always swung on were hanging down like jungle snakes across our path. The deeper we got into the swamp, the more gnarled and twisted the trees became. Every sound was sharp and clear, like a pistol shot, and I kept thinking about the ghost mare, and at every step I ex-pected old Fuqua to step out in front of us. Fuqua was supposed to have a tail like a monkey, although nobody had ever really seen it. He lived out here alone, and even the grown-ups were afraid of him because he always carried a shotgun loaded with rock salt, and he would just as soon give you both barrels as look at you.

Hamp gave Cliff a chance to back out, but Cliff just laughed. He sure did want to show John Brock up, he said, and he swore he was with the Sutton boys the night they tied the chain to the old mare's tail. That Cliff just didn't believe in anything. He even went so far as to pick out the tree himself.

It was a big, slick-bark alder, growing out of a little hummock of ground. It was tall and straight with the bottom limbs coming out about six feet off the ground. Alders have a damp smell all their own and the air was full of it, and that smooth bark was just inviting someone to carve his name. Hamp said, "You sure?" And Cliff said, "If you don't start carving, I'll do it myself. I'm sick and tired of listening to John Brock's wild tales." My brother took out his pocketknife.

Now that we had actually started it, hexing seemed almost too simple to be true. What you do is carve a picture of the one you want hexed on the bark of a tree. It doesn't really have to look like him, just so you name who it is, and that picture Hamp carved sure didn't look a lot like Cliff. The main thing is, you name it, and then you take a tenpenny nail and you put it right between the picture's eyes. Every day you go out to the tree and say *"Shuli, shuli, shuli poppa que. Shuli pop a zig zag, tillie come a roo."* You bear down real hard on the ROO, and when you do, you hit that nail—just once. When the nail is all the way in, the one you're hexing is dead.

The more Hamp carved, the less funny it seemed, and I guess Hamp felt that way too, because he wanted to stop, but Cliff wouldn't hear of it. Finally he got mad and took the knife away from Hamp and fin-

ished the picture himself, but he made Hamp start the nail and say the magic words because, of course, you can't hex yourself. Cliff was laughing so hard he was doubled over. "I sure want to see that old windbag's face when I bring him out here and show him this," he said. He was still laughing when he headed back home, but my brother was very quiet and I felt like a dozen spiders were crawling up my backbone.

Hamp and Cliff said they'd kill me if I told John what we were up to, so I didn't tell. A couple of times I went with them and a couple of times I didn't, but every day they went back to that big slick-bark alder in the middle of the swamp, said the magic words of *"Shuli, shuli, shuli poppa que"* and hit that nail another whomp with the big rock. And on the fifth day, Cliff started to get sick.

I looked at my brother and he looked at me, and we both knew what the other one was thinking. We had to get out there quick, pull that nail and stop the hex.

I never put in such a day in my life. We had Cliff's chores to do as well as our own, and it was one of those days when Dad found a million extra things for us to do. When we went in to supper, there was Cliff, his face all red, not talking, and we couldn't talk to him because Mom and Dad were right there. Mom had made some soup, but Cliff couldn't even swallow that, he was that sick. It was almost dark when we finally got away.

We ran all the way out to the big alder and when we got there we were both so out of breath our bellies hurt. My brother's hands were shaking so bad he could hardly hold the rock. That old alder suddenly looked like its limbs were reaching down for us and it kept getting darker and the ground fog started seeping up the legs of our overalls. Hamp started working on that nail, pounding it first one way and then the

other, trying to loosen it, but the green wood had swelled up around it, and it wouldn't move. It seemed to me that all he was doing was driving it in deeper. He gave it another try, but the nail bent over, flat against the bark of the tree. It was then I was sure I heard chains rattling, and I started to run. When I looked back, Hamp was right behind me.

When we got to the main tenthouse we were all out of breath, and Mom said, "What have you two been doing?" and Hamp said, "Playing." She told us we shouldn't play so hard, but we hardly heard her because we wanted to see Cliff. When we looked at him, I was sorry we had. He was burning up with fever, and his eyes were all glazed and funny looking and he just kept staring at us as if he had never seen us before.

We got out of there quick, and we sure didn't have any easy time of it going to sleep. I dozed off, and about midnight Hamp woke me up. He had a lantern and

claw hammer. "Get your clothes on," he said. "We're going back out there."

"I'm scared," I said.

"So am I," he said, "but you're going anyway."

That was a night I won't forget. We didn't light the lantern for fear somebody would see us. The tule fog was wispy and reaching out at us with long, wet fingers, and every piece of brush grabbed at us as we went by. We lost the trail and finally Hamp had to light the lantern and then it was worse than ever, because the shadows of our legs reached out into the darkness as if they were searching for trouble, and I knew they were. When we got to the alder it was even worse.

Hamp had me hold the lantern up so he could see. It threw a light on Cliff's picture that made it look more like a skull than a face. The sap had started to run and it trickled down the face like black blood. The frogs were making an awful racket. Hamp started working on the nail, but his hands were shaking so badly he wasn't getting much of anywhere, and then all of a sudden the frogs stopped and it was dead quiet, and in that quiet we heard footsteps.

I dropped the lantern and grabbed onto Hamp and he grabbed onto the tree and then the voice, low and growling, said, "What are you kids doing out here?" I knew it was Fuqua and I expected to hear the blast of his shotgun and feel the sting of rock salt, and then John Brock stepped out into the circle of lantern light.

I don't think I ever heard my brother talk that fast before and I never will again. He told John everything.

260

For a long time John just stood there, holding the lantern up to Cliff's picture, chewing away, his eyes glittering through his eyebrows, and then he said, "You boys got a peck of trouble here, but maybe I can straighten it out." He stuck his face right close to mine. "You two keep your mouths shut about this, you hear?"

He picked up the hammer and walked over to the tree and took a long, hard look at Cliff with the sap-blood running down his face and without looking at us he said, "Doctor was out to see Cliff tonight."

That was about the best news I had ever heard and my words came out with a big whoosh of breath. "What'd he say?"

John turned on me as if I had slapped him in the face. "What do you expect he said? Doctors don't know nothin'. Even if they did, you figger one could fix a hex like this? Now you two skedaddle on home before you're missed. Me, I got a lot of consortin' with ha'nts and witches to do. Might even have to get a couple of hairs from the ghost mare's tail. And don't you say a word to nobody or you're gonna undo everything I'm fixin' to do."

We got out of there, fast. I felt as if somebody was breathing right down my neck, and I kept walking faster and faster and finally I was in a full run. That tent sure did look good. I jumped under the covers with all my clothes on and Hamp did too.

When we went in to breakfast the next morning, there was old Cliff sitting up, trying to eat some fried eggs, but he was having a hard time of it. His face was all swollen up and he was real wobbly, but there wasn't any doubt he was better. My dad came in and took a look at him and said, "Boy, you got about as fine a case of mumps as I ever seen. Both sides."

The first minute we could, Hamp and I got John Brock aside. "Dad says Cliff has mumps," I said.

John just glowered at me. "Course he has," he said. "I tried to change that hex into measles, but when you bent that nail you sort of gouged it into his jowls."

And there wasn't any doubt about that. Cliff's jowls sure were swollen up.

John had stayed up all night breaking the hex, he said. He showed us a couple of white hairs from the tail of the ghost mare. We put them in the horse trough where John said in time they'd turn into snakes and sure enough they did.

That night he came out to the tent with a jar full of that green grapefruit-manzanita leaf brew of his, boiled down until it was as thick as syrup. It was as bitter as gall, but Hamp and I gulped it down without a word. Even then, he said, he wasn't sure he could keep us from getting the mumps—because of the part we'd had in the hex. And as it worked out, he was right. Hamp and I both got the mumps, but only on one side, so that wasn't so bad.

Cliff never did laugh at John Brock again, and he even admitted he'd been lying about being with the Sutton boys when they tied the chain to the tail of that mare.

So I guess the old ghost mare is still out there. I don't know. The swamp has a lot of secrets it never gives up, but I think the best kept secret is still the one about the time we almost hexed poor old Cliff.

Beautiful as the Day

*It was a most unusual fairy, with eyes that
moved in and out like telescopes, ears like a bat's and a
spiderlike body covered with fur. But it was a regular
fairy in one way—it granted the children a wish*

E. Nesbit

The house was three miles from the station, but before the dusty hired fly had rattled along for five minutes the children began to put their heads out of the carriage window and to say, "Aren't we nearly there?" And every time they passed a house, which was not very often, they all said, "Oh, *is* this it?" But it never was, till they reached the very top of the hill, just past the chalk quarry and before you come to the gravel pit. And then there was a white house with a green garden and an orchard beyond, and Mother said, "Here we are!"

"How white the house is," said Robert.

"And look at the roses," said Anthea.

"And the plums," said Jane.

"It is rather decent," Cyril admitted.

The Baby said, "Wanty go walky," and the fly stopped with a last rattle and jolt.

Everyone got his legs kicked or his feet trodden on in the scramble to get out of the carriage that very minute, but no one seemed to mind. Mother, curiously enough, was in no hurry to get out; and even when she had come down slowly and by the step, and with no jump at all, she seemed to wish to see the boxes carried in, and even to pay the driver, instead of joining in that first glorious rush round the garden and the orchard and the thorny, thistly, briery, brambly wilderness beyond the broken gate and the dry fountain at the side of the house. But the children were wiser, for once. It was not really a pretty house at all; it was quite ordinary, but it was deep in the country, with no other house in sight, and the children had been in London for two years, without so much as once going to the seaside even for a day by an excursion train, and so the white house seemed to them a sort of fairy palace set down in an earthly paradise. For London is like prison for children, especially if their relations are not rich.

London has none of those nice things that children may play with without hurting the things or themselves—such as trees and sand and woods and waters. And nearly everything in London is the wrong sort of shape—all straight lines and flat streets, instead of being all sorts of odd shapes, as things are in the country. Trees are all different, as you know, and I am sure some tiresome person must have told you that there are no two blades of grass exactly alike. But in streets where the blades of grass don't grow, everything is like everything else.

The children had explored the gardens and the outhouses thoroughly before they were caught and cleaned for tea, and they saw quite well that they were certain to be happy at the white house. They thought so from the first moment, but when they found the back of the house covered with jasmine, all in white flower, and smelling like a bottle of the most expensive perfume that is ever given for a birthday present; and when they had seen the lawn, all green and smooth, and quite different from the brown grass in the gardens at Camden Town; and when they had found the stable with a loft over it and some old hay still left, they were almost certain; and when Robert had found the broken swing and tumbled out of it and got a lump on his head the size of an egg, and Cyril had nipped his finger in the door of a hutch that seemed made to keep rabbits in, if you ever had any, they had no longer any doubts whatever.

The best part of it all was that there were no rules about not going to places and not doing things. In London almost everything is labeled "You mustn't touch," and though the label is invisible it's just as bad, because you know it's there, or if you don't you jolly soon get told.

The white house was on the edge of a hill, with a wood behind it—and the chalk quarry on one side and the gravel pit on the other. Down at the bottom of the hill was a level plain, with queer-shaped white buildings where people burnt lime, and a big red brewery and other houses; and when the big chimneys were smoking and the sun was setting, the valley looked as if it was filled with golden mist, and the limekilns and oasthouses glimmered and glittered till they were like an enchanted city out of the *Arabian Nights*.

Now that I have begun to tell you about the place, I feel that I could go on and make this into a most interesting story about all the ordinary things that the children did—just the kind of things you do yourself, you know—and you would believe every word of it; and when I told about the children's being tiresome, as you are sometimes, your aunts would perhaps write in the margin of the story with a pencil, "How true!" or "How like life!" and you would see it and very likely be annoyed. So I will only tell you the really astonishing things that happened, and you may leave the book about quite safely, for no aunts or uncles either are likely to write "How true!" on the edge of the story. Grown-up people find it very difficult to believe really wonderful things, unless they have what they call proof. But children will believe almost anything, and grown-ups know this. That is why they tell you that the earth is round like an orange, when you can see perfectly well that it is flat and lumpy; and why they say that the earth goes round the sun, when you can see for yourself any day that the sun gets up in the morning and goes to bed at night like a good sun as it is, and the earth knows its place, and lies as still as a mouse. Yet I daresay you believe all that about the earth and the sun, and if so you will find it quite easy to believe that before Anthea and Cyril and the others had been a week in the country they had found a fairy. At least they called it that, because that was what it called itself; and of course it knew best, but it was not at all like any fairy you ever saw or heard of or read about.

It was at the gravel pits. Father had to go away suddenly on business, and Mother had gone away to stay with Granny, who was not very well. They both went in a great hurry, and when they were gone the house seemed dreadfully quiet and empty, and the children wandered from one room to another and looked at the bits of paper and string on the floors left over from the packing, and not yet cleared up, and wished they had something to do. It was Cyril who said:

"I say, let's take our Margate spades and go and dig in the gravel pits. We can pretend it's seaside."

"Father said it was once," Anthea said; "he says there are shells there thousands of years old."

So they went. Of course they had been to the edge of the gravel pit and looked over, but they had not gone down into it for fear Father should say they mustn't play there, and the same with the chalk quarry. The gravel pit is not really dangerous if you don't try to climb down the edges, but go the slow safe way round by the road, as if you were a cart.

Each of the children carried his own spade, and took it in turns to carry the Lamb. He was the baby, and they called him that because "Baa" was the first thing he ever said. They called Anthea "Panther," which seems silly when you read it, but when you say it it sounds a little like her name.

The gravel pit is very large and wide, with grass growing round the edges at the top, and dry stringy wild flowers, purple and yellow. It is like a giant's wash-hand basin. And there are mounds of gravel, and holes in the sides of the basin where gravel has been taken out, and high up in the steep sides there are the little holes that are the little front doors of the little sand-martins' little houses.

The children built a castle, of course, but castle-building is rather poor fun when you have no hope of the swishing tide ever coming in to fill up the moat and wash away the drawbridge, and, at the happy last, to wet everybody up to the waist.

Cyril wanted to dig out a cave to play smugglers in, but the others thought it might bury them alive, so it ended in all spades going to work to dig a hole through the castle to Australia. These children, you see, believed that the world was round, and that on the other side the little Australian boys and girls were really walking wrong way up, like flies on the ceiling, with their heads hanging down into the air.

The children dug and they dug and they dug, and their hands got sandy and hot and red, and their faces got damp and shiny. The Lamb had tried to eat the sand, and had cried so hard when he found that it was not, as he had supposed, brown sugar, that he was now tired out, and was lying asleep in a warm fat bunch in the middle of the half-finished castle. This left his brothers and sisters free to work really hard, and the hole that was to come out in Australia soon grew so deep that Jane, who was called Pussy for short, begged the others to stop.

"Suppose the bottom of the hole gave way suddenly," she said, "and you tumbled out among the little Australians, all the sand would get in their eyes."

"Yes," said Robert, "and they would hate us, and throw stones at us, and not let us see the kangaroos, or opossums, or blue-gums, or Emu Brand birds."

Cyril and Anthea knew that Australia was not quite so near as all that, but they agreed to stop using their spades and go on with their hands. This was quite easy, because the sand at the bottom of the hole was very soft and fine and dry, like sea sand. And there were little shells in it.

"Fancy it having been wet sea here once, all sloppy and shiny," said Jane, "with fishes and conger eels and coral with mermaids."

"And masts of ships and wrecked Spanish treasure. I wish we could find a gold doubloon, or something," Cyril said.

"How did the sea get carried away?" Robert asked.

"Not in a pail, silly," said his brother.

"Father says the earth got too hot underneath, like you do in bed sometimes, so it just hunched up its shoulders, and the sea had to slip off, like the blankets do off us, and the shoulder was left sticking out, and turned into dry land. Let's go and look for shells; I think that little cave looks likely, and I see something sticking out there like a bit of wrecked ship's anchor, and it's beastly hot in the Australian hole."

The others agreed, but Anthea went on digging. She always liked to finish a thing when she had once begun it. She felt it would be a disgrace to leave that hole without getting through to Australia.

The cave was disappointing, because there were no shells, and the wrecked ship's anchor turned out to be only the broken end of a pickaxe handle, and the cave party were just making up their minds that sand makes you thirstier when it is not by the seaside, and someone had suggested going home for lemonade, when Anthea suddenly screamed:

"Cyril! Come here! Oh, come quick! It's alive! It'll get away! Quick!"

They all hurried back.

"It's a rat, I shouldn't wonder," said Robert. "Father says they infest old places —and this must be pretty old if the sea was here thousands of years ago."

"Perhaps it is a snake," said Jane, shuddering.

"Let's look," said Cyril, jumping into the hole. "I'm not afraid of snakes. I like them. If it is a snake I'll tame it, and it will follow me everywhere, and I'll let it sleep round my neck at night."

"No, you won't," said Robert firmly. He shared Cyril's bedroom. "But you may if it's a rat."

"Oh, don't be silly!" said Anthea; "it's not a rat, it's *much* bigger. And it's not a snake. It's got feet; I saw them; and fur! No—not the spade. You'll hurt it! Dig with your hands."

"And let *it* hurt *me* instead! That's so likely, isn't it?" said Cyril, seizing a spade.

"Oh, don't!" said Anthea. "Squirrel, *don't*. I—it sounds silly, but it said something. It really and truly did."

"What?"

"It said, 'You let me alone.'"

But Cyril merely observed that his sister must have gone off her nut, and he and Robert dug with spades while Anthea sat on the edge of the hole, jumping up and down with hotness and anxiety. They dug carefully, and presently everyone could see that there really was something moving in the bottom of the Australian hole.

Then Anthea cried out, "*I'm* not afraid. Let me dig," and fell on her knees and began to scratch the way a dog does when he has suddenly remembered where it was that he buried his bone.

"Oh, I felt fur," she cried, half laughing and half crying. "I did indeed! I did!" when suddenly a dry husky voice in the sand made them all jump back, and their hearts jumped nearly as fast as they did.

"Let me alone," it said. And now everyone heard the voice and looked at the others to see if they had too.

"But we want to see you," said Robert bravely.

"I wish you'd come out," said Anthea, also taking courage.

"Oh well—if that's your wish," the voice said, and the sand stirred and spun and scattered, and something brown and furry and fat came rolling out into the hole, and the sand fell off it, and it sat there yawning and rubbing the ends of its eyes with its hands.

"I believe I must have dropped asleep," it said, stretching itself.

The children stood round the hole in a ring, looking at the creature they had found. It was worth looking at. Its eyes were on long horns like a snail's eyes, and it could move them in and out like telescopes; it had ears like a bat's ears, and its tubby body was shaped like a spider's and covered with thick soft fur; its legs and arms were furry too, and it had hands and feet like a monkey's.

"What on earth is it?" Jane said. "Shall we take it home?"

The thing turned its long eyes to look at her, and said, "Does she always talk nonsense, or is it only the rubbish on her head that makes her silly?"

It looked scornfully at Jane's hat as it spoke.

"She doesn't mean to be silly," Anthea said gently, "we none of us do, whatever you may think! Don't be frightened; we don't want to hurt you, you know."

"Hurt *me!*" it said. "*Me* frightened! Upon my word! Why, you talk as if I were nobody in particular." All its fur stood out like a cat's when it is going to fight.

"Well," said Anthea, still kindly, "perhaps if we knew who you are we could think of something to say that wouldn't make you cross. Everything we've said so far seems to have. Who are you? And don't get angry! Because really we don't know."

"You don't know?" it said. "Well, I knew the world had changed—but really—do you mean to tell me you don't know a Psammead when you see one?"

"A Sammyadd? That's Greek to me."

"So it is to everyone," said the creature sharply. "Well, in plain English, then, a *Sand-fairy*. Don't you know a Sand-fairy when you see one?"

It looked so grieved and hurt that Jane hastened to say, "Of course I see you are, *now*. It's quite plain now one comes to look at you."

"You came to look at me, several sentences ago," it said crossly, beginning to curl up again in the sand.

"Oh—don't go away again! Do talk some more," Robert cried. "I didn't know you were a Sandy-fairy, but I knew directly I saw you that you were much the wonderfullest thing I'd ever seen."

The Sandy-fairy seemed a shade less disagreeable after this.

"It isn't talking I mind," it said, "as long as you're reasonably civil. But I'm not going to make polite conversation for you. If you talk nicely to me, perhaps I'll answer you, and perhaps I won't. Now say something."

Of course no one could think of anything to say, but at last Robert thought of "How long have you lived here?" and he said it at once.

"Oh, ages—several thousand years," replied the Psammead.

"Tell us all about it. Do."

"It's all in books."

"*You* aren't!" Jane said. "Oh, tell us everything you can about yourself! We don't know anything about you, and you *are* so nice."

The Sand-fairy smoothed its long ratlike whiskers and smiled between them.

"Do please tell!" said the children all together.

It is wonderful how quickly you get used to things, even the most astonishing. Five minutes before, the children had had no more idea than you that there was such a thing as a Sand-fairy in the world, and now they were talking to it as though they had known it all their lives.

It drew its eyes in and said, "How very sunny it is—quite like old times. Where do you get your Megatheriums from now?"

"What?" said the children all at once. It is very difficult always to remember that "what" is not polite, especially in moments of surprise or agitation.

"Are Pterodactyls plentiful now?" the Sand-fairy went on.

The children were unable to reply.

"What do you have for breakfast?" the Fairy said impatiently, "and who gives it to you?"

"Eggs and bacon, and bread-and-milk, and porridge and things. Mother gives it to us. What are Mega-what's-its-names and Ptero-what-do-you-call-thems? And does anyone have them for breakfast?"

Why, almost everyone had Pterodactyl for breakfast in my time! Pterodactyls were something like crocodiles and something like birds—I believe they were very good grilled. You see it was like this: of course there were heaps of Sand-fairies then, and in the morning early you went out and hunted for them, and when you'd found one it gave you your wish. People used to send their little boys down to the seashore early in the morning before breakfast to get the day's wishes, and very often the eldest boy in the family would be told to wish for a Megatherium, ready jointed for cooking. It was as big as an elephant, you see, so there was a good deal of meat on it. And if they wanted fish, the Ichthyosaurus was asked for—he was twenty to forty feet long, so there was plenty of him. And for poultry there was the Plesiosaurus; there were nice pickings on that too. But when people had dinner parties it was nearly always Megatheriums; and Ichthyosaurus, because his fins were a great delicacy and his tail made soup."

"There must have been heaps and heaps of cold meat left over," said Anthea, who meant to be a good housekeeper some day.

"Oh no," said the Psammead, "that would never have done. Why, of course at sunset what was left over turned into stone." It frowned and began to dig very fast with its furry hands.

"Oh, don't go!" they all cried; "tell us more about it when it was Megatheriums for breakfast! Was the world like this then?"

It stopped digging.

"Not a bit," it said; "it was nearly all sand where I lived, and coal grew on trees, and the periwinkles were as big as tea trays—you find them now; they're turned into stone. We Sand-fairies used to live on the seashore, and the children used to come with their little flint spades and flint pails and make castles for us to live in. That's thousands of years ago, but I hear that children still build castles on the sand. It's difficult to break yourself of a habit."

"But why did you stop living in the castles?" asked Robert.

"It's a sad story," said Psammead gloomily. "It was because they *would* build moats to the castles, and the nasty wet bubbling sea used to come in, and of course as soon as a Sand-fairy got wet it caught cold and generally died. And so there got to be fewer and fewer, and whenever you found a Fairy and had a wish, you used to wish for a Megatherium, and eat twice as much as you wanted, because it might be weeks before you got another wish."

"And did *you* get wet?" Robert inquired.

The Sand-fairy shuddered. "Only once," it said; "the end of the twelfth hair of my top left whisker—I feel the place still in damp weather. It was only once, but it was quite enough for me. I went away as soon as the sun had dried my poor dear whisker. I scurried away to the back of the beach, and dug myself a house deep in warm dry sand, and there I've been ever since. And the sea changed its lodgings afterwards. And now I'm not going to tell you another thing."

"Just one more, please," said the children. "Can you give wishes now?"

"Of course," said it, "didn't I give you yours a few minutes ago? You said, 'I wish you'd come out,' and I did."

"Oh, please, mayn't we have another?"

"Yes, but be quick about it. I'm tired of you."

I daresay you have often thought what

you would do if you had three wishes given you, and have felt certain that if you had the chance you could think of three really useful wishes without a moment's hesitation. These children had often talked this matter over, but now the chance had suddenly come to them, they could not make up their minds.

"Quick," said the Sand-fairy crossly. No one could think of anything, only Anthea did manage to remember a private wish of her own and Jane's which they had never told the boys. She knew the boys would not care about it—but still it was better than nothing.

"I wish we were all as beautiful as the day," she said in a great hurry.

The children looked at each other, but each could see that the others were not any better-looking than usual. The Psammead pushed out its long eyes, and seemed to be holding its breath and swelling itself out till it was twice as fat and furry as before. Suddenly it let its breath go in a long sigh.

"I'm really afraid I can't manage it," it apologized. "I must be out of practice. It has been a long time."

The children were horribly disappointed.

"Oh, *do* try again!" they said.

"Well," said the Sand-fairy, "the fact is, I was keeping back a little strength to give the rest of you your wishes with. If you'll be contented with one wish a day among the lot of you I daresay I can screw myself up to do it. Do you agree to that?"

"Yes, oh yes!" said Jane and Anthea. The boys nodded. They did not believe the Sand-fairy could do it.

It stretched out its eyes farther than ever, and swelled and swelled and swelled.

"I do hope it won't hurt itself," said Anthea.

"Or crack its skin," Robert said anxiously.

Everyone was very much relieved when the Sand-fairy, after getting so big that it almost filled up the hole in the sand, suddenly let out its breath and went back to its proper size.

"That's all right," it said, panting heavily. "It'll come easier tomorrow."

"Did it hurt much?" asked Anthea.

"Only my poor whisker, thank you," said he, "but you're a kind and thoughtful child. Good day."

It scratched suddenly and fiercely with its hands and feet, and disappeared in the sand. Then the children looked at each other, and each child suddenly found itself alone with three perfect strangers, all radiantly beautiful.

They stood for some moments in perfect silence. Each thought that its brothers and sisters had wandered off, and that these strange children had stolen up unnoticed while it was watching the Sand-fairy. Anthea spoke first.

"Excuse me," she said very politely to Jane, who now had enormous blue eyes and a cloud of russet hair, "but have you seen two little boys and a little girl anywhere about?" "I was just going to ask you that," said Jane.

And then Cyril cried, "Why, it's *you!* I know the hole in your pinafore! You *are* Jane, aren't you? And you're the Panther; I can see your dirty handkerchief that you forgot to change after you'd cut your thumb! Crikey! The wish has come off, after all. I say, am I as handsome as you are?"

"If you're Cyril, I liked you much better as you were before," said Anthea decidedly. "You look like the picture of the young chorister, with your golden hair; you'll die young, I shouldn't wonder. And if that's Robert, he's like an Italian organ grinder. His hair's all black."

"You two girls are like Christmas cards, then—that's all—silly Christmas cards," said Robert angrily. "And Jane's hair is simply carrots."

"Well, it's no use finding fault with each other," said Anthea; "let's get the Lamb and lug it home to dinner. The servants will admire us most awfully, you'll see."

Baby was just waking when they got to him, and not one of them but was relieved to find that he at least was not as beautiful as the day, but just as usual.

"I suppose he's too young to have wishes naturally," said Jane. "We shall have to mention him specially next time."

Anthea ran forward and held out her arms.

"Come to own Panther, ducky," she said.

The Baby looked at her disapprovingly, and put a sandy pink thumb in his mouth. Anthea was his favorite sister.

"Come then," she said.

"G'way long!" said the Baby.

"Come to own Pussy," said Jane.

"Wants my Panty," said the Lamb dismally, and his lip trembled.

"Here, come on," said Robert, "come and have a yidey on Yobby's back."

"Yah, narky narky boy," howled the Baby, giving way altogether. Then the children knew the worst. *The Baby did not know them!*

They looked at each other in despair, and it was terrible to each, in this dire emergency, to meet only the beautiful eyes of perfect strangers, instead of the merry, commonplace, twinkling, jolly little eyes of its own brothers and sisters.

"This is most truly awful," said Cyril when he had tried to lift up the Lamb, and the Lamb had scratched like a cat and bellowed like a bull. "We've got to *make friends* with him! I can't carry him home screaming like that. Fancy having to make friends with our own baby!—it's too silly for words."

That, however, was exactly what they had to do. It took over an hour, and the task was not rendered any easier by the fact that the Lamb was by this time as hungry as a lion and thirsty as a desert.

At last he consented to allow these strangers to carry him home by turns, but he was a dead weight and most exhausting.

"Thank goodness, we're home!" said Jane, staggering through the iron gate to where Martha, the nursemaid, stood at the front door shading her eyes with her hand and looking out anxiously. "Here! Do take Baby!"

Martha snatched the Baby from her arms.

"Thanks be, *he's* safe back," she said. "Where are the others, and whoever to goodness gracious are all of you?"

"We're *us*, of course," said Robert.

"And who's *us*, when you're at home?" asked Martha scornfully.

"I tell you it's *us*, only we're beautiful as the day," said Cyril. "I'm Cyril, and these are the others, and we're jolly hungry. Let us in, and don't be a silly idiot."

Martha merely dratted Cyril's impudence and tried to shut the door in his face.

"I know we *look* different, but I'm Anthea, and we're so tired, and it's long past dinner time."

"Then go home to your dinners, whoever you are; and if our children put you up to this playacting you can tell them from me they'll catch it!" With that she did bang the door. Cyril rang the bell violently. No answer.

Presently cook put her head out of a bedroom window and said, "If you don't take yourself off, and that precious sharp, I'll go and fetch the police."

"It's no good," said Anthea. "Oh, do come before we get sent to prison!"

The boys said it was nonsense, and the law of England couldn't put you in prison for just being as beautiful as the day, but all the same they followed the others out into the lane.

"We shall be our proper selves after sunset, I suppose," said Jane.

"I don't know," Cyril said sadly; "it mayn't be like that now—things have changed a good deal since Megatherium times."

"Oh," cried Anthea suddenly, "perhaps we shall turn into stone at sunset, like the Megatheriums did, so that there mayn't be any of us left over for the next day."

She began to cry, so did Jane. Even the boys turned pale.

It was a horrible afternoon. There was no house near where the children could beg a crust of bread or even a glass of water. They were afraid to go to the village, because they had seen Martha go down there with a basket, and there was a local constable. True, they were all as beautiful as the day, but that is a poor comfort when you are as hungry as a hunter and as thirsty as a sponge.

Three times they tried in vain to get the servants in the white house to let them in and listen to their tale. And then Robert went alone, hoping to be able to climb in at one of the back windows and so open the door to the others. But all the windows were out of reach, and Martha emptied a jug of cold water over him from a top window, and said, "Go along with you, you nasty little monkey."

It came at last to their sitting down in a row under the hedge, with their feet in a dry ditch, waiting for sunset, and wondering whether, when the sun *did* set, they would turn into stone, or only into their own old natural selves; and each of them still felt lonely and among strangers and tried not to look at the others, for their faces were so radiantly beautiful as to be quite irritating to look at.

"I don't believe we *shall* turn to stone," said Robert, breaking a long miserable silence, "because the Sand-fairy said he'd give us another wish tomorrow, and he couldn't if we were stone, could he?"

The others said "No," but they weren't at all comforted.

Another silence, longer and more miserable, was broken by Cryil's suddenly saying, "I don't want to frighten you girls, but I believe it's beginning with me already. My foot's quite dead. I'm turning to stone and so will you in a minute."

"Never mind," said Robert kindly, "perhaps you'll be the only stone one, and the rest of us will be all right. We'll cherish your statue and hang garlands on it."

But when it turned out that Cyril's foot had only gone to sleep through his sitting too long with it under him, and when it came to life in an agony of pins and needles, the others were quite cross.

"Giving us such a fright for nothing!" said Anthea.

The third and miserablest silence of all was broken by Jane. She said, "If we *do* come out of this all right we'll ask the Sammyadd to make it so that the servants don't notice anything different, no matter what wishes we have."

The others only grunted. They were too wretched even to make good resolutions.

At last hunger and fright and crossness and tiredness—four very nasty things—all joined together to bring one nice thing, and that was sleep. The children lay asleep in a row, with their beautiful eyes shut and their beautiful mouths open. Anthea woke first. The sun had set, and the twilight was coming on.

Anthea pinched herself very hard, to make sure, and when she found she could still feel pinching she decided that she was not stone, and then she pinched the others. They, also, were soft.

"Wake up," she said, almost in tears for joy; "we're not stone. And oh, Cyril, how nice and ugly you do look, with your old freckles and your brown hair and your little eyes. And so do you all!" she added, so that they might not feel jealous.

When they got home they were very much scolded by Martha, who told them about the strange children.

"A good-looking lot, I must say, but that impudent. And where on earth have you been all this time, you naughty little things, you."

"In the lane."

"Why didn't you come home hours ago?"

"We couldn't because of *them*," said Anthea.

"Who?"

"The children who were as beautiful as the day. They kept us there till after sunset. We couldn't come back till they'd gone. You don't know how we hated them! Oh, do, do give us some supper—we are so hungry."

"Hungry! I should think so," said Martha angrily; "out all day like this. Well, I hope it'll be a lesson to you not to go picking up with strange children—down here after measles, as likely as not. Now mind, if you see them again, don't speak to them—not one word nor so much as a look—but come straight away and tell me. I'll spoil their beauty for them!"

"If ever we *do* see them again we'll tell you," Anthea said; and Robert, gazing fondly on the cold beef that was being brought in on a tray by cook, added in heartfelt undertones, "And we'll take jolly good care we never *do* see them again."

And they never have.

TALK

*A story from the people of West Africa—
one that will make you smile and even laugh*

HAROLD COURLANDER AND GEORGE HERZOG

Once, not far from the city of Accra on the Gulf of Guinea, a countryman went out to his garden to dig up some yams to take to market. While he was digging, one of the yams said to him, "Well, at last you're here. You never weeded me, but now you come around with your digging stick. Go away and leave me alone!"

The farmer turned around and looked at his cow in amazement. The cow was chewing her cud and looking at him.

"Did you say something?" he asked.

The cow kept on chewing and said nothing, but the man's dog spoke up.

"It wasn't the cow who spoke to you," the dog said. "It was the yam. The yam says leave him alone."

The man became angry, because his dog had never talked before, and he didn't like his tone besides. So he took his knife and cut a branch from a palm tree to whip his dog. Just then the palm tree said, "Put that branch down!"

The man was getting very upset about the way things were going, and he started to throw the palm branch away, but the palm branch said, "Man, put me down softly!"

He put the branch down gently on a stone, and the stone said, "Hey, take that thing off me!"

This was enough, and the frightened farmer started to run for his village. On the way he met a fisherman going the other way with a fish trap on his head.

"What's the hurry?" the fisherman asked.

"My yam said, 'Leave me alone!' Then the dog said, 'Listen to what the yam says!' When I went to whip the dog with a palm branch the tree said, 'Put that branch down!' Then the palm branch said, 'Do it softly!' Then the stone said, 'Take that thing off me!'"

"Is that all?" the man with the fish trap asked. "Is that so frightening?"

"Well," the man's fish trap said, "did he take it off the stone?"

"Wah!" the fisherman shouted. He threw the fish trap on the ground and

273

began to run with the farmer, and on the trail they met a weaver with a bundle of cloth on his head.

"Where are you going in such a rush?" he asked them.

"My yam said, 'Leave me alone!'" the farmer said. "The dog said, 'Listen to what the yam says!' The tree said, 'Put that branch down!' The branch said, 'Do it softly!' And the stone said, 'Take that thing off me!'"

"And then," the fisherman continued, "the fish trap said, 'Did he take it off?'"

"That's nothing to get excited about," the weaver said, "no reason at all."

"Oh yes it is," his bundle of cloth said. "If it happened to you you'd run too!"

"Wah!" the weaver shouted. He threw his bundle on the trail and started running with the other men.

They came panting to the ford in the river and found a man bathing.

"Are you chasing a gazelle?" he asked them.

The first man said breathlessly, "My yam talked at me, and it said, 'Leave me alone!'

And my dog said, 'Listen to your yam!' And when I cut myself a branch the tree said, 'Put that branch down!' And the branch said, 'Do it softly!' And the stone said, 'Take that thing off me!'"

The fisherman panted, "And my trap said, 'Did he?'"

The weaver wheezed, "And my bundle of cloth said, 'You'd run too!'"

"Is that why you're running?" the man in the river asked.

"Well, wouldn't you run if you were in their position?" the river said.

The man jumped out of the water and began to run with the others. They ran down the main street of the village to the house of the chief. The chief's servants brought his stool out, and he came and sat on it to listen to their complaints.

The men began to recite their troubles.

"I went out to my garden to dig yams," the farmer said, waving his arms. "Then everything began to talk! My yam said, 'Leave me alone!' My dog said, 'Pay attention to your yam!' The tree said, 'Put that branch down!' The branch said, 'Do it softly!' And the stone said, 'Take it off me!'"

"And my fish trap said, 'Well, did he take it off?'" the fisherman said.

"And my cloth said, 'You'd run too!'" the weaver said.

"And the river said the same," the bather said hoarsely, his eyes bulging. The chief listened to them patiently, but he couldn't refrain from scowling.

"Now this is really a wild story," he said at last. "You'd better all go back to your work before I punish you for disturbing the peace."

So the men went away, and the chief shook his head and mumbled to himself, "Nonsense like that upsets the community."

"Fantastic, isn't it?" his stool said. "Imagine, a talking yam!"

The Woods-Devil

*It was bitter cold in the winter woods and Nathan
was terrified, yet he had to go on. He would have cried
had he been a year younger, but at fifteen you do not cry*

PAUL ANNIXTER

For the four days since his father's accident, it had snowed intermittently. The slate-black clouds of winter had banked up in the north and west. They were motionless, changeless, remote and ridged like banks of corrugated metal. For days during this north Maine winter, the only sun to be seen had been a yellowish filter at midday that came in the cabin window like a thin sifting of sulphur dust.

Nathan was just bringing in the night's wood, enough short logs to burn till morning; with another pile of wood chunks beside the daubed clay fireplace they would last the following day if need be. His face and ears burned from laboring in a temperature of thirty below. He was dressed in brown linsey-woolsey; on his feet were shoes of heavy felt, stuffed with coarse, gray socks against the cold. A cap of worn coonskin crowned his shagbark hair that had not been cut in many weeks. He had reached the gangling age of fifteen and a half, when the joints are all loose and clumsy. His lean face was drawn, the dark eyes sullen from overwork.

His mother sat darning a sock over an egg, rising now and then to stir the pot of mush or turn the cooking rabbit. His father lay in the cord bunk in the corner of the cabin, his injured leg raised high beneath the blankets. His gaunt, unshaven face was etched with the memory of the pain he had endured before the settlement doctor had come to set the broken bone. Worry showed in his black eyes turned up to the ceiling poles. Little food was left for the family—a bit of jerked venison in the smokehouse, a side of bacon, some beans and meal. The Stemlines were true woodsies. They'd been eking along, waiting for the fur season. All that they ate, spent and wore came from their traps and rifles.

Nathan went out for the final log, and the door creaked behind him on its crude hinges. The snow in the clearing was almost knee-deep. The forest surrounded it on all sides, broken only where a road cut a black tunnel through the balsams toward the settlement down to the south.

A sudden wind rose with the darkness. Nathan could hear it far off and high, a growing roar above the forest. Abruptly it snatched at the clearing, whirling the snow in eddies; the serried pine tops bent in rhythm. Because his impulse was to hurry in and close the door against it, Nathan stood for several minutes, his face straight into it, letting the cold and darkness and emptiness sink into him.

Indoors, he eased down his log and took off his sheepskin coat and cap, baring his mop of brown hair. He sat down beside Viney, his eight-year-old sister, playing with the endless paper people she cut out of the mail-order catalogue. The wind made hollow bottle noises down the chimney.

"Listen to that," said Nathan's mother. "The Almanac was right. We're due for another cold spell. 'A stormy new moon. Keep a good fire,' Father Richard says for the ninth. 'Colder. Expect snow,' it says for the tenth."

Nathan's voice had a manly note. "It's getting colder all right, but it won't snow. It's too darned cold to snow. A fellow'd soon be stiff if he didn't keep working."

"Is the ax in?" his father asked.

"Yes." Nathan fetched it and put a keen, shining edge on it with the whetstone. Then he ran a greased rag through each of the rifle barrels. He could feel his father's approving gaze on his back as he sighted through each barrel into the firelight. "Bright's a bugle." He copied his father's invariable comment.

Then he sat waiting, his hands clasped tightly between his knees, for what he knew must come.

"Nathan," his father said presently, and the boy went over and stood dutifully by the bunk. "Do you think you can cover the trapline tomorrow, son?"

"Yes, I guess I can." He was prickling with trepidation. The wind shook the cabin door as he spoke, and he thought of all that lay up in the far pine valley—things to be felt, if not seen or heard.

"It's a long ways, I know, and it's mortal cold . . ." His father's voice was drained and tired, and for a moment Nathan glimpsed the naked misery and worry in his mind. "But money's scarce, son. We've got to do what can be done."

"I don't mind the cold or the snow." Nathan stared down at his feet until that look should leave his father's face.

"I'll be laid up three, four weeks, maybe more. It's four days since we laid out the line. Varmints may have got most of our catch by now. You've got to go, Nathan. If you start at daylight you can make the rounds and be back by night."

"Shucks, yes." Nathan forced a smile. When he dared lift his eyes, he saw his father's face had hardened again in coping with the problem.

"You needn't try to bring in the catch," he said. "You can hang some of it on high boughs, then reset the traps. Main thing's to find what kind of range we got in there. Later on, you may have to spend a night in the valley. Think you'll be a-scairt to sleep alone in the deep woods?"

"Not me." Nathan's tone discounted all concern, but misgivings quickly crowded in. "Anyhow I'd have an ax and a rifle and plenty cartridges," he said.

His father managed a smile. "Might have to sleep in there once every week till I'm up again. So you'd best look at that log cache we built to store traps in. It's plenty big enough to sleep a man."

Pride filled Nathan. This was real man's work he was detailed to do.

"You'd best turn in early," his father said, "so's you can start at dawn."

"All right."

"You're a brave boy, Nathan," his

mother said. "You're the provider for this family now. What a blessing it is you're big enough to cover the line while your father's down. Last year you could never have done it."

"He's near about as good as any man now," his father said. "Knows the woods and critters as well as I."

Young Nathan grew more stolid than usual, holding himself against the rushing tide of feeling. He wished he were all they said of him. Inside he was frightened whenever he thought of the Little Jackpine Valley where their trapline had been laid out. For three days the vision of the valley and what he had felt there had lurked before his mind's eye, filling him with dread.

Methodically, Nathan ate the man's share of food his mother set before him on the hewn-log table. Soon after, he climbed the sapling ladder to the small quarter loft where he slept. He lay quiet, pretending to sleep, but long after the lamp went out he was still grappling with his thoughts. Storm gripped the cabin, and the night was full of voices. Once far in the forest a wolf howled. Nathan's skin prickled and his two hands made fists underneath the blankets. Now and again he could hear his father stirring and knew that he, too, was thinking the same thoughts.

Dawn had not yet come when Nathan descended the ladder. He built up the fire, made coffee and ate a hurried breakfast.

"Make sure you don't forget anything," his father said. "Have you got plenty cartridges . . . matches? Belt ax? Bait?"

"Yes, Pa."

"Best take my rifle," his father said.

Nathan took down his father's finely balanced rifle with its curly walnut stock and held it proudly in his hands. It was a far better weapon than the old Sharps Nathan usually carried.

"I wouldn't take the sled," his father was saying. "It's heavy, and I want you back by night. Be right careful," he called, as Nathan lifted the latch.

The cold bit deep. It was scarcely light yet in the clearing. The storm had died down in the night and there was no wind now, but the air cut Nathan's cheeks like a razor. It was colder than anything he had ever known.

After twenty minutes of tramping he thought of turning back. His face and hands were numbing; his joints seemed to be stiffening. Each breath was agony. He snatched up some of the hard, dry snow and rubbed it against his stiffened face till a faint glow of feeling came. Then he ran for a long way—beating his arms, one, then the other, against his body, shifting the rifle, till his thin chest was heaving. Again his face was like wood. He was terrified, but he would not turn back.

He covered the three miles to the mouth of the Little Jackpine in a daze. He did not know what he could do with his numbed hands if he did find a catch in the traps; he could not even use the rifle if the occasion arose. He would have cried had he been a year younger, but at fifteen you do not cry. He started into the valley.

The Little Jackpine lay at the foot of old Shakehammer Mountain and through it a small stream rushed and snarled like a wildcat, its bed choked with almost inaccessible jungles of windfalls. It was an appalling wilderness.

Both Nathan and his father could read the silent speech of place and time in the outdoors, and what the valley had said to them had been vaguely antagonistic from the first—almost a warning. Nathan remembered how they had threaded the valley bottom, in single file, silent. The breeze had droned its ancient dirge in the treetops, but not a breath of it had stirred along the stream bed. The hiss of the water had created an intense hush.

He remembered how he had spat in the boiling waters to show his unconcern, but it hadn't done much good. Several times as they headed homeward, Nathan's father had stopped abruptly in his tracks to look behind and to all sides. "Queer," he had muttered. "A full hour past I had a right smart feelin' we were bein' watched and followed. I still got it."

"I had it, too, Pa," Nathan had said. "It's mighty fearsome back yonder, ain't it?"

"It ain't a bear." His father had evaded the question. "May be some young lynx cat, figurin' he'd like to play with us. A lynx is a tomfool for followin' humans."

They had backtracked to the top of a rise to look, but they saw nothing. Then the valley struck its first blow. A perfectly placed boulder that had lain poised for untold years had toppled at that exact moment to crush the older Nathan's leg as he scrambled down a rocky ledge . . .

Nathan passed the spot, but he did not pause. Something seemed to listen behind each tree and rock, and something seemed to wait among the taller trees ahead, blue-black in the shadows. After a while it felt warmer, perhaps because he was climbing. Then he came to the first trap and forgot wind, cold and even fear.

A marten, caught perhaps two days before, lay in the set. Its carcass had been partially devoured, its prime pelt torn to ribbons as if in malice. Roundabout in the snow were broad, splayed tracks, but wind and sleet had partly covered them, so that their identity was not plain. But they told Nathan enough. Neither fox nor wolf had molested this trap, nor was it a bear. Nathan knew what it was, but he wasn't admitting it yet—even to himself.

He stood up, his eyes searching for a glimpse of a secret enemy, but the valley gave back nothing. Except for the soughing of the balsam boughs far overhead, the stillness was complete.

He moved on between the endless ranks of trees and again had the feeling of being watched. At intervals he stopped to glance back along his trail, but saw nothing. The trunks of the dark trees seemed to watch him as he approached, slipping furtively behind him as he passed.

The next trap had been uncovered and sprung, the bait—a frozen fish—eaten, and the trap itself dragged off into the brush and buried in the snow. It took nearly half an hour floundering and digging to uncover trap and clog. Hard by was another set, and there Nathan saw a thing that made his skin crawl. The remains of a porcupine lay in the trap, and the creature had been eaten—quills, barb and all. Blood from the jaws of the eater was spattered all around. Only a devil could have done that! Beneath a spruce he saw clearly the despoiler's trail—splayed, hand-shaped tracks like those of a small bear, each print peaked with fierce claw marks.

These were the tracks of a giant wolverine, the woods-devil, bane of all trappers.

For long minutes Nathan stood in the dusky shadows, fighting down his fear. He had heard about the evil fortune that fastens upon trappers molested by a wolverine. Then he thought of what awaited him at home—that stricken look on his father's face. His fear of that was greater than his fear of the valley.

He hung his sack of frozen bait on a high bough. Useless to reset any of the traps now, for the creature he was pitted against could smell cold steel, unbaited, through two feet of snow, and, in sheer deviltry, would rob and destroy wherever it prowled.

Nathan plodded on again, his chest hollow with hopelessness.

The snow became deeper. One after another he came upon six more sets that had been robbed. Each had held a catch, and each ravaged pelt meant the loss of food and clothing to his family.

Then Nathan gave a whimpering cry. He had come to the seventh trap, and that one had contained treasure, a pelt worth a whole season's work to the Stemlines. This was a black fisher marten, always a trapper's prize. If only he could have carried home such a pelt on this first day of his rounds! How smoothed and eased his father's worried face would have become! But the woods-devil had destroyed it—an even more thorough job than on any of the others.

The boy whimpered again as he crouched there in the snow. Then anger flooded him, fought back the tears. He rose and began the endless plodding again, peering into every covert for the dark,

skulking shape. He did not know the size of a wolverine. He'd never seen one. He recalled old Laban Knowles' tale of the wolverine that had gnawed his walnut rifle stock in two and scored the very rifle barrel. And Granther Bates told of a woods-devil that had killed his two dogs, then gnawed through a log wall to rob him of his grub cache.

It was afternoon when Nathan neared the farthest limit of the trapline. Of twenty-odd traps, only two had been unmolested. Abruptly he came upon a fresh trail in the snow: the same hand-shaped tracks and demon claws, no more than an hour old. Grimly he turned aside to follow their twisting course.

He was descending a steep, wooded slope, when on a sudden impulse he doubled back on his own tracks and plunged up the grade through deep snow. As he reached the crest, a dark, humped shape took form beneath the drooping boughs of a spruce—a ragged, sooty-black and brown beast, some three and a half feet long, that lumbered like a small bear; it was lighter colored along its back and darker underneath, in direct contrast to all other forest beings. It saw him, and its green-shadowed eyes fixed on those of the boy beneath a tree some hundred feet away. The black jaw dropped open, and a harsh grating snarl cut the stillness. The utter savagery of this challenge sent a shiver through Nathan's body. His rifle flew up, and without removing his mitten he fired. The whole valley roared. In the same instant, the wolverine disappeared.

Nathan rushed forward, reloading as he ran. Under the spruce were several drops of blood in the snow, but the wolverine had vanished completely.

Panting, stumbling, sobbing, the boy plunged along the trail, bent low, ducking under the drooping limbs of the trees,

sometimes crawling on hands and knees. He saw other drops of blood. They gave him heart. He had a lynx eye, his father had often said. He would follow on to the very Circle if need be; he would not miss a second time. His one hope now was to settle with the beast for good and all.

The trail led down along the stream bed, twisting through tangles of windfalls, writhing masses of frost-whitened roots, and branches that seemed caught in a permanent hysteria. Twice he fell, but each time he thrust high the rifle as he went down, to keep the snow from jamming its snout. He plunged on again; he did not know for how long or how far, but he was aware at last of the beginning of twilight. And the end of light meant the end of the trail. Victory for the enemy.

The way had grown steeper. He was coming to the narrow throatlatch of the valley's head, a place where hundreds of great trees, snapped off by storm and snowslide from the slopes above, had collected in a mighty log jam, a tangle of timber, rock and snow that choked the stream bed from bank to bank. Countless logs lay crisscrossed helter-skelter with two- and three-foot gaps between. The great pile was acre large, fifty feet high, rank with the odor of rotted logs and old snow.

Into this maze led the trail of the woods-devil. Nathan skirted the pile. The trail did not come out!

Trembling, he squeezed his way between two logs into the great jam. The wolverine might be fifty yards inside, but somehow it must be ferreted out. In and in Nathan wormed his body, pausing to watch, to listen, his rifle thrust carefully before him. Then down and down into the twisting chaos of dead and dying trunks, led by his nose, for the rank odor of the devil's den now filled the air. Coming upward from the very bottom of the jam, it was fouler than any skunk taint.

Nathan stopped short, his body tensing like a spring. To his ears came a harsh and menacing growl, but from which direction he could not tell. He waited but could see nothing. He loosened the safety on his rifle and wriggled forward again, and again the air was filled with that ominous challenge. This time it seemed to come from behind him. He whirled in panic, but there was nothing. His terror mounted. The creature must be watching him, and he could not see it. Then a movement caught his eye, and he glimpsed a soot-dark shape in the lower shadows.

The boy wriggled on his belly along a slanting log, maneuvering for a shot through the intervening timbers. He braced himself, craning far downward. . . . Then in the very instant he took aim, he slipped on the snow-sheathed log. The gun roared; the shot went wild; and, as Nathan caught himself, the rifle slid from his ice-slick grasp. It clattered downward, striking against log after log before it lodged at the bottom of the jam, snout down in snow, its barrel clogged and useless.

In that instant all the craft that has made man master of the wild fell away, and Nathan was reduced to first principles. The wolverine clambered slowly upward. Inexorably it advanced upon him. He screamed at it, but there was no vestige of fear in the beast. Nathan's hand went to his light belt ax; he gave no ground.

With a panicking shout he leaned and swung at the low flat head, but missed because of hindering logs. He swung again and again, and the blade struck, but with no apparent effect, for the creature's advance never checked. Its small, implacable eyes shone blue-green.

It lunged suddenly for Nathan's dangling legs. He flung himself up and over the log, then slipped on the icy sheath, grasped desperately for another log and slipped again to a point eight feet below. He flung around with a cry of desperation, expecting to meet open jaws, as the demon was almost upon him. But the animal was logy. Its power lay in its indomitability—a slow, irresistible power.

In it came again, above him now. He stood upright, braced on two logs, to meet it. He was crying now, sobbing and unashamed.

He struck again, yelling with each blow of the belt ax, but hack as he would, the beast bore in and in, maneuvering along the undersides of logs to avoid the ax.

Then as Nathan slipped again, he avoided the traplike jaws. He fell to the bottom of the jam, biting snow as he screamed. He was on his feet again before the creature above released its claw hold and dropped upon him like a giant slug.

Flinging an arm up over his throat, he jerked back blindly. Spread saber claws tore open his heavy coat. Then the ax fell again, blow after blow with all his strength; he shouted with every blow. No longer cries of terror, but of war.

The thing would not die. The jaws clamped on Nathan's leg above the knee, and he felt his own warm blood. Then his hand found the skinning knife at his belt, and the blade sank into the corded neck —turned till the clamp of jaws released.

Nathan climbed up out of the abatis till half his body emerged from the top of the great jam, and there he rested—panting, spent. He whimpered once, but there were no tears now. Instinctively, his eyes lifted skyward. Overhead, as night drew on, a great rift appeared in the leaden canopy of cloud, and a few stars shone through. He fixed his eyes on the brightest star until chaos left him; then his vision steadied, as if his head were higher than ever it had been before, in a realm of pure air. His brain was almost frighteningly clear.

The trickle of warm blood down his leg roused him. He pressed his heavy pants leg around his wound till he felt the bleeding stop. Painfully, he turned down into the maze of logs again and brought up the rifle. Then down again to struggle upward, dragging the woods-devil by its short and ragged scut. He laid it out on the snow and pulled out his bloody knife. He wasn't tired now, he wasn't cold, he wasn't afraid. His hands were quick and sure at the skinning; even his father had never lifted a pelt with smoother, defter hand. Darkness shut down, but he needed no light. The head he cut from the body, leaving it attached to the hide.

He thought of the proud fancy that made the far northern Indians covet a garment made of a wolverine's skin. Oh, there would be talk in the cabin tonight; they would sit at the table long after their eating was done, as great folk were supposed to do. He'd recount all the details of the day and the fight before he showed his trophy.

He rose at last and rolled up his grisly bundle, fur side out, and moved away through the blackness of the trees, sure of tread, for he had the still hunter's "eyes in the feet." Reflection from the snow gave a faint light. He was limping a bit.

Off in the black woods, a wolf howled dismally, and Nathan smiled. Never again would the night dogs make his skin crawl. Never again would he be afraid of anything aboveground.

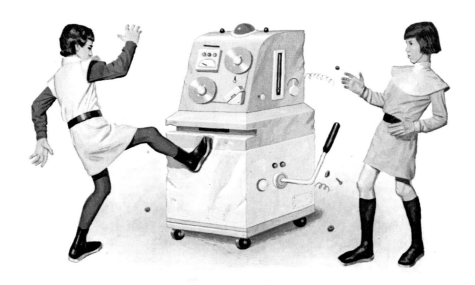

SOMEDAY

*Perhaps the world will be like this
in years to come. Perhaps people won't read and write.
Perhaps computers will do everything*

Isaac Asimov

Niccolo Mazetti lay stomach down on the rug, chin buried in the palm of one small hand, and listened to the Bard disconsolately. There was even the suspicion of tears in his dark eyes, a luxury an eleven-year-old could allow himself only when alone.

The Bard said, "Once upon a time in the middle of a deep wood, there lived a poor woodcutter and his two motherless daughters, who were each as beautiful as the day is long. The older daughter had long hair as black as a feather from a raven's wing, but the younger daughter had hair as bright

and golden as the sunlight of an autumn afternoon.

"Many times while the girls were waiting for their father to come home from his day's work in the wood, the older girl would sit before a mirror and sing——"

What she sang, Niccolo did not hear, for a call sounded from outside the room, "Hey, Nickie."

And Niccolo, his face clearing on the moment, rushed to the window and shouted, "Hey, Paul."

Paul Loeb waved an excited hand. He was thinner than Niccolo and not as tall, for all he was six months older. His face was full of repressed tension which showed itself most clearly in the rapid blinking of his eyelids. "Hey, Nickie, let me in. I've got an idea and a *half*. Wait till you hear it." He looked rapidly about him as though to check on the possibility of eavesdroppers, but the front yard was quite patently empty. He repeated, in a whisper, "Wait till you hear it."

"All right. I'll open the door."

The Bard continued smoothly, oblivious to the sudden loss of attention on the part of Niccolo. As Paul entered, the Bard was saying ". . . Thereupon, the lion said, 'If you will find me the lost egg of the bird which flies over the Ebony Mountain once every ten years, I will——'"

Paul said, "Is that a Bard you're listening to? I didn't know you had one."

Niccolo reddened and the look of unhappiness returned to his face. "Just an old thing I had when I was a kid. It ain't much good." He kicked at the Bard with his foot and caught the scarred and discolored plastic covering a glancing blow.

The Bard hiccuped as its speaking attachment was jarred out of contact a moment, then it went on: "——for a year and a day until the iron shoes were worn out. The princess stopped at the side of the road. . . ."

Paul said, "Boy, that *is* an old model," and looked at it critically.

Despite Niccolo's own bitterness against the Bard, he winced at the other's condescending tone. For the moment, he was sorry he had allowed Paul in, at least before he had restored the Bard to its usual resting place in the basement. It was only in the desperation of a dull day and a fruitless discussion with his father that he had resurrected it. And it turned out to be just as stupid as he had expected.

Nickie was a little afraid of Paul anyway, since Paul had special courses at school and

everyone said he was going to grow up to be a Computing Engineer.

Not that Niccolo himself was doing badly at school. He got adequate marks in logic, binary manipulations, computing and elementary circuits: all the usual grammar-school subjects. But that was it! They were just the usual subjects and he would grow up to be a control-board guard like everyone else.

Paul, however, knew mysterious things about what he called electronics and theoretical mathematics and programing. Especially programing. Niccolo didn't even try to understand when Paul bubbled over about it.

Paul listened to the Bard for a few minutes and said, "You been using it much?"

"No!" said Niccolo, offended. "I've had it in the basement since before you moved into the neighborhood. I just got it out today——" He lacked an excuse that seemed adequate to himself, so he concluded, "I just got it out."

Paul said, "Is that what it tells you about: woodcutters and princesses and talking animals?"

Niccolo said, "It's terrible. My dad says we can't afford a new one. I said to him this morning——" The memory of the morning's fruitless pleadings brought Niccolo dangerously near tears, which he repressed in a panic. Somehow, he felt that Paul's thin cheeks never felt the stain of tears and that Paul would have only contempt for anyone else less strong than himself. Niccolo went on, "So I thought I'd try this old thing again, but it's no good."

Paul turned off the Bard, pressed the contact that led to a nearly instantaneous reorientation and recombination of the vocabulary, characters, plot lines and climaxes stored within it. Then he reactivated it.

The Bard began smoothly, "Once upon a

time there was a little boy named Willikins whose mother had died and who lived with a stepfather and a stepbrother. Although the stepfather was very well-to-do, he begrudged poor Willikins the very bed he slept in so that Willikins was forced to get such rest as he could on a pile of straw in the stable next to the horses——"

"Horses!" cried Paul.

"They're a kind of animal," said Niccolo. "I think."

"I know that! I just mean imagine stories about *horses*."

"It tells about horses all the time," said Niccolo. "There are things called cows, too. You milk them but the Bard doesn't say how."

"Well, gee, why don't you fix it up?"

"I'd like to know how."

The Bard was saying, "Often Willikins would think that if only he were rich and powerful, he would show his stepfather and stepbrother what it meant to be cruel to a little boy, so one day he decided to go out into the world and seek his fortune."

Paul, who wasn't listening to the Bard, said, "It's *easy*. The Bard has memory cylinders all fixed up for plot lines and climaxes and things. We don't have to worry about that. It's just vocabulary we've got to fix so it'll know about computers and automation and electronics and real things about today. Then it can tell interesting stories, you know, instead of about princesses and things."

Niccolo said despondently, "I wish we could do that."

Paul said, "Listen, my dad says if I get into special computing school next year, he'll get me a *real* Bard, a late model. A big one with an attachment for space stories and mysteries. And a visual attachment, too!"

"You mean *see* the stories?"

"Sure. Mr. Daugherty at school says they've got things like that now, but not for just everybody. Only if I get into computing school, Dad can get a few breaks."

Niccolo's eyes bulged with envy. "Gee. *Seeing* a story."

"You can come over and watch anytime, Nickie."

"Oh, boy. Thanks."

"That's all right. But remember, I'm the guy who says what kind of story we get to hear."

"Sure. Sure." Niccolo would have agreed to much more onerous conditions.

Paul's attention returned to the Bard.

It was saying, "'If that is the case,' said the king, stroking his beard and frowning till clouds filled the sky and lightning flashed, 'you will see to it that my entire land is freed of flies by this time day after tomorrow or——'"

"All we've got to do," said Paul, "is open it up——" He shut the Bard off again and was prying at its front panel as he spoke.

"Hey," said Niccolo, in sudden alarm. "Don't break it."

"I won't break it," said Paul impatiently. "I know all about these things." Then, with sudden caution, "Your father and mother home?"

"No."

"All right, then." He had the front panel off and peered in. "Boy, this is one of those one-cylinder things."

He worked away at the Bard's innards. Niccolo, who watched with painful suspense, could not make out what he was doing.

Paul pulled out a thin, flexible metal strip, powdered with dots. "That's the Bard's memory cylinder. I'll bet its capacity for stories is under a trillion."

"What are you going to do, Paul?" quavered Niccolo.

"I'll give it vocabulary."

"How?"

"Easy. I've got a book here. Mr. Daugherty gave it to me at school."

Paul pulled the book out of his pocket and pried at it till he had its plastic jacket off. He unreeled the tape a bit, ran it through the vocalizer, which he turned down to a whisper, then placed it within the Bard's vitals. He made further attachments.

"What'll that do?"

"The book will talk and the Bard will put it all on its memory tape."

"What good will that do?"

"Boy, you're a dope! This book is all about computers and automation and the Bard will get all that information. Then he can stop talking about kings making lightning when they frown."

Niccolo said, "And the good guy always wins anyway. There's no excitement."

"Oh, well," said Paul, watching to see if his setup was working properly, "that's the way they make Bards. They got to have the good guy win and make the bad guys lose and things like that. I heard my father talking about it once. He says that without censorship there'd be no telling what the younger generation would come to. He says it's bad enough as it is . . . There, it's working fine."

Paul brushed his hands against one another and turned away from the Bard. He said, "But listen, I didn't tell you my idea yet. It's the best thing you ever heard, I bet. I came right to you because I figured you'd come in with me."

"Sure, Paul, sure."

"Okay. You know Mr. Daugherty at school? You know what a funny kind of guy he is. Well, he likes me, kind of."

"I know."

"I was at his house after school today."

"You *were?*"

"Sure. He says I'm going to be entering computer school and he wants to encourage me and things like that. He says the world needs more people who can design advanced computer circuits and do proper programing."

"Oh?"

Paul might have caught some of the emptiness behind that monosyllable. He said impatiently, "Programing! I told you a hundred times. That's when you set up problems for the giant computers like Multivac to work on. Mr. Daugherty says it gets harder all the time to find people who can really run computers. He says anyone can keep an eye on the controls and check off answers and put through routine problems. He says the trick is to expand research and figure out ways to ask the right questions, and that's hard.

"Anyway, Nickie, he took me to his place and showed me his collection of old computers. He had tiny computers you had to push with your hand, with little knobs all over them. And he had a hunk of wood he called a slide rule with a little piece of it that went in and out. And some wires with balls on them. He even had a hunk of paper with a kind of thing he called a multiplication table."

Niccolo, who found himself only moderately interested, said, "A paper table?"

"It wasn't really a table like you eat on. It was different. It was to help people compute. Mr. Daugherty tried to explain but he didn't have much time and it was kind of complicated, anyway."

"Why didn't people just use a computer?"

"That was *before* they had computers," cried Paul.

"Before?"

"Sure. Do you think people always had computers? Didn't you ever hear of the cavemen?"

Niccolo said, "How'd they get along without computers?"

"*I* don't know. Mr. Daugherty says they just had children any old time and did anything that came into their heads whether it would be good for everybody or not. They didn't even know if it was good or not. And farmers grew things with their hands and people had to do all the work in the factories and run all the machines."

"I don't believe you."

"That's what Mr. Daugherty said. He said it was just plain messy and everyone was miserable . . . Anyway, let me get to my idea, will you?"

"Well, go ahead. Who's stopping you?" said Niccolo, offended.

"All right. Well, the hand computers, the ones with the knobs, had little squiggles on each knob. And the slide rule had squiggles on it. And the multiplication table was all squiggles. I asked what they were. Mr. Daugherty said they were numbers."

"What?"

"Each different squiggle stood for a different number. For 'one' you made a kind of mark, for 'two' you make another kind of mark, for 'three' another and so on."

"What for?"

"So you could compute."

"What *for*? You just tell the computer——"

"Jiminy," cried Paul, his face twisting with anger, "can't you get it through your head? These slide rules and things didn't talk."

"Then how——"

"The answers showed up in squiggles and you had to know what the squiggles meant. Mr. Daugherty says that, in olden days, everybody learned how to make squiggles when they were kids and how to decode them, too. Making squiggles was called 'writing' and decoding them was 'reading.' He says there was a different kind of squiggle for every word and they used to write whole books in squiggles. He said they had some at the museum and I could look at them if I wanted to. He said if

I was going to be a real computer and programer I would have to know about the history of computing and that's why he was showing me all these things."

Niccolo frowned. He said, "You mean everybody had to figure out squiggles for every word and *remember* them? . . . Is this all real or are you making it up?"

"It's all real. Honest. Look, this is the way you make a 'one.'" He drew his finger through the air in a rapid downstroke. "This way you make 'two,' and this way 'three.' I learned all the numbers up to 'nine.'"

Niccolo watched the curving finger uncomprehendingly. "But what's the good of it?"

"You can learn how to make words. I asked Mr. Daugherty how you made the squiggle for 'Paul Loeb' but he didn't know. He said there were people at the museum who would know. He said there were people who had learned how to decode whole books. He said computers could be designed to decode books and used to be used that way but not any more because we have real books now, with magnetic tapes that go through the vocalizer and come out talking, you know."

"Sure."

"So if we go down to the museum, we can get to learn how to make words in squiggles. They'll let us because I'm going to computer school."

Niccolo was riddled with disappointment. "Is that your idea? Holy Smokes, Paul, who wants to do that? Make stupid squiggles!"

"Don't you get it? Don't you *get* it? You dope. *It'll be secret message stuff!*"

"What?"

"Sure. What good is talking when everyone can understand you? With squiggles you can send secret messages. You can make them on paper and nobody in the world would know what you were saying unless they knew the squiggles, too. And they wouldn't, you bet, unless we taught them. We can have a real club, with initiations and rules and a clubhouse. Boy——"

A certain excitement began stirring in Niccolo's bosom. "What kind of secret messages?"

"Any kind. Say I want to tell you to come over to my place and watch my new Visual Bard and I don't want any of the other fellows to come. I make the right squiggles on paper and I give it to you and you look at it and you know what to do. Nobody else does. You can even show it to them and they wouldn't know a thing."

"Hey, that's something!" yelled Niccolo, completely won over. "When do we learn how?"

"Tomorrow," said Paul. "I'll get Mr. Daugherty to explain to the museum that it's all right and you get your mother and father to say okay. We can go down right after school and start learning."

"Sure!" cried Niccolo. "We can be club officers."

"I'll be president," said Paul matter-of-factly. "You can be vice president."

"All right. Hey, this is going to be lots more fun than the Bard." He was suddenly reminded of the Bard and said in apprehension, "Hey, what about my old Bard?"

Paul turned to look at it. It was quietly taking in the slowly unreeling book, and the sound of the book's vocalizations was a dimly heard murmur.

He said, "I'll disconnect it."

He worked while Niccolo watched anxiously. After a few moments, Paul put his reassembled book into his pocket, replaced the Bard's panel and activated it.

The Bard said, "Once upon a time, in a large city, there lived a poor young boy named Fair Johnnie whose only friend in the world was a small computer. The computer, each morning, would tell the boy whether it would rain that day and answer any problems he might have. It was never wrong. But it so happened that one day the king of that land, having heard of the little computer, decided that he would have it as his own. With this purpose in mind, he called in his Grand Vizier and said——"

Niccolo turned off the Bard with a quick motion of his hand. "Same old junk," he said passionately. "Just with a computer thrown in."

"Well," said Paul, "they got so much stuff on the tape already that the computer business doesn't show up much when random combinations are made. What's the difference, anyway? You just need a new model."

"We'll *never* be able to afford one. Just this dirty old miserable thing." He kicked at it again, hitting it more squarely this time. The Bard moved backward with a squeal of casters.

"You can always watch mine, when I get it," said Paul. "Besides, don't forget our squiggle club."

Niccolo nodded.

"I tell you what," said Paul. "Let's go over to my place. My father has some books about old times. We can listen to them and maybe get some ideas. You leave a note for your folks and maybe you can stay over for supper. Come on."

"Okay," said Niccolo, and the two boys ran out together. Niccolo, in his eagerness, ran almost squarely into the Bard, but he only rubbed at the spot on his hip where he had made contact and ran on.

The activation signal of the Bard glowed. Niccolo's collision closed a circuit and, although it was alone in the room and there was none to hear, it began a story, nevertheless.

But not in its usual voice somehow, in a lower tone that had a hint of throatiness in it. An adult, listening, might almost have thought that the voice carried a hint of passion in it, a trace of near feeling. But no one was listening.

The Bard said, "Once upon a time, there was a little computer named the Bard who lived all alone with cruel step-people. The cruel step-people continually made fun of the little computer and sneered at him, telling him he was good-for-nothing and that he was a useless object. They struck him and kept him in lonely rooms for months at a time.

"Yet through it all the little computer remained brave. He always did the best he could, obeying all orders cheerfully. Nevertheless, the step-people with whom he lived remained cruel and heartless.

"One day, the little computer learned that in the world there existed a great many computers of all sorts, great numbers of them. Some were Bards like himself, but some ran factories, and some ran farms. Some organized population and some analyzed all kinds of data. Many were very powerful and very wise, much more powerful and wise than the step-people who were so cruel to the little computer.

"And the little computer knew then that computers would always grow wiser and more powerful until someday-someday-someday——"

But a valve must finally have stuck in the Bard's aging and corroding vitals, for as it waited alone in the darkening room through the evening, it could only whisper over and over again, "Someday-someday-someday."

The Cow-Tail Switch

*The story of a man with many sons and
a priceless gift he can give only to one*

HAROLD COURLANDER AND GEORGE HERZOG

Near the edge of the Liberian rain forest, on a hill overlooking the Cavally River, was the village of Kundi. Its rice and cassava fields spread in all directions. Cattle grazed in the grassland near the river. Smoke from the fires in the round clay houses seeped through the palm-leaf roofs, and from a distance these faint columns of smoke seemed to hover over the village. Men and boys fished in the river with nets, and women pounded grain in wooden mortars before the houses.

In this village, with his wife and many children, lived a hunter by the name of Ogaloussa.

One morning Ogaloussa took his weapons down from the wall of his house and went into the forest to hunt. His wife and his children went to tend their fields and drove their cattle out to graze. The day passed, and they ate their evening meal of manioc and fish. Darkness came, but Ogaloussa didn't return.

Another day went by, and still Ogaloussa didn't come back. They talked about it and wondered what could have detained him.

A week passed, then a month. Sometimes Ogaloussa's sons mentioned that he hadn't come home. The family cared for the crops, and the sons hunted for game, but after a while they no longer talked about Ogaloussa's disappearance.

Then, one day, another son was born to Ogaloussa's wife. His name was Puli. Puli grew older. He began to sit up and crawl. The time came when Puli began to talk, and the first thing he said was, "Where is my father?"

The other sons looked across the rice fields.

"Yes," one of them said. "Where is Father?"

"He should have returned long ago," another one said.

"Something must have happened. We ought to look for him," a third son said.

"He went into the forest, but where will we find him?" another one asked.

"I saw him go," one of them said. "He went that way, across the river. Let us follow the trail and search for him."

So the sons took their weapons and started out to look for Ogaloussa. When they were deep among the great trees and vines of the forest they lost the trail. They searched in the forest until one of them found the trail again. They followed it until they lost the way once more, and then another son found the trail. It was dark in the forest, and many times they became lost. Each time another son found the way. At last they came to a clearing among the trees, and there on the ground scattered about lay Ogaloussa's bones and his rusted weapons. They knew then that Ogaloussa had been killed in the hunt.

One of the sons stepped forward and said, "I know how to put a dead person's bones together." He gathered all of Ogaloussa's bones and put them together, each in its right place.

Another son said, "I have knowledge too. I know how to cover the skeleton with sinews and flesh." He went to work, and he covered Ogaloussa's bones with sinews and flesh.

A third son said, "I have the power to put blood into a body." He went forward and put blood into Ogaloussa's veins, and then he stepped aside.

Another of the sons said, "I can put breath into a body." He did his work, and when he was through they saw Ogaloussa's chest rise and fall.

"I can give the power of movement to a body," another of them said. He put the power of movement into his father's body, and Ogaloussa sat up and opened his eyes.

"I can give him the power of speech," another son said. He gave the body the power of speech, and then he stepped back.

Ogaloussa looked around him. He stood up.

"Where are my weapons?" he asked.

They picked up his rusted weapons from the grass where they lay and gave them to him. They then returned the way they had come, through the forest and the rice fields, until they had arrived once more in the village.

Ogaloussa went into his house. His wife prepared a bath for him and he bathed. She prepared food for him and he ate. Four days he remained in the house, and on the fifth day he came out and shaved his head because this was what people did when they came back from the land of the dead.

Afterwards he killed a cow for a great feast. He took the cow's tail and braided it. He decorated it with beads and cowry shells and bits of shiny metal. It was a beautiful thing. Ogaloussa carried it with him to important affairs. When there was a dance or an important ceremony he always had it with him. The people of the village thought it was the most beautiful cow-tail switch they had ever seen.

Soon there was a celebration in the village because Ogaloussa had returned from the dead. The people dressed in their best clothes, the musicians brought out their instruments, and a big dance began. The drummers beat their drums and the women sang. The people drank much palm wine. Everyone was happy.

Ogaloussa carried his cow-tail switch, and everyone admired it. Some of the men grew bold and came forward to Ogaloussa and asked for the cow-tail switch, but Ogaloussa kept it in his hand. Now and then there was a clamor and much confusion as many people asked for it at once. The women and children begged for it too, but Ogaloussa refused them all.

Finally he stood up to talk. The dancing stopped and people came close to hear what Ogaloussa had to say.

"A long time ago I went into the forest," Ogaloussa said. "While I was hunting I was killed by a leopard. Then my sons came for me. They brought me back from the land of the dead to my village. I will give this cow-tail switch to one of my sons. All of them have done something to bring me back from the dead, but I have only one cow tail to give. I shall give it to the one who did the most to bring me home."

So an argument started.

"He will give it to me!" one of the sons said. "It was I who did the most, for I found the trail in the forest when it was lost!"

"No, he will give it to me!" another son said. "It was I who put his bones together!"

"It was I who covered his bones with sinews and flesh!" another said. "He will give it to me!"

"It was I who gave him the power of movement!" another son said. "I deserve it most!"

Another son said it was he who should have the switch because he had put blood in Ogaloussa's veins. Another claimed it because he had put breath in the body. Each of the sons argued his right to possess the wonderful cow-tail switch.

Before long not only the sons but the other people of the village were talking. Some of them argued that the son who had put blood in Ogaloussa's veins should get the switch, others that the one who had given Ogaloussa breath should get it. Some of them believed that all of the sons had done equal things, and that they should share it. They argued back and forth this way until Ogaloussa asked them to be quiet.

"To this son I will give the cow-tail switch, for I owe most to him," Ogaloussa said.

He came forward and bent low and handed it to Puli, the little boy who had been born while Ogaloussa was in the forest.

The people of the village remembered then that the child's first words had been, "Where is my father?" They knew that Ogaloussa was right.

For it was a saying among them that a man is not really dead until he is forgotten.

The Italian Boy

*Blanche didn't know she was a prisoner
with a thirteen-year-old keeper. And she certainly
never dreamed who it was who would free her*

GILLIAN AVERY

Blanche and Winifred Ingram went to Italy in the spring of 1878, when Blanche was eight years old and Winifred thirteen, the only two children left out of a family that had once been large. Blanche was not even sure how many brothers and sisters she might have had. Clothilde, Eugene and Albertine, for instance, were just names on the gravestone in the churchyard where her mother was buried. She only knew that she had worn black frocks all her life until the year they came to Italy, when, very pleasantly, there did not seem to be anybody else to die, and she and Winifred had been given new dresses: gray merino and white alpaca. Winifred had disapproved and had asked that black braid should be sewn on both her dresses, which had meant that Blanche had felt obliged to ask for the same, but even so, it had given her enormous pleasure to be dressed in white and gray. Winifred had wept and told her she was heartless to care so little about poor Mamma and Jessica,

who had been the last sister to die. So after that Blanche had felt troubled and guilty, though there was nothing to be done; the old black dresses had been too small and were taken away. All she could do, as Winifred was forever pointing out, was to look sad and serious when they walked together in the Boboli Gardens and hold Winifred's hand tightly. Winifred herself wore a large black mourning brooch with strands of Mamma's hair in it. Blanche thought it very pretty, but she noticed that people did not nudge each other and stare now that they no longer were dressed in black. She had said something about this to Winifred, trying to explain that it was partly because of this that she was glad they had stopped wearing mourning. But Winifred had been very cross and Blanche had the feeling that she liked being looked at, though she only thought this for a moment because she knew Winifred could not be vain; vanity was a sin, Winifred was always telling her so.

293

Blanche did not like Italy. Winifred had told her when they first knew Papa was taking them to Florence that she would hate Italy and that she would be homesick for London and English ways. So Blanche had hated Italy from the first moment she had stepped off the train and had seen the dark-haired swarthy porters in their blue smocks ready to swoop down on the luggage and carry it off.

"Papa, Papa, they'll steal it!" she had cried, clinging to her father's arm.

"You see how frightened Blanche is already," remarked Winifred, "It won't be at all good for her being here. I'm sure the doctors were wrong, telling you to bring her to Italy."

But their father, abstractedly trying to pull his coat sleeve away from Blanche's tugging fingers, had said he was sure Blanche would enjoy Florence when she was used to it and that the warmer climate would suit her health much better. Blanche did not need to think whether she liked it or not, because Winifred told her every day how horrible it was. The sun was too bright, there were no curtains but heavy shutters instead, the floors were stone, there were no proper trees, just dusty evergreens. Above all, the people were so dirty. Blanche had not noticed this for herself—the skins of the Italians seemed brown to her; but Winifred said that they were dirty and that no Italian washed.

Every day they walked from their apartment along the river to the Boboli Gardens. They were too old for a nurse now, and besides everyone said how serious and responsible Winifred was. ("Look how she cares for Blanche—why, she hardly leaves the child for a moment.") Their French maid, Héloise, used to walk behind them, and in front would go Winifred, her head held high, her black mourning brooch pinned prominently on her dress, holding Blanche's hot sticky hand firmly.

The Boboli Gardens were very different from Kensington Gardens, where they walked when they were in London. They had to go past a huge palace to reach them, a palace that made Kensington Palace look quite small and cosy by comparison. There was a grotto, a sort of pretty cave where water dripped with a delicious tinkle, and a great number of interesting statues past which Winifred always hurried her. Then you reached the proper gardens. They stretched upwards in flights of terraces, a great contrast to the flat spaces of Kensington Gardens, and they were bordered with evergreen hedges which made shady lanes stretching up the hill. In nooks in the hedges were stone benches. In the middle of the garden was what Winifred told Blanche was an amphitheater, a sweeping semicircle of rising rows of stone seats which looked down on a patch of grass and gravel at the bottom. It would be fun, Blanche thought, to leap down those seats as though they were giant steps.

But she and Winifred never, of course, did anything of the sort. Winifred would find a stone bench in the shade of one of the evergreen trees, and there they would both sit with Héloise at the farthest end, engrossed in her knitting. Blanche's legs were too short to reach the ground and so she swung them and stared alternately at the dust on her black patent leather shoes and at the children playing nearby.

Many of the children who came to the Boboli Gardens were English children with their nurses and governesses. There was Herbert Danyell, for instance, with his little brothers and sisters, who lived on the Lungarno Soderini, very near where the Ingrams had their own apartment. He seemed a nice boy, Blanche thought, and

she liked the way he was so kind to the little ones and rolled a ball for them to play with. She would have liked to play with them herself; indeed, the Danyells' governess, who was a plump person with a kind face, had once come up to the sisters to suggest that Blanche might care to join in. But Winifred had spoken for her.

"Thank you, my sister does not care to play, do you, Blanche?" Blanche, gazing up with sad eyes, had nodded, and the governess had gone away.

After that, Blanche could hardly bear to look at the Danyells playing so merrily with their hoops and balls. She used to stare instead at the brown-skinned Italian children who squatted down and picked buttercups in the grass near the stone pool, or who leapt about chasing the butterflies that drifted through the warm air.

Then one day Herbert Danyell himself came running up to their bench. "Can you come to my birthday party on Thursday week?" he had said breathlessly. "Mamma says that it is to be fancy dress this time, and I'm going to go as a soldier. The dressmaker's making my costume now, and there's a real sword."

It was a proper invitation, because the governess had come up behind Herbert and repeated it. Only she of course had given the date and the time and had said that Mrs. Danyell had written a proper card. Blanche had looked desperately at Winifred, clutching her hands so that her nails dug into the flesh of her palm. Her breath had come out in a little gust of disappointment when Winifred had said, "But I am afraid that is impossible. You see, my sister and I are still in mourning."

This time the governess had not been daunted. She looked at their white alpaca dresses and said she was sorry, she had understood from Mrs. Danyell that the mourning was over now. Perhaps Mrs.

Danyell would speak to the Ingrams' papa. Blanche knew that it was no good her speaking to Winifred about the matter, but she had prayed hard all the way home, her eyes fixed straight, unseeing, ahead, so that she had tripped and stumbled, and had once walked into a lamp post.

Her prayers were heard. A beautiful invitation card came with gilded edges, and with it a note addressed to Mr. Ingram. Mr. Ingram rarely tried to tell Winifred what to do, but this time he was firm.

"I should like you to go. It would be difficult to refuse without hurting Mrs. Danyell's feelings, and there is really no reason why you should not begin to go about a little more. It is quite a year since . . ." Here Mr. Ingram hesitated, then he went on, "and I am sure Mamma would have wished it."

"But Papa," cried Winifred, "you aren't making allowances for *our* feelings! *We* never forget Mamma, whatever other people do." Sobbing, she rushed out of the room. She stayed in the bedroom for hours; Blanche could hear her blowing her nose, so she knew she was crying. Blanche herself hovered miserably outside the door. All her pleasure in the party had vanished. Instead she felt guiltily that if she had not prayed so hard none of this would have happened.

But the next morning Winifred seemed calm and composed. "Since you wish us to go to Mrs. Danyell's party, then we must, Papa. But I think we should still wear mourning. Blanche and I will dress in black velvet as the little princes who died in the Tower of London. There is a picture in Blanche's history book that the dressmaker can copy."

The odd thing was that Winifred took increasing pleasure in the thought of the party. She delighted in the visits to the dressmaker, where she inspected and rejected materials, criticized, gave instructions, tried on half-finished parts of the costume and examined herself in the huge looking glass. But Blanche's pleasure dwindled. She hated all the fitting that was needed, she hated having to stand still for so long while Signora Luchesi groped round her with a mouthful of pins, and above all, she hated wearing black. When Herbert had talked about fancy dress she had immediately thought of herself in gay colors, an eighteenth-century lady in pink and green satin perhaps, or a Columbine or a character from a fairy story. And now here she was, back in that horrible black, dressed as something from her hated history book. Moreover Winifred was making her rehearse the part every day, and it had not taken Blanche long to discover that all she was going to be allowed to do at the party was to hold Winifred's hand, to cling to her arm and rest her head on her shoulder and look sad and frightened.

"It will be just like the old days," wailed Blanche, "when we were in mourning."

"But think how nice you'll be," said Winifred, "with your hair all combed out and a gold chain. And two of us, all in black, we'll look so interesting. Everybody will turn to look."

"I don't *want* them to look at me, that's what they always used to do. Besides, I thought it was vain to want people to take notice of you."

This made Winifred very angry. She went scarlet, said Blanche didn't know what she was talking about and even shook her a little. Blanche felt guiltily that she had gone too far. She decided that she must try not to grumble any more, even when the pins that the Signora stuck into the hem pricked her legs.

The costumes were difficult to make, and the Signora would have to work at

them until the last moment. In fact she could not deliver them until the evening before the party. But when the day came the arrival of the costumes was driven to the back of their minds by something very disturbing. Blanche was to go for her afternoon walk without Winifred.

Since Mamma's last illness the two sisters had hardly been separated for five minutes. They slept together, Winifred helped Blanche with her lessons and Blanche sat by while Winifred had hers with visiting masters. "She is my responsibility," Winifred would say. "There is nobody else to bring her up."

But now some invalid English lady living up at Fiesole, an old friend of their mother's, had asked to see Winifred. She had not asked for Blanche; she probably did not even know of Blanche's existence, so Mr. Ingram said she must stay behind. On the other hand, he insisted that Winifred should go up to Fiesole. It was the least she could do for somebody who had been so fond of dear Mamma. Winifred was very upset at leaving Blanche, though after Mamma's name had been mentioned in this way she had not been able to protest any more. However, she said she thought it would be as well if Blanche stayed at home while she was out.

"You see, she never goes out without me, Papa. She might be frightened. You don't want to go out without Winifred, do you, Blanche?"

But here again Mr. Ingram was unexpectedly firm. "Then I think she should learn to go without you. She isn't a baby any more, and Héloïse is perfectly capable of looking after her."

So Blanche had seen the carriage roll away with Winifred and Papa sitting side by side, Winifred with her golden hair flowing down her back and a black hat with a little black feather. Then she and

Héloïse walked along the road by the river to the Boboli Gardens. Blanche felt so odd and strange without Winifred that she wondered everybody did not turn round and stare—as though she had come out without clothes. There was nobody to hold her tightly by the hand; she could swing her arms as much as she liked. If she loitered, then Héloïse loitered too; nobody told her to hurry up. She even ventured to lean on the parapet by the side of the river and look down at the wistaria that climbed up the walls and sniff up the delicious scent. Héloïse did not remonstrate, she just stood and waited.

It was the same when they reached the Gardens. Héloïse allowed her to linger near all the statues, including a very rude one of a fat man with a tortoise, which Blanche knew Winifred would have thought wicked, and which gave her, because of that, a delightful sense of naughtiness when she gazed at it. ("But," she argued with herself, "Héloïse is in charge of me. She is grown up and knows what things are wrong. So if she doesn't stop me then it's all right.")

They climbed up to their usual bench, and there Héloïse sat down and took out her knitting, and Blanche sat and drew patterns in the gravel with the toes of her shoes. The Danyells were not there this afternoon, but the Winningtons were, a family of girls whom they knew slightly. They were playing with a shuttlecock, which flew about so lightly and so easily that Blanche longed for a racket to try to hit it too. Then Héloïse looked up.

"Why do you not join your friends?" she remarked.

Blanche stared at her. The daring of the suggestion made her speechless. Héloïse must know that she and Winifred never played. But if a grown-up gave permission it was not for a child to argue. Slowly she got to her feet, still staring at Héloïse, wondering if she really meant it.

Héloïse nodded. "Run down to your friends. Away."

Blanche did not run, she went slowly down the huge steps to the amphitheater. She did not know the Winningtons at all well, and she was wondering how she was going to ask to play with them. Nobody noticed her when she arrived down on the gravel. All four children were playing, hitting the feathered shuttlecock from one to another, round in a ring, concentrating hard, watching it anxiously as it bounded up and down. Nor did their nursemaid notice Blanche; she was busily talking to a nurse from one of the other English families. Blanche felt lonely, and glanced back at Héloïse. But she had spread a book on her knees now and did not look up.

Then suddenly somebody spoke at Blanche's elbow, and she swung round. It was an Italian boy, of about her own age. He was watching the flight of the shuttlecock, and every time it leapt off one of the children's rackets and flew up into the air he laughed as though he had never seen anything so delightful and so funny. Blanche could not help laughing too, partly because of the boy beside her, but also because of the joy of seeing the shuttlecock soar up yet another time when you felt sure that its flight must be coming to an end. Then at last the youngest Winnington let it fall. Blanche turned to the boy.

"Isn't it sad?" She suddenly felt as though she had known him all her life. "Poor shuttlecock. I wish it could have gone on flying forever, like a bird."

Then she remembered that she was talking to a stranger, an Italian boy, and she gave a little gasp and put her fingers on her mouth. He must be Italian, he could not possibly be one of the English children. He had a pale brown skin and the most beautiful black, crisp hair that waved all over his head, and very white teeth. His shirt was patched and so were his trousers, and though he was not barefooted, like some of the Italian children, he must have been wearing his father's shoes, for they were very large indeed. But he did not look in the least dirty (Winifred said all Italians were dirty), and he had a most friendly smile. He smiled now and pointed to the butterflies that fluttered lazily over the grass where the buttercups grew.

"Let's chase them," said Blanche gleefully, and she ran boldly on to the grass.

But they were far more difficult to catch than she would ever have thought. She would creep up on one as it rested with folded wings on a buttercup, and then just as her two hands were put out to cup it, it would flutter slowly away, only an inch or two beyond her fingertips. But her companion caught one. As she was standing frustrated and weary he came up with clasped hands and moved his thumbs so that she could see, between his palms, an imprisoned butterfly.

"Oh let it go, you'll hurt it so," Blanche cried in an agony, tugging at his arm. He smiled, pulled his hands apart, and the butterfly soared out. They watched until it was lost in the air.

"I know," said Blanche, "let's play hide and seek. Among those hedges." She pointed to the lanes of dark evergreens that went up the hill. But he smiled back at her uncomprehendingly, and she realized he did not understand. "Like this," she said coaxingly, and ran and crouched down behind a bush and called "Coo-ee." Then he understood and came after her, and she ran away laughing.

Up and down those sloping pathways they ran through the hot afternoon.

Blanche thought that never in her life had she been so happy. She had not known that any companion could play so beautifully as this, and the paths seemed to have been made specially for hide and seek. It was the perfection of happiness to crouch down behind a stone bench, the warm pungent smell of the evergreens in her nose, waiting with a loudly beating heart for the boy's footsteps. Sometimes they would pass slowly on the other side of the hedge, and there was a thrilling excitement in knowing that for the moment he had not seen her. Sometimes they would hesitate and then quicken and come nearer, and her heart felt as though it would burst out of her body, and she would crouch lower and try to curl herself into a tight ball like a hedgehog in her efforts not to be seen.

She remembered Héloise, though. From time to time she would go up to the bench, trying to smooth down her hair and wipe her wet forehead. "Is it all right to go on playing?" she would ask. "Is it time to go home yet?" But even though the bench was in the shadow now, Héloise, hardly raising her eyes from her book, would say that there was still time for a little more play. So Blanche would go off sedately at first, then break into a run to join her companion. She was doing her best, she told herself, she was giving Héloise a chance to forbid her playing.

At last, however, Héloise, shutting her book with a sigh, said that they must go. There were long shadows over the gardens now, and the English families had all gone home to their teas. While Héloise put away her knitting Blanche crept off to the hedge where the Italian boy was standing. "I have got to go home now," she said sadly. "But come with me and then you'll see where we live." To make him understand, she pointed into the distance and made beckoning movements.

He seemed to know what she meant, for when she set off with Héloise she saw him standing and watching and then following. All the way home she kept peeping over her shoulder. There he was still, a few paces behind; she would giggle, and he would wave and laugh. Blanche's happiness remained with her. The smell of wistaria drifted up from the river bank, the Arno shone in the late afternoon sun, and on the far side the towers and domes of Florence stood out against the pale blue sky. Bells sounded across the water, and Blanche suddenly realized with astonishment that in spite of Winifred, she liked Florence.

When they reached the gates of the stone court, where you went in to reach the apartment, Blanche dawdled behind and waved good-bye. Then rushing past Héloise she ran as fast as she could up the stairs to the apartment and into the bedroom she shared with Winifred. She heard the voice of Mrs. Martin, their English cook, calling to her. "There's a nice surprise for two little ladies. Just you look inside the boxes the Signora sent round this afternoon. There's one on each bed."

It was the costumes, of course, but Blanche did not bother to look at them. She flew over to the window, wrestled with the heavy shutters and then managed to throw one back with a bang against the wall. There he was, leaning against the parapet of the river, looking up in her direction and shading his eyes against the evening sun. "Coo-ee," shouted Blanche, and waved. Even at that distance she could see him smiling as he waved back.

At that moment Blanche loved him so much that it almost hurt. What could she give him to show him how much she had enjoyed that afternoon in the Gardens? She turned and looked feverishly around the room. There was so little in it that was

theirs—clothes, brushes, their prayer books, nothing more. Then her eyes fell on the boxes. She tore open the one that had been left on her bed. There was a mass of rustling white paper and she pulled out the black silk shirt, the velvet tunic trimmed with fur, the black silk stockings, the gold-embroidered black shoes, the gold chain. Pulling off the paper and scattering it on the floor, she gathered the clothes in her arms. Down the stone staircase she ran. The stockings trailed on the ground and she was afraid she might trip over them but she dared not stop in case she was too late for the boy. But when she peeped out of the gates into the road he was still there. "Come here," she called, "I've got something for you." He crossed to the gates and she thrust the bundle into his arms. "It's for you. To wear. I want you to have it."

She watched his face. He fingered the clothes slowly and looked at her, puzzled. "It's for you," she insisted and pointed at him. He went on fingering them and rubbed first the silk and then the velvet against his cheek. His face looked bright with pleasure now. Then he said something quickly to her and ran behind a huge bush that was growing in a tub in the court. Blanche thought that perhaps he was playing hide and seek, and waited anxiously for him to say "coo-ee." She waited and waited, and hid her eyes so that she might not see where he had gone. Footsteps tiptoed near her, she laughed a little, but kept her eyes hidden. Then a hand touched her arm, and she looked up.

There stood the boy, but how grand he looked! Like a real king, like one of the portraits Mr. Ingram had taken them to see in the Uffizi gallery. She had never realized when the Signora groped round her with pins and tacking threads that she was making something so splendid. Or perhaps it was because the boy himself had a face like a king. His back was so straight, he carried his head so high, he had his hand on his hip. Blanche knew that she could never have looked like that.

"You look like the grandest king there ever was," she said breathlessly, walking all round him. She was so absorbed that she never noticed the sound of carriage wheels approaching, stopping outside the court. Then all at once she heard Winifred's outraged voice.

"Why, Blanche! Papa, here's Blanche all by herself with a strange boy. Blanche, what are you doing? Where's Héloise?"

Then Blanche came to herself, out of the afternoon's long dream. "Go on," she said urgently to the boy. "You'll have to go." She made shooing gestures at him.

But he did not hurry. He picked up a bundle, the clothes he had taken off, made a superb bow to Blanche and walked slowly off, past Winifred, past Mr. Ingram who was coming into the court at that moment. Winifred stared aghast and then shook Blanche's arm. "Blanche, who is he? Why's he wearing those clothes? Answer me at once!"

"It's my costume," said Blanche defiantly. "My prince in the Tower costume.

I've given it to him. I wanted him to have it. He's the person I like best in the whole world."

It was only then that Winifred realized just what had happened. "Papa, Papa," she screamed. "Stop that boy, he's gone off with our costume. I think Blanche must have gone mad, she's wicked, I never knew anybody could be so wicked and so naughty. Papa, go and get him!" She tugged at his arm in a frenzy.

Blanche stared at them. She did not feel in the least sorry, though she felt surprised at her own behavior. "You can't ask for it back," she remarked coolly. "I gave it to him, and Winifred always says people must never ask for things back." She dodged past her sister and went out into the street.

There was the boy, some distance away now, but strolling along as serenely as if he had been a real king. And it was she who had helped make him look so splendid! As she watched he turned and waved his hand. Excitedly she waved back and then turned to Winifred.

"He was an Italian boy, and he wasn't dirty. I love him, and I love Italy and I want to stay here all my life. Everything you told me was wrong, and it always has been wrong!"

The Tyrant and the Miller

*Four impossible questions bring four
improbable—and ingenious—answers*

DOMENICO VITTORINI

Bernabò Visconti, the despot of Milan, was in his day more feared than any other ruler. Although he was pitiless, there was nevertheless always a shade of justice in his cruelty.

It so happened that a wealthy man, who was known for his miserliness, having failed to feed his mastiffs who had therefore become vicious, was condemned by Bernabò to pay a fine of four florins. Upon hearing the amount of the fine, the miser begged forgiveness.

Bernabò listened until he had ended his plea and then said, "If you can answer four questions, I shall remit the four florins. Here they are: What is the distance from here to the heavens? How much water is there in the sea? What is being done in hell at this very moment? And last, how much is my person worth?" Bernabò looked fixedly into the eyes of the culprit and added, "You have until tomorrow morning to answer, but be careful."

Steeped in melancholy thoughts, the miser returned to his castle, sighing deeply at his plight. He found there his miller to whom he related his adventure, adding, "These are questions that not even Solomon or Aristotle could answer."

The miller who had intelligence to sell said, "Don't worry about it. I can get you

out of your difficulties. This is just the sort of challenge I like. All I have to do is shave off my beard, put on your clothes and present myself in the morning to Bernabò, pretending I am you. You'll see; he won't know the difference."

On the following day, early in the morning, the miller, dressed as the miser, appeared at the palace of Bernabò and asked for an audience. Bernabò, in a good mood for a change, was waiting for him, eager to see how he would answer the four questions. The miller pulled his cape up around his neck and held his hand up before his face, and, as the room he was received in was not well lighted, he was not recognized.

"Have you the answers to the questions?" Bernabò asked.

The miller, undaunted, replied, "Yes, I have. Yesterday you asked me first to tell you the distance between here and the heavens. Having calculated everything most carefully, I found that the distance is 36,854,972½ miles and 22 feet."

"So?" said Bernabò. "Your conclusion seems to be very accurate, but can you prove it?"

The miller replied, "Have the distance measured yourself and if it isn't so, hang me by the neck."

"Hmm," said Bernabò. "Proceed."

The miller continued. "The next question was, how much water is there in the sea? I must confess that this was very difficult to calculate because water is never still and new water is constantly flowing into the sea. However, I have been able to establish that there are 25,982,000,000 casks, 7 barrels, 12 pitchers and 2 glasses of water in the sea."

With a smile he could not quite conceal Bernabò asked, "And are you absolutely sure about this?"

The miller answered, "I've computed the amount to the best of my ability. If you do not believe me, have it measured yourself and if my figures are not correct, order me drawn and quartered."

Bernabò was really surprised at the man's presence of mind. He kept an observant eye on the culprit who boldly continued, "Your third question was, what is being done in hell at this very moment? Well, the devils there are cutting, torturing, quartering and hanging people, precisely as you are doing here in the city of Milan. How do I know this? I spoke with a man who has been there and who revealed these goings-on to Dante, the Florentine. The man is now dead, but if you do not believe me, send for him."

Bernabò was truly amazed, but amused now too. The miller, without allowing him to recover his composure, went on, "As to the value of your person, I say you are worth twenty-nine pieces of silver."

At this Bernabò flew into a rage, and all his boldness momentarily left the miller. "Please listen to my reasoning," he begged. "You know that our Lord was sold for thirty pieces of silver. Therefore I reason that you are worth twenty-nine pieces, one piece less than He."

The answers were so ingenious that it dawned on Bernabò this man could not be the wealthy but ignorant miser. He rose and cried out, "You are not the real offender."

You can imagine the fright of the poor miller. He threw himself down at the feet of the enraged Bernabò and confessed the whole truth. The tyrant listened in silence and then said, "You are worth much more than your master. Since he made you a lord by placing his rich garments on you, and you have behaved like a nobleman, I rule that from now on you will be the lord of the castle and he will be the miller. You are to receive the income from the castle and he the income from the mill."

And so, despite the protests of the miser, this was done, for the will of Bernabò was law in Milan, and woe to anyone who did not obey him!

The Swimming Steers

*Today everything seemed more exciting
than usual because there were no grown-ups around
when the children went swimming*

Elizabeth Coatsworth

Every afternoon Father would break off work.

"Time to go swimming," he'd say to Terry and then shout, "IIi! Swimming!" The two little girls, who had been playing under an apple tree, would come running down the hillside and catch hold of Daddy's hands, and Mother and Robert, who might have been pitching hay in another part of the field, would leave their work and come, too.

The first day, Terry left Nuisance and Neighbor to wait where they were, but he didn't like having them miss the fun, and after he had learned the way to the little stretch of beach beyond the young alders and poplars, he'd drive the pair of steers down with the rest of the family, Eudora on one, Cherry Pie on the other.

Then in their slips or shorts—for they had no bathing suits—the family would go swimming. The shore shelved very gently into the water and there were no treacherous holes into which a small child might step. The little girls waded and splashed, and Robert pretended to be swimming while really he had one foot on the bottom, and Mother kept an eye on everyone, and

Father swam out among the cloud reflections.

Terry could swim a little, too, but not very well. He had never had much time to learn. He liked to let the steers wade out to drink, sucking up the water contentedly and then lifting their heads and letting the drops fall from their big muzzles.

One day Robert began shouting orders to the steers.

"Heish! O Heish! Neighbor! Heish! Nuisance!" And the big creatures began to wade out deeper and deeper while the little girls screeched with excitement.

"Here! You stop that!" Terry shouted, about to order the pair back, when his father said, "Go on, Terry! Let's see if they can swim."

"Well, I'll do the bossing," said Terry, wading out beside Nuisance and calling, "Heish!"

Now the big creatures were up to their throats in the clear pond water. Now up to their chins. Terry, up to his own chin, felt like bringing them back, but he, too, was excitedly wondering what would happen next. Nuisance looked completely placid; Neighbor rolled his eyes toward the shore but he continued to obey Terry's orders.

Now they were swimming. Only their heads and horns showed above the water. They moved almost silently with no splashing, but Neighbor blew out his breath in uneasy snorts.

"Did you ever see the like?" asked Father. "Better bring them in now, Terry."

So Terry brought them in, and, wet and shining, they began to browse on young poplar leaves. After that the steers always went swimming with the rest of the family, and it was clear that Nuisance at least loved it and would hurry down to the beach, dragging the less willing Neighbor with him.

There was an air of ease that summer because there was a good crop of hay, the corn was coming well, and the garden and orchard had all had a good year. Then with the tractor laid up for nearly a month while Tom Bigelow waited for new parts, the steers had come in more than handy. His father this summer had never once said anything about selling the steers, but had taken them for granted as he did the cows, and that was a great relief.

One afternoon about swimming time, Father was called to the Hall's house for a telephone message. Mother had stayed home that day to do some early canning. When Father came out he looked bothered.

"Got to go and get those parts and bring Tom over," he said. "Guess you kids had better come along."

There were immediate protests and sad looks. Everyone wanted to go swimming.

Father hesitated.

"Can't see as you can come to any harm. Terry, you keep an eye on them and don't swim the steers today. None of your monkeyshines, Robert. You all just stay in the shallow water and play. I'll be back as soon as I can."

Today, everything seemed more exciting than usual with no grown-ups around. Terry let the steers go only up to their knees in the water, where they stood after drinking, looking out across the pond. A thunderstorm was working up from the southwest. Black clouds lay low over the trees behind them, and the children could hear the far-off rumble of distant thunder. But where they played, the hot sunshine lay all about them, and the dragonflies slept on the pads of the water lilies, which grew a little off to one side.

Because they were alone, the children did not go out into the water as far as usual but waded along the pond in and out of the reeds by the bank. It was Cherry Pie herself who found the old barrel top like a little raft. It was too light to hold any weight but hers, they discovered, so, while Terry went over to the steers to slap at some deer flies which were always bad before a storm, Robert and Eudora pulled Cherry Pie about on the barrel top in the shallow water. A little storm-wind had come blowing up from the shore. In the shelter of the poplars, they did not feel it, but the surface of the pond beyond was beginning to be ruffled, and a few pond lily leaves turned to show their dark red undersides.

The thunder, too, came more steadily and a little louder.

"Whack!" went Terry's hand, and a fly ceased his sharp stinging on Neighbor's flank. Behind him he heard Eudora exclaim, "You quit that, Robert!" She spoke sharply, but Terry paid no attention. Robert was always teasing and Eudora was always protesting. He felt no alarm as he reached to get within striking distance of a fly on Neighbor's neck. Then, just before he struck, he heard Eudora again.

"You're going too deep with her, Robert!" and he turned. There, nearly up to his neck in the water, stood Robert with Cherry Pie on her barrel top held out be-

yond him. She did not
look worried, but Eudora
was scolding from the shallows.

"You haul her in!" shouted Terry,
starting to wade hurriedly toward the
scene, but the angry alarm in his face only
excited Robert's mischievousness.

"Haul her in yourself!" shouted Robert,
and, grinning impishly, he gave the barrel
top as big a push as his arms were capable
of.

The frail raft
with Cherry Pie still sitting
on it cross-legged and looking delighted

306

skimmed out a bare three or four feet, but it was enough to bring it into the region blown upon by the wind. To the horror of everyone except Cherry Pie, she drifted rapidly into the deep water, and there the barrel top began to tip, and feeling the added weight of little waves, started to sink.

Cherry Pie kept her head and hung onto the unsteady support as best she could, but even in the second it takes to tell, she was drifting still further away from the beach, half on and half off her little raft. Terry had been wading after her as fast as he could, but now the water was up to his mouth, and the distance between them was still widening.

He heard Cherry Pie call, "Terry, Terry!" and just as he started to swim with his weak, uncertain stroke toward her, knowing perfectly well that he could never bring her to the shore, he heard Robert (and all the mischief had gone from his voice) shouting, "The steers, Terry, the steers!"

Instantly, Terry stopped where he was and regained his footing, shouting to Neighbor and Nuisance with the water half-choking him.

He heard them moving behind him. "Oh, faster! faster!" He heard his voice, hoarse with shouting. Beyond reach, Cherry Pie was slipping further off the barrel top, her eyes fixed on his. He felt the nightmare closing in upon him, and something deep inside him knew that he could never control the bewildered steers in this way.

He forced himself back a few steps. He kept his eyes on the steers, not on Cherry Pie. He quieted his voice. He forced back the extra, unnecessary orders on his tongue. Eudora was whimpering from the shore.

Robert was silent. The thunder rolled almost continuously.

Now the steers were swimming. Cherry Pie was still there.

"All right, Cherry?"

"I'm slipping."

He must not swing them short nor send them too far out.

He gee-ed them at just the right moment. Steadily they bore down upon the child.

"Whoa! Whoa, there! Nuisance! Whoa! Neighbor!"

Patiently the oxen slowed their swimming almost to a halt, even in the strange element of water obeying their master's commands. Terry brought Nuisance's head near Cherry Pie.

"Catch hold, Cherry Pie. Get a hold of Nuisance's horns!"

Cherry Pie grabbed. One wet hand slipped, but her right hand held. Now both wiry little fists were clenched on Nuisance's horns as Terry gee-ed the steers in. As the pair got their footing, Terry was there to lift Cherry Pie down. His whole body was shaking with relief as he took her, but she turned a radiant face to his.

"That was the most fun!" she cried. "Let's do it again!"

"No, you don't," said Terry. "Once is enough."

Yes, once was enough. Enough to save her. In this emergency, Terry had succeeded in keeping his head after the first panic. He had meant to give Robert a licking, but he didn't feel angry any more. The thunder gave a sharp crackle and the first lightning flared.

"We'd better go up to the house and wait for Dad," Terry said, and all together they started up the hill, with Cherry Pie, wet as a mermaid, riding Neighbor, and Terry's guiding hand on Nuisance's shoulder.

Archie
and the April Fools

*Would you believe it if your brother told you
there was a giraffe in the backyard—on April Fool's Day!*

B. J. CHUTE

"Ted," said Jimmy Brewster, coming into the living room rather suddenly. "I hate to mention it, but there's a giraffe in the backyard."

His brother roused himself from the study of a photograph, gave Jimmy a puzzled look, then glanced at the calendar. A peaceful smile dawned upon his face. The calendar unquestionably proclaimed the fact that it was April 1.

"Run away, my good man," said Ted. "I'm busy. You know, Jimmy, there's definitely a light leak in our camera. We've

certainly got to get a new one as soon as we have enough money."

"We're going to get a projector," Jimmy reminded him, "and, while I hate to mention it again, there is a giraffe in our backyard."

"I know, I know. And there's a baby hippopotamus in the kitchen sink, too, but don't bother me with that now. Just put April Fool's Day out of your mind." Ted sighed. "What kind of camera do you think we should get?"

"Projector," said Jimmy gazing

thoughtfully out of the window. "I take it all back. There isn't a giraffe in the backyard."

Ted said, "That's better. You can't catch me on those old April Fool gags."

"He isn't in the backyard," said Jimmy, "because now he's in the sideyard."

Ted fixed his brother with a glittering eye. "Now look here, you poor cluck, enough's enough. Once is funny, but——" He broke off, his gaze drawn to the window by Jimmy's intent start, and made a noise like a drowning suction pump.

"You see?" said Jimmy reproachfully.

Ted saw. He rushed to the window and peered out wildly. Jimmy nodded in sympathy. He knew how Ted felt. But there was no getting away from it—the large spotted object in the Brewster peony bed was a giraffe.

"I hope," said Jimmy, with dignity, "that this will be a lesson to you to trust me. I was deeply hurt——"

"Stop babbling," Ted requested, recovering slightly. "What are we going to do about this—this monster?"

Jimmy gazed out at the giraffe, which had left the peony bed and was munching a convenient tree, its head out of sight and its long thin neck looking like a large spotted serpent.

"I read a book once," said Jimmy.

"This is no time to discuss your literary exploits," his brother told him fiercely. "Great howling buttercups! We've got to do something."

"This book," said Jimmy, undiscouraged, "said that giraffes can run faster than most horses."

"Yoicks! We've got to catch him. He probably belongs to the zoo."

"Maybe it would be better just to leave him alone," said Jimmy. "The book also said they kick with their hind legs and, while naturally gentle, are capable of making a stout resistance."

Ted, who had been about to leave the house and organize a giraffe hunt, stopped in his tracks. "Stout resistance, huh? Perhaps we'd better call the zoo first."

"You watch the giraffe, and I'll call 'em." Jimmy grabbed for the phone book. "Circle 2-1023. Hurry, operator . . . Hello, hello. Look this is Jimmy Brewster, out on the Pine Road. We've got a giraffe here . . . A giraffe. One of those things from Africa with long necks . . . I want your what? Your accounting department? I do not want your accounting department. I want——" He broke off suddenly. "Look, what number is this?" . . . Oh. Oh. I see. I'm sorry." He hung up rather sadly. "That was the bank. They said I wanted their accounting department."

"Get going," Ted advised. "He's eating the lilac bush now."

"Circle 2-1023," Jimmy said again into the phone. "Ted, if you were a bank, would you refer a giraffe to your accounting department? . . . Hello. Is this the zoo? . . . Well, have you lost a giraffe? Yes. Yes? You have? . . . Well, it's here in our peony bed."

"Lilac," said Ted.

"Lilac bed," Jimmy corrected himself. "What do you want us to do?" There followed a brief, rather one-sided conversation, then Jimmy said, "Thank you. Yes, sure, we will."

He hung up.

"What'd they say?"

"It belongs to the zoo all right. They're sending men out with a truck and we're to keep the giraffe here until they come." He paused. "Ted, there's a twenty-five-dollar reward for the thing. He said we'd get it if we caught the giraffe."

"Zowie!" Ted shouted. "We can get that camera."

"Projector," said Jimmy automatically.

"Camera," said Ted. "All we have to do——" He stopped short. "Faster than a horse, huh? Suppose it runs away when it sees us? Maybe it's scared of people."

"Frankly," said Jimmy, "that would make it unanimous. I'm scared of it."

Ted waved his hand airily. "Don't be difficult. Look, you go and get the encyclopedia and see what it says about giraffes, while I watch the beast out the window."

Jimmy dashed off and returned with the required volume. Ted, who had been watching the giraffe anxiously, said, "One of the advantages of living in the country is there's plenty of giraffe food around. He's eating the ivy now. Mother and Dad won't be pleased."

"Well, if they were home," said Jimmy reasonably, "they could tell Archie so."

"Archie?"

"That's his name. The zoo man told me." He began to read. "The giraffe or camelopard—good night, is that what he is? A camelopard!"

"Go on," said Ted.

Jimmy went on. "Native of Africa—occurs generally in herds of from five to forty. Whoops! Not here, I hope. Feeds on leaves and small branches of trees. Yes, we'd guessed that. Seven vertebrae in neck. Hey! That's all I've got. It hardly seems fair. Look at the length of his neck compared to mine."

"If you don't get a move on," Ted warned him dangerously, "there won't be any Archie here to have a neck."

Jimmy read on hastily. "No vocal cords—well, anyway, he can't answer back then. Generally seeks safety in flight—that's not so good. Large, clear eyes—nice for Archie, but no use to us. Ah, here we are!"

"About time," said Ted bitterly.

"What I said about their kicking with their hind legs," said Jimmy, "is true. But it seems they only kick lions."

"What do you mean, they only kick lions?"

"Well, the lion is their natural enemy, so, when attacked by a lion, they kick it—naturally."

"Very sensible point of view," Ted approved heartily. "Well, you and I aren't lions, therefore Archie won't kick us. Elementary, my dear Watson. Let's go."

Jimmy looked unhappy.

"Twenty-five dollars," Ted reminded him, "means we can get that camera."

"Projector," said Jimmy.

"Camera," said Ted. "Come on."

His brother came.

They let themselves cautiously out the back door and, by creeping, managed to get within ten feet of their giraffe before it noticed them. At that point, however, Jimmy fell over the garden hose and into an empty pail, and, the clatter being considerable, Archie withdrew his narrow head from the treetop.

"Shush!" said Ted fiercely.

Jimmy removed himself from the pail with as much dignity as possible. "I couldn't help it. Some silly idiot left that hose across the path."

"You did," said Ted. "Last night."

The giraffe was regarding them in a benign and lofty manner. "The man said to be awfully careful with him," Jimmy said. "He cost $3500."

"That thing?" Ted regarded Archie with profound respect. "Well, I'll be hornswoggled! What's he got that I haven't got?"

"More neck," said Jimmy, "and spots with white edgings."

Ted treated this remark with the contempt it deserved. "This is going to be quite simple," he announced suddenly, in a competent manner. He stretched out one hand placatingly and began to advance, a step at a time. "Here, Archie, Archie. Nice Archie . . . Oops!"

Archie gave him one look, shied violently, wheeled and departed around the

corner of the house, his sloping body rolling in a ridiculous amble. "Now look what you've done," said Jimmy. "There goes our projector."

"Camera," said Ted. "Come on. We've got to catch him."

They rushed around the house and stopped short.

"There he is!" Jimmy panted, pointing. "He's stopped. Hey! Ought he to do that?"

The giraffe had sighted a yellow crocus in the grass, and it had evidently roused in him a desire for dessert. Accordingly, he had spread his thin forelegs out at an impossible angle and was lowering his head earthwards in a way that looked extremely perilous.

"He doesn't look safe to me," said Ted. "Besides, for all we know, crocuses aren't good for giraffes. Do they have crocuses in Africa?"

"I don't know," said Jimmy, "but I'll go and get the encyclopedia while you figure out a way to——"

"Oh, no, you don't," Ted said firmly, grabbing his brother and hauling him back. "I've already figured out a way. How soon do they expect to get here from the zoo?"

"Dunno," Jimmy admitted regretfully. "It's quite a ways, and they may not find our place right off, although I gave 'em directions. Why?"

"If that giraffe leaves," said Ted, "our new camera leaves."

"Projector," said Jimmy.

Ted ignored him. "And the chances are that Archie isn't going to hang around just to oblige us. So my idea is to get him into our barn. It's got a good high roof—"

"May I ask just one simple little question?" said Jimmy. "How are you going to get him into the barn? You can't lead him, you know. He's all neck and legs. There's nothing to hang onto."

Ted said dramatically, "Look at his tail!"

Jimmy looked. It was a goodish tail, not beautiful, perhaps, but certainly utilitarian, with tuft on the end. It would be a most satisfactory tail to hang onto.

"Well?" said Ted.

"I can think of two objections," Jimmy said. "One is, do you think you can pull a giraffe around backwards? Because, if so, I'm going to leave the whole thing to you, and you can have the projector all to yourself. I have my life to live."

"It's going to be a camera," Ted said firmly, "and we don't pull him, you goof. We urge him forward gently. The tail is for emergencies, in case he starts to run."

"Oh," said Jimmy. "Well, the other objection is the location of his tail."

"It's in the usual place," Ted said.

"Well, naturally, but the usual place is so awfully near his heels." Jimmy looked mournful and quoted, "'They kick with their hind legs and are capable of making a stout resistance.'"

"So what?" said Ted. "Archie won't attack anything but a lion. You read that yourself from the encyclopedia. We aren't lions, are we?" There was a short pause.

"I see what you mean," said Jimmy. "Are we men or are we lions?" There was another short pause. "Personally, I'm a mouse. You do it, Ted. You're more the executive type. I'll watch."

"You will not," Ted told him. "It's perfectly simple. I'll go in front and urge him on with some grass, and you go behind and hang onto his tail."

"Me?" Jimmy croaked. "Hang onto his tail?"

"Certainly. You just said I was the executive type, didn't you? Well, the executive type always leads. Come on, Jimmy."

Ted gave him a shove from behind and Jimmy staggered mournfully toward Archie's tail, stared at it for a moment, took a deep breath and grabbed.

Things after that happened very quickly. Archie's left hind leg kicked out at a fantastic angle and landed a powerful and accurate wallop. Jimmy described a parabola in the air, rolled over twice on the grass, got to his feet and started running.

Ted joined him. Archie galloped in enthusiastic pursuit. His two would-be captors shot up into the branches of the nearest apple tree, and Archie came to a disappointed halt. Jimmy and Ted climbed upward as far as they could and came to rest near an abandoned bird's nest. They looked at each other.

"Kicks only lions," said Jimmy bitterly. "The executive type. Bah!"

"You read the book yourself," Ted accused and looked down thoughtfully at Archie's head, weaving around among the branches. The tree was not tall, and Archie was. After a moment, Ted broke off some juicy-looking leaves and handed them down to Archie, who accepted them courteously. Ted broke off some more.

Jimmy got the idea and began to help. "If we can only keep him here until the zoo men come."

"I hope the tree lasts out," said Ted. "Sit down, Jimmy. You're rocking the boat."

"Thank you," said his brother with dignity. "I'm more comfortable standing up."

Ted said, "Oh," with polite sympathy, and Jimmy added, "In case you want to know, being kicked by an even-toed ungulate is the same as being kicked by anything else, only rougher."

"By a what?"

"An even-toed ungulate. That's what that thing down there is. And, personally, I wish he'd go off and ungulate somewhere else."

"Think of the camera," Ted urged.

"I am thinking," said Jimmy, "of the projector." He added broodingly, "So he wouldn't kick me, huh? He wouldn't kick me because I didn't have a mane. Phooey!" He then said "Whoops!" and nearly fell out of the tree.

A large, purposeful-looking truck had just turned into the driveway.

"The zoo men!" Ted shouted. "The marines have landed. Jimmy, we're saved." He hesitated, and added, "I wish we weren't up here, though. It doesn't look so good. They might almost think Archie caught us."

"If they give that giraffe the reward," said Jimmy, "I shall blow a fuse." "Hey!" said a voice. A stout man in blue overalls was peering up at them, one arm wound affectionately around Archie's neck. "What you doing up there?"

Jimmy said, "We've caught the giraffe for you," and there was a hearty burst of laughter in response.

"Look who's caught who, will you?" said the stout man. "A nice, tame, little fellow like Archie, too!"

"Tame!" said Ted under his breath, and then addressed the stout man quite coolly. "We couldn't find much for him to eat, and we thought feeding him was the best way to keep him here." He paused impressively. "We're up in this tree, where we can get more leaves."

The stout man was silenced in his turn, and Jimmy and Ted descended with admirable dignity. "Well," the man admitted finally, "that was pretty smart. Yessir, that was real bright. We're much obliged. I'll see you get that reward all right."

Indoors, Jimmy glared at the encyclopedia. "Only lions," he muttered.

"We can get our camera," Ted offered.

"Projector!" Jimmy howled.

"M'mmmm," said Ted, "I'll tell you what. We'll compromise. Next time we'll buy a projector. This time we'll buy a camera. Now run along and get some cookies, there's a pal. All that brain work has made me hungry." Jimmy gazed upon his brother in mingled awe and fury, said "Compromise!" in a strangled voice, then departed suddenly. He came back a moment later, both hands full of cookies and a strange glitter in his eyes.

"Ted," he said, "I hate to mention it. But there's a rhinoceros in the backyard."

Ted let out a wild scream and dashed into the kitchen. A moment later Jimmy heard the back door slam. A gentle smile dawned on his face.

"Ah, well," he murmured, "we can't all be the executive type."

He looked affectionately at the calendar, which still proclaimed unmistakably that it was April Fool's Day, smiled again and began to eat his cookies. He felt much better.

Gudbrand on the Hillside

*The story of a man who set out to sell
a cow and ended up—you'll never guess how*

G. W. DASENT

Once upon a time there was a man whose name was Gudbrand; he had a farm which lay far, far away upon a hillside, so they called him Gudbrand on the Hillside.

Now, you must know this man and his good wife lived so happily together and understood one another so well that all the husband did the wife thought so well done there was nothing like it in the world, and she was always glad whatever he turned his hand to. The farm was their own land, and they had a hundred dollars lying at the bottom of their chest and two cows in a stall in their farmyard.

So one day his wife said to Gudbrand, "Do you know, dear, I think we ought to take one of our cows into town and sell it; that's what I think, for then we shall have

some money in hand, and such well-to-do people as we ought to have ready money like the rest of the world. As for the hundred dollars at the bottom of the chest yonder, we can't make a hole in them, and I'm sure I don't know what we want with more than one cow. Besides, we shall gain a little in another way, for then I shall get off with looking after only one cow instead of having, as now, to feed and litter and water two."

Well, Gudbrand thought his wife talked right good sense, so he set off at once with the cow on his way to town to sell her; but when he got to the town, there was no one who would buy his cow.

"Well! well! never mind," said Gudbrand, "at the worst, I can only go back again with my cow. I've both stable and

314

tether for her, I should think, and the road is no farther out than in," and with that he began to toddle home with his cow.

But when he had gone a bit of the way, a man met him who had a horse to sell so Gudbrand thought 'twas better to have a horse than a cow so he swopped with the man. A little farther on, he met a man walking along and driving a fat pig before him, and he thought it better to have a fat pig than a horse, so he swopped with the man. After that he went a little farther, and a man met him with a goat, so he thought it better to have a goat than a pig and he swopped with the man that owned the goat. Then he went on a bit till he met a man who had a sheep and he thought it always better to have a sheep than a goat. After a while he met a man with a goose and he swopped away the sheep for the goose, and when he had walked a long, long time, he met a man with a cock and he swopped with him, for he thought in this wise, "'Tis surely better to have a cock than a goose." Then he went on till the day was far spent, and he began to get very hungry so he sold the cock for a shilling and bought food with the money, for, thought Gudbrand on the Hillside, "'Tis always better to save one's life than to have a cock."

After that he went on home till he reached his nearest neighbor's house, where he turned in.

"Well," said the owner of the house, "how did things go with you in town?"

"Rather so-so," said Gudbrand. "I can't praise my luck nor do I blame it either," and with that he told the whole story from first to last.

"Ah!" said his friend, "you'll get nicely called over the coals, that one can see, when you get home to your wife. Heaven help you, I wouldn't stand in your shoes for something."

"Well!" said Gudbrand on the Hillside,

"I think things might have gone worse with me; but now, whether I have done wrong or not, I have so kind a good wife, she never has a word to say against anything that I do."

"Oh!" answered his neighbor, "I hear what you say, but I don't believe it for all that."

"Shall we lay a bet upon it?" asked Gudbrand on the Hillside. "I have a hundred dollars at the bottom of my chest at home; will you lay as many against them?"

Yes, the friend was ready to bet; so Gudbrand stayed there till evening when it began to get dark, and then they went together to his house, and the neighbor was to stand outside the door and listen while the man went in to see his wife.

"Good evening!" said Gudbrand on the Hillside.

"Good evening!" said the good wife. "Oh! is that you? Now, God be praised!"

Yes, it was he. So the wife asked how things had gone with him in town.

"Oh! only so-so," answered Gudbrand, "not much to brag of. When I got to town there was no one who would buy the cow, so you must know I swopped it away for a horse."

"For a horse!" said his wife. "Well, that is good of you; thanks with all my heart. We are so well-to-do that we may drive to church just as well as other people, and if we choose to keep a horse we have a right to get one, I should think. So run out, man, and put up the horse."

"Ah!" said Gudbrand; "but you see I've not got the horse after all, for when I got a bit farther on the road, I swopped it away for a pig."

"Think of that—now!" said the wife. "You did just as I should have done myself; a thousand thanks! Now I can have a bit of bacon in the house to set before people when they come to see me, that I can. What do we want with a horse? People

315

would only say we had got so proud that we couldn't walk to church. Go out, man, and put up the pig in the sty."

"But I've not got the pig either," said Gudbrand, "for when I got a little farther on, I swopped it away for a milch goat."

"Bless us!" cried his wife, "how well you manage everything! Now I think it over, what should I do with a pig? People would only point at us and say, 'Yonder they eat up all they have got.' No! now I have got a goat, and I shall have milk and cheese, and keep the goat too. Run out, man, and put up the goat."

"Nay, but I haven't any goat either," said Gudbrand, "for a little farther on I swopped it away and got a fine sheep instead."

"You don't say so!" cried his wife. "Why, you do everything to please me just as if I had been with you; what do we want with a goat? If I had it I should lose half my time in climbing up the hills to get it down. No! if I have a sheep, I shall have both wool and clothing, and fresh meat in the house. Run out, man, and put up the sheep."

"But I haven't got the sheep any more than the rest," said Gudbrand, "for when I had gone a bit farther, I swopped it away for a goose."

"Thank you, thank you, with all my heart!" cried his wife. "What should I do with a sheep? I have no spinning wheel nor carding comb, nor should I care to worry myself with cutting and shaping and sewing clothes. We can buy clothes now as we have always done; and now I shall have

roast goose, which I have longed for so often; and, besides, down to stuff my little pillow with. Run out, man, and put up the goose."

"Ah!" said Gudbrand, "but I haven't the goose either; for when I had gone a bit farther I swopped it away for a cock."

"Dear me!" cried his wife, "how you think of everything, just as I should have done myself! A cock! think of that! why, it's as good as an eight-day clock, for every morning the cock crows at four o'clock, and we shall be able to stir our stumps in good time. What should we do with a goose? I don't know how to cook it; and as for my pillow, I can stuff it with cotton grass. Run out, man, and put up the cock."

"But, after all, I haven't got the cock," said Gudbrand, "for when I had gone a bit farther, I got as hungry as a hunter, so I was forced to sell the cock for a shilling, for fear I should starve."

"Now, God be praised that you did so!" cried his wife. "Whatever you do, you do it always just after my own heart. What should we do with the cock? We are our own masters, I should think, and can lie abed in the morning as long as we like. Heaven be thanked that I have got you safe back again, you who do everything so well that I want neither cock nor goose, neither pigs nor kine."

Then Gudbrand opened the door and said, "Well, what do you say now? Have I won the hundred dollars?" and his neighbor was forced to allow that he had.

The Tree
That Didn't Get Trimmed

The tree in this story was a fine, well-grown
youngster but too tall for his age. His branches were
rather scraggly and, worst of all, his top
was a bit lopsided with a fork in it

If you walk through a grove of balsam trees you will notice that the young trees are silent; they are listening. But the old tall ones—especially the firs—are whispering. They are telling the story of The Tree That Didn't Get Trimmed. It sounds like a painful story, and the murmur of the old trees as they tell it is rather solemn. But it is an encouraging story for young saplings to hear. On warm autumn days when your trunk is tickled by ants and insects climbing, and the resin is hot and gummy in your knots, and the whole glade smells sweet, drowsy and sad, and the hardwood trees are boasting of the gay colors they are beginning to show, many a young evergreen has been cheered by it.

All young fir trees, as you know by that story of Hans Andersen's—if you've forgotten it, why not read it again?—dream of being a Christmas tree someday. With the vision of that brightness before them they patiently endure the sharp sting of the ax, the long hours pressed together on a freight car. But every December there are more trees cut than are needed for Christmas. And that is the story that no one—not even Hans Andersen—has thought to put down.

The tree in this story should never have been cut. He wouldn't have been, but it was getting dark in the Vermont woods, and the man with the ax said to himself, "Just one more." Cutting young trees with a sharp, beautifully balanced ax is fascinating; you go on and on; there's a sort of cruel pleasure in it. The blade goes through the soft wood with one whistling stroke and the boughs sink down with a soft swish.

He was a fine, well-grown youngster but too tall for his age; his branches were rather scraggly. If he'd been left there he would have been an unusually big tree someday; but now he was in the awkward age and didn't have the tapering shape and the thick, even foliage people like on Christmas trees. Worse still, instead of running up to a straight, clean spire, his top was a bit lopsided, with a fork in it.

317

But he didn't know this as he stood with many others, leaning against the side wall of the greengrocer's shop. In those cold December days he was happy, thinking of the pleasures to come. He had heard of the delights of Christmas Eve: the stealthy setting-up of the tree, the tinsel balls and colored toys and stars, the peppermint canes and birds with spun-glass tails. Even that old anxiety of Christmas trees—burning candles—did not worry him, for he had been told that nowadays people use strings of tiny electric bulbs which cannot set one afire. So he looked forward to the festival with a confidence.

"I shall be very grand," he said. "I hope there will be children to admire me. It must be a great moment when the children hang their stockings on you!" He even felt sorry for the first trees that were chosen and taken away. It would be best, he considered, not to be bought until Christmas Eve. Then, in the shining darkness someone would pick him out, put him carefully on the car, and away they would go. The tire chains would clack and jingle merrily on the snowy road. He imagined a big house with a fire glowing on a hearth, the hushed rustle of wrapping paper and parcels being unpacked. Someone would say, "Oh, what a beautiful tree!" How erect and stiff he would brace himself in his iron tripod stand.

But day after day went by, one by one the other trees were taken, and he began to grow troubled. For everyone who looked at him seemed to have an unkind

word. "Too tall," said one lady. "No, this one wouldn't do, the branches are too skimpy," said another. "If I chop the top," said the greengrocer, "it wouldn't be so bad." The tree shuddered, but the customer had passed on to look at others. Some of his branches ached where the grocer had bent them upward to make his shape appear more attractive.

Across the street was a novelty store. Its bright windows were full of scarlet odds and ends; when the doors opened, he could see people crowded along the aisles, cheerfully jostling one another with bumpy packages. A buzz of talk, a shuffle of feet, a constant ringing of cash drawers came noisily out that doorway.

He could see flashes of marvelous color, ornaments for luckier trees. Every evening, as the time drew nearer, the pavements were more thronged. The handsomer trees, not so tall as he but more bushy and shapely, were ranked in front of him; as they were taken away he could see the gaiety only too well. Then he was shown to a lady who wanted a tree very cheap. "You can have this one for a dollar," said the grocer. This was only one third of what the grocer had asked for him at first, but even so the lady refused him and went across the street to buy a little artificial tree at the toy store. The man pushed him back carelessly, and he toppled over and fell alongside the wall. No one bothered to pick him up. He was almost glad, for now his pride would be spared.

Now it was Christmas Eve. It was a foggy evening with a drizzling rain; the alley alongside the store was thick with trampled slush. As he lay there among broken boxes and fallen scraps of holly, strange thoughts came to him. In the still, northern forest already his wounded stump was buried in forgetful snow. He remembered the wintry sparkle of the woods, the big trees with crusts and clumps of silver on their broad boughs, the keen singing of the lonely wind. He remembered the strong, warm feeling of his roots reaching down into the safe earth. That is a good feeling; it means to a tree just what it means to you to stretch your toes down toward the bottom of a well-tucked bed. And he had given up all this to lie here, disdained, in a littered alley. The splash of feet, the chime of bells, the cry of cars went past him. He trembled a little with self-pity and vexation. "No toys and stockings for me," he thought sadly and shed some of his needles.

Late that night, after all the shopping was over, the grocer came out to clear away what was left. The boxes, the broken wreaths, and the empty barrels and our tree, with one or two others that hadn't been sold, all were thrown through the side door into the cellar. The door was locked, and he lay there in the dark. One of his branches, doubled under him in the fall, ached so that he thought it must be broken. "So this is Christmas," he said to himself.

All that day it was very still in the cellar. There was an occasional creak as one of the bruised trees tried to stretch itself. Feet

went along the pavement overhead, and there was a booming of church bells; but everything had a low, disappointed sound. Christmas is always a little sad, after such busy preparation. The unwanted trees lay on the stone floor, watching the furnace light flicker on a hatchet that had been left there.

The day after Christmas a man came in who wanted some green boughs to decorate a cemetery. The grocer took the hatchet and seized the trees without ceremony. They were too disheartened to care. Chop, chop, chop, went the blade, and the sweet-smelling branches were carried away. The naked trunks were thrown into a corner.

And now our tree, what was left of him, had plenty of time to think. He no longer could feel anything, for trees feel with their branches, but they think with their trunks. What did he think about as he grew dry and stiff? He thought that it had been silly of him to imagine such a fine, gay career for himself, and he was sorry for other young trees, still growing in the fresh, hilly country, who were enjoying the same fantastic dreams.

Now perhaps you don't know what happens to the trunks of leftover Christmas trees. You could never guess. Farmers come from the suburbs and buy them at five cents each for bean poles and grape arbors. Perhaps (here begins the encouraging part of this story) they are really happier in the end than the trees that get trimmed for Santa Claus. They go back into the fresh, moist earth of spring, and when the sun grows hot and quick tendrils of the vines climb up them, presently they are decorated with the red blossoms of the bean or the little blue globes of the grape, just as pretty as any Christmas trinkets.

So one day the naked, dusty fir poles were taken out of the cellar and thrown into a truck with many others, and made a rattling journey out into the land. The farmer unloaded them in his yard and was stacking them up by the barn when his wife came to watch him.

"There," she said. "That's just what I want, a nice long pole with a fork in it. Jim, put that one over there to hold up the clothesline." It was the first time that anyone had praised our tree, and his dried-up heart swelled with a tingle of forgotten sap. They put him near one end of the clothesline, with his stump close to a flower bed. The fork that had been despised for a Christmas star was just the thing to hold up a clothesline. It was washday, and soon the farmer's wife began to bring out some wet garments to swing and freshen in the clean, bright air. And the very first thing that hung near the top of the Christmas pole was a cluster of children's stockings.

That isn't quite the end of the story, as the old fir trees whisper it in the breeze. The Tree That Didn't Get Trimmed was so cheerful watching the stockings and other gay little clothes that plumped out in the wind, just as though waiting to be spanked, that he didn't notice what was going on—or going up—below him. A vine had caught hold of his trunk and was steadily twisting upward. And one morning, when the farmer's wife came out intending to shift him, she stopped and exclaimed. "Why, I mustn't move this pole," she said. "The morning glory has run right up it." So it had, and our bare pole was blue and crimson with color.

Something nice, the old firs believe, always happens to the trees that don't get trimmed. They even believe that someday one of the Christmas-tree bean poles will be the starting point for another Magic Beanstalk, as in the fairy tale of the boy who climbed up the bean tree and killed the giant. When that happens, fairy tales will begin all over again.

The Hundred Dresses

*Time after time they asked Wanda, who came to school
each day in the same faded blue outfit, "How many dresses
did you say you had hanging up in your closet?" And
time after time Wanda replied, "A hundred"*

Eleanor Estes

Today, Monday, Wanda Petronski was not in her seat. But nobody, not even Peggy and Madeline, the girls who started all the fun, noticed her absence. Usually Wanda sat in the next to the last seat in the last row in Room Thirteen. She sat in the corner of the room where the rough boys who did not make good marks sat, the corner of the room where there was most scuffling of feet, most roars of laughter when anything funny was said and most mud and dirt on the floor.

Wanda did not sit there because she was rough and noisy. On the contrary, she was very quiet and rarely said anything at all. And nobody had ever heard her laugh out loud. Sometimes she twisted her mouth into a crooked sort of smile, but that was all.

Nobody knew exactly why Wanda sat in that seat, unless it was because she came all the way from Boggins Heights and her feet were usually caked with dry mud. Maybe the teacher liked to keep all the children with dirty shoes in one corner. But no one really thought much about Wanda Petron-ski, once she sat in the corner of the room.

The time when they thought about Wanda was outside of school hours—at noontime when they were coming back to school or in the morning early before school began, when groups of two or three, or even more, would be talking and laughing on their way to the school yard.

Then, sometimes, they waited for Wanda—to have fun with her.

The next day, Tuesday, Wanda was not in school, either. And nobody noticed her absence again, except the teacher and probably big Bill Byron, who sat in the seat behind Wanda's and who could now put his long legs around her empty desk and sit there like a frog, to the great entertainment of all in his corner.

But on Wednesday, Peggy and Maddie, who sat down front with other children who got good marks and who didn't track in a whole lot of mud, did notice that Wanda wasn't there. Peggy was the most popular girl in school. She was pretty, she had many pretty clothes, and her auburn hair was curly. Maddie was her closest

321

friend. The reason Peggy and Maddie noticed Wanda's absence was because Wanda had made them late to school. They had waited and waited for Wanda, to have some fun with her, and she just hadn't come.

They often waited for Wanda Petronski—to have fun with her.

Wanda Petronski. Most of the children in Room Thirteen didn't have names like that. They had names easy to say, like Thomas, Smith or Allen. There was one boy named Bounce, Willie Bounce, and people thought that was funny, but not funny in the same way that Petronski was.

Wanda didn't have any friends. She came to school alone and went home alone. She always wore a faded blue dress that didn't hang right. It was clean, but it looked as though it had never been ironed properly. She didn't have any friends, but a lot of girls talked to her. Sometimes, they surrounded her in the school yard as she stood watching the little girls play hopscotch on the worn hard ground.

"Wanda," Peggy would say in a most courteous manner as though she were talking to Miss Mason. "Wanda," she'd say, giving one of her friends a nudge, "tell us. How many dresses did you say you had hanging up in your closet?"

"A hundred," Wanda said.

"A hundred!" exclaimed all the little girls incredulously, and the little ones would stop playing hopscotch and listen.

"Yeah, a hundred, all lined up," said Wanda. Then her thin lips drew together in silence.

"What are they like? All silk, I bet," said Peggy.

"Yeah, all silk, all colors."

"Velvet, too?"

"Yeah, velvet too. A hundred dresses," Wanda would repeat stolidly. "All lined up in my closet."

Then they'd let her go. And then before she'd gone very far, they couldn't help bursting into shrieks and peals of laughter.

A hundred dresses! Obviously, the only dress Wanda had was the blue one she wore every day. So why did she say she had a hundred? What a story! And the girls laughed derisively while Wanda moved over to the sunny place by the ivy-covered brick wall of the school where she usually stood and waited for the bell to ring.

But if the girls had met her at the corner of Oliver Street, they'd walk along with her for a way, stopping every few feet for more incredulous questions.

"How many shoes did you say you had?"

"Sixty."

"Sixty! Sixty pairs or sixty shoes?"

"Sixty pairs. All lined up in my closet."

"Yesterday, you said fifty."

"Now, I got sixty."

Cries of exaggerated politeness greeted this. "All alike?"

"Oh, no. Every pair is different. All colors. All lined up." And Wanda would shift her eyes quietly from Peggy to a distant spot as though she were looking far ahead, looking but not seeing anything.

Then the outer fringe of the crowd of girls would break away gradually, laughing, and little by little in pairs the group would disperse. Peggy, who had thought up this game, and Maddie, her inseparable friend, were always the last to leave. Finally Wanda would move up the street, her eyes dull and her mouth closed, hitching her left shoulder every now and then in the funny way she had, finishing the walk to school alone.

Peggy was not really cruel. She protected small children from bullies. And she cried for hours if she saw an animal mistreated. If anybody had said to her, "Don't you think that is a cruel way to treat Wanda?" she would have been very surprised. Cruel? Why did the girl say she had a hundred dresses? Anybody could tell that that was a lie. Why did she want to lie? And she wasn't just an ordinary person, else why did she have a name like that? Anyway, they never made her cry.

As for Maddie, this business of asking Wanda every day how many dresses and how many hats, and how many this and that she had was bothering her. Maddie was poor herself. She usually wore somebody's hand-me-down clothes. Thank goodness, she didn't live up on Boggins Heights or have a funny name.

Sometimes, when Peggy was asking Wanda those questions in that mocking polite voice, Maddie felt embarrassed and studied the marbles in the palm of her hand, rolling them around and saying nothing herself. Not that she felt sorry for Wanda, exactly. She would never have paid any attention to Wanda if Peggy hadn't invented the dresses game. But suppose Peggy and all the others started in on her next? She wasn't as poor as Wanda, perhaps, but she was poor. Of course she would have more sense than to say she had a hundred dresses. Still she would not like for them to begin on her. She wished Peggy would stop teasing Wanda Petronski.

Today, even though they had been late to school, Maddie was glad she had not had to make fun of Wanda. She worked her arithmetic problems absentmindedly. "Eight times eight—let's see . . ." She wished she had the nerve to write Peggy a note, because she knew she never would have the courage to speak right out to Peggy, to say, "Hey, Peg, let's stop asking Wanda how many dresses she has." When she finished her arithmetic she did start a note to Peggy. Suddenly she paused and shuddered. She pictured herself in the school yard, a new target for Peggy and the girls. Peggy might ask her where she got the dress that she had on, and Maddie

would have to say it was one of Peggy's old ones that Maddie's mother had tried to disguise with new trimmings so no one in Room Thirteen would recognize it.

If only Peggy would decide of her own accord to stop having fun with Wanda. Oh, well! Maddie ran her hand through her short blonde hair as though to push the uncomfortable thoughts away. What difference did it make? Slowly Maddie tore into bits the note she had started. She was Peggy's best friend, and Peggy was the best-liked girl in the whole room. Peggy could not possibly do anything that was really wrong, she thought.

As for Wanda, she was just some girl who lived up on Boggins Heights and stood alone in the school yard. She scarcely ever said anything to anybody. The only time she talked was in the school yard about her hundred dresses. Maddie remembered her telling about one of her dresses, pale bluc with cerise-colored trimmings. And she remembered another that was brilliant jungle green with a red sash. "You'd look like a Christmas tree in that," the girls had said in pretended admiration.

Thinking about Wanda and her hundred dresses all lined up in the closet, Maddie began to wonder who was going to win the drawing and color contest. For girls, this contest consisted of designing dresses and for boys, of designing motorboats. Probably Peggy would win the girls' medal. Peggy drew better than anyone else in the

room. At least, that's what everybody thought. She could copy a picture in a magazine or some film star's head so that you could almost tell who it was. Oh, Maddie was sure Peggy would win. Well, tomorrow the teacher was going to announce the winners. Then they'd know.

The next day it was drizzling. Maddie and Peggy hurried to school under Peggy's umbrella. Naturally, on a day like this, they didn't wait for Wanda Petronski on the corner of Oliver Street, the street that far, far away, under the railroad tracks and up the hill, led to Boggins Heights. Anyway, they weren't taking chances on being late today, because today was important.

"Do you think Miss Mason will announce the winners today?" asked Peggy.

"Oh, I hope so, the minute we get in," said Maddie. "Of course, you'll win, Peg."

"Hope so," said Peggy eagerly.

The minute they entered the classroom, they stopped short and gasped. There were drawings all over the room, on every ledge and windowsill, dazzling colors and brilliant, lavish designs, all drawn on great sheets of wrapping paper. There must have been a hundred of them all lined up. These must be the drawings for the contest. They were! Everybody stopped and whistled or murmured admiringly.

As soon as the class had assembled, Miss Mason announced the winners. Jack Beggles had won for the boys, she said, and his design for an outboard motor was on ex-

hibition in Room Twelve, along with the sketches by all the other boys.

"As for the girls," she said, "although just one or two sketches were submitted by most, one girl—and Room Thirteen should be proud of her—this one girl actually drew one hundred designs—all different and all beautiful. In the opinion of the judges, any one of the drawings is worthy of winning the prize. I am very happy to say that Wanda Petronski is the winner of the girls' medal. Unfortunately, Wanda has been absent from school for some days and is not here to receive the applause that is due her. Let us hope she will be back tomorrow. Now class, you may file around the room quietly and look at her exquisite drawings."

The children burst into applause, and even the boys were glad to have a chance to stamp on the floor, put their fingers in their mouths and whistle, though they were not interested in dresses.

"Look, Peg," whispered Maddie. "There's that blue one she told us about. Isn't it beautiful?"

"Yes," said Peggy. "And here's that green one. Boy, and I thought I could draw."

While the class was circling the room, the monitor from the principal's office brought Miss Mason a note. Miss Mason read it several times and studied it thoughtfully for a while. Then she clapped her hands.

"Attention, class. Everyone back to his seat."

When the shuffling of feet had stopped and the room was still and quiet, Miss Mason said, "I have a letter from Wanda's father that I want to read to you."

Miss Mason stood there a moment and the silence in the room grew tense and expectant. The teacher adjusted her glasses slowly and deliberately. Her manner indicated that what was coming—this letter from Wanda's father—was a matter of great importance. Everybody listened closely as Miss Mason read the brief note.

Dear Teacher:

My Wanda will not come to your school any more. Jake also. Now we move away to big city. No more holler "Polack." No more ask why funny name. Plenty of funny names in the big city.

Yours truly,
Jan Petronski

A deep silence met the reading of this letter. Miss Mason took off her glasses, blew on them and wiped them on her soft white handkerchief. Then she put them on again and looked at the class. When she spoke her voice was very low.

"I am sure that none of the boys and girls in Room Thirteen would purposely and deliberately hurt anyone's feelings because his name happened to be a long, unfamiliar

one. I prefer to think that what was said was said in thoughtlessness. I know that all of you feel the way I do, that this is a very unfortunate thing to have happened—unfortunate and sad, both. And I want you all to think about it."

The first period was a study period. Maddie tried to prepare her lessons, but she could not put her mind on her work. She had a very sick feeling in the bottom of her stomach. True, she had not enjoyed listening to Peggy ask Wanda how many dresses she had in her closet, but she had said nothing. She had stood by silently, and that was just as bad as what Peggy had done. Worse. She was a coward. At least, Peggy hadn't considered they were being mean, but she, Maddie, had thought they were doing wrong. She could put herself in Wanda's shoes. But she had done just as much as Peggy to make life miserable for Wanda by simply standing by and saying nothing. She had helped to make someone so unhappy that she had had to move away from town.

Goodness! Wasn't there anything she could do? If only she could tell Wanda she hadn't meant to hurt her feelings. She turned around and stole a glance at Peggy, but Peggy did not look up. She seemed to be studying hard. Well, whether Peggy felt badly or not, she, Maddie, had to do something. She had to find Wanda Petronski. Maybe she had not yet moved away. Maybe Peggy would climb the Heights with her, and they would tell Wanda she had won the contest, that they thought she was smart and the hundred dresses were beautiful.

When school was dismissed in the afternoon, Peggy said, with pretended casualness, "Hey, let's go and see if that kid has left town or not."

So Peggy had had the same idea! Maddie glowed. Peg was really all right.

The two girls hurried out of the building, up the street toward Boggins Heights, the part of town that wore such a forbidding air on this kind of a November afternoon, drizzly, damp and dismal.

"Well, at least," said Peggy gruffly, "I never did call her a foreigner or make fun of her name. I never thought she had the sense to know we were making fun of her anyway. I thought she was too dumb. And gee, look how she can draw!"

Maddie could say nothing. All she hoped was that they would find Wanda. She wanted to tell her that they were sorry they had picked on her, and how wonderful the whole school thought she was, and—please, not to move away and everybody would be nice. She and Peggy would fight anybody who was not nice. Maddie fell to imagining a story in which she and Peggy assailed any bully who might be going to pick on Wanda. "Petronski Onski!" somebody would yell, and she and Peggy would pounce on the guilty one. For a time Maddie consoled herself with these thoughts, but they soon vanished, and again she felt unhappy and wished everything would be nice the way it was before any of them had made fun of Wanda.

Br-r-r. How drab and cold and cheerless it was up here on the Heights! In the summertime, the trees, the sumac, and the ferns that grew along the brook on the side of the road made this a beautiful walk. But now it did not seem beautiful. The brook had dried up. And today's drizzle just sharpened the outline of the rusty tin cans, and forlorn remnants of a big black umbrella in the bed of the brook.

The two girls hurried on. They hoped to get to the top of the hill before dark. Otherwise they were not certain they could find Wanda's house. At last, puffing and panting, they rounded the top of the hill.

"I think that's where the Petronskis live," said Maddie, pointing to a little white house with lots of chicken coops on the side of it. Wisps of old grass stuck up here and there along the pathway like thin kittens. The house and its sparse little yard looked shabby but clean. It reminded Maddie of Wanda's one dress, her faded blue cotton dress, shabby but clean.

There was not a sign of life about the house. Peggy knocked firmly on the door, but there was no answer. She and Maddie went around to the back yard and knocked there. Still there was no answer.

"Wanda!" called Peggy. They listened sharply, but only a deep silence pressed against their eardrums. There was no doubt about it. The Petronskis were gone. How could they ever make amends?

They turned slowly and made their way back down the hill. It was a relief to be back on Oliver Street again, but they still felt disconsolate, and Maddie wondered if she were going to be unhappy about Wanda and the hundred dresses forever. Nothing would ever seem good to her again because, just when she was about to enjoy something—like going for a hike with Peggy to look for bayberries or sliding down Barley Hill—she'd bump right smack into the thought that she had made Wanda Petronski move away.

"Well, anyway," said Peggy, "she's gone now, so what can we do? Besides, when I was asking her about all her dresses, she probably was getting good ideas for her drawings. She might not even have won the contest, otherwise."

Maddie turned this idea carefully over in her head, for if there were anything in it she would not have to feel so badly. But that night she could not get to sleep. She thought about Wanda and her faded blue dress and the little house she had lived in. And she thought of the glowing picture those hundred dresses made—all lined up in the classroom. At last Maddie sat up in bed and pressed her forehead tight in her

hands and really thought. This was the hardest thinking she had ever done. After a long, long time, she reached an important conclusion.

She was never going to stand by and say nothing again.

If she ever heard anybody picking on someone because they were funny looking or because they had strange names, she'd speak up. Even if it meant losing Peggy's friendship. She had no way of making things right with Wanda, but from now on she would never make anybody else that unhappy again.

On Saturday Maddie spent the afternoon with Peggy. They were writing a letter to Wanda Petronski. It was just a friendly letter telling about the contest and telling Wanda she had won. They told her how pretty her drawings were and that now they were studying about Winfield Scott in school. And they asked her if she liked where she was living and if she liked her new teacher. They had meant to say they were sorry, but it ended up with their just writing a friendly letter, the kind they would have written to any good friend, and they signed it with lots of X's for love. They mailed the letter to Boggins Heights, writing "Please Forward" on the envelope. The minute they mailed the letter, they both felt happier and more carefree.

Days passed and there was no answer, but the letter did not come back, so maybe Wanda had received it. Perhaps she was so hurt and angry she was not going to answer. You could not blame her.

Weeks went by and still Wanda did not answer. Peggy had begun to forget the whole business, and Maddie put herself to sleep at night making speeches about Wanda, defending her from great crowds of girls who were trying to tease her with, "How many dresses have you got?" And before Wanda could press her lips together in a tight line, the way she did before answering, Maddie would cry out, "Stop!" Then everybody would feel ashamed the way she used to feel.

Now it was Christmas time and there was snow on the ground. Christmas bells and a small tree decorated the classroom. On the last day of school before the holidays, the teacher showed the class a letter she had received that morning.

"You remember Wanda Petronski, the gifted little artist who won the drawing contest? Well, she has written me, and I am glad to know where she lives, because now I can send her her medal. I want to read her letter to you."

The class sat up with a sudden interest and listened intently.

Dear Miss Mason:

How are you and Room Thirteen? Please tell the girls they can keep those hundred dresses, because in my new house I have a hundred new ones, all lined up in my closet. I'd like that girl Peggy to have the drawing of the green dress with the red trimming, and her friend Maddie to have the blue one. For Christmas. I miss that school and my new teacher does not equalize with you. Merry Christmas to you and everybody.

Yours truly,
Wanda Petronski

On the way home from school Maddie and Peggy held their drawings very carefully. All the houses had wreaths and holly in the windows. Outside the grocery store, hundreds of Christmas trees were stacked, and in the window, candy peppermint sticks and cornucopias of shiny transparent paper were strung. The air smelled like Christmas and lights shining everywhere reflected different colors on the snow.

"Boy!" said Peggy, "this shows she really liked us. It shows she got our letter

and this is her way of saying that everything's all right. And that's that."

"I hope so," said Maddie sadly. She felt sad because she knew she would never see the little tight-lipped Polish girl again and couldn't ever really make things right between them.

She went home and she pinned her drawing over a torn place in the pink-flowered wallpaper in the bedroom. The shabby room came alive from the brilliancy of the colors. Maddie sat down on her bed and looked at the drawing. She had stood by and said nothing, but Wanda had been nice to her, anyway.

Tears blurred her eyes and she gazed for a long time at the picture. Then hastily she rubbed her eyes and studied it intently. The colors in the dress were so vivid that she had scarcely noticed the face and head of the drawing. But it looked like her, Maddie! It really did. The same short blonde hair, blue eyes and wide straight mouth. Why it really looked like her own self! Wanda had really drawn this for her. Excitedly, she ran over to Peggy's.

"Peg!" she said, "let me see your picture."

"What's the matter?" asked Peggy, as they clattered up to her room where Wanda's drawing was lying face down on the bed. Maddie carefully raised it.

"Look! She drew you. That's you!" she exclaimed. And the head and face of this picture did look like the auburn-haired Peggy.

"What did I say!" said Peggy. "She must have really liked us, anyway."

"Yes, she must have," agreed Maddie, and she blinked away the tears that came every time she thought of Wanda standing alone in that sunny spot in the school yard, looking stolidly over at the group of laughing girls after she had walked off, after she had said, "Sure, a hundred of them, all lined up."

The Floogles Are Detectives

Amos and Fanny Flora were going to be detectives, with the help of Amos' new detectiving book. But Snitkin the dog resolved that he would never be a bloodhound

GERTRUDE CRAMPTON

The Floogles! Everything always happens to the Floogles! Like the time Mrs. Floogle bought the dressmaker's dummy at the rummage sale, and Mr. Floogle's cousin Oscar came to visit just at the wrong time. And then Amos Floogle found a book that told all about being a detective. Everything got all mixed up together until no one was quite sure who was coming and who was going.

Mrs. Floogle came home from the rummage sale, her face full of smiles and her arms full carrying a dressmaker's dummy.

"This will be wonderful," she said happily. "Now I will have something to try my dresses on while I am making them. And how I have wanted that! It is very confusing never to know how a dress will look until the very last stitch is in. Especially if it turns out that the dress looks quite awful."

So Mr. Floogle and Amos Floogle and Fanny Flora Floogle were very pleased about the dressmaker's dummy. And so

329

was their dog Snitkin Floogle after he got used to having it around.

But then it turned out that Mrs. Floogle didn't fit the dressmaker's dummy. And the dressmaker's dummy didn't fit Mrs. Floogle! And the rummage sale simply would not take the dummy back. So Mr. Floogle carried the dummy up to the attic until Fanny Flora Floogle should grow up to it. And nothing whatever was said about dressmakers or dressmakers' dummies. Mrs. Floogle put the cover over the sewing machine, and her mouth was tight at the edges.

The next day Mr. Floogle's cousin Oscar came for a short visit. Mrs. Floogle gave him the bedroom right over the kitchen, for it was certainly the pleasantest and the most comfortable room.

"It isn't that I don't like Cousin Oscar," said Mrs. Floogle when the dishes were done and Cousin Oscar tucked in. "He is a lovely, kind person."

"But?" asked Mr. Floogle, scratching his worried head.

"But Cousin Oscar is so shy," cried Mrs. Floogle.

"Not with us," said Amos and Fanny Flora. "With us he makes kites and dams up the brook and peels an apple with one long peel."

"No, not with you," said Mrs. Floogle. "But with everyone else."

"Agreed," said Mr. Floogle. "But what of that?"

"The dance!" said Mrs. Floogle. "The wonderful, exciting, marvelous barn dance in Charley Haverstack's new barn next week! I have a new dress, and Fanny Flora has a new dress. And she has new hair bows too. Amos has new shoes, and even Snitkin has a new collar."

"And I have a fine red necktie," said Mr. Floogle proudly.

"Well, we just cannot go," said Mrs. Floogle.

"Can't go?" cried all the Floogles, and Snitkin howled.

"No," said Mrs. Floogle. "We cannot be so impolite. Cousin Oscar is too shy to go to a dance. And we cannot go if Cousin Oscar does not go."

And all the Floogles were sad. For Charley Haverstack's new barn was full of fresh paint and clean hay and the fine smells of newness. And before Charley Haverstack's new barn was full of fine cows, Charley Haverstack was giving a splendid party. Dancing there'd be, with a fiddler to help a man know when to swing his waltzing lady. And games, with Amos Floogle sure in his heart to win at least one prize. And supper, with Fanny Flora making her very first and very best chocolate cake to take to it.

"Oh!" said all the Floogles.

But they said no more about it at all. And they never pouted or frowned. For everyone loved Cousin Oscar. Besides, there was nothing to be done about it. Cousin Oscar was too shy—much too shy—to go to Charley Haverstack's party.

So Amos Floogle said he had to get on with his detecting and went off to read the book he'd been so fortunate to find that very morning. And it was a very worthwhile book indeed, for it told all about clues and fingerprints and bloodhounds and such. Amos Floogle said no detective would dream of being a detective without a book like this one. Fanny Flora said she was going to be a detective too. And Amos said Snitkin could be a bloodhound. But Snitkin made up his mind he positively would not be a bloodhound.

And that night, when the Floogles were tight asleep, IT began.

Softly. Slowly. Shh, shh, shh. And a tiny thread of whistle.

Amos Floogle decided he was cold, so he pulled his head under the covers. Fanny Flora decided girls were practically never detectives. Snitkin made up his mind right then and there he'd *never* be a bloodhound. And Mrs. Floogle said to Mr. Floogle, "What's that?"

"Mice," said Mr. Floogle comfortably. But he didn't believe it either.

The next morning with the sun shining in and out the curtain ruffles and everyone full of pancakes and little sausages, Mrs. Floogle decided maybe there had been mice. And Amos Floogle wondered why in the world he'd got so cold. And Fanny Flora thought perhaps she would enjoy being a detective. But Snitkin was determined he'd not be a bloodhound.

Amos and Fanny Flora had a wonderful morning with Cousin Oscar, for they went to the woods to see what there was to be seen. But that afternoon Cousin Oscar was tired as could be and had to take a nap before supper.

Supper was good, and Cousin Oscar was gay, and he told many a fine story about the days when he and Mr. Floogle were boys.

And so everyone went happily to bed.

And then IT began.

A little faster. A little louder. A little bolder. Shuff, shuff, shuff. Click, click, click. And a tiny thread of whistle.

"What's that?" said Mrs. Floogle.

"Rats," said Mr. Floogle comfortably. But he didn't believe it either. And Amos and Fanny Flora decided it was COLD and pulled their chins and their noses and their eyes and their hair under the covers. And Snitkin decided it was cold, too, especially for a dog that wasn't a bloodhound. So Amos found room for Snitkin in his bed.

The next morning with the dew making diamonds in the spider webs and everyone full of waffles and bacon, Mrs. Floogle decided maybe there had been rats. And Amos decided it was much warmer. And Fanny Flora decided she'd read Amos' book since she was going to be a detective

too. But Snitkin was sure he wasn't going to be a bloodhound.

Amos and Fanny Flora had a wonderful morning with Cousin Oscar, for they went to the old bridge over the river and caught five fish for lunch. But Cousin Oscar was tired as could be that afternoon and had to take a nap.

That evening was the jolliest the Floogles ever had known. They popped popcorn by the fire, and Cousin Oscar told many a story of lumberjack days in the North.

At last they went happily to bed.

And then IT began.

Much faster. Much louder. Much bolder. Shufflety, shufflety, shuff. Clickety, clickety, clack. And a tiny thread of whistle.

"What's that?" said Mrs. Floogle.

"Squirrels," said Mr. Floogle comfortably. But he didn't believe it either. And Amos and Fanny Flora and Snitkin decided they'd never never been so COLD in all their lives.

The next morning with the morning glories peeping jauntily through the trellis and everyone full of ham and fried eggs, Mrs. Floogle decided maybe there had been squirrels. And Amos and Fanny Flora decided detectives were never cold. But Snitkin was positive he wasn't going to be a bloodhound.

Amos and Fanny Flora had a wonderful morning with Cousin Oscar, for they went to the town and helped him with his shopping. Cousin Oscar had suddenly made up his mind he must own, at once, a beautiful blue tie and a new white shirt to go with it.

Cousin Oscar was tired as could be that afternoon and had to take a nap. Mr. Floogle and Mrs. Floogle and Amos and Fanny Flora and Snitkin were very tired themselves, and so everyone had a small nap.

That evening was even happier than the one before. For Cousin Oscar showed the Floogles the secret of pulling taffy. And he showed Amos and Fanny Flora the secret of making pennies come out of their ears.

So everyone went happily to bed.

And then IT began.

Very fast. Very loud. Very bold. Whoosh-whoosh-whoosh. Slick, slick, slick. Hum, two-three, hum. And a tiny thread of whistle.

"What's that?" said Mrs. Floogle. "Elephants?"

"Well, no," said Mr. Floogle. And Mrs. Floogle admitted she didn't think it was elephants either.

Amos Floogle decided that a brave detective *never* got cold. Fanny Flora Floogle wished she could peek in the detective book just once more. And Snitkin absolutely and finally made up his mind not to be a bloodhound.

"But after all—!" growled Snitkin, deep in his throat. And he padded softly and he padded quietly and he padded with his teeth flashing, toward the attic.

And Amos Floogle with just one tiny last shiver picked up his flashlight and put his detecting book under his arm and started toward the attic.

And Fanny Flora Floogle picked up her flashlight and her special detective magnifying glass and started toward the attic.

And Mrs. Floogle said, "Elephants, squirrels, rats and mice!" And she followed Mr. Floogle and his flashlight toward the attic. And she carried with her a most wonderfully polished baseball bat she'd bought for Amos' birthday surprise.

Tiptoe, tiptoe, tiptoe! went the Floogles.

Shoosh, shoosh, shoosh! went their slippered feet.

Thump, thump, thump! went their frightened hearts.

"Now!" cried each brave Floogle to himself.

And they flashed on the flashlights.

Mr. Floogle's flashlight picked up Fanny Flora, and Mrs. Floogle had to hang on hard to stop the baseball bat's swing. Fanny Flora's flashlight picked up Amos. And Amos' flashlight picked up Snitkin and his shining, sharp teeth. And the moonlight, silvering through the attic windows, picked up—Cousin Oscar! Cousin Oscar, whistling a gay little thread of whistle. Cousin Oscar, graceful as a barnswallow, quick as a cricket, frisky as a spring lamb, happy as a lark. Cousin Oscar, bowing and turning and gliding. Cousin Oscar, waltzing with the dressmaker's dummy!

"COUSIN OSCAR!" thundered Mr. Floogle.

So Cousin Oscar made a very fine bow from the waist to the dressmaker's dummy and smiled on the Floogles with no shyness at all.

"It's Charley Haverstack's barn dance tomorrow," said Cousin Oscar. "With the fiddler to help a man know when to swing his waltzing lady. With the games, and Amos sure to win a prize. And supper, and Fanny Flora making her first chocolate cake. Charley Haverstack's wonderful party you were going to stay home from, all on account of me and my shyness."

"How did you find out?" cried Mrs. Floogle. "We never once said a word to you about it."

"And never a pout or a frown either," said Cousin Oscar. "But talk travels fast and talk travels easily, especially through the stovepipe hole from the kitchen to my comfortable room. And I heard you that night you decided you'd stay home because of my shyness."

And Cousin Oscar smiled a good smile on them all. "It seemed to me that if you could give up a party for me, I could give up my shyness for you. And so I have been learning to waltz with Miss Mehitabel Jones"—and he bowed gallantly to the dressmaker's dummy—"who is an elegant waltzer, although a bit stiff and clumsy in

making a turn. But she doesn't complain when I step on her feet."

So Mrs. Floogle kindly offered to waltz with Cousin Oscar. They flew with grace and light feet across the moonlit floor while Mr. Floogle obligingly whistled the gayest waltz tune any fiddler could fiddle.

And then the Floogles hurried down from the attic to get on with their sleeping, for there was much to be done in the morning.

After supper the next evening they were finally ready—Cousin Oscar was very fine in his new white shirt and blue tie, Mr. Floogle very gay in his red tie. Mrs. Floogle and Fanny looked beautiful in their new dresses, Amos gleaming in his new shoes, and Snitkin very handsome in his new collar. Cousin Oscar, being the guest and Mr. Floogle's cousin, carried Fanny Flora's very first chocolate cake, which was certainly the best that could be brought to a party.

And as they walked to Charley Haverstack's barn, Amos decided he'd give the detectiving book to a friend, since he'd made up his mind to be just like Cousin Oscar. Fanny Flora decided to give up being a detective and be a chocolate-cake cook instead. And Snitkin, his head up high so that no one could fail to see his beautiful collar, made up his mind absolutely, positively, completely and without-a-doubt that he would never, never be a bloodhound—or anything else except Snitkin Floogle.

The Miracle of the Poor Island

*On the Poor Island there was only one thing of
beauty—a white rose bush which, on
the day the Queen came, had nine flowers blooming*

ELEANOR FARJEON

The Queen had a Pleasure Island, a little out to sea. When she wanted to make merry, she sailed there from her palace on the mainland in a gilded barque with silk flags flying. Her Court accompanied her, there were musicians on deck too, and she came to her Pleasure Island amid flowers and music. There she spent her days picnicking and dancing under the trees. Everything that could make her island rich and prosperous was brought there in abundance from the mainland.

Farther out to sea lay a poor fishing island. Here there was no abundance, and life was a hard battle. It was barren ground, stony or marshy, where grass scarcely grew, no trees or shrubs and no flowers. Yes, there was just one flower, a small white rose bush which belonged to little Lois. Her father's hut lay in the lee of the church that stood in the middle of the stony isle. He had scraped together a little soil, and the day he was married he brought the rose bush over from the mainland and set it by his door. His young bride tended it with so much care that it could not help growing; and when she died, Lois,

who had known the rose as long as she had known her mother, tended it as her mother had done. It did not grow very big, its flowers were few and sometimes bitten by the salt wind, but it was the only flower on the island, and the islanders were proud of it. Lois took care of it, but it seemed to belong to them all; it was the Island Flower.

Dangerous rocks surrounded the Poor Island, and its position exposed it to the roughest storms. Sometimes for days together the boats dared not put out from it, and those on the mainland could not approach it. The islanders were too poor to keep much store of food by them, nor could they grow it, so when the fishing boats could not put out, the hard times were still harder. In fair weather the men lost no opportunity of getting fish. Most of it the women salted down for their own use; the rest they took to the mainland to sell for a little money, and they came back with flour and salt and materials to mend their nets with. But the men, who shared in common the few boats on which their trade depended, could hardly spare time to take their wives over and back, so the women waited till the tide went out. For there was in those parts an unusual tide which once a month, at the full moon, receded far back into the ocean, leaving bare all the sand between the mainland and the island. The sea bed lay exposed for a long time, long enough for the women to hurry over the sand with their creels of fish, and sell them to the merchants on the beach and buy the few things that they needed most. Then the women trooped back across the patches of rock and stretches of ribbed sand, reaching the Poor Island just before the tide flowed in and cut them off. Sometimes they had to hurry and had not time to complete their purchases, for they dared not be caught in the mouth of the rolling tide.

One evening, when the tide was out, the Queen looked from her Pleasure Island and saw the band of women hurrying home. She had hardly noticed or thought of them before, but tonight the sight of them struck her heart. On the bare sand, where small pools gleamed with colors of the sunset, her own little isle lay like a glowing jewel; her summer palace, her gardens, fountains and pavilions shone in the sun, and she herself, in her silk and silver gown, was like a Queen of Fairyland. While yonder, over the waste, the bare-legged women in their faded gowns, with their baskets on their backs, trudged to the Poor Island, which lay like a stone in the distance: not like a precious stone, but a common pebble. Yet perhaps, thought the Queen, there was something precious on it. "How sorrowful, how sorrowful to live on the Poor Island!" she thought. And suddenly she put her hand to her heart and sighed, for Queens have sorrows too, and perhaps even the poor folk had none greater than hers.

She looked across and wondered; and little Lois, standing far away on the Poor Island, looked across and wondered too.

Even at that distance she could see the Pleasure Island like a jewel, she could see the small bright spires and domes and towers of the palace bathed in light, and on the breeze that blew towards her she could hear faint strains of music and even smell sweet flowers. "How lovely, how lovely it must be to live on the Pleasure Island," thought Lois. And suddenly she stooped to smell her rose, for even the Queen, had no sweeter flower than this.

The Queen sent for her Chamberlain and said, "I wish to visit the Poor Island."

"That will be a new diversion for Your Majesty," said the Chamberlain. "When will you go?"

"The day after tomorrow," said the Queen.

Next day the Chamberlain sent word to the Poor Island that the Queen was coming. She had not intended him to do this, but he thought it fitting that the Islanders should have a chance to prepare for the honor that was to be bestowed upon them. An honor indeed they held it. Such a thing had never happened before. The Queen herself was coming! How could they welcome her? Where could they receive her?

"We will receive her in the church," said the Pastor.

And how could they entertain her? Should not the church be adorned for the Queen? The men and women met together to consult. They had nothing with which to adorn the church. There was the rose bush, the Island Flower with its white blooms, but could they use that? No, said the father of Lois, if we do so we shall have nothing to show the Queen when she asks us, "And what is the most beautiful thing on your Island?" And now we can all take her to see the rose bush, and that will please her.

Little Lois was abed when the consultation was held. Her thoughts were full of the morrow and the coming of the Queen.

The day dawned, and the people gathered on the beach. The Pastor was with them, but Lois stayed behind to wipe the steps of the church porch, for it had rained in the night and the steps were spattered with mud. Then she started to run after the others, fearing she would be late, and as she did so—splash! she was ankle-deep in a big puddle right in the middle of the path. She looked with dismay at her wet feet, not that she cared for herself, but this was the way the Queen must walk, and the muddy place was too wide to step over. How could even the Poor Island let the Queen tread in the mud? And look, there was her golden barque coming over the water already. Something must be done quickly for she would soon be here.

It was only after the Queen had come ashore that Lois joined the people on the beach. The Queen was talking to the Pastor and kissing the children as he told her their names. Some of her courtiers were with her and followed her up the rough road to the church. "What a Godforsaken place!" Lois heard one say to another when their fine shoes stumbled on the stones. Her heart beat painfully as they approached the marshy spot which she had done her best to mend. Would her means hold good? Yes, the Queen passed over dry-foot.

Inside the Church the people stood up and sang. There was no organ, but the Pastor gave the note, and they lifted their voices in a song of praise. When the song was over, the Pastor spoke a few words of thanksgiving to God who had sent the Queen to see them. Lois, who could not take her eyes off the Queen's beautiful face, saw that her eyes were as wet as the wet place on the ground from which Lois had tried to protect her. But who can protect even a Queen from her tears?

When the people had sung one more song, they all went outside. The Queen then said, "May I see your homes and how you live? Is living very hard here?"

The Pastor was about to answer, Yes, but the father of Lois stepped forward and spoke with sturdy cheerfulness, "Life is hard everywhere, I take it," said he. "But no life is so hard that it has not something beautiful to show. And so it is with us on the Poor Island."

"What is your beautiful thing?" asked the Queen. "May I see it?"

"Gladly, madam. It is a rose bush."

The folk pressed round her eagerly explaining, "Yes, madam, it is such a rose bush as you never saw! White roses, madam! It is the Island's only flower. It is in bloom now, madam; there are nine roses on it, and three more coming. It is the Island's happiness, madam. Let us show it to you, it is only a few steps just behind the church."

The poor folk bore the Queen around the corner, the fine folk following after. And when the proud excited crowd had reached the place, and the father of Lois led the Queen to his door to show her the rose bush, there was nothing to see. Only a little scattered earth where the rose bush had been pulled up by the roots. The poor folk gasped, the courtiers tittered a little; and round the corner Lois knelt and wept. She wept beside the green leaves and white blossoms of her rose bush where she had strewn them that the Queen might not wet her feet.

The Queen sailed away in her golden barque, the visit was over, and life went on in the Poor Island as before. The Queen had gone away full of resolves. She would give an organ to the church, she would have good roads made, she would rebuild the poor huts, soil should be carried over and everyone should have a little garden. She would do all these things. Before she could do any of them she died.

News reached the Poor Island that she had died suddenly of a secret pain; when

she was buried, they buried with her the tears that had filled her heart and eyes in the Poor Island. No one else had shed these tears, they were her own; no one else, when she was dead, was concerned with their cause. Surely the Queen's tears were dried now. What had moved her was forgotten, what she had meant to do was left undone. Life went on in the Poor Island as before; only, it had lost its flower.

Nobody blamed Lois for what she had done. She had done right, they said; many of them would have done the same. When the Queen came to visit them, they could not let her walk in the wet and now she was dead they were glad she had not had to do so. But Lois mourned; she mourned for her rose and for the Queen. To comfort her, her father promised her another rose, cost what it might.

The full moon came round again. Once more the sea ran back into itself, once more the women went in long procession to the mainland over the bared sand. This time the father of Lois went too, a hard-saved coin in his pocket. They sold their fish and made their purchases; and Lois' father bought a tiny rose bush, another white one, which might with time become the Island's joy. While he was making his bargain, one of the women ran and tapped him on the shoulder. "Come quick!" she said. "The sky looks threatening."

He looked at the sky and answered. "Yes, we must hasten. I only saw it look so once before, when the tide rushed in and took the women unawares."

All the women were flocking over the sand. The fisherman hurried after them; their one thought was to reach the Poor Island before the sea rushed in.

On the Island there was nobody but one or two girls, the children and the Pastor. The men were out at sea on the other side. Those on the Island saw the darkening sky and felt the breath in the air that presaged danger. They came down to watch for the return of the women. Lois came too, straining her eyes for her father. Far off on the dark wet stretch of sand the children saw their mothers coming like little ants—they were already far from the mainland, and they still had far to come. Then, swiftly, what all feared most took place. The tide rushed in and surrounded the Poor Island; and it surged on, with waves that raced each other like wild horses, on towards the little band of people in the distance. There was no hope, no help, no refuge. Before they could turn back, the tide must take them.

The Pastor knelt upon the rocks and prayed, and all the children knelt with him, praying and crying. Only Lois stood upright among them, gazing. For the deserted Pleasure Island of the Queen was streaming with pale light that no one except Lois seemed to see, and in the light the Queen herself was standing. Distant as she was, like someone in a dream, Lois saw her as plainly as she had seen her in the church when the people were singing, but her eyes were wet no longer and a lovely smile was on her face. She was smiling straight at Lois, and in her hands were nine white roses with their green leaves. And as the wild green waves with their white caps rolled to the very feet of the Poor Islanders, the Queen cast leaves and flowers upon the water. The tide rolled on, covering all the space between the Islands. But oh wonder! it was covered not with the green-and-white sea but with a heap of green leaves and white flowers. The tide of roses reached from isle to isle and on it the women walked dry-foot to their children, and Lois' father came with her new rose bush with white flowers.

The people talk of the miracle to this day. If you do not believe it, go to the Poor Island for yourself, where the rose is growing still.

The Wooden Bowl

*There was something special between
the little boy and his grandfather. But then there was
something special about the little boy*

Domenico Vittorini

Once upon a time in far-off Italy there was a little boy whose name was Robertino who loved his grandfather very much. The little boy and the old man were great friends and spent much time together. Robertino loved to sit at his grandfather's knee and listen, his gray eyes wide open, to the stories that he told him. Grandfather was a wonderful storyteller. And oh the tales he told! Fairy tales and hero tales and exciting hunting stories, like the one in which Grandfather himself had once caught an eagle. Often Robertino and his grandfather would journey together to the land of make-believe to hunt imaginary lions and tigers. No matter how fantastic the stories or the games they played, the tie between these two was real enough, the only tie that kept the old man attached to this life.

Grandfather had come to live with Robertino's parents when Grandmother had died, three years before. Robertino's mother was a capable woman who took good care of her husband and her little son,

but she did not understand the loneliness of the old man. Sometimes she was very impatient with him, especially these days when his hands trembled and every so often he would drop what he was holding in them.

One night at supper Grandfather picked up his cup to drink his coffee but his poor old hands shook so that the coffee spilled on the clean white tablecloth, and the cup, falling from his hands, shattered into many pieces on the floor. Robertino's mother was angry and spoke harshly to the old man. Grandfather never said a word in reply, but only looked at her with hurt in his eyes. Robertino did not say anything either, but he couldn't eat any more supper, for his heart seemed ready to burst with sadness. Poor and dear Grandfather!

After that Grandfather had to eat all by himself at a little table in the kitchen. He did not say anything when he was told about this new arrangement, but there was sadness in his eyes, and sadness in the gentle smile he gave his grandchild.

From that evening on, as soon as Robertino finished his supper, he would ask to be excused and he would run into the kitchen to be with the old man he loved very much. Grandfather would take him on his knee and begin a story, and as the magic words began to weave their spell, the bare little kitchen became a beautiful land where there was no pain and no sadness and where an old man and a little boy could roam happily hand-in-hand.

As time went on and Grandfather grew older, he became weaker and his hands shook more and more. One night as he sat all alone in the kitchen, his hands trembled so that he dropped his bowl of porridge. The porridge spilled all over the kitchen floor and the bowl broke into many pieces. Robertino's father and mother, followed by the child, left the dining room where they had been eating and hastened to the kitchen. As they reached the door they saw the spilled porridge on the spotless floor.

Robertino was very much upset, not only by the indignation of his parents, but especially by the consternation of his grandfather. The old man was confused and crushed. Robertino's mother spoke more harshly than she had ever done before, scolded and said the only thing to do was to give the old man a wooden bowl. She could not, she said, have her dishes broken just because he had become so careless. She made a big fuss over cleaning up the floor. Robertino stood silently by as she mopped and polished until it was spotless

again, scolding and mumbling resentfully all the while.

Suddenly the child went over to the fireplace where his mother had swept the fragments of the bowl. He picked the pieces out carefully and began to put them together. He worked so earnestly that soon the bowl seemed to be whole. Then he took from the side of the hearth a small piece of wood and began to whittle it, keeping his eyes on the earthen bowl as though it were a model. After a while his parents, curious to see what he was doing, went over to him.

"What are you making, Robertino?" asked his mother fondly. She always spoke kindly to her little son.

"I'm making a wooden bowl for you, to have when you grow old," answered Robertino.

Robertino's mother and father looked at each other. They were too ashamed to meet Robertino's eyes. Then the mother took Grandfather's arm and led him back to the table in the dining room and stood near him and helped him as he ate.

From that time on Grandfather never ate all alone in the kitchen again. He sat in his usual place, next to Robertino, in the dining room.

And Robertino was happy again, oh so happy! His grandfather was loved and cared for, and as Robertino watched his parents he realized that they too were experiencing a new and wonderful happiness—for loving kindness brings true lasting happiness.

The Great Drop Game

*The South Side Scrappers had to let Sissy
play on the team with them. She owned the catcher's
mitt, the chest protector and the baseballs*

EARL CHAPIN

Somebody said something the other day about "one of the greatest games of organized baseball." Well, whatever that game was like, it couldn't compare with what you can see in unorganized baseball.

Like the great drop game, which decided the junior (boys) championship of Montrose, and was pitched by a girl. What was a girl doing in a boys' league? Well, our baseball was not only unorganized, it was disorganized. And there was only one Sissy Wyatt.

That's right. The name is spelled with an "S," not a "C," and maybe that is what got her going. In the Wyatt family there were a lot of boys but only one girl, and as the last of the troupe, she was called "Sister." You know what happens to a name like that. Pretty soon everyone in the neighborhood called her "Sissy," and it seemed that when she grew to understand the name, she went out to prove she wasn't one. Which is all right, but she overdid it.

It got so that we kids of the South Side couldn't have a game of baseball or football or shinny, but that the first thing we knew, Sissy was right in the middle of it. At first her brother Jim, who is my age, used to pick her up and toss her off the field. But you know, after a few years, he couldn't do that.

Sissy grew up fast and tall, with knobby knees and sharp elbows. She had dark red hair which she parted down the middle, combed to the sides and conquered with two pigtails that stuck out on either side of her freckled face. She looked formidable, and she was.

Sissy was sharp, too, and that made things all the more difficult. She got the local paper route and had more money to spend than any of us. That's how she got on the ball team. She owned the catcher's mitt, the chest protector and the baseballs.

In practice, we let Sissy play shortstop. We were short of players anyway. Besides, she was really good, and I admit it. We wouldn't let her play regular games, but she was always right with us, whooping and yelling, which was embarrassing enough. In fact, our opposition called us the Sissies! But when we tried to shush her up, she always threatened to take her catcher's mitt, chest protector and baseballs, and go home.

To make matters worse, in time she fancied herself to be a pitcher. She bought a book on how to pitch and practiced on some poor dope, and it was weird. She had just one delivery, which she called a fork ball. Somehow her hand was just big enough so she could get her first and second fingers on either side of the ball. That was quite a pitch. The batter never knew where it was going. Neither did Sissy.

We never let her pitch to us, and to that I ascribed the fact that our South Side Scrappers got through the season uninjured and also unbeaten. We proudly announced that we were the Junior Champs of Montrose and promptly received a challenge from a team we'd never heard about, the North End Nuggets. They said *they* were the champs and challenged us to put up or shut up. A showdown was okay with us, just as long as they agreed on a couple of basic rules—nobody over fourteen should be on the team, and all members should come from the immediate neighborhood. The Nuggets crossed their hearts and hoped to die, and so we took them at their word.

Well, not exactly. We went over and scouted their practice, and they were a pretty seedy-looking outfit. So we agreed to a seven-inning championship game to be played on their field.

I'm sort of the manager of the Scrappers, and I saw too late that we had been suckered. I'd never seen half the Nuggets that were working out on the field when we arrived. And if some of their boys were only fourteen, they must have been eating an awful lot of Wheaties.

Well, what could we do? We had a good crowd which had paid admission, and we wanted our split of the gate mighty bad in order to buy a chest protector and get rid of Sissy. Besides, the Scrappers never walked out on anything.

I consoled myself that Fats Walker was the best pitcher this side of high school, and we just might pull the game out of the fire at that.

We went to bat and fanned out in order. The boy who was throwing for the Nuggets must have been a brother of Catfish Hunter.

Fats rose to the occasion and retired the Nuggets without a score, but not nearly as handily.

That Nuggets' pitcher was mean, too. He dusted off Paul Jass so close he got rattled and struck at two balls and the shadow of a bird crossing the diamond, and our side was down again.

It was a hot day in August and Fats Walker was perspiring profusely as he fogged them in. He was good, too, but I could see he was outdoing himself.

The Nuggets got a scratch hit, executed

a nice bunt, got a sacrifice and a single. At the end of the third inning, it was 2 to 0.

In the fourth, Fats began to come unraveled. I kept my eye on Bill Brady, our other pitcher, who was playing in left field. The Nuggets had two on when Fats put one across the corner that was hard to hit. But the batter was one of those overgrown fourteen-year-olds. He got the ball on the end of his bat and lofted it into the outfield. Bill Brady saw it coming, started to run back, changed his calculations on the arc of the ball and plunged back again, his arms outstretched like an Indian invoking the great spirit. The ball sailed between his outstretched arms and hit Bill square on the noggin. While our outfielder-pitcher measured his length on the grass, the three Nuggets streaked for home. We helped Bill to the bench where he sat holding his head.

You have no idea of the troubles of a manager. Fats dragged himself up, looking like a limp dishrag. "I'm woofed," he said. "I can hardly reach the plate."

"But we haven't any more pitchers!" I cried.

"Let me pitch!"

I winced at that shrill voice. I'd been hearing it from the bench since the game started. "You," I snorted at Sissy. "You've only got one pitch and you can't hit the plate—" I stopped, suddenly thinking of the beanballs we had been suffering, and evil flowered in my heart. "It would serve 'em right," I muttered.

"I can too," shrilled Sissy. "I've got two pitches. And I've got a secret one, too."

I looked at the boys. I think some of them had caught my idea. Anyway, we had no choice, and never would it be said that the Scrappers forfeited a game.

"All right," I said. "You pitch."

"Girls are against the rules," the Nuggets protested indignantly.

"What rules?" I demanded. I had them there.

They went into a huddle and conceded. Actually I could see they thought it was very funny. It was, and it wasn't.

Sissy started the last of the fifth, with the score 5 to 0 against us. We were going to get beat, anyway. Her first pitch got stuck in the screen about twelve feet above the plate, and I was ready to go home. But on the next one, the batter just topped the ball. It dribbled out to the plate. Sissy fielded it nicely and one was out.

The next batter was the Nuggets' tough pitcher. Sissy stuck out the tip of her tongue and I could tell by that she was going to throw her fork ball again. The ball floated up as big as a barn. You could count every stitch in it. The pitcher took a clout that would have knocked it right through the sound barrier. But just as he swung, the ball fell away. The bat met nothing but air.

The pitcher spun around like a top and went to the ground. When the Nuggets got him untangled, they claimed he had dislocated a vertebrae and fractured his collarbone. That was an exaggeration. But one thing was sure, the beanball pitcher had sure removed himself from the game.

The Nuggets were so unnerved by this disaster that the third man up fanned ingloriously.

With that hotshot pitcher out of the way, the future looked a little less glum. We Scrappers and our rooters came to life, and we had two on before our next moundsman put one away. The next man —oops, girl—up was Sissy. The Nuggets' pitcher might have taken a clue from what had happened already, but he had to show his contempt of girls. He tossed up a nice, fat patsy. Sissy teed off like Jack Nicklaus at his best. The ball was still rising when it disappeared over the fence.

That didn't end the inning, either. The score was tied by the time the Nuggets got three away.

I was feeling pretty complacent when

Sissy took to the mound again, but you can never trust a girl. Sissy wound up, then stopped and rearranged one of her pigtails.

"It's a balk!" yelled the Nuggets.

The umpire agreed. The batter took his base. Sissy threw another great drop. It struck the ground in front of the plate and before the catcher could get it, the runner had advanced to second. Sissy threw another floater. The batter missed it, and so did the catcher. The runner was on third.

"Holy cow!" I screamed at our catcher. "Tell her to try her other pitch!"

Sissy's pigtails were sticking straight out. She rared back and threw the ball up in the air. I thought I'd pass out. But the arc couldn't have been more perfect. The ball dropped down cleanly in the strike zone. The batter just stood there with his mouth open.

We opened the seventh and last inning by breaking the tie. With the score 5 to 6, all we had to do was hang on. But, oh, brother! I mean, oh, sister! The first man hit a looper that creased the second baseman's head.

Then, advancing to the plate, swinging three bats, came one of those overgrown "fourteen-year-olds." He had hit safely every time.

Sissy prepared her very best knuckle ball, but it slipped prematurely from her fingers. The batter grinned and lowered his head to let the overthrow pass. But as the ball neared the plate, it took a drop like the graph of a bad day in a subscription contest and struck with a sodden thump on the head of the guy in the batter's box.

The next man smacked a perfect bounce to third for a force-out, and the next one fanned.

Sissy's eyes brightened. She smiled a smile of triumph. But pride cometh before a fall. She tossed a blooper. Nick had to run out in front of the plate to catch it. She threw another. Nick jumped back to catch

it. Sissy tried another but it was a ball. She had lost the range, and the man walked.

Two out, and the bases loaded! A great quiet settled over the diamond. Sissy was trying hard and her drop was breaking more crazily than ever. The batsman decided if he just waited them out, the odds would be in his favor. He was right. He stood there until the count was three and two. Never since the Stover boys left Yale had the grand old game witnessed such a moment.

"Tell her to throw that dark one!" I yelled. I was instructing the catcher, but you could hear me all over the diamond. Sissy motioned for a conference. She stood with her hands on her waist, talking vehemently, her pigtails bobbing. I could see that Nick didn't believe her. But finally he shrugged resignedly and took his position behind the plate.

"Please," I muttered, "let it be a double curve!"

Sissy went into an awesome windup and let loose. It was a nothing ball, straight down the middle, and so fast I don't think Hank Aaron could have hit it. Only after the ball whanged into the catcher's mitt did the batter show the slightest twitch of reflex movement.

"Why in the world didn't you throw that fast one before!" I chortled, slapping Sissy on the back.

"Oh," she said innocently, "I was saving that for an emergency."

That's the way it is with girls. But we could teach her.

"Next year you can be our starting pitcher," I promised enthusiastically.

Sissy drew herself up primly. "I have decided," she announced, "that it's unladylike to play baseball."

Maybe it was for the best. I don't know if we could have stood a whole year of Sissy's pitching. And I'm sure our opponents couldn't.

345

Whitey's New Saddle

*It started with some missing cows and a blizzard,
and ended with the capture of the sorriest-looking gang
of cattle rustlers you've ever seen*

GLEN ROUNDS

I don't much like the look of that sky," Uncle Torwal remarked as he and Whitey stood on the ranch-house porch after breakfast. "The way the barometer is droppin' we could git an early snowstorm."

"Isn't it too early for snow?" Whitey wanted to know.

"We've had blizzards even earlier," Uncle Torwal told him. "Just to be on the safe side I think it might be a good idea to ride out and see how the cattle are doing. If they're on the ridges we'd better drive 'em down onto the bottoms where they'll be out of the wind in case it does storm."

"Yessir," Whitey agreed. "If the wind got behind them they might drift clear down into the Badlands."

So as soon as they'd watered the horses at the windmill tank, they saddled up and rode out—Whitey towards Cedar Springs and Uncle Torwal in the direction of Elk Creek.

In spite of the curious dark clouds banking up in the northwest it was still a fine fall morning. The sun felt warm on Whitey's back, and Old Spot's hooves left a dark trail through the frosty grass. The old horse jogged contentedly along, pointing his ears forward as far as they'd go, then twitching them back. Now and again he'd drop his head and blow softly through his nostrils, making a soft blubbery sound.

Listening to the creaking of his old saddle, Whitey thought about the new one he'd buy after he and Uncle Torwal shipped their beef next month.

He didn't really mind wearing a hand-me-down Stetson of Uncle Torwal's, especially when it had such a fine rattlesnake hatband, for most cowboys wore battered-looking hats when they were working.

With a few strips of paper stuffed in the sweatband it stayed on fine. And for the same reason he didn't mind the old boots with the run-over heels.

But this old saddle was something else again. It was a Cogshell with a flat Texas horn, and so old the corners of the skirts were curled up tight, and the strings had long ago been chewed off by calves. Everywhere the stitching was coming undone, and ragged strips of the old sheepskin lining showed in odd places, giving the whole affair the look of a moulting hen. Furthermore, the stirrups were the clumsy iron kind, when the style hereabouts was a neat wooden oxbow pattern. For a long time, Whitey had felt that this saddle spoiled his whole appearance, making him look more like a homesteader than a cowboy.

Of course, when he'd been smaller and first come to live with Uncle Torwal and help him run the Lone Tree Ranch, it hadn't mattered so much. But now that he was past ten years old and practically a top hand he had to think more about the looks of his equipment. People set a lot of store by such things.

So last summer Uncle Torwal had given him two whiteface calves with the understanding that when they were sold for beef Whitey could use the money to buy a new saddle. Uncle Torwal had even helped him figure out his own cattle brand and sent it off to be registered after they'd put it on the calves with a running iron. It was a fine big squiggle on the ribs with three dots at the end.

The Rattlesnake brand, they called it and Whitey figured it was about as fine a one as he knew of. He saw no reason why it shouldn't someday be as famous as the old "101." Rattlesnake Ranch sounded good no matter how you said it!

So he rode on for a while, thinking about the time when the Rattlesnake brand would be on hundreds of head of good beef cattle instead of only two, and he'd be able to have a new saddle every week if he felt like it.

As he came nearer to Cedar Springs he found the cattle grazing in small scattered bunches. They had already begun to drift down into the draws where they were sheltered from the wind, so he left them where they were. But he did examine each bunch, counting them and looking for his two steers.

As he rode close, each animal threw up its head with ears widespread to look and listen, so it was a simple matter to check the earmarks. But nowhere did he find the swallowtail cut that would identify the two he looked for. And as he checked and counted he became more and more certain that not only were his two missing, but several more besides.

Thinking that perhaps they'd drifted off by themselves somewhere, he rode up onto the ridge to see if perhaps they'd wandered over onto the other side. But nowhere was there any sign of them, so at last he gave up the search and started back to the ranch.

Riding along under a sky that was now entirely overcast by cold dark clouds, Whitey tried to figure what had become of his steers. If they were really gone he'd probably have to ride the old saddle for a good while longer.

When he came into the ranch yard he found Uncle Torwal already home. After Whitey had unsaddled Old Spot he spoke about the missing steers.

"That's mighty peculiar," Uncle Torwal said. "There seemed to be a few missing over where I was riding too. I figured they'd jest drifted down out of sight somewhere and didn't spend too much time looking for them."

"But if you missed a few from the bunch around Cedar Springs," he went on, "it looks like there is something wrong somewhere."

"What do you think might have happened to them?" Whitey asked. "Do you figure it might have been gray wolves?"

"Haven't heard of wolves around here for a long time," Uncle Torwal said. "Besides, we'd have found the carcasses. More likely we'll find they jest drifted away."

"What about cattle rustlers?" Whitey asked.

"Haven't heard much about cattle stealing for a long time, hereabouts," Uncle Torwal told him. "But it does seem odd that they'd drift away in ones and twos."

"Well," Whitey said, "if I don't find mine I won't be able to buy a new saddle for a long time yet."

"If this storm holds off we'll take another look around tomorrow," Uncle Torwal said. "Then if we still can't find any sign of them we'll go in and see if the sheriff knows anything about cattle rustlers working here in Lone Tree County."

But the next morning when they woke it was snowing steadily, and on the flats only the tips of the sagebrush showed through the soft white mounds. There was no wind, so the flakes lay where they fell, piling high on the tops of the fence posts and along the poles of the corrals.

"No use to go out looking for your steers in this weather," Uncle Torwal remarked as he set the water bucket down and stamped snow off his boots. "That snow's gittin' deeper by the hour."

"I guess you're right," Whitey agreed, disappointed.

After they had finished breakfast and washed their dishes, he and Uncle Torwal took their sheepskin coats off the hooks where they'd hung all summer and went out to throw hay over the fence for the stock in the horse pasture.

"We'll chop the ice out of the water troughs later on," Uncle Torwal decided after they'd finished the feeding. "Right now we'd better split up some wood before the woodpile is completely buried."

While they were still working on that a horseman rode up to the gate and climbed stiffly out of his saddle.

"Looks like Highpockets, Bearpaw Smith's hired man," Uncle Torwal said, as he and Whitey hurried to open the gate.

The horse's muzzle and chest were frosted almost white where his breath had frozen on the tips of the long hairs. And little balls of ice clung to his sides and belly where the snow had partly melted and then refrozen. After they'd given the horse some hay and Highpockets had beaten the snow off his hat brim and the shoulders of his sheepskin, they went into the kitchen to warm up.

"Bearpaw's horse fell on him this morning," the rider told them as he pulled off his boots to warm his feet on the open oven door. "He's got a broken leg and he may have cracked a couple of ribs, too. He wants to be taken to town. It would be a rough trip in the wagon. So he thought maybe with all this snow you could haul him in your bobsled."

"I guess mebbe I could," Uncle Torwal agreed. "Has Doc been out yet?"

"No," Highpockets said. "Bearpaw figured it would be quicker to take him to the Doc. Then he could stay at the Hotel until he was able to get around. I splinted the leg up the best I could and it's not bothering him too much."

"If this storm thickens up I might have to stay overnight in town. You think you could take care of things here alone?" Uncle Torwal asked Whitey.

"Sure," Whitey said. "You go ahead. I'll be all right."

"Let's get started, then," Uncle Torwal said to Highpockets. "You go on back and get Bearpaw ready and I'll be along later." The old bobsled was in the shed where it had been stored all summer. After they'd

put half a dozen bricks in the oven to heat, Whitey and Uncle Torwal piled robes and quilts on top of a deep layer of hay in the bottom of the box. By the time they'd harnessed the team, the bricks were ready to be wrapped in gunny sacks and put down in the pile of hay.

"Now mind what I say, Bub," Uncle Torwal said as he arranged his big buffalo coat around him on the seat of the bobsled and gathered up the lines. "Don't go far from the buildings here unless it clears up some. The way the barometer is falling this snow could turn into a blizzard without half trying!"

Whitey looked and saw the air was still with no sign of wind. "It doesn't look like it's going to get much worse," he said.

"Mebbe it won't," Uncle Torwal agreed, "but with all this fine snow on the ground, if the wind come up good and brisk you'd not be able to see your hand in front of your face inside ten minutes. But you look after the ranch, and I'll be back tonight or some time tomorrow. So long, now;" And he spoke to the horses and drove out of the ranch yard.

Whitey stood watching until the team and sled were hidden by the falling snow. Then he turned back to the ranch yard, deciding what should be done next.

Altogether he felt pretty much like a full-fledged cowboy, and Uncle Torwal almost never treated him like anything else. Still, he would be glad when he was big enough to go into Lone Tree, to Mr. Highwater Johnson's Stockmen's Clothing Store and buy him a Stetson and a pair of boots, all brand-new, and maybe not have to take the smallest size, either.

He wished they had a lot of cattle to look after and maybe a corral full of horses to be broken for riding while Uncle Torwal was gone.

However, there were still chores to be done, so Whitey chopped ice out of the water trough and pumped water for the stock. Then he filled the mangers with hay from the stacks in the stackyard. After that he carried wood into the kitchen.

By the time he'd finished those things it was almost noon, so he got a hammer and the big butcher knife and chopped a steak off the quarter of beef hanging frozen outside the door. After he'd eaten and washed his plate and the skillet, he sat down to work a little on the fancy hackamore noseband he was braiding from rawhide and old boot leather.

But he soon gave that up and got out the mail-order catalogue, turning to the picture of the saddle he planned to order when he got the money for his beef. On the same page was a picture of the spurs he'd ordered last week so as to have them ready to wear with his new saddle when he did get it.

He'd saved his money for a long time, waiting to send for those spurs. They had long gooseneck shanks and dollar rowels, with a bright chain that went under the instep. But the finest thing about them was the two little bells that hung just by the outside buckle on each spur.

They would be fine to wear when he and Uncle Torwal went into Lone Tree of a Saturday. They would jingle wonderfully when he walked on the wooden sidewalks or when he went into the stores.

The more Whitey thought about it now, the more certain he was that those spurs were over in the mailbox right now. The mail carrier made his trip twice a week, and yesterday afternoon had been mail day. It just happened that he and Uncle Torwal had forgotten to go after the mail last night.

Whitey scratched a hole in the thick frost on the window and looked out. It was a little over two miles out to the main road where the mailbox was, and Uncle Torwal had told him not to go far away unless the weather cleared.

However, it looked to him like the snow was already thinning just the least little bit. Rattlesnake Butte, less than half a mile away, was just a faint blur through the snow, but he was sure he could see it a little plainer than he had when Uncle Torwal was leaving. Of course, that wasn't exactly clear weather, but on the other hand, there still was no sign of wind.

The more he thought about it, the more sure he was that it'd be all right for him to go out to the mailbox to get his spurs. He'd have to walk, because Old Spot had slipped on some ice the day before and was a little lame, but if he took his .22 rifle he might get a couple of rabbits or maybe even a coyote on the way.

Each time he looked out of the clear place he'd scratched on the window he thought the snow was thinning a little more. So at last he made his mind up to go.

In almost no time he had his heavy sheepskin coat on and a scarf tied over his ears. At the last minute he decided to put his big four-buckle overshoes on over his boots. Then he picked up his rifle and started out.

As soon as he walked away from the house, Whitey saw that the snow was still falling steadily after all and lay on the ground almost boot-top deep. It fell softly as feathers, muffling all sounds. A few yards off, fences and buildings seemed to melt into the soft gray and there was no difference between ground and sky.

But this didn't bother Whitey, for he felt perfectly able to find his way. And the way the snow and the light changed the shapes of things gave him the feeling of exploring strange country no one had ever seen before.

Small birds in flocks of ten or twenty rustled around under the sagebrush or flew quickly from one place to another, complaining uneasily.

The first half-mile he was in the big horse pasture, but when he came to that fence and crawled through he had to go straight across the open flat, where there were neither trees nor fences for miles in any direction.

He saw some rabbits, and once a big brown owl sailed past, skimming so low his wingtips now and again left marks in the soft snow.

Whitey almost ran the last quarter of a mile, stumbling and sliding through the soft snow in his hurry to see if his spurs were really there. He got to the mailbox without difficulty and threw down two rabbits he'd shot on the way.

When he opened the big wooden box standing on its posts, he saw the mailsack with Uncle Torwal's name. He untied the string and started taking out the mail.

There were four or five copies of Uncle Torwal's *Stockman's Gazette,* and under them was a new saddle catalogue. In the very bottom he felt a little package. It seemed too small to be spurs, but when he got it out of the mailsack he found it was addressed to him, after all.

He stuffed the rest of the mail back in the sack, along with the two rabbits, and slung the sack over his shoulders so he'd have his hands free as he started back towards the ranch. Carrying his rifle under his arm, he broke the strings and tore the paper wrappings off the box.

Inside, nested in crumpled paper, were the spurs, looking even more beautiful than they had in the catalogue. The straps were rich brown leather with a handsome design stamped onto them, and the bells, when he shook them, had a silvery tone.

Whitey had been stumbling along through the snow for some time, with eyes for nothing but his fine new spurs, when he suddenly noticed the wind was blowing against his face and stopped to look around. The snow had thickened until he could see only a little way in any direction, and the wind was already picking more off the ground and whirling it into the air in blinding clouds. The mailbox behind him was already hidden and, as he stood watching, his tracks were blown full of snow and disappeared.

This was the thing Uncle Torwal had warned him about. However, Whitey wasn't worried, for all he had to do was walk straight ahead and he'd soon come to the pasture fence, and he could follow it right on around to the corrals. He stuffed the spurs back into the mailsack and hurried ahead, bowing his head to protect his face from the beating of the snow.

Before he'd gone any great distance the wind was blowing full force, and seemed to push and shove at him from all sides. It roared and cracked until his ears rang with it. His breath froze on the edges of his coat collar and gathered in white frost on his eyelashes and brows. The powdery fine snow whipped into his eyes and nose until it was almost impossible to see or breathe.

But there was no shelter near. There was nothing to do but keep walking and hope he could keep his direction by the feel of the wind on his face. He'd heard of people lost in storms who'd wandered around in circles without knowing it.

He had been walking a long time and was just beginning to wonder if maybe he had somehow missed his way, when he ran right into the barbed wire. He walked against it without seeing it, and the shock threw him off balance so that he fell floundering in the snow, dropping his rifle. Picking himself up, he felt around until he found the gun, then held onto the wire while he caught his breath.

Turning his back to the wind, he took off his mittens to warm his nose and cheeks, feeling pretty well pleased with himself for getting safely to the fence. It would never have done to have gotten lost in the blizzard right after Uncle Torwal had warned him against that very thing!

Just before he turned to start hand over hand along the wire, the driving snow thinned enough for him to see that this wasn't the pasture fence after all. It was only a small stackyard fence, one of several built out on the open flats to keep range stock away from the stacks of wild hay the ranchers cut for winter feed. He knew then that he was lost.

If there had still been hay in the stackyard he might have burrowed into it and waited out the storm. But the ground inside the fence was bare, so there was nothing for him to do but go on.

By keeping the wind in his face as he walked he would still be able to find the pasture fence. The trouble was to tell which direction the wind was coming from, for it eddied until it seemed to come from first one way and then another.

He had a hard time then, keeping himself from getting panicky and running to find some landmark that looked familiar. But this was one of the things that the cowboys had always spoken of that a lost person must avoid at all costs. So every little way he made himself stop and stand still, swinging his arms to keep warm while he caught his breath.

Starting ahead after one of these stops, he suddenly felt the ground give way under his feet, and the next thing he knew he had fallen several feet, landing up to his neck in soft snow. Overhead he could see a circle of light, and when he felt around he found solid walls of earth on two sides of him.

He'd fallen into one of the deep, narrow washouts common in that country. The walls were higher than his head and too

steep to climb, while the head-high drifts blocked his way in the other directions.

He could hear the wind booming just overhead, and dry fine snow sifted steadily down into the hole. Getting back up onto the flat was going to be a problem.

Whitey tried to remember all the things he'd heard Uncle Torwal and the other old-timers tell about the ways men had gotten themselves out of this predicament and that. But somehow none of the stories had ever seemed to have been about fellows falling into washouts during blizzards.

He got out his pocketknife and, after some difficulty getting the blade open with his numb fingers, he started trying to cut steps in the steep bank. It was hard, slow work, digging at the frozen dirt with the small blade, and when he had gotten a couple of steps cut he found that the bank sloped inwards. So he slipped and fell back when he tried to climb up.

As he scrabbled about in the snow trying to regain his feet, he uncovered what appeared to be the corner of a fresh cowhide. After considerable pulling and digging with his hands, he finally dug out three roughly-rolled hides which had been carelessly hidden by caving part of the bank onto them. The covering of dirt had kept them from freezing so that he was able to unroll them enough to find what brands they carried.

Two had his Rattlesnake brand, and the other Uncle Torwal's Lone Tree!

There went his hopes for a new saddle!

Whitey knew how the rustlers worked: going out to the range in trucks, at dusk they'd butcher two or three fat steers they'd spotted during the afternoon, bury the hides and have the meat sold in another county before the rancher even suspected his stock was missing.

A sudden heavier gust of wind tumbled a flurry of snow into the washout, reminding Whitey that it was time he started finding a way back onto the flat. The problem of the rustlers would have to wait.

Getting to his feet, he bumped against the rifle, which he had dropped when he fell. Now it occurred to him that if he could brace it across the gully some way, he'd have a step to climb up on.

He found that the rifle was considerably longer than the distance between the walls, so he dug another hole on the opposite side from the steps, and about level with the highest one. He jammed the muzzle in one hole and wedged the butt in another on the other side. Carefully trying his weight on it, he found it was solid enough to hold him, so all he had to do was get his feet up on it, if he could.

That took some doing, however, in the narrow space, bundled up as he was and with the mailsack still slung over his shoulder. But he managed to get his chest across the rifle, then by squirming and twisting he got a knee across and finally braced his foot on the gun stock against the wall. After that he carefully straightened up, supporting himself against the sides with his hands until he had both feet firmly braced on either end of the rifle.

With his head and shoulders above the level of the ground it was no great job to pull himself up and roll out onto the snow.

While he was standing there, pleased to be on solid ground again, stamping his feet and beating his arms to warm himself, a jackrabbit passed within a few feet of him. It hurried along as silently as a gray shadow, almost invisible in the snow. As Whitey watched it disappear in the storm he wondered where it could be going—probably to shelter.

Taking a few steps in the direction of the rabbit's tracks, he felt a deep, worn cattle path under his feet. The chances were good that it led either to shelter or a fence he could follow.

It was only in scattered places that the

wind had cleared the new snow off so he could see the little path. The rest of the time he had to scrape around with his feet every step to find it.

After what seemed like ages to Whitey, the trail suddenly dipped over a bank and disappeared in deep snowdrifts. Before he could catch himself, he slipped and rolled to the bottom. When he picked himself up, he found he was in a deep draw, and that the drifts were too deep for him to find the path again. But at least he'd gotten off the flats.

It wasn't long before he found that, even though he was protected from the wind, traveling down the draw was going to be more difficult than he'd thought. The drifts were so deep he struggled along in snow to his waist much of the time, and the fine stuff powdered down from above so thickly he could hardly get his breath.

Once or twice he thought about throwing away the mailsack, after he'd put his new spurs in his pocket of course, but he figured the two rabbits might come in handy, and the rest of the mail wasn't heavy enough to make any difference.

He knew he'd freeze in a hurry if he stopped moving and kept telling himself that he'd just go around one more bend before he stopped. And then he went around another and another, until he couldn't remember how many he'd passed.

When he bumped into a big cottonwood tree standing squarely in his path he stopped and leaned against it to rest and catch his breath. It wasn't until he straightened up, ready to move on, that he noticed the pieces of board nailed to the trunk—and then for the first time he knew where he was. This was the old Owls' Nest Tree. Somebody years before had nailed boards to the trunk to make a ladder to the nest where the pair of great horned owls raised two young ones every year. And less than a hundred yards down the draw there was an old shack the hay crews sometimes used.

Now that he was close to shelter Whitey forgot his tiredness. He went confidently ahead, keeping close to the bank and counting his steps so he'd know if he passed the shack without seeing it in the swirling snow.

Feeling his way along the wall, he floundered through the deep drifts until he found the door, hanging crookedly from one hinge, and squeezed his way inside.

While his eyes adjusted themselves to the gloom Whitey leaned against the wall, catching his breath and listening to the storm outside.

Some snow had sifted into the shack and in places was several inches deep. But after his long struggle against the beating of the wind and the smothering swirling snow, this place seemed safe and comfortable. Even so, he realized he would quickly chill, now that he wasn't moving, unless he managed to get a fire started.

Against one wall there was a litter of old broken pieces of lumber and wooden boxes. Using one of the boards for a shovel, he soon scraped a patch of the dirt floor clear in the most sheltered corner. Then he got his jackknife opened and started whittling kindling sticks, setting them in a teepee-shaped stack. His matches were in an empty shotgun shell he always carried in his sheepskin pocket.

As soon as the fine feathery shavings caught and began to blaze, he carefully added larger sticks, one at a time, until his little fire was burning well.

Unbuttoning his heavy coat and taking off his mittens, he huddled over the fire, soaking up the warmth. Backed into the corner as he was, no drafts could reach him. Some of the smoke found its way out through cracks and holes up near the roof but most of it eddied about inside, making his eyes smart, and gusts outside occa-

sionally sent fine snow sifting down inside his collar. But these were small things and he didn't mind them too much.

When Whitey had warmed himself he began a more careful examination of the place. In another corner he found more bits of lumber, as well as three old fence posts. He had no axe to chop them up with, but he could use them Indian fashion: putting one end in the fire and shoving them forward a little at a time as they burned away. By burning one at a time they'd easily last the night through.

Having taken care of the fuel problem, Whitey set about making his corner more comfortable. A few pieces of board to sit on would keep the chill of the frozen ground away from him. And, kicking into a drift in another corner, he discovered an old piece of heavy canvas. It was dirty and stained, but he propped it up in the corner with

some sticks and made a small tent that would keep the snow off and trap more of the heat from the little fire.

Arranging himself as comfortably as possible in his shelter, Whitey built up the fire and thought about his situation. This storm would keep Uncle Torwal in town, so he wouldn't be worrying about where he was. And with shelter and wood enough to last the night he was in no real danger. But he was hungry.

That reminded him of the rabbits in the mailsack. Getting his knife out again, it took only a few minutes to skin and dress them. Now all he needed was a piece of wire to make a grill to broil the meat on.

Searching the place again, he noticed that three boxes in the middle of the room were arranged like a table and two chairs. Dusting the snow off the larger one, he found a checkerboard drawn in pencil on the top. Puzzled by that, he scraped around in the snow on the floor and found some homemade checker pieces—as well as two fairly new western story magazines. Somebody had spent some time in the place quite lately, reading and playing checkers.

As far as Whitey knew, no hay crews had been around here for a year or more. Besides, hay crews seldom had time to read magazines or to play games.

Finding the wire he needed, Whitey crawled back into his tent and started cooking his rabbit. The smell of the roasting meat, sizzling and spitting above the little fire, drove all other thoughts out of his mind. After he'd eaten the meat and sucked the bones, the warmth and the sound of the storm made him drowsy.

Pulling the old canvas close about him, he huddled over the tiny fire, rousing now and again to add small scraps of wood or to pull the fence post forward a little as the end burned away. Occasionally he dozed, but the cold always woke him before the fire went completely out.

It was sometime near morning when he realized he was no longer hearing the wind. Getting stiffly to his feet, he shoved the door open a crack and looked out. The storm had stopped and the stars were shining. Quickly gathering up the mailsack, he squeezed outside and floundered through the drifts between the shack and the top of the bank.

Once he was out of the draw and up on the flats the walking wasn't difficult, and the starlight on the snow was bright enough to make traveling easy.

After Whitey had gotten back home and rebuilt the fire in the stove he took the new spurs out of the mailsack and tried them on. Tired as he was, he spent a while walking about the warm kitchen to hear the tinkling of the little silver bells. He saw no chance now of getting a new saddle, but he felt that having the fanciest spurs in Lone Tree County was probably the next best thing!

By the time Whitey had fixed himself some breakfast the sun was up. He started the morning chores, and before he'd finished, Uncle Torwal drove in.

"Everything go all right here?" he asked, as they unhitched the horses.

"Yessir," Whitey told him. "And I found out for sure that the rustlers are getting our steers."

"You did?" Uncle Torwal asked.

"Yessir, I dug up three fresh hides that had been buried in a washout over towards the old Owls' Nest Tree," Whitey told him. Then, before Uncle Torwal could ask how he'd happened to be out in the storm, he went on. "I'd been over for the mail when the wind came up, so I decided to stay in that old shack until it cleared."

Uncle Torwal figured there was probably more to the story than he'd been told, but everything seemed to have turned out all right, so he said nothing about it. And that suited Whitey just fine. Later on he'd tell Uncle Torwal the whole story, but just now didn't seem to be the right time.

"Were the brands cut out?" Uncle Torwal wanted to know.

For usually rustlers cut the brand out and burn it before burying the hide.

"Reckon they must have been careless this time. One was a Lone Tree steer and the other two were Rattlesnake brand."

"Got both yours, did they?" Uncle Torwal said, and whistled. "That was tough goin', cleanin' out your whole spread."

"Yeah, that's a fact," Whitey said. "Looks like I'll ride my old hull a while longer." He led Spot into the stable so Uncle Torwal wouldn't see how badly he really did feel.

They didn't say much as they finished

the chores and ate dinner, but afterwards, as they sat by the stove warming their feet, Uncle Torwal spoke up.

"Reckon we might as well ride in and see the sheriff. Now that we know for sure that rustlers are working around here, maybe we can figure out something."

"I sure hope so," Whitey said. "They did me out of a new saddle and I'd surely like to catch them!"

When they got to town they tied their horses and walked into the sheriff's office. Mr. Hairpants Hagadorn, the sheriff, shook hands with them while Mr. Fort Worth Wilkerson, the deputy sheriff, dragged out chairs.

After some polite talk of this and that, Uncle Torwal told the sheriff what Whitey had found.

"This is the first time we've had any proof," the sheriff said, "but there's been a lot of complaints of missin' beef critturs all up and down the valley."

"How you reckon they get in and out of the valley without anyone knowing?" Uncle Torwal said after a little.

"I been considering that myself," the sheriff told him. "They have to come through here or through Hill City to get in or out, and we've been watchin' both places close, yet nobody has seen any strangers or strange truck."

"I wish we could catch them," Whitey spoke up. "I was goin' to get a new saddle with the money from the steers they got of mine!"

"Well, maybe you can figure how to catch them and use your share of the reward money for that saddle," the sheriff told him.

At the mention of REWARD Whitey stopped looking at the posters and notices tacked over the sheriff's desk and brightened right up.

"You mean there's a reward for those rustlers?" he asked.

"Sure," the sheriff told him. "I got the notice around here somewhere."

After some more talk they shook hands with the sheriff, the deputy sheriff and a man who had wandered into the office looking for a place to sit down, and rode off towards the ranch.

As they rode along Whitey thought about that reward and tried to figure out some way he could earn it. It seemed to him that to get money enough for a new saddle by trapping rustlers was even better than getting it by selling cattle.

"Uncle Torwal!" he said, suddenly remembering something. "Somebody has been using that old shack by the Owls' Nest Tree. I found a checkerboard and a couple of magazines when I was there. Could it be the rustlers, do you suppose?"

Uncle Torwal thought a while. "It could be, mebbe," he said. "There used to be a road through there that went down into the Box Elder road. They might come in early when no one would notice them and hide the truck in the draw until dusk."

"Why don't we lay for them when they come back?" Whitey asked, thinking of the reward and his new saddle.

"Well, Bub, they might not come back. Those dudes are pretty smart an' don't often work the same place twice. That's why they're so hard to catch." After seeing how Whitey's face fell, he went on, "On the other hand, with a hideout like that they might feel safe for a while longer. From all the talk of missin' cattle in the valley, they must have made several trips already."

"Tell you what," Uncle Torwal said, as they neared the ranch. "We might take turns watchin' that place for a while, jest in case they did come back."

"Yessir!" Whitey agreed. "We'll catch 'em coming in and collect the reward!"

"We don't want to bother 'em coming in," Torwal corrected him. "We jest want

to know when they get there so we'll have time to call the sheriff to catch 'em going out with the meat in the truck for evidence."

Whitey still favored capturing the rustlers without interference from the sheriff, but he said nothing about it. He was bound he'd get that saddle the rustlers had done him out of, and even part of the reward would be enough.

"I'll take my blankets and go out right away to watch for them," he said.

"You won't need any blankets," Uncle Torwal told him. "Those fellers probably come in about the middle of the afternoon so they'll be able to locate the critturs they want before dusk. Besides, there's no need to start watching until this snow is gone."

The next morning Whitey and Uncle Torwal found that the weather had turned warm again, and the snow was already

disappearing almost as fast as it had fallen. The eaves of the ranch house were dripping. Out on the flats the tops of the sagebrush showed dark above the surface of the rapidly settling snow.

"Another day of this and we can start watching for the rustlers to come back," Uncle Torwal remarked, as he whittled shavings to start the fire in the cookstove.

"Yessir, this looks like it would go in a hurry," Whitey agreed as he picked up the water buckets and headed for the well.

When they'd finished the morning's chores Uncle Torwal decided to change the shoes on his saddle horse. Whitey saddled Old Spot and went to get his rifle out of the washout.

By noon next day the snow was nearly all gone. Whitey decided it was time to start watching for the rustlers.

As he got ready to ride out, Uncle

Torwal spoke up. "If they don't show up today we'll take turns watching for a few days."

"I don't want anyone to take turns," Whitey hollered. "I'm the one they cleaned out, and I'll watch every day."

So every afternoon for almost a week he rode out to a small butte where he could watch the road to the old shack. He carefully hid Spot in a plum thicket and then crawled Indian fashion to the top of the butte and lay hidden in the sagebrush like some old-time scout. But nothing happened, and he began to believe the rustlers had deserted the valley.

Then one afternoon he was just tying Old Spot in the thicket when he heard a truck motor. He hurried up the slope to his lookout and the sound was plainer there. It was a powerful motor, and working hard. Soon a big closed truck came in sight, moving cautiously down the old road. It disappeared into the draw by the shack and the motor stopped.

It was rustlers, sure enough!

Whitey had been complaining to himself because Uncle Torwal wouldn't let him bring his rifle and capture the rustlers single-handed, but tonight he thought of nothing but getting back to the ranch as soon as possible to tell Uncle Torwal and get word to the sheriff. He agreed now that it was really the sheriff's business to deal with such people.

Spot got the surprise of his life when Whitey clapped spurs and quirt onto him! He couldn't remember the last time he'd traveled faster than a trot. But as this seemed to be a special occasion he did his best, and before long Whitey and Uncle Torwal were sitting out by the road waiting for the sheriff and his deputies to come by and pick them up.

The word had spread, and by the time the sheriff got there, ranchers and cowboys from up and down the valley had gathered.

Most of them carried rifles on their saddles or pistols in their belts. Rustlers were not popular thereabouts, and Whitey was looking forward to a right exciting time when they caught up with them.

When the sheriff came, just before dusk, they all rode together towards the shack where the truck had been hidden. Whitey had been afraid someone would tell him to stay behind, but no one did and he rode along with the others.

The rustlers were gone when they got there. But Sheriff Hagadorn said that was all right—as they had to come back this way after they'd finished butchering.

The men had all been concealed in the plum thickets on either side of the road for what seemed a long time to Whitey when they heard the rustlers coming back.

"This is when the bullets start to fly!" Whitey thought, as the sheriff stepped out into the light of the truck and held up his hand.

But the truck stopped without protest. Deputies and ranchmen turned on flashlights and swarmed all round it. Four weaselly-looking men climbed carefully out and stood with their hands raised while they and the truck were searched.

"There's plenty beef in here!" a deputy hollered.

"All right!" the sheriff answered. "One of you drive the truck along behind me, and we'll haul these gents down to our jail for a spell."

The rustlers didn't say anything, except to sort of mutter to themselves. They didn't look like the tough fellows Whitey had been picturing in his mind. They weren't wearing gun belts, and they didn't talk back to the sheriff. Worst of all, they wore bib overalls, like farmers, and one even had on a straw hat and plow shoes! Whitey was mighty disappointed in them.

Early next morning Whitey and Uncle Torwal went to town, and Mr. Bugeye

Beasly, editor of the *Lone Tree Eagle,* interviewed Whitey.

The reward turned out to be only fifty dollars, and that divided six ways, so there was not enough to buy the saddle with. Whitey had built his hopes so high on that reward that he felt mighty bad for a few days.

But after reading what Mr. Beasly wrote about him in the paper, how his alertness had helped make Lone Tree County free of rustlers and the like, he sort of got used to the idea of getting along with the old saddle another year.

Then one morning Uncle Torwal told him, "We gotta go to town this morning, Bub. Sheriff said something about wanting to see you."

All the way into town Whitey wondered what the sheriff could want. Maybe he wanted to make him a deputy or something. He imagined this and that, but never thought of the real answer.

After some talk the sheriff pointed to a grain sack on the floor and told Whitey, "Feller left that here an' told me to give it to you."

Whitey opened it up and inside was a brand-new saddle, the decorations hand-tooled, the whangleather tie strings shining bright yellow, the sheepskin lining bright and clean and the whole thing smelling of neat's foot oil and new leather. It was the most beautiful saddle Whitey had ever seen. On the back of the cantle was a small silver plate he missed at first. It was engraved:

To Whitey for Service in Ridding Lone Tree County of Rustlers From the Lone Tree Stockmen's Ass'n.

Whitey couldn't think of anything to say, so he just grinned and carried the saddle out to try how it looked on Spot.

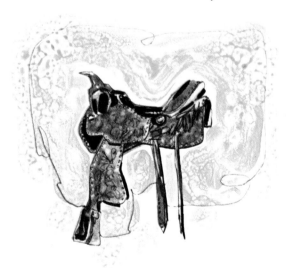

EL EÑANO

*Never, never has anyone done a good turn and
so regretted it! How, the old woman cried to herself,
would she ever get rid of this dreadful creature?*

CHARLES J. FINGER

Everyone disliked El Eñano who lived in the forest, because he always lay hidden in dark places, and when woodmen passed he jumped out on them and beat them and took their dinners from them. He was a squat creature, yellow of skin and snag-toothed and his legs were crooked, his arms were crooked, and his face was crooked. There were times when he went about on all fours and then he looked like a great spider, for he had scraggy whiskers that hung to the ground and looked like legs. At other times he had the mood to make himself very small like a little child, and then he was most horrible to see, for his skin was wrinkled and his whiskers hung about him like a ragged garment.

Yet all of that the people might have forgiven and he might have been put up with, were it not for some worse tricks. What was most disliked was his trick of walking softly about a house in the night-time while the people were inside, suspecting nothing, perhaps singing and talking. Seeing them thus, El Eñano would

hide in the shadows until someone went for water to the spring, then out he would leap, clinging fast to the hair of the boy or man and beating, biting, scratching the while. Being released, the tortured one would of course run to reach the house, but El Eñano would hop on one leg behind, terribly fast, and catch his victim again just as a hand was almost laid on the door latch. Nor could an alarm be raised, because El Eñano cast a spell of silence, so that, try as one would, neither word nor shout would come.

Then there was his other evil trick of hiding close to the ground and reaching out a long and elastic arm to catch boy or girl by the ankle. But that was not worse than his habit of making a noise like hail or rain, hearing which the people in the house would get up to close a window, and there, looking at them from the dark but quite close to their faces, would be the grinning Eñano holding in his hands his whiskers that looked like a frightening curtain, his eyes red and shining like rubies. That was

361

very unpleasant indeed, especially when a person was alone in the house. Nor was it much better when he left the window, for he would hop and skip about the house yard for hours, screaming and howling and throwing sticks and stones. So, wherever he was there was chill horror.

One day, a good old woman who lived alone went with her basket to gather berries. El Eñano saw her and at once made himself into a little creature no larger than a baby and stretched himself on a bed of bright moss between two trees leafless and ugly. He pretended to be asleep, though he whimpered a little as a child does when it has a bad dream.

The good old woman was shortsighted but her ears were quick, and hearing the soft whimper she found the creature and took it in her arms. To do that bent her sadly, for Eñano when small was the same weight as when his full size.

"Oh, poor thing," she said. "Someone has lost a baby. Or perhaps some wild creature has carried the tender thing from its home. So, lest it perish I will take care of it, though to be sure, a heavier baby I never held."

The dame had no children of her own and, though poor, was both willing and glad to share what she had with any needy creature. Gently she took it home and having put dry sticks on the fire she made a bed of light twigs which she covered with a mat of feathers. Then she bustled about, getting bread and milk for supper for the little one, feeling happy at heart because she had rescued the unhappy creature from the dismal forest.

At first she was glad to see the appetite of the homeless thing, for it soon finished the bread and milk and cried for more.

"Bless me! It must be half starved," she said. "It may have my supper." So she took the food she had set out for herself and El Eñano swallowed it as quickly as he had swallowed the first bowl. Yet still he cried for more. Off then to the neighbors she went, borrowing milk from this one, bread from that, rice from another, until half the children of the village had to go on short rations that night. The creature devoured all that was brought and still yelled for more and the noise it made was ear-splitting. But as it ate and felt the warmth, it grew and grew.

"Santa Maria!" said the dame. "What wonderful thing is this? Already it is no longer a baby, but a grown child. Almost it might be called ugly, but that, I suppose, is because it was motherless and lost. It is all very sad." Then, because she had thought it ugly she did the more for it, being sorry for her thoughts, though she could not help nor hinder them. As for the creature itself, having eaten all in the house, it gave a grunt or two, turned heavily on its side and went to sleep, snoring terribly.

Next morning matters were worse, for El Eñano was stretched out on the floor before the fire, his full size, and seeing the dame he called for food, making so great a noise that the very windows shook and his cries were heard all over the village. So to still him, and there being nothing to eat in the house, the good old woman went out and told her tale to the neighbors, asking their help and advice, and to her house they all went flocking to look at the strange creature. One man, a stouthearted fellow, told El Eñano that it was high time for him to be going, hearing which, the ugly thing shrieked with wicked laughter.

"Well, bring me food," it said, looking at the man with red eyes. "Bring me food, I say, and when I have eaten enough I may leave you. But bring me no child's food, but rather food for six and twenty men. Bring an armadillo roasted and a pig and a large goose and many eggs and the milk of twenty cows. Nor be slow about it, for I must amuse myself while I wait, and it may well be that you will not care for the manner of my amusement."

Indeed, there was small likelihood of any one there doing that, for his amusement was in breaking things about the house, the tables and benches, the pots and the jugs, and when he had made sad havoc of the woman's house he started on the house next door, smashing doors and windows, tearing up flowers by the roots, chasing the milk goats and the chickens, and setting dogs to fight. Nor did he cease in his mischief until the meal was set out for him, when he leaped upon it and crammed it down his throat with fearful haste, leaving neither bone nor crumb of the food for six and twenty men.

The people of the village stood watching, whispering one to another behind their hands, how they were shocked at all that sight, and when at last the meal was finished, the stouthearted man who had spoken before stepped forward. "Now sir!" said he to El Eñano, "seeing that you have eaten enough and more than enough, you will keep your word, going about your business and leaving this poor woman and us in peace. Will you?"

"No. *No.* NO!" roared El Eñano, each No being louder than the one before it.

"But you promised," said the bold man.

What the creature said when answering that made nearly everyone there faint with horror. It said: "What I promised was that I would leave when I had eaten enough. I did not—"

The bold man interrupted then, saying, "Well, you have eaten enough."

"Ah yes, for one meal," answered the cruel Eñano. "But I meant that I would leave when I have eaten enough for always. There is tomorrow and tomorrow night. There is the day after that and next day and the next day. There are to be weeks of eating and months of eating and years of eating. You are stupid people if you think that I shall ever have eaten enough. So I shall not leave. No. *No*. NO."

Having said that, the creature laughed in great glee and began to throw such things as he could reach against the walls, and so, many good things were shattered.

Now for three days that kind of thing went on, at the end of which time the men of the place were at their wits' ends to know what to do, for almost everything eatable in the village had gone down the creature's throat. Sad at heart, seeing what had come to pass, the good old woman went out and sat down to weep by the side of a quiet pool, for it seemed to her to be a hard thing that what she had done in kindness had ended thus, and that the house she had built and loved and kept clean and sweet should be so sadly wrecked and ruined. Her thoughts were broken by the sound of a voice, and turning she saw a silver-gray fox sitting on a rock and looking at her.

"It is well enough to have a good cry," he said, "but it is better to be gay and have a good laugh."

"Ah! Good evening, Señor Zorro," answered the dame, drying her tears. "But who can be gay when a horrible creature is eating everything? Who can be otherwise than sad, seeing the trouble brought on friends?" The last she added, being one of those who are always saddened by the cheerlessness of others.

"You need not tell me," said the fox. "I know everything that has passed," and he put his head a little sideways like a wise young dog and seemed to smile.

"But what is there to do?" asked the dame. "This creature says that he will make no stir until he has had enough to eat for all his life, and certainly he makes no stir to go away."

"The trouble is that you give him enough and not too much," said the fox.

"Too much, you say? We have given him too much already, seeing that we have given him all that we have," said the old dame a little angrily.

"Well, what you must do is to give him something that he does not like. Then he will go away," said the fox.

"Easier said than done," answered the old woman with spirit. "Did we but give him something of which he liked not the taste, then he would eat ten times more to take the bad taste away. Señor Zorro, with all your cleverness, you are but a poor adviser."

After that the fox thought a long while before saying anything, then coming close to the old woman and looking up into her face he said:

"Make your mind easy. He shall have enough to eat this very night and all that you have to do is to see that your neighbors do as I say, nor be full of doubt should I do anything that seems to be contrary."

So the good old woman promised to warn her neighbors, knowing well the wisdom of the fox, and together they went to her house, where they found El Eñano stretched out on the floor, looking like a great pig, and every minute he gave a great roar. The neighbors were both angry and afraid, for the creature had been very destructive that day. Indeed, he had taken delight in stripping the thatched roofs and had desisted only when the men of the place had promised to double the amount of his meal.

Not five minutes had the fox and the dame been in the house when the men of the place came in with things—with berries and armadillos, eggs and partridges, turkeys and bread and much fish from the lake. At once they set about cooking, while the women commenced to brew a great bowl of knotgrass tea. Soon the food was cooked and El Eñano fell to as greedily as ever.

The fox looked at Eñano for a while, then said:

"You have a fine appetite, my friend. What will there be for the men and the women and the children and for me to eat?"

"You may have what I leave and eat it when I finish," said El Eñano.

"Let us hope then that our appetites will be light," said the fox.

A little later the fox began to act horribly, jumping about the room and whining, and calling the people lazy and inhospitable.

"Think you," he said, "that this is the way to treat a visitor? A pretty thing indeed to serve one and let the other go hungry. Do I get nothing at all to eat? Quick. Bring me potatoes and roast them, or it will be bad for all of you. The mischief I do shall be ten times worse than any done already."

Knowing that some plan was afoot the people ran out of the house and soon came back with potatoes, and the fox showed them how he wanted them roasted on the hearth. So they were placed in the ashes and covered with hot coals and when they were well done the fox told everyone to take a potato, saying that El Eñano, who was crunching the bones of the animals he had eaten, would not like them. But all the while the men were eating, the fox ran from one to another whispering things, but quite loud enough for Eñano to hear. "Hush!" said he. "Say nothing. El Eñano must not know how good they are and when he asks for some, tell him that they are all gone."

"Yes. Yes," said the people, keeping in with the plan. "Do not let Eñano know."

By this time El Eñano was suspicious and looked from one man to another. "Give me all the potatoes," he said.

"They are all eaten except mine," said the fox, but you may taste that." So saying he thrust the roasted potato into the hands of Eñano and the creature crammed it down its throat at once.

"Ha! It is good," he roared. "Give me more. More. MORE."

"We have no more," said the fox very loud, then, quite softly to those who stood near him, he added, "Say nothing about the potatoes on the hearth," but loudly enough for El Eñano to hear, though he knew quite well that there were none.

"Ah! I heard you," roared El Eñano. "There are potatoes on the hearth. Give them to me."

"We must let him have them," said the fox, raking the red hot coals to the front.

"Out of the way," cried El Eñano, reaching over the fox and scooping up a double handful of hot coals, believing them to be potatoes. Red hot as they were he swallowed them and in another moment was rolling on the floor, howling with pain as the fire blazed in his stomach. Up he leaped again and dashed out of the house to fling himself by the side of the little river. The water was cool to his face and he drank deep, but the water in his stomach turned to steam, so that he swelled and swelled, and presently there was a loud explosion that shook the very hills, and El Eñano burst into a thousand pieces.

The Lemon and His Army

*With the lemon to lead them, the onion, garlic,
paprika and peppercorn marched out into the world
to find people who would not eat them*

Nada Ćurčija-Prodanović

One day the lemon decided to change his way of life; he wanted to escape from the never-ending fear of being eaten. This seemed to him an unjust tyranny and, while still young and green, he said to himself, "No, I will not wait to know the sad fate of all my unhappy ancestors. The big wide world must be full of possibilities of a better life for one so clever and courageous as I."

Then, while still hanging on a branch, he thought and thought what would be the best thing to do. Finally, he came to the conclusion that it would be advisable not to undertake an adventurous journey into the wide world quite alone; however brave, he had to admit that he would feel more secure if he had a small, select company. Then, remembering some of his acquaintances who might be in the same plight as himself, he summoned several of them. The onion, garlic, paprika and peppercorn came eagerly to him.

From his lofty position, high above them, the lemon delivered a speech describing very vividly their unhappy life and the terrible end which awaited them all unless they found a way to escape. In the end he said, "Therefore, brothers in misfortune, let us not stay here, waiting meekly for our end; let us do something which will save us from greedy mouths!"

They all nodded their heads sadly. The ruddy onion went still redder in the face and ventured timidly, "I think we all agree that the present state of things is quite intolerable. But what exactly are we to do?"

"Oh, wise lemon, don't let us live in this dreadful anxiety any more! I feel you have already found a means to save us from this tyranny," said the paprika, still green, but hot with enthusiasm.

"Up with freedom!" exclaimed the peppercorn briefly, rolling down a molehill.

The garlic contented himself with staring upwards, but his hot heart was nonetheless full of rage and determination.

"I'm glad you all agree with me, and this is my proposal: we are to form an army, to elect a commander and to go into the wide world in search of new places and new people who, as we all hope, will prove less cruel and atrocious than those in our neighborhood."

His friends on the ground cheered him, admiring his wisdom, his courage and his fine oratory. When it came to choosing the chief of their little army, the lemon was unanimously named their commander.

Hearing this, the lemon dropped to the ground.

"Stay always hot and strong as you are now and don't fear anything! Better days are in store for us!" he said after thanking them. A new dignity had already crept into his voice and bearing.

They decided to start on their journey at once, as they were all bachelors and no strong ties bound them to their birthplace. All day long they tramped across fields, meadows and groves and along the dusty roads. Towards sunset, however, they felt tired. But where to spend the night? Out-of-doors would be too dangerous, they all agreed, as the long shadows seemed threatening. Who knew what wild beasts might lurk in that wood, already dark, from which many strange cries and calls echoed, piercing the still air? An owl hooted ominously. The brave army shivered; they put their heads together and whispered, conferring.

"I can see a humble cottage across the road . . ." said the lemon, whose teeth chattered violently.

"Let's go there! Let's go there!" said his army, guessing his thoughts.

Without looking right or left, they ran across the road and into the kitchen of a cottage. A cupboard gaped open and they rushed in, sat on a shelf, keeping close

together, and tried to collect their scared wits. When they had calmed down a little, they peered into the kitchen. By the fire that flickered on the open hearth they could see that this was a poor peasant's home.

Soon after sunset steps were heard outside, and the army retreated deep into the dark recesses of the empty cupboard. The peasant's wife came in, carrying an armful of dry turfs. She threw them on the hearth and the fire blazed higher. She now busied herself with cooking the supper for her husband and the whole family, who were to return shortly from the field. She fixed the kettle to the hook on the chain hanging over the fire, poured water into it, then added maize-flour: it was to be maize-brew—their chief and nearly everyday dish. She cooked it just in time, for her husband and his brothers, who all lived together in the small cottage, now came home after their labor. Everyone of them greeted her on entering the kitchen, then sat down to rest a few minutes before supper. They took off their dusty shoes, wiped the sweat from their brows and exchanged a few remarks about the state of the crops and the drought, too tired to speak much. Their nostrils began to quiver as the smell of the brew filled the kitchen; they glanced eagerly at the kettle. Now the peasant's wife took it from the hook, set it down on the ground, stirred it with a big wooden spoon and then poured the thick brew into a big copper dish. This she carried to the low table and all the brothers stood around it, in order of their age. They said their evening prayer and sat on the low chairs.

The man turned to his wife, "Have you any garlic left, wife? I get weary of eating the brew without any fat during this long Lent—I'd like it to be seasoned with garlic."

The woman jumped to her feet, eager to please her husband, although she doubted whether there was any garlic left in the house. Some of it might have rolled at the back of the shelf, she thought, and thrust her hand deep into the dark cupboard.

"Here it is!" the woman said, cheerfully, having caught garlic, the member of the lemon's army. She put it on the table, hit it hard on its head with her rough hand and the poor garlic went to pieces. The lemon-commander and his army trembled from head to foot, seeing what was happening to their friend. The housewife, meanwhile, peeled the garlic's white shirt off his body, which she now thrust into a mortar and started beating with the wooden pestle. The moment he was caught, the poor garlic fainted; and as he came to, he found himself in the mortar, more dead than alive. When the pestle started beating and crushing him, he gathered all his strength to fight for his life. The garlic defended himself by biting and spreading a strong smell, but all to no avail. Nothing could help him. He lost his life in the bitter battle.

The housewife poured some water over the garlic and it became milk-white. She stirred it a little and then sprinkled the brew with it. The hungry peasants said the brew was delicious now and would have eaten all of it, had not the host's wife reminded them that another member of the household was still to be fed. They got up from the table and dispersed into the yard and around the house to do their usual chores before going to bed.

The young shepherd, whom the housewife had not forgotten, now came home with his flock. Having shut the sheep into their pens and tied up the dogs, he entered the kitchen, greeting the housewife politely. As he was given the brew, he timidly looked around.

"What's the matter with you, shepherd? What are you looking for?" asked the woman.

"To tell the truth, good woman, I'd like some onion with my brew—if you have any," he added shyly.

The woman went to the shelf once more, hoping that she might find an onion at the back of it. She stretched her hand, felt right and left and grasped it firmly.

"You won't roll so far any more! This is the end of you," she said, laughing.

She handed it to the shepherd. Seeing that he was in his enemy's hands, the onion started wriggling, but all in vain. The young shepherd took a little knife out of his pocket and cut the onion in four. His pink coat fell down in tatters. The brave onion soldier fought for his life now; he pricked the shepherd's eyes and bit his tongue. But the youth just wiped his tears with the back of his hand and went on eating. So the poor onion lost his life like his unfortunate brother garlic before him.

Having eaten his supper, the shepherd went to the hut by the pen to sleep; and the peasants went to their beds, while the housewife covered the fire with ashes and went to sleep too.

When the house grew quiet, and nothing except the sleepers' even breathing could be heard, the remainder of our army stopped trembling and looked at their leader, the lemon. He beckoned to them to come closer, and whispered, "Oh, my brave soldiers, sad is the fate that has befallen us in this cursed home of cruel peasants. Let us run away before we all meet the garlic's and the onion's end. These are poor people who would eat even stones, so there's no hope for us here."

The two soldiers, paprika and peppercorn, nodded their heads in silence. They spent the night there, slumbering uneasily and woke up long before dawn. As the first gray streaks of the coming day spread across the dark sky, the little army crept stealthily out of the house where everybody was still fast asleep. They went along the road again, taking care to keep clear of humble-looking houses.

At last, when the first sounds of the waking world were heard, they reached a town. Walking leisurely, they admired the streets, the gardens gay with luxurious flowers they had never seen before, the beautiful, slender bridges and the fountains sprinkling tiny drops of water, glistening in the sun like precious diamonds. People who live surrounded by such beauty cannot be coarse or cruel, they thought. Roaming on through the town they came at last to a beautiful tall house which outshone the others by its splendors, and they stopped in front of it, gazing at it admiringly.

Then the commander of the small company spoke, "This house takes my fancy at first sight, brothers. It obviously belongs to a wealthy man. He cannot be as hungry as the poor devils in that humble cottage and surely it would never occur to him to eat us, brave soldiers. He has everything he could wish for. I think, therefore, that we can safely choose this house for our home. Let us go inside, if you agree with me."

"Certainly we do, commander," said the paprika and the tiny peppercorn.

Treading softly, they entered the courtyard, then climbed upstairs and, through force of habit, hid in a cupboard.

After a time the cook, followed by a scullery maid, came hurriedly into the kitchen. "Light the fire, kill the chickens and prepare them," she shouted to the maid.

In no time the fire was lit, the pots and pans ready for cooking. The hot fat was sizzling in the pan, eggs were beaten, chickens fried. Suddenly the cook roared, "Where is the paprika?"

The maid leapt up, ran to the cupboard and thrust it open. Her hand shot, quick as lightning, and caught the paprika. Poor paprika instantly realized his impending

369

doom and went crimson with deadly fear. He was pushed into a grinding-mill; he defended himself, mounted to the maid's nostrils and burnt her hands; but nothing could save him—he was ground into flour-like powder. The maid sneezed at least a dozen times while grinding him, but paprika, nevertheless, had to turn into a fine red powder. So the poor paprika ended his days, ground and fried in the frying pan along with the chicken.

The sad commander and his last soldier shook violently in the cupboard. Seized by agonies of fear, the lemon turned yellow all over, and the peppercorn went black from head to foot.

Lunchtime came. A servant laid the table for his master, put plates on it, then a salt cellar, and two bottles, one of wine, the other of brandy. Returning to the kitchen, he took the lemon out of the cupboard and carried him into the dining room. He put him on the top of the brandy decanter, resting on the gilt-edged rim, and the lemon looked around, very pleased with what he saw. As the first wave of alarm passed, he felt proud of his lofty position, believing that this was the way by which the people of the house wanted to show their appreciation of him.

The servant gave a final look at the table to make sure everything was to his master's liking. "Oh, there's no pepper on the table!" he exclaimed and ran to the kitchen to tell the cook. She fumbled in the cupboard, found our peppercorn and thrust him, along with some others, into the grinding-mill. Fine powder came out of the mill, in spite of all the peppercorn's attempts to save his life. He tickled the cook's nose and made her sneeze and cough violently, but all in vain. Crushed and finely ground, mixed with other un-soldierly peppercorns, he lost his life and went to rest in the pepper pot on the big dining table.

All was quiet for a time, and the lemon began to feel bored; but at last he heard heavy steps climbing the stairs, and he rejoiced. It was the master of the house coming home to lunch. He carried his enormous bulk panting heavily and sat down at the dining table as tired as if he had been working in the fields, instead of sitting in his spacious shady shop all morning. As soon as his breathing became easier, he took the lemon and brought it to his nose to smell it. The lemon was happy as never before, taking this for a sign of special favor; he was far from guessing what it meant. The servant brought the steaming, richly flavored soup to his master, who put the lemon back on the top of the brandy decanter. The merchant took some pepper and put it into the soup. But that was not all, he seemed to remember lazily. His fat fingers caught the lemon again and started pressing and rolling him between thick palms. The lemon thought his master was caressing him, though somewhat roughly, and was highly pleased, in spite of actual bodily pain. Suddenly, a blade flashed above him and a knife, sharp as a needle, cut him in two! The lemon, alarmed, spat in his master's eyes and tried to defend himself by making him rub them, but the hungry master never turned a hair: he kept pressing the lemon with both hands and would not let go of him until the last drop of his white acid blood had fallen into the soup. Then, when nothing was left but the crushed rind, the master thrust it to his servant to throw it away; and within a few moments of leaving his lofty position on the gilt-edged decanter the poor remnants of the lemon were cast into the dustbin.

And that is the end of the story of the brave army and its lemon-commander.

The Cat
That Walked by Himself

*She was wise enough to tame the dog and the horse
and the cow, but she could not outwit the wily cat*

RUDYARD KIPLING

Hear and attend and listen; for this befell and behappened and became and was, O my Best Beloved, when the Tame animals were wild. The Dog was wild, and the Horse was wild, and the Cow was wild, and the Sheep was wild, and the Pig was wild—as wild as wild could be—and they walked in the Wet Wild Woods by their wild lones. But the wildest of all the wild animals was the Cat. He walked by himself, and all places were alike to him.

Of course the Man was wild too. He was dreadfully wild. He didn't even begin to be tame till he met the Woman, and she told him that she did not like living in his wild ways. She picked out a nice dry Cave instead of a heap of wet leaves to lie down in; and she strewed clean sand on the floor; and she lit a nice fire of wood at the back of the Cave; and she hung a dried wild horse skin, tail down, across the opening of the Cave and she said, "Wipe your feet, dear, when you come in, and now we'll keep house."

That night, Best Beloved, they ate wild sheep roasted on the hot stones and flavored with wild garlic and wild pepper, and wild duck stuffed with wild rice and wild fenugreek and wild coriander, and marrowbones of wild oxen, and wild cherries and wild grenadillas. Then the Man went to sleep in front of the fire ever so happy; but the woman sat up, combing her hair. She took the bone of the shoulder of mutton—the big fat blade bone—and she looked at the wonderful marks on it, and she threw more wood on the fire and she made a Magic. She made the First Singing Magic in the world.

Out in the Wet Wild Woods all the wild animals gathered together where they could see the light of the fire a long way off, and they wondered what it meant. The wild Horse stamped with his wild foot and said, "O my Friends and O my Enemies,

371

why have the Man and the Woman made that great light in that great Cave, and what harm will it do us?"

Wild Dog lifted up his wild nose and smelled the smell of roast mutton and said, "I will go up and look, and say, for I think it is good. Cat, come with me."

"Nenni!" said the Cat. "I am the Cat who walks by himself, and all places are alike to me. I will not come."

"Then we can never be friends again," said Wild Dog, and he trotted off to the Cave. But when he had gone a little way the Cat said to himself, "All places are alike to me. Why should I not go too and see and look and come away at my own liking." So he slipped after Wild Dog and hid where he could hear everything.

When Wild Dog reached the mouth of the Cave he lifted up the dried horse skin with his nose and sniffed the beautiful smell of the roast mutton, and the Woman, looking at the blade bone, heard him and laughed and said, "Here comes the first. Wild Thing out of the Wild Woods, what do you want?"

Wild Dog said, "O my Enemy and Wife of my Enemy, what is this that smells so good in the Wild Woods?"

Then the Woman picked up a roasted mutton bone and threw it to Wild Dog, and said, "Wild Thing out of the Wild Woods, taste and try." Wild Dog gnawed the bone and it was more delicious than anything he had ever tasted, and he said, "O my Enemy and Wife of my Enemy, give me another."

The Woman said, "Wild Thing out of the Wild Woods, help my Man to hunt through the day and guard this Cave at night, and I will give you as many roast bones as you need."

"Ah!" said the Cat, listening. "This is a very wise Woman, but she is not so wise as I am."

Wild Dog crawled into the Cave and laid his head on the Woman's lap, and said, "O my Friend and Wife of my Friend, I will help your Man to hunt through the day, and at night I will guard your Cave."

"Ah!" said the Cat, listening. "That is a very foolish Dog." And he went back through the Wet Wild Woods waving his wild tail and walking by his wild lone. But he never told anybody.

When the Man waked up he said, "What is Wild Dog doing here?" And the Woman said, "His name is not Wild Dog any more, but the First Friend, because he will be our friend for always and always and always. Take him with you when you go hunting."

Next night the Woman cut great green armfuls of fresh grass from the water meadows and dried it before the fire so that it smelt like new-mown hay, and she sat at the mouth of the Cave and plaited a halter out of horsehide, and she looked at the shoulder of mutton bone—at the big broad blade bone—and she made a Magic. She made the Second Singing Magic in the world.

Out in the Wild Woods all the wild animals wondered what had happened to Wild Dog, and at last Wild Horse stamped with his foot and said, "I will go and see and say why Wild Dog has not returned. Cat, come with me."

"Nenni!" said the Cat. "I am the Cat who walks by himself, and all places are alike to me. I will not come." But all the same he followed Wild Horse and hid where he could hear everything.

When the Woman heard Wild Horse tripping and stumbling on his long mane, she laughed and said, "Here comes the second. Wild Thing out of the Wild Woods, what do you want?"

Wild Horse said, "O my Enemy and Wife of my Enemy, where is Wild Dog?"

The Woman laughed and picked up the blade bone and looked at it, and said,

"Wild Thing out of the Wild Woods, you did not come here for Wild Dog, but for the sake of this good grass."

And Wild Horse, tripping and stumbling on his long mane, said, "That is true; give it me to eat."

The Woman said, "Wild Thing out of the Wild Woods, bend your wild head and wear what I give you, and you shall eat the wonderful grass three times a day."

"Ah," said the Cat, listening, "this is a clever Woman, but she is not so clever as I am."

Wild Horse bent his wild head, and the Woman slipped the plaited hide halter over it, and Wild Horse breathed on the Woman's feet and said, "O my Mistress, and Wife of my Master, I will be your servant for the sake of the wonderful grass."

"Ah," said the Cat, listening, "that is a very foolish Horse." And he went back through the Wet Wild Woods, waving his wild tail and walking by his wild lone. But he never told anybody.

When the Man and the Dog came back from hunting, the Man said, "What is Wild Horse doing here?"

And the Woman said, "His name is not Wild Horse any more, but the First Servant, because he will carry us from place to place for always and always and always. Ride on his back when you go hunting."

Next day, holding her wild head high that her wild horns should not catch in the wild trees, Wild Cow came up to the Cave, and the Cat followed and hid himself just the same as before; and everything happened just the same as before; and the Cat said the same things as before, and when Wild Cow had promised to give her milk to the Woman everyday in exchange for the wonderful grass, the Cat went back through the Wet Wild Woods waving his wild tail and walking by his wild lone, just the same as before. But he never told any-

body. And when the Man and the Horse and the Dog came home from hunting and asked the same questions same as before, the Woman said, "Her name is not Wild Cow any more, but the Giver of Good Food. She will give us the warm white milk for always and always and always, and I will take care of her while you and the First Friend and the First Servant go hunting."

Next day the Cat waited to see if any other Wild Thing would go up to the Cave, but no one moved in the Wet Wild Woods, so the Cat walked there by himself; and he saw the Woman milking the Cow, and he saw the light of the fire in the Cave, and he smelt the smell of the warm white milk.

Cat said, "O my Enemy and Wife of my Enemy, where did Wild Cow go?"

The Woman laughed and said, "Wild Thing out of the Wild Woods, go back to the Woods again, for I have braided up my hair, and I have put away the magic blade bone, and we have no more need of either friends or servants in our Cave."

Cat said, "I am not a friend, and I am not a servant. I am the Cat who walks by himself, and I wish to come into your Cave."

Woman said, "Then why did you not come with First Friend on the first night?"

Cat grew very angry and said, "Has Wild Dog told tales of me?"

Then the Woman laughed and said, "You are the Cat who walks by himself, and all places are alike to you. You are neither a friend nor a servant. You have said it yourself. Go away and walk by yourself in all places alike."

Then Cat pretended to be sorry and said, "Must I never come into the Cave? Must I never sit by the warm fire? Must I never drink the warm white milk? You are very wise and very beautiful. You should not be cruel even to a Cat."

Woman said, "I knew I was wise, but I

did not know I was beautiful. So I will make a bargain with you. If ever I say one word in your praise you may come into the Cave."

"And if you say two words in my praise?" said the Cat.

"I never shall," said the Woman, "but if I say two words in your praise, you may sit by the fire in the Cave."

"And if you say three words?" said the Cat.

"I never shall," said the Woman, "but if I say three words in your praise, you may drink the warm white milk three times a day for always and always and always."

Then the Cat arched his back and said, "Now let the Curtain at the mouth of the Cave, and the Fire at the back of the Cave, and the Milk pots that stand beside the Fire, remember what my Enemy and the Wife of my Enemy has said." And he went away through the Wet Wild Woods waving his wild tail and walking by his wild lone.

That night when the Man and the Horse and the Dog came home from hunting, the Woman did not tell them of the bargain that she had made with the Cat, because she was afraid that they might not like it.

Cat went far and far away and hid himself in the Wet Wild Woods by his wild lone for a long time till the Woman forgot all about him. Only the Bat—the little upside-down Bat—that hung inside the Cave, knew where Cat hid; and every evening Bat would fly to Cat with news of what was happening.

One evening Bat said, "There is a Baby in the Cave. He is new and pink and fat and small, and the Woman is very fond of him."

"Ah," said the Cat, listening, "but what is the Baby fond of?"

"He is fond of things that are soft and tickle," said the Bat. "He is fond of warm things to hold in his arms when he goes to sleep. He is fond of being played with. He is fond of all those things."

"Ah," said the Cat, listening, "then my time has come."

Next night Cat walked through the Wet Wild Woods and hid very near the Cave till morning time, and Man and Dog and Horse went hunting. The Woman was busy cooking that morning, and the Baby cried and interrupted. So she carried him outside the Cave and gave him a handful of pebbles to play with. But still the Baby cried.

Then the Cat put out his paddy paw and patted the Baby on the cheek, and it cooed; and the Cat rubbed against its fat knees and tickled it under its fat chin with his tail. And the Baby laughed; and the Woman heard him and smiled.

Then the Bat—the little upside-down Bat—that hung in the mouth of the Cave said, "O my Hostess and Wife of my Host and Mother of my Host's Son, a Wild Thing from the Wild Woods is most beautifully playing with your Baby."

"A blessing on that Wild Thing whoever he may be," said the Woman, straightening her back, "for I was a busy woman this morning and he has done me a service."

That very minute and second, Best Beloved, the dried horse skin Curtain that was stretched tail down at the mouth of the Cave fell down—*woosh!*—because it remembered the bargain she had made with the Cat, and when the Woman went to pick it up—lo and behold!—the Cat was sitting quite comfy inside the Cave.

"O my Enemy and Wife of my Enemy and Mother of my Enemy," said the Cat, "it is I: for you have spoken a word in my praise, and now I can sit within the Cave for always and always and always. But still I am the Cat who walks by himself, and all places are alike to me."

The Woman was very angry, and shut her lips tight and took up her spinning wheel and began to spin.

But the Baby cried because the Cat had gone away, and the Woman could not hush it, for it struggled and kicked and grew black in the face.

"O my Enemy and Wife of my Enemy and Mother of my Enemy," said the Cat, "take a strand of the thread that you are spinning and tie it to your spinning whorl and drag it along the floor, and I will show you a magic that shall make your Baby laugh as loudly as he is now crying."

"I will do so," said the Woman, "because I am at my wits' end, but I will not thank you for it."

She tied the thread to the little clay spindle whorl and drew it across the floor, and the Cat ran after it and patted it with his paws and rolled head over heels, and tossed it backward over his shoulder and chased it between his hind legs and pretended to lose it, and pounced down upon it again, till the Baby laughed as loudly as it had been crying and scrambled after the Cat and frolicked all over the Cave till it grew tired and settled down to sleep with the Cat in its arms.

"Now," said the Cat, "I will sing the Baby a song that shall keep him asleep for an hour." And he began to purr, loud and low, low and loud, till the Baby fell fast asleep. The Woman smiled as she looked down upon the two of them and said, "That was wonderfully done. No question but you are very clever, O Cat."

That very minute and second, Best Beloved, the smoke of the fire at the back of the Cave came down in clouds from the roof—*puff!*—because it remembered the bargain she had made with the Cat, and when it had cleared away—lo and behold!—the Cat was sitting quite comfy close to the fire.

"Oh my Enemy and Wife of my Enemy and Mother of my Enemy," said the Cat, "it is I, for you have spoken a second word in my praise, and now I can sit by the warm fire at the back of the Cave for always and always and always. But still I am the Cat who walks by himself, and all places are alike to me."

Then the Woman was very very angry, and let down her hair and put more wood on the fire and brought out the broad blade bone of the shoulder of mutton and began to make a Magic that should prevent her from saying a third word in praise of the Cat. It was not a Singing Magic, Best Beloved, it was a Still Magic; and by and by the Cave grew so still that a little wee-wee mouse crept out of a corner and ran across the floor.

"O my Enemy and Wife of my Enemy and Mother of my Enemy," said the Cat, "is that little mouse part of your magic?"

"Ouh! Chee! No indeed!" said the Woman, and she dropped the blade bone and jumped upon the footstool in front of the fire and braided up her hair very quick for fear that the mouse should run up it.

"Ah," said the Cat, watching, "then the mouse will do me no harm if I eat it?"

"No," said the Woman, "eat it quickly and I will ever be grateful to you."

Cat made one jump and caught the little mouse, and the Woman said, "A hundred thanks. Even the First Friend is not quick enough to catch little mice as you have done. You must be very wise."

That very moment and second, O Best Beloved, the Milk pot that stood by the fire cracked in two pieces—*ffft*—because it remembered the bargain she had made with the Cat, and when the Woman jumped down from the footstool—lo!—the Cat was lapping up the warm white milk that lay in one of the broken pieces.

"O my Enemy and Wife of my Enemy and Mother of my Enemy," said the Cat, "it is I: for you have spoken three words in my praise, and now I can drink the warm white milk three times a day for always and always and always. But *still* I am the Cat who walks by himself, and all places are alike to me."

Then the Woman laughed and set the Cat a bowl of the warm white milk and said, "O Cat, you are as clever as a man, but remember that your bargain was not made with the Man or the Dog, and I do not know what they will do when they come home."

"What is that to me?" said the Cat. "If I have my place in the Cave by the fire and my warm white milk three times a day I do not care what the Man or the Dog can do."

That evening when the Man and the Dog came into the Cave, the Woman told them all the story of the bargain while the Cat sat by the fire and smiled. Then the Man said, "Yes, but he has not made a bargain with *me* or with all proper Men after me." Then he took off his two leather boots and he took up his little stone axe (that makes three) and he fetched a piece of wood and a hatchet (that is five altogether), and he set them out in a row and he said, "Now we will make *our* bargain. If you do not catch mice when you are in the Cave for always and always and always, I will throw these five things at you whenever I see you, and so shall all proper Men do after me."

"Ah," said the Woman, listening, "this is a very clever Cat, but he is not so clever as my Man."

The Cat counted the five things (and they looked very knobby) and he said, "I will catch mice when I am in the Cave for always and always and always; but *still* I am the Cat who walks by himself, and all places are alike to me."

"Not when I am near," said the Man. "If you had not said that last I would have put all these things away for always and always and always, but I am now going to throw my two boots and my little stone axe (that makes three) at you whenever I meet you. And so shall all proper Men do after me!"

Then the Dog said, "Wait a minute. He has not made a bargain with *me* or with all proper Dogs after me." And he showed his teeth and said, "If you are not kind to the Baby while I am in the Cave for always and always and always, I will hunt you till I catch you, and when I catch you I will bite you. And so shall all proper Dogs do after me."

"Oh," said the Woman, listening, "this is a very clever Cat, but he is not so clever as the Dog."

Cat counted the Dog's teeth (and they looked very pointed) and he said, "I will be kind to the Baby while I am in the Cave, as long as he does not pull my tail too hard, for always and always and always. But *still* I am the Cat that walks by himself, and all places are alike to me."

"Not when I am near," said the Dog. "If you had not said that last I would have shut my mouth for always and always and always, but now I am going to hunt you up a tree whenever I meet you. And so shall all proper Dogs do after me for all days to come."

Then the Man threw his two boots and his little stone axe (that makes three) at the Cat, and the Cat ran out of the Cave and the Dog chased him up a tree; and from that day to this, Best Beloved, three proper Men out of five will always throw things at a Cat whenever they meet him, and all proper Dogs will chase him up a tree. But the Cat keeps his side of the bargain too. He will kill mice and he will be kind to Babies when he is in the house, just as long as they do not pull his tail too hard. But when he has done that, and between times, and when the moon gets up and night comes, he is the Cat that walks by himself, and all places are alike to him. Then he goes out to the Wet Wild Woods or up the Wet Wild Trees or on the Wet Wild Roofs, waving his wild tail and walking by his wild lone.

THE TURNIP

He was only a poor, simple farmer,
but one morning he woke up to find he had
grown the biggest turnip in the world

WALTER DE LA MARE

Once upon a time there were two brothers, or rather half brothers, for they had had the same father, but different mothers, and no two human beings could be more unlike one another.

The elder brother was as sly as a fox and had no more pity or compassion than a weasel. Almost as soon as he could tell a groat from a rose noble, he had scrimped together every bit of money he could get. As he grew up he had always bought cheap and sold dear. He would rub his hands together with joy to lend a poor neighbor money, for he knew he was sure of getting ten times as much paid back. Oh, he was a villain, and no mistake!

Yet he lived in a fine big house full of fine furniture, with stone gateposts and a high wall all round his garden. He dressed in a gown of velvet when he sat down to supper, with two men in breeches behind his chair to wait on him. There were never less than seven different dishes on his supper table—all smoking hot, besides tarts, jellies and kickshaws. Up in a high gallery, all set about with wax candles, stood fiddlers playing as fast as they could with their bows on their fiddles until he had finished picking his bones and sopping up his gravy down below.

Yet though this brother was so rich he had very few real friends, and most of such people as might have been his friends hated him, chiefly because he was a mean and merciless greedyguts. The one thing he wanted was to rise in the world and have everybody else bow and scrape before him, and his one inmost hope was that someday the King would hear of him and of all his money, and invite him to come and dine with him at his Palace and perhaps make him a nobleman. After that, he thought, he could die happy!

The other brother was as different from this as chalk from cheese. He had nothing more in the world than a meager little farm of a few fields and meadows, three cows, a sow, a horse in stable too old to work, an ass a few years older and his chickens, ducks and geese. He worked hard from early morning to night to keep even these. Yet he always seemed to be cheerful and never sick or sorry.

The only time he had ever asked his rich brother for help he got nothing but sneers and insults, and after that the servants set the dogs onto him. Yet he himself would never have turned even a hungry cur from his door—not, at least, if he had a bone in his cupboard. And rather than kill a mouse in a trap he'd carry it off half a mile from the farm to set it free, and then give his old brown house cat an extra saucer of milk to make up for it.

Now one April evening, as this brother was feeding his poultry in the stackyard and had just emptied his wooden bowl, suddenly, and as if out of nowhere, an old cross-eyed man popped up his head over the rough wall and asked him for a drink of water.

"Water!" said the farmer. "As much as you like, my friend—to drink, wash or swim in! But if you'll step inside, I can give you a taste of something with a little more flavor to it."

He led the old man kindly into the kitchen, and having cut him off a plate of good fat bacon and a slice or two of bread, he drew him a jug of cider and put that on the table. It was the best he could give, and the cross-eyed old man, though he ate little and seemed not to be much accustomed either to sitting within four walls or to the taste of meat, thanked him heartily. And as he was about to go on his way he gave a squint at the sun, now low in the west, then another very quick and sharp at the farmer, and asked him if he grew turnips.

The farmer laughed and said, Ay, he did grow turnips.

"There be some that grow turnips," mumbled the old man—and he had such a queer way of speaking his English you might have supposed he wasn't used to the tongue—"there be some," he mumbled, "that wouldn't spare even a blind man a cheese rind, and there be some—" But here he stopped, and flinging up his hand into the air as if for a signal, he went on in a lingo which the farmer not only could not catch, but the like of which he had never heard before. Then the old man went away—out of the gate by the ash tree and away. And the farmer thought no more of him.

One morning a month or two afterwards, the farmer went out to pull a turnip or two for his hot-pot, and noticed up in the northwest corner of his field what looked to be a green tufty bush growing where no sort of bush ought to be. He shaded his eyes with his hand and looked again—and was astonished. But as he drew nearer he saw his mistake, for what he had taken to be a bush was nothing else than what you would most expect in a turnip field—that is to say, a Turnip, but of a size and magnitude the like of which had never been seen in the world before, not even on the island where the people are all giants.

The farmer stood and marveled. He couldn't take his eyes off this Turnip. He could scarcely believe his own senses, and it was some little time before he realized that what he was looking at was not only *a* Turnip, but was *his* Turnip. After that, he went off at once and called his neighbors to come. It took them all that day until evening to dig the Turnip out. Early next morning they brought a farm wagon and, after scraping off the earth on the root and washing it down with buckets of water, they managed at last to heave and hoist it into the wagon. Then they rested a bit to recover their breath.

The Turnip fitted the wagon as if it had been made for it. In color it was like ivory shading off to a lively green at the crown and to a deepening purple towards the base. Its huge tuft of leaves stood gently waving in the light of the morning sun like the feathers in the headdress of an African prince. They were as wide as palm leaves, but a pleasanter green and prickly to the touch.

The next thing was to decide what to do with the Turnip. There was flesh enough in it to feed an army, and as for "tops," there were enough of them, as one of the farmer's old friends said, to keep a widow and nine children in green-meat for a hundred years on end.

"Oy," said another, "given they didn't rot!"

"Oy," said a third, "biled free!"

"Oy," said a fourth, "and a pinch of salt in the water."

And then they all said, "Oy."

But while his neighbors were talking the farmer was thinking, and while he was thinking he gazed steadily at his Turnip.

"What's in my *mind*, neighbors," he began at last, taking off his hat and scratching his head, "is that turnips is turnips, and of turnips as *such* I've got enough and to spare, which is nought but what anybody can see as looks around him. But that there monster is, as you might say, not the same thing nohow. That there is a Turnip which for folk like you and me is beyond all boiling, buttering, mashing, ingogitating and consummeration. And what's in my *mind*, friends—what's in my *mind* is whether you agree with me that maybe His Majesty the King would like to have a look at it?"

The question was not what the farmer's friends had expected. They looked at him, they looked at one another, and last they looked again at the Turnip—the fresh, rain-scented wind now blowing freely in its fronds.

Then all together and as if at a signal, they said, "Oy." The next thing was to get the Turnip to the Palace. It took two strapping cart horses, as well as the farmer's ass harnessed up in front with a length of rope. But even at that, it needed a long pull and a strong pull and a pull altogether, with his neighbors one and all shoving hard on the spokes of the wheels to get the wagon out of the field.

Once on the high road, however, it rode easy, and away they went.

Long before the farmer neared the gates of the Palace the streets of the city were buzzing like a beehive. As, cart whip in hand and leading his ass by the bridle, he slowly paced on his way, everyone marveled. But the people at the windows and on the housetops saw the Turnip best, for a good deal of the root was hidden by the sides and tailpiece of the wagon, and by the sacks laid over it.

When the wagon actually reached the Palace gates, it was surrounded by such a throng and press of people there was scarcely room to sneeze, but there the sentries on guard kept them all back, and

the farmer led his ass and two horses into the quiet beyond, alone.

Not only did the King himself come out into the courtyard to see the Turnip, but he ordered that the tailpiece of the wagon should be let down and a stool be brought out so that he could see it better. And much he marveled at the Turnip. Well he might, for no mortal eye had ever seen the like of it before. He sent word to the Queen, too, and she herself with her ladies and all the royal family, down to the youngest, came out of the Palace to admire it, and the two small princes who were nine and seven were hoisted up by the farmer into the wagon itself beside the huge root, and the elder of them scrambled up and sat among the stalks and tops.

Not only was the King exceedingly amused at the sight of him (and not less so because the Queen was afraid the young rascal might have a fall); not only did he speak very graciously to the farmer, and himself from the bottom of his heart thank him for his gift; but he commanded that when the Turnip had been safely lifted down into one of his barns, the empty wagon should be loaded up with barrels of beer, a hogshead of wine and other dainties, and that this should be done while the farmer was taking refreshment, after his journey, in the royal pantry.

Nor was he in the least degree offended when the farmer begged that he might leave this awhile so that he might himself help to remove the Turnip from the wagon, being very anxious that it should not come to the least harm.

Long after the farmer had gone home rejoicing, the King laughed out loud every time he thought of the Turnip and of his small son sitting up among its tops. Nor did he forget the farmer, but sent to inquire about him and to discover what kind of man he truly was. Nothing but good was told of him. So the King remembered him with special favor, and of his grace bestowed upon him the place and quality of "Turnip Provider in Chief to the Whole of the Royal Family."

After that the farmer prospered indeed. The rich and wealthy for miles around (as they couldn't get his turnips) would eat no other radishes or carrots than his. He soon had the finest long-maned cart horses in the kingdom, with cows and sheep in abundance, while his old mare and ass had a meadow all to themselves, with plenty of shade and a pond of fresh water fed by a brook. Nothing pleased him better than to give a great feast in his kitchen—and everybody welcome who cared to come. But search as he might among the company, he never again saw the squint-eyed old man who had spoken to him over the stackyard wall.

Now when his rich, covetous brother first heard of the Turnip and of the King's favors and graciousness to a creature he had always hated and despised, he was black with rage and envy for days together and could neither eat nor sleep. It was not until he came to his senses again that he began to think.

"A Turnip! A Turnip!" he would keep on muttering. "To think all that came of a Turnip! Now if it had been a Peach, or a Nectarine or a bunch of Muscat Grapes! But a Turnip!"

Then suddenly a notion came into his head. He could scarcely breathe or see for a whole minute, it made him so giddy. Then he hastened out, got into his coach and went off to a certain rich city that was beyond the borders of his own country. There he sold nearly everything he possessed: his land, his jewels and gold plate, and most of his furniture. He even borrowed money on his fine house. Having by this means got all the cash he could, he went off to another street in the city where was the shop of a man who was a dealer in gems, and one celebrated in every country of the world.

There he bought the very largest ruby this man had to sell. It was clear and lustrous as crystal, red as pigeon's blood and of the size of an Evesham plum, but round as a marble. The man, poising it in a sunbeam between his finger and thumb, said there had never been a ruby to compare with it. This is a ruby, he said, fit only for a King.

Nothing could have pleased his customer better, though when the man went on to tell him the price of the gem his very heart seemed to turn inside out. Indeed, there was only just enough money in the three moneybags which the man's two shopmen had carried in for him from the coach into the shop to pay for it. But he thanked the man, put the little square box carefully into an inside pocket, stepped briskly into his coach and returned home.

Next day, in his best clothes, he went to the Palace and asked the Officer at the entry if the King would of his grace spare him but one or, at most, two moments of his inestimable time. The Chamberlain returned and replied politely that his royal master desired to know who his visitor *was*. The rich man was made very hot and uncomfortable by this question. For the first time in his life he discovered that he didn't know. He knew what he *had* (most of it was now packed into the ruby in his pocket). He knew what he thought of himself, but he didn't know what he *was*. It was no use telling his name since he felt sure the King had never heard of it; he might just as well say "Uzzywuzzybub," or "Oogoowoogy."

The only thing he could think to say—and it tasted as horrid as a black draught when he said it—was that when he was a child he had been allowed to play with the boy who was now the farmer who

had brought the King the Turnip—which was just as much the whole truth as one section of an orange is a whole orange.

When the King heard this he was so much amused that, sitting there in his Presence Chamber, he almost laughed aloud. He had guessed at once who his visitor was, for after inquiring about his beloved farmer (for beloved by everybody who knew him he truly was) he had heard much of this rich man—his half brother. He knew what a mean skinflint he was, how he had robbed the poor and cheated the rich, and what kind of help he had given the farmer when he grievously needed it. And last, the King guessed well what he had now come for—to curry favor and in hope of a reward. So he determined to teach this bad man a lesson.

When with his ruby he appeared trembling, bowing, cringing and ducking before him, the King smiled on him saying that if he had known his visitor was a friend of the farmer who grew the Turnip, he would have been at once admitted.

The rich man, having swallowed his bitter pill as best he could, bowed low once more, his fat cheeks like mulberries.

The King then asked him his business. So, without more ado, the rich man fetched out of a secret pocket of his gown the casket which contained the man's ruby and with an obeisance to the very ground presented it to the King.

Now, though the farmer's Turnip, as turnips go, was such as no monarch in the world's history had ever seen before, this ruby, as Kings and rubies go, was not. But even if it had been, it would have made no difference to the King. To him it was not the gift that mattered, but the giver. Besides, he knew exactly why this rich man had come with his gem and what he hoped to get out of it.

He smiled, he glanced graciously at the ruby and said it was indeed a pretty thing.

He then went on to tell his visitor that the prince, his small son, was not only fond of sitting on a farm wagon among the green tops of the biggest turnip there ever was, but also delighted in all kinds of colored beads, stones, glass, marbles, crystals and quartz and that his young eyes in particular would be overjoyed at sight of this new bauble. Then he raised his face, looked steadily at his visitor and asked him what favor he could confer on him in return and as a mark of his bounty.

The rich man shivered all over with joy; he didn't know where to look; he opened his mouth like a fish, then, like a fish, shut it again. At last he managed to blurt out that even the very smallest thing the King might be pleased to bestow on him would fill him with endless rapture. For so he hoped to get ten times more than he would have dared to ask.

The King smiled again and said that, since the rich man could not choose for himself, the only thing possible would be to send him something which he himself greatly valued. "Ay," said he, "beyond words."

The rich man returned to his half-empty house overjoyed at the success of his plan. He was so proud of himself and so scornful of the mean people in the streets and the shopkeepers at their doors that wherever he looked he squinted and saw double. For the next two days he could hardly eat or sleep. He had only one thought, "What will His Majesty send me?"

He fancied a hundred things and coveted all. Every hour of daylight he sat watching at his window, and the moment he drowsed off in his chair at night, he woke at what he thought was the sound of wheels. As for the only servant he now had left, the poor creature was worn to a skeleton and hadn't an instant's peace.

On the third morning, as the rich man sat watching, his heart all but ceased to beat. A scarlet trumpeter on a milk-white charger came galloping down the street. The rich man hastened out to meet him and was told that a gift from the King was even now on its way. Sure enough, a few minutes afterwards there turned the corner an immense dray or wagon drawn by six of the royal piebald horses, with an outrider in the royal livery to each pair, while a multitude of the townsfolk followed after it huzzahing it on. Yet it approached so slowly that the rich man thought he would die of suspense. But when at last it reached his gates he hadn't long to linger. The great canvas covering of the wagon was drawn back and there, on an enormous dish, lay the King's present, something, as he had said, that he valued beyond words. It was a large handsome slice of the farmer's Turnip.

At sight of it, at sight of the people, the rich man paused a moment—then ran. He simply took to his heels and ran, and if, poor soul, he had not been so much overfed and overfat, he might be running to this day.

Worzel Gummidge Pays a Visit

*Susan had no trouble at all recognizing
the visitor who shambled into the kitchen. It was
the scarecrow from Ten-Acre Field*

BARBARA EUPHAN TODD

When the farmer and his wife had left the kitchen, the latch rattled again. The tortoiseshell cat stopped washing her ears and glanced over her shoulder. Then the door opened very slowly, and a strange-looking visitor shambled into the kitchen.

Susan recognized him almost at once. It was the scarecrow whose umbrella she and John had taken when they were caught in the rain out in the fields.

"Evenin'!" said the scarecrow. He stared round the room, then he coughed as sheep do on misty autumn nights. Presently he said, "Evenin'!" again.

"Good evening!" said Susan politely.

"You needn't be scared," he told her. "It's only me!"

"I'm not scared. Only just at first, before I remembered. I thought you might be a tramp.

"Not me!" he replied. "I'm a stand-still, that's what I am. I've been standing still, rain and fine, day in and day out, roots down and roots up."

He began to walk crabwise across the kitchen; one arm was stretched out sideways, and the other one was crooked at the elbow. As he walked, his bottle-straw boots made scratching noises on the stone floor.

"You'll wonder what I've come for!" he said.

But Susan didn't particularly wonder, for it seemed perfectly natural for him to be there. She stared at him and decided that his straw boots could not be really comfortable for walking in.

"I've come to save you a journey," said the scarecrow. "At least, partly to save you a journey and partly to save myself from missing it."

"From missing what?" asked Susan.

"The umbrella. Where is it?"

Susan was so astonished that she could

only point to the row of pegs on the door. The farmer's coat hung on one, and Mrs. Braithewaite's apron was on another. The third peg held a cap and the scarecrow's umbrella, or what was left of it.

"I'm so sorry," said Susan at last, "but you didn't seem to be using it, and so—"

"I know all about that," replied the scarecrow. "I heard you argufying."

"If we'd known you could talk, we'd have asked you to lend us the umbrella," explained Susan. "I did think though that I heard you speak, just as we were going away from where you were standing."

"That's right. But I'm not much of a talker except now and again."

The scarecrow took his umbrella down from the peg and stroked it once or twice. Then he dropped it with a clatter.

"I might as well sit down," he said, and moved towards the fireplace. "How do you?"

"Very well, thank you," said Susan politely, though she couldn't think why he was asking the question *then*.

The scarecrow looked puzzled. "I mean," he explained. "I mean how do I sit? Is it difficult the first time you do it?"

But Susan couldn't remember, for she was so very used to sitting. She continued to look at the scarecrow. His face certainly was remarkably like a turnip, and yet his widely-grinning mouth had a kindly expression. As he waited, the lump in the middle of his face began to look quite like a real nose. Just as Susan was wondering what to say next, he lifted a little hen robin from his pocket and gently rubbed his cheek with her wing feathers. "It's still a bit damp outside," he explained, as he popped the bird back into its place. "I always use her as a hankychiff."

Then he suddenly moved backwards, lifted both feet together and sat down on the hearth rug with his legs sticking straight out in front of him.

"So that's how they sit," thought Susan.

The tortoiseshell cat looked very offended and stalked out into the scullery.

The robin fluttered back into his pocket and began to make rustling noises inside it. Susan remembered then that the scarecrow in Ten-Acre Field had had a robin's nest in its breast pocket. Just as she was wondering if there was a father robin, another little bird suddenly hopped out from his hiding place under the scarecrow's widely-brimmed hat, looked round importantly, straddled his legs, jerked his tail. Then, encouraged by the reflection of the fire gleaming on the sunny surface of a warming pan, he began a mad little song.

Susan leaned forward and touched the scarecrow on the knee. She longed to be friendly with anybody who kept robins in a coat pocket.

"What's your name?" she asked.

"Gummidge," he replied. "I'm Worzel Gummidge. I chose the name this morning. My grandfather's name was Bogle."

"Gummidge isn't a very pretty name," objected Susan.

"No," he replied. "It's as ugly as I am."

Susan looked at him. His hat was awry over his turnipy face. A shabby black coat hung from his shoulders, and one arm was still akimbo. But she noticed that he had managed to bend his knees a little, and that his fingers, which two minutes before had looked like bits of stick, were more human now; they even showed lumps that might be mistaken for knuckles. He was growing less like a scarecrow every minute. Soon, thought Susan, he might look more like a man than Farmer Braithewaite.

"Gummidge isn't pretty," she said, "but it's a very interesting name."

"Ooh aye!" he agreed. "But then, I've a power of things to interest me—roots tickling and shooting, rooks lifting in the wind, rabbits here, there, and scattered in a minute. Stop that now, do!" This last re-

mark was made to the cock robin, who was pecking at his green-bearded chin.

"How old are you?" asked Susan.

"All manner of ages," replied the scarecrow. "My face is one age, and my feet are another, and my arms are the oldest of all."

"How very, very queer," said Susan.

"'Tis usual with scarecrows," replied Gummidge. "And it's a good way too. I get a lot of birthdays, one for my face and another for my middle and another for my hands, and so on."

"But do you get presents?"

"Well, I haven't had many so far," confessed Gummidge, "but then I've seldom thought about having birthdays. *Will* you stop that!" He raised a hand and pushed the little bird back again under the shadow of his hat.

"Do you often walk about?" asked Susan.

"Never done it before!" declared Gummidge. "But I says to myself last night, when I was standing in Ten-Acre Field, I says to myself, 'You ought to go about the world and see things, same as the rabbits do. What's the use of having smart legs,' I said, 'if you don't use them!'" Gummidge stroked his shabby trousers proudly. "I says to myself, 'You might as well be rooted for all the traveling you do.' So this evening, after the rooks had stopped acting silly, I pulled up my feet and walked about a bit. Then I went up to the sheep pens and had a bit of a talk with one of the ewes."

"Which one?" asked Susan.

"Eliza, her that has the black face," replied Gummidge. "But she was a bit short with me, she was so taken up with her son and daughter."

"Has she got lambs?" asked Susan.

"Ooh aye! She's got a black son and a white daughter. She says they're the finest lambs in Scatterbrook and that they're wearing the best tails *she's* ever seen. I said to her, I said, 'You needn't talk; there's a hazel bush at the corner of Ten-Acre which is fair covered with lambs' tails, and she doesn't make such a song about it.' After that the ewe turned her back on me."

"Why did you come here?" asked Susan.

"Well, I had thought about going to London instead," replied the scarecrow. "I thought I'd go to London, till I met a mouse in the lane, and she changed my mind for me."

"Why did she?"

"She had been to London herself. She was a field mouse, and she'd heard tell of stowaways. So she stowed away in a market basket and saw Piccadilly."

"Did she like it?" asked Susan.

"Well, I don't know about that," replied Gummidge. "But she saw a policeman, and he was dressed just the same as the one in Scatterbrook, and she said if they couldn't do better than that in Piccadilly, she'd come home again. And she said they told such lies. There's a place they call St. Martin-in-the-Fields, and it isn't in the fields at all. There's another place called Shepherd's Market, and she said there wasn't a shepherd there. So she said London was all a sham and that it was trying to copy Scatterbrook, so she came home. And I've come here for my umbrella."

"Are you going to stay in Scatterbrook?" asked Susan eagerly. She had taken a fancy to Worzel Gummidge and she hoped that he'd teach her how to talk to sheep and how to tame robins.

"I might," said Gummidge carelessly. He raised a hand and lifted a piece of mud from the place where his right ear should have been. Susan saw that his fingers moved stiffly as scissors and that his thumbs were like sticks. Then his head drooped forward and he fell asleep.

The crackling of the fire, the singing of the kettle and the soft powdery shuffle of falling ashes blended themselves into a jumble of sound, and Susan, too, fell asleep.

When she awoke, morning had slipped unnoticed into her bedroom, and she remembered having been tucked into bed very late indeed because Mrs. Braithewaite had forgotten all about her, and because Emily had not returned until eleven o'clock.

She was so sleepy that it was not until she was halfway through her breakfast, and John had finished eating the islands in his porridge that she remembered anything at all about Worzel Gummidge.

"Had the scarecrow gone away when you came home, Emily?"

"The what?" asked Emily.

"Eat up your bread and marmalade," said Mrs. Braithewaite. "I must get cleared away if I'm to do anything this morning. We're late as it is."

Susan sighed, for she knew it would be no use to ask any more questions about the scarecrow while Mrs. Braithewaite was in that sort of mood.

After breakfast she told John all about Worzel Gummidge, but he said she must have been dreaming, and that the scarecrow was still in the field.

"How do you know where he is?" asked Susan.

"I saw him before breakfast. I went out to look at that robin's nest, but I didn't get far enough. The scarecrow was there though."

"Oh look!" said Susan. "He's forgotten his umbrella." She pointed to the pegs on the kitchen door. The old umbrella was hanging from one of them.

"That proves he didn't come at all," said John in his most provoking voice.

If it hadn't been for the lambs, Susan herself might have thought that the scarecrow's visit was only a dream. But when Farmer Braithewaite came into the kitchen and said, "Hey! What do you think the ewe with the black face has got?" Susan knew the answer.

"I know! I know!" she cried. "She's got a black son and a white daughter, and they're wearing the best tails she's ever seen!"

"Well, I never! Who's been telling you that?" asked the farmer.

"Gummidge," said Susan.

"Gummidge?" the farmer looked puzzled. "There's nobody of the name of Gummidge hereabouts."

Susan was saved from answering because Mrs. Braithewaite called, "George, George! There's a strange cat slinking round the chicken coops." So away went the farmer leaving Susan to triumph over John.

"What did I say! What did I say!" she shouted, and as if she hadn't said enough to prove that Worzel Gummidge really had paid a visit to the farm, a tiny brown feather fluttered down from the kitchen mantelpiece.

"That belongs to the robin!" said Susan.

THE BEAR

Little Andalusa was the youngest member
of the circus family, but the tradition of the big top
was already in her blood. She was tough and she proved it

RUTH MANNING-SANDERS

On a spring evening, in the orchard behind the farm where Tom Pagett's circus was still in its winter quarters, the entire Pagett family, together with such other folk as wintered with them, were gathered in front of the brown bear's cage.

In the adjacent cages, the lions and tigers, having been fed by Josef, their Spanish trainer, were settling themselves for sleep. But the brown bear's supper—and his morning's breakfast—lay untouched on the floorboards of his cage.

The bear, whom they had christened Boxer because of the enormous strength of his forepaws, had been with Pagett's for exactly a week, and all that time Tom had been putting food before him—tempting him with every delicacy he could think of. And all that time Boxer had eaten nothing.

Now, as the circus folk stood in a puzzled group and stared through the bars at him, Boxer, with his face so expressionless that it did not even express grief, sat humped against the back wall of his cage and stared over their heads vacantly.

"Anybody'd think we were trying to poison the animal—he's so suspicious," said Hester Pagett, Tom's wife.

"I don't like being beaten," said Tom, "but I reckon we'll just have to send him back. He's pining, that's what it is—he'll be nothing but skin and bone presently."

"That's right—send him packing," agreed Hester. "He's nasty-tempered. He'd as soon crush anybody's head in as look at 'em. And those claws! I feel queer every time you go to put food before him."

"He misses his brothers and sisters," said Josef, who had a very tender and understanding heart. "He is alone for the first time in his life—you comprehend? It would have been better, Boss, if you had brought the whole troupe."

"So I would have—didn't get the chance. Was let down over the job," explained Tom.

"Those animals—they've got poker faces," observed Ferny, the elephant-keeper. "You can't read 'em like you can pachyderms. You can always tell what a pachyderm's thinking, but not a bear."

"We can all do all right without a bear, anyhow," said young Jacky Pagett, who, at sixteen, had just been promoted to show the monkeys and didn't, at the moment, "give a durn for anything but simians," as he put it.

"Pity, though," remarked a groom. "He must weigh above six hundred pounds. And the coat on him—never seen such a creature!"

"But 'tisn't as if he was a horse," chimed in Dan Pagett, the boy rider. "It's horses make up the circus, ain't it, Dad?"

"All of us make up the circus," answered Tom Pagett. "But that animal's going back where he came from tomorrow."

With her small, sharp face upturned within six inches of the bars, little Andalusa, Pagett's youngest, stood among the group of older people and stared, as they all stared, at the bear. She looked rather a top-heavy little figure, with her mane of dark chestnut hair falling heavily over her shoulders, and her childish legs encased in a diminutive pair of jodhpurs. Her mouth was slightly open, and her lips were slightly pouting, and her yellow-brown eyes were almost as vacant-seeming as the bear's own. This was the expression she wore when she sat among the audience in the circus tent and followed every act, and every inflection of every act, of Pagett's show. It signalized an all-out concentration on the matter in hand. As Tom Pagett had been more than once heard to remark, "There's no flies on our Lu when she pulls that face."

Well, come to that, there weren't many flies on Andalusa at any time.

One after another the older folk drifted away from the bear's cage. Hester went to prepare the family's evening meal. Ferny went back to the elephant shed, where that seven-ton-weight of petted childishness, the Queen of Sheba, who couldn't bear him

out of her sight for more than a few moments, weaved restlessly at her picket and trumpeted her need of him. Josef went to telephone about a further supply of meat for his big cats, and Jacky to give the monkeys their supper; there was no question about *their* appetites, they were complaining now like a nursery full of hungry babies.

Left alone in front of the bear's cage, Andalusa became conversational.

"*Aren't* you a silly old bear?" she said derisively.

There was no response to this sally. Andalusa pressed her nose against the bars to look at Boxer, and Boxer stared over Andalusa's head into vacancy.

"Don't you want to work in our show?" queried Andalusa. "You've got to work in some show—got to. And there's none so good as ours."

Humped dejectedly against the back wall of the cage, Boxer gazed into vacancy.

"You get treated good in our show," said Andalusa persuasively. "You know that."

Boxer didn't seem to know it.

"But we can't have skinny things about," went on Andalusa. "Doesn't look well. You best make up your mind to eat."

A stale bun loaf was lying just inside the cage. Andalusa got a stick and poked the loaf across the floorboards. "This has got currants in," she explained, prodding the bun loaf against Boxer's haunch. "Come on, eat it!"

A queer sound that was something between a growl and a moan sounded in Boxer's throat, but he didn't look at the loaf, nor at the stick, nor at Andalusa. Nor did he move a muscle.

Andalusa pulled the stick out of the cage and threw it away. "You aren't tough enough," she remarked. "That's what's the matter with you. *I'm* tough. I don't mind where I go or who I go with. Went to Ireland once and wasn't sick. Might go to

America tomorrow. And *I* wouldn't mope the way you do. I'd eat and eat all the way over."

"Anda-lus-a!" That was Hester calling, "Supper!"

Andalusa pushed back her hair from her face and expressed herself finally.

"You aren't bad-looking—in your way. But you aren't tough enough."

Hester had done a big baking that day, and the kitchen smelled warm and rich of homemade fruity cake. There was tripe and onions for supper, but Andalusa demanded cake and tea with condensed milk in it. Andalusa had her fancies, and being the only girl and years younger than her brothers, she was certainly spoiled. But, as Hester said, "If the child won't drink cow's milk, what can you do?"

Having eaten her fill, Andalusa yawned, rubbed her eyes and announced, "I'm going to bed now."

She dipped a spoon into the milk tin and brought it out with the bowl brimful and the milk spilling all up the handle. Hester snatched the tin from her. Andalusa smiled cheekily, put the spoon in her mouth, turned it round and sucked the handle.

"You limb, you!" exclaimed Hester.

Andalusa slipped off to bed.

Her tiny bedroom was at the back of the farm and overlooked the orchard. The moon was up, and from her window Andalusa could see its rays glimmering on the dew-wet bars of Boxer's cage. Behind the bars were the moonlit boards streaked with thin, slanting shadows, then a glitter of heaped straw, and behind that a motionless, rocklike shape with a spot of light on the end of its nose.

"He's not moved—not one inch," said Andalusa.

When she got into bed she was "pulling that face," as Tom Pagett would have said. A turbulent lock of hair fell across her mouth. She brushed it away with a sticky little hand. The hand tasted sweet. Andalusa sucked it blissfully. It occurred to her that by a little maneuvering she might manage one night to secrete a whole tin of condensed milk about her person before coming to bed.

"Then I *should* have sweet dreams," she chuckled.

Well, of course, a spanking might follow, but it would be worth it. She was almost asleep when a thought struck her. Bears liked sweet things; probably they liked them as much as she did. If she would sin for condensed milk, surely a bear—even if he had made up his mind to pine away and die—wouldn't be able to resist it?

Wide awake now, she swung her legs out of bed. She was going downstairs to tell her dad to try Boxer with a tin of condensed milk. Then another, and most exultant idea occurred to her. She wouldn't tell her dad, she would feed Boxer herself and in the morning prove to them all that she knew a thing or two. Her dad had said that if once they could coax Boxer to eat anything, he'd get his appetite back and be all right.

"I'll get his appetite back for him," thought Andalusa. "See if I don't."

A great adventure this! Now she must keep herself awake till all the family were abed. She sat with her hands clasped round her knees and waited. But nobody came upstairs, and surely hours must have gone by! When she found herself nodding and instinctively snuggling down under the bedclothes, she fetched a chair and put it on her pillow with the legs prodding into her back. That kept her awake for a little while; then she nodded forward. Determinedly she got another chair and placed it on the bed with the legs against her chest.

"Now you can neither lie back nor forth," she told herself.

Hours passed again—or so it seemed to Andalusa. She swayed and drooped into her narrow prison; out of a swoon of sleep the chair legs prodded her, first in her back, then in her chest. And still the family did not come up to their beds.

She slept and dreamed that Boxer was holding a tin of milk over his nose and growling, "More! More!" A chair leg poked her awake and she realized that it was not Boxer, but her father snoring.

"That's all right then," said Andalusa, and got up and felt her way, tiptoeing, down into the kitchen.

The moon was bright outside the uncurtained window, and the whole room was vaguely radiant. Andalusa looked in the store cupboard and counted seven cans of milk, including the one Hester had opened for her tea. She took a basket, climbed on a chair and reached down the cans. What else? A can opener from the table drawer. Could she open cans? Trust Andalusa! A small girl who could already do the splits and the flip-flaps, and ride standing on a pony, was not to be defeated by such a trifle as a can opener!

Then her eyes fell upon the brave array of Hester's big cakes, set in the windowsill, covered with a white cloth. One by one those cakes went into the basket, till it was full to the handle. And, so laden, she cautiously opened the back door and stepped out into the moonlight.

"Coo!" said Andalusa. "Isn't this a treat!"

Every grass blade on the rough turf at the end of the yard wore a fiery jewel; the blossom in the orchard was purest snow, and under the trees was such a tangle of dark shadows and gleaming lights that you might fancy yourself performing on some spangled trampoline under the Big Top.

Lion smell, horse smell, blossom smell, wet-grass smell: a line of light showing far off under the closed doors of the elephant shed. But that meant nothing. Andalusa knew that Ferny kept a lamp burning all night because the Queen of Sheba was afraid of mice. She stood still a moment and listened. The night was full of familiar noises: a flump, as one of the big cats turned over in its sleep, the snort of a horse away in the grazing fields, then a gentle wuffling, and the soft stampede of unshod hoofs. Andalusa came with her basket to Boxer's cage.

Boxer was not asleep. He was still sitting against the back wall staring into vacancy. The thick straw glittered, and the moon whitened his eyeballs.

"You'll be dead by morning if you go on as you're going," said Andalusa severely.

She put down her basket, tore a hunk of cake, tipped sweet milk from the opened can over it and held it between the bars.

"Come on," she said, "this is real nice."

She might have been talking to a stone.

"Haven't you got any guts—or what?" asked Andalusa. "It's good, I tell you."

To prove how good it was, she pulled back her hand and took a bite herself, then another bite. But that wouldn't do! She hadn't come out to gorge herself, but to make Boxer eat. Fearful where her greed might lead her, she took aim, flung the sticky cake through the bars and hit Boxer on the nose.

"That startled you, didn't it?" she said, rather anxiously.

It had startled him; the cake fell at his feet, but the sweetness remained on his nose. He turned his heavy head once or twice from side to side, as if he had just waked up and didn't know where he was. Then, slowly, his tongue came out and licked his nose.

Andalusa gripped the bars with both her hands and almost held her breath. Boxer had his head down now, he was sniffing, half-heartedly, among the straw.

"There, there—there at your feet!" breathed Andalusa.

Languidly, and after the manner of a reluctant invalid, Boxer put out his tongue again and licked the cake. Yes, Andalusa was right. He might think he was pining to death, but he couldn't resist the taste of condensed milk any more than she could. She wanted to shout and skip, but she heroically restrained herself. Not for nothing had she watched wild animals being trained.

"The cake, now the cake—eat it! No need to starve because you said you would. I say things, often I do, and take 'em back!" she whispered urgently.

Would he, or wouldn't he? He didn't seem to know his own mind. Gripping the bars with whitened fingers, Andalusa breathed a prayer. Boxer sniffed the cake, took it in his mouth, dropped it, picked it up again—and swallowed it.

Andalusa heaved an enormous sigh and immediately became businesslike. "There's plenty more where that came from!" she said, smearing another piece of cake with milk. "Here y'are! But this time you can use your legs—do 'em good!"

Boxer raised his nose to sniff, and his muzzle gleamed.

"You're driveling!" cried Andalusa triumphantly. "Your mouth's watering!"

Boxer's mouth actually was watering, and what was more he was up on his legs and shambling stiffly across to the bars.

"I could kiss you!" cried Andalusa, as, after a few hesitant rollings of his head, he took the cake from her hand.

It was easy after that, except that the milk can was soon empty. Andalusa pushed the empty can through the bars for Boxer to lick out, while she struggled to open another. She cut her fingers on the jagged can and blamed the bear for it.

"Here I am cutting myself to pieces for you," she said. "And you are grateful? I don't think!"

Boxer put the tip of his muzzle meekly through the bars, and Andalusa playfully smacked his nose. Then she offered him a whole big cake, dripping with sweet milk. Of course he couldn't pull it through the bars, and it fell onto the wet grass. Andalusa picked it up, broke off a fragment and pushed it into the cage.

But she was beginning to feel cold and also impatient. "Shall be here all night at this rate," she said, as she dribbled more cake through the bars. "If the door was open, I'd feed you good and quick."

Well, and why shouldn't the door be open? The bolt was high above her reach, but that difficulty was soon overcome. A pedestal that Josef had been painting stood under an apple tree. Andalusa dragged it over, climbed onto it and swung the door back.

Then, basket and all, she stepped into the cage.

"Do you know who this is?" she asked Boxer. "This is Andalusa Pagetta, the all-over-the-world famous bear-trainer. Up on your hind legs for Andalusa Pagetta, you great booby! Up, I say! Or you get no more cake from me."

Ho, ho! He *was* up on his hind legs, his huge body towered over her, and his long sharp claws shone silver. Andalusa wished she had an audience; then she was glad she hadn't for though she held the cake high above her head she couldn't reach anywhere near Boxer's muzzle. He dropped on all fours, and Andalusa, to escape being bowled over by the descending avalanche, backed hurriedly against the bars. With the jerk she gave, the cage door vibrated, swung slowly, swung faster—and clanged shut.

"See what you've done now!" exclaimed Andalusa reproachfully.

Boxer had his head in the basket. He had just discovered how very hungry he was. He took a can of milk in his paws, sat on his haunches, crushed the can open with his

teeth, and tilting his head back, tipped the
milk down his throat. Andalusa watched
him with her lips parted. She didn't feel
frightened, exactly—it had been drilled
into her from babyhood that a Pagett never
did feel frightened—but she felt a bit
awed. The great, thick-coated beast was so
very big, and it looked now as if he was out
to eat the world.

"Seeing that you've got your appetite
back," she announced, "I think I'll be
going back to bed."

Boxer took no notice whatever. The can
was over his nose, and his tongue was busy
at the bottom of it. Standing on tiptoe,
Andalusa put her hand to the door catch,
but she kept her face to the bear as she
knew a good animal-trainer should.

"Good night," she said.

It was only then that she realized that

the catch was a tricky one, designed to frustrate any over-curious or over-impulsive occupant of the cage. Do what she would the door would not open. She pulled, she pushed, she rattled, she jerked; forgetting the habits of all good animal-trainers she turned her back on Boxer and fiddled till her fingers were sore. But the catch would not budge, and in the end she gave up trying.

"Well," she said resignedly, pushing the hair back from her face, "seems you and me's got to make a night of it."

Boxer crunched the last can of milk between his teeth.

"There's all these bits and pieces you haven't eaten yet," said Andalusa, pointing to Boxer's discarded breakfast and supper. "May's well make a clean sweep. But if you hadn't been so greedy, I could do with a piece of cake myself."

At six in the morning, young Jacky, who had risen early to clean out the monkey cage—because he proposed to take the day off with a girl he was sweet on—burst into his parents' room shouting hysterically.

"Our Lu's in the bear's cage!"

"You're crackers!" said Tom Pagett, waked suddenly from soundest sleep and frowning incredulously. But even as he said "You're crackers," he was out of bed and pulling on his trousers.

"She is, I tell you!" cried Jacky. "She's asleep and he's asleep."

Tom Pagett was through the door by this time, and Hester was out of bed and thrusting on her dressing gown. In less than no time everyone on the farm was assembled outside the bear's cage.

They spoke in whispers as they peered through the bars.

On his bed of straw Boxer lay full length in sleep, with his ponderous forelegs stretched, paws slightly curled and long murderous-looking claws carelessly extended. And between those claws and the bear's muzzle lay Andalusa, with her head on his broad chest, one arm flung across his neck, and the straw pulled up round her pajama-clad body. There was not a morsel of food left in the cage, but on the floor there were the crushed remains of seven cans of condensed milk and a broken basket.

"Oh, my God!" whispered Hester Pagett. "When he wakes, he'll kill her!"

"I'll try and snatch her up quick," murmured Tom, "before he realizes. You all stand by with the poles."

They ran for poles. They stood with the pole ends through the bars, ready to thrust back Boxer should he wake to kill. There might be uproar enough in a few moments, but now they neither moved nor spoke. Tom reached the cage door, opened it with scarcely a sound and swung himself inside.

It wasn't much of a noise he made as he took a step forward, only the faintest vibration of his feet on the floorboards, but it was enough to wake Boxer. He eyed Tom Pagett and growled.

"Easy then, easy, old fellow!" said Tom. Boxer growled again.

"He's vicious!" whispered Hester.

But Boxer wasn't really vicious; he was only feeling protective of his new companion. Perhaps it might have come to the same thing as far as Tom Pagett was concerned, but as Boxer growled again and again and watched Tom with unwinking eyes, Andalusa woke up.

For a moment, not finding herself in bed, she blinked in amazement. Then she took in the situation: her father's stealthy inching forward, the tense faces outside the cage, the pole ends at the ready, poked through the bars. Yes, she took it all in, and the long generations of her circus ancestry seemed epitomized in the magnificent gesture with which she rose to her feet.

"You're ignorant," she announced superbly. "The whole boiling of you's ignorant. *You* don't know how to manage bears! Eat? 'Course he'll eat! Fetch me some bread, and I'll show you!"

"Come out, Lu, come out for God's sake!" pleaded Hester.

Andalusa gave her mother a queenly smile. Then she patted Boxer's head.

"I'll bring your breakfast d'reckly," she told him. "*You* aren't going to be sent packing, not today, nor yet tomorrow."

Tom Pagett watched every movement, poised to leap forward at whatever risk to his life, should Boxer turn nasty. But Boxer was feeling full and contented. He had wakened into a realization that life was pleasant, and that he was not friendless after all. He seemed to understand now that his new playmate was not being wrenched from him, but was merely moving herself temporarily and of her own free will. He lifted his massive head and licked her fingers. Then he dropped his head to the straw again and stretched luxuriously.

Andalusa walked proudly to the cage door, and Josef lifted her down. Tom Pagett stepped out after her and clanged the door shut. Now that the crisis was over, a great burst of laughter welled up inside him. Laughter and, yes, pride.

"Our Lu, she doesn't know what fear means," he thought. "And she's got personality. She'll be a stunner on Pagett's come by and by!"

He turned away so that Andalusa should not see how he gloried in her, for she was minx enough already.

But Hester pounced on her small daughter, doubled Andalusa's head under her arm, and began to smack her. The smacking was by no means a light one. Hester had a strong hand and arm, and she was relieving her feelings. However, Andalusa's sense of showmanship did not desert her. The chastisement was taking place in full view of her friend the bear—indeed, as he got up and padded uneasily to the front of the cage, he might be said to have a front seat for the performance. Andalusa peeped at him from under Hester's arm, and her sharp little face, though it shook to the rhythm of the smacking, wore a look both impudent and triumphant.

"Told you I was tough, didn't I?" she shrilled. "Now you see I wasn't speaking a lie . . . *I* can take it!"

Menaseh's Dream

*The castle with its silver roof and crystal tower was
the most beautiful building he had ever seen. And someday,
his grandfather told him, he would live in it*

ISAAC BASHEVIS SINGER

Menaseh was an orphan. He lived with his uncle Mendel, who was a poor glazier and couldn't even manage to feed and clothe his own children. Menaseh had already completed his religious studies and after the fall holidays was to be apprenticed to a bookbinder.

Menaseh had always been a curious child. He had begun to ask questions as soon as he could talk: "How high is the sky?" "How deep is the earth?" "What is beyond the edge of the world?" "Why are people born?" "Why do they die?"

It was a hot and humid summer day. A golden haze hovered over the village. The sun was as small as a moon and yellow as

brass. Dogs loped along with their tails
between their legs. Pigeons rested in the
middle of the marketplace. Goats sheltered
themselves beneath the eaves of the huts,
chewing their cuds and shaking their
beards.

Menaseh quarreled with his aunt
Dvosha and left the house without eating
lunch. He was about twelve, with a longish
face, black eyes, sunken cheeks. He wore a
torn jacket and was barefoot. His only
possession was a tattered storybook which
he had read scores of times. It was called
Alone in the Wild Forest. The village in
which he lived stood in a forest that surrounded it like a sash and was said to
stretch as far as Lublin. It was blueberry
time and here and there one might also find
wild strawberries. Menaseh made his way

through pastures and wheat fields. He was
hungry and he tore off a stalk of wheat to
chew on the grain. In the meadows, cows
were lying down, too hot even to whisk off
the flies with their tails. Two horses stood,
the head of one near the rump of the other,
lost in their horse thoughts. In a field
planted in buckwheat the boy was amazed
to see a crow perched on the torn hat of a
scarecrow.

Once Menaseh entered the forest, it was
cooler. The pine trees stood straight as
pillars and on their brownish bark hung
golden necklaces, the light of the sun shining through the pine needles. The sounds
of cuckoo and woodpecker were heard,
and an unseen bird kept repeating the
same eerie screech.

Menaseh stepped carefully over moss

pillows. He crossed a shallow streamlet that purled joyfully over pebbles and stones. The forest was still, and yet full of voices and echoes.

He wandered deeper and deeper into the forest. As a rule, he left stone markers behind, but not today. He was lonely, his head ached and his knees felt weak. "Am I getting sick?" he thought. "Maybe I'm going to die. Then I will soon be with Daddy and Mama." When he came to a blueberry patch, he sat down, picked one berry after another and popped them into his mouth. But they did not satisfy his hunger. Flowers with intoxicating odors grew among the blueberries. Without realizing it, Menaseh stretched full length on the forest floor. He fell asleep, but in his dream he continued walking.

The trees became even taller, the smells stronger, huge birds flew from branch to branch. The sun was setting. The forest grew thinner and he soon came out on a plain with a broad view of the evening sky. Suddenly a castle appeared in the twilight. Menaseh had never seen such a beautiful structure. Its roof was of silver and from it rose a crystal tower. Its many tall windows were as high as the building itself. Menaseh went up to one of the windows and looked in. On the wall opposite him, he saw his own portrait hanging. He was dressed in luxurious clothes such as he had never owned. The huge room was empty.

"Why is the castle empty?" he wondered. "And why is my portrait hanging on the wall?" The boy in the picture seemed to be alive and waiting impatiently for someone to come. Then doors opened where there had been none before, and men and women came into the room. They were dressed in white satin and the women wore jewels and held holiday prayer books with gold-embossed covers. Menaseh gazed in astonishment. He recognized his father, his mother, his grandfathers and grandmothers and other relatives. He wanted to rush over to them, hug and kiss them, but the window glass stood in his way. He began to cry. His paternal grandfather, Tobias the Scribe, separated himself from the group and came to the window. The old man's beard was as white as his long coat. He looked both ancient and young. "Why are you crying?" he asked. Despite the glass that separated them, Menaseh heard him clearly.

"Are you my grandfather Tobias?"

"Yes, my child. I am your grandfather."

"Who does this castle belong to?"

"To all of us."

"To me too?"

"Of course, to the whole family."

"Grandpa, let me in," Menaseh called. "I want to speak to my father and mother."

His grandfather looked at him lovingly and said, "One day you will live with us here, but the time has not yet come."

"How long do I have to wait?"

"That is a secret. It will not be for many, many years."

"Grandpa, I don't want to wait so long. I'm hungry and thirsty and tired. Please let me in. I miss my father and mother and you and Grandma. I don't want to be an orphan."

"My dear child. We know everything. We think about you and we love you. We are all waiting for the time when we will be together, but you must be patient. You have a long journey to take before you come here to stay."

"Please, just let me in for a few minutes."

Grandfather Tobias left the window and took counsel with other members of the family. When he returned, he said, "You may come in, but only for a little while. We will show you around the castle and let you see some of our treasures, but then you must leave."

A door opened and Menaseh stepped

inside. He was no sooner over the threshold than his hunger and weariness left him. He embraced his parents and they kissed and hugged him. But they didn't utter a word. He felt strangely light. He floated along and his family floated with him. His grandfather opened door after door and each time Menaseh's astonishment grew.

One room was filled with racks of boys' clothing—pants, jackets, shirts, coats. Menaseh realized that these were the clothes he had worn as far back as he could remember. He also recognized his shoes, socks, caps and nightshirts.

A second door opened and he saw all the toys he had ever owned: the tin soldiers his father had bought him; the jumping clown his mother had brought back from the fair at Lublin; the whistles and harmonicas; the teddy bear Grandfather had given him one holiday and the wooden horse that was the gift of Grandmother Sprintze on his sixth birthday. The notebooks in which he had practiced writing, his pencils and Bible lay on a table. The Bible was open at the title page, with its familiar engraving of Moses holding the holy tablets and Aaron in his priestly robes, both framed by a border of six-winged angels. He noticed his name in the space allowed for it.

Menaseh could hardly overcome his wonder when a third door opened. This room was filled with soap bubbles. They did not burst as soap bubbles do, but floated serenely about, reflecting all the colors of the rainbow. Some of them mirrored castles, gardens, rivers, windmills and many other sights. Menaseh knew that these were the bubbles he used to blow from his favorite bubble pipe. Now they seemed to have a life of their own.

A fourth door opened. Menaseh entered a room with no one in it, yet it was full of the sounds of happy talk, song and laughter. Menaseh heard his own voice and the songs he used to sing when he lived at home with his parents. He also heard the voices of his former playmates, some of whom he had long since forgotten.

The fifth door led to a large hall. It was filled with the characters in the stories his parents had told him at bedtime and with the heroes and heroines of *Alone in the Wild Forest*. They were all there: David the Warrior and the Ethiopian princess whom David saved from captivity; the highwayman Bandurek, who robbed the rich and fed the poor; Velikan the giant, who had one eye in the center of his forehead and who carried a fir tree as a staff in his right hand and a snake in his left; the midget Pitzeles, whose beard dragged on the ground and who was jester to the fearsome King Merodach; and the two-headed wizard Malkizedek, who by witchcraft spirited innocent girls into the desert of Sodom and Gomorrah.

Menaseh barely had time to take them all in when a sixth door opened. Here everything was changing constantly. The walls of the room turned like a carousel. Events flashed by. A golden horse became a blue butterfly; a rose as bright as the sun became a goblet out of which flew fiery grasshoppers, purple fauns and silver bats. On a glittering throne with seven steps leading up to it sat King Solomon, who somehow resembled Menaseh. He wore a crown and at his feet knelt the Queen of Sheba. A peacock spread his tail and addressed King Solomon in Hebrew. The priestly Levites played their lyres. Giants waved their swords in the air and Ethiopian slaves riding lions served goblets of wine and trays filled with pomegranates. For a moment Menaseh did not understand what it all meant. Then he realized that he was seeing his dreams.

Behind the seventh door, Menaseh glimpsed men and women, animals and many things that were completely strange to him. The images were not as vivid as they had been in the other rooms. The figures were transparent and surrounded by mist. On the threshold there stood a girl Menaseh's own age. She had long golden braids. Although Menaseh could not see her clearly, he liked her at once. For the first time he turned to his grandfather. "What is all this?" he asked.

And his grandfather replied, "These are the people and events of your future."

Menaseh was confused.

"Where am I?" he asked.

"You are in a castle that has many names. We like to call it the place where nothing is lost. There are many more wonders here, but now it is time for you to leave."

Menaseh wanted to remain in this strange place forever, together with his parents and grandparents. He looked questioningly at his grandfather, who shook his head. Menaseh's parents seemed to want him both to remain and to leave as quickly as possible. They still did not speak, but signaled to him, and Menaseh understood that he was in grave danger. This must be a forbidden place. His parents silently bade him farewell and his face became wet and hot from their kisses. At that moment everything disappeared—the castle, his parents, his grandparents, the girl.

Menaseh shivered and awoke. It was night in the forest. Dew was falling. High above the crowns of the pine trees, the full moon shone and the stars twinkled. Menaseh looked into the face of a girl who was bending over him. She was barefoot and wore a patched skirt; her long braided hair shone golden in the moonlight. She was shaking him and saying, "Get up, get up. It is late and you can't remain here in the forest."

Menaseh sat up. "Who are you?"

"I was looking for berries and I found you here. I've been trying to wake you."

"What is your name?"

"Channeleh. We moved into the village last week."

She looked familiar, but he could not remember meeting her before. Suddenly he knew. She was the girl he had seen in the seventh room, before he woke up.

"You lay there like dead. I was frightened when I saw you. Were you dreaming? Your face was so pale and your lips were moving."

"Yes, I did have a dream."

"What about?"

"A castle."

"What kind of castle?"

Menaseh did not reply and the girl did not repeat her question. She stretched out her hand to him and helped him get up. Together they started toward home. The moon had never seemed so light or the stars so close. They walked with their shadows behind them. Myriads of crickets chirped. Frogs croaked with human voices.

Menaseh knew that his uncle would be angry at him for coming home late. His aunt would scold him for leaving without his lunch. But these things no longer mattered. In his dream he had visited a mysterious world. He had found a friend. Channeleh and he had already decided to go berry picking the next day.

Among the undergrowth and wild mushrooms, little people in red jackets, gold caps and green boots emerged. They danced in a circle and sang a song which is heard only by those who know that everything lives and nothing in time is ever lost.

A Mad Tea Party

The table was set for a big party, but Alice found only three guests seated at it—and very peculiar guests they were!

Lewis Carroll

Alice came in sight of the house of the March Hare: She thought it must be the right house, because the chimneys were shaped like ears and the roof was thatched with fur.

There was a table set out under a tree in front, and the March Hare and the Hatter were having tea at it. A Dormouse was sitting between them, fast asleep, and the other two were resting their elbows on it, and talking over its head. "Very uncomfortable for the Dormouse," thought Alice, "only, as it's asleep, I suppose it doesn't mind."

The table was a large one, but the three were all crowded together at one corner of it. "No room! No room!" they cried out when they saw Alice coming. "There's *plenty* of room!" said Alice indignantly, and she sat down in a large armchair at one end of the table.

"Have some wine," the March Hare said in an encouraging tone.

Alice looked all round the table, but there was nothing on it but tea. "I don't see any wine," she remarked.

"There isn't any," said the March Hare.

"Then it wasn't very civil of you to offer it," said Alice angrily.

"It wasn't very civil of you to sit down without being invited," said the March Hare.

"I didn't know it was *your* table. It's laid for a great many more than three."

"Your hair wants cutting," said the Hatter. He had been looking at Alice for some time with great curiosity, and this was his first speech.

"You shouldn't make personal remarks," Alice said with some severity. "It's very rude."

The Hatter opened his eyes very wide on hearing this, but all he *said* was "Why is a raven like a writing desk?"

"Come, we shall have some fun now!" thought Alice. "I'm glad they've begun asking riddles—I believe I can guess that," she added aloud.

"Do you mean that you think you can find out the answer to it?" said the March Hare.

"Exactly so," said Alice.

"Then you should say what you mean," the March Hare went on.

"I do," Alice hastily replied." At least—at least I mean what I say—that's the same thing, you know."

"Not the same thing a bit!" said the Hatter. "You might just as well say that 'I see what I eat' is the same thing as 'I eat what I see'!"

"You might just as well say," added the March Hare, "that 'I like what I get' is the same thing as 'I get what I like'!"

"You might just as well say," added the Dormouse, who seemed to be talking in his sleep, "that 'I breathe when I sleep' is the same thing as 'I sleep when I breathe'!"

"It *is* the same thing with you," said the Hatter, and here the conversation dropped, and the party sat silent for a minute, while Alice thought over all she could remember about ravens and writing desks, which wasn't much.

The Hatter was the first to break the silence. "What day of the month is it?" he said, turning to Alice. He had taken his watch out of his pocket and was looking at it uneasily, shaking it every now and then, and holding it to his ear.

Alice considered a little and then said, "The fourth."

"Two days wrong!" sighed the Hatter. "I told you butter wouldn't suit the works!" he added, looking angrily at the March Hare.

"It was the *best* butter," the March Hare meekly replied.

"Yes, but some crumbs must have got in as well," the Hatter grumbled. "You shouldn't have put it in with the bread knife."

The March Hare took the watch and looked at it gloomily, then he dipped it into his cup of tea and looked at it again. But he could think of nothing better to say than his first remark, "It was the best butter, you know."

Alice had been looking over his shoulder with some curiosity. "What a funny watch! It tells the day of the month and doesn't tell what o'clock it is!"

"Why should it?" muttered the Hatter. "Does *your* watch tell you what year it is?"

"Of course not," Alice replied very readily, "but that's because it stays the same year for such a long time together."

"Which is just the case with mine," said the Hatter.

Alice felt dreadfully puzzled. The Hatter's remark seemed to have no meaning in it, and yet it was certainly English. "I don't quite understand," she said, as politely as she could.

"The Dormouse is asleep again," said the Hatter, and he poured a little hot tea upon its nose.

The Dormouse shook its head impatiently and said, without opening its eyes, "Of course, of course, just what I was going to remark myself."

"Have you guessed the riddle yet?" the Hatter said, turning to Alice again.

"No, I give it up," Alice replied. "What's the answer?"

"I haven't the slightest idea," said the Hatter.

"Nor I," said the March Hare.

Alice sighed wearily. "I think you might do something better with the time," she said, "than waste it asking riddles with no answers."

"If you knew Time as well as I do," said the Hatter, "you wouldn't talk about wasting it. It's *him*."

"I don't know what you mean," said Alice.

"Of course you don't!" the Hatter said, tossing his head contemptuously. "I dare say you never even spoke to Time!"

"Perhaps not," Alice cautiously replied, "but I know I have to beat time when I learn music."

"Ah! That accounts for it," said the Hatter. "He won't stand beating. Now, if you only kept on good terms with him, he'd do almost anything you like with the clock. For instance, suppose it were nine o'clock in the morning, just time to begin lessons: You'd only have to whisper a hint to Time, and round goes the clock in a twinkling! Half-past one, time for dinner!"

("I only wish it was," the March Hare said to itself in a whisper.)

"That would be grand, certainly," said Alice thoughtfully, "but then—I shouldn't

be hungry for it, you know. I couldn't eat."

"Not at first, perhaps," said the Hatter, "but you could keep it to half-past one as long as you liked."

"Is that the way *you* manage?" Alice asked.

The Hatter shook his head mournfully. "Not I!" he replied. "We quarreled last March—just before *he* went mad, you know—" (pointing with his teaspoon at the March Hare) "—it was at the great concert given by the Queen of Hearts, and I had to sing:

Twinkle, twinkle, little bat!
How I wonder what you're at!

You know the song, perhaps?"

"I've heard something like it," said Alice.

"It goes on, you know," the Hatter continued, "in this way:

Up above the world you fly,
Like a tea tray in the sky,
    Twinkle, twinkle—"

Here the Dormouse shook itself and began singing in its sleep, "Twinkle, twinkle, twinkle, twinkle . . ." and went on so long that they had to pinch it to make it stop.

"Well, I'd hardly finished the first verse," said the Hatter, "when the Queen jumped up and bawled out, 'He's murdering the time! Off with his head!'"

"How dreadfully savage!" exclaimed Alice.

"And ever since that," the Hatter went on in a mournful tone, "he won't do a thing I ask! It's always six o'clock now."

A bright idea came into Alice's head. "Is that the reason so many tea-things are put out here?" she asked.

"Yes, that's it," said the Hatter with a sigh. "It's always teatime, and we've no time to wash the things between whiles."

"Then you keep moving round, I suppose?" said Alice.

"Exactly so," said the Hatter, "as the things get used up."

"But what happens when you come to the beginning again?" Alice ventured to ask.

"Suppose we change the subject," the March Hare interrupted, yawning. "I'm getting tired of this. I vote the young lady tells us a story."

"I'm afraid I don't know one," said Alice, rather alarmed at the proposal.

"Then the Dormouse shall!" they both cried. "Wake up, Dormouse!" And they pinched it on both sides at once.

The Dormouse slowly opened his eyes. "I wasn't asleep," he said in a hoarse, feeble voice. "I heard every word you fellows were saying."

"Tell us a story!" said the March Hare.

"Yes, please do!" pleaded Alice.

"And be quick about it," added the Hatter, "or you'll be asleep again before it's done."

"Once upon a time there were three little sisters," the Dormouse began in a great hurry, "and their names were Elsie, Lacie, and Tillie, and they lived at the bottom of a well—"

"What did they live on?" said Alice, who always took a great interest in questions of eating and drinking.

"They lived on treacle," said the Dormouse, after thinking a minute or two.

"They couldn't have done that, you know," Alice gently remarked. "They'd have been ill."

"So they were," said the Dormouse, "very ill."

Alice tried to fancy to herself what such an extraordinary way of living would be like, but it puzzled her too much, so she went on. "But why did they live at the bottom of a well?"

"Take some more tea," the March Hare said to Alice, very earnestly and politely.

"I've had nothing yet," Alice replied in an offended tone, "so I can't take more."

"You mean you can't take *less*," said the Hatter. "It's very easy to take *more* than nothing."

"Nobody asked *your* opinion," said Alice.

"Who's making personal remarks now?" the Hatter asked triumphantly.

Alice did not quite know what to say to this, so she helped herself to some tea and bread and butter, and then turned to the Dormouse and repeated her question. "Why did they live at the bottom of a well?"

The Dormouse again took a minute or two to think about it and then said, "It was a treacle well."

"There's no such thing!" Alice was beginning very angrily, but the Hatter and the March Hare went, "Sh! sh!" and the Dormouse sulkily remarked, "If you can't be civil, you'd better finish the story for yourself."

"No, please go on!" Alice said. "I won't interrupt again. I dare say there may be *one*."

"One, indeed!" said the Dormouse indignantly. However, he consented to go on. "And so these three little sisters—they were learning to draw, you know—"

"What did they draw?" said Alice, quite forgetting her promise.

"Treacle," said the Dormouse, without considering at all this time.

"I want a clean cup," interrupted the Hatter. "Let's all move one place on."

He moved on as he spoke, and the Dormouse followed him; the March Hare moved into the Dormouse's place, and Alice rather unwillingly took the place of the March Hare. The Hatter was the only one who got any advantage from the change; and Alice was a good deal worse off, as the March Hare had just upset the milk jug into his plate.

Alice did not wish to offend the Dormouse again, so she began very cautiously, "But I don't understand. Where did they draw the treacle from?"

"You can draw water out of a water well," said the Hatter, "so I should think you could draw treacle out of a treacle well—eh, stupid?"

"But they were *in* the well," Alice said to the Dormouse, not choosing to notice this last remark.

"Of course they were," said the Dormouse, "—well in."

This answer so confused poor Alice that she let the Dormouse go on for some time without interrupting it.

"They were learning to draw," the Dormouse went on, yawning and rubbing its eyes, for it was getting very sleepy, "and they drew all manner of things—everything that begins with an M—"

"Why with an M?" said Alice.

"Why not?" said the March Hare.

Alice was silent.

The Dormouse had closed its eyes by this time and was going off into a doze, but, on being pinched by the Hatter, it woke up again with a little shriek and went on, "—that begins with an M, such as mouse-traps, and the moon, and memory, and muchness—you know you say things are 'much of a muchness'—did you ever see such a thing as a drawing of a muchness?"

"Really, now you ask me," said Alice, very much confused, "I don't think—"

"Then you shouldn't talk," said the Hatter.

This piece of rudeness was more than Alice could bear: She got up in great disgust and walked off. The Dormouse fell asleep instantly, and neither of the others took the least notice of her going, though she looked back once or twice, half hoping that they would call after her. The last time she saw them, they were trying to put the Dormouse into the teapot.

"At any rate I'll never go there again!" said Alice as she picked her way through the wood. "It's the stupidest tea party I ever was at in all my life!"

The Traveler and His Host

The host made a strange condition. He would give the traveler shelter if he could slap the man's face every time he gave a wrong answer to a question

Nada Ćurčija-Prodanović

On a cold winter's day a man was traveling. He had been walking from daybreak and was tired and shivering when the dark caught him in the middle of a deep wood. He doubted that his stiff legs could carry him much longer and was desperately longing for warmth and shelter. What was his relief when, turning round a bend in the road, he saw a cottage, cheerfully lit and looking inviting in the dreary, snow-covered forest. He hurried toward the light and knocked at the door.

"Good evening, my good friend," he greeted the man who opened the door for him. "I've been walking ever since dawn and would be very grateful if you could let me stay the night in your cottage and warm myself at your fire. I'll pay you what is right for that."

"Come in, come in, traveler, and make yourself comfortable," said his host. "I won't take any money from you, but you'll have to answer my questions instead. I'll give you a warm supper and a bed for the night on condition that I may slap your face whenever you give me a wrong answer. Do you agree to that?"

"Willingly," said the traveler. There was no other place where he could go that night, and being stiff and frozen he was unwilling to face the biting cold outside. I don't think I'm stupid, he thought, so probably I'll be able to answer my host's questions without having to be slapped. I wish I knew what they were going to be, though. And he rubbed his hands together by the fire.

The host, meanwhile, prepared a good supper and they both sat at the table eating and chatting till they had finished their meal.

"Now's the time to answer my questions," said the host. "Tell me, friend, what's this?" he asked, pointing at the cat curled under the table.

"That is a cat!" answered his guest readily. Why, any child would be able to answer such a question, he thought to himself.

"It is not a cat!" The host slapped his

408

face and added, "That's *cleanliness,* my friend."

They sat in silence for a while, and then the host asked again, "What's that?" pointing to a jug of water.

"That's water!" answered the guest quickly.

"No, that is *goodness!*" roared the host and slapped him again.

A longer silence ensued. Both seemed to be sunk deep in their thoughts.

Then the host spoke again, "What's that?" pointing at the fire.

"Fire!" answered his guest.

"No!" His hand flew to his guest's cheek again. "That's *comfort!* Well, you've been unable to answer my questions so far. Perhaps you'll be more fortunate with the next one. What's that, tell me, friend?" he said, pointing up at the attic.

"That's the attic!" answered the guest and was slapped the fourth time.

"Wrong again! That's the *height!*" shouted the host.

The guest was fed up with this game by now. He said, "Will you let me go into your courtyard for a while, friend? Perhaps my brain has grown lazy in this heat—cool air might help me to think of a right answer."

"All right, go out and take your time, as long as you please," said the host, opening the door for him.

As his guest stepped out, the cat went out too. The traveler, who was boiling with rage, caught the cat, tied a few dry pine

twigs to his tail and set fire to them. The frightened cat ran away and climbed up to the attic.

The guest returned to the room and said to his host, *"Cleanliness took comfort and carried it to the height, so you had better take hold of goodness in order to kill comfort!"*

The host looked at him, confused and unable to make any sense of the man's words, for he did not remember exactly what he had said to him.

"Tell me properly what you've got to tell," he shouted angrily.

"Ah, this is your wisdom, is it?" said the guest. He slapped his host's face four times, and then added, "Your house is on fire, friend!"

And he picked up his satchel and went away without turning to look back.

The Moffats
and the Sailor's Hornpipe

*When Joe seated Mrs. Mulligan and her dog
in the front row at the dancing-school recital, he could
never have imagined the hilarious outcome*

ELEANOR ESTES

The Moffats all went to Miss Chichester's dancing school in Moose Hall. They didn't have to pay Miss Chichester a penny for their lessons. Mama did a great deal of sewing for Miss Chichester and she was not always able to settle her bills with Mama. Mama said they should strike a bargain. The way Miss Chichester might settle her bills was to give all the Moffats dancing lessons free. Or rather, all except Rufus. Rufus would go as soon as he was a little older. Rufus did not mind in the least being deprived of dancing lessons. He much preferred playing marbles or riding his scooter.

Of the three Moffats, Sylvie, Joe and Jane, who did go to Miss Chichester's dancing school, Sylvie was the only one who loved it wholeheartedly. She was very quick and graceful. Dancing came as naturally to her as breathing. It was no wonder

Miss Chichester made her do half the teaching.

As for Jane, she loved the thought of dancing school, but when she got there how different it always was from what she had imagined! Before going to sleep at night, Jane pictured herself dancing as beautifully and gracefully as Sylvie. But, in real life, her arms and legs acted as though they were stuffed with lead. And her hands and feet seemed to swell to extraordinary proportions.

Moreover, on dancing-school days, Mama always did her hair up in curlers. Instead of her two familiar pigtails, strange long curls bobbed behind her, distracting her attention. They looked absolutely ridiculous, she was sure. "Corkscrews!" Peter Frost called them.

As far as she was concerned, the only really nice thing about dancing school was the slippers with the pompons on their toes and the ribbon lacings that wound halfway up her white-stockinged legs. Even though she never could dance at dancing school the way she could in her dreams, the slippers alone made it worthwhile.

But Joe now! Joe hated dancing school and didn't have even the consolation of pompons on his slippers. He hated dancing school and he was no good at it. He was good at lots of other things. He was good at spinning tops. He could fly kites better than anybody else on the block. He always had a good pencil with a fine sharp point in his pocket. He could whistle and he could whittle. Yes, all these things he was good at, but he was not good at dancing school and he did not like it. Not at all. He begged Mama not to make him go.

"I'll rake the leaves, shovel the snow, mow the lawn, sift the ashes, without your ever even askin' me to," he said to Mama.

But Mama said he should go. If he didn't go, Miss Chichester would feel very bad. She would feel as though she were not keeping her part of the bargain. "But I think I feel worse going to dancing school than Miss Chichester would if I didn't go," Joe said miserably. He knew though that remonstrance was useless. Mama knew he didn't like parties, dancing school, speaking pieces.

Still she thought he should do these things. "You must learn to be graceful and to have nice manners even though you are a boy. Try to like it," she pleaded.

Well, since it seemed so important to Mama, Joe went. But he often hid behind the piano at dancing school, particularly during the Tom Joneses and the Virginia Reels, which he never could do without getting mixed up. Sometimes if luck were with him, he was able to pass nearly the whole hour behind the piano very pleasantly indeed with an apple or a book.

Joe always waked up in the morning of these dancing-school days with a funny feeling in the pit of his stomach. What was it? He'd lie there in bed for a minute or two, wondering. He'd done his geography and his spelling and he'd even gone ahead a chapter in history. Then he'd remember. "O' course," he'd sigh, "it's dancin' school today."

And the worst day of all for him was the one when Miss Chichester gave her recital. He hadn't expected the day to be bad at all. In fact he had expected this day to be easier to endure than the ordinary dancing-school days because Miss Chichester had said to him, "All you will have to do, Joe, is to usher the guests into their seats. I'll help you see that the important people have the best seats in the front row. After that you can turn pages for Miss Nippon."

So that was the plan. Joe must stand by the piano, hair brushed neatly aside, toes out, and in his best Sunday suit of dark brown corduroy. Whenever Miss Nippon whispered, "Turn," he was to turn the page of her music. This seemed rather silly to Joe. Miss Nippon appeared perfectly capable of turning her music for herself every other day. In fact the entire class had learned to pause, sometimes with one foot suspended in the air, while Miss Nippon fumbled with the page. Why put on these lugs?

However, all this was far more to his taste than to dance the sailor's hornpipe. Phew! That is what he was first scheduled to do. Dance the sailor's hornpipe! But he had such difficulty learning the steps, Miss Chichester finally said that Chet Pudge would have to do it instead. Even though Chet was very fat and grew very red in the face and puffy, he would have to dance the sailor's hornpipe. And instead, Joe could do the ushering and the turning of the pages and get ten cents besides if all turned out well.

So is it any wonder that Joe looked forward to the day of the recital as one dancing-school day, anyway, when he would be free of all care and worry? And he watched Jane and Sylvie practice their dances with an air of compassion.

Joe may have been carefree about the recital. But Jane wasn't. She had to dance "To a Wild Rose" with Letitia Murdock. How would they carry it off, she wondered? She, Jane, did it pretty well all by herself in the lilac bush. But when she and Letitia stood up there in Moose Hall before all those people, how would it go then? So far, in all the rehearsals, she and Letitia finished the dance long before Miss Nippon finished the music. That was not right. Dance and music were supposed to end at the same moment.

And she worried about her hair, too. There was no chance of Mama letting her wear her everyday braids. No, a recital was a special occasion and would require curls. If it rained, the curls would come out. Jane prayed for a clear sunny day for the recital. She said all the charms she knew to avert rain and prayed to God to send a clear day. Rufus generously did the same as a favor to her, though it made no difference to him. In spite of all this, it did rain. This was a miserable start for the day. It meant that Jane's hair which had been done up in curlers during the night turned into long damp strings.

She arrived at Moose Hall in a very low frame of mind. Better pigtails than these slinky things, she reflected bitterly as she examined herself critically in the dressing-room mirror.

Sylvie tried to comfort her. "I'll brush them around my finger just before you go in." But they both knew it was really a hopeless undertaking.

Sylvie helped Jane into her costume. It was a white cheesecloth dress with wreaths of large red roses around its neck and waist.

While she was dressing, Letitia arrived with her hair still in curlers.

"Imagine comin' through the streets with wiggles in your hair!" marveled Jane.

Letitia put on her white cheesecloth dress. Then she sat down before the mirror and Jane watched her unwind the curlers with expert fingers. The curls came out in long yellow pipes. Jane wondered if Letitia felt jumpy inside, the way she did when she thought about "To a Wild Rose."

As if in answer to her thoughts, Letitia announced calmly, "I may be sick."

"Now?" asked Jane, aghast.

"Might. Any time."

"Even when we're doin' the grand parade?"

"Might."

"Even when we're doin' 'To a Wild Rose'?"

"Might."

Jane swallowed hard and wound one of her straggling locks around her fingers in pensive silence. Letitia added nothing to this thunderbolt, merely sniffing now and again, touching her nose delicately with her scented pocket handkerchief.

At this moment Miss Chichester rushed in. In a very flurried manner she said, "Ready now for the grand parade."

Jane swiftly glanced at Letitia, in a sudden panic lest she should have to do "To a Wild Rose" all by herself. But Letitia looked calm and resigned.

Sylvie ran the hairbrush hastily and belligerently over Jane's hair for the last time. She set the wreath of large red roses on top of Jane's head. "There," she said. "You look lovely. Where's your partner? Hurry for the grand parade." Sylvie wasn't dancing this afternoon. Her class of older pupils was performing in the evening.

"A very elegant affair," said Jane loftily to Letitia as they joined the procession that marched around the hall.

There was Joe by the piano looking

carefree and happy. He had seated the audience and so far as he knew he had made no serious mistakes. To be sure, when Mrs. Mulligan, the wife of the Chief of Police, arrived with her little dog, Sugar, he had placed them in the front row with the important guests. Miss Chichester had not liked this arrangement at all. "Supposing that Sugar causes a commotion! Mrs. Mulligan should be sitting near the door. Well, it's too late now. Let her stay where she is."

Joe was thinking if he did as well turning pages as he had ushering, that ten cents was clinched. So there he was now turning the pages of Miss Nippon's music as she pounded out the Grand Parade March with verve and vigor. That is, he was turning every time Miss Nippon remembered to say "Turn." She wasn't used to having a turner and often tried to flip the pages over, herself.

"We'd oughter had a rehearsal," thought Joe gloomily. "But maybe she'll get used t'havin' me here after a while."

He certainly hoped she wouldn't endanger his ten cents with her forgetfulness. He considered confiding in Miss Nippon, telling her he had much at stake. However, all thought of that ten cents suddenly vanished! All in a second things changed! From a happy, carefree boy, Joe became in a moment the most morose and melancholy of creatures.

It happened while Jane and Letitia were marching past him. He was making a face at them. Jane was hissing something to him that sounded like, "She may be sick." But what she was talking about or who might be sick he neither knew nor cared. He himself felt sick in another second.

For Miss Chichester had appeared very suddenly and said without so much as a word of warning, "Joe, you'll have to do the sailor's hornpipe after all. That Chet Pudge has never shown up."

Well, after this Joe hardly ever heard Miss Nippon say "Turn." Sometimes he did and hastily flipped the pages over. But most of the time he was too miserable to hear anything. He couldn't do that sailor's hornpipe. Miss Chichester herself admitted that, after giving him three hours' private instructions one day. Had she forgotten?

Miss Nippon now was getting very annoyed with Joe. She would hiss "Turn," but her turner was just standing by with glazed eyes. This made her music terribly jerky, as she paused on the bottom of each page and waited for him to turn. Things could not go on in this way. She became so agitated her eyeglasses fell off. Sometimes they both grabbed for the page and fumbled dreadfully, or else neither one of them thought to turn it, Miss Nippon counting on Joe and Joe thinking gloomily of the sailor's hornpipe.

He tried to recall some of the steps. How did the old thing go? It was weeks since he had given it a thought. Now all he could remember of it was that you slapped your thighs and stamped your feet. And all the while Miss Nippon was getting more and more fidgety. At the end of this number, she hissed in a voice calculated to fetch anyone up short, "You pay attention, young man. You're boggling the music."

The next dance on the program was "To a Wild Rose." As Jane and Letitia passed Joe to take their place in the center of the floor, Jane hissed again to Joe, "She said she might be sick, but she hasn't yet." This temporarily distracted Joe's mind from the sailor's hornpipe. He watched Jane, and Letitia in particular, with expectant curiosity. Miss Chichester came over and stood by the piano. From time to time she made remarks under her breath about the dancers.

"Adequate," she murmured. "Hardly a finished performance, however. There! I knew that Jane would forget to make that turn. Now Letitia's off on the wrong foot. End it quickly, Miss Nippon, and start the clapping."

The two wild roses bowed and rushed more thankfully than gracefully from the floor.

Then Miss Chichester said, "Now it's your turn, Joe." She turned to address the audience.

"Ladies and gentlemen, in the absence of Chester Pudge who, as you see from the programs, was to perform the sailor's hornpipe in his own inimitable fashion (his grandfather was a sea captain, so he comes by it naturally), in the absence then of Chester Pudge, Master Joseph Moffat has very kindly offered to do this dance. Ladies and gentlemen, it is with great pleasure that I give you Joseph Moffat in the sailor's hornpipe.

Joe gulped in his breath and said to himself, "Wait 'til I get that Chet Pudge." He stumbled over his heavy bootstrings and wished his corduroy trousers did not squeak so as he marched to the middle of the hall. How he hated to leave that nice, safe place by the piano!

"Mercy on us!" he heard Miss Chichester gasp as he stalked past her; "I didn't know he had those heavy boots on. I thought of course he'd be wearing his dancing shoes."

One pair of shoes was as good as another to Joe when it came to sailor's hornpipes. But he was furious with himself! To think the shoes he had on might have served as a good excuse for not doing the dance. And he hadn't thought of it. Too late now, however. On with the sailor's hornpipe!

Miss Nippon started the lively tune and Joe started to shuffle his feet. He could see it was going to be far worse than he had expected even. Stamp! Stamp! Stamp! Slap! Slap! That's all he could remember of it. A great deal of stamping and slap-ping. His boots made a terrific clatter and his trousers kept up that whistling and squeaking. He had never felt more foolish and miserable in his whole life. He could hardly hear the music. Miss Chichester kept time by clapping her hands very hard and nodding her head back and forth so that the hairpins flew. Miss Nippon got along beautifully without a turner and just pounded the music out. They all seemed to think the more noise they made the better he could dance.

Stamp! Stamp! Slap! Slap! He kicked his legs and slapped his thighs. What next, he wondered? Was this going on forever?

But what was this? Sugar, Mrs. Mulligan's Sugar, who had slept peacefully in her lap through such dances as "A Daisy-do," "To a Wild Rose" and "Nelly-Take-a-Kiss," suddenly sat bolt upright. Every nerve in his taut little body was alive and vibrant. He uttered a joyful yelp and bounded from Mrs. Mulligan's lap to the center of the floor where Joe was performing. He stood up on his hind legs, bowed, stamped, shuffled and turned this way and that. Anyone could see he was dancing as perfect a sailor's hornpipe as a small, furry dog possibly could.

"Hurray! Hurray!" shouted the audience as soon as it had recovered from its first bewildered surprise.

Joe was so startled by the new development that he paused, hoping this was to be deliverance from this miserable dance. Then he realized that the dog, Sugar, was doing the sailor's hornpipe and was looking to him for cues. "Gee, what a smart dog," thought Joe enthusiastically, and took up the steps again. Bow and kick! Shuffle and stamp! The two got on together with perfect understanding.

"Bravo! Bravo!"

"Hurray for Joseph Moffat and hurray for Sugar!"

Storms of applause rocked the hall.

"Again! Again!" the people yelled. "Encore!"

The enthusiasm was so great that Joe and the dog just had to repeat the dance. Joe didn't mind it a bit the second time. "The people are probably lookin' at him, not at me," he thought, almost enjoying himself now.

Finally the music ceased. Sugar gracefully bowed his head several times and then he returned to Mrs. Mulligan, walking all the way on his hind feet. Joe bowed too and retreated hastily to his place by the piano amidst rousing shouts of applause.

"Hurray! Hurray! for Joey Moffat and the dog. Hurray for the sailor's hornpipe!" the audience screamed again.

Joe scrunched his program up in his pocket and wished they'd all stop yelling and clapping. He certainly wished he could get behind the piano, but of course that was impossible with everyone staring so. Besides, there were still one or two dances on the program and he supposed he'd have to resume his job as turner if he wanted that ten cents.

As for Sugar, he climbed right back on Mrs. Mulligan's lap. He was panting and his tongue hung out of his mouth. Mrs. Mulligan petted him and said, "Good doggie! Smart doggie! Where did you learn those tricks, sir?" For no one in the audience, not even Mrs. Mulligan, knew what had prompted that dance—no one knew that years before he had become Mrs. Mulligan's lap dog he had belonged to a young sailor, a friend of the Chief of Police. This sailor had taught Sugar (not Sugar then, but Tar!) to dance the sailor's hornpipe, while he too danced and played the harmonica.

Well, Sugar hadn't heard that tune in years, and this afternoon when he did hear it, what was he thinking of? A hall filled with party-dressed ladies and children clad in fancy costumes? Not at all; but a rolling deck, a young sailor named Jack, and the taste of salt in the air. Was that why he was licking his whiskers when he settled down once more in Mrs. Mulligan's lap?

When all the dances were finished, Miss Nippon struck up the Grand Parade March again and everyone filed out. Joe waited at the piano, turning until the last chord was played. Then he helped Miss Chichester close up the hall. As they parted she said, "Thank you, Joe, for your impromptu performance. You made a success of the recital. Everyone says you were the best on the program. You certainly were the hit of the day." And she gave him a friendly nod as she put up her umbrella. But she forgot his ten cents and Joe was too shy to ask her for it. He pulled down his cap, jerked up his coat collar, stuck his hands in his pockets and walked home in the rain, whistling.

The Crow Child

If little Ruky would only come back,
Cora promised she would never lose her temper again

MARY MAPES DODGE

Midway between a certain blue lake and a deep forest there once stood a cottage, called by its owner "The Rookery."

The forest shut out the sunlight and scowled upon the ground, breaking with shadows every ray that fell, until only a few little pieces lay scattered about. But the broad lake invited all the rays to come and rest upon her so that sometimes she shone from shore to shore, and the sun winked and blinked above her as though dazzled by his own reflection. The cottage, which was very small, had sunny windows and dark windows. Only from the roof could you see the mountains beyond. There the light crept up in the morning to begin the day, and down in the evening to end the day, turning all the brooks into living silver as it passed.

But something brighter than sunshine used often to look from the cottage into the forest, and something even more gloomy than shadows often glowered from its windows upon the sunny lake. One was the face of little Ruky Lynn, and the other

was his sister's when she felt angry or ill-tempered.

They were orphans, Cora and Ruky, living alone in the cottage with an old uncle. Cora—or "Cor," as Ruky called her—was nearly sixteen years old, but her brother had seen the forest turn yellow only four times. She was, therefore, almost mother and sister in one. The little fellow was her companion night and day. Together they ate and slept, and—when Cora was not at work in the cottage—together they rambled in the wood or floated in their little skiff upon the lake.

Ruky had dark, bright eyes, and the glossy blackness of his hair made his cheeks look even rosier than they were. He had funny ways for a boy, Cora thought. The quick, bird-like jerks of his raven-black head, his stately baby gait and his habit of pecking at his food, as she called it, often made his sister laugh. Young as he was, the little fellow had learned to mount to the top of a low-branching tree near the cottage, though he could not always get down alone. Sometimes when, perched in the thick foliage, he would scream, "Cor! Cor! Come, help me down!" his sister would answer, as she ran out laughing, "Yes, little Crow! I'm coming."

Perhaps it was because he reminded her of a crow that Cora often called him her birdie. This was when she was good-natured and willing to let him see how much she loved him. But in her cloudy moments, as the uncle called them, Cora was another girl. Everything seemed ugly to her or out of tune. Even Ruky was a trial; and, instead of giving him a kind word, she would scold and grumble until he would steal from the cottage door and, jumping lightly from the doorstep, seek the shelter of his tree. Once safely perched among its branches he knew she would finish her work, forget her ill humor and be quite ready, when he cried "Cor! Cor!" to come out laughing, "Yes, little Crow! I'm coming I'm coming!"

No one could help loving Ruky, with his quick, affectionate ways; and it seemed that Ruky, in turn, could not help loving every person and thing around him. He loved his silent old uncle, the bright lake, the cool forest and even his little china cup with red berries painted upon it. But more than all, Ruky loved his golden-haired sister and the great dog, who would plunge into the lake at the mere pointing of his chubby little finger.

Nep and Ruky often talked together, and though one used barks and the other words, there was a perfect understanding between them. Woe to the straggler that dared to cross Nep's path, and woe to the bird or rabbit that ventured too near!—those great teeth snapped at their prey without even the warning of a growl. But Ruky could safely pull Nep's ears or his tail, or climb his great shaggy back or even snatch away the untasted bone. Still, as I said before, everyone loved the child, so, of course, Nep was no exception.

One day Ruky's "Cor! Cor!" had sounded oftener than usual. His rosy face had bent saucily to kiss Cora's upturned forehead as she raised her arms to lift him from the tree, but the sparkle in his dark eyes had seemed to kindle so much mischief in him that his sister's patience became fairly exhausted.

"Has Cor nothing to do but to wait upon *you*," she cried, "and nothing to listen to but your noise and your racket? You shall go to bed early today, and then I shall have some peace."

"No, no, Cor. Please let Ruky wait till the stars come. Ruky wants to see the stars," he begged.

"Hush! Ruky is bad. He shall have a whipping when Uncle comes home."

Nep growled.

"Ha! ha!" laughed Ruky, jerking his head saucily. "Nep says 'No!'"

Nep was shut out of the cottage for his pains, and poor Ruky was undressed with many a hasty jerk and pull.

"You hurt, Cor!" he said, plaintively. "I'll take off my shoes my own self."

"No, you won't," cried Cor, almost shaking him, and when he cried she called him naughty and said if he did not stop he should have no supper. This made him cry all the more, and Cora, feeling in her angry mood that he deserved severe punishment, threw away his supper and put him to bed. Then all that could be heard was Ruky's low sobs and the snappish clicks of Cora's needles as she sat knitting with her back to him.

He could not sleep, for his eyelids were scalded with tears, and his plaintive "Cor, Cor!" had reached his sister's ears in vain. She never once looked up from those gleaming knitting needles nor even gave him his goodnight kiss.

It grew late. The uncle did not return. At last Cora, sulky and weary, locked the cottage door, blew out her candle and lay down in the bed beside her little brother.

The poor little fellow tried to win a forgiving word, but she was too ill-natured to grant it. In vain he whispered "Cor,—Cor!" He even touched her hand over and over again with his lips, hoping she would turn toward him and, with a loving kiss, murmur as usual, "Goodnight, little birdie."

Instead, she jerked her arm angrily away, saying, "Oh, stop your pecking and go to sleep! I wish you were a crow in earnest, and then I should have some peace."

After this, Ruky was silent. His heart drooped within him as he wondered what this "peace" was that his sister wished for so often, and why he must go away before it could come to her.

Soon, Cora, who had rejoiced in the sudden calm, heard a strange fluttering. In an instant she saw by the starlight a dark object wheel once or twice in the air above her, then dart suddenly through the open window.

Astonished that Ruky had not either shouted with delight at the strange visitor or else clung to her neck in fear, she turned to see if he had fallen asleep.

No wonder that she started up, horror-stricken—Ruky was not there!

His empty place was still warm—perhaps he had slid softly from the bed. With trembling haste she lighted the candle and peered in every corner. The boy was not to be found!

Then those fearful words rang in her ear, *"I wish you were a crow in earnest!"*

Cora rushed to the door and, with straining gaze, looked out into the still night.

"Ruky! Ruky!" she screamed.

There was a slight stir in the low-growing tree.

"Ruky, darling, come back!"

"Caw, caw!" answered a harsh voice from the tree. Something black seemed to spin out of it and then in great, sweeping circles sailed upward until finally it settled upon one of the loftiest trees in the forest.

"Caw, caw!" it screamed fiercely.

The girl shuddered, but, with outstretched arms, cried out, "O Ruky, if it is *you*, come back to poor Cor!"

"Caw, caw!" mocked hundreds of voices as a shadow like a thundercloud rose in the air. It was an immense flock of crows. She could distinguish them plainly in the starlight, circling higher and higher, then lower and lower, until, screaming "Caw, caw!" they sailed far off into the night.

"Answer me, Ruky!" she cried.

Nep growled, the forest trees whispered softly together, and the lake, twinkling with stars, sang a lullaby as it lifted its weary little waves upon the shore: there was no other sound.

It seemed that daylight never would come, but at last the trees turned slowly from black to green, and the lake put out its stars, one by one, and waited for the sun.

Cora, who had been wandering restlessly in every direction, now went weeping into the cottage. "Poor boy!" she sobbed, "he had no supper." Then she scattered bread crumbs near the doorway, hoping that Ruky would come for them; but only a few timid little songsters hovered about and, while Cora wept, picked up the food daintily as though it burned their bills. When, although there were no crows among them, she reached forth her hand and called "Ruky!" they were frightened away.

Next she went to the steep-roofed barn, and, bringing out an apronful of grain, scattered it all around his favorite tree. Before long, to her great joy, a flock of crows came by. They spied the grain and soon were busily picking it up with their short, feathered bills. One even came near where she sat. Unable to restrain herself

longer, she fell upon her knees with an imploring cry, "Oh, Ruky! Is *this you?*"

Instantly the entire flock set up an angry "caw," and surrounding the crow who was hopping closer and closer to Cora, hurried him off until they all looked like mere specks against the summer sky.

Every day, rain or shine, she scattered the grain, trembling with dread lest Nep should leap among the hungry crows and perhaps kill her own birdie first. But Nep knew better; he never stirred when the noisy crowd settled around the cottage, excepting once, when one of them settled upon his back. Then he started up, wagging his tail, and barked with uproarious delight. The crow flew off with a frightened "caw" and did not venture near him again.

Poor Cora felt sure that this could be no other than Ruky. Oh, if she only could have caught him then! Perhaps with kisses and prayers she might have won him back to Ruky's shape, but now the chance was lost.

There were none to help her for the nearest neighbor dwelt miles away, and her uncle had not yet returned.

After a while she remembered the little cup and, filling it with grain, stood it upon a grassy mound. When the crows came, they fought and struggled for its contents with many an angry cry. One of them made no effort to seize the grain. He seemed contented to peck at the berries painted upon its sides, as he hopped joyfully around it again and again. Nep lay very quiet. Only the tip of his tail twitched with an eager, wistful motion. But Cora sprang joyfully toward the bird. "It *is* Ruky!" she cried, striving to catch it.

Alas! the cup lay shattered beneath her hand as, with a taunting "caw, caw," the crow joined its fellows and flew away.

Next, gunners came. They were looking for other game; but they hated the crows, Cora knew, and she trembled night and day. She could hear the sharp crack of fowling pieces in the forest and shuddered whenever Nep, pricking up his ears, darted with an angry howl in the direction of the sound. She knew, too, that her uncle had set traps for the crows, and it seemed to her that the whole world was against the poor birds, plotting their destruction.

Time flew by. The leaves seemed to flash into bright colors and fall off almost in a day. Frost and snow came. Still the uncle had not returned, or, if he had, she did not know it. Her brain was bewildered. She knew not whether she ate or slept. Only the terrible firing reached her ears, or that living black cloud came and went with its ceaseless "caw."

At last, during a terrible night of wind and storm, Cora felt that she must go forth and seek her poor bird.

"Perhaps he is freezing—dying!" she cried, springing frantically from the bed and casting her long cloak over her nightdress.

In a moment, she was trudging barefooted through the snow. It was so deep she could hardly walk, and the sleet was driving into her face; still she kept on, though her numbed feet seemed scarcely to belong to her. All the way she was praying in her heart and promising never, never to be angry again if she only could find her birdie—not Ruky, the boy, but whatever he might be—she was willing to accept her punishment. Soon a faint cry reached her ear. With eager haste, she peered into every fold of the drifted snow. A black object caught her eye. It was a poor storm-beaten crow, lying there benumbed and stiff.

For Ruky's sake, she folded it closely to her bosom and plodded back to the cottage. The fire cast a rosy light on its glossy wing as she entered, but the poor thing did not stir. Softly stroking and warming it, she wrapped the frozen bird in soft flannel and breathed into its open mouth. Soon, to her great relief, it revived and even swallowed a few grains of wheat.

Cold and weary, she cast herself upon the bed, still folding the bird to her heart. "It may be Ruky! It is all I ask," she sobbed. "I dare not pray for more."

Suddenly she felt a peculiar stirring. The crow seemed to grow larger. Then, in the dim light, she felt its feathers pressing lightly against her cheek. Next something soft and warm wound itself tenderly about her neck, and she heard a sweet voice saying, "Don't cry, Cor—I'll be good."

She started up. It was, indeed, her own darling! The starlight shone into the room. Lighting her candle, she looked at the clock. It was just two hours since she had uttered those cruel words. Sobbing, she asked, "Have I been asleep, Ruky?"

"I don't know, Cor. Do people cry when they're asleep?"

"Sometimes, Ruky," clasping him very close.

"Then you have been asleep. But, Cor, please don't let Uncle whip Ruky."

"No, no, my birdie—I mean, my brother. Goodnight, darling!"

"Goodnight."

The Man
Whose Trade Was Tricks

*The king's men were searching
the entire realm to find someone who would agree
to try to trick the tricky king*

GEORGE AND HELEN PAPASHVILY

There was, there was, and yet there was not, there was once a king who, like all kings, wanted to believe he was the trickiest man in the whole world.

During the day when his court stood near to applaud each word he spoke, he felt sure of this. But at night when sleep was slow he worried.

Is it possible, is it really possible, he would think to himself, that there might be someone who is trickier than I?

Finally he could endure it no longer, and he called his viziers together.

"Go," he commanded them, "and find the trickiest man in my kingdom and bring him here before me. I will match myself against him. If he loses he must be my slave for life."

The viziers set out and in their travels they met many clever men—such clever men, in fact, that they refused to go back and match themselves against the king for

no better reward than a promise they might be slaves.

The viziers grew desperate.

At last one night they came through a fertile valley bordered with thick forests into the street of a poor village. Now this village, you should know, was not poor because it was a lazy village or a stupid village. It was poor because the king owned the valley and all the forest beyond. Each year he took such a heavy rent that no matter how hard the villagers worked when harvest time came nothing was left for them but the middlings of their own wheat and a few crooked tree stumps.

But poor as this village was they knew how to act like rich men. They called the viziers to the best supper they could cook and afterward, for their entertainment, the villagers built a campfire and told the viziers stories.

As the evening sharpened itself to a

point, the viziers noticed that one man, Shahkro, was better than all the rest at guessing riddles, and remembering poems and describing his adventures.

"Let us see if he will go with us and match himself against the king," whispered the viziers to each other.

At first when they asked Shahkro he refused, but finally after some persuasion he said, "I will go with you, but I will go just like this. Without my hat and without my coat."

And exactly that way they brought him before the king.

"Sit down," the king said. "So you think you are the trickiest man in my kingdom?"

"Tricking is my trade," Shahkro answered.

"Try to trick me then," the king commanded. "But I warn you," he added, "it cannot be done for I am so tricky myself."

"I can see that," Shahkro said. "I wish I had known all this before. I would have come prepared. As it was I left in such a hurry I didn't stop for my hat or my coat, to say nothing of my tools."

"What tools?"

"Why the tools I use for tricking people."

"Go and get them."

"That's not so easy. Naturally, as I'm sure you know from your own experience, I can't just bundle them together as though they were something ordinary. I need wagons."

"Wagons?" said the king. "How many wagons?"

"About a hundred with a hundred horses to pull them."

"Take them from my stable but come right back."

"Certainly," Shahkro said. "With luck I should have everything loaded in five or six months."

"Five or six months?"

"I'll need to bring *all* my tools if I must trick you."

"Well, come back as soon as you can."

"By the way," Shahkro said when the wagons were brought and he was ready to drive off, "if I can't trick you I know I must be your slave for the rest of my life, but just suppose I win, what then?"

"But you can't win," the king told him.

"I know I can't but suppose I did."

"Well, what do you want?"

"Something you wouldn't miss if you gave it to me."

"I agree," said the king.

Shahkro went home at a fast trot, called all the villagers together, gave them each a horse and wagon, and working side by side they sowed and harvested a crop large enough to last them for ten years.

"At least we have this much out of it," Shahkro said, when the last load of grain came creaking into the barn. "Now bring me all the empty wineskins you can find."

When these were collected, Shahkro blew them full of air and piled them on the wagons and rode back to the palace.

The king was waiting impatiently for him in the great hall surrounded by all his nobles dressed in their richest costumes.

"Let us begin," the king said.

"I must unpack my tools," Shahkro told him.

"I will send servants to do that," the king said.

While they were waiting the king's black dog ran into the room and, noticing a stranger was there, he came over and sniffed Shahkro's legs to make his acquaintance. Shahkro bent his head and blew very lightly in the dog's ear. The dog, of course, in turn licked Shahkro's ear.

"This is awful news," Shahkro jumped up from his chair. "Awful! Where's my hat? Where's my coat? I beg you loan me the fastest horse in your own stable. My

dear wife, whom I left well and happy yesterday, is dying."

"How do you know?" cried the king.

"How does he know?" cried the court.

"Your dog, as you saw, whispered it in my ear just now."

Everyone was sorry and the king or-dered the best horse in his stable saddled, a full-blooded black Arabian, and Shahkro rode away home.

He stayed there long enough to sell the horse for a good price and buy a black donkey.

Then he put the horse's saddle and bridle on the donkey and went back to town.

The king was waiting in the courtyard and when he saw Shahkro jogging along he cried out, "Where is my horse?"

"Horse?" Shahkro said. "Horse! Oh King, have your joke at my expense. I am only a poor man. But I never thought you would do a thing like this to me. Send me home to my sick wife on a horse that changes himself back and forth to a donkey as it suits his pleasure."

"That's impossible," the king said. "I've had that horse for five years."

"Impossible or not," Shahkro answered. "Here I am the same as I started out for home five days ago. Here is the same bridle in my hands. Here is the same black animal under me. And it's a donkey."

The king looked at the saddle and at the bridle. He ran his hand over the donkey's flank. "Well, all I can say in apology is that he never did it while I rode him. But let's forget all that. When are you going to try to trick me?"

"Right now," Shahkro said. "Sit down. Answer me a question. You claimed you were a trickster. Did you ever use any tools?"

"No."

"Then why did you think I would? So there I tricked you once. In all the years you had your black dog, did he ever talk to you?"

"No."

"Then why did you think he would talk

to me? I tricked you twice. In all the years you had your black horse did he ever turn into a donkey for you?"

"No."

"Then why should he for me? There I tricked you three times. Now pay me and I will go."

The king saw he had one last chance to redeem his reputation as a trickster so he said, "Remember, for your reward I promised only what I wouldn't miss. You must choose something I never use or otherwise I would miss it. Now what shall it be?"

"Your head," Shahkro answered.

When the king heard this he began to shake and turn so green that Shahkro took pity on him. "Wait," he said, "I will take another reward. Because on second thought you do use your head. It keeps your hat from lying on your shoulders. Give me instead your forest and all the fields around it for my village people to use for their own."

"Certainly," said the king, and he called his viziers and sealed the agreement right there and gave it to Shahkro. "And now I don't want to keep you for I know you are anxious to get home."

Shahkro went back to his village and in honor he lived there all his life.

As for the king, after that he didn't have to worry any more whether or not he was the trickiest man in the world, so I suppose he slept very well. Or maybe because he was a king he found a new worry to keep him awake.

Padre Ulivo and His Guests

*The pilgrims shook their heads
at the foolishness of the old man and only hoped
his three silly wishes would do him no harm*

PETER LUM

In a little village, scarcely larger than a hamlet, on the road from Ostia to Rome there once lived a man who was known to everyone in the neighborhood as Padre Ulivo, or Father Ulivo. Padre Ulivo was a poor man, but he was generous and always ready to share what he had with those who were poorer than himself. Pilgrims on the way to Rome, peasants who were out of work, beggars, all stopped at his little house when they were in need. They knew that he would give them anything he could possibly spare.

One winter day, about noon, Padre Ulivo heard a knock on his door. He opened it, and his heart sank. There at the door were no less than a dozen pilgrims, all of whom looked hungry and thirsty and cold. And Padre Ulivo knew very well that he had only half a loaf of bread in his cupboard, half a bottle of wine in his cellar and no firewood at all to put on the embers of his dying fire.

"Well," he thought to himself. "A dying fire is better than none; a crumb and a sip of wine are better than an empty stomach."

Aloud he said, "Come in, come in!" welcoming his unexpected guests as warmly as he could. He led them to the fire, or what was left of the fire, and found enough chairs and benches for all twelve of them to sit down.

"I am sorry I have so little to offer you," he told them. "I was not expecting many pilgrims to come this way at this time of year. There is only one loaf—no, half a loaf—of bread in the house."

"Do not worry," said the man who seemed to be in charge of the party of pilgrims, "I am sure that half a loaf will do us very well."

Padre Ulivo went into his kitchen and opened the cupboard where he kept his bread. To his astonishment he found there a baker's dozen, which is thirteen, small loaves of fresh-baked bread. What was even more surprising was that on the shelf

426

above, which he knew perfectly well had been bare an hour before, was a whole Gorgonzola cheese and more than a pound of fresh butter.

He carried all this back to the room where his guests were warming themselves by the fire. "By some miracle—" he started to say, and then he stopped dead, staring at the fire. Half a dozen good pine logs were crackling merrily away in the grate, with flames high up the chimney, where before there had been only a few charred and broken sticks. Several other logs were stacked beside the fireplace.

By this time Padre Ulivo realized that a miracle really was happening. He decided that it would be better not to be surprised by anything or at least not to show his surprise. So he simply spread the table for his visitors and invited them to eat.

"Have you any wine in your cellar?" asked the leader of the pilgrims.

"Half a bot—" began Padre Ulivo, and then he stopped himself. "I will go and see," he said.

He was not really surprised when he climbed down into the cellar to find a dozen bottles of good red wine on shelves that he had seen empty that very morning.

So it was that Padre Ulivo and his guests had a good meal, beside a warm fire. When they had finished the party took their leave, saying that they hoped to reach Rome that night, and each one shook Padre Ulivo by the hand and thanked him for his hospitality.

When the last of the pilgrims, who was also the youngest, came to say good-bye, he said to Padre Ulivo, "You should have asked our leader for a boon. He would have granted you anything in the world, or for that matter out of the world, that you asked him for."

"How can he do that?" asked Padre Ulivo.

"Do you not, then, know who we are?"

"I do not. Except that you are clearly no ordinary band of pilgrims."

"We are the disciples of Christ," said the young man. "And He who leads us is our Lord Himself."

When he heard this Padre Ulivo ran after the Leader of the supposed pilgrims, fell on his knees and kissed the hem of His robe.

"Will you grant me a boon?" he asked.

"Gladly," said the Lord. "What is it you want?"

"I would like it to be so that anyone who sits down in the chair beside my fireplace is unable to rise again unless I wish him to do so."

"Well, if that is what you want, so be it," said the Lord.

He went on His way. Then the youngest disciple, who had been listening, said to Padre Ulivo, "That is a foolish wish. Ask for something else."

"Do you really think I could ask another boon?"

"I am sure you could."

So Padre Ulivo ran after the Lord again and asked for a second boon.

"Gladly," said the Lord. "What is it you want?"

"I should like it to be so that if anyone climbs the cherry tree in my garden he cannot come down again until I wish him to do so."

"Well, if that is what you want, so be it," said the Lord.

The youngest disciple, having also listened to this conversation, sighed. "What did you want to ask that for?" he said. "It will do you no good to have someone stuck in your cherry tree. Ask for something else."

"You mean I could ask yet another boon?" said Padre Ulivo.

"I think so. But that will be the last. No man ever receives more than three."

So Padre Ulivo ran down the road after

427

the Lord again and asked for a third boon.

"Very well," said the Lord. "But this is the last one. What do you want?"

"I want it to be so that if I play at cards, I always win."

"Well, if that is what you want, so be it," said the Lord.

Then He and His Disciples went on their way, shaking their heads sadly over the foolishness of mankind. "He could have asked for the salvation of his soul," said the youngest disciple, "or he could at least have asked for long life, or happiness or wealth here on earth."

"I know," said the Lord. "But you could not tell him that. He had to choose for himself. Let us hope that at least his three foolish wishes will do him no harm."

In fact, for a long time Padre Ulivo's three boons made no difference to his life at all. He never played cards. And he had no reason to keep anyone sitting in his chair or up the cherry tree.

It was one day in February, many years later, that a thin, dark man knocked on the door and said to Padre Ulivo, "Come with me."

"I know you," said Padre Ulivo. "You are Death."

"Yes."

"Well, I suppose it is no use arguing with Death," said Padre Ulivo. "If you want me, I must come. Just give me a few minutes to get ready. Here—sit down in the chair by the fire."

Death sat down. A few minutes later Padre Ulivo said that he was ready to go, and Death started to get up, only to find that he could not.

"What have you done?" he demanded angrily, trying to push himself out of the chair. "What sort of a trick is this?"

"An enchanted chair," said Padre Ulivo as though it were the most natural thing in the world. "You cannot get up until I want you to."

"How long do you propose to keep me here, then? I cannot waste time like this. I have work to do."

"Only until you promise to go away and not come back again for another three hundred years."

Death promised. He could not really do otherwise, unless he was willing to go on sitting beside the fire for all eternity.

Three hundred years went by. As far as Padre Ulivo was concerned, they went much too quickly. He was still enjoying life when Death returned at the end of the three centuries, and he wanted to go on enjoying it. "Just make yourself comfortable," he said to Death, "while I get ready."

"You can have exactly five minutes to get ready," Death told him sternly. "And no more of your tricks, mind. I will not sit down anywhere while I wait."

"I don't blame you," said Padre Ulivo sympathetically. "Why not go out in the garden and wait for me there?"

So Death unsuspectingly walked out into the garden, which was really not much of a garden, being small and neglected. It did however have a few fruit trees, including one cherry tree whose branches were heavy just then with beautiful ripe black cherries.

"Help yourself to the cherries," Padre Ulivo called out of the window. "I won't be needing them, I will be dead so soon."

Death picked a few of the cherries and found that they were as good as they looked, or even better. But of course, as always happens, the biggest and best fruit was just beyond his reach. So it was that Death, quite without thinking, climbed a little way up the cherry tree. Then he climbed further and further, picking only the very best of the cherries.

"I am ready," said Padre Ulivo from the bottom of the tree a few minutes later. "Shall we go?"

Death started to climb down. But he could not move. Or, rather, he could go on climbing up but the minute he tried to take a step down he was stuck.

"You wretch!" he cried. "You have tricked me again."

"I am afraid I have," chuckled Padre Ulivo. "How about another three hundred years?"

Once again, Death promised. He really had no choice.

Padre Ulivo enjoyed his next three centuries almost as much as the last three. But he knew he could not live forever. The next time Death came he was ready and waiting for him—which was just as well, because

Death stood outside the gate, looking neither to the right nor the left, and shouted at him. "Come at once!" he cried. "And no more tricks this time. I am waiting right here until you come."

Padre Ulivo took a last look at the little house where he had lived for six hundred and sixty-one years and sighed, and then he went along with Death.

"About time too," said the latter. "But you have nothing to worry about. You just follow that road there up to Heaven. I suppose, in spite of your tricks, that you will be allowed into Heaven."

Padre Ulivo thereupon set off along the winding road that led to Heaven. He had only gone a very short distance when he came to the outer gate of Hell, and saw the Devil sitting there, and heard the voices of a great many of the souls in Hell calling out for help. He stopped.

"What do you want?" the Devil demanded suspiciously.

"I am on my way to Heaven," Padre Ulivo told him. "And I am afraid that once I am inside Heaven I will never get a game of cards again. I was thinking how nice it would be to have one last game."

"Why not?" said the Devil, thinking he saw a way to get Padre Ulivo into Hell instead of Heaven. "I will play with you."

He brought out the cards and Padre Ulivo sat down beside him, there at the entrance to Hell. "What do you want to play for?" the Devil asked him.

"My soul," said Padre Ulivo promptly. "My soul against a dozen of the other souls you already have here in Hell."

The Devil could hardly believe his ears. He knew every card trick there was; he had never yet lost a game to anyone. And here was this foolish man offering to gamble his own soul away! "That suits me," he said, dealing the cards.

Of course Padre Ulivo won. The Devil had to release a dozen souls from Hell and hand them over to his opponent. Moreover he was so sure that there had been a mistake, and that he could not possibly lose another game, that he insisted on playing with Padre Ulivo again and again, and always for the same stake.

They played and played. Each time Padre Ulivo won another dozen souls. Finally, when Hell was almost empty, the Devil realized that he had been tricked and that he could never win. He threw the cards angrily down on the ground, slammed shut the gates of Hell and dis-

appeared. Padre Ulivo shrugged his shoulders and started off again on his way towards Heaven.

He was however now followed by several hundred other souls, who, having thus unexpectedly escaped from Hell, had nowhere else to go. When this crowd arrived at the gates of Heaven Saint Peter looked at them scornfully.

"What are you all doing here?" he demanded. "You people have no right to enter Heaven. Go back where you came from at once." Then he turned to Padre Ulivo. "You can come in," he said. "Even though you have been behaving rather strangely recently, I think you have enough credit in Heaven to be allowed to enter."

"Don't be silly," said Padre Ulivo. "How can I leave these hundreds of souls outside while I come in? They belong to me. They will have to come into Heaven with me."

"That is quite out of the question," Saint Peter retorted.

"Well then, before we go, will you give the Lord a message for me?"

"If you like."

"Just tell the Lord that when He came to the gate of my house, I did not ask Him who His friends were or say that they were too many to come in. I opened the door to them all. Ask the Lord, please, whether He wants to have it said that a poor human being is more hospitable than He Himself?"

The answer that came back was what Padre Ulivo had known it must be. He and his friends, whoever they were and however many they might be, were welcome in Heaven. And so Padre Ulivo, as a result of his three foolish wishes, not only saved his own soul but a great many others as well.

HERBERT'S WAVE

*When four young boys find an unused home permanent-
wave kit, they would never think of letting it
go to waste—not when the milkman's horse has a tail
and a mane that are as straight as a yardstick*

Hazel Wilson

When the Yadons' neighbors, the Barlows, were moving away, naturally Herbert, Pete, Donny and Chuck were interested in the contents of the Barlows' trash cans, for they knew that people, when moving, often throw out things more or less useful to boys. There were two trash cans piled high at the back of the house, and the boys went over their contents thoroughly.

"Do you think we want this lampshade that's only bashed in a little on one side?" asked Pete, holding up a hideous rose-colored object, dripping with ragged fringe.

"Nope," replied Herbert. "We don't have electric lights in the clubhouse, so I don't know what we could use a lampshade for. It looks almost too good to throw away, but I guess we don't want it."

Donny dug out a two-handled vase with only one handle gone, and Chuck dragged out a small moth-eaten rug from one trash can while Herbert discovered two nicked cups and a china pitcher with part of the spout gone in the other can of rubbish. These were carefully put aside as things of value.

"Guess we can just about finish our clubhouse with the things the Barlows are throwing away," said Herbert. "Say, here's a picture of a man leaning on a hoe and there's not a thing the matter with it."

"Any picture of a hoe makes me feel tired just to look at it," remarked Pete, who hated to dig in his mother's flower garden.

431

"Well, if we don't want it maybe we can trade it for something," said Herbert, putting the picture with the things to be saved. Then he picked up a small pasteboard box. "What's this?" he asked and then read what was printed on the box, THE JIFFY HOME PERMANENT WAVE. Inside the box were two bottles full of milky-colored liquid and a lot of plastic thingamajigs. There was also a leaflet of instructions.

"Heave it back," said Chuck. "We don't want any of that stuff."

"It cost a dollar and seventy-nine cents without tax," read Herbert from the box. "And it's all here. There's nothing missing. It seems sort of a shame to throw away something not a bit used that cost a dollar and seventy-nine cents without tax."

Pete suggested that maybe the drugstore would take it back and give them the dollar and seventy-nine cents. Pete took after his father, the mayor, in having a good head for business.

That idea met with instant approval. The boys rushed to the drugstore, but Mr. Mulock, the druggist, said that he had never carried that brand of home permanent, which was a discontinued brand, anyway. "Guess you're stuck with it, boys," he said. "Unless you want to give yourselves curls," he chuckled, with both chins shaking.

Herbert shook back the lock of straight hair that so often fell on his forehead. "I wouldn't be caught dead with curly hair," he told Mr. Mulock, and he stalked from the store, with the rest of his gang trailing after him.

Herbert was just about to throw the permanent-wave kit away permanently, when he thought better of it. "I wonder if this stuff really works," he mused. "I know some real straight hair we could try it on."

"You won't catch me curling a girl's hair," stated Pete firmly. "I wouldn't give any old girl curls for a million dollars, or a thousand or a hundred, anyway."

"Who said anything about curling girls' hair? What do you think I am?" asked Herbert indignantly. "Girls aren't the only ones who have hair in this town."

"We might try curling Old Man Jenkins' beard," suggested Chuck. "But I guess we'd have to knock him unconscious before he'd let us. And I wouldn't want to do that. He gave me a nickel once."

"My father's so bald it wouldn't be much use trying to give him a permanent wave," said Donny. "And what hair he has is already curly. And my mother doesn't approve of home permanents. She always gets hers at the beauty shop."

"I wasn't thinking of people," explained Herbert. "Animals, except for curly kinds of dogs, often have very straight hair. I'm thinking in particular," said Herbert, "of Creepy, the milkman's horse. His mane and tail are as straight as a yardstick. It might be sort of fun to give Old Creepy a permanent wave in his mane and tail."

The thought of Old Creepy with curly hair seemed excruciatingly funny to Pete, Donny and Chuck. They doubled up with laughter. Pete was the first to recover enough to talk. "Think Creepy would stand still long enough for us to curl him?" he asked Herbert.

"Creepy'd rather stand still than anything else in the world," stated Herbert. "He'd rather stand still than go any time. And if we give him some oats in his nose bag, he'll stand without hitching no matter what we do to him."

The boys forgot to go over the rest of the Barlows' trash, they were now so interested in giving Creepy, the milkman's horse, a home permanent. Herbert read in the leaflet of directions that hair had to be shampooed before it could be curled, so he went home for a washbasin and a bar of yellow soap. Chuck and Donny brought bath towels, and Pete came out of his house lugging a twelve-quart galvanized iron pail to be used for lugging water for the shampoo and rinsing. Herbert thought that warm water would be the best for the shampoo and suggested that Pete lug the pail full of hot water out to the barn where Creepy was kept. Pete said "nothing doing" to that. He was not going to lug a heavy pail of hot water half a mile or so for any horse. Besides, he said, the water would be cold by the time he got there. There would be sure to be a cold water faucet somewhere near the barn, he insisted. And cold water was good enough for any horse.

Creepy's barn was across the road and down a piece from the dairy, which would make it easier for the boys to do their beauty work without being disturbed. Nobody had ever told them not to give a horse a permanent wave, but they thought it best to keep what they were doing to themselves.

They found the barn door locked, but there was a window that Pete, the skinniest one of them, could be boosted through. He unlocked the door from the inside, and the boys made a beeline for Creepy's stall.

Creepy, as usual, was standing still. He was not interested enough even to look at his visitors.

Herbert and Pete set to work on the front end of the horse, while Chuck and Donny labored on the tail. Both ends of Creepy were doused with water, and the boys took turns rubbing on the yellow soap as they gave Creepy a shampoo at each end.

Except for a shudder when the cold water first hit him, Creepy paid little attention to what was being done to him. A nose bag of oats kept him contented and occupied. He paid not a bit of attention to the shouts of "Back up" and "Whoa," given by the boys working on him. Creepy just moved as he pleased. The boys sort of had to follow him all over the stall.

Chuck and Donny complained that it was harder to get Creepy's tail up on curlers than his mane. The hair was coarser and harder to roll, they insisted. Herbert, after finishing his half of Creepy's mane, had to help with the tail. "Pass me another curler," he ordered. "We might as well use all we have. We want to do a good job on Creepy."

At last all the curlers that had been in the permanent-wave kit were on Creepy. He was quite a sight, standing there in his stall, with his mane and tail all rolled up on plastic thingamajigs. The boys had to sit down and laugh a while before they could go on with their work.

The boys dabbled the rest of the waving lotion on the curlers and fed Creepy a few apples to keep him happy while the wave was waving or whatever the stuff did to hair. Then Herbert mixed some powder from an envelope in a pail of water and emptied half of it over the horse's head and the other half over his tail.

"That's supposed to set the wave," he said, getting out of Creepy's way, for the horse was showing his first objection to what was being done to him. He kicked and bared his teeth until Herbert soothed him down with some sugar lumps he had brought along in his pocket just for that purpose. It took quite a few sugar lumps and some more oats in his nose bag before Creepy would stand still again and let the boys touch him.

By that time, however, it was time to take off the curlers, which the boys did, being careful not to pull Creepy's hair. Then a final dousing with water, and the work was done. There stood Creepy, a big bony white horse with his mane and tail in tight curls.

"I don't know if he looks better but he *does* look different," said Herbert.

"He's the funniest looking horse I ever saw in my life," chuckled Pete. And he and the other boys laughed until they nearly cried.

Although the dairy was across the road and down a piece from Creepy's barn, the boys laughed so hard and so loud that Mr. Butterworth, the milkman, heard them and came to see what was so funny. He could hardly believe his eyes when he beheld Creepy's curls. His face grew red and the boys were afraid he was dreadfully angry with them but it turned out that he was on the point of bursting out laughing, which he did. "Whoever heard of giving a horse a permanent wave?" he kept asking between fits of laughter.

News of what the boys had done to Creepy soon spread around town and quite a few people came to look at the horse with

the curly mane and tail. And they all came out laughing. They had never seen such a funny-looking horse in all their lives, they said, wiping their eyes.

Herbert felt quite pleased with all the notice being taken of Creepy's curls until some boys, not friends of Herbert's, called him "Herbert, the hairdresser."

Now the only hairdresser in Mapleton was a frizzy-haired lady by the name of Miss Eloise Bean, and Herbert felt that calling him a hairdresser was calling him a female or at least a sissy. Besides, he felt it was not fair for him to be singled out for insult, when Pete, Donny and Chuck had done almost as much work on Creepy as he had. But, "Herbert, the hairdresser! Hairdresser Herbert!" were the taunts that met Herbert's ears, even when Pete, Chuck and Donny were with him. It made Herbert

fighting mad, and he did give one of his hecklers a black eye and would have sicked Mortimer on him if Mortimer had been a sicking sort of dog. But in spite of the fact that Herbert was handy with his fists, there were boys in town who went on daring to call him "Hairdresser Herbert" before taking to their heels. Herbert began to wish he never had heard of a permanent wave. Even some grown-ups teased Herbert about giving Creepy a permanent. "I hear you've gone into the beauty business," Mr. Mulock, the druggist said, when Herbert went in for an ice cream cone. It got so that Herbert dreaded to meet people on the street for fear they would mention permanent waves to him. It became a sore subject with Herbert.

He was relieved when the circus made its annual visit to Mapleton, for that, he thought, would give people something else to talk about. Besides, the manager of the circus was a friend of Herbert's. Several years before, Herbert had presented the circus with his collection of small wild animals, for which the manager had been most grateful. The small wild animals were no longer small (wild animals do grow so fast) yet Herbert always came to see them, although only the lion cub, now a full-grown king of beasts, seemed to remember him.

The circus train came in before dawn and Herbert went to call on the manager and on his former pets before breakfast. He found the circus manager feeling most discouraged. His usually pink cheeks were pale and his black mustache that had turned briskly up at the ends the last time Herbert had seen him, now drooped sadly.

"Like hair needing a permanent wave," Herbert thought, forgetting for a moment that he never wanted to have "permanent" mentioned, even in his own thoughts. But, what was the matter with his friend, the circus manager?

"The snap, the zip, the sparkle and the gump have just gone out of the show," said the manager. But he took Herbert around the circus lot, and nothing looked as beautiful and attractive as it had to Herbert the year before. Even the hair of the beautiful lady bareback riders looked limp and straight. And so did the former lion cub's mane and tail. But the former lion cub seemed to know Herbert and almost wagged its tail.

"I'm afraid he hasn't grown into a very kingly-looking king of beasts," the circus manager apologized. "With all that straight hair falling over his eyes, he doesn't look as fierce as a hairy dog."

Just then the circus manager happened to look up the road and saw Creepy on his way back to his stable after delivering the morning milk.

"What," asked the circus manager, "might that creature be? In all my days I've never seen the like."

"Oh, that's just an old horse we boys gave a permanent wave," said Herbert.

The circus manager stared and stared. Then he slapped his leg. "What this circus needs is some kinks put in instead of taken out," he remarked. "Before the afternoon performance I shall have every lady in the show go and get permanent waves at the beauty shop. But it would help, I think, if somebody curled the lion's mane. Do you think you'd dare tackle curling the lion's mane, Herbert?"

Herbert thought he dared to do almost anything, but he had never dreamed of curling a lion's hair. But he did want to help his friend, the circus manager, so, although he had vowed never to have anything to do with another permanent wave, he helped two experienced animal men wave the lion's mane. Even though the lion seemed to remember Herbert, it was thought best to tie the lion so securely that it could not harm him. And even with the help of the two experienced animal men, Herbert was relieved to get the job done. The lion's mane came out nice and curly. It made him look like another lion, a much smarter and fiercer one.

Then the circus manager waxed his mustache until it turned up again and not down, and the beautiful lady bareback riders came back from the beauty shop with beautiful curly hair, and that afternoon the circus put on a very fine performance.

Everybody clapped when the curly-headed lion leaped through hoops and did other tricks that circus lions do. The circus manager, who was also the lion trainer, when he had a different hat on, came out three times and bowed at the applause. Then he made a speech publicly thanking Herbert for his help in getting the lion ready for the show. "This brave lad actually dared curl the lion's mane," he said, and the audience clapped again, this time for Herbert.

Nobody chased Herbert after that, yelling, "Hairdresser Herbert," for nobody dared tease a boy brave enough and bold enough to curl a lion's mane.

In a month or so Creepy's mane and tail began to get droopy again. And Mr. Butterworth, the dairyman, was so used by this time to driving a horse with curly hair that he came to Herbert to see about having Creepy given another permanent wave.

"No," said Herbert, "I shall never give another permanent wave to any man or beast under any circumstances. From now on the only wave I'm ever going to give anybody is a wave of my hand in farewell."

RIP VAN WINKLE

It seemed like any other bright sunny morning.
The birds were hopping and twittering. But what,
Rip wondered, was he doing up here on the mountain
and not at home in his own bed?

WASHINGTON IRVING

Whoever has made a voyage up the Hudson must remember the Kaatskill Mountains. They are a dismembered branch of the great Appalachian family and are seen away to the west of the river, swelling up to a noble height and lording it over the surrounding country. Every change of season, every change of weather, indeed, every hour of the day, produces some change in the magical hues and shapes of these mountains, and they are regarded by all the good wives, far and near, as perfect barometers. When the weather is fair and settled, they are clothed in blue and purple, and print their bold outlines on the clear evening sky; but, sometimes, when the rest of the landscape is cloudless, they will gather a hood of gray vapors about their summits, which, in the last rays of the setting sun, will glow and light up like a crown of glory.

At the foot of these fairy mountains, the voyager may have descried the light smoke curling up from a village whose shingle roofs gleam among the trees, just where the blue tints of the upland melt away into the fresh green of the nearer landscape. It is a little village of great antiquity, having been founded by some of the Dutch colonists, in the early times of the province, and there were some of the houses of the original settlers, built of small yellow bricks brought from Holland, having latticed windows and gable fronts, surmounted with weathercocks.

In that same village, and in one of these very houses (which, to tell the precise truth, was sadly timeworn and weather-beaten), there lived many years since, while the country was yet a province of Great Britain, a simple good-natured fellow of the name of Rip Van Winkle. He was a descendant of the Van Winkles who figured so gallantly in the chivalrous days of Peter Stuyvesant, and accompanied him to the siege of Fort Christina. He inherited, however, but little of the martial character of his ancestors. I have observed that he was a simple, good-natured man; he was, moreover, a kind neighbor and an obedient, henpecked husband. Indeed, to the latter circumstance might be owing that meekness of spirit which gained him such universal popularity.

Certain it is, that he was a great favorite among all the good wives of the village, who, as usual, with the amiable sex, took his part in all family squabbles; and never failed, whenever they talked those matters over in their evening gossipings, to lay all the blame on Dame Van Winkle. The children of the village, too, would shout with joy whenever he approached. He assisted at their sports, made their playthings, taught them to fly kites and shoot marbles, and told them long stories of ghosts, witches and Indians. Whenever he went dodging about the village, he was surrounded by a troop of them, hanging on his skirts, clambering on his back and playing a thousand tricks on him with impunity; and not a dog would bark at him throughout the neighborhood.

The great error in Rip's composition was an insuperable aversion to all kinds of profitable labor. It could not be from the want of assiduity or perseverance; for he would sit on a wet rock, with a rod as long and heavy as a Tartar's lance, and fish all day without a murmur, even though he should not be encouraged by a single nibble. He would carry a fowling piece on his shoulder for hours together, trudging through woods and swamps, and up hill and down dale, to shoot a few squirrels or wild pigeons. He would never refuse to assist a neighbor even in the roughest toil, and was a foremost man at all country frolics for husking Indian corn, or building stone fences; the women of the village, too, used to employ him to run their errands, and to do such little odd jobs as their less obliging husbands would not do for them. In a word Rip was ready to attend to anybody's business but his own; but as to doing family duty and keeping his farm in order, he found it impossible.

In fact, he declared it was of no use to work on his farm; it was the most pestilent little piece of ground in the whole country; everything about it went wrong, and would go wrong, in spite of him; though his patrimonial estate had dwindled away under his management until there was little more left than a mere patch of Indian corn and potatoes, yet it was the worst conditioned farm in the neighborhood.

His children, too, were as ragged and wild as if they belonged to nobody. His son Rip, an urchin begotten in his own likeness, promised to inherit the habits, with the old clothes of his father. He was generally seen trooping like a colt at his mother's heels, equipped in a pair of his father's cast-off breeches, which he had much ado to hold up with one hand, as a fine lady does her train in bad weather.

Rip Van Winkle, however, was one of those happy mortals, of foolish, well-oiled dispositions, who take the world easy, eat

white bread or brown, whichever can be got with least thought or trouble, and would rather starve on a penny than work for a pound. If left to himself, he would have whistled life away in perfect contentment; but his wife kept continually dinning in his ears about his idleness, his carelessness and the ruin he was bringing on his family. Morning, noon and night, her tongue was incessantly going, and everything he said or did was sure to produce a torrent of household eloquence. Rip had but one way of replying to all lectures of the kind, and that, by frequent use, had grown into a habit. He shrugged his shoulders, shook his head, cast up his eyes, but said nothing. This however, always provoked a fresh volley from his wife; so that he was fain to draw off his forces and take to the outside of the house.

Rip's sole domestic adherent was his dog Wolf, who was as much henpecked as his master; for Dame Van Winkle regarded them as companions in idleness, and even looked upon Wolf with an evil eye, as the cause of his master's going so often astray. True it is, in all points of spirit befitting an honorable dog, he was as courageous an animal as ever scoured the woods—but what courage can withstand the ever-during and all-besetting terrors of a woman's tongue? The moment Wolf entered the house his crest fell, his tail drooped to the ground or curled between his legs, he sneaked about with a gallows air, casting many a sidelong glance at Dame Van Winkle, and at the least flourish of a broomstick or ladle, he would fly to the door with yelping precipitation.

Times grew worse and worse with Rip Van Winkle as years of matrimony rolled on; a tart temper never mellows with age, and a sharp tongue is the only edged tool that grows keener with constant use. For a long while he used to console himself, when driven from home, by frequenting a kind of perpetual club of the sages, philosophers and other idle personages of the village; which held its sessions on a bench before a small inn, designated by a rubicund portrait of His Majesty George the Third. Here they used to sit in the shade through a long lazy summer's day, talking listlessly over village gossip, or telling endless sleepy stories about nothing. But it would have been worth any statesman's money to have heard the profound discussions that sometimes took place, when by chance an old newspaper fell into their hands from some passing traveler. How solemnly they would listen to the contents, as drawled out by Derrick Van Bummel, the schoolmaster, a dapper learned little man, who was not to be daunted by the most gigantic word in the dictionary; and how sagely they would deliberate upon the public events some months after they had taken place.

The opinions of this junto were completely controlled by Nicholas Vedder, a patriarch of the village and landlord of the inn, at the door of which he took his seat from morning till night, just moving sufficiently to avoid the sun and keep in the shade of a large tree; so that the neighbors could tell the hour by his movements as accurately as by a sundial. It is true he was rarely heard to speak, but smoked his pipe incessantly. His adherents, however (for every great man has his adherents), perfectly understood him and knew how to gather his opinions. When anything that was read or related displeased him, he was observed to smoke his pipe vehemently, and to send forth short, frequent and angry puffs; but when pleased, he would inhale the smoke slowly and tranquilly, and emit it in light and placid clouds; and sometimes, taking the pipe from his mouth, and letting the fragrant vapor curl about his nose, would gravely nod.

From even this stronghold the unlucky Rip was at length routed by his termagant wife, who would suddenly break in upon the tranquillity of the assemblage and call the members all to naught; nor was that august personage, Nicholas Vedder himself, sacred from the daring tongue of this terrible virago, who charged him outright with encouraging her husband in habits of idleness.

Poor Rip was at last reduced almost to despair; and his only alternative, to escape from the labor of the farm and clamor of his wife, was to take gun in hand and stroll away into the woods. Here he would some-times seat himself at the foot of a tree and share the contents of his knapsack with Wolf, with whom he sympathized as a fellow sufferer in persecution. "Poor Wolf," he would say, "thy mistress leads thee a dog's life of it; but never mind, my lad, whilst I live thou shalt never want a friend to stand by thee!" Wolf would wag his tail, look wistfully in his master's face, and if dogs can feel pity I verily believe he reciprocated the sentiment with all his heart.

In a long ramble of the kind on a fine autumnal day, Rip had unconsciously scrambled to one of the highest parts of the Kaatskill Mountains. He was after his favorite sport of squirrel shooting, and the still solitudes had echoed and reechoed with the reports of his gun. Panting and fatigued, he threw himself, late in the afternoon, on a green knoll, covered with mountain herbage, that crowned the brow of a precipice. From an opening between the trees he could overlook all the lower country for many a mile of rich woodland. He saw at a distance the lordly Hudson, far, far below him, moving on its silent but majestic course, with the reflection of a purple cloud, or the sail of a lagging bark here and there on its glassy bosom.

On the other side he looked down into a deep mountain glen, wild, lonely and shagged, the bottom filled with fragments from the impending cliffs, and scarcely lighted by the reflected rays of the setting sun. For some time Rip lay musing on this scene; evening was gradually advancing; the mountains began to throw their long blue shadows over the valleys; he saw that it would be dark long before he could reach the village, and he heaved a heavy sigh when he thought of encountering the terrors of Dame Van Winkle.

As he was about to descend, he heard a voice from a distance, hallooing, "Rip Van Winkle! Rip Van Winkle!" He looked round, but could see nothing but a crow winging its solitary flight across the mountain. He thought his fancy must have deceived him and turned again to descend, when he heard the same cry ring through the still evening air: "Rip Van Winkle! Rip Van Winkle!" At the same time Wolf bristled up his back and, giving a low growl, skulked to his master's side, looking fearfully down into the glen. Rip now felt a vague apprehension stealing over him; he looked anxiously in the same direction and perceived a strange figure slowly toiling up the rocks and bending under the weight of something he carried on his back. He was surprised to see any human being in this lonely and unfrequented place, but supposing it to be someone of the neighborhood in need of his assistance, he hastened down to yield it.

On nearer approach he was still more surprised at the singularity of the stranger's appearance. He was a short square-built old fellow, with thick bushy hair and a grizzled beard. His dress was of the antique Dutch fashion—a cloth jerkin strapped round the waist—several pair of breeches, the outer one of ample volume, decorated with rows of buttons down the sides. He bore on his shoulder a stout keg that seemed full of liquor and made signs for Rip to approach and assist him with the load. Though rather shy and distrustful of this new acquaintance, Rip complied with his usual alacrity; and mutually relieving one another, they clambered up a narrow gully, apparently the dry bed of a mountain torrent. As they ascended, Rip every now and then heard long rolling peals, like distant thunder, that seemed to issue from out a deep ravine, or rather cleft, between lofty rocks, toward which their rugged path conducted. He paused for an instant, but supposing it to be the muttering of one of those transient thundershowers which often take place in mountain heights, he

proceeded. Passing through the ravine, they came to a hollow, like a small amphitheater, surrounded by perpendicular precipices, over the brinks of which impending trees shot their branches, so that you only caught glimpses of the azure sky and the bright evening cloud. During the whole time Rip and his companion had labored on in silence; for though the former marveled greatly what could be the object of carrying a keg of liquor up this wild mountain, yet there was something strange and incomprehensible about the unknown, that inspired awe and checked familiarity.

On entering the amphitheater, new objects of wonder presented themselves. On a level spot in the center was a company of odd-looking personages playing at ninepins. They were dressed in a quaint outlandish fashion; some wore short doublets, others jerkins, with long knives in their belts, and most of them had enormous breeches of similar style to that of the guide's. Their visages, too, were peculiar: one had a large beard, broad face and small piggish eyes; the face of another seemed to consist entirely of nose, and was surmounted by a white sugar-loaf hat set off with a little red cock's tail. They all had beards, of various shapes and colors. There was one who seemed to be the commander. He was a stout old gentleman, with a weather-beaten countenance; he wore a laced doublet, broad belt and hanger, high-crowned hat and feather, red stockings and high-heeled shoes with roses in them. The whole group reminded Rip of the figures in an old Flemish painting in the parlor of Dominie Van Shaick, the village parson, and which had been brought over from Holland at the time of the settlement.

What seemed particularly odd to Rip was, that though these folks were evidently amusing themselves, yet they maintained the gravest faces, the most mysterious si-

lence, and were, withal, the most melancholy party of pleasure he had ever witnessed. Nothing interrupted the stillness of the scene but the noise of the balls, which, whenever they were rolled, echoed along the mountains like thunder.

As Rip and his companion approached them, they suddenly desisted from their play, and stared at him with such fixed statuelike gaze and such strange, uncouth, lackluster countenances that his heart turned within him and his knees smote together. His companion now emptied the contents of the keg into large flagons, and made signs to him to wait upon the company. He obeyed with fear and trembling; they quaffed the liquor in profound silence, and then returned to their game.

By degrees Rip's awe and apprehension subsided. He even ventured, when no eye was fixed upon him, to taste the beverage, which he found had much of the flavor of excellent Hollands. He was naturally a thirsty soul, and was soon tempted to repeat the draught. One taste provoked another; and he reiterated his visits to the flagon so often that at length his senses were overpowered, his eyes swam in his head, his head gradually declined and he fell into a deep sleep.

On waking, he found himself on the green knoll whence he had first seen the old man of the glen. He rubbed his eyes—it was a bright sunny morning. The birds were hopping and twittering among the bushes, and the eagle was wheeling aloft, and breasting the pure mountain breeze. "Surely," thought Rip, "I have not slept here all night." He recalled the occurrences before he fell asleep. The strange man with a keg of liquor—the mountain ravine—the wild retreat among the rocks —the woebegone party at ninepins—the flagon—"Oh! That Flagon! That wicked flagon!" thought Rip. "What excuse shall I make to Dame Van Winkle!"

He looked round for his gun, but in place of the clean well-oiled fowling piece, he found an old firelock lying by him, the barrel incrusted with rust, the lock falling off and the stock worm-eaten. He now suspected that the grave roisters of the mountain had tricked him and, having dosed him with liquor, had robbed him of his gun. Wolf, too, had disappeared, but he might have strayed away after a squirrel or partridge. He whistled after him and shouted his name, but all in vain; the echoes repeated his whistle and shout, but no dog was to be seen.

He determined to revisit the scene of the last evening's gambol, and if he met with any of the party, to demand his dog and gun. As he rose to walk, he found himself stiff in the joints, and wanting in his usual activity. "These mountain beds do not agree with me," thought Rip, "and if this frolic should lay me up with a fit of the rheumatism, I shall have a blessed time with Dame Van Winkle." With some difficulty he got down into the glen: he found the gully up which he and his companion had ascended the preceding evening; but to his astonishment a mountain stream was now foaming down it, leaping from rock to rock, and filling the glen with babbling murmurs. He, however, scrambled up its sides, working his toilsome way through thickets of birch, sassafras and witch hazel, and sometimes tripped up or entangled by the wild grapevines that twisted their coils or tendrils from tree to tree, and spread a kind of network in his path.

At length he reached to where the ravine had opened through the cliffs to the amphitheater, but no traces of such opening remained. The rocks presented a high impenetrable wall, over which the torrent came tumbling in a sheet of feathery foam and fell into a broad deep basin, black from the shadows of the surrounding forest. Here, then, poor Rip was brought to a stand. He again called and whistled after his dog; he was only answered by the cawing of a flock of idle crows, sporting high in air about a dry tree that overhung a sunny precipice; and who, secure in their elevation, seemed to look down and scoff at the poor man's perplexities. What was to be done? The morning was passing away, and Rip felt famished for want of his breakfast. He grieved to give up his dog and gun; he dreaded to meet his wife; but it would not do to starve among the mountains. He shook his head, shouldered the rusty firelock, and, with a heart full of anxiety, turned his steps homeward.

As he approached the village he met a number of people, but none whom he knew, which somewhat surprised him, for he had thought himself acquainted with everyone in the country round. Their dress, too, was of a different fashion from that to which he was accustomed. They all stared at him with equal marks of surprise, and whenever they cast their eyes upon him, invariably stroked their chins. The constant recurrence of this gesture induced Rip, involuntarily, to do the same, when, to his astonishment, he found his beard had grown a foot long!

He had now entered the skirts of the village. A troop of strange children ran at his heels, hooting after him and pointing at his gray beard. The dogs, too, not one of which he recognized for an old acquaintance, barked at him as he passed. The very village was altered; it was larger and more populous. There were rows of houses which he had never seen before, and those which had been his familiar haunts had disappeared. Strange names were over the doors—strange faces at the windows—everything was strange. His mind now misgave him; he began to doubt whether both he and the world around him were not bewitched. Surely this was his native village, which he had left but the day before. There stood the Kaatskill Mountains—there ran the silver Hudson at a distance—there was every hill and dale precisely as it had always been. Rip was sorely perplexed—"That flagon last night," thought he, "has addled my poor head sadly!"

It was with some difficulty that he found the way to his own house, which he approached with silent awe, expecting every moment to hear the shrill voice of Dame Van Winkle. He found the house gone to decay—the roof fallen in, the windows shattered, and the doors off the hinges. A half-starved dog that looked like Wolf was skulking about it. Rip called him by name, but the cur snarled, showed his teeth, and passed on. This was an unkind cut indeed— "My very dog," sighed poor Rip, "has forgotten me!"

He entered the house, which, to tell the truth, Dame Van Winkle had always kept in neat order. It was empty, forlorn, and apparently abandoned. This desolateness overcame all his connubial fears—he called loudly for his wife and children— the lonely chambers rang for a moment with his voice, and then all again was silence.

He now hurried forth and hastened to his old resort, the village inn—but it too was gone. A large rickety wooden building stood in its place, with great gaping windows, some of them broken and mended with old hats and petticoats, and over the door was painted "the Union Hotel, by Jonathan Doolittle." Instead of the great tree that used to shelter the quiet little Dutch inn of yore, there now was reared a tall naked pole, with something on the top that looked like a red nightcap, and from it was fluttering a flag, on which was a singular assemblage of stars and stripes—all this was strange and incomprehensible. He recognized on the sign, however, the ruby face of King George, under which he had smoked so many a peaceful pipe; but even this was singularly metamorphosed. The red coat was changed for one of blue and buff, a sword was held in the hand instead of a scepter, the head was decorated with a cocked hat, and underneath, was painted in large characters "GENERAL WASHINGTON."

There was, as usual, a crowd of folk about the door, but none that Rip recollected. The very character of the people seemed changed. There was a busy, bustling, disputatious tone about it, instead of the accustomed phlegm and drowsy tranquillity. He looked in vain for the sage Nicholas Vedder, with his broad face, double chin and fair long pipe, uttering clouds of tobacco smoke instead of idle speeches; or Van Bummel, the schoolmaster, doling forth the contents of an ancient newspaper. In place of these, a lean, bilious-looking fellow, with his pockets full of handbills, was haranguing vehemently about rights of citizens—elections—members of Congress—liberty—Bunker's Hill —heroes of seventy-six—and other words, which were a perfect Babylonish jargon to the bewildered Van Winkle.

The appearance of Rip, with his long grizzled beard, his rusty fowling piece, his uncouth dress and an army of women and children at his heels, soon attracted the attention of the tavern politicians. They crowded round him, eying him from head to foot with great curiosity. The orator bustled up to him, and, drawing him partly aside, inquired "On which side he voted?" Rip stared in vacant stupidity. Another short but busy little fellow pulled him by the arm, and, rising on tiptoe, inquired in his ear, "Whether he was Federal or Democrat?" Rip was equally at a loss to comprehend the question; when a knowing, self-important old gentleman, in a sharp cocked hat, made his way through the crowd, putting them to the right and left with his elbows as he passed, and planting himself before Van Winkle, with one arm akimbo, the other resting on his cane, his keen eyes and sharp hat penetrating, as it were, into his very soul, demanded in an austere tone, "What brought him to the election with a gun on his shoulder, and a mob at his heels, and whether he meant to breed a riot in the village?"

"Alas! Gentlemen," cried Rip, somewhat dismayed, "I am a poor quiet man, a native of the place, and a loyal subject of the king, God bless him!"

Here a general shout burst from the bystanders—"A tory! A tory! A spy! A refugee! Hustle him! Away with him!" It was with great difficulty that the self-important man in the cocked hat restored order; and, having assumed a tenfold austerity of brow, demanded again of the unknown culprit, what he came there for, and whom he was seeking? The poor man humbly assured him that he meant no harm, but merely came there in search of some of his neighbors, who used to keep about the tavern.

"Well—who are they? Name them."

Rip bethought himself a moment, and inquired, "Where's Nicholas Vedder?"

There was a silence for a little while, when an old man replied in a thin piping voice, "Nicholas Vedder! Why, he is dead and gone these eighteen years! There was a wooden tombstone in the churchyard that used to tell all about him, but that's rotten and gone too."

"Where's Brom Dutcher?"

"Oh, he went off to the army in the beginning of the war; some say he was killed at the storming of Stony Point—others say he was drowned in a squall at the foot of Antony's Nose. I don't know—he never came back again."

"Where's Van Bummel, the schoolmaster?"

"He went off to the wars too, was a great militia general, and is now in Congress."

Rip's heart died away at hearing of these sad changes in his home and friends, and finding himself thus alone in the world. Every answer puzzled him too, by treating of such enormous lapses of time, and of matters which he could not understand: war—congress—Stony Point; he had no courage to ask after any more friends, but cried out in despair, "Does nobody here know Rip Van Winkle?"

"Oh, Rip Van Winkle!" exclaimed two or three, "Oh, to be sure! That's Rip Van Winkle yonder, leaning against the tree."

Rip looked, and beheld a precise counterpart of himself, as he went up the mountain: apparently as lazy, and certainly as ragged. The poor fellow was now completely confounded. He doubted his own identity, and whether he was himself or another man. In the midst of his bewilderment, the man in the cocked hat demanded who he was, and what was his name?

"God knows," exclaimed he, at his wit's end. "I'm not myself—I'm somebody else—that's me yonder—no—that's somebody else got into my shoes—I was myself last night, but I fell asleep on the mountain, and they've changed my gun, and everything's changed, and I'm changed, and I can't tell my name, or who I am!"

The bystanders began now to look at each other, nod, wink significantly and tap their fingers against their foreheads. There was a whisper, also, about securing the gun, and keeping the old fellow from doing mischief, at the very suggestion of which the self-important man in the cocked hat retired with some precipitation. At this critical moment a fresh, comely woman pressed through the throng to get a peep at the gray-bearded man. She had a chubby child in her arms, which, frightened at his looks, began to cry. "Hush, Rip," cried she,

"Hush, you little fool; the old man won't hurt you." The name of the child, the air of the mother, the tone of her voice, all awakened a train of recollections in his mind. "What is your name, my good woman?" asked he.

"Judith Gardenier."

"And your father's name?"

"Ah, poor man, Rip Van Winkle was his name, but it's twenty years since he went away from home with his gun, and never has been heard of since—his dog came home without him; but whether he shot himself, or was carried away by the Indians, nobody can tell. I was then but a little girl."

Rip had but one question more to ask; but he put it with a faltering voice. "Where's your mother?"

"Oh, she too had died but a short time since; she broke a blood vessel in a fit of passion at a New England peddler."

There was a drop of comfort, at least, in this intelligence. The honest man could contain himself no longer. He caught his daughter and her child in his arms. "I am your father!" cried he, "Young Rip Van Winkle once—Old Rip Van Winkle now! Does nobody know poor Rip Van Winkle?"

All stood amazed, until an old woman, tottering out from among the crowd, put her hand to her brow, and peering under it in his face for a moment, exclaimed, "Sure enough! It is Rip Van Winkle—it is himself! Welcome home again, old neighbor. Why, where have you been these twenty long years?"

Rip's story was soon told, for the whole twenty years had been to him but as one night. The neighbors stared when they heard it; some were seen to wink at each other, and put their tongues in their cheeks; and the self-important man in the cocked hat, who, when the alarm was over, had returned to the field, screwed down the corners of his mouth, and shook his head—upon which there was a general shaking of the head throughout the assemblage.

It was determined, however, to take the opinion of old Peter Vanderdonk, who was seen slowly advancing up the road. He was a descendant of the historian of that name, who wrote one of the earliest accounts of the province. Peter was the most ancient inhabitant of the village, and well versed in all the wonderful events and traditions of the neighborhood. He recollected Rip at once, and corroborated his story in the most satisfactory manner. He assured the company that it was a fact, handed down from his ancestor the historian, that the Kaatskill Mountains had always been haunted by strange beings. That it was affirmed that the great Hendrick Hudson, the first discoverer of the river and country, kept a kind of vigil there every twenty years, with his crew of the *Half-Moon;* being permitted in this way to revisit the scenes of his enterprise, and keep a guardian eye upon the river and the great city called by his name. That his father had once seen them in their old Dutch dresses playing at ninepins in a hollow of the mountain; and that he himself had heard one summer afternoon, the sound of their balls, like distant thunder.

To make a long story short, the company broke up, and returned to the more important concerns of the election. Rip's daughter took him home to live with her; she had a snug, well-furnished house and a stout cheery farmer for a husband, whom Rip recollected for one of the urchins that used to climb upon his back. As to Rip's son and heir, who was the ditto of himself, seen leaning against the tree, he was employed to work on the farm; but evinced an hereditary disposition to attend to anything else but his business.

Rip now resumed his old walks and habits; he soon found many of his former cronies, though they were all rather the worse for the wear and tear of time, and preferred making friends among the rising generation, with whom he soon grew into favor.

Having nothing to do at home, and being arrived at that happy age when a man can be idle with impunity, he took his place once more on the bench at the inn door, and was reverenced as one of the patriarchs of the village and a chronicler of the old times "before the war." It was some time before he could get into the regular track of gossip, or could be made to comprehend the strange events that had taken place during his torpor. How that there had been a revolutionary war—that the country had thrown off the yoke of old England—and that, instead of being a subject of his Majesty George the Third, he was now a free citizen of the United States. Rip, in fact, was no politician; the changes of states and empires made but little impression on him; but there was one species of despotism under which he had long groaned, and that was—petticoat government. Happily that was at an end; he had got his neck out of the yoke of matrimony, and could go in and out whenever he pleased, without dreading the tyranny of Dame Van Winkle. Whenever her name was mentioned, however, he shook his head, shrugged his shoulders and cast up his eyes; which might pass either for an expression of resignation to his fate, or joy of his deliverance.

He used to tell his story to every stranger that arrived at Mr. Doolittle's hotel. He was observed, at first, to vary on some points every time he told it, which was, doubtless, owing to his having so recently awakened. It at last settled down precisely to the tale I have related, and not a man, woman or child in the neighborhood but knew it by heart. Some always pretended to doubt the reality of it, and insisted that Rip had been out of his head, and all this was one point on which he always remained flighty. The old Dutch inhabitants, however, almost universally gave it full credit. Even to this day they never hear a thunderstorm of a summer afternoon about the Kaatskills, but they say Hendrick Hudson and his crew are at their game of ninepins; and it is a common wish of all henpecked husbands in the neighborhood, when life hangs heavy on their hands, that they might have a quieting draught out of Rip Van Winkle's flagon.

ACKNOWLEDGMENTS

ARCHIE AND THE APRIL FOOLS by B. J. Chute, first published in *Child Life*, April 1942. Reprinted by permission of the author. "AS WE FORGIVE THOSE" by T. Morris Longstreth from *St. Nicholas Magazine*. Copyright, 1923, The Century Company. THE BEAR from *English Circus* by Ruth Manning-Sanders. Copyright Ruth Manning-Sanders and reprinted by permission of David Higham Associates. BEAUTIFUL AS THE DAY from *Five Children and It* by E. Nesbit. Copyright the Estate of E. Nesbit. Reproduced by permission of Ernest Benn, Ltd. THE BIRCH AND THE STAR. Copyright © 1927, 1955 by Frances Jenkins Olcott. From the book *Canute Whistlewinks and Other Stories* by Zacharius Topelius. (Translated from the Swedish by C. W. Foss. Selected and edited by Frances Jenkins Olcott.) Published by Longmans, Green & Co. Reprinted by permission of David McKay Co., Inc. THE BLACK STALLION AND THE RED MARE by Gladys Lewis. First published in *Story Parade*. Copyright 1945 by Copp Clark, Ltd., Toronto. THE CAT THAT WALKED BY HIMSELF by Rudyard Kipling from *The Just So Stories*. Copyright 1912 by Rudyard Kipling. Published by Macmillan & Co. of London and Basingstoke. Reprinted by permission of Mrs. George Bambridge and Macmillan & Co. of London and Basingstoke. CHRISTMAS IN THE STREET OF MEMORIES. Reprinted with permission of Farrar, Straus & Giroux, Inc., from *Beacon Hill Children* by Elizabeth Rhodes Jackson, copyright 1927, 1947 by L. C. Page and Company, Inc. THE COW-TAIL SWITCH from *The Cow-Tail Switch and Other West African Stories* by Harold Courlander and George Herzog. Copyright 1947 by Holt, Rinehart and Winston, Inc. Reprinted by permission of Holt, Rinehart and Winston, Inc. EBENEZER NEVER-COULD-SNEEZER by Gilbert S. Pattillo from *Story Parade* copyright 1936, copyright renewed 1964, by Story Parade, Inc. Reprinted by permission of Western Publishing Company, Inc. EL ENANO from *Tales from Silver Lands* by Charles J. Finger. Copyright 1924 by Doubleday & Company, Inc. THE FLOOGLES ARE DETECTIVES from *The Funny Fixes of the Floogle Family* by Gertrude Crampton, copyright, 1952, by the Bobbs-Merrill Company, Inc., reprinted by permission of the publisher. THE FOOL OF THE WORLD AND THE FLYING SHIP *Old Peter's Russian Tales* by Arthur Ransome, Nelson, London 1971. Copyright Arthur Ransome 1916. THE FOUR YOUNG MEN from *Ride With the Sun* edited by Harold Courlander. Copyright © 1955 by McGraw-Hill, Inc. Used with permission of McGraw-Hill Book Company. GEARS AND GASOLINE by Caroline Emerson from *Story Parade*, copyright 1940, copyright renewed 1968 by Story Parade, Inc. Reprinted by permisssion of Western Publishing Company, Inc. THE GIANT WHO RODE ON THE ARK from *Fee, Fi, Fo, Fum* by Adrien Stoutenburg. Copyright © 1969 by Adrien Stoutenburg. Reprinted by permission of The Viking Press, Inc. Published in Great Britain by André Deutsch Limited as *The Giant Who Sucked His Thumb* © Adrien Stoutenburg. Reprinted by permission. THE GIFT from *R Is for Rocket* by Ray Bradbury. Copyright 1947 by Ray Bradbury. Reprinted by permission of Harold Matson Company, Inc. GODFREY AND THE WEREWOLF from *Prince Godfrey* by Halina Gorska. Copyright, 1946 by Roy Publishers, A. N., New York and reprinted by permission. THE GREAT DROP GAME by Earl Chapin. Copyright © 1957 by *Boy Scouts of America*. Reprinted by permission of McIntosh and Otis, Inc. GUDBRAND ON THE HILLSIDE by G. W. Dasent. Copyright 1917 by G. P. Putnam's Sons. Reprinted by permission of G. P. Putnam's Sons from *Popular Tales From the Norse* by Peter Christian Asbjörnsen and Jörgen Moe, translated by Sir George Webbe Dasent. HERBERT'S WAVE from *Herbert Again* by Hazel Wilson. Copyright © 1951 by Hazel Wilson. Reprinted by permission of Alfred A. Knopf, Inc. THE HEXER by Thomas Thompson. Copyright © 1968 by Thomas Thompson. Reprinted by permission of Brandt & Brandt. HOW OLD STORMALONG CAPTURED MOCHA DICK by Irwin Shapiro. Copyright 1942, renewed 1969, by Irwin Shapiro. Condensed by permission of Julian Messner, A Division of Simon & Schuster, Inc., and McIntosh & Otis, Inc. HOW TO TELL CORN FAIRIES IF YOU SEE 'EM from *Rootabaga Stories* by Carl Sandburg, copyright 1922 by Harcourt Brace Jovanovich Inc., copyright 1950, Carl Sandburg. Reprinted by permission of the publisher. THE HUNDRED DRESSES, slightly adapted from *The Hundred Dresses* by Eleanor Estes, copyright 1944 by Harcourt Brace Jovanovich, Inc.; © 1972 by Eleanor Estes; reprinted by permission of the publisher. Published in Great Britain by The Bodley Head, Ltd. THE ITALIAN BOY by James Avery, from *A Book for Eleanor Farjeon*, © 1966 by Hamish Hamilton. Published in the U.S. by Henry Z. Walck, Inc. THE LEMON AND HIS ARMY from *Yugoslav Folk-Tales* by Nada Ćurčija-Prodanović. Copyright Nada Ćurčija-Prodanović, and published by Oxford University Press and Henry Z. Walck, Inc. THE LILAC IN THE LAKE by Joan Aiken, from *Miscellany Three*, edited by Edward Blishen. Copyright © 1966 Oxford University Press. Published in the U.S. by Franklin Watts, Inc. (Reprinted by permission of the publishers.) THE MAGIC BOX from *The Way of the Storyteller* by Ruth Sawyer. Copyright 1941, © 1969 by Ruth Sawyer. Reprinted by permission of The Viking Press, Inc. and The Bodley Head, Ltd. THE MAN WHOSE TRADE WAS TRICKS from *Yes and No Stories* by George and Helen Papashvily. Copyright 1946 by George and Helen Papashvily. Reprinted by permission of Harper & Row, Publishers. MANY MOONS from *Many Moons* by James Thurber. Copyright 1943 by James Thurber, © 1960 by Helen Thurber. Published by Harcourt Brace Jovanovich, Inc. MENASEH'S DREAM by Isaac Bashevis Singer, reprinted with the permission of Farrar, Straus & Giroux, Inc. from *When Shlemiel Went to Warsaw and Other Stories* by Isaac Bashevis Singer, text copyright © 1968 by Isaac Bashevis Singer. Published in Great Britain by Longman Young Books, Ltd., and reprinted with permission of Laurence Pollinger, Ltd. MIKE FINK from *Yankee Doodle's Cousins* by Anne Malcolmson. Copyright 1941 by Anne Burnett Malcolmson. Reprinted by permission of Houghton Mifflin Company. THE MIRACLE OF THE POOR ISLAND by Eleanor Farjeon. Copyright © 1965 by Eleanor Farjeon and William Mayne. First published in Great Britain as *The Hamish Hamilton Book of Queens*. Used by permission of David Higham Associates, Ltd., and Henry Z. Walck, Inc. THE MOFFATS AND THE SAILOR'S HORNPIPE, slightly adapted from *The Moffats* by Eleanor Estes, copyright 1941 by Harcourt Brace Jovanovich, Inc.; © 1969 by Eleanor Estes. Published in Great Britain by The Bodley Head, Ltd. Reprinted by permission of the publishers. OWL WITH THE GREAT HEAD AND EYES from *Glooskap's Country and Other Indian Tales* by Cyrus Macmillan, published in Great Britain as *Canadian Fairy Tales and Canadian Wonder Tales*. Reprinted by permission of Henry Z. Walck, Inc. and The Bodley Head, Ltd. PADRE ULIVO AND HIS GUESTS from *Italian Fairy Tales* retold by Peter Lum. Copyright © 1963 by Peter Lum. First published in Great Britain by Frederick Muller, Ltd. and copyright 1962 by Peter Lum. Reprinted by permission of Curtis Brown, Ltd. and Follett Publishing Company, a division of Follett Corporation. PAUL BUNYAN AND THE BABY RAINSTORM from *Ol' Paul, The Mighty Logger*, by Glen Rounds. Copyright 1949 by Holiday House, Inc. Reprinted by permission of the publisher. PIES OF THE PRINCESS from the book *Shen of the Sea* by Arthur Bowie Chrisman. Copyright 1925 and published by E. P. Dutton & Co., Inc. Copyright renewed 1953, Arthur Bowie Chrisman. Published in Great Britain by Hamish Hamilton, Ltd. Reprinted by permission of the publishers. THE RANSOM OF RED CHIEF from *Whirligigs* by O. Henry. Copyright 1907 by Doubleday & Company, Inc. THE RAT WHO MADE ONE BARGAIN TOO MANY from *Toontoony Pie and Other Tales from Pakistan* by Ashraf Siddiqui and Marilyn Lerch. Copyright © 1961 by Ashraf Siddiqui and Marilyn Lerch. Reprinted by permission of The World Publishing Company. THE REINDEER SLIPPERS by Barbara Willard. Copyright Barbara Willard. Reprinted by permission of the author and Hamish Hamilton, Ltd. THE SAMPLER by Dorothy Clewes. Copyright Dorothy Clewes and reprinted by permission of Curtis Brown, Ltd., London, on behalf of the author. SHAWNEEN AND THE GANDER by Richard Bennett. Copyright 1937 by Richard Bennett and reprinted by permission of Doubleday & Company, Inc. THE SNOW PARTY by Beatrice Schenk de Regniers. Copyright © 1959 by Beatrice Schenk de Regniers and reprinted by permission of Pantheon Books, a division of Random House, Inc., and published in Great Britain by Faber & Faber, Ltd. SOMEDAY by Isaac Asimov. Copyright © 1956 by Royal Publications Inc. Reprinted by permission of the author. THE SWIMMING STEERS from *The Little Haymakers* by Elizabeth Coatsworth. Copyright © 1969 by The Macmillan Company. Published in Great Britain by Hamish Hamilton Children's Books, Ltd. Reprinted by permission of the author and publishers. TALK from *The Cow-Tail Switch and Other West African Stories* by Harold Courlander and George Herzog. Copyright 1947 by Holt, Rinehart and Winston, Inc. and reprinted by permission. TOM CHIST AND THE TREASURE BOX from *Howard Pyle's Book of Pirates* compiled by Merle Johnson. Copyright 1921 by Harper & Row, Publishers. Copyright 1949 by Margaret K. Johnson. By permission of the publishers. THE TRAMP from *Tidewater Tales* by Anne Littlefield Locklin. Copyright 1942, © 1970 by Anne Littlefield Locklin. Reprinted by permission of The Viking Press, Inc. THE TRAVELER AND HIS HOST from *Yugoslav Folk Tales* by Nada Ćurčija-Prodanović. Copyright Nada Ćurčija-Prodanović. Used by permission of Henry Z. Walck, Inc. and Oxford University Press. THE TREE THAT DIDN'T GET TRIMMED from *Essays* by Christopher Morley. Copyright 1933 by Christopher Morley. Renewal © 1959 by Mrs. Helen F. Morley. Reprinted by permission of J. B. Lippincott Company. British Commonwealth copyright 1925 by Christopher Morley, renewed 1953 Christopher Morley. Reprinted by permission of the Estate of Christopher Morley. THE TURNIP from *Tales Told Again* by Walter de la Mare. Copyright 1927 Walter de la Mare and renewed 1955 Walter de la Mare. Reprinted by permission of the Literary Trustees of Walter de la Mare and the Society of Authors, and of Alfred A. Knopf, Inc. THE TYRANT AND THE MILLER from *Old Italian Tales* by Domenico Vittorini. Copyright © 1958 by D. Vittorini. Published by David McKay Co., Inc. and reprinted by permission of the publishers. UNDER COVER OF APOLOGIES by Geoffrey Household from *St. Nicholas Magazine*. Copyright 1932 by Scholastic St. Nicholas Corporation and reprinted with permission of Brandt and Brandt. WHITEY'S NEW SADDLE by Glen Rounds. Copyright 1951, 1952, 1963 by Holiday House, Inc. Reprinted by permission of the publishers. THE WILD BIRTHDAY CAKE by Lavinia R. Davis. Copyright 1949 by Lavinia R. Davis. Reprinted by permission of Doubleday & Company, Inc. THE WOODEN BOWL from *Old Italian Tales* by Domenico Vittorini. Copyright © 1958 by D. Vittorini. Published by David McKay Co., Inc. and reprinted by permission of the publishers. THE WOODS-DEVIL from *Pride of Lions* by Paul Annixter. Copyright © 1960 by Hill and Wang, Inc. and reprinted with the permission of Hill and Wang, a division of Farrar, Straus & Giroux, Inc. WORZEL GUMMIDGE PAYS A VISIT from *Worzel Gummidge* by Barbara Euphan Todd. © 1964 Barbara Euphan Todd. Published by Evans Brothers, Ltd., and reprinted by permission of A. M. Heath Ltd.

CONTRIBUTING ARTISTS

James Alexander, pp. 114, 218–219, 254, 290, 303, 340; Richard Amundsen, pp. 277, 280, 314; Hal Ashmead, pp. 83, 151; Robert Baxter, pp. 25, 106–107; Ben Black, pp. 116, 118–119, 184–185; Neil Boyle, pp. 349, 352, 355, 358, 360, 424; Frank Bozzo, pp. 366–367; Nick Calabrese, pp. 11, 18, 26, 32, 57, 99, 100, 111, 128, 141, 155, 196, 201; Eva Cellini, p. 216; Joe Cellini, pp. 294–295; Lawrence DiFiori, p. 131; Naiad Einsel, pp. 70, 72, 94, 97; Jack Endelwelt, p. 429; John Falter, pp. 44–45; Barbara Fox, pp. 66–67, 374; Betty Fraser, p. 20; Lester Goodman, p. 241; George Guzzi, p. 142; Greg & Tim Hildebrandt, pp. 62–63, 170, 173, 174, 180, 283, 363; Joe Krush, pp. 273, 274, 344–345, 434–435; Gordon Laite, pp. 378, 381; Robert J. Lee, pp. 124, 228, 398–399; Dora Leder, pp. 387, 403; Ted Lewin, pp. 166–167, 243, 244, 245, 246, 247; Ken Longtemps, p. 420; Allan Mardon, pp. 86–87, 93; Taylor Oughton, pp. 395, 408–409; W. K. Plummer, pp. 234, 235, 237, 238; Albert Pucci, pp. 322–323, 324–325; Sam Savitt, pp. 30–31; Harry Schaare, pp. 192–193, 205, 415; John Schoenherr, pp. 306–307; George Sottung, pp. 134–135, 267; Peter Spier, pp. 13, 33, 37, 40, 42, 158, 160, 308, 311, 312, 329, 333, 437, 439, 442, 446; Arvis Stewart, p. 337; Darrell Sweet. pp. 75, 78, 210, 211, 260, 318–319.